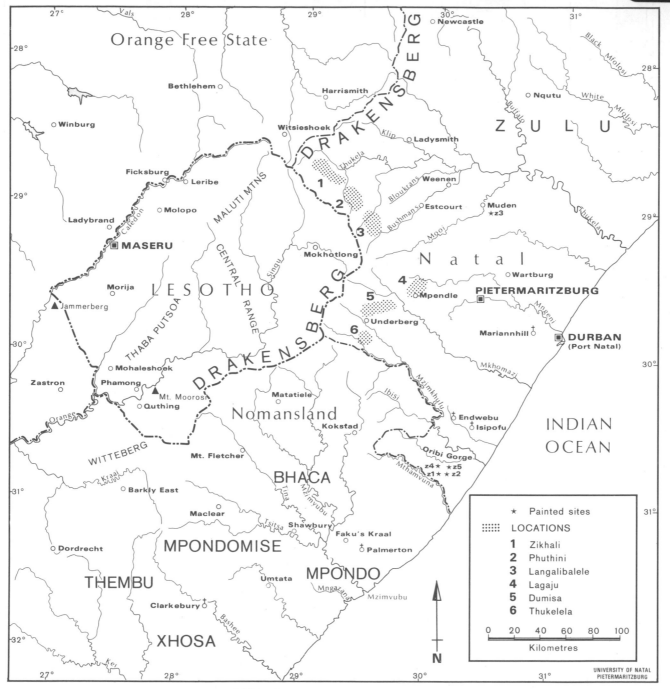

Orange Free State

○ Newcastle

ZULU

○ Winburg

Bethlehem ○

○ Harrismith

DRAKENSBERG

Witsieshoek

○ Nqutu

Ficksburg

○ Leribe

Ladysmith ○

Weenen ○

1

2

○ Molopo

Estcourt ○

Muden ○
★z3

Ladybrand ○

MALUTI MTNS

3

MASERU ▣

Mokhotlong ○

N a t a l

LESOTHO

Morija ○

4

○ Wartburg

Mpendle ○

PIETERMARITZBURG ▣

CENTRAL RANGE

▲ Jammerberg

THABA PUTSOA

5

DRAKENSBERG

6

Underberg ○

Marianhill ○

DURBAN ▣
(Port Natal)

Mohaleshoek ○

Zastron

Phamong ○

▲ Mt. Moorosi

○ Quthing

Matatiele ○

Nomansland

Kokstad ○

Endwebu ○
Isipofu ○

INDIAN
OCEAN

WITTEBERG

Mt. Fletcher ○

Oribi Gorge

BHACA

z4 ★   ★ z5
z1 ★   ★ z2

○ Barkly East

Maclear ○

Shawbury ○

Faku's Kraal ○

Palmerton ○

MPONDOMISE

Dordrecht ○

THEMBU

Umtata ○

MPONDO

Clarkebury ○

XHOSA

★ Painted sites

▦ LOCATIONS

1 Zikhali
2 Phuthini
3 Langalibalele
4 Lagaju
5 Dumisa
6 Thukelela

0   20   40   60   80   100

Kilometres

N

UNIVERSITY OF NATAL
PIETERMARITZBURG

MAP 2: SOUTHERN NATAL

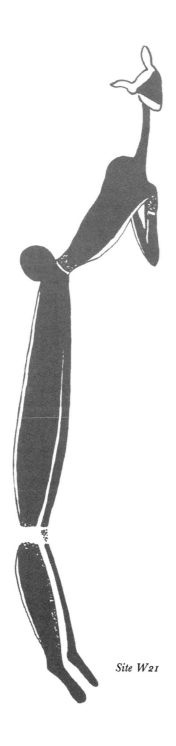

Site W21

People of the Eland

Site Q12

*This beautiful group of eland in a variety of attitudes was painted on the ceiling of
an overhanging slab of rock. The panel was becoming obliterated by water seepage,
and has now been removed for safe keeping to the Natal Museum.*

People of the Eland

Rock Paintings of the Drakensberg Bushmen

as a reflection of their life and thought

Patricia Vinnicombe

University of Natal Press
Pietermaritzburg

1976

ISBN   0 86980 054 X

The opinions expressed in this book are those
of the author and do not necessarily reflect
those of the bodies who sponsored the research.

COPYRIGHT ACKNOWLEDGEMENTS

The University of Natal Press acknowledges with thanks permission given by those listed below to use copyright material. Details of individual publications are given in the chapter references and the bibliography.

Books of Africa (Pty) Ltd, Cape Town
Botswana Government Printer, Gaborone
Carnegie Corporation of New York, New York
Free Press, United States of America
Government Printer, Pretoria
Hogarth Press Ltd., London
Humanities Press, United States of America
Human Sciences Research Council, Pretoria
International African Institute, London
Journal of the Royal Anthropological Institute, London
MacDonald and Company (Publishers) Ltd, London
Martin Secker & Warburg Ltd., London
Maskew Miller, Ltd., Cape Town

Merlin Press Ltd., London
Natal Mercury, Durban
Natal Museum, Council of; Pietermaritzburg
Natal Witness (Pty) Ltd., Pietermaritzburg
Oxford University Press, Oxford
Routledge & Kegan Paul, Ltd., London
Royal Society of South Africa, Rondebosch
South African Journal of Science, Marshalltown
South African Museum, Cape Town
University of Cape Town, Rondebosch
University of Chicago Press, Chicago
Wildlife Society of Southern Africa, Durban
Witwatersrand University Press, Johannesburg

Printed by
HAYNE & GIBSON LIMITED
"*The Press at Kingsmead*"
DURBAN
SOUTH AFRICA
1976

THIS BOOK IS NUMBER <u>595</u>

This is a limited edition of 1000 numbered copies, of which numbers 1 to 100 are collectors' editions, specially bound and autographed.

Numbers 101 to 120 are presentation copies, and numbers 121 to 1000 are the standard edition.

Site G3

Contents

Site B4

Sponsors and Subscribers

The very generous support of the following sponsors and subscribers made the publication of this book possible:

SPONSORS

Barnby, H. G.
Gravett, Miss I. M.
Greenacre Remembrance Foundation
Institute for the Study of Man in Africa.
Levitt, Robert E.
Pierson, Victor L.
Renaud, C. L.
Smuts Memorial Fund.
South African Permanent Building Society.
Swan Fund, the James A.
Vinnicombe, Mr & Mrs F. J.
Vinnicombe, Mr & Mrs J. W.

SUBSCRIBERS

Abbott, Professor C. W.
Abro, Mr & Mrs Mel.
Africana Book Collectors.
Africana Study Group.
Allsopp, Miss R. J.
Amson, Mrs H.
Ancient Africa Club.
Balinsky, Dr D.
Barrett, Professor A. M.
Bradlow, F. R.
Brown, D. C.
Butcher, M. R.
Campbell, Mr & Mrs John.
Campbell, Mrs N.
Carbutt, Mr & Mrs Hugh.
Catzel, Dr P.
Chutter, Rev Canon and Mrs J. B.

Clark, Mrs E.
Clark, Dr John.
Clark, M.
Clement-Smith, Mr & Mrs A.
Collett, L. H.
Cope, Professor A. T.
Craig, Mr & Mrs C. B.
Dart, Professor R. A.
Dold, Mrs D. F.
Duane, Mrs I. W.
Durban Alumnus Association.
Ermert, E. A.
Evans, R. J.
Flamand, J.
Historical Association, Pietermaritzburg.
Hoehn, G. C.
Hughes, Mr & Mrs W. H.
Johnson, Townley.
Kass & Watkins.
Kelsall, Miss L. M.
Lawson, Mrs C. M.
Lee, D. N.
Lund, Mr & Mrs K. S.
MacArthur, Advocate Neil M.
MacDonald, J. D.
McGregor, Mrs L. C.
McKenzie, Miss S.
McLaren, Mr & Mrs G.
Malan, B. D.
Maritzburg Ramblers Club.
Martin, Mrs A. M.
Mason, Professor R. J.
Matter, Mrs V.
Meintjes, Mrs J.
Milne, D. G.
Mogg, V.
Mokhotlong Mountain Transport (Pty) Ltd.
Moodley, Miss S.
Moore, Miss G.

Nagy, Mr & Mrs P. de F.
Natal & East Griqualand Milk Producers' Union
Neilson, Mrs N.
Nissen, Mr & Mrs C.
Oberem, W. F.
Ordman, Dr & Mrs David.
Orford, Mr & Mrs J. L.
Pager, H.
Palframan, Mrs Phyllis
Parkin, John.
Parnell, F. I.
Punt, Dr W. H. J.
Rabinowitz, H.
Rae, John.
Renaud, Miss D.
Richards, Dr & Mrs R.
Roberts, Mrs K. L.
Robertson, Mrs E. J.
Roulston, Mr & Mrs N.
Slotow, Dr & Mrs M.
Smits, Drs L. G. A.
South African Archaeological Society, Witwatersrand Centre.
Spence, G. V.
Stanley, Mr & Mrs D.
Stretton, S.
Sutherland, Mrs D. A. M.
Thurston, Mr & Mrs N. L.
Underberg/Himeville Women's Institute.
Van der Riet, A. W. G.
Van Proosdij, Mr & Mrs J.
Vaughan, Mr & Mrs I.
Walker, L. A.
Webb, Professor C. de B.
Welbourne, R. G.
Witte, Dr H. H.
Woodhouse, H. C.
Wright, J. B.

Illustrations

The scale shown in the illustrations is in centimetre units unless otherwise stated. In a few cases inches as well as centimetres are included in photographs.

In the black-and-white illustrations the following colour codes are used:

Black   ■   Light red   ▨

Dark red   ▦   Orange   ▨

Areas of white are outlined with a continuous or broken line.

Orthography and Terminology

Professor T. E. Cope and Mr D. N. Bang of the Department of Bantu Languages at the University of Natal, kindly checked the spelling of proper names of people and places, and in the text the presently accepted Zulu orthography has been followed. These spellings and their former more familiar counterparts include:

abaThwa	*in place of*	Abatwa
Bhaca		Baca
Lotheni		Loteni
Mkhomazi		Umkomaas
Mkhomazana		Umkomazana
Mngeni		Umgeni
Mzimkhulu		Umzimkulu
Mzimvubu		Umzimvubu
Mzumbi		Umzumbi
Ngcaphayi		Ncapaai
Nhlazane		Unshlasaan
Phuti		Baputi
Thembu		Tembu
Thukela		Tugela
Xhosa		Xosa

The spelling of Bushman words has been adapted to conform to the orthography more familiar to Western readers. Diacritical signs denoting clicks, which are present in most Bushman words, have been omitted except in the case of the term *n!ow* in order to avoid confusion with the English word *now*.

The designations *Bushman*, *Hottentot*, *Bantu* and *African* will no doubt prove unacceptable to some readers. Scholars are now replacing the term *Bushman* with *San*, but the former is still in common usage and will be more readily understood by the majority of readers. It does not yet come easily to me to refer to San paintings, San beliefs, or a Kung San instead of a Kung Bushman. I have therefore, perhaps erroneously, elected to retain a term which will, in time, undoubtedly become archaic.

The word *Hottentot* is popularly used to refer to cattle-keeping peoples of Khoisan stock, but it is now being replaced by *Khoikhoi*. There were very few pure Khoikhoi left by the mid-nineteenth century, and the Hottentots referred to in this book are more correctly Coloured people of mixed descent. They were, however, predominantly Khoikhoi, and were generally called Hottentots by the white colonists. For the purposes of the history chapter, I have continued this usage.

The word *African* implies any of the indigenous peoples of Africa and therefore, strictly speaking, includes Bushmen (San) and Hottentots (Khoikhoi) as well. In this book, however, it is used exclusively to refer to Southern African negroes and therefore excludes the Khoisan peoples. Use of the term *Bantu* to refer to a particular population group has fallen into disfavour: academics use it rather to denote a group of related languages. However, to write of 'a Bantu-speaking man hotly pursuing a San' is somewhat ludicrous and, since it is not always known whether the Bantu-speaker was of Nguni or Sotho stock, it is impossible to refer to him by a more specific designation. I have, therefore, used the term *African*, and occasionally *Bantu*, to fill this awkward gap in our daily terminology.

Lesotho has been used with reference to the present independent kingdom of that name, although it was known as Basutoland for the greater part of the period under review.

Site U3

Preface

This book, even more than most, is the result of the combined efforts of a great number of people. The gathering of facts from the paintings as well as from published and unpublished sources, the thinking that has gone into the interpretation of these facts, and the labour of getting the results committed to paper in an intelligible form have, all along, been very much a communal affair. It has involved many people in many walks of life in several different countries.

For a start, the work I have done would have been impossible without my parents' farm as a base from which to operate and from which to draw resources. I was born and brought up in the shadow of the Drakensberg with painted rock shelters as part of my extensive childhood playground. Learning to speak Zulu at the same time as learning to speak my mother tongue, walking or riding rather than travelling by modern conveyances, and absorbing veld lore as an integral part of one's background, have all been inestimable advantages in carrying out the fieldwork.

Education entailed going away to boarding school and, at Girls' High School in Pietermaritzburg, art teachers encouraged my interest in rock paintings. Later, at the University of the Witwatersrand where I trained as an occupational therapist, my lecturers included Professors Raymond Dart and Phillip Tobias, who were engaged in exciting research on the Kalahari Bushmen. Jean Humphreys, an active member of the South African Archaeological Society, was the first to teach me the value of accurate tracings of rock paintings as opposed to freehand copies, and from then on, the stage was set for a more scientific approach to my hobby.

Between 1954 and 1956 I visited Britain, and the interest taken by such people as Dr C. A. Burland and Dr K. P. Oakley of the British Museum, led to an exhibition of some of my tracings at the then Imperial Institute in London. A considerable amount of publicity attended the exhibition, which only served to make me acutely conscious of my ignorance of the subject. I went to the Abbé Henri Breuil, doyen of prehistorians in Europe, for help and direction.

> 'Don't come to me for advice, my girl. I am an old man now, and my methods and approach are outmoded. You are young, vigorous, energetic. You just go ahead and do the job. Develop new ideas, new techniques. It doesn't matter how you do it, as long as you do it to the best of your ability. And when you have gathered the facts, then you can make a start on interpreting the material. At this stage, nobody knows more than you do.'

With these words this remarkable man presented a challenge and imbued me with a sense of commitment which is with me still. I returned to South Africa and did as he said.

A lecture to the Natal section of the Mountain Club in 1957 resulted in my meeting the late Professor J. D. Krige, who encouraged me to apply for an *ad hoc* grant from the National Council for Social Research, now incorporated into the Human Sciences Research Council. At first I took unpaid leave from my post as an occupational therapist at Addington Hospital in Durban, then later, with the offer of an increased grant, regretfully resigned in order to work on recording rock paintings full time. At a subsequent meeting of the South African Association for the Advancement of Science where I presented a preliminary report on the fieldwork, Professor Dart recommended that, in order to continue the project, I should be paid a salary commensurate with what I had previously been earning. The Human Sciences Research Council generously provided funds until my marriage in 1961.

During the period 1958-1961, my work was supervised by Mr B. D. Malan of the Historical Monuments Commission, and it was through his perceptive direction that I first embarked on a programme of numerical analysis. Dr C. A. Schoute-Vanneck helped me work out an initial scheme for objectively quantifying a variety of significant factors that could be abstracted from a detailed study of the paintings, and later, at my first married home in Ghana,

Dr Nick Jago and Dr Paul Ozanne launched me into the complexities of storing, retrieving and cross-comparing data by means of the punched card system. The volume of material which had been collected in the field was immense, and the task of analysis and collation overwhelming. Once again I applied to the Human Sciences Research Council for financial assistance, and the award of a Senior Bursary enabled me to continue the work first in Cambridge, England, and later in Dar-es-Salaam, Tanzania. Here the quantitative analysis of the paintings was completed, and a start made on writing the history chapter. A return visit to South Africa gave me the opportunity to conclude investigations in the Natal Archives where documentary evidence helped explain details in many of the historical paintings.

Back in England again, I was awarded a Research Fellowship by Clare Hall, Cambridge, a newly established post-graduate College. This has provided me with access to the magnificent library facilities in Cambridge, as well as a quiet haven in which to work. But above all, being a member of Clare Hall has given me the opportunity to discuss a wide spectrum of problems with scholars and specialists from many fields, and this, in turn, has given me the confidence to write what I have written in *People of the Eland*. On a more material level, Clare Hall has also contributed towards travelling and typing expenses, for all of which I am immensely grateful.

Archaeological fieldwork in Lesotho undertaken jointly with my husband, Patrick Carter, during the years 1969, 1970 and 1974 has been generously supported by the James A. Swan Fund, administered by the Pitt-Rivers Museum, University of Oxford. The period of my research tenure in Cambridge has therefore been interspersed with frequent return visits to the Drakensberg; the excavation and field survey programme, apart from adding considerably to our knowledge of the Mountain Bushmen, has enabled me to check details necessary for the completion of the book. Our sincere appreciation goes to Bernard Fagg for his active assistance and encouragement in this project.

My current sojourn in Natal to see *People of the Eland* through the press has been made possible by the Emslie Horniman Trust, a fund administered by the Royal Anthropological Institute of Great Britain and Ireland. Without this, the problems of transmitting scripts, galleys, blocks and layout designs backwards and forwards between two continents would have been immense.

The first chapter of this book was written in Ghana in 1962 and the last was completed in Lesotho in 1970. Because the writing has been spread over a period of eight years, the discerning reader will no doubt detect inconsistencies in style and viewpoint. Since 1970 other pertinent publications have appeared, in particular *Ndedema* by Harald Pager, *Art on the rocks of Southern Africa* by Lee and Woodhouse, and papers in journals by David Lewis-Williams. While revising and 'polishing' sections of the script before final submission to the publisher, I have been able to include only brief references to these works.

When the book was finally completed, it was obvious that to publish without ample illustrations was to present conclusions without the supporting evidence. The only solution to satisfactory publication was to find a subsidy. Applications to the larger grant-giving bodies in Britain and America met with little success; nothing was left but to make a public appeal, and the only public which had any sympathy for the cause of rock paintings in South Africa was the South African public. The University of Natal Press undertook the onerous task of publishing the book, and the appeal was launched with an exhibition of tracings in Pietermaritzburg organised jointly by Tim Maggs and Valerie Leigh. The public began to respond, including many people who had, at one time or another, had some contact with my work. Then the community of Underberg rallied generously; these were the people among whom I had been born and brought up, the people who had shared and helped in the field work, who had fed me information, supplied me with transport, stimulated me with their interest. They felt in some way that the book was theirs as well as mine, and so it is. Diana Nagy and Peggy Roulston in particular, played a key part in rousing local interest and in co-ordinating the fund-raising effort. Recognition is given elsewhere to the many who have contributed financial aid.

Before I married, my fieldwork was heavily dependent on friends and acquaintances who, at their own expense, spent leaves and vacations with me in the mountains. They carried heavy equipment and provisions, trudged many miles searching the krantzes for rock-paintings, and willingly took a share in the time-consuming camp chores. The hard work was not without compensations, and the experiences we shared will always be remembered as among the happiest of my life. Those who helped during field trips include:

Don Allison
Fiona Barbour
Victor Biggs
Dennis Bird
Anne Bullivant
Keith Burridge
Mr and Mrs Edgar
   Calderpotts
Marina Cippico
Patrick Carter
Ian Cuthbert
Richard and Peggy Evans
Andy and Norah Farnden
Donald Gibbs
Isabelle Gravett
Cedric and Margaret Green
Allan and Joy Greenway
Jean Hewlett
Betty Hodkinson
Frances Hoedemaker
Clayton Holliday
Stephen Kass
Kearsney College
   Archaeological Society

Nora Kirk
Neil Lee
Tim Lovell-Hewitt
Stoffel Louw
Jimmy McInnes
Tom McLean
Tim and Val Maggs
Jim Mangan
Allan and Angela Manning
Lura and Michael Mason
Don Morrison
Paul and Diana Nagy
Margaret and Bert Nash
Bill Northcott
Harald and Shirley Pager
Lorna Peirson
Vic Pierson
Jean and David Poynton
Hyme Rabinowitz
'Doc' Schoute-Vanneck
Moira Soffe
Mr and Mrs G. K. Sprot
Audrey Treleaven
John Vinnicombe

Gedys and Avie Vinnicombe
Penny Vowles
Ray Walsh
Des and Jeannie Watkins
John Webb

Edrid, Elizabeth and
   Richard Wedgwood
Mrs Ivy Wilson
Bert and Diana Woodhouse
John Wright

In addition to the above, Lea Mguni and Stali Zondi, who have worked with my family for longer than I have been alive, have been devoted assistants whenever their services were called upon.

Especial thanks are due to Jean Hewlett (now Meintjes), Lorna Peirson, Elizabeth Wedgwood, Clayton Holliday, Cedric and Margaret Green for the many hours they have spent diligently assisting with tracing; Patrick Carter for undertaking much of the photography, Victor Pierson for developing and printing numerous rolls of film at minimal cost, and Diana Nagy for enthusiastic encouragement throughout the project. In the Natal Archives, Angela Manning and Mr C. Evans helped in the laborious task of searching through newspapers. Allan Manning provided a copying machine, Betty Hodkinson typed out relevant passages and Babsie Bambus translated documents from Dutch into English. John Wright, who was also searching the Archives for information on the Bushmen for a master's thesis, generously shared his findings, and I am indebted both to him and to Professor Colin Webb for reading and commenting on various drafts of the historical chapter.

Professor Edmund Leach, Professor Ralph Bulmer, Professor Isaac Shapera, Dr Peter Ucko and Dr Michael Jackson also read and criticised various chapters, particularly those relating to anthropology, and many of the points they discussed stimulated new waves of productive thinking on my part. To David Buxton, who scrutinised the final chapters for sense and readability, and who prevented me from committing misleading phrases and grammatical errors to print, I am especially indebted. Adrian du Plessis, Garth Sampson and Charles Turner suggested the re-ordering of some chapters and their contents, while Theya Molleson, Tim Maggs, Roger Summers, David Lewis-Williams and Lucas Smits have read and corrected sections of the typescript and galley-proofs. There are many, too, whose specialist knowledge has already been acknowledged in the text. Among these are Tom McClean, Major G. Tylden, Dr O. Leistner, Dr O. Hilliard and Professor A. W. Bayer.

In the early stages of typing and re-typing drafts, Caroline Etches and my cousins Avonal and Jocelyn Vinnicombe were especially industrious. Avonal Vinnicombe (now Pyetan) also made the preliminary drawings of several of the maps that were finally prepared for block-making by Bruno Martin and Raymond Poonsamy of the Department of Geography, University of Natal. Also at the final stages, Brigid Kelsey patiently helped with the laborious chore of checking and standardising bibliographical references.

Gedys Vinnicombe, Hans Witte, Moira Soffe, Neil Lee, Harald Pager, Lorna Marshall, Des Watkins, the South African Museum, the Museums of Man and Science and the Société des Missions Evangéliques in Paris have provided illustrations with no benefit to themselves other than an acknowledgement. Permission to quote passages from previously published works has been granted by a large number of publishers and organisations which are listed separately.

The facilities afforded by the Natal Museum, and the willing assistance at all times given by the Director and staff, have been of great help throughout the project.

The late Dr Killie Campbell kindly lent a Rolleiflex camera for use in the field and, more recently, Peter Narracot of the Pitt-Rivers Museum, Oxford, photographed many of the facsimile copies reproduced here as half-tone illustrations.

The original tracings from which the blocks in this book have been made are housed in the Natal Museum where they can, on request, be made available to any member of the public.

Map references for the sites listed in the appendix have intentionally been omitted, but anyone planning to carry out further recording or research may obtain detailed information from the Archaeology Department of the Natal Museum, Pietermaritzburg, or from the Archaeological Data Recording Centre at the South African Museum, Cape Town.

The printers of this book, Hayne and Gibson Ltd of Kingsmead, Durban, have been both patient and meticulous in their execution of a complex task. The close co-operation between printer and author has been particularly appreciated, and especial thanks are due to the management and staff for their sympathetic handling of the many technical problems that have arisen. The University of Natal Press, too, has had many difficulties to contend with. In particular, Professor C. W. Abbott, Mrs H. Cook, Mr P. E. Patrick and Miss M. P. Moberly have spent a great deal of time and energy in editing the script, checking the proofs and planning the layout. Mrs A. J. Neilson of the University Library painstakingly compiled the index. I thank them all most sincerely for their interest.

The greatest debt of all I have left till the last, and this is to my family. This project, which has extended over a quarter of a century, would have been impossible without the special understanding and co-operation given at all times by my parents and brother. They have allowed me the freedom to do what I really wanted to do, yet at the same time have provided the stability that has been such a comfort to fall back upon. Mountain trips with my brother John, a true man of nature, are always unforgettable episodes packed with action, practicality and humour.

More recently my husband, Patrick Carter, has taken over the role of encouraging, even bullying me, to complete the tedious painting analysis and to commit my views to paper. He has at all times supported my work both in the field and at home with unstinting enthusiasm, has worked many hours in the darkroom on my behalf, has sat laboriously pressing buttons of a calculating machine while I sang out interminable sets of figures, and has read and re-read scripts, ruthlessly deleting the subjective and the sentimental. Although I sometimes resented being taken away from my beloved Drakensberg, it is through his influence that I have been able to see the paintings in the wider perspective which has been essential to a deeper understanding of their significance.

During the trying period associated with the final production of this book, my young son Gavin has been a much needed link with the lighter, brighter side of life. His abounding vitality, keen observation and unfettered thinking have acted as a great tonic; may his enquiring mind never be blunted by complacency.

The date of publication of *People of the Eland* coincides with the commemoration of Dr Bleek's death exactly a hundred years ago. Shortly before he died, Dr Bleek wrote that the demonstrable connection between Bushman paintings and Bushman mythology could hardly be valued sufficiently:

> *It gives at once to Bushman art a higher character, and teaches us to look upon its products not as the mere daubing of figures for idle pastime, but as an attempt, however imperfect, at a truly artistic conception of the ideas which most deeply moved the Bushman mind and filled it with religious feeling.*

If *People of the Eland* serves in some small measure to stimulate interest in the oldest of South Africa's art forms, the effort that went into it will have been worth-while. My main aim has been to demonstrate that the Bushman rock paintings are concerned not so much with the commonplace, material aspects of life, but with the deeper philosophies which govern relationships between man and the world he lives in, between man and man, and between man and the Creator Spirit.

Patricia Vinnicombe
West Ilsley
Underberg

January, 1975

Site F19

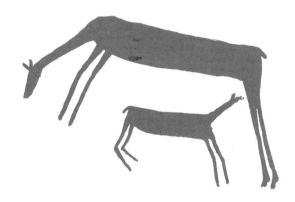

Site F6

1 The Setting

'It was a place enclosed with hills and precipices, and there was one pass, and it was constantly filled with a freezingly cold mist so that none could pass through it.'

From a legend related in 1873 by a Mountain Bushman named Qing.[1]

Area defined

The area with which this survey of rock paintings is mainly concerned lies along the foothills of the Drakensberg escarpment in the Republic of South Africa, and extends westwards of that range to include eastern Lesotho. Situated between 28° 50′ to 29° 47′ east of the meridian, and 29° 20′ to 30° 19′ south of the equator, this area incorporates the magisterial districts of Mpendle, Underberg and Pholela in the province of Natal, Mount Currie and part of Matatiele in the East Griqualand region of the Cape Province, and sections of the Qacha's Nek and Mokhotlong districts in Lesotho. The mountainous terrain, well-watered by numerous streams, is drained by the Mkhomazi, Mzimkhulu, and Mzimvubu rivers which run their comparatively short and rapid courses eastwards to the Indian Ocean, while the tributaries west of the watershed unite to form the Orange river flowing into the Atlantic Ocean. (See endpapers and maps)

Geology and Physiography

The Drakensberg or Dragon Mountain was originally called *Khahlamba* by the Bantu-speakers, a name said to mean 'the row of upward-pointing spears', or 'a rough bony object'[2]. This great escarpment was formed in Triassic times when enormous volumes of liquid lava from a series of volcanic fissure eruptions buried the earlier sandy sediments to a depth of thousands of feet. Through the millennia, this basalt crown has been eroded into deeply incised gorges and gulleys, and the indented and still receding façade now stands frowning guard along the eastern borders of Lesotho. Below, the undulating grass-clad terrain of Natal and East Griqualand, ribbed by the supporting buttresses of the austere lava wall and rutted by the rapidly flowing rivers, drops away in a series of steps towards the Indian Ocean only a hundred miles away. In the valleys thus dissected, the original pre-volcanic sediments are again exposed. Forming a foundation ledge to the dark basaltic crags and spurs of the High Berg, is a conspicuous wind and water-laid deposit of fine-grained yellow Cave Sandstone, so called because it is frequently undercut when weathered. Varying in thickness from three hundred to eight hundred feet, this richly coloured, weather-streaked deposit forms a prominent terrace at some distance from the High Berg but parallel to it, and is now generally referred to as the Little Berg. Immediately below the Cave Sandstone lie the Red Beds, shales of a rose-pink to purplish hue, which weather rapidly and thus intensify the shelving appearance of the sandstone bands. Below this again are numerous alternations of sandstone with doleritic intrusions producing stony ridges or dykes which are bounded by zones of metamorphosed or indurated shale. Chert, chalcedony and agate derived from the amygdaloidal lavas of the High Berg, together with the indurated shale and sandstone, were all well suited to the needs of a Stone Age community. In addition, the weathered sandstone ledges or 'krantzes' provided ample shelter and suitable painting surfaces for the aboriginal inhabitants of the area, the San or Bushmen as they are commonly called. So identified were they with this environment that the early colonists referred to the Little Berg as the 'Bushman's Terrace'.[3]

Figure 1

Cultivated fields on the farm West Ilsley, *Underberg. The view looks out across what used to be known as the Hartebeest Flats towards the Drakensberg, sprinkled with the first snowfall in autumn. On the left is Rhino's Horn (High Berg), in the centre Garden Castle (Little Berg). In the foreground of the picture, immediately beyond the belt of introduced trees, there is a narrow gorge at the head of which is evidence of a Bushman camp-site. Stone artefacts lie strewn around, and an incompletely made digging stone was found lying in the lee of an overhanging rock. The photograph is taken from the top of a band of sandstone in which there are three painted sites (L 32, 33, 34), and the slopes in front of the shelters are littered with scrapers and debris from making stone tools.*

Photo: Gedys Vinnicombe

Present economy and communications

Less than a century ago the last of the nomadic hunter-gatherer Bushmen were finally driven from the foot of the Drakensberg by the inevitable encroachment of pastoralists and agriculturalists. Today the area supports a prosperous mixed farming community, whose chief products are beef, milk, mutton, wool and potatoes. The commercial centres of Underberg, Bulwer, Matatiele and Swartberg are connected by rail to the provincial capital of Pietermaritzburg and the seaport of Durban, and road communications are improving rapidly.

In East Griqualand the farmlands extend as far as the Lesotho border, while in Natal the Government has far-sightedly proclaimed a chain of forestry, nature and game reserves along the base of the escarpment. Wilderness areas provide additional protection against development, so ensuring that some of the finest scenery in all of southern Africa will be preserved in much the same unspoilt state that the hunter-gatherers knew it. Trout-fishing and mountain holiday resorts increase in popularity; and the attractions of an invigorating climate and magnificent natural setting are considerably enhanced by the many rock paintings left by the former Bushman inhabitants.

West of the Drakensberg watershed lies Lesotho, a high, broken country of unending hills and valleys; bleak, desolate, windswept and rugged. Where the headwaters of the Orange river have eroded through the overlying lava, they have gouged deeply into the colourful sandstones and shales to form immensely tortuous gorges characteristically lined with innumerable rock shelters. Basotho settlement of the area is of a comparatively recent date, and the permanent peasant communities are limited to the more sheltered valleys where arable land is available. The overhanging rocks that once sheltered the Bushmen are now used to shelter stock, and some of them are seasonally inhabited by Basotho herdsmen. During the summer months, their cattle, horses and goats are taken to graze on the high plateau bordering on the escarpment, but the winter snows oblige them to retreat again to the protection of the valleys.

Because of the great mountain barrier, communication between Natal and Lesotho is difficult. Some of the mountain passes are traversed by steeply zig-zagging bridle paths, and until one of these was negotiated by powered transport little more than a decade ago, all trade goods were conveyed to and fro by pack animals. Long before the advent of commercial enterprise, however, these trails had already been blazed by the Bushmen. When the hunters began augmenting their diet with domestic stock stolen from Bantu-speaking pastoralists and from white settler farmers, they would retreat over the passes in the high escarpment with their booty and then take refuge in the inaccessible hinterland where their pursuers were loath to follow.

The most negotiable passes in the area of the rock painting survey are the Mohlesi and Sani on the headwaters of the Mkhomazi river, and the Thamatuwe and Bushman's Nek passes on the southern tributaries of the Mzimkhulu river. At this point the austere natural barrier between Natal and Lesotho comes to an end, and the main mountain massif veers westwards then southwards to enclose the headwaters of the Tsoelike river, a tributary of the Orange. Hemmed in by mountains on all sides, but with relatively easy winter access to the sweeter veld of the Orange river valley, the catchment basin of the Tsoelike river is one of the richest grazing areas in Lesotho. Judged by the great number of painted shelters found along the course of this river, it must have been a popular haunt of the Bushmen and probably once supported plentiful game. West of the Tsoelike river the high basalt continuation of the Drakensberg can be traversed via Letiba's Nek, from which the terrain once again drops away to the valley of the Orange river below. The boundary between East Griqualand and Lesotho is formed by a sandstone continuation of the Little Berg, which also becomes the watershed between the Tsoelike and Mzimvubu rivers. Today a vehicle track connects the rail-head at Matatiele with trading stores at Ramatseliso and Sehlabathebe on the Lesotho heights, and still further south a serviceable road cuts through a break in the sandstone escarpment at Qacha's Nek.

But these are developments of the twentieth century. Until less than one hundred years ago, the area was unscathed by commercial progress but boasted a sufficiently varied natural vegetation to sustain an abundance of wild life, and to provide an adequate living for scattered hunter-gatherer bands.

Climate and vegetation

The climate and vegetation of Natal and East Griqualand, lying between the great escarpment and the Indian Ocean, are largely regulated by altitude. Three distinct belts are recognisable; the sub-tropical Lowveld occupying a narrow band along the coast, the Middleveld with ridges of grassland and patches of temperate forest intersected by valleys covered with thornveld or scrub, and the mountainous Highveld running parallel with the Drakensberg escarpment which in places reaches heights of more than eleven thousand feet above sea level.

The area of the rock art survey falls largely within the Highveld

Figure 2a

Winter. *View overlooking the Orange River from Ramathlama's shelter, with the Central Range of the Maluti Mountains in the background. This inaccessible site was formerly used as a hiding place by Bushman stock rustlers. Paintings in the shelter include domestic animals as well as warriors with spears and shields, and the occupation debris contains cattle bones in association with stone implements.*

Figure 2b

Summer. *A thunder storm brewing over one of the many painted shelters at the foot of the Cave Sandstone on* Belleview *farm, East* Griqualand. *The scene showing European soldiers firing at a herd of eland (Figure 40) is on the exposed face of rock on the left. Higher up the valley, and just out of sight in this photograph, is a large overhang providing excellent shelter, but it contains no paintings. The site was nevertheless occupied by Bushmen for a long period of time. The 'Later Stone Age' deposit reaches a depth of 2⅓ metres in places, and has produced dates ranging from* A.D. *1135 to 6,700* B.C.

region where the climate shows marked seasonal variation. The warm summer days are frequently interrupted by sudden and often violent thunder storms which can bring devastating hail, while the dry winters are frosty with occasional falls of snow. Although the days are often clear and sunny, there is marked diurnal variation, with temperatures frequently falling to below freezing at night. The vegetation is predominantly open grassland with patches of residual forest in the more protected gulleys. Dependent upon the amount of trace elements retained in the soil, the grassland is divided into sweet, mixed, and sour veld. Sweet veld, which in Natal and East Griqualand is limited to the lower-lying river valleys, provides the richest grazing and retains its nutritive value throughout the year, whereas mixed veld produces good grazing for only eight out of twelve months. Sour veld, though very nutritious in early summer, soon becomes unpalatable as the season advances, and is therefore of only limited value as sustenance for animals. The greater part of the survey area is covered by sour veld, with a basin of mixed veld in the vicinity of Swartberg, Matatiele and Mount Fletcher in East Griqualand, extending to include the Tsoelike valley around Ramatseliso and Sehlabathebe in Lesotho. The vegetation on top of the escarpment is alpine in character, with short grass and scrubby heaths that are virtually devoid of nutriment.[4-7] Between the Cave Sandstone level of approximately six thousand feet and the heaths above nine thousand feet, there is a band of 'sweet sour veld' which grows on the steep slopes overlying the basalt. Here the soils are less leached than on the lower-lying sandstone, and the vegetation they support is more sustaining. The staff of the Drakensberg Game and Forestry Reserves have observed that, as the winter advances, the larger game animals move up to these levels to graze. Here they remain until forced down by the winter snow which usually covers the top of the Berg for two or three months. Late winter is a crucial period for animals as they lose condition rapidly on the frosted veld, and, when survival is largely dependent upon spring rains, a drought can be calamitous. Present farmers in the Highveld districts encourage the growth of succulent new grass as early as possible by burning off the old dry veld, a habit that was also practised by the former Bushman hunters in order to attract game.[8,9]

At a casual glance the vast expanses of open grassland characteristic of the Highveld, lusciously green in summer but bronze and brittle in winter, appear botanically very uniform. Closer inspection nevertheless reveals a great variety of plant species most of which have perennial underground organs with annual above-ground parts. The Mountain Bushmen, like the hunter-gatherers who still live in the desert regions of South West Africa and Botswana, must have possessed an intimate knowledge of plant-life, both edible and poisonous, as this was the mainstay of their economy.[10]

The harsh winter months would certainly have been the most lean for humans and animals alike, and although little is known of the movements of game animals before they were restricted by settlement, there is little doubt that the majority migrated in winter from the sour Highveld down towards the sweeter Middleveld where the vegetation was more sustaining. For the hunter-gatherers too, who of necessity followed the game, the lower-lying temperate forests and bushveld would have produced many varieties of fruits, roots and tubers not obtainable at the higher altitudes. It may therefore be safely assumed that, before the interference of pastoralists and agriculturalists, game and its predators, including man, would have frequented the sour Highveld in numbers only during the summer when the vegetation was tempting to the palate. Because it has poorer grazing, poorer soil and a colder climate than the surrounding areas, the sour Highveld was one of the last areas to be permanently settled by white farmers and was therefore one of the last refuges of the ousted Bushman.

Fauna

The larger fauna of Natal and East Griqualand have been drastically reduced since European settlement, and now survive for the most part only in game reserves.

Little is known of the early distribution of wild animals in the Highveld region, but references by travellers and sportsmen, and the painted records left by the Bushman hunters, indicate that there were many more species than are found today.

Captain Allen Gardiner, a missionary who visited the area of this survey in October 1835, has left the earliest written record of indigenous game.

On the Ngwangwana and Mzimkhulu rivers, Gardiner mentions seeing eland, gnu or black wildebeest, large herds of hartebeest, a lioness with four young cubs, jackal, coveys of partridges, and plentiful duck in the rivers. Towards the headwaters of the Mzimvubu river, the numbers of gnu increased and they became the most common animal seen, but as the party turned away from the open veld at the foot of the Drakensberg and began to traverse more broken terrain, Gardiner remarked, 'The gneu have now entirely deserted us, this country being ill adapted for their wild racing'.[11]

Captain A. W. Drayson, resident in Natal between 1847 and 1849, describes the herds of elephant then found in the sub-tropical forests, the hippopotami and crocodiles in the rivers, the buffalo and hartebeest that roamed the plains in large numbers, and the eland that grazed among the foothills of the Drakensberg. In addition to the many species of antelope, including bushbuck, duiker, steenbuck, oribi and rhebuck, he mentions wild-pigs, warthogs, leopards and the spotted hyena. Ostriches, he said, were sometimes to be seen on the plains below the Drakensberg mountains, and a farmer near the headwaters of the Mngeni river told how 'quaggas' (a name also applied to Burchell's and Mountain Zebras by early colonists) occasionally grazed within sight of his house.[12]

Several records left by early settlers refer to annual migrations of game into the uplands of Natal; herds of eland, blesbok, wildebeest, quagga and zebra, with the attendant lions, would descend the mountains from the high Orange Free State plateau during winter in search of grazing in the Thukela basin, returning to the Free State again in summer.[13-17] From Giant's Castle southwards the grazing again becomes sour, which was doubtless an effective barrier to the southerly movement of herbivorous animals. Another basin of mixed veld on the upper reaches of the Mzimvubu in East Griqualand carried large herds of game which were probably also attracted from the neighbouring sour veld during winter.[18] Major D. B. Hook records having shot lion, wild boars, hartebeest, numerous wildebeest and a zebra in this area in 1864.[19]

Blesbok and wildebeest have recently been re-introduced to the game parks with great success, and at Giant's Castle and its environs an estimated 600–800 eland survive. In the seclusion of the mountains other smaller antelope have managed to escape the ravages of recent man, and rhebuck, oribi, and very occasionally klipspringer can still be seen bounding effortlessly up the steep slopes. Dassies or rock rabbits (*Procavia capensis*) scuttle for cover among the stones when disturbed, and troops of baboons raucously bark their claim to the precipitous krantzes. At night, antbears, hares, porcupines and numerous small rodents emerge from their forms and warrens to feed, while other nocturnal carnivorous animals, jackals, cats, genets and mongooses, prowl about in search of prey. The abundant and varied bird-life includes game species such as guinea-fowl, bustards, wild duck, geese, seasonal quail and partridge, and the eggs of these birds too, are good eating. In the rivers where introduced trout now thrive, yellow-fish and barbel were indigenous, and shy otters can sometimes be glimpsed.

Among the food resources exploited by the Bushmen were lizards and grasshoppers, as well as seasonal swarms of locusts and winged termites. Termite eggs, often referred to as Bushman rice, were excavated from subterranean nests, and the produce of the wild honey bee was also much sought after.[20]

This then was the setting enjoyed by the early Bushman inhabitants of the area. The weathered sandstone krantzes offered comfortable shelter, usually with an ample and easily accessible water supply. In good seasons there was an abundance of game, with suitable resources near at hand for the manufacture of tools and weapons, snares and poisons. Cured and softened animal skins provided protection against the cold, while a variety of edible fruits and tubers were relatively easy to collect. When conditions were favourable, life was not a perpetual struggle, and whatever the motive, pleasure or purpose, the Bushman found time to express his life and his thoughts in dancing, singing, miming and story-telling, and in executing the paintings which still adorn the walls of his now deserted haunts.

The Bushmen

The physical characteristics of the Bushmen, also known as the San or Khoisan peoples, are too well known to require further detailed discussion here,[21] but since there are very few first-hand descriptions of the Bushmen who inhabited the Drakensberg region, one such account is worth relating.

In 1863, a visitor to Natal heard of a farmer living on the upper reaches of the Thukela river who, having lost some live-stock, followed the traces into a deep kloof in the mountains. Here he came upon a family of Bushmen driving three of his sheep towards the escarpment, whereupon he shot the two men, and took a woman and two children back to his farm to be trained as servants. The visitor was curious to see these 'remnants of an almost extinct race', and found the unfortunate captives confined in an outhouse, squatting on the floor, and looking 'anything but amiable'. The prisoners were brought out for closer inspection. The woman, who measured only four feet one inch in height, had a light yellowish skin colour, with sparse tufts of woolly hair on her head. She had broad cheek-bones, a sharp pointed chin, thin projecting lips,

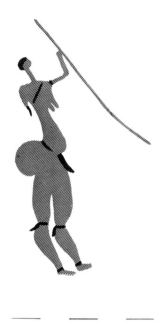

Figure 3a

This cast of a Khomani Bushwoman from the Gemsbok Park shows the steatopygea (large buttocks) and lordosis (hollow back) typical of the Khoisan peoples. The woman wears a pubic apron of tanned skin. Copyright: *South African Museum Collection.*

Figure 3b

Rock-paintings of Bushwomen on Mpongweni Mountain (site G3) show that physical features often thought to be stylised by the Bushman artists are in fact very true to nature.

7

Figure 4

'Kingking', a Bushman from southern Lesotho aged about twenty years. He wears drop ear-rings and the type of skin cloak or kaross illustrated in many of the paintings.

Drawn by Rev. Francois Maeder in 1844, and reproduced here by kind permission of the Société des Missions Evangéliques in Paris.

a flat nose which appeared to be little more than two orifices in the head, and her eyes were narrowed into slits by heavily folded lids. Her spine had an exaggeratedly inward curve so that her stomach was correspondingly protuberant, and she boasted the peculiar accumulations of fat on the buttocks and on the thighs known as steatopygia and steatomeria. (Figures 3a and b). The visitor then remarked that their language was 'almost without words except clicks', and that for anthropological science 'these people should be preserved'. But like the game which had once been

abundant, he feared they were doomed to be 'cleared from the face of the earth by the rifle'.[22]

Among the records of the Société des Missions Evangéliques in Paris, there is an excellent drawing of a young Bushman named 'Kingking', probably pronounced with a double click. It was made in 1844 by a missionary, François Maeder, at Morija in Lesotho. Although there is no further information accompanying the drawing, a later article by Maeder mentions that he had seen two Bushmen who had been taken captive by the Basotho following an outbreak of cattle-stealing between Thaba Morena and Maphutseng. The drawing may therefore be a portrait of one of the prisoners.[23] It is known that Bushmen from southern Lesotho also raided cattle from Natal on occasions, and the drawing made by Maeder is no doubt typical of the Bushmen who inhabited the mountain regions and who became such an annoyance to the early European settlers.[24] (Figure 4.)

References

1. Orpen 1874.
2. Doke and Vilakazi 1948.
3. King 1951, see *Drakensberg* in index; Malan 1955; Natal Regional Survey Vol. I, 1951: 30-41. C.S.O. 35, No. 4, 24/3/1856.
4. Scott 1957: 30-41; Niddrie 1951: 42-66.
5. Acocks 1953.
6. Killick 1963.
7. Edwards 1967.
8. Drayson 1858: 110.
9. J. Shepstone Papers, Box 4: 63-5, Natal Archives.
10. Story 1958.
11. Gardiner 1836: 320, 326, 328, 350, 352.
12. Drayson 1858: 59, 63, 119.
13. Barter 1852: 69, 82, 89.
14. Gray 1851: 36.
15. Mann 1859: 160, 163.
16. Orpen 1908: 97.
17. Statement by Hans Naude 1914, Witwatersrand University Library Archives.
18. Sanderson 1860.
19. Hook 1908: 127, 336.
20. Ellenberger 1953: 97.
21. Schapera 1930: 51-59; Tobias 1964; Dart 1937.
22. Anderson 1887 (1): 6, 12-14.
23. Maeder 1884.
24. I am indebted to Rev. Brutsch of Maseru for drawing my attention to the above reference, and also for showing me a copy of the portrait of Kingking which is reproduced with the kind permission of the Société des Missions Evangéliques in Paris.

Figure 5 *Site W21*

2 Hunters on Horseback
A history of the eastern Bushmen

Early contacts with Bantu-speakers and Europeans

The history of the Bushmen in the eastern region of southern Africa has, in the past, been marked by a paucity of factual information coupled with an emotionally charged quality of tragedy that characterises most treatises on broken peoples.[1] It is difficult indeed to reconstruct their story from the partial documents left by their arch-enemies, the white settlers, but it is the purpose of this chapter to draw from this unavoidably one-sided documentation in an attempt to describe the conditions under which the hunter-gatherers found themselves living in the 19th century, and to evaluate how they reacted to the changing situation. The evidence is balanced by incorporating, wherever possible, the painted documents left by the Bushmen themselves.

The early history of the Bushmen belongs to the period before events were recorded in writing, and therefore has to be reconstructed from archaeological sources. Until recently, archaeological studies were mainly concerned with the typological classification of the 'Later Stone Age' artefacts with which the Bushmen were associated, but a start has now been made on interpreting their former occupation sites in relation to the preceding 'Middle Stone Age' as well as in terms of environment, resources, exploitation patterns and seasonal activities.[2-4] As yet, however, most information on this aspect of Bushman life is too tentative to be included as historical fact.

Although the economy of the hunter-gatherer Bushmen had been affected by contact with pastoral Hottentots (Khoikhoi) in the southern and western Cape since at least 300 A.D.,[5] it was in the central and eastern regions of South Africa that the loosely bonded and mobile Bushman bands met their most formidable opposition and challenge. The highly institutionalised and settled Bantu-speaking communities of negroid origins slowly but inexorably pushed their way southwards into the midst of the Bushman hunting grounds, bringing with them not only large herds of sheep and cattle, but also a knowledge of iron-working and agriculture. The nature of the confrontation which commenced at least a millennium ago in some areas,[6] is clouded in obscurity, but was probably a combination of extermination, retreat, absorption and acculturation.

The extent of extermination inflicted by the immigrant Africans on the indigenous Bushman population will never be known, but it has in the past been assumed that the hunters were obliged to retreat to the refuge of the mountains as more and more Africans settled in the areas most suited to tillage and grazing.[7] Recent archaeological finds, however, indicate that Bushmen had elected to live in some of the mountain areas of their own free will and volition for thousands of years before the advent of the Bantu-speakers,[8] and it has not yet been convincingly demonstrated whether there was, in fact, a marked increase in the mountain population at any given time during the prehistoric period. In

9

Figure 6 *Site Z7*

Part of a group of fragmentary battle-axes in thick white pigment painted on top of earlier antelope in red. There are also remnants of antelope in white which have not been included in this illustration.

addition to the inevitable hostility that must have existed between hunter and pastoralist, there is strong evidence for a certain amount of fraternisation, trade and clientship between the two groups,[9,10] and Bushwomen were much sought after by the Bantu as wives.[11-17] Hybrid skeletons found in archaeological contexts,[18, 19] as well as residual Khoisanoid features among many south-eastern Bantu[20] and the incorporation of clicks into their language,[21,22] bear out this process of racial admixture. The cultural diffusion was very much a two-way process, for there is also a marked Bantu influence in the remnant Bush dialects recorded from the eastern Transvaal and the Transkei[23]: Particularly after the widespread upheavals caused by the Shaka wars early in the 19th century, it is probable that the traditional mode of life of most of the hunter-gatherers living to the east of the great escarpment had been modified to a greater or lesser extent by the selective incorporation of new technologies and alien concepts.

Interesting evidence of this acculturation can be seen in a painted rock shelter on the farm *Waterfalls* near Paddock in the Alfred district of Natal. This part of the coastal area was settled by Bantu-speakers at an early date, and the shelter contains traditional hunter paintings of antelope in dark red, overpainted by a series of battle-axes executcd in a thick dirty-white pigment.[24] (Figure 6)

Rock-paintings depicting both Bantu-speakers and Bushmen in the same scene usually accentuate the different weapons used — assegai, shield and stick as opposed to bow, quiver and arrow; and the difference in size between the robust and muscular Bantu is contrasted with the diminutive and slender Bushman. (See Figure 7). The few such painted scenes within the survey area are unfortunately very fragmentary (Figures 28, 51), but others better preserved have been recorded from the eastern Cape.[25] The Bantu-speakers' impression of the Bushman hunters likewise singles out differences in stature and weapons, as evidenced by the records collected by Canon Callaway when working among Zulus who were settled near Richmond in the Mkhomazi valley over a century ago. There follows a literally-translated account of the Bushmen, who were known to the Zulu as umuThwa in the singular, abaThwa in the plural:

The Abatwa are very much smaller people than all other small people; they go under the grass, and sleep in anthills; they go in the mist; they live in the upcountry in the rocks; they have no village of which you may say, 'There is a village of Abatwa'. Their village is where they kill game; they consume the whole of it, and go away. That is their mode of life.

But it happens if a man is on a journey, and comes suddenly on an Umutwa, the Umutwa asks, 'Where did you see me?' But at first through their want of intercourse with the Abatwa, a man spoke the truth, and said. 'I saw you in this very place'. Therefore the Umutwa was angry, through supposing himself to be despised by the man; and shot him with his bow, and he died. Therefore it was seen that they like to be magnified; and hate their littleness. So then when a man met with them, he saluted the one he met with, 'I saw you!' (This is a literal translation of the traditional Zulu greeting 'Sa ku bona', hence the play on words). The Umutwa said 'When did you see me?' The man replied, 'I saw you when I was just appearing yonder. You see yon mountain; I saw you then, when I was on it'. So the Umutwa rejoiced, saying, 'O, then I have become great'. Such, then, became the mode of saluting them.

They are dreaded by men; they are not dreadful for the greatness of their bodies, nor for appearing to be men; no, there is no appearance of manliness; and greatness there is none; they are little things which go under the grass. And a man goes looking in front of him, thinking, 'if there come a man or a wild beast, I shall see'. And, forsooth, an Umutwa is there under the grass; and the man feels when he is already pierced by an arrow; he looks, but does not see the man who shot it. It is this then that takes away the strength, for they will die without seeing the man with whom they will fight. On that account then, the country of the Abatwa is dreadful; for men do not see the man with whom they are going to fight. The Abatwa are fleas, which are unseen whence they came; yet they tease a man; they rule over him, they exalt themselves over him until he is unable to sleep, being unable to lie down and unable to quiet his heart; for the flea is small; the hand of a man is large; it is necessary that it should lay hold of something which can be felt. Just so are the Abatwa; their strength is like that of the fleas which have mastery in the night, and the Abatwa have mastery through high grass, for it conceals them; they are not seen. That then is the power with which the Abatwa conquer men, concealment, they [lie in] wait for men; they see them for their part, but they

Figure 7

A Bushman named 'Punch', and a Zulu compared. This photograph, taken by the late H. C. B. Wylde-Brown of Weenen, shows the differences between Khoisanoid and South African Negro physical types very clearly. Note the height of the Bushman in relation to the double-barrelled gun. There was a Bushman survivor in the Greytown district until the turn of this century, but it is not known whether this portrays the same man.[54]

Photograph reproduced from the collection of the late M. C. Burkitt, Cambridge.

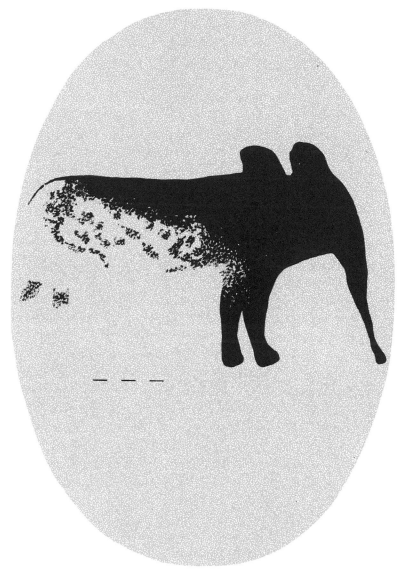

Figure 8 *Site Z6*

This fragmentary elephant in dark red is painted in a narrow gully on the farm Rockfontein in the Ixopo district. Bantu-speaking peoples in the nearby Mkhomazi valley used to act as intermediaries between the Port Natal ivory traders and the Bushman hunters who had perfected the art of killing elephant with poisoned assegais.

are not seen. The bow with which they shoot beast or man, does not kill by itself alone; it kills because the point of their arrow is smeared with poison, in order that as soon as it enters, it may cause much blood to flow; blood runs from the whole body, and the man dies forthwith. But that poison of theirs, many kinds of it are known to hunters of the elephant. That then is the dreadfulness of the Abatwa, on account of which they are dreaded.[26]

The fact that salutation did take place, and that the Zulu acknowledged certain terrain as being 'the country of the Abatwa', perhaps explains the surprising lack of reference to Bushman depredations among early African traditions. The later European arrivals, completely lacking in courtesy towards the aboriginals, and ruthlessly ignoring land claims, were subjected to reprisals on their stock almost immediately.

Early European settlement

Apart from sporadic visits by shipwrecked Portuguese, Dutch and English mariners, some of whom remained on the coast and were absorbed by local clans, the first permanent European settlement of Natal began in 1824.[27] A group of traders established themselves on the present site of Durban and bartered guns, cloth, beads, wire and sundry domestic merchandise in exchange for ivory, skins and horns. Through the intermediary of Bantu-speakers with whom they had direct connection it was not long before profitable but indirect relations were established with groups of hunter Bushmen living in the Natal uplands,[28,29] and paintings of elephants and elephant-hunting in the Drakensberg may perhaps be related to Bushman contacts with the ivory trade.

In a secluded kloof on a small tributary of the Mkhomazi river near Ixopo, there is a fragmentary painting in red of an elephant with ears flapping angrily, but if the tusks were ever shown, they have now faded away. This area is not far from where the Nhlangwini settled under chiefs Fodo and Dumisa, who were among those who bartered ivory with the Durban traders. Tradition has it that Dumisa, having been dispossessed by the Shaka wars, attached himself to a group of wandering Bushmen and from them learned the art of hunting elephant with poisoned assegais.[30-32] Dumisa was, therefore, both well equipped and well situated to provide a link between the traders and the inland Bushmen. (Figure 8)

High in the mountains on the farm *Bundoran* on a northern tributary of the Lotheni river, a dramatic scene painted on the rocks

Figure 9 *Site B12*
The elephant hunt on Bundoran, *upper Lotheni.*

shows eleven small and naked hunters surrounding a large bull elephant. Some of the humans flee before the elephant's extended trunk, while others seem to protect themselves behind branches held in their hands. More figures run up from the rear, some carrying sticks and what may be slightly curved bows. Two hunters squatting above the elephant apparently thrust long-handled flexible spears into the spine immediately behind the head of the animal, although these lines could possibly be interpreted as harpoons or ropes. The position and attitude of the two squatting figures indicates that they are on a higher level than their prey, which may have been in a pit or defile. An exudate from the elephant's trunk suggests that it is bleeding, or perhaps trumpeting violently. (Figure 9)

Another elephant, apparently associated with paintings of mounted horsemen, is depicted on the southern slopes of Sangwana Mountain in the Underberg district (Figure 62), and on the northern aspect of the same mountain there is a rhinoceros, another animal whose horns were much in demand by the traders. (Figure 10)

Although it is questionable whether the open grassland of the Natal Highveld was ever the natural habitat of elephants and rhinos, it is known that continual hunting sometimes drives animals to an unnatural environment.[33] Elephant bones were recovered in a patch of bush in the Njasuthi valley of the Drakensberg,[34] and wounded elephants certainly sought refuge in the mountains when pursued by hunters. An aged informant, Mgcamuse Nyide, was able to show Mr. A. T. McClean where an elephant was killed on the farm *Duart Castle* on the Hlatimba river in the 1860s. Tradition held that the elephant had been shot somewhere on the middle reaches of the Mkhomazi river, and the wounded animal, pursued by African hunters for several days, wandered further and further up the valley. Whenever the animal halted to rest, the hunters would open up its wounds with spears, causing heavy bleeding. The elephant finally crossed over Mohrotia Mountain into the Hlatimba valley, and there collapsed and died from loss of blood.[35]

It must, however, remain a matter of conjecture whether the elephant and rhinoceros paintings in the Drakensberg were painted by Bushmen who actually saw these animals in that area, or who hunted them elsewhere and then returned to the rock shelters to record what they had seen. Although it is uncertain whether the painters of these scenes were involved with the ivory trade in any way, it is an historical fact that Bushmen living within the survey area bartered ivory for European goods between the years 1830-1850,[36] and this contact, albeit indirect, may have extended as far back as the sixteenth century when the Portuguese were collecting tusks from the Zululand coast.[37]

The Natal traders were soon followed by missionaries, and one of these zealous men, Captain Allen Gardiner, was the first European to traverse and make observations in the survey area. In a vain attempt to reach the Cape yet avoid the hostile Xhosa during the 1835 Cape Frontier war, Gardiner headed inland. For a time, he followed the waggon tracks made by a party of Boers who had visited Natal on a 'Kommissie trek' or exploratory expedition with 14 waggons the year before,[38] and having gained a favourable impression, had returned to the Cape to collect their families.[39] Gardiner's cavalcade consisted of twelve people, including his waggon-driver Dick King, with two waggons, 51 draught oxen, calves for slaughtering, and riding horses. Once he had passed beyond the territory of the Nhlangwini on the Mkhomazi river, the country appeared deserted, with no signs whatever of habitations or agriculture although game was plenteous. It caused Gardiner considerable surprise therefore, when crossing a stream between the present Bamboo Mountain and Garden Castle, to come upon human footprints in the sand. From these it was evident that two persons, accompanied by a dog, had recently forded the stream, and he concluded that they were Bushmen.

Quite unwittingly, Gardiner had the previous day camped next to a Bushman habitation at a place on the Pholela river which he named Agate Vale.[40] An accurate sketch in his book records the details. In the background is the distinctive mountain now known as Hodgson's Peaks, and in the foreground, an outspanned waggon and his tent which is pitched near a large boulder.

Today, the vicinity of Gardiner's camp is strewn with stone artefacts of Bushman manufacture, and on the rough, undercut side of the boulder next to which he outspanned, there are rock paintings: eland, fragmentary hunters, and a bizarre hairy figure spread-eagled above a kneeling group. (Figure 225). But these signs of human activity obviously escaped Gardiner's attention — unless, of course, they were executed after his visit.

On the krantzes near the summit of Mpongweni Mountain shown on the left of Gardiner's camp scene there is another famous painted rock shelter (G3), and no doubt even while Gardiner was at work

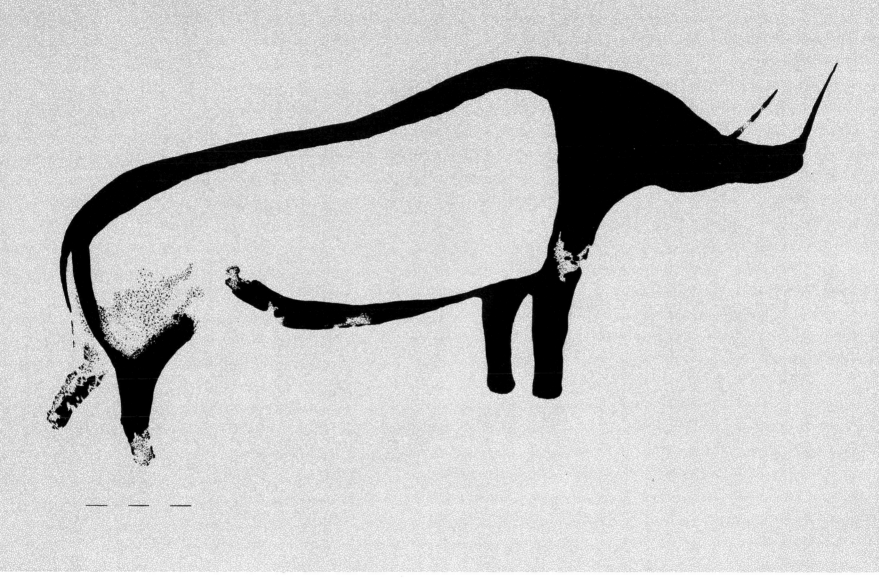

Figure 10 *Site 78*
A rhinoceros in faded black painted on Sangwana Mountain, near Underberg.

On stone by T.M. Haynes.   Printed by C. Hullmandel.

THE GIANT'S CUP from AGATE VALE.

Published by W Crofts Chancery Lane

Figure 11a

Allen Gardiner's drawing of the Giant's Cup, now named Hodgson's Peaks, was made in October 1835. His two waggons are outspanned on the flats in a bend of the upper Pholela river, and a tent is pitched in front of the large boulder at centre left. On the undercut surface of this boulder (Site G2), there are paintings, some of which are reproduced in Figure 225. Mpongweni Mountain rises on the left, and the famous site containing paintings of men spearing fish from small craft is situated in the band of krantzes near the summit. See Figure 63. On the right is Ndhloveni Mountain (Scafel), on the northern and eastern aspect of which there are also many painting sites.

16

Figure 11b

The accuracy of Gardiner's drawing reproduced opposite is verified by a recent photograph taken upstream of Cobham *Forestry Station on the* Pholela. *The only liberty Gardiner took was to use stones from a higher level as foreground.*

Photo: Gedys Vinnicombe.

on his sketch, Bushmen were observing his every movement from secluded vantage points. Gardiner did, in fact, pass very close to a shelter on Bamboo Mountain which lies in the direction of the footprints he described, and where there is a faded painting of just such a scene as Gardiner's cavalcade must have presented (Site H3). Riding out in front are horsemen prospecting the route, while the team of oxen drawing the covered waggon is led by a 'voorloper'. Bringing up the rear are a number of cattle driven by other horsemen. Could this be a record, as seen through the eyes of a Bushman, of the first entry of the white man into his domain?

Gardiner traversed the Drakensberg foothills in the month of October, and noted that in places the grass had been burnt. This had doubtless been set alight by Bushmen to attract game to the new spring grass, and in the vicinity of the Ndawana river, he found the remains of a hunter's repast — a few burnt sticks methodically arranged near the skull of an eland.[41-43] Beyond this, in a valley overlooked by a peak which Gardiner named Cavernglen Mountain, now known as Mount Fred, the travellers unexpectedly came across a well-beaten track and numerous traces of horses and cattle:

> Following the winding footpath for about half a mile further up the valley, we suddenly reached the mouth of a cavern, formed by a huge slab of rock jutting out from the precipice, the interior of which had been ingeniously partitioned off by trunks and branches of trees, so as to form separated rooms or compartments. Marks of fire were everywhere visible: remnants of mats, bunches of Indian corn, cooking bowls, a head-plume and armlet of hair, with several other articles, but more especially the traces of horses, sufficiently proved who had been the late occupants of this singular place of refuge. It could have been no other than a party of Amakosa [Xhosa], who had retreated into this mountain fastness; and a more well-chosen place for defence it is scarcely possible to conceive.
>
> The cave itself could contain at least one hundred persons; and from the irregularity of approach and the numerous masses of rock lying detached about its mouth, its very existence might long have been concealed, while in the immediate neighbourhood there is good and ample pasturage for a numerous herd of cattle.[44, 45]

Gardiner may well have been correct in his deduction that the cave had been visited by refugee Xhosa, but it is equally possible that the inhabitants were Bushmen. If so, it is interesting to note the presence of horses and cattle at this date, 1835. In 1846, a Boer named Jacobus Uys encountered cattle-owning Bushmen in East Griqualand who were riding horses stolen from between the Kraai and Orange rivers in 1837.[46] It may well be that a band of Bushmen who raided cattle and horses from the eastern Cape had already taken up residence on the upper reaches of the Mzimvubu by the time of Gardiner's visit there. Only with caution therefore, should rock-paintings depicting horse and cattle raids in Natal be associated with the arrival of the Boers in that Colony in 1837.

The interpretation given by Bushmen to their first incredulous view of waggons has been recorded from several areas. Some thought they were a terrestrial form of the strange white things that came out of the sea (sailing ships).[47] Others imagined they were animals that left a strange spoor, and speculated on what type of young they bred.[48, 49]

In the Cape, a broken-down waggon was thought by a Bushman to be a missionary's pack-ox with a broken leg. Since it had been standing stationary in the veld for a long time, and he observed it did not eat any grass, he was afraid it would soon die of hunger if it was not led elsewhere.[50] Similar impressions were recorded from the Masarwa Bushmen in the Lake Ngami region of Botswana. Their description was roughly this:

> We thought the waggons were big animals. There were many oxen going before, and as we thought, these big animals going after .... They looked like elephants, but they were white. We watched them a long time, and then we saw that some of them stopped. There was not much rain that year, and the grass was not good. The oxen were thin, and then they died. Many died before they got to the lake, and sometimes we had some of the flesh. At last one day, we saw the white men take all the cattle away from this animal, and leave it on the veld. We were afraid to go near it. We thought it had been left to graze, but then we saw that its feet did not move. Some of us got near then, and we looked in. There were lots of things inside, but we Bushmen did not know their uses, and so we left them. We found some dry meat, which we took. .... After a time, all the cattle died of sickness, and the white men got sick and died too .... We Bushmen never killed any of these people, but we took their cattle and ate them. The waggons died on the veld, and some of them were burnt.[51]

One Bushman admitted that the first time he and his people saw a waggon, they had run away from it for a whole night, thinking it was a terrible monster. They always jumped over the spoor, and would not touch the wheel tracks on any account.[52]

In the waggon group painted on Bamboo Mountain, the procession follows along a bleached line in the rock. It is difficult to determine whether this was painted intentionally to represent a track, or whether the artist incorporated a natural mark on the rock into his composition. Clearly, however, the spoor left by the vehicle was a source of fascination.

Figure 12 *Site H3, Bamboo Mountain*

In 1835, Captain Gardiner and his party travelled along the foot of Bamboo Mountain. He had with him covered waggons, trek oxen, cattle for slaughtering, and riding horses. This scene represents just such a party, with a voorloper *leading the oxen, mounted scouts with brimmed hats carrying guns over shoulders, and a rider driving the cattle at the rear. Parts of the group are unfortunately very faint, but the cavalcade apparently follows a track. The scene measures 89 cms from one end to the other, and is painted in black, orange and white.*

On his homeward journey through what is now Mount Currie District, Gardiner travelled past the Bokberg. Near the summit of this mountain there is a shelter containing another painting of a waggon, which indicates what may be wheel spokes. There are trek oxen on either side of the waggon shaft, but the complete span has unfortunately been erased by drip marks on the rock (Figure 13a).

In 1910, Trooper A. D. Whyte reported another faint painting of a waggon and a span of oxen on a farm on the Ndawana river, but I have been unable to locate it; possibly it has now disappeared altogether.

As the Bushmen watched Gardiner and his party toil their way laboriously up hill and down dale, the waggons capsizing in rocky streams and the men being kicked by oxen, it is difficult to know whether their reactions were predominantly amusement or bewilderment. Another rock painting of a waggon on the farm *Kilmun*, also within view of Gardiner's route, contains an element of caricature: a bearded figure wearing a wide-brimmed hat and wielding a whip sits in front of the covered waggon, trying to urge on a very dejected-looking animal being hauled along by a 'voorloper'. One wonders whether this might be a portrait of Gardiner's waggon-driver, Dick King, who afterwards became famous for his desperate ride to relieve the siege of Durban. Or is it a portrait of a Boer who was soon to follow, seeking pastures new?

It may be disputed whether any of the paintings of covered waggons depict Gardiner's visit to the Drakensberg in 1835, as they could equally represent other missionaries, traders or farmers of that period. It is certain, however, that they record, with a considerable amount of faithful detail, the intrusion of an entirely alien technology into the hunting grounds of the Bushmen during the mid-nineteenth century.[53]

References

1. A notable exception is the 1971 publication by J. B. Wright, *Bushman Raiders of the Drakensberg*, 1840-1870. Since the presentation of his thesis to the University of Natal in 1968, my own chapters have been abbreviated in order to avoid excessive duplication of detail.
2. Carter 1970 a, b.
3. Deacon 1972.
4. Parkington 1971.
5. Schweitzer & Scott 1973.
6. Phillipson 1969: 43.
7. Willcox 1956: 27; Davies 1951: 28.
8. Carter 1970 b.
9. Brookes & Webb 1965: 3.
10. Ergates 1905; McKenzie 1946.
11. Rock paintings vividly illustrating the rape of small, light-coloured Bushwomen by robust, dark-skinned African men were recorded from the Upper Mooi river by the late Col. E. Meinertzhagen (unpublished diary 1910), but recent attempts to relocate the site in the Kamberg area have not been successful.
12. Bryant 1929: 22.
13. Stanford 1958: 45.
14. Walton 1956a: 26-32; 1956b.
15. Stow 1905: 190, 229.
16. How 1962: 13.
17. Ellenberger 1912: 12.
18. Murray 1933.
19. Wells 1934; Galloway 1935-6; Beaumont 1967.
20. de Villiers 1968: 186-192.
21. Bourquin 1951.
22. Greenberg 1966: 66-84.
23. Lanham & Hallowes 1956; Anders 1935.
24. See also p. 37
25. Stow 1930: Pl. 28, 35, 36, 62 etc.
26. Callaway 1868: 353-5.
27. Brookes & Webb 1965: 4-6.
28. Isaacs 1836: 43, 75, 185.
29. MacKeurtan 1930: 157.
30. See also p. 104.
31. Gardiner 1836: 313.
32. Isaacs 1836: 185, 197.
33. Stevenson-Hamilton 1954: 77.
34. Personal communication, W. Barnes, 3/1/1967.
35. Personal communication, A. T. McClean, 28/1/1967.
36. See p. 32; also Wright 1971: 33, 62.
37. Boxer 1959; 69-70.
38. Fynn 1950: 230.
39. Gardiner 1836: 311.
40. McKenzie (1946), incorrectly identifies Agate Vale with the Mkhomazana river. Gardiner's very faithful illustration, however, is clearly drawn from the Pholela valley. Hodgson's Peaks, named after Thomas Hodgson who was accidentally shot in their vicinity in 1862, was originally named Giant's Cup by Gardiner in 1835.
41. Gardiner 1836: 343.
42. Drayson 1858: 110.
43. J. Shepstone Papers, Box 4, p. 63-5.
44. Gardiner 1836: 345.
45. I have not yet re-located the shelter described by Gardiner, therefore am unable to say whether or not it contains rock-paintings. Judging from the elevation of Gardiner's drawing of Cavernglen Mountain which is situated immediately south-west of Ramatseliso Nek, the site must have been on the Umtai or possibly the Mngeni tributaries of the Mzimvubu. It is noteworthy that, at a later date, other Drakensberg shelters which had recently been inhabited by Bushmen were described as being separated into compartments or stalls (See p. 78, 48).
46. Natal No. 2: 106; see also p. 29.
47. Alexander 1838 (2): 20.

Figure 13a *Site R6* (above)

Covered waggon in a shelter near the summit of the Bokberg, Mount Currie district. The complete span of oxen has unfortunately been erased by drip marks down the face of the rock.

Figure 13b *Site J21* (below)

A waggon driver wielding a whip urges along a tired ox. In the same shelter, there is the faded remains of another covered waggon with solid wheels, drawn by two oxen.

48. Sparrman 1876 (2) : 34.
49. Chapman 1868 (1) : 82.
50. Alexander 1838 (2) : 20.
51. Dornan 1917 : 84.
52. Alexander, *op. cit.*
53. The paintings of waggons in Natal and East Griqualand, though obviously of recent date, are very faint indeed, which suggests that the later paintings lacked adequate binding properties. This is in contrast to the waggon and coach paintings found in the Koue Bokkeveld in the Cape, where the medium of the later subjects seems to have the same retentive quality as that used in the earlier paintings (Johnson, Rabinowitz & Sieff 1959).
54. H. C. B. Wylde-Brown also took excellent photographs of rock paintings, but unfortunately his family did not retain his records. The original of the photograph reproduced here, which was in the album of the late M. C. Burkitt of Cambridge who visited South Africa in 1927, bears no caption other than: 'A Bushman — Punch — supposed to be aged 106, compared to a Zulu.' The estimated age of the Bushman is no doubt exaggerated. Mr. Wylde-Brown's daughter, Mrs M. Runwick, remembers seeing Punch when she was a young girl in the Weenen district, but she was unable to furnish any additional information.

A Bushman with the nickname Ruiter survived near Greytown until the turn of this century, but I have been unable to establish whether there was any connection between Punch and Ruiter. Ruiter spent his last years sheltering under half an iron tank on a vacant plot in Greytown near the present corner of Pine and Bell street, and was issued with provisions by the magistrate. He is remembered by early residents as being very small and wrinkled, but no-one knows his background. The voortrekker ancestors of Mr W. K. van Rooyen, of Greytown, brought a 'tame' Bushman with them when they arrived in Natal, as did other settlers (see Currlé 1910). It is possible, therefore, that old Ruiter was brought into Natal and subsequently abandoned by his employers, or he may have been a local survivor of a more numerous Bushman band that once inhabited the koppies in the vicinity of Muden where painted rock shelters have been recorded. (Site Z3; see also Farnden 1965).

For information on the Greytown Bushman, I am indebted to Mrs R. Wilson of *Glenside*, Underberg, and to Mrs J. M. Tatham, and Neish and Stella Tatham, who kindly made copies of notes by Mr A. Harris, Mrs C. Oliver, and Mr W. K. van Rooyen, all of Greytown.

Figure 14 *Site M7*

These armed and mounted settlers are painted on the boundary between Natal and East Griqualand. Notice the boots, the powder horns swinging from the waist, and the stirrup hanging below the stomach of the horse.

22

Boer and British Settlement

Prologue:

We were riding on an elevated spur of the Drakensberg near the Mooi river, when a Boer suddenly reined up his horse, and exclaimed;

"Cess, kek die spoor von verdamt Boschmon!"

Jumping off his horse, he examined the ground, and then said: "A man it is; one naked foot, the other with a veldschoen". The whole party immediately became intensely excited, they scattered in all directions like a pack of hounds in cover; some galloped to the nearest ridge, others followed on the spoor, all in search of the Bushman.

"He has not long gone", said one of my companions; "be ready".

"Ready for what?" I inquired.

"Ready to shoot the schelm."

"Would you shoot him?" I asked.

"Just so as I would a snake."[1, 2]

In December 1837, the Voortrekkers crossed the Drakensberg to explore the farming potential of Natal, and the permanent settlement which resulted hastened the end of the Mountain Bushmen. Already well accustomed to handling commandos against stock thieves, the Boers had been physically and mentally tempered by the rigours of frontier life, and when it came to protecting their 'rights' and their 'property', they believed in firm action. Almost immediately they ran into trouble with the Bushmen. Depredations on the farmers' stock commenced not six months after their arrival, and the familiar pattern of raid and retaliation, with which the Boers had had to contend in the Cape, dogged them to their new Republic. This friction is usually attributed to the Bushmen's resentment of intrusion into their hunting preserves, their lack of the pastoralist's concept of ownership, and their failure to distinguish between wild and domestic animals[3-7]. Prior to the Shaka wars, however, the land settled by the Boers had all been occupied by cattle-owning Bantu-speakers who had apparently remained on comparatively amicable terms with the Bushmen.[8] The introduction of domestic animals by the Boers was therefore nothing new to the Natal Bushmen, but whatever understanding they had reached with the black pastoralists was not extended to the white settlers. Aboriginal land claims had been ruthlessly disregarded ever since European settlement of the Cape in 1652, and by the time the Boers arrived in Natal almost two centuries later, antipathy was apparently already widely aroused.[9] When the farmers went on their annual hunts into the foothills of the Drakensberg to shoot game for curing as biltong,[10] they inevitably upset the Bushmen living within that area, but the situation was obviously complicated by factors other than the rights of a few scattered bands of Bushmen. Many of the raids against the Natal Boers were organised from great distances away, and tribes in addition to the Bushmen were involved. To what extent these depredations can be attributed to personal vendettas against the white intruders, or simply to lawless banditti, is difficult to assess. It is well established that many of the Bantu-speakers who had been rendered homeless by the chaotic events preceding the Great Trek, adopted cattle rustling as a way of life,[11] and the settlers' herds which often grazed unattended over vast areas of unfenced country became an obvious object of cupidity.

The only documentation available on the eastern Bushmen dates from this period of conflict. It is therefore biased in the extreme, consisting principally of bitter complaints of stock theft followed by official reports on the measures taken to retrieve the stolen property. The details are tediously repetitive. The Bushmen usually raided under cover of darkness or bad weather and retreated to the mountains with herds of up to 300 cattle and horses. The farmers were invariably caught unawares, and often did not detect the losses until many hours or even days had elapsed. When they followed the trail of the stolen stock, usually assisted by Africans and later by contingents of British soldiers or police, they seldom met with success. At best they would return with a few animals that had strayed from the herd, and usually they never so much as caught sight of the thieves. On the few occasions when the farmers did overtake the depredators, their feeling of frustrated impotence was aggravated by the Bushman's habit of maliciously stabbing the animals to death rather than allowing them to fall into the hands of their owners. Between 1840 and 1872, the heyday of the raids, there are only five recorded instances of the Bushmen being surprised and wounded, captured or killed by punitive parties, but no doubt many exploits were never accounted for officially.

The Bushmen connected with stock thefts in Natal can be divided into two main groups: those who harassed farmers living on the northern tributaries of the Thukela and who retreated over the escarpment towards northern Lesotho and the Orange Free State, and those who raided farms on the southern Thukela, the Mngeni and the Mkhomazi.[12] The latter group of Bushmen retreated with their booty to the upper reaches of the Mkhomazi, Mzimkhulu and Mzimvubu rivers as well as to the eastern and southern regions of Lesotho. This is exactly the area covered by the present survey. A count of the paintings located within these river valleys establishes that a high proportion of the animals depicted are domestic rather than wild, and it is here rather than in the more northern parts of the escarpment that scenes relating to the period of settlement by white colonists have been found. The stock raids as such are therefore very relevant to the paintings, and for this reason, details of selected incursions are included in this text. The purpose is not to give a chronological inventory of all the depredations reported, but rather to set the atmosphere in which the later Bushman artists executed their work, and to abstract information which sheds light on their way of life at this time.

By December 1840 the Boers had suffered nine consecutive thefts from the Weenen and Mkhomazi districts, and more than 700 head of cattle and 50 horses were reported missing. Eventually the Volksraad, desperately trying to impose some control on the unruly Boers, could ignore the demands for retribution no longer, and a full-scale commando of 260 mounted men was organised. The spoor of the stolen animals had always led in the same direction, southwards and westwards, and by enlisting the help of local Africans, the Boers had established that the robbers were a group of 'plundering and bloodthirsty' Bushmen who lived in caves not far from the kraals of the Bhaca chief Ngcaphayi on the sources of the Mzimvubu river. Ngcaphayi was known to be a daring and warlike freebooter whose tribe was strengthened by deserters from the Zulu, and who made raids on all the surrounding tribes. The people of Ngcaphayi were reported to participate in, if not organise, these raids by the Bushmen, and their incursions led them as far afield as the Cape frontier, as well as to the Natal Boers.[13] The commando, after singing psalms and praying that they be granted strength, power and understanding to perform their duty, sallied across the Mzimkhulu river. *En route* southwards, their numbers were swelled by about 100 members of the Nhlangwini under chief Fodo, on the understanding that they would receive a share of the booty. Faku, chief of the Pondo, confirmed that Ngcaphayi was in league with the Bushmen who, it was said, took possession of the horses captured from the Boers, while the cattle were retained by the Bhaca. Without further ado, the Boers turned in vengeance on the Bhaca. When the commando withdrew, they left some 150 Bhaca dead in the field, and took with them a booty of 3 000 head of cattle as well as great flocks of sheep and goats and seventeen 'apprentice' children to work as servants. The Bushmen, who were thought to have been responsible for the initial thefts, escaped without injury.

During the attack on Ngcaphayi, Fodo and his Nhlangwini were left in the rear, and misunderstanding later arose about their share of the booty. The Boers also suspected Fodo of complicity with the Bushmen, as the stolen stock must have been driven through his territory with his full knowledge. This may well have been true, since the Nhlangwini are known to have had trading alliances with the Bushmen only six years beforehand.[14] In any event, Fodo denied all knowledge of the thefts, which enraged the Boers, and as a punishment they tied him to a waggon wheel and flogged him with twenty-five lashes on the back.[15]

The Boer aggressions had far-reaching repercussions, not only in establishing antagonism among those Africans who were allies of the Bushmen, but also in precipitating British intervention in their affairs. Although there were other reasons involved, it is usually forgotten that the Bushmen played an important if indirect role in bringing about the downfall of the Boer Republic in Natal.[16]

The Republic submitted to the Crown in 1843, but the new Government was a long time taking over control. Meanwhile, the Volksraad continued to govern, and the Bushmen continued to harry the farmers. In 1842 the Commandant-General dedicated himself anew to seek out the kraals of the Bushmen who were 'on a par with vermin in destruction and rapacity', but few details of these activities survive.[17]

On the farm *Beersheba* in Mount Currie district, East Griqualand, there is a highly descriptive but poignant cartoon, as seen through the eyes of the Bushmen themselves, of one of these punitive commandos. The wide-brimmed hats, beards, flint-lock muzzle-loader guns and powder horns leave little doubt as to the identity of the majority of the pursuers. Riders with long feathers in their hats or no headgear at all, or who carry assegais, are possibly Boer retainers known as 'agterryers'. Many of these were Hottentot or Bushman captives brought by the Boers to Natal.[18] (Figure 15)

The picture illustrates, with much faithful detail, a mounted commando of about 27 men who have caught up with a band of some 16 Bushmen making off with a troop of horses and cattle. An indistinct and headless carcase of an ox near the centre of the group where various items of paraphernalia lie around, suggests that the Bushmen had probably stopped for a meal when they were surprised by the irate owners of the stolen stock. Some of the farmers

Figure 15a   *Site M9*

The commando scene on Beersheba farm, East Griqualand. Irate farmers fire on Bushmen who have raided horses and cattle. (See text for full description; also Willcox 1963, Plate 3, for colour photograph of same scene). The total height of the scene is 110 cm.

Tracing made in 1960 with assistance from Lorna Peirson and Jean Hewlett.

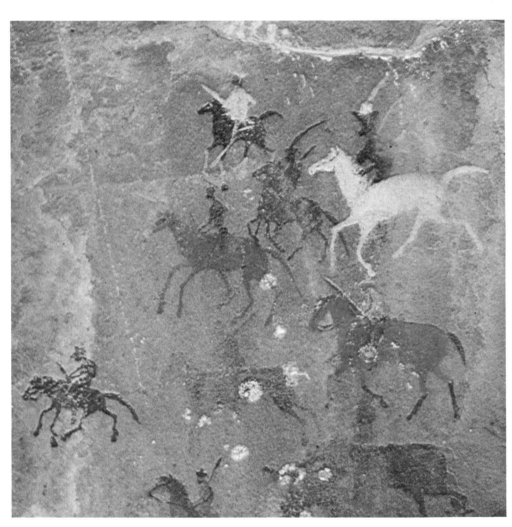

Figure 15b

A photograph of the lower left part of the scene shown as a tracing in Figure 15a. Horsemen have dismounted in order to fire at Bushman depredators. The central Bushman, who holds a bow, has apparently suffered a double wound: the lines of fire from the Boers' rifles strike an arm and a leg. The paintings to the right are very faint as a result of water seepage. (See also Lee and Woodhouse 1970, Figures 246, 247, 248.)

Figure 15c

Photographic detail of horsemen in upper section of scene. Most of the riders wear hats, some decorated with long feathers, but the black figure on a red horse at centre left is bare-headed and bare-legged and does not carry a gun. The other horseman on a red mount is apparently European; he wears a white slouch hat and black trousers, and his gun rests on the pommel of the saddle. In the original painting, details of white buttons on his pink jacket are visible on close inspection. Notice the bearded figure with a spear over his shoulder at lower left. Some of the paintings are in danger of becoming obliterated by a chemical deposit resulting from water seepage.

dismount to take careful aim, others, Boer fashion, shoot directly from the saddle. Long white streaks issuing from the barrels mark the flight of the bullets; some of these lead to somersaulting or upturned Bushmen who were obviously left as dead or dying. All is chaos. Dejected and bewildered cattle mill around, some apparently wounded, while others are already straying homewards. Beyond the melée of cattle and horses, naked Bushmen with bows and hunting bags in hand flee for their lives, legs extended as far as they will go, and with heads turned over their shoulders to watch the line of fire. But the pursuers do not have it all their own way. Near the animal carcase where one unfortunate Bushman already lies dead, a comrade has turned on the farmers, and with bow in hand, has directed six arrows in quick succession against the guns. Lines radiating upwards from the heads of the Bushmen suggest arrows carried in a fillet for rapid and easy access.

While it is certain that not all successful exploits against the Bushmen were recorded in official documents, there are written accounts of three episodes which could be associated with this graphic painting, one of which corresponds with the details more convincingly than the others.

Early in January, 1847, a commando of 17 Boers and five Cape Mounted Riflemen overtook and fired upon a party of seven Bushmen driving stolen stock up a tributary of the Lotheni river.[19] No casualties were reported,[20] and neither the site, the details, nor the numbers depicted in the painted group coincide with this incident.

Another episode took place in February 1852 when 300 cattle, stolen from a farm on the Bushman's river, were hotly pursued.[20] All were retaken except one cow which the Bushmen had killed and were eating when they were surprised. No mention is made of fatalities, and from the curt account in the local newspaper,[21] it is not clear who participated in the chase, nor where the encounter took place. The Bushmen were apparently not much daunted by the proceedings, for after losing the first capture, they promptly returned and carried off a large herd of horses. The painting on *Beersheba* shows both cattle and horses among the captured stock, and the Bushmen have certainly suffered fatalities. An added point of uncertainty is that in both 1847 and 1852, commandos would have included Cape Mounted Riflemen as well as Boers. Although the painted scene at first sight appears to represent men in uniform, the details do not bear out this interpretation. The uniform of the Cape Mounted Riflemen consisted of black trousers and a dark green stable jacket, whereas the Bushmen depicted black jackets and red trousers, or conversely red jackets and black trousers, in what is apparently a completely random choice of colour. (See also Figures 14, 39, 40)

The majority of the commando wear slouch hats and ride with long stirrups typical of the Boers, and in addition, the Boers trained their horses to stand still when the reins hung down on the ground. By contrast, the British cavalry always held the reins looped over the arm. The Bushman artist has represented all the dismounted horses in this scene with reins hanging down. Furthermore, all the guns depicted are long-barrelled flint-lock muskets known as 'roers' by the Boers. When the flint struck the frizzen, a flash of smoke from the pan resulted, which was accentuated in old and well-worn guns. As early as 1835, the Cape Mounted Riflemen were issued with short-barrelled percussion lock carbines, from which no flash from the pan would be visible. In the painted scene, it will be noted that an upward puff of smoke exploding in front of the marksmen's heads is in each case clearly represented. It would seem, therefore, that the majority of details are in support of the commando consisting of Boers accompanied by their 'agterryers'.[22]

It is of note that part of the evidence presented by the Boers in justification of their attack on the Bhaca under Ngcaphayi reads:

> One of our patrols overtook some Bushmen with stolen stock, of whom several were killed, and they were mostly accompanied by Kaffirs, one of whom the patrol caught who belonged to Ncaphayi . . . ; the patrol on this occasion also followed the spoor to within sight of Ncaphayi's kraals.

Since Ngcaphayi resided on the Mzimvubu river in what is now East Griqualand, the painting on *Beersheba* might well have been on the route of this commando.

The minutes of the Volksraad record that Jacobus Uys was scheduled to lead a commando against the Bushmen on the 20th April, 1840, and he subsequently reported the result on the 8th June. This was approved by the Raad, but since the full report cannot be found, the possible link between the Uys commando and the painted scene must remain conjectural.[23] The date of the painting can, however, almost certainly be limited to within the period 1836-1845 when the Boers ran their own affairs in Natal, and is more likely to be associated with the earlier years than the later.

Carefully guarded documents containing the exploits of the pioneers of European settlement in Natal against the Bushmen, written in faded ink on yellowing paper, can still be perused within the brick and concrete walls of the Government Archives in the Province's capital city. Of no less historical interest is the unprotected record, faithfully delineated in paint by an unknown hand, on the rocks of a hidden gully on the Gongununu river in East Griqualand.

A touching addendum to the commando scene was provided by the Gilson brothers, owners of the property on which the paintings occur, when in 1945 they located a Bushman skeleton in a crouched position in a niche between boulders near the shelter.[24] The body had apparently not been intentionally buried. The facts behind the death of this Bushman can only be conjectural, but a number of possibilities readily spring to mind. Did the skeleton belong to one of the victims of the commando? Was the artist perhaps one of those fatally wounded? Was the scene he recorded with such poignant and precise detail the last thing he did before he crawled away and died in a niche among the rocks, his compatriots having fled for their lives?

The British take over

It was not until the end of 1845 that settled institutions of government under a Lieutenant-Governor were established by the British in Natal. By this time the Boers were thoroughly dismayed at the lack of protection against Africans and Bushmen alike, and with their dislike of British rule, were beginning to gravitate back across the Drakensberg into the interior.[25]

The first despatches sent by the new Lieutenant-Governor of Natal to the Governor of the Cape contained a request for more troops to deal with the Bushman problem.[26] The new régime had scarcely taken breath before reports came in of raids, including one on a farm in the present Elandskop district when the Bushmen made off with about forty horses.[27] A later theft of cattle from property in the Mkhomazi valley was followed up the north bank of the Mzimkhulu river by a combined party of farmers and Africans. From the smallness of the footprints, it was judged that the stock had been driven by a group of from two to four Bushmen. High in the mountains, the tracks turned southwards towards Faku's territory, and the chase was abandoned.[28] The following month, March 1846, the Bushmen delivered another blow in the Elandskop district when their objective was again horses.[29] The Boers were galled by these

Figure 16 *Site M9*

The Beersheba *commando scene is painted in the small overhang in the shadow on the right. Scale is indicated by a human figure standing outside the shelter, and another figure crossing the Gongununu stream. A Bushman skeleton was found in the scrub near the overhang.*
Round the corner made by the stream, and out of sight in this picture, another larger rock shelter shows signs of previous occupation. Stone artefacts and fragments of bone and pottery lie strewn on the ashy floor. In summer, the sides of this secluded glen are blue with Agapanthus *flowers.*

Photo: Gedys Vinnicombe.

losses and complained bitterly to the authorities, but the impecunious and ill-equipped government, realising that it lacked the means to effectively prevent the robberies, tried to foist the responsibility onto chief Faku of the Pondo.[30] After repeated requests to restore the stolen property or surrender the culprits, Faku eventually protested that he held no authority over the Bushmen, and had no means of either pursuing or punishing them.[31]

Meanwhile, some enlightening information was obtained by two Boers, Jacobus and Dirk Uys, when they journeyed across Pondoland in June 1846. While outspanned among mountains about nine waggon-days' journey from Pietermaritzburg,[32] their camp was visited by a Bushman leader named Mdwebo[33] and his son Qinti, accompanied by about 30 followers, who were all mounted and armed. Amongst the horses, the Uys brothers recognised three of their own; two that had been stolen nine years previously between the Kraai and Orange rivers near the Witteberg in the Cape Colony, and one six years previously at the Mkhomazi river, Natal. They also identified two cows belonging to the farmer who had lost stock from the Mkhomazi valley a few months previously, as well as three snaffle bridles taken at the same time. More stock could be discerned on a distant hill in the direction from which the Bushmen had come. The two farmers, accompanied by a Hottentot waggon-driver who acted as interpreter, pretended that they were associated with the Transkei missionaries rather than with the Natal Boers, and thereby avoided any confrontation.

Mdwebo, whose band included a number of Africans, said his people had no fixed place of residence, but that they wandered about from place to place. They were eager to exchange ivory for pots, tinderboxes, guns and ammunition. One of the Bushmen carried a soldier's musket, at this date almost certainly a flint-lock, but in addition they requested detonating caps. When asked for what purpose, the Bushmen claimed to own a percussion rifle, at that time not in common use among civilians,[34] which was said to have been obtained from a murdered trader.[35, 36]

This evidence, if dependable, indicates that by 1846 certain of the Mountain Bushmen had developed far beyond a simple Stone Age existence. They owned horses and were accomplished riders, they were acquainted with various European trade goods, and they possessed and apparently understood the use of different types of fire-arms. With Bantu-speaking adherents, they were banded together under a recognised leader, and had been organising widespread stock raids for at least nine years.

The Boers were not unaware of the extent of these forays, for prior to their attack on Ngcaphayi in 1840, they claimed that the Bushmen residing among the Bhaca plundered the Cape borders as well as the Natal farmers.[37] Similar views were expressed in a Boer newspaper early in 1845 when a robbery in the Thukela area was thought to have been committed by a gang of Bushmen from the Witteberg.[38]

Like the North American Indians, the Mountain Bushmen were quick to appreciate the advantages of horses and fire-arms, and there is much evidence of their eagerness to acquire mounts during the period of early European settlement in Natal. In addition to the thefts already cited, the Boer leader Andries Pretorius was obliged to abandon one of his farms when 22 horses were stolen in one fell swoop,[39] and on a night in June 1846, a party of four Bushmen with only one horse between them made a determined attempt to make good their needs by breaking into a locked stable on the Bushman's River. They eventually resorted to digging out the door frame, but the noise awoke a farmhand who frightened them off by firing a gun. Thus thwarted, the aspirant equestrians retreated towards a drift on the upper Mkhomazi river.[40]

Apart from stock raids, another problem that vexed the newly established government was the influx of Africans into the farming areas previously thought to be uninhabited. Andries Pretorius aired the grievances of his people in a series of letters to the authorities. In addition to the fear of being swamped by an 'ocean of Kaffirs', he claimed that between 1 000 and 1 200 head of cattle had been taken from the Boers since their arrival in Natal in 1838, and as a direct result of Bushman depredations, all the farms south of the Mkhomazi river and west of the road leading northwards to the Orange Free State had been deserted. Since Uys had actually seen stolen animals in the possession of certain Bushmen, Pretorius hoped that decisive steps would be taken 'to rid us once and for all of this cancer'. His letter to the Lieutenant-Governor reads:

> Let the males who may resist be killed, and the others placed in the service of the people, that they may thereby be brought to civilisation instead of subsisting by plunder and murder. By doing so, much good will be effected . . . .
>
> I place every confidence in your Honour, that you will go to work deliberately, firmly, and with activity, so that time which is costly for Natal will not be lost.[41, 42]

It was not long before the attitude of the new régime was put to the test. In September, fresh traces of Bushmen were observed on a footpath between the Thukela river and the source of the Mkhomazi.[43] Being forewarned, the farmers were able to thwart an attempt to make off with their cattle, but the thieves did not disperse, for later an African suddenly came upon a party of about ten marauders from whom he narrowly escaped. Despite the reference to 'Bushmen' in the report, three of the party were identified as members of a Bantu-speaking tribe said to be recognisable by the distinctive skin caps they wore.[44] This is further evidence of the hybrid nature of the Bushman bands at this time.

It was presumably this band of mixed peoples who struck at a farm in the Karkloof area a few days later, and successfully drove off 38 oxen and eight horses. Obliged to follow the spoor on foot because all their mounts had been taken, the owners of the stock found the track which led towards the upper Mkhomazi valley littered with animals stabbed to death or cruelly maimed, and the chase was finally abandoned because of a snowstorm. The unfortunate farmers, whose whole means of subsistence had been lost, appealed to the Lieutenant-Governor for help and protection.[45]

A commando of about 30 men was immediately ordered out, the Government offering to provide tents and to pay tariff for each horse and waggon employed. The Bushmen in Faku's territory were suspected, and Jacobus Uys who had lately seen them there, offered to accompany the commando. Nevertheless, a sufficient force could not be mustered as all the horses were in poor condition following on the winter. In any case, the Government was still hopeful of obtaining redress for the robberies from Faku without itself incurring effort or expense. As an interim measure, a small party under Jacobus Uys was sent off to find out where the robbers lived.

The mission, led by Uys, was instructed to establish friendly communications with the Bushmen, and to persuade them to settle in a permanent location. Although Uys was given strict injunctions to avoid all hostilities, the proposed commando was held in readiness to act, if necessary, on the information obtained.[46, 47] It was, therefore, with no great hope of success that the reconnaissance 'peace mission' set out to parley with the Bushmen in the spring of 1846.[48, 49]

The interpreter for the party of four was John Shepstone, a newcomer to Natal then only nineteen years of age, who was destined to play a leading role in future campaigns against the Bushmen. His reminiscences of this errand, written in the shaky hand of old age, provide some invaluable though frustratingly incomplete details.[50,51]

Travelling westwards from the present situation of Ixopo town, John Shepstone describes the country as wild and full of game, specifically mentioning buffalo, lion and herds of eland. In East Griqualand, the party came upon traces of Bushmen. Impromptu huts, erected in small patches of forest and consisting of no more than a few branches tied together with grass rope, showed no attempt at comfort. The sides were open, and the top, though roughly covered with grass, was not sufficient to withstand the rain. They also saw signal fires and found patches of burnt grass, a sure indication, claimed Shepstone, of the presence of Bushmen, but the hunters themselves kept out of the way.

Eventually, after several weeks, the mission glimpsed human beings in the distance, and after waving, Shepstone and Uys rode up unarmed. They found about four Bushmen all well armed with bows ready strung and with a good supply of poisoned arrows in the sheaths that hung from their shoulders. Shepstone was able to exchange a few words with the Bushmen in the Xhosa language, which they understood, and while the conversation was taking place, several other armed Bushmen joined the party. The Europeans, who felt decidedly uncomfortable in what could have proved a hostile situation, uneasily suggested that the Bushmen should accompany them back to where their camp was pitched on the Ibisi river. This the Bushmen gladly did, and on arrival at the camp, one of the hunters moved into an open space and began signalling with a small skin cloak which he had tied round his neck. When asked what he was doing, he replied that he was telling his comrades upon the hillside that the visiting party was friendly, and that they could come down. Although Shepstone could see no-one, six or seven more Bushmen soon joined the original party. Their old chief, Mdwebo, was also present, therefore the Government representatives opened the subject of their mission without further ado. They requested the Bushmen to abandon their nomadic habits, and to settle instead in a specific part of the country which the Government would set aside for their use. The Bushmen politely replied that it would be impossible for them to comply with this request; not only did they like the roving life, but their livelihood depended upon following the migrations of game. After being given presents of such items as rugs, beads and knives, the Bushmen invited the European contingent to see where their women and children were camped only about a mile distant.

Shepstone described the Bushmen as small but active people, the tallest of the men being no more than five feet. In conversation

Figure 17 *Site P5*

The hunter on the left appears to be signalling with a skin cloak (1:1 detail from the scene reproduced in Figure 153).

Figure 18

Seated figures are working with arrows, while bows, quivers, bags and a skin cloak lie near at hand. This is part of a group of exfoliated paintings south of the survey area. The shelter is in East Griqualand near the Lesotho border at Qacha's Nek. John Shepstone saw Bushmen in East Griqualand licking their arrows to make the poison adhere firmly, and this activity is probably depicted at lower left.

their eyes were restless, giving the impression of always being on the alert, and when game was sighted (Shepstone mentions jackals and buck), they would rush off in pursuit and invariably secure it. Shepstone also saw the Bushmen applying poison to their arrows; in order to smooth it off and make it adhere firmly, they would lick it with their tongues with no ill effect.[52] (Figure 18). The only form of clothing seen among the Bushmen was a simple covering made from the skins of small antelope, but none were sewn together to make a larger blanket or kaross. One of the women, on being questioned about strips of eland hide seen hanging up, demonstrated how they could be used for food in an emergency. She first threw the hide into the fire to make it crisp, and after cooling it, pounded it into powder with a stone. She mixed the resultant meal with water in a small pot, and while the mixture

boiled on an open fire, stirred it until a thick gelatinous substance was produced. This was eaten as a meat substitute.[53]

Jacobus Uys, who gives additional information on the mission, reported a total of fourteen men in the band, no less than nine of whom carried European fire-arms. These guns, it was ascertained, had been bartered from Dick King, the trader in Port Natal who had accompanied Gardiner on his inland trip in 1835.[54] The guns had been exchanged for horses, the rate being one horse for one gun. In addition, the Bushmen had traded 50 elephant tusks for gunpowder and lead.[55]

These reports, based on one of the few non-hostile contacts ever made between Europeans and the aboriginal hunters of Natal and Pondoland, provide an invaluable insight into contemporary conditions among the Bushmen. Their contacts were many. Not only were they conversant with the Xhosa language, so proving close contact with their Nguni neighbours, but they were also actively engaged in the European arms and ivory trade, exchanging tusks and stolen horses for guns and ammunition. In the daily or seasonal course of events, they built rude huts, used pots for cooking, and during the spring at least, wore but scant skin clothing. They also practised grass-burning to attract game, yet despite the apparent abundance of wild life, a constant supply of fresh meat was not always available, and emergency rations had to be resorted to in times of need. They could also convey messages from a distance by signalling with skin cloaks or with smoke, an observation independently confirmed by a Thembu fugitive who lived among the Bushmen for some years.[56] But of their paintings there is no mention, and a golden opportunity to obtain answers to some of the questions which sorely perplex the student of art and anthropology today was irretrievably lost.

Since the old chief Mdwebo is again mentioned in these accounts, the party of Bushmen interviewed must have been members of the same group as that seen by Jacobus Uys and his brother three months previously. It seems anomalous that at that time, during the winter, the Bushmen were mounted and in possession of stolen stock, yet in the spring no reference is made to either horses or cattle. In fact, Shepstone expressed the opinion that the Bushmen he saw were not stock thieves. A possible explanation is that the Bushmen's activities were seasonal, living on the proceeds of the chase during the summer and on the proceeds of stock raids during the leaner winter months. Countering this explanation is the fact that a list of all the documented thefts shows them to have been more frequent during summer than winter.[57] It is uncertain, therefore, whether the lack of incriminating evidence during the spring encounter was due to genuine innocence or clever management on the part of the Bushmen, who were doubtless fully aware of the presence of Europeans in their area long before the actual meeting took place. It is known from later evidence that the Pondoland Bushmen not only bartered the animals they stole for other effects, but that they also had an arrangement whereby their stock was kraaled among the neighbouring Bhaca.[58] It may well be, therefore, that their animals were simply elsewhere while the mission was parleying, and the spring season was always the time of year when Bushmen were enticed from a sedentary way of life back to their traditional hunting and gathering.[59]

One positive outcome of the 'peace' mission was that two of the Bushmen agreed to accompany Uys and Shepstone back to Pietermaritzburg to see the Lieutenant-Governor in person. One of these Bushmen represented Mdwebo, while the other represented Qangi, an old Bushman whose band habitually linked up with Mdwebo. Unfortunately there is no record of the negotiations that followed, nor of the Bushmen's reaction to what they saw in the colony's capital. After a fortnight, they were given more presents and were sent back with an invitation to Mdwebo to pay a visit to the seat of Government, a request with which he did in fact comply eight months later.[60-63]

The Lieutenant-Governor was obviously in a cleft stick. On the one hand the Boers threatened to leave Natal unless active measures were taken to stop the cattle thefts, while on the other, the Government was disinclined and ill-equipped to repress the aggressions by force.[64] The Lieutenant-Governor's two-pronged approach to the problem reflected his quandary. During the same month that he interviewed the Bushman envoys, he authorised the expenditure of £116.19.8¾ for the establishment of a temporary military barracks to check their depredations. The peace mission to the Bushmen cost only £44.11s.[65]

The site selected for the military post was the farm of old Van Vuuren on the Boesmansrand near Elandskop, and the Boers hailed the decision with enthusiastic co-operation. They offered to accompany patrols until the soldiers were acquainted with the footpaths and knew the spots from which to reconnoitre, and Andries Pretorius made the usual practical, if wily, suggestions. He advised that, while keeping watch for the approach of thieves, the patrols should never climb to the hill-tops, as silhouetted against the sky they would

easily be detected and avoided by the sharp-eyed Bushmen. The soldiers should give the impression that they were hunters rather than an armed force, and should take especial care to camouflage their bright arms which reflected the sun and could be seen from a great distance. He also recommended that Africans living in the neighbourhood should be instructed to report the movements of the Bushmen. If this were done, Pretorius said, the farmers who had lost all hope would be encouraged to remain in Natal, and the Boer exodus would be halted.[66, 67]

The Bushmen were not deterred by these preparations. In December, more than 24 cattle were driven from a farm in the Karkloof area. The trail, which included the footprints of three Bushmen and two Africans, led first towards the Mooi river, and thence to a spot near the source of the Mkhomazi known as *The Stable*.[68] The farmers and Africans who followed the traces found stabbed animals on the way, but heavy rains hampered further pursuit. It was therefore proposed that, with the next full moon, a party of about twenty Boers and a few British dragoons should endeavour to recover the cattle.[69] Walter Harding, the Crown Prosecutor, was put in charge of the commando, and was accompanied by John Shepstone who had latterly returned from the 'peace mission' to the Bushmen. Further re-inforcements were obtained from chief Lugaju, but whereas the rest of the commando was mounted, the auxiliaries were on foot and armed only with assegais.[70]

Meanwhile, forty-eight more oxen were taken from a property on the Mooi river. Yet again, the Mkhomazi was the destination, and after finding a partly eaten beast on the tracks, the farmers located twenty-six of the stolen oxen hidden in thick bush.[71]

Walter Harding and his party were immediately alerted, and without delay, two patrols set out in an attempt to intercept the robbers and to guard the passes leading over the mountains at the sources of the Mkhomazi. Although tremendous rains flooded the rivers and caused considerable inconvenience, this meant that the retreat of the thieves was also barred. On a tributary of the Lotheni river, one of the patrols surprised a party of seven Bushmen with the stolen oxen. When they found they were being overtaken, the thieves began stabbing the cattle, but dispersed when fired upon from long range. No casualties were reported, and the Bushmen fled into the mountains where it was impossible to follow.

Despite continuous rain, Harding, acting on the advice of Andries Pretorius, determined to continue the chase under the guise of a hunting party. But the Boers were discontented. In addition to the trying weather, they complained that their horses were fatigued, that they had harvests to reap, and that the Bushmen who had escaped would soon return to steal more cattle. They felt they had a right to government protection without having to participate themselves, and they resented that the British dragoons were paid for their services, whereas the farmers received nothing.[72-75] The commando soon broke up, and the members turned homeward.

In the upper reaches of the Lotheni river, overlooking a tributary locally known as the Xalweni, there is a sandstone shelter containing a painted group of twenty-two horses and riders all determinedly heading in the same direction. Harding's force to the upper Lotheni consisted of five Cape Mounted Riflemen and seventeen Boers, a total of twenty-two.[76] Although not all the horsemen visible in the scene are convincingly European, the close correspondence between the painted scene and the documentation, both in respect of venue and numbers, suggests that the Bushman artist may well have witnessed and depicted the Harding commando of early January, 1847. (Figure 19)

News of Harding's success against the Bushmen evoked at least one unexpected response. While the British forces were again on the offensive, this time against chief Fodo of the Nhlangwini who had attacked and killed some Bhaca, a Bushman chief named Yele visited the military camp on the Mkhomazi river. Yele had heard of the recent expedition against the Bushmen on the upper reaches of the Mkhomazi, and was afraid he might suffer similar punishment. Yele wished to make it clear that he had been living near the mouth of the Mzumbi river for the past eight years, that his band of ten men including some 'Bushman kaffirs', had all married 'kaffir' women, that they bred cattle, cultivated the ground, and only occasionally went on hunting trips. He mentioned that Qangi, the old Bushman chief who usually wandered about the country with Mdwebo, also wanted to join his settlement. Yele was assured of his safety, and because it was thought that the services of his people might prove useful to Government in future operations against the robber Bushmen, he was asked to visit the Lieutenant-Governor in Pietermaritzburg.[77, 78] Although there is no record of either Yele or Qangi having done so, in May 1847 Mdwebo presented himself at the capital. This may have been as a result of consultations with Yele and Qangi, but may also have been in response to the invitation carried back to him by his envoy in November of the previous year. The object of Mdwebo's visit was formally to request a perma-

nent place to settle within the Colony, and he was directed to locate himself near the mouth of the Mzimkhulu river. The report mentions that this terrain was already occupied by another band of Bushmen who had begun to cultivate ground and keep domestic stock; presumably this refers to the heterogeneous people under Yele.[79] The only other official reference to this settlement was made when the first taxes were collected from natives living in the Mkhomazi and Mzimkhulu divisions of Natal in December 1849, when Theophilus Shepstone reported:

> A kraal of Bushmen also presented their taxes, and as they have been quietly residing in the District for upwards of ten years and regularly till the ground under a native chief, I received them.[80]

Whether or not Mdwebo and his people ever made the adjustment to a more settled way of life is uncertain. His son, at any rate, continued to roam about the countryside. In 1848, a year after his father was granted a location, he was mentioned as a participant in a marauding party that visited the Mngeni river,[81] and in 1852, he gave evidence to H. F. Fynn in Pondoland.[82] However, the name of a mission station called Endwebu in Location No. 8 on the upper Mzumbi river suggests that the old man, with at least some of his followers, may have succumbed to the process of civilisation.

The archival records point to the considerable amount of acculturation that had taken place among some of the Natal Bushmen by the middle of the nineteenth century. While strong Khoisan strains may perhaps still be detected among the present Bantu-speaking inhabitants of the numerous Locations near the mouths of the Mzumbi and Mzimkhulu rivers, the Bushmen, as a distinct entity, have been completely absorbed. An abundance of 'Later Stone Age' sites nevertheless testifies to the fact that this lowland terrain bordering on the sea had been inhabited by hunter-gatherers long before the arrival of Bantu-speakers,[83, 84] and a rock shelter excavated at the turn of the century yielded Bushmanoid remains from a considerable depth.[85] There are also several rock painting sites in this area (Z1, 2, 4, 5, 7, 8, 9), one of which symbolises in visual form the imposition of iron age on stone age: a series of battle-axes are superimposed on earlier paintings of buck.[86] Domestic animals, however, are nowhere represented. Whether this suggests that the rock paintings were essentially related to a hunting economy and became redundant after the adoption of pastoralism, is a matter of debate and speculation.

Figure 19 *Site B7, upper Lotheni*

In January 1847, a commando of twenty-two horsemen led by Walter Harding surprised and fired at a party of Bushmen in the upper Lotheni. There are twenty-two horses in this scene. Some of the riders have faded completely.

The existence of these paintings first came to my notice through a copy made by the late Mary Young in the early 1930's and now housed in the Natal Museum. The

shelter was subsequently re-located by Don Allison, great-grandson of Captain Albert Allison who led a commando against the Bushmen in 1869.

The tracing reproduced here was made in 1959, and comparison with the copy made thirty years previously shows little or no deterioration.

References

NOTE: For abbreviations used for official manuscripts see p. 368.

1. Captain A. W. Drayson, in Wood 1874: 299.
2. The archaic Afrikaans in this quotation has been left as it appears in the original text which was written by a British soldier.
3. Bleek 1924: vii.
4. Stow 1905: 39, 215.
5. Walker 1957: 34.
6. Willcox 1956: 29.
7. Willcox 1963: 21.
8. See p. 10.
9. Marks 1972.
10. Drayson 1858: 110.
11. Lye 1967.
12. S.N.A. 1/1/1, No. 29, 4/7/1849.
13. *Natal No. 1*: 370.
14. See p. 12.
15. *Natal No. 1*: 390; C.S.O. 19, p. 70, 28/9/1849.
16. Cory 1926 (4): 121.
17. *Natal No. 1*: 150, 403.
18. Dart 1923-26; Currlé 1910.
19. See pp. 34, 35.
20. See Wright 1971: 106.
21. *Natal Independent*, 26/2/1852.
22. I am indebted to Major G. Tylden for information and useful discussion on the identification of the members of this commando.
23. *Natal No. 1*: 42, 46.
24. This skeleton was taken to the Natal Museum, Pietermaritzburg, but can no longer be located. The Gilson brothers described the bones as being small, like those of a juvenile, yet the teeth were heavily abraded like those of an older person.
25. *Natal No. 2*: xix.
26. Cory 1926 (4): 207.
27. *Natalier* 26/12/1845.
28. C.S.O. 11(2), No. 168, 18/2/1846.
29. C.S.O. 11(2), No. 174, 15/3/1846.
30. *Natal No. 2*: 109-110.
31. C.S.O. 11(2), p. 197-200, 9/10/1846.
32. The name of the mountain where the Uys brothers camped is given as Blesboksberg in one document, and Bokboksberg in another, and was said to be south of the Tafoela river. Although these place-names no longer apply, the mountains could possibly be the Bokberg in the Mount Currie district, East Griqualand, where there is a drawing of an ox-drawn waggon (site R6). The Bokberg, near Tafelkop, is not far from the sources of the Ibisi river where Mdwebo and his band were again encountered by J. Uys three months later (See p. 30).
33. The name of this Bushman leader is variously spelt Debu, Dwebu, Umdwebo, Mdwebu and Mdwebo.
34. Tylden 1957; personal communication March 1968.
35. *Natal No. 2*: 106, 109.
36. Fynn Papers No. 19 25/9/1850, 1/10/1852.
37. *Natal No. 1*: 370.
38. *Natalier*, 1/1/1845.
39. C.S.O. 37(1), No. 34, 6/8/1846.
40. C.S.O. 11(2), p. 175, 3/7/1846.
41. C.S.O. 37(1), 16/7/1846.
42. C.S.O. 34, 6/8/1846.
43. The fact that a footpath already existed between these two river systems at this date suggests that a route along the contours of the Little Berg was habitually used by Bushmen. Eland too, as opposed to other game, prefer to move across steep ground by following contours rather than gradients. (Personal communication C. W. Abbott, 1973).
44. C.S.O. 11(2), p. 188, 17/9/1846.
45. *Natal No. 2*: 107.
46. G. H. 1321, No. 69.
47. *Natal No. 2*: 6, 7.
48. Bulpin 1953: 141.
49. Willcox 1956: 38.
50. See also Willcox 1956: 34-38.
51. Wright 1971: 60-61.
52. Bushman arrow poison is cardiotoxic and therefore acts through the blood stream, not through the digestion.
53. J. Shepstone Papers, 'Reminiscences of the Past', pp. 63-65, and J. Shepstone Papers, Box No. 3, no pagination.
54. See p. 20.
55. Wright 1971: 62.
56. Stanford 1910.
57. Wright 1971: 62, 202.
58. See p. 60.
59. Stanford 1910.
60. C.S.O. 11(2), p. 201, 9/10/1846.
61. T. Shepstone Papers, diary: 20/10/1846.
62. Willcox 1956: 33.
63. C.S.O. 11(1), No. 12, 12/3/1847.
64. G. H. 1321, No. 69, 9/11/1846.
65. C.S.O. 11(2), p. 202, 4/11/1846.
66. C.S.O. 11(2), p. 109, 21/8/1846.
67. C.S.O. 37(2), No. 123, 19/9/1846.
68. An 1863 map of Natal made by Captain Grantham, marks *Bushman's Stable* on one of the branches of the Nzinga river, a tributary of the Mkhomazi. A barn-like shelter containing rock-paintings on the farm *Maylands* in the Nzinga valley may be the spot referred to, or it may possibly be another unusually large rock-shelter, much used by hunters in the early days, situated near the summit of Mulungane Mountain on the farm *Surprise*. (Personal communication, A. T. McClean, 1959).
69. C.S.O. 11(2), p. 203, 11/2/1846.
70. C.S.O. 45(1), No. 62, 1/1/1847.
71. C.S.O. 45(1), No. 52, 20/1/1847.
72. *Patriot*, 1/1/1847.
73. *Natal Witness*, 25/12/1846; 8/1/1847.
74. C.S.O. 45(1), No. 58, 59, 61 & 52: 8 9 10 & 20/1/1847.
75. John Shepstone Papers, Box 4, 'Reminiscences of the Past,' p. 66.
76. *Natal Witness* 8/1/1847.
77. Without stating references, Bulpin (1953: 61) records that a party of Bushmen under Hele were active elephant hunters on the middle

reaches of the Mzimkhulu river, and that they supplied ivory to H. F. Fynn. In a personal communication (13/10/1966) Bulpin agrees that Hele and Yele are probably one and the same person.

78. C.S.O. 11(1), No. 12, 12/3/1847.
79. T. Shepstone papers, diary: 26/5/1847; B.P.P. No. 980.
80. C.S.O. 20(1), No. 42, 17/12/1849.
81. C.S.O. 11(2), No. 68, 12/6/1848.
82. Fynn Papers, 1/10/1852.
83. Schoute-Vanneck & Walsh 1959, 1960, 1961.
84. Brien 1932.
85. Bazley 1905.
86. See also p. 10.

Figure 20   *Site H2*

Figures carrying bundles of spears or arrows lead and drive two horses laden with meat. The men have two knobs each on their heads, wear flaps or tassels tied below the knees, and have slender thongs or skin aprons hanging fore and aft.

This block of stone is part of the frieze shown in Figure 24 and was removed to the Natal Museum in 1910. Abrasion marks have caused superficial damage. The scale is in centimetres and the paintings are bright orange and black.

Photo: Laura Kelsall.

The Establishment of Military and Police Posts

Early in 1847 the military post on Van Vuuren's farm on the Eland's river in the present Boston area was completed. It soon became known as Van Vuuren's Post,[1] and was manned by a detachment of Cape Mounted Riflemen (C.M.R.). The contingent, consisting of six Coloured men of mixed descent under the command of a British officer, was instructed to make frequent patrols, and in the event of a theft, to assist farmers in the retrieval of their stock.

The cavalrymen's first call to action was in June 1847 when a daring robbery took place from property only one hour's ride from the capital, and but two gun-shot's distance from the house of no less a person than the Boer leader Andries Pretorius.[2] The spoor of hastily driven cattle and horses was recognised by Pretorius' nephew who reported the theft to the Post, where he was joined in the pursuit by four C.M.R. They soon came upon stray horses and oxen, and knew they were hot on the trail when they found the carcass of a freshly killed ox concealed in a patch of bush. The following day the patrol overtook ten horses recently abandoned by the thieves, some of which were loaded with saddles of raw meat covered over with pieces of skin. After recovering all but one of Pretorius' cattle, the pursuing party was obliged to return because of the fatigued condition of their mounts, and the Bushmen got away with only three horses.[3, 4]

Despite the prompt recovery of most of his stock, Pretorius was galled and disgusted by the fact that the British Government had not only previously attempted to make a peace treaty with the Bushmen who had robbed him, but had even given them *presents!* An added point of resentment was that the recently proclaimed Swartkop Location, which bordered Pretorius' property and had been established much against his will, had proved totally ineffective in acting as a buffer between settled farmers and raiding Bushmen. Pretorius pointed out that the thieves had ridden for three or four hours across terrain thickly populated by Africans who, since they did nothing to intercept the stolen stock, must have been tacitly acquiescing in the thefts.[5] Pretorius became increasingly incensed by the inertia and lack of co-operation of the British authorities, and in disgust, he finally left Natal with a party of dissident Boers.[6]

Figure 21 *Site W23*
A horse laden with strips of meat is led by a figure carrying a spear. Note the knobbed head-dress with a flap hanging at the back of the neck.

In August 1847 the contingent at Van Vuuren's Post again took action. During a thunderstorm, sixteen cattle and two horses were taken from near the Post, and were subsequently hidden in thick bush. When this was searched, all the cattle were retrieved alive, and the slaughtered remains of one of the horses was found while the other carried a saddle of meat. The thieves, however, got clear away without even being seen.[7]

The official records of these operations are of particular interest because of the mention of Bushmen using horses to carry meat. Paintings which clearly depict this usage have been found on Bamboo mountain and on *Kilmun* farm in the Underberg district, and on the Tsoelike river in eastern Lesotho (sites H2, J21, W23). In each case the horses are being led, and the load is shown as a protuberance on the back with strips of meat or hide hanging down in uneven strips below the belly of the pack animal. (Figures 20, 21, 217)

It was soon realised that the post on Van Vuuren's farm was not well located, for stock thefts from the Bushman's River and Karkloof areas continued unchecked. The thieves seemed to single out particular farms for their attention, probably because they were conveniently located for a quick get-away, and in one of these raids, no less than 63 horses were driven away.[8, 9] The trail of the stolen animals was clearly shown by well-trodden grass and the usual litter of stabbed and abandoned animals. When the Boers appealed to Government for assistance, four men of the Cape Corps were sent to investigate.[10] The track led across the open grassland towards the Drakensberg, then at the foot of the escarpment it wheeled southwards, following the contours of the dissected valleys. Between the Mkhomazi and Mzimkhulu rivers, the pursuers found the remains of six horses. These generally lay at the top of steep ascents, where they had probably dropped from the fatigue of over-driving, and had then been peremptorily despatched. The spoor, followed for several days, was at last obliterated by heavy rains. Yet again, the Bushmen won the round.[11, 12]

It is of interest that two depictions of upside-down or dead horses have been found within the survey area, one in a tributary of the Mzimkhulu (K1), and the other on the headwaters of the Mzimvubu (Q21). Both sites are in the direction taken by the stock thieves. (Figure 22)

Because of the recurrent raids on farms in the Bushman's River area, a new military post was established near the present town of Estcourt, and from December 1847, the temporary premises at Van Vuuren's Post were 'to let'.[13] In an additional attempt to provide adequate machinery to cope with the Bushman menace, the Natal Native Police Corps was recruited from among the African population 'for the protection of Her Majesty's subjects from the robberies they suffer from the Bushmen inhabiting the lower range of the Drachenberg Mountains'.[14] Theophilus Shepstone was appointed Captain-in-Chief, with John Shepstone and James Melville as Lieutenants.[15] By the middle of the year, the Corps was sufficiently well trained to commence operations, and a detachment under Melville was called upon to investigate a minor theft. Depredators had picked and scattered fruit on a vacated farm on the Mngeni river, and had lifted a goat from an African's kraal on the Eland's river. The official directions were 'to follow up the traces of the Bushmen and to endeavour to apprehend them, and should they resist, to fire upon them'.[16] Although the culprits were not found, enquiries in the neighbourhood revealed that the robbers were five in number, and that they were a part of Mdwebo's tribe, one of them answering the description of Mdwebo's son. These Bushmen were reported to be living on the Ibisi river west of the Mzimkhulu, the same area where they had previously been encountered by Uys.[17, 18]

In July, a contingent of the Native Police re-occupied the deserted barracks at Van Vuuren's. They were instructed to patrol the vicinity, acquaint themselves thoroughly with the Bushman paths, and report on suitable situations for the erection of permanent protective posts. Strategic sites on the upper Bushman's river and on the Spioen Kop dividing the headwaters of the Mngeni from the Mkhomazi had already been suggested.[19] The patrolling instructions were no sooner issued than they were revoked because of other pressures,[20] and almost immediately a large robbery of 100 cattle took place not seven miles from the military post on the Bushman's river.[21, 22] A Hottentot herdsman reported the loss, and a contingent of the 45th Regiment accompanied by a guide immediately set off on an arduous pursuit. The party was obliged to split when the spoor divided, but despite very rough terrain, they held the trail for three days, noticing that the Bushman foot-prints became very numerous along the base of the Drakensberg. Thawing snow combined with steep inclines finally impeded the progress of the horses altogether, and the dejected party returned to base after five days absence, having found only carcasses of animals and one live bullock.[23, 24]

Realising the error of procrastination, the Colonial Office now sent an officer with about fifty men of the Natal Native Police Corps to the Bushman's River Post for patrolling duty. A line of march parallel with the Drakensberg mountains between Bushman's river and the Thukela was chosen, and by continually patrolling the countryside and thus cutting across the Bushman paths, it was hoped that the 'plagues of Bushmen' would be driven out or captured.[25]

It was, however, a vain hope. Indeed, when the cattle thieves returned, their objective was again a farm very near the Bushman's River Post. When news of this daring robbery of 200 cattle and four horses filtered through to the public, the local newspaper remarked, 'Poor England's protection of the Colonies is a contemptible thing. Britain may beat a Bonaparte, but can't beat a Bushman . . . . !'[26]

A party of Cape Mounted Riflemen and a contingent of Native Police, accompanied by a farmer, immediately rode off towards the mountains, and at nightfall came across cattle straying back along the spoor. Before sunrise the next morning, they were on the

Figure 22 *Site Q14, upper Mzimvubu*

A troop of horses is driven towards a natural recess in the shelter wall which suggests an overhang. Within the recess, seated women clap their hands in delight. Above, right, one of the horses has collapsed from fatigue, and below (inset), is a painting of another dead horse from a shelter overlooking the headwaters of the Mzimkhulu river (site K1). This horse has apparently been stabbed in the rump, where strokes of paint suggest gushing blood.

41

tracks again, and soon found stabbed beasts and another that had apparently fallen down a ravine. The spoor took the same direction as the previous theft, and then led to a pass in the mountains over which the animals had apparently been driven. Because the army regulars had insufficient rations and had received no instructions to proceed over the mountains, they returned to headquarters, leaving Lieutenant Melville with his Native Police and the farmer, Philip Nel, to continue up the pass.[27] After reaching the watershed, the party followed the spoor for three or four days along the course of a river running in a westerly to north-westerly direction. *En route*, they found a total of thirty-four carcasses and thirteen live animals which had been left behind by the thieves or had wandered from the drove. At this crucial juncture, Melville fell violently ill, and had to be carried back down the escarpment. Philip Nel, with Sergeant Klaas and fourteen of the Native Police, continued the chase, and after crossing over a ridge of mountains, probably the Black mountains, followed the spoor across extensive table-lands on top of the escarpment. Not far from the headwaters of the Mzimkhulu river, Nel turned back to find out how Melville was faring, and reported having seen a mare and foal grazing, as well as traces of numerous other horses. He also came across the freshly killed carcass of one of the stolen oxen from which the hide and flesh had been carried away, and from the nature of the country, felt sure he was not far from the Bushmen's habitation.

Meanwhile Klaas, left near the source of the Mzimkhulu, sent out a scouting party who, on climbing to a vantage point, glimpsed some Bushmen on an opposite hill. The Police surrounded the hill under cover of darkness, and at dawn stealthily ascended, hoping to take the robbers by surprise. The Bushmen, however, had fled. Their footprints were followed down the escarpment to the Natal side of the Berg,[28] where the tracks turned northwards towards the Mkhomazi river. During the afternoon, the Bushmen were again sighted on the summit of a steep stony hill. The Native Police ascended in an oblique direction, while the Bushmen, standing on the edge of a precipice, rolled stones down upon them, demanding why people of the same nation as themselves should come to retake cattle stolen from Europeans. They did not steal from Blacks, so why should the Blacks pursue them? On gaining the top of the hill, the Police found stray cattle and saw several Bushmen on foot scrambling down precipitous places where it was impossible to follow or even get near them. There were also three mounted Bushmen driving some cattle down a very difficult path, whom they hotly pursued. The Bushmen, realising they would be unable to get away with their booty, set about maliciously stabbing the animals with their assegais, then escaped. Altogether, about twenty animals were found killed, but an equal number of live cattle and six horses were rounded up by the Police. Klaas and his men camped for the night on the hill, making a large fire near the stock and lying in wait in case the Bushmen returned. Nothing happened, and the following morning they found a deserted Bushman kraal with pots and calabashes lying around. It was situated between the sources of the Mkhomazi and Mzimkhulu rivers, five or six hours on horseback from the nearest African kraal on the Mkhomazi river. Klaas also stated that the people he saw were apparently all Bushmen with the exception of one African, whom he recognised as having been amongst a party of Bushmen sent to the seat of Government some time previously with a present of ivory from Mdwebo. He had also seen this same man on subsequent occasions in Pietermaritzburg.[29, 30]

The stock re-taken from the Bushmen proved to be the proceeds of four different raids from the Bushman's river area. These had taken place at roughly six-monthly intervals over a period of eighteen months.

A re-appraisal of the follow-up details of these successive raids reveals an interesting progression of increasingly complicated manoeuvres on the part of the Bushmen. None of the cattle from the first robbery in July 1847 were recovered despite concerted efforts by the farmers.[31] No other details survive. In December 1847, the clear and undisguised trail of a large troop of horses which had been driven along the base of the Drakensberg was followed by four men of the Cape Corps almost a week after the theft occurred. Somewhere between the Mkhomazi and the Mzimkhulu rivers the spoor was obliterated by heavy rains, and the pursuit was abandoned.[32] In July 1848, another theft of cattle was followed in the same direction. This time, the Bushmen tried the ruse of dividing the spoils to confuse the trackers, and then driving the animals over very rough terrain. Despite this precaution, however, the trail was held, and again, only the intervention of the weather forced the pursuers to retire.[33] By December 1848, the Bushmen had become wary of driving their booty straight to their haunts. Although the circuitous route taken on this occasion cannot be reconstructed with any precision, it is certain that the Bushmen withdrew over the escarpment, possibly through the pass now known as Langalibalele's, and thence inland towards the present Mokhotlong area in Lesotho. Part of the spoils were then apparently driven over the

Black mountains, and back down the escarpment between the headwaters of the Mkhomazi and Mzimkhulu rivers. Here the Bushmen themselves were seen, as well as their habitation. It is not clear from the written account whether they were living in a rock shelter or in constructed shelters, but the presence of domestic utensils suggests that the site was more than a simple transit camp.

The indications, therefore, are that a party of Bushmen who rode horses and grazed cattle were living at the foot of the Drakensberg in the vicinity of the Mkhomazi and Mzimkhulu rivers during the years 1847 and 1848. That they were not an isolated band completely unaware of the outside world is suggested by their contact with Mdwebo's Bushmen in Faku's territory, and with western civilisation in Pietermaritzburg. These Bushmen, with at least one African adherent, participated in repeated stock thefts from the Bushman's river area, and in order to avoid the increasing danger of detection, finally resorted to driving the stolen animals first over the high escarpment, and thence back to the terrain along the foothills. A similar pattern was repeated in 1862,[34] which suggests that their occupation of these remote valleys persisted until that time. During the later period, however, when pressures increased, Bushman occupation of the eastern side of the escarpment was probably intermittent or seasonal, their principal habitat being the inaccessible gorges of the Orange river system.

The paintings from this area support the archival evidence very closely. On the headwaters of the Orange river near its junction with the Mokhotlong tributary, there is a rough basalt rock shelter which contains a scatter of stone artefacts as well as fragmentary paintings. Those that are still recognisable show a mounted horseman, head decorated with a feather and riding at great speed, driving a mixed troop of horses and cattle.

In the grasslands below the Drakensberg immediately south-west of this terrain, there are four painting sites (G3, H1, H2 and J21) where details of stock raids are depicted; and other shelters in the vicinity, all within the Mkhomazi and Mzimkhulu catchment area, contain numerous paintings of cattle and horsemen. (See Table 4)

Two of the stock raid scenes actually show cattle and horses being driven towards an encampment (Figures 24, 210), and the best preserved of the groups, removed from Bamboo mountain on the upper Mzimkhulu and now housed in the Natal Museum, includes details worthy of close consideration. (Figures 20, 24, 25, 26, 240)

In the centre of the eight-foot long scene, a shelter or enclosure is represented by an encircling line. Tasselled skin bags hang suspended on branches, and rounded objects with flat bases, perhaps quern stones or pots, are scattered around. Within the shelter, women squat with babies in their arms, all looking expectantly towards the right. Other figures, sticks in hand, walk towards a large herd of cattle and horses approaching from the right. These are triumphantly driven by five mounted men and one on foot, all wearing knobbed decorations on their heads, and one has a handsome spotted skin cape flying from his shoulders. Bringing up the rear are two horses, one led and one driven, both heavily laden with meat.

Archival reports made between Sunday 17th and Thursday 21st of December 1848 immediately come to mind. High on the headwaters of the Mzimkhulu and Mkhomazi rivers there were traces of numerous horses, and the freshly killed carcass of an ox was found from which the hide and flesh had been carried away. Bushmen were then seen driving cattle, some on horseback and some on foot, and the following day, their kraal was located with utensils lying scattered around. The area in which these observations were made is the same as the area in which the paintings occur.[34, 35]

Three months later, again in the upper Mzimkhulu terrain, John Shepstone reported seeing shelters recently occupied, and specifically mentioned the presence of domestic animals among the paintings. He also estimated from the traces he saw, that the Bushmen had about thirty horses in their possession. Twenty-three are depicted in the raid scene on Bamboo mountain.

To the left of the domestic animals and definitely part of the same scene, there is an enigmatic extension to the composition. Decorated human figures, some with spots of red falling from their heads, drive and entice a large unidentifiable animal towards the encampment, to which it is connected by a rope-like line. By analogy with similar paintings explained by Bushmen from the Cape region,[36] a rain-making rite is possibly being enacted. According to this interpretation, initiated sorcerers, some bleeding from the nose, lead a rain animal over the land, and numerous small strokes surrounding the group suggest that rain, which would obliterate the traces of the stolen stock, has successfully been evoked.

The Bushmen were widely recognised by Africans as powerful 'rain-doctors',[37] and there are repeated references in the archival records to those in pursuit of the Bushmen having to turn back because of the spoor being washed out by rain, or because of swollen rivers, snow-storms or generally unfavourable weather conditions.

In addition, a Natal newspaper actually carried a report that, on being closely chased by a party of Africans on a certain occasion, the Bushmen had been obliged to resort to magic, and had summoned a torrential downpour of rain by blowing a blast on an eland horn.[38]

The stock raid scene referred to above was taken from a shelter near the summit of Bamboo mountain, which was known to the Bantu as *Mvuleni*, meaning 'The Place of Rain'. In its original situation, the painting was orientated so that the 'rain animal' with its power to wash away the tell-tale tracks was led in from the direction of the farm-lands to the south-east, while the horses and cattle were driven from the escarpment to the north-west. These details correspond to a remarkable degree with the documented evidence which dates the events depicted by the Bushmen to the years 1847 and 1848. (Figures 24, 25, 26, 240)

Back at Bushman's river camp, Lieutenant James Melville, deeply disappointed at having been compelled by illness to withdraw from the chase after the Bushmen, resumed operations. Because there were at least 115 head of cattle and four horses from the last robbery alone unaccounted for, Melville felt convinced that a division of the spoils had taken place, and that the remainder of the booty would be found at a permanent Bushman kraal rumoured to be 'where the Orange river leaves the Mountain'. The prevalent view at this time was that somewhere in the rugged hinterland there was a large and permanent settlement of Bushmen, and if only this could be found and destroyed, the stock-theft problem would be solved. Melville therefore begged leave from the authorities to proceed again on commando with volunteer farmers and selected police, each to be armed with at least twenty-five rounds of cartridges.[39]

The Lieutenant-Governor approved, but in his opinion, the seat of the trouble was in Faku's territory. He sent word to the British Agent, Henry Fynn, that an armed force was about to take action against the 'plundering Bushmen' and that Faku was expected to assist.[40] A commando of as many men of the Cape Corps as could be made available, about one hundred Native Police, and thirty or forty farmers would, it was hoped, take 'vigorous measures to check these depredations'.[41]

However, due to much indecision as to which route the commando should take and lack of co-operation on the part of the farmers, the plan fell through,[42-44] and within a few weeks, the cattle thieves struck again. On the 18th February, 1849, seventy-

Figure 23   *Site H2*

The shelter on Bamboo mountain (Mvuleni) from which the paintings shown opposite were expertly quarried in 1910.

Photo: Pat Carter.

Figure 24   *Site H2*   (above)

Bamboo Mountain stock raid. On the left, a 'rain animal' is being led towards a Bushman encampment where women and children are sitting. On the right, a herd of cattle and horses are driven by mounted Bushmen, followed by two horses laden with meat. (See also Figures 26, 240). This photograph was taken in situ *before the group was removed to the Natal Museum in 1910. The full length of the scene is approximately 244 centimetres.*

Figure 25   *Site H2*   (below)

Detail of the cattle and horses. Photographed in situ, *1910.*

Photos 24 and 25 by kind permission of Natal Museum.

45

nine head of cattle were reported stolen from a farm just two hours' ride from Pietermaritzburg. In an attempt to intercept the thieves, the Lieutenant-Governor immediately ordered one body of Native Police directly to the site of the robbery, and another to the Spioen Kop.[45] It was reported that African women visiting a kraal between the head-waters of the Mngeni and Mooi rivers had actually seen the thieves driving the cattle in a great hurry, some on horseback and some on foot,[46] but the intercepting parties under John Shepstone and James Melville could find no traces to follow.[47] While scouting around the upper Mkhomazi, one of the patrols came across animal tracks, but whether of buffalo or cattle they could not tell. The spoor was already several days old, and since the river was swollen, it was impossible to investigate further. The two parties finally joined forces, but since they knew the Lieutenant-Governor had been in communication with Faku, they were uncertain whether they should endeavour to locate the Bushman kraals with or without the assistance of that chief. They wrote to headquarters for instructions, and while awaiting an answer, they milled around the area between the Mkhomazi and Mzimkhulu rivers where their movements were still hampered by bad weather. Here their suspicions were aroused by the precipitate flight of the inhabitants of an African kraal where there were a large number of ox-hides.[48] In addition, a small patrol sent out by the farmer whose stock had been taken, learned that an African headman named Matshinkwana, living on the south bank of the Mkhomazi, had in his possession many cattle supposed to have been traded from Bushmen in payment for lodging. The farmer suggested that if Matshinkwana's co-operation with the thieves could be established, the Bushmen could easily be dealt with by the simple expedient of confiscating Matshinkwana's cattle and refusing to return them until he had delivered the Bushmen to the authorities.[49] The Government did not, apparently, act on this advice, but the hint of trade and other dealings of convenience between Africans living in the Mkhomazi valley and the Bushmen in the mountains beyond is significant.[50] (Figure 39)

Meanwhile, rumours were heard of a party of Bushmen living at or near Dronk Vlei in the present Creighton area. Although Melville had no evidence that they were responsible for any of the thefts, he hoped to capture them. Fortunately for the Bushmen, enquiries from chief Mdushane who lived nearby elicited the information that they had moved south of the Mzimkhulu after the spring planting season, and because the river was in spate, pursuit was out of the question.

Melville felt that if decisive action was to be taken against the Bushmen, further means should be put at his disposal. He therefore wrote again to headquarters, making five basic requests: tents for protection against the rain, pack oxen to carry the provisions, further supplies of ammunition because much had been rendered useless while crossing flooded rivers, replacements of the men who had fallen lame, and additional riding horses with forage to feed them. It is clear from Melville's correspondence that he was under the impression that the stolen stock had been driven over a pass near the sources of the Mooi river, but that the Bushmen had again descended the escarpment to the sources of the Mzimkhulu as on the previous raid.[51] However, before Melville could put any plans into action, he again fell ill, and returned to Pietermaritzburg leaving the police force under the command of Lieutenant John Shepstone.[52]

Meanwhile, the Bushmen were not as irresolute as their pursuers. They took positive advantage of the bad weather, and in heavy mist and rain, again made off with a large herd of cattle belonging to Henry Ogle on the Bushman's river. Although the robbery was not detected for some time, Sergeant Klaas, who was left in charge of the remainder of the Native Police in the absence of the European sergeants, went in pursuit from the nearby Bushman's river camp. By the time he reached the mountains, the Bushmen were so far ahead that he decided it was useless to continue. The police found 3 oxen killed, and judged from the spoor that not more than 50 had been stolen. Whether there had again been a division of the spoils, or whether the losses originally estimated at 240 had been exaggerated, is not clear.[53, 54]

John Shepstone, still camped on the Mkhomazi river, soon received news of the robbery. Guided by one of the police, Shepstone and his men followed up the river to within a day's march of the Bushman kraal which had previously been located by Sergeant Klaas. Although they could find no trace of the recent robbery, they did come across the spoor of the cattle taken a month before and which had previously been confused with buffalo spoor. Following this trail up the south bank of the Mkhomazi, then across a ridge to a tributary of the Mzimkhulu, Lieutenant John Shepstone reports:[55]

> On the 19th [March, 1849] I continued following up the spoor and after carrying it through the remaining branches of the Umzimkhulu, it turned up the mountain. On the 18th, 19th, 20th and 21st we were covered by a dense fog which rendered it impossible to see more than fifty yards before us. We com-

Figure 26 *Site H2*

Detail of the figures sitting in the shelter reproduced in full in Figure 24. Tasselled bags hang from the ceiling of huts or skerms built within the shelter, as well as from forked branches apparently carried in for that purpose. Women sit with children on their laps, and around the periphery of the shelter are what may be grinding stones. Cattle have been tethered to knobbed sticks, and at far right, a cow with a calf has been tied to a partition. Below, a calf sucks from its mother's udder, and straps hanging from the lower partition may be other tethering ropes. The tall figure standing near a child in the centre of the group carries a long knobbed stick as well as multi-pronged artefacts similar to those often carried by horsemen. (Figure 29). The male figures have skin flaps or similar decorations below the knee, and wear knobbed head-dresses which may be bladders attached to the hair. The women have feathers or tassels hanging from the crown of their heads. The paintings are in black and bright orange.

menced the ascent of the Drakensberg on the spoor about 11 a.m. and after winding along its side without halting except for the men to load, as we fully expected to find the Bushmen on the top, we reached the summit about 4 p.m., where to our great disappointment we found they had left the position some time previous. From the general appearance of the top of the mountain, it was evidently a place used as a residence by the Bushmen, there were two large caves the walls of which were covered with paintings of scenes of animals both wild and domestic. Many of the stones were still covered with grease from the cattle they had killed. There were two cattle hides, quantities of bones and horns, heads of horses and cattle the former of which had been roasted in the fire and appeared to have been used for food. The quantity of wild vegetable which had been dug in the mountain to be used as food also showed it to have been more than a temporary abode. The grass was much eaten down all over the top of the mountain apparently chiefly by horses, the traces of which we saw in great abundance, but from where they were kept at night, I should estimate the number in the possession of this party to be about 30.

The 20th and part of the 21st I remained in the mountain endeavouring to find the spoor so as to pursue it further, but it was so scattered and the grazing traces so numerous that I could not succeed. I have omitted to mention that at the principal cave there was a small spring of water in which we found two short pieces of wood tied together covered with a substance very like the poison they use on their arrows. The water looking green and otherwise suspicious, caused the men to examine it before using. On the 21st I descended on my return. My own provisions were exhausted some days previous so that I had to live on meat alone like the men, with the exception of a cup of coffee in the morning. The country I traversed would be quite impracticable to waggons from the depth and number of the morasses and muddy rivulets forming the sources of the larger rivers. It took me eight days hard marching fully 25 miles a day the shortest route across country to reach this place on my return, having been out in all 37 days.[56]

I have to report that the men were most cheerful and well behaved during the whole of my march, and their disappointment at finding the supposed Bushman's stronghold evacuated was evidenced by their countenances when they reached the summit. During the ascent, I found it necessary to continue in front of them to prevent the strongest from out-running the main body, and fearing also that if they fell in with any women or children of the Bushmen in their excited state, they would butcher them indiscriminately.

This communiqué is of interest in that it is one of the few which actually describes a rock shelter currently inhabited by Bushmen, and is also the first known reference to rock paintings in the Drakensberg.

Unfortunately, the details of Shepstone's route are somewhat perplexing, and it is not possible to identify the sites referred to with any certainty. The report gives the impression that the main escarpment was ascended and that the shelters and signs of domestic animals were found on the summit. This is unlikely, since suitable shelters seldom occur in the basalt, and grazing on top of the escarpment is of inferior quality. It is probable that Shepstone did not, in fact, climb beyond the Little Berg, for in his later reminiscences he recalled that dry Protea wood provided good coals for cooking, and this vegetation is limited to the Cave Sandstone zone. On Shepstone's own admission the terrain was thickly covered by mist throughout his stay in the mountains, and this circumstance would have caused confusion even to one well acquainted with the area, which Shepstone was not.[57] Since specific mention is made of the upper tributaries of the Mzimkhulu river in Shepstone's report, it is probable that the shelters he described are among the sites recorded in this vicinity, where 'paintings of scenes and animals both wild and domestic' can still be viewed today.

In the stock raid scene from Bamboo mountain on the upper Mzimkhulu, where there are two adjacent painted shelters (H2 & H3), the stolen animals are being driven towards a partitioned shelter or enclosure within which cattle, some with calves, are tethered. That the Bushmen of the upper Mzimkhulu and Mkhomazi area had kept stock in their possession for a period of at least eighteen months was proved by the identification of the animals retrieved by Klaas and his men three months before Shepstone's expedition.[58] In addition, the use of some type of kraal or stabling arrangement such as is shown in the painting is confirmed by Shepstone's observation that the horses were kept in a specific place at night, and a later account, 1858, refers to 'a Bushmen's cave in which there were stalls for horses' on the upper Mkhomazi.[59]

By the middle of the nineteenth century therefore, the Bushmen of the upper Mkhomazi and Mzimkhulu rivers, no doubt influenced by their Bantu-speaking adherents, had modified their hunter-gatherer economy by the adoption of stock keeping. Although Shepstone does not specify the particular domestic animals he saw painted, the use of the plural suggests both cattle and horses. It is therefore unlikely that the paintings he saw in March 1849 were executed before 1838 when stock raids in Natal commenced, and when horses were introduced to the area in any numbers.[60] The period during which the paintings were executed is thus limited to within ten years, 1838 – 1848, and this dating may safely be applied to at least some of the paintings of domestic animals that decorate the rocks of the upper Mzimkhulu and Mkhomazi valleys. (Figures 24, 27, 39)

Figure 27 *Site G3*

The proceeds of a stock raid, Mpongweni Mountain. Notice the two saddled horses, and the naked drovers who wear hats and carry arrows or spears in bags on their backs.
(For colour reproduction of part of scene, see Willcox 1963, Plate 36).

References

1. In 1965, Mrs H. R. Lindsay, former resident of the farm *Rossie* which was once part of *Van Vuuren's Post*, showed me the remains of an old building on that property. The surrounding hills, the adjacent natural bush, the fresh-water spring and three distinct mounds now overgrown with rank grass, all agreed very well with the description of the military post written over a century before (C.S.O. 5, p. 22, 20/4/1847). The three heaps of rubble no doubt represent the burnt brick stable, the barracks for the rank and file, and the quarters for the sergeant in command. While clearing the grass to take measurements of the stone foundations, we located a heavy iron hinge near the doorway of the building presumed to be the stable, and fragments of broken china around the 'barracks' bore testimony to the occupation of bygone years. At a little distance away, in what is now a wattle plantation, there are five or six graves marked by heaps of stones.

   Other interesting relics are to be found on an adjacent farm *Elandshoek* owned by Mr John Black. Here a grassy south-facing slope between two clumps of bush is pitted with about twenty-five circular depressions roughly six feet in diameter. These possibly represent former game traps. It is of interest that in March 1840, one L. P. Meyer petitioned the Volksraad that the *Boschejemankaffers* in the vicinity of his property should be prevented from digging big holes to trap game, because his son had recently been killed in such a pit (N1, p. 33). A search among the registration files of the Lands and Survey Department in Pietermaritzburg unfortunately threw no light on the whereabouts of this farm, but the Boston and Elandskop districts were among those settled by the Boers at an early date.
2. Part of Andries Pretorius' house still stands. The building is now an African school in Edendale, a suburb of Pietermaritzburg (J. Clark. *Natal Witness* 26/5/1964).
3. C.S.O. 45(1), No. 65, 27/11/1847.
4. *Natal Witness* 16/7/1847.
5. *Natal Witness* 30/7/1847.
6. Brookes & Webb 1965: 62.
7. C.S.O. 5, No. 42, 27/8/1847.
8. *Patriot*, 6/8/1847.
9. C.S.O. 45(1), No. 66, 26/11/1847.
10. C.S.O. 45(1), No. 64, 65, 66: 23, 26 & 27 /11/1847.
11. *Natal Witness* 10/12/1847.
12. Stalker 1912: 28-9.
13. *Natal Witness* 3 & 31/12/1847.
14. *Natal No. 2*: Appendix.
15. *Natal Witness* 29/2/1848, 7/7/1848.
16. C.S.O. 45(2), No. 74, 5/6/1848.
17. C.S.O. 11(2), No. 68, 12/6/1848.
18. C.S.O. 44(2), No. 53, 26/6/1848.
19. C.S.O. 2296, No. 58, 3/7/1848.
20. C.S.O. 2296, No. 170, 19/8/1848.
21. C.S.O. 44(2), No. 53, 26/6/1848.
22. C.S.O. 2296, Nos. 58, 170, 3/7 & 19/8/1848.
23. *Natal Witness* 21/7/1848.
24. C.S.O. 5, Nos. 80, 81, 11/8/1848.
25. C.S.O. 5, No. 76, 26/8/1848.
26. *Natal Witness* 22/12/1848.
27. Unfortunately, insufficient details are given to identify this pass with any certainty. It was probably at the headwaters of the Bushman's river, possibly Langalibalele's Pass.
28. The descent must have been made somewhere between the Mzimkhulu and Mkhomazi rivers, possibly down the Sani Pass.
29. C.S.O. 49(1), No. 65, 4/1/1849.
30. C.S.O. 44(1), No. 8, 22/12/1848.
31. *Patriot*, 6/8/1847.
32. *Natal Witness* 10/12/1847.
33. C.S.O. 5, No. 80, 81, 11/8/1848.
34. See p. 42.
35. C.S.O. 44(1), No. 8, 22/12/1848; C.S.O. 49(1), No. 65, 4/1/1849.
36. Bleek in Orpen 1874.
37. Willcox 1963: 20.
38. *Natal Independent*, 16/1/1851.
39. C.S.O. 44(1), No. 8, 22/12/1848.
40. C.S.O. 2296, No. 431, 28/12/1848.
41. C.S.O. 2296, No. 476, 25/1/1849.
42. C.S.O. 45(2), No. 78, 27/12/1848.
43. C.S.O. 25(1), Nos. 4 & 5, 18 & 19/1/1849.
44. *Natal Witness* 9/2/1849.
45. C.O. 2296, No. 519, 18/2/1849.
46. C.S.O. 14(3), No. 158, 20/2/1849.
47. C.S.O. 14(3), No. 158, 20/2/1849.
48. C.S.O. 49(1), p. 176, 28/3/1847.
49. C.S.O. 14(3), No. 158, 20/2/1849.
50. See p. 52 for reference to an African member of a Bushman band from the upper Mkhomazi.
51. C.S.O. 49(1), No. 71, 4/3/1849.
52. C.S.O. 49(1), No. 70, ?/3/1849.
53. C.S.O. 6(1), No. 9, 12/3/1849.
54. C.S.O. 6(1), No. 12, 8/3/1849.
55. C.S.O. 49(1), No. 73, 28/3/1849.
56. It is difficult to reconcile this assertion with the actual mileage from the sources of the Mzimkhulu river to Pietermaritzburg, which is a distance of about 100 miles.
57. J. Shepstone Papers, Box 4, p. 56-7.
58. See p. 42.
59. See p. 78.
60. For cautionary note, see p. 18

The Buffer Locations

During the early winter of 1848, a party of Boers returned over the northern Drakensberg in the vicinity of Oliviershoek to re-occupy their Natal farms. Not only did they find them settled by Africans when they arrived, but on the way, all fifteen of their horses were stolen. The farmers were reduced to pursuing the thieves on foot, but the only evidence they found was the entrails of a pig which had been used for carrying water. A fall of snow caused them considerable discomfort by numbing their feet, and one of the party had to be carried home. The spoor led towards the Witzieshoek area to which some of Langalibalele's tribe had fled when they escaped the tyranny of the Zulu chief Mpande. Jacobus Uys, whose previous dealings with the Bushmen have been recorded, was amongst the farmers who returned. He made further enquiries and elicited the information that two Bushmen had been seen amongst Langalibalele's people. One of them had a gun, and during a skirmish against the Zulus he had killed four of the enemy with one shot. This so impressed Langalibalele's people that the Bushmen were urged to obtain more guns in exchange for oxen. It was also confirmed that during their flight over the mountains with the first of Langalibalele's refugees, the two Bushmen had taken some pigs from a farm, and had apparently subsequently used the entrails of these animals as a container for water.

In his report, Jacobus Uys urged the authorities to remove all the Africans who had settled in the Klip river area; this was good country for European cattle farmers, and if the refugees were allowed to remain, they were bound to provoke further attacks by the Zulu chief Mpande in which the Europeans would inevitably be involved.[1] In order to prevent this very real possibility, and to pacify the Boers, the Natal Government resolved to remove the refugee tribes from the Klip river, and to place them in prescribed locations as near to the Drakensberg as they could inhabit. This would leave the rich farming areas in the vicinity of the Thukela, Bloukrans and Bushman's rivers free for European settlement, and at the same time form a buffer zone between the settled farmers and the stock-thieving Bushmen.[2]

The scheme was eventually implemented, but not without a considerable amount of resentment on the part of the Africans concerned. Chiefs Langalibalele and Daman were particularly rebellious, but were finally bullied into submission by a show of force which included severe corporal punishment, the impounding of vast herds of cattle, and the destruction of crops and kraals. This was all done in order to 'preserve the dignity of the Government.'[3-7] The Native Police force under command of John Shepstone and James Howell, who had replaced the invalid Melville, were instructed to 'fire upon and kill' anyone attempting to re-occupy the land they had been forced to vacate. The same drastic punishment was to be meted out to anyone caught stealing cattle. Howell's reaction is revealing: 'I could shoot a dozen Bushmen without compunction, but I do not like killing a kaffir merely because he will not vacate the country.'[8,9] It is of interest that the name J. Howell is listed as donor of a Natal Bushman's hunting kit to the British Museum in 1872, but there is no record of how or where the weapons were obtained.[9]

The institution of the buffer locations along the foot of the Drakensberg naturally resulted in increasing hostility between the Africans and the Bushmen. Whereas they had formerly lived together on comparatively amicable terms and the few reported thefts had been on a relatively petty scale,[10,11] from this time onwards the Bushmen did not distinguish between the herds of the Europeans and those of the Blacks.

The Bushmen themselves told the Africans that they did not wish to molest them, but that they were in the way, and until they went out of it, their cattle would be taken.[12]

Chief Zikhali, who was loyal to the Natal government throughout the re-location troubles, was amongst the first to suffer, but his people pursued the Bushmen so vigorously and promptly on each occasion that they were able to regain all their cattle.[13] The Bushmen nevertheless continued to make daring attacks, as a result of which Zikhali was supplied with ten stand of Government arms and sixty rounds of ball cartridge for each musket, and was promised a reward of cattle for any authentic information he could obtain on the haunts of the Bushmen.[14-16]

While the measures for establishing the Drakensberg locations were being carried out, rumours of Bushman activity continued. It was reported that fires had been seen on the Nhlazane mountain, that a Bushman had been caught stealing mealies from a farm on the Upper Mngeni, and that a Bushman hut built in the same vicinity at the beginning of summer was stocked with boiled meat, mealies and tobacco.[17-20] The rumours seemed justified when in June 1849, more than 240 cattle and 7 horses were taken from property on the

Thukela river.[21, 22] Outraged farmers in the vicinity were eager to pursue the robbers whose haunts had reputedly been located by Zikhali's people, but volunteers for the commando dwindled because of jealousies as to who should take command, and the plan was dropped.[23]

Co-incident with a report from Fynn in Pondoland saying that the Bushmen from the sources of the Mzimvubu were out 'hunting', stock again disappeared from a farm on the Bushman's river early in August, 1849. A combined party of Cape Mounted Riflemen under Lieutenant Mills and Native Police Corps under James Howell, with two farmers, hopefully set out in pursuit. After following a clear trail along the base of the Drakensberg for three days, they were summarily halted by an exceptionally heavy snow-fall which successfully interrupted the chase, and caused heavy losses among stock and game alike.[24]

Shortly after this episode, some members of the Native Police successfully captured a Bushman whom they sighted when on patrol. The prisoner turned out to be a known deserter from the Cape Mounted Rifles. In the 1830's this regiment had enlisted about 50 full-blooded Bushmen,[25] and the deserter confessed to having come from a Bushman kraal in the mountains where there were reputedly about 500 head of cattle. It was hoped that he could be persuaded to guide a commando back to the Bushman haunts which were said to be about eight days' march from the Post, but again, efforts to raise sufficient men to participate failed. It is not known what became of the Bushman captive.[26, 27]

Towards the end of 1849, one of the Boers living on the Bushman's river lost four horses, and since he had already suffered heavy losses three times previously, he asked permission to vacate his property in preference for a farm on the Klip river where he hoped he could 'escape from the Bushmen'.[28] Almost as if to clinch matters, the Bushmen immediately returned to his farm and drove off another 55 head of cattle. The desolate farmer carried news of the theft to the military post at nine o'clock at night, and notwithstanding mist and rain, ten Cape Mounted Riflemen under a European Lieutenant immediately started in pursuit. The spoor wound and doubled among the hills, but this time the pursuers were not misled; they abandoned the confused trail and took a short-cut directly to a pass in the escarpment known to be used by the Bushmen. After nineteen hours hard riding, they glimpsed the cattle and one Bushman on top of a prominence. Dismounting, they scaled the rocks on foot and retook all but two of the cattle. The latter were found dismembered and grilling on a fire, but there was no sign of the culprits.[29]

In order to afford better protection against the Bushmen in the future, the Natal Native Police Corps stationed on the Bushman's river near the military post, were removed to a more strategic position on the Spioen Kop. Officered by Lieutenants John Shepstone and James Howell, the men built their own headquarters consisting of simple mud huts.[30] In addition to the re-siting of the Police Post, some of Langalibalele's people were persuaded to build their kraals in key positions near the principal passes and drifts across rivers known to have been used by Bushmen. For this service they were paid 15 cows per annum by the Government.[31, 32] The Bushmen nevertheless continued to harass and harry the intruders, but were less successful in getting away with cattle from the Africans than from the Europeans.[33-35] Since they failed to dislodge their opponents by inroads on personal property, the Bushmen were reduced to making night attacks on the kraals of the African guards, and Mavuka and Christian, petty chiefs under Langalibalele who had been stationed high up the Bushman's river, suffered several demoralising incidents. Then in December 1850, the Bushmen seized an opportunity when all but Christian's wife and a herdboy were away, to swoop down from the mountains and retreat with a drove of cattle. The herdboy fled with the news to Christian, who hastily assembled ten men and went in pursuit. The ensuing details differ slightly in the extant accounts, but it seems that three of the party who were well in advance caught up with the thieves in the pass, probably the one now known as Langalibalele's, and when near enough, hurled an assegai. Five of the Bushmen continued to drive off the cattle while five more remained to hold their ground. Concealed behind rocks, they showered arrows and stones down on their assailants, striking one on the shin with a stone, and another on the collar-bone with an arrow. The wound, however, was not fatal as the arrow did not penetrate sufficiently deeply for the poison to take effect. (Figure 28)

When the remainder of the pursuing party came in sight, the defenders withdrew, taking the cattle with them. According to an account given by Christian and reported in the local press, the Bushmen, finding themselves doggedly followed, 'had then to resort to their black arts. They blew a blast on an eland horn, and immediately the rain descended in torrents. Christian and his party having thus their courage cooled for the pursuit, returned to their kraals for shelter.' The next morning being fine, they set out again with renewed confidence, and after tracking the robbers over the Drakensberg, camped the night. Starting out on the trail again at dawn, one of the men smelt smoke. Investigating the cause, they

Figure 28 *Site G3*

Bushmen with bows and arrows at the ready draw up a defence against pursuing Bantu who carry shields. The Bantu have thrown knobbed sticks and spears at the Bushmen, and while the Bushmen return a shower of poisoned arrows, a member of their party quickly drives off the cattle. The Bushmen wear knobbed head-dresses and carry arrows in quivers on their backs as well as what may be a fillet of arrows on their heads. Poor quality sandstone has unfortunately caused some of the cattle to exfoliate. The length of the scene from left to right is 66 cm.

found four Bushmen and one Mosotho sitting round a large fire at the foot of an overhanging precipice, evidently preparing for the day's march. The only possible approach to the shelter was from the side where the cattle were standing, a fortunate circumstance for the attackers, for thus screened, they were able to creep up closely without being observed. Barring all retreats save a precipitous slope, Christian's men suddenly sprang up, beating their shields and shouting a war cry. Pandemonium broke out. In trying to escape, three of the Bushmen were stabbed, one fatally, as he did not get more than a yard or two from the fire. The Mosotho, stunned by a blow on the head from a stone, went rolling down the steep incline, but regained sufficient consciousness to catch hold of tufts of grass. Righting himself, he made off, bleeding profusely from the wound on his head.

Twenty of the twenty-eight stolen cattle were recovered, as well as a horse belonging to the Cape Mounted Riflemen and branded C.M.R. Christian had reason to feel well pleased with the success of the affray, but on returning to his kraal on the Bushman's river, he found his wife dead, with two assegai wounds in her back and one from a poisoned arrow. Shortly afterwards, the Bushmen again attacked Christian's kraal during the night and wounded a boy. Thoroughly unnerved by these events, the families quit their stations and sought protection from the Military Post. Christian and Mavuka were subsequently provided with fifteen stand of arms and the necessary ammunition in order to guard the pass in their charge more effectively.[36-38]

The Bushmen, however, seemed determined to dislodge the obstacles in their way, for the following autumn they descended on a herd of African-owned cattle grazing on the upper Mngeni, and killed the two attendants. The first intimation of the robbery was when these boys failed to return to their homes in the evening, and a search party the following day found their bodies stabbed, and the cattle gone.[39]

It is small wonder then, that when 150 head of cattle were taken from chief Lugaju's kraals on the Mngeni river the following year, the 300 men who pursued as far as the Mkhomazi, turned back for fear of witchcraft when they found a baboon's head impaled on a stick. The Bushmen had a powerful reputation for sorcery among the Africans,[40] and the same year, some women who had gone to collect firewood were greatly perturbed not so much by an outrage committed against them, as by the threatened consequences. Suddenly surprised by a party of mounted Bushmen, the women fled in alarm, but one, heavily pregnant and therefore unable to run, was seized and killed. Ripping open her body, the Bushmen were reported to have taken out the child, shouting to the women who escaped, 'This we will take home and burn and bewitch, and trouble, pain and sorrow shall then befall you.'[41]

In March 1852, chief Mdushane who resided on the middle reaches of the Mzimkhulu, was goaded into action after a double robbery. Accompanied by some of his followers, Mdushane pursued the thieves into the mountains for four days, and towards evening, caught up with them at their kraals on the sources of the Mzimvubu river. The robbers had just killed an ox, but fled on Mdushane's approach, leaving the carcass and the remaining cattle in his possession. The Bushmen returned during the night and fired on his camp, but without doing any damage. Next morning, Mdushane, on the offensive again, captured ten horses from the Bushmen. These were handed over to the Government on his return to Pietermaritzburg, where the majority were claimed by the colonists.[42]

A gang of timber-sawyers later gave warning that a large party of Bushmen had congregated in the mountains near the sources of the Mngeni and Mooi rivers,[43] an observation of particular interest in that the season was mid-winter. It is therefore possible that the Bushmen who had been living on the high Lesotho plateau during the summer months had been obliged, either by necessity or by habit, to seek shelter and sustenance at lower-lying altitudes during the harsh winter months.

Meanwhile, an unexpected turn of events on the Cape frontiers caused the Natal Native Police Corps to be disbanded in 1851, and the post on the Spioenkop to be evacuated. During the war against the Xhosa towards the end of 1850, many of the African police and Coloured Cape Mounted Riflemen turned traitor to the Government and went over to the enemy.[44, 45] This was attributed to the 'perilous policy of training uncivilised tribes in the use of arms, giving them physical powers before they have the requisite moral influence of civilisation'. A Natal newspaper had previously written of the 'humiliation of an obligation to barbarians for protection'.[46, 47] Despite the sentiments voiced, however, greater stress was placed on locating Africans in strategic positions for the protection of European farmers. In the event of a theft, these Africans were to take prompt action under European command, for which they would be paid a daily wage as long as their services were required — an arrangement which undoubtedly placed far less strain on the coffers of the Government than the maintenance of a permanent force.[48]

The net around the Bushmen was closing in more tightly. The Natal Government's expediential policy of creating buffer locations and of contriving to set the African population against the Bushmen was taking effect. The Bushmen, realising that this strategy would seriously hinder their raids against the European intruders, tried desperately but in vain to dislodge and demoralise the African guards and levies. But in the long run, the Government threat of brute force on the one hand, and the promise of material gain on the other, spoke louder than traditional morality; the implementation of law and order 'to preserve the dignity of the Government' and the rewards of cash and cattle compromised the Africans' inherent diplomacy and courtesy towards the aboriginal inhabitants. At this point of the mid-nineteenth century, the balance swung decisively against the Bushmen, a swing which was given added momentum by events in Nomansland on the southern borders of Natal.

References

1. C.S.O. 12(2) p. 148, 13/6/1848.
2. *Natal No. 3*: 99.
3. C.S.O. 20(1), Nos. 7, 8, 10, 15, 24, 30/4/1849.
4. C.S.O. 21(1), No. 36, 5/9/1849.
5. C.S.O. 21(1), No. 37, 20/9/1849.
6. C.S.O. 49(2), No. 84, 25/9/1849, Nos. 97 & 91, 10 & 15/10/1849.
7. *Natal No. 3*: 197 - 201.
8. S.N.A. 1/1/2, No. 103, 23/8/1849.
9. C.S.O. 49(2), No. 84, 25/9/1849.
10. C.S.O. 12(2) p. 148, 13/6/1848.
11. C.S.O. 11(2), No. 68, 12/6/1848.
12. C.S.O. 21(1), No. 1, 9/1/1851.
13. C.S.O. 20(1), No. 7, 15/4/1849.
14. *Natal No. 3*; 14.
15. C.S.O. 20(1), No. 28, 28/6/1849.
16. C.S.O. 3(1), No. 68, 28/6/1849.
17. C.S.O. 51(1), No. 85, 14/4/1849.
18. C.S.O. 20(1), No. 19, 8/6/1849.
19. C.S.O. 49(2), No. 78, 3/7/1849.
20. C.S.O. 2296, No. 620, 11/4/1849.
21. C.S.O. 25(1), No. 21, 18/6/1849.
22. C.S.O. 2238, No. 201, 28/9/1849.
23. C.S.O. 25(1), Nos. 21, 22 & 29, 18 & 22/6/1849, 8/9/1849.
24. S.N.A. 1/1/2, No. 101, 10/8/1849.
25. Tylden 1950; see also Gray 1849: 156, who mentions that the Bushmen near the Winterberg were under a chief named Vlux, formerly a soldier of the Cape Corps.
26. S.N.A. 1/1/2, Nos. 101, 103: 10 & 23/8/1849.
27. C.S.O. 6, Nos. 23, 24; 15 & 20/8/1849.
28. C.S.O. 45(1), No. 70, 18/10/1849.
29. *Natal Witness* 16 & 23/11/1849.
30. J. Shepstone Papers, Box 4.
31. C.S.O. 20(1), No. 7, 15/4/1849.
32. C.S.O. 3(2), No. 102, 10/8/1850.
33. C.S.O. 49(2), No. 121, 5/3/1850.
34. C.S.O. 15(2), No. 85, 27/4/1850.
35. C.S.O. 51(2), No. 94.
36. C.S.O. 49(2), Nos. 139 & 143. 29/12/1851 & 5/1/1851.
37. *Natal Independent* 16/1/1851.
38. J. Shepstone Papers, Box 4, p. 80-1.
39. Ergates 1905.
40. See p. 57.
41. C.S.O. 28(2), No. 71, 18/5/1852.
42. C.S.O. 21(4), No. 168 & 177, 25/3 & 20/4/1852.
43. *Natal Independent* 9/6/1853.
44. Walker 1963: 349-50.
45. Walker 1957: 250-1.
46. *Natal Independent* 1/8/1850.
47. *Natal Independent* 20/2/1851.
48. C.S.O. 21(1), No. 56, 30/7/1851.

Figure 29 *Site L37*

Seated figures with accoutrements lying around appear to hold a discussion centred on cattle, one of which is near a kraal or enclosure. It is uncertain what the forked objects represent—they may be the same as the weapons sometimes carried by horsemen. (See Figure 82 and page 273)

Figure 30 *Site J10*
Hunters carrying bows, arrows, quiver and a brush or fly-switch, accompanied by dogs.

Nomansland

According to a treaty signed with the Cape Government in 1844, Faku, chief of the Pondo, was given jurisdiction over a large tract of country south of the Mzimkhulu river extending from the sea to the Drakensberg mountains. He was made responsible for seizing all persons suspected of having committed offences against the British, and for delivering them to the nearest authority. In addition, any stolen cattle, horses or other property traced to within his territory had to be returned or fully compensated for.[1]

As early as 1846, after a theft from the Mkhomazi area, the Natal Government called upon Faku to put this treaty into effect with regard to the Bushman stock thieves who had been traced west of the Mzimkhulu and thus within his domain.[2]
Faku finally replied:

> The Bushmen are wild bucks who fly from rock to rock; they are things that run wild and I hold no authority over them. I do not recognise them in any way . . . . I have nothing at all to do with them, nor have I the means of pursuing them or punishing them.[3]

The British Agent among the Xhosa corroborated this assertion, and pointed out that it would be quite impossible for Faku, with not a mounted man in his country, to apprehend the wandering Bushmen who were all well mounted. Mandela, chief of the Mpondomise who lived outside the treaty area, was also approached. His people were understood to have some connection with the Bushmen living in the mountains near Clarkebury mission station, but Mandela gave a similar reply to Faku, describing the Bushmen as 'wild animals who prowl about the wild country'.

In 1848, Henry Francis Fynn, former ivory trader in Natal, was appointed British Resident among the Pondo. He reported almost total lack of control among the many tribes living within the territory nominally under Faku's jurisdiction, with the result that internecine feuds were waged continually.[4, 5]

The treaty of 1844 was obviously a farce. Nevertheless, in December 1848, after a large number of stock was taken from the Bushman's river, the Natal Government asked Fynn to enlist Faku's co-operation in an attack against the Bushmen.[6] In order to provide more effective assistance, Fynn moved to the northern part of Faku's territory, and during the months that he awaited the arrival of the forces from Natal that never materialised,[7] Fynn busied himself with collecting further information about the Bushmen and their alleged robberies. His evidence points to the existence of an interesting 'clientship' between Bantu-speakers and Bushmen in what is now the Transkei area, and clearly others than the Bushmen were implicated in the raids against the Natal farmers.

After the death of Ngcaphayi who had been punished by the Boers for his participation in stock thefts, the Bhaca split into two sections, one under the regency of Mamjucu, Ngcaphayi's widow, and the other under her son Mchithwa. Mchithwa and his brother Bhekezulu lived on the outposts of their territory high up the Mzimvubu river, and it was generally known among the Pondo that the Bushmen residing near the headwaters of the Mzimvubu stole cattle from Natal. The Bushmen used a drift across the river about eight miles from the furthermost Bhaca kraals, and were in the habit of selling the tails of the cattle they slaughtered to the Bhaca who used them for ornamental dress. Early in 1849 the Bushmen returned from Natal with about twenty head of cattle bearing European brands. The Bushmen slaughtered three of these, and their Bhaca neighbours joined in the festivities, dancing and drinking beer with the Bushmen. Some of the Bhaca visitors were seen returning to their kraals across the river carrying meat, and the following day they came back to the Bushmen for further supplies.[8]

The remainder of the cattle were kept at the Bushman kraals for four nights when they were collected by some of Hans Lochenberg's people. Hans Lochenberg, son of a notorious freebooter, elephant hunter and fugitive from justice, was himself of mixed descent and had about 200 followers.[9] It was specifically noted that some of these people wore hats, an observation that can possibly be related to paintings of stock raids associated with drovers who wear hats. (Figures 27, 31). The Bushmen were seen to accompany Lochenberg's people with the cattle, and after eight days' absence, the Bushmen returned with dogs purchased in exchange for the cattle. (Figure 30). On another occasion, they exchanged cattle for corn. Lochenberg himself was alleged to have obtained two horses from the Bushmen, but he later denied this accusation, and produced a Bushman who resided among the Bhaca to witness his innocence.[10,11] There was apparently a strong alliance between Lochenberg, Mchithwa and the Bushmen, and it was rumoured that they planned to unite and together occupy the country on the upper Mzimvubu.

Figure 31 *Site W21*

Drovers, one wielding a whip and another wearing a hat, separate cattle from horses. The Bushman stock raiders were in the habit of trading stolen cattle to their Bantu neighbours, but kept the horses themselves. In the rock shelter, the paintings are orientated so that the cattle are driven towards Ramatseliso Nek, a pass leading to the upper reaches of the Mzimvubu, while the horses face upstream the Tsoelike river towards the Sehlabathebe basin in Lesotho. At the upper left there are two fat-tailed sheep, and three others, reproduced in Figure 85, are further to the left. Above the horses on the right, and at the same level to the left but not included in this block, a series of horizontal lines suggest an element of landscape. They possibly represent a track or a river. The original composition is in black, grey, orange and white.

58

Figure 32 *Site W21*

A photograph of part of the scene reproduced on the opposite page. Vandalism in the form of scratching, and the recent application of commercial paint, has been omitted from the tracing on the left.

Photo: Pat Carter.

Through his intelligence system, Fynn learned that some of Lochenberg's followers had set themselves up as agents between the Pondo and the Bushmen. It was cited that a Pondo client obtained a cow in exchange for a roll of tobacco which the agent transmitted to the Bushman vendor. The commission received by the agent was another roll of tobacco plus a garden hoe. The cow itself was not directly handed over, but had to be fetched by the client from a hiding place on the understanding that he would slaughter it immediately lest it be seen by the British Resident.[12]

Fynn sent a spy to the Bhaca kraals on the upper Mzimvubu who confirmed that there was a party of Bushmen living nearby. Taking two Bhaca as guides, the spy then walked up the Mzimvubu river through uninhabited country for six or seven hours, where he found another Bushman kraal. The only occupants were four women and a sick man, who said that their cattle were taken care of by Bhekezulu, Mchithwa's brother. On the opposite side of the river a second Bushman kraal could be seen where twenty or thirty cattle and five horses were grazing.

On establishing the participation of the Bhaca in the stock thefts, Fynn demanded that the Bushman thieves should be captured and the stolen cattle handed over, but the principal men of the tribe declared it impossible to make immediate prisoners of the Bushmen because they had gone away to hunt. When Fynn's envoy visited Mamjucu, co-regent of the Bhaca, to insist on punitive action, she stated that Mchithwa had openly declared that the Bushmen were not to be molested on any account; if she defied her son and took the Bushmen by force, she would not only cause dissension among her own people, but would also be opposed by Mandela whose tribe had intermarried among the Bushmen. This in turn would invoke the displeasure of Hans Lochenberg who was quoted as having said: 'The Bushmen and Mandela's people are under my feet. Anyone who molests them will find me fighting in their cause.'

Fynn's envoy then visited Mchithwa who, throughout the interview and on subsequent occasions, displayed a very aggressive attitude. It was learned that his brother Bhekezulu had returned from a visit over the mountains to the Sotho country at the beginning of 1849, bringing with him thirty cattle. Before going, he claimed to have given orders that the Bushmen should no longer make use of his kraals for their cattle, but that they should in future build their own. He admitted that the Bushmen did in fact have large grazing kraals nearby.

While Fynn's emissary was still delivering warnings that the Bhaca would lay themselves open to attack from the Natal Government if they continued to harbour stolen stock, a report came in that the Bushmen who had been out 'hunting' had just arrived with yet more cattle from Natal, and that these had been secreted in a forest near Mchithwa's kraal.[13]

By the end of April, 1849, Fynn still did not know whether a force from Natal was arriving or not, yet from his emissaries as well as other witnesses, he knew that three lots of cattle had been driven to the source of the Mzimvubu river since the beginning of the year. The dates of their arrival among the Bhaca are only approximately recorded, but can almost certainly be related to thefts from the Bushman's river area which took place during the months December, February and March. Part of the spoils from these same raids were traced to Bushman haunts on the upper Mzimkhulu, which confirms the pursuers' suspicions that the booty was divided, and suggests a certain amount of contact and co-operation between the Bushmen of the Mzimvubu and Mzimkhulu areas.[14] Later, Fynn wrote to the Natal Government saying 'the Bushmen are out hunting again', and this coincided with another theft from the Bushman's river at the beginning of August.[15,16]

When Fynn heard that the Bhaca had had the effrontery to continue receiving stolen animals even after negotiations to make good the previous misdeeds had commenced, he sent for Mchithwa, demanding an explanation and insisting that he should immediately seize and deliver the Bushmen. Mchithwa again evaded the issue by saying he was afraid of the Bushmen's poisoned arrows, and he suggested that the British Resident should perform the task himself. Fynn's response was decisive. He promptly arrested Mchithwa, and called upon Faku to punish the Bhaca and those of Mandela's and Lochenberg's people who were implicated in the thefts. The result was that two hundred and fifty-one cattle were impounded, of which ninety were forwarded to Natal. The majority of these were awarded to a farmer residing on the Mngeni river who had lost stock the previous February.[17-19] Mchithwa promised that if he was given his freedom and allowed to return to his people, he would capture the Bushmen and call upon his tribe to make restitution. To give added encouragement to this measure, and to prevent the Bushmen from finding asylum among the Bantu-speakers, Fynn offered a reward of four head of cattle for each Bushman prisoner produced. His report of May, 1849, noted that ten head of cattle had already been expended in that service. Whether this implies that one of three prisoners was a juvenile worth only two cattle is not clear, nor is it stated what became of the captives.[20]

The result of Fynn's attack on the Bhaca and Mandela's people was a vehement protest from the missionaries east of the Kei river. They maintained that the Bhaca were innocent, and that the Bushmen responsible for the thefts were not those near the Bhaca but others who lived three days' journey away on the headwaters of the Mzimvubu river.[21] Fynn on the other hand, who had long experience of native laws and custom and was a fluent linguist, felt there was a very strong case against the accused. He was also satisfied that the several bands of Bushmen living at various points on the Mzimvubu river and its tributaries were all implicated in the thefts to a greater or lesser extent.[22, 23]

After the settlement of Natal by whites, Mdwebo and his band had slowly withdrawn from the middle Mkhomazi area where they had originally lived, and had placed themselves in clientship to the Bhaca. This band, which also had contacts with the acculturated Bushmen under Yele near the mouth of the Mzumbi,[24] habitually roamed the country between the Ngeli mountains and the Mzimkhulu river. Mdwebo was also related to a small band under Nqabayo whose home range included the Tina river, a southern branch of the Mzimvubu. Another band called the Mbaklu were said to have once lived near the sources of the Mzimvubu, but it was not known what had become of them. In any event, the upper Mzimvubu was currently occupied by a large band known as the Thola Bushmen with whom Mdwebo and his allies were at enmity. The Thola hunted the plains at the foot of the Drakensberg escarpment, the Mvenyane tributary of the Mzimvubu being specifically mentioned as one of their haunts,[25] but they never went further seawards than the Ngeli mountains. Their territory also extended northwards over the Drakensberg escarpment into the eastern tributaries of the Orange river. Bushmen other than the Thola, and with whom the Bushmen living among the Bhaca 'apparently had occasional contact, occupied the Orange river valley itself, presumably within Lesotho, but the name by which this band was known has not been recorded.[26] From this and other indications in the archival evidence there appears to have been a network of contact between individual groups of Bushmen extending from the Tsitsa river in the south to the Bushman's river in the north, and from the Orange river in the west to the Indian Ocean in the east; in all, a considerable extent of country covering some 150 miles in each direction.[27]

When Fynn began his investigations into the Natal stock thefts, he sent spies to the separate bands of Bushmen occupying the Ngeli mountains and the upper Mzimvubu on the pretext of enquiring whether they had any ivory for sale. Later entries in his diary suggest that he maintained watch on their movements, for on the 23rd June 1849 he notes that 'the Bushmen residing with the Bhaca had recently visited the upper Bushmen at the Sanguu [Sinqu or Orange river] and a cow had been killed for them'. It is probable that they had gone to warn their compatriots of danger of an attack from Natal, for in July Fynn learned that the Bushmen living on the Orange river were on the alert, and had killed a horse prior to moving further away.[28] This indicates that during the mid-nineteenth century at least, there was a certain amount of cohesion between the Mzimvubu Bushmen and those living over the mountains in what is now Lesotho, as well as with the Bushmen of the upper Mzimkhulu, all of whom raided cattle from as far afield as the Bushman's river in Natal. These factors are significant in that similarities noted in the subject matter and style of the paintings in these areas may legitimately be ascribed to cultural contact, if not cultural homogeneity, among the Bushmen living there.

After the intervention of the missionaries in Fynn's handling of affairs in Nomansland, more and more evidence was produced to exonerate the peoples originally accused and punished for the stock thefts. Fynn, who was thus placed in an invidious position, requested the Natal government to institute a full enquiry to clarify the situation. When this eventually took place most of the statements initially made to Fynn were refuted in the presence of Walter Harding, who led the enquiry. It was said that many of the witnesses were intimidated by Hans Lochenberg, whose brother also acted as Harding's not altogether impartial interpreter.[29, 30] However, whilst sifting through the prevaricating and circumlocutory evidence, Harding saw a golden opportunity for further successful action against the robber Bushmen. His informants supported the missionaries in attributing the thefts to the Thola, who were described as 'wild Bushmen riding on horses' who dwelt in the rugged foothills of the Drakensberg mountains. Mandela of the Pondomise and the Bushman chief Mdwebo, who had been directly accused of the theft of Ogle's cattle from the Bushman's river, joined in deflecting the blame, and expressed their willingness to guide a force from Natal to the hide-outs of the real culprits.[31]

It was said that the Thola, under Biligwana, consisted of a mixture of about 200 Bushmen, Hottentots and runaway servants, and that large herds of cattle, sheep and goats plundered from Natal, as well as from the Cape borders, were in their possession. It was also claimed that many of the Thola were armed with guns, and for this reason, neither Mandela nor Mdwebo were willing to attack them without the backing of a European force.[32, 33]

Harding therefore strongly urged the Government to act vigorously, and to send a force of thirty to forty burghers without delay. Volunteers to go on commando against the Bushmen were immediately called for, but the response was once again most disappointing.[34-36] At this crucial point, a new Lieutenant-Governor was appointed to Natal, and Harding was recalled to the seat of Government in Pietermaritzburg.

Harding's departure from Nomansland did not, however, ease the tense situation created by Fynn's accusation and the enquiry that followed. Mdwebo's Bushmen felt let down when their offer to guide a commando to the thieves in the mountains was not taken up, although a statement by Qinti, Mdwebo's son, suggests that their principal motivation was to enlist help in attacking the Thola against whom they were waging a personal feud. Biligwana's Bushmen had apparently initiated the trouble by killing a man of Nqabayo's band, after which Mdwebo united with his ally Nqabayo in a retaliatory attack. The result was several fatalities, as well as the capture of stock and a gun. Qinti claimed that this was the stock seen by the Uys brothers in Mdwebo's possession in 1846, when Nqabayo's son had been carrying the gun. Qinti also maintained that Biligwana and his sons were among the enemy killed, after which defeat the remainder of Biligwana's followers joined the Thola.[37-39] If this information is correct, it is difficult to understand why Biligwana was still referred to as leader of the Thola. Whatever the truth of the story, Mdwebo's band was not on the best of terms with the Thola, and apart from wanting to settle old grudges, they were only too ready to expose the Thola as a guilty party in order to clear themselves from suspicion as participants in the stock thefts. (Figures 33a, 33b)

Mdwebo's Bushmen accordingly enlisted the help of four armed Hottentots, and set off on an expedition towards the Drakensberg on their own account, despite the season being mid-winter. After passing a large vlei with abundant water-fowl, they surprised and shot some Bushmen among the mountains, but found no cattle. Arriving at the Orange river, they followed the eastern branches upwards through rugged and precipitous country which they noted was but scantily supplied with game. They did, however, come across many rudely constructed stone kraals with numerous bullocks' heads lying about. Then, at a point almost parallel with the sources of the Mzimkhulu river, they surprised an inhabited kraal.[40] Despite a determined resistance, four of the resident Bushmen, including their chief Mjinga, were killed, and eighteen prisoners

Figure 33a   *Site W23*

Opponents use knobbed sticks to settle a dispute. No physical distinction is drawn between the combatants, and some of them wear the knobbed head-dress that was favoured by the Bushmen who were involved in stock theft. (See Figures 26, 28)

were taken — one man, nine women and eight children. In the kraal, the marauding party found gear from a horse-waggon, and other European articles such as bridles, iron pots and copper ladles. There was also an enclosure made of stakes driven into the ground, wattled by strips of hide from the slaughtered cattle, and with the interstices well filled with skulls and horns. The whole place was littered with bones, which gave the impression that hundreds of animals had been destroyed on the same spot. Mdwebo's Bushmen learned that there were other Bushman kraals higher up the river, but a heavy fall of snow prevented further offensive action. They therefore turned homewards with their prisoners and twenty-one head of captured cattle, and several horses. The Thola prisoners maintained that at the time of the attack, most of the men of their party were on a foraging expedition to Natal.[41-43]

This information coincided with a daring raid on a farm in the immediate neighbourhood of the Bushman's river military post in July.[44-46] The newly appointed Lieutenant-Governor lamented that Harding's request for a force to chastise the Bushmen had not been met and, realising that attempts to guard Natal's frontiers against the stock thieves were both difficult and futile, resolved to apply pressure on chief Faku of the Pondo yet again. To put this into effect, he sanctioned a commando not exceeding fifty men, to be led by Walter Harding.[47] It seems that no more than about a dozen co-operative burghers could be found, but with this small force Harding sallied forth to Pondoland.[48] His instructions were to demand from Faku, in terms of the former treaty, full restoration of all the stock stolen from Natal and traced into his territory, totalling about 1 000 animals. Faku was also to use his 'best exertions to seize and deliver all persons reasonably suspected of having committed thefts', and if he pleaded inability to do this, Harding was to assist him.[49-52]

Unfortunately, the official report of this mission cannot be traced in the Natal records, but it seems that Harding duly demanded the 1 000 head of cattle from Faku which, through Fynn's not inconsiderable influence, were eventually collected. The seizure of those 'reasonably suspected of having committed the thefts' was another matter. Fynn, who knew very well that the force under Harding's command was inadequate to achieve any success, pointed out that the various bands of Bushmen could at all times find asylum either with Mandela or with the Bhaca who openly protected the Bushmen, and their intelligence system was such that the approach of Harding's party was widely known long before he reached Faku's country.[53]

Figure 33b *Site W23*
A fight between Bushmen. The weapons used by both sides are short bows and arrows.

The missionaries with whom Harding communicated were firmly of the opinion that Mdwebo's Bushmen were innocent, and that solely the Thola were responsible for the stock thefts from Natal. They believed that Mdwebo's Bushmen had acquired colonial cattle only indirectly as a result of their initial attack on the Thola some time between 1843 and 1845. Harding was quick to point out that, according to Uys's evidence, animals stolen in 1846[54] had been seen in the possession of Mdwebo's Bushmen, and this was *after* their attack when the stock was reputedly captured.[55, 56] Notwithstanding Harding's doubts as to the innocence of Mdwebo's band, he does not seem to have taken any direct action against them, but simply demanded the cattle and prisoners they had taken on their recent raid against the Thola.[57] Not all the prisoners, however, could have been handed over, for the local newspaper reported Harding's return to Pietermaritzburg with a thousand head of Faku's cattle and only four or five of the initial eighteen Bushmen captives. These unfortunate people were subsequently distributed among members of the expedition, presumably as servants.[58, 59] A year later a Natal businessman requested permission to send two Bushman children to his partner in England.[60] It was presumably these children, a boy aged 14 and a girl of 16 years, described as orphans originating from an area towards the sources of the Orange river, who were exhibited in London in 1853. They had been in England since 1851, in the care of a Mr George.[61] It is stated that he 'civilized' the children, but it is not known what finally became of them.

It was rumoured that, cut to the quick by the loss of so much stock, Faku fell upon the Bushmen in vengeance and exterminated many of them.[62] Faku also realised that he had nothing to gain and everything to lose by his former treaty with the British. He therefore sent word, via Fynn, that he could not continue to be held responsible for 'the acts of wolves', and he begged the Natal Government to take his country under their management and themselves control the people within it.[63]

Feeling that it was unjust to accept both Faku's country and his livestock, the Lieutenant-Governor resolved to return 600 of the confiscated cattle, promising that the remainder would follow when the complete cession of his territory was concluded.[64] However, with part of his wealth restored, Faku felt differently about giving away his land, and supported by the missionaries, he repudiated his previous request. Although envoys were sent to settle the differences, the new land treaty agreed upon was never ratified by the Colonial Office.[65, 66]

The upper Mzimvubu continued to be a Nomansland administered by no particular authority, and therefore became a haven not only for Bushmen, but also for refugees and remnants of former chiefdoms, as well as individual freebooters, opportunists, racketeers and renegades of all castes and colours. The Bushmen became pawns and scapegoats at the hands of unprincipled profiteers, and irrespective of who were responsible for the stock raids, the Bushmen were always blamed.

During this lawless period in Nomansland, an increasing liaison developed between the hunter Bushmen and landless people of mixed blood who were generally referred to as 'Hottentots'. In about 1850, a body of between forty and fifty of these discontented 'Hottentots' who had rebelled against the Cape Government, located themselves with the Bushmen under Mdwebo on the Tina and Mzimvubu rivers. Their leader, Martinus, was a wily impostor who went about the countryside forcing the inhabitants to slaughter cattle or goats for him, often rejecting the proffered meat as not being of a high enough quality to match his own superior rank. This practice led to his arrest, yet even while he was Fynn's prisoner, he continued to intimidate the Bushmen, threatening them with lightning from heaven, and declaring that he could at any moment release himself from his fastenings by divulging the secret routes used for stealing cattle. Martinus was taller than the Bushmen, commented Fynn, and wore scanty European clothing, and for these reasons they looked up to him as 'a White Man to whom the greatest respect is due'. After serving his detention in Pietermaritzburg, Martinus returned to his people and incited further disorders. Some Bushmen joined him, but most of Mdwebo's band refused to participate. The mixed Hottentot-Bushman party then terrorised the countryside, marauding and plundering cattle and horses, and were reported to be moving towards Natal. Hulley, a lay preacher among the Bhaca, confirmed that various groups of Hottentots and Bushmen had recently fallen back to the mountain caves, and that a united attack was feared.[67-69] This caused quite a stir in Natal, especially when it was rumoured that the marauders had taken refuge between the Mzimkhulu and Mkhomazi rivers. The chiefs located at the foot of the Drakensberg north of this area were warned of the intruders, and instructed to apprehend them. It was feared that the rebel Hottentot band would league themselves with Bushmen known to inhabit the mountains immediately beyond Langalibalele's domain on the Bushman's river, and that six Hottentot deserters from the nearby military post would also join them. John Shepstone was despatched to investigate the rumours,

Figure 34

Magaditseng, Kenegha Poort, Mount Fletcher district.
In 1851, Chief Mchithwa of the Bhaca, a patron of the Bushmen, was killed by a poisoned arrow which penetrated his abdomen. He had been pursuing cattle stolen from the upper Mzimvubu.

but they proved to be unfounded.[70-73]

Back on the Mzimvubu where raids and counter-raids had become the order of the day, some Bushmen stole cattle from the Bhaca. They were immediately pursued by none other than chief Mchithwa, himself a former champion of the Bushmen. During the chase, a poisoned arrow hit Mchithwa in the thigh, but after cutting out the flesh around the wound, he still followed on. A second arrow penetrated his abdomen and this proved fatal, a paradoxical end for a man who had initially refused to capture his Bushman clients because he feared their poisoned arrows.[74-76] (Figure 34.) Those Bushmen under Mdwebo who had not been involved in the affray swiftly moved south of the Mthatha river, doubtless to seek refuge from possible retaliation, but the following year (1852), Mdwebo's son Qinti testified that his band was again living with and under the protection of the Bhaca.

The Rev. Albert Schweiger, a missionary on the Kei river during the early years of this century, recorded from oral sources how the Xhosa chief Rarabe, having initially obtained his land from a Hottentot chief in exchange for skins, tobacco and dogs, then set about exterminating the Bushmen. There is an interesting story of

Bushmen holding as hostage some of Rarabe's men who had killed game in their territory, in retaliation for which the Bushmen made reprisals on the Xhosa stock. This evoked vicious counter-attacks in which the Xhosa ambushed entire groups of Bushmen in their shelters, slaughtering them mercilessly and burning the dreaded quivers full of poisoned arrows. Despite this traditional antagonism, however, there were still aged Africans living on the Kei river between 1908 and 1912, who had seen Bushmen and claimed to have traded with them.[77, 78]

A similar example of the dual relationship between Bushmen and Bantu-speakers is evident from a statement made in 1884 by a converted stock-thief named Silayi. Himself a Thembu, he said that on the Tsitsa river (immediately south of the Tina where Lochenberg and Mandela grazed their ill-gotten herds), many of his people were still on comparatively friendly terms with the Bushmen in the 1850s, despite their thieving propensities. There was enough give and take, it seems, for the occasional misdemeanour, once punished or recompensed, to be forgiven. Apart from the advantage of being able to add to their herds at very little cost by bartering with the Bushman stock-thieves, the Bantu held the aboriginal hunters in high repute as rain-makers, and they were much in demand during the dry seasons.[79-81] Silayi tells how he and a Hottentot companion were introduced to a clan of Bushmen living in the mountains in the Maclear district through the medium of a Bush-Hottentot half-caste. The old Bushman leader, apparently none other than Mdwebo's ally Nqabayo, supplied the visitors with five young men, and together they set out along the foot of the Drakensberg bent on stock theft. When near the sources of the Kraai river, the Bushmen complained that the novices would merely be a hindrance, and the party split. Not to be outdone, however, Silayi and his friends persevered, and drove off a fine troop of horses belonging to a Boer. When they returned with their booty to the Tsitsa river, they fell foul of the Thembu chief who objected to the theft. Taking some of the stolen horses with them, the three men defected to the Bushmen who were then living in a different part of the mountain. They were given bows and arrows and received into the band which mustered forty-three men and sported three flint-lock guns. Following on successful stock raids to the Wodehouse district, the band moved down river but were repelled by the Thembu and driven back to the Drakensberg. Further thefts provoked an attack from the Boers. When cornered in their cave, the Bushmen defended themselves fiercely with bows and arrows, but the Boers nevertheless succeeded in wounding three of their number. Fortunately for the Bushmen, night intervened, and under cover of darkness, they drove the stolen animals further into the mountains and escaped.

Silayi took the daughter of his Hottentot friend as a wife, and after living three years among the Bushmen, he was able to give considerable insight into their way of life. In the foothills of the Drakensberg, he said, there was no necessity to construct huts, for they all slept together in one cave. He described the jubilation with which the women and children greeted the men on their return from a successful raid, and how, according to custom, the women besmeared themselves from the rumen of the slaughtered oxen, afterwards washing in the nearest stream. The Bushmen used fires and sticks stuck into the ground as signals, and they were also able to convey messages by waving the skin cloaks they wore. The leader of the band prepared and distributed arrow poison which was made by boiling ingredients of vegetable origin in a clay pot until a black-looking jelly was produced. Paintings were made from natural ochres obtained from the ground, and some pigments were prepared at the fire. Silayi commented that the people of Nqabayo's band could paint very well.

After leaving the Bushmen and returning to his own people, Silayi heard that the band had been severely punished in about 1858 when they misguidedly stole stock from their Nguni neighbours, and very few survived this attack. Old Nqabayo and his daughter escaped, and with a few men and two boys, first took refuge under

Figure 35

Part of a poorly preserved herd of cattle in dark red from Mangolong East, Mount Fletcher district. Disturbances and disputes over cattle were rife in this area between 1840 and 1870.

another Nguni chief, and later went back to the mountains around the sources of the Mzimvubu river. The 'Hottentot' subsequently joined the Griqua under Adam Kok.[82, 83]

It was also in 1858 that Robert Speirs, a Natal farmer from near Dargle, followed up a stock theft across the Mzimkhulu into Nomansland. He visited Hulley, a lay evangelist at Shawbury mission, for advice on how to retrieve his stolen animals. Hulley's comments on the volatile relationships between the various racial groups agree well with Silayi's statement.

All along the base of the Drakensberg in Nomansland there were petty chiefs who collaborated with the Bushmen in stock thieving, and only a short time previously, had been punished by Faku who deprived them of about 3 000 head of cattle. This was several years after the punishment instigated by Fynn in 1849, and suggests that, after having been heavily fined by the Natal Government, Faku was making some attempt to inhibit the depredations. Presumably when these people were attacked by Faku, they in turn fell upon the Bushmen, when the likes of Nqabayo's band were broken up.

The mountains beyond the more settled peoples were generally referred to as Lisawana's Mountains. Lisawana, brother of the Phuti chief, Moorosi, was reputedly the leader of a group of Bushmen, and Hulley knew that cattle belonging to chief Lugaju in Natal had been stolen in 1855 by a combined party of Hottentots, Africans and Bushmen under Lisawana. This party subsequently broke up, but the Hottentots returned a few months later and attacked their old allies, taking about ninety head of cattle that had been Lisawana's share under the joint foray. (Figure 40)

Speirs himself visited these rebel Hottentots, and found among them a European, Thomas Heron, who confirmed that the Hottentots had raided Lisawana several months previously. No doubt to make good these losses, Lisawana, with about twelve Bushmen and two Basotho, set off towards the Orange river, and returned with thirteen horses from the Cape Colony. At the same time, another party went towards Natal and returned with cattle. The Cape Frontier Armed and Mounted Police followed the horses into Moorosi's territory, and this chief was accused of conniving at the theft. Pressured by the police, Moorosi provided guides to locate the Bushmen under his brother Lisawana, but Speirs heard that the party had been led on a wild goose chase into the depths of the Drakensberg, whereas in reality the culprits were sheltering among the Thembu and Bhaca at the base.[84] Another report by one of the

police present on that occasion states that after holding court, Moorosi ordered a fine, and although many of the horses were recovered, the Bushmen themselves were never seen.[85]

Because Lisawana's party had five or six guns and knew how to use them well, Speirs was advised not to attempt a reprisal without sufficient backing, but his attempts to enlist armed assistance from among Africans as well as Hottentots failed. Thwarted at every turn by involved excuses and lengthy procrastinations, Speirs summarised the situation in Nomansland thus:

> So there it stands. Faku will not have it, Natal does not claim it, and parties of thieves and robbers do just what they like with it.[86]

At this time Governor Sir George Grey embarked on an active 'civilizing' policy along the north-eastern frontiers of the Cape Colony. This resulted in the rebellious Hottentots who had been expelled from the Cape settlements being driven further towards the borders of Natal.[87] In February 1859, it was reported that the Hottentots were living on the Ibisi river where Mdwebo's Bushmen had previously roamed. The magistrate of the upper Mkhomazi division centred at Richmond went to investigate, and found about fifty people with at least ten stand of firearms and a waggon. They lived in reed shelters, and had brought with them a large number of horses, including some from the Orange river. Other Hottentots were located on the Mthamvuna river as well as among the Bhaca on the Mzimvubu. A regular communication was reported to exist between these several settlements and the Hottentot communities of Natal, the Cape Colony and the Orange Free State. The following year it was rumoured in alarm that the Hottentots, whose bands included known rebels from the Cape Colony and little clans of Bushmen, had sent a deputation to Adam Kok requesting reinforcements so that a system of plundering Natal's outlying farms could be organised.[88-90]

By 1860, therefore, the association between 'Bushmen' and 'Hottentots' in Nomansland was apparently well established. Both peoples were of predominantly Khoisan stock, and both peoples herded cattle, rode horses, and hunted with the bow and arrow[91] as well as with European firearms. The distinction between 'Bushman' and 'Hottentot', at all times based on confused criteria, must have become increasingly difficult to detect. It is for these reasons that possible 'Hottentot' influence on some of the Drakensberg rock paintings cannot be entirely eliminated, although if it existed at all, it was undoubtedly minimal.[92]

Figure 36

A site on York *farm in the Ongeluk's Nek valley shows warriors carrying three different types of shields, pictorial proof of the heterogeneous mixture of peoples who had invaded the Bushmen's terrain in so-called Nomansland by 1864.*

Above, cattle are the cause of a dispute between warriors carrying heavy spears and another protecting himself with an oval shield of the type used by the southern Nguni. For the sake of clarity, fragmentary black paint between the second and third figures has been omitted from this copy. (See also Figures 37, 38.)

In the hinterland to the north and west of Nomansland, many of the peoples scattered by the Shaka wars and the upheavals of the Mfecane were being welded together by chief Moshoeshoe. As the Sotho kingdom grew and expanded, it is reported that more and more Bushmen spilled down the mountains into Nomansland.[93] It was not long, however, before the Basotho followed them there.

In 1858 Moshoeshoe sent his son Nehemiah to establish a claim to the land on the upper Mzimvubu still not under the jurisdiction of any recognised authority.[94] When the Basotho descended the Drakensberg and settled on the hill country below, they disturbed great flocks of duck from the extensive marshes in that vicinity. This, according to tradition, is the origin of the name Matatiele, meaning *the duck have flown*.[95] Little is known of the Bushmen's reactions to the arrival of the Basotho, but rock paintings in the Ongeluk's Nek valley show warlike Basotho with spears and shields, and cattle are also depicted. (Figures 36, 37, 38). Even if the Bush-

men put up a certain amount of resistance to the intruders, they had no ultimate chance of survival. Want of land was causing friction on all sides, and more and more eyes turned hungrily towards this so-called 'uninhabited' country.[96] The Griqua, with a strong Hottentot or Khoi strain in their ancestry, were being hounded from their terrain to the west of the present Orange Free State.

In 1859, an exploratory party under their leader Adam Kok made an epic trek by ox-waggon across southern Lesotho, descending the escarpment at Qacha's Nek. The Natal Government was doubtless somewhat surprised, for they had themselves been seeking a direct route through the mountains for some years without success. Not realising the immensely rugged nature of the terrain, they imagined that the passage pioneered by Kok would not only open up trade, but would also be a means of 'extirpating' the Bushmen who had their 'hiding places at the roots of the Drakensberg'.[97-99]

The following year, 1860, the farmers of the Upper Mngeni presented a memorandum on the Bushman problem to Governor Sir George Grey when he was on a visit to decide the future of Nomansland. It was said he instructed Sir Walter Currie, commander of the Frontier Police Force, 'to give the Bushmen the benefit of his best attentions', and he also granted Nomansland to the Griqua, hoping they would act as a civilising influence and a buffer against Basotho infiltration.[100, 101]

This caused no little dissension since Natal claimed part of the terrain as a result of the treaty with Faku; and the Bhaca, the Pondo and the Basotho under Nehemiah, son of Moshoeshoe, all resented the intrusion of yet another people. Feuds, attacks and thefts

Figure 37 York *farm, Ongeluk's Nek*
A warrior wearing horns or feathers on his head stands concealed behind a large hour-glass shaped shield. He carries a long-handled spear with broad blade. The painting is in black, and the shield, including stick, measures 16 cm.

Photo: Pat Carter.

Figure 38 York *farm, Ongeluk's Nek*
Basotho warriors carrying indented shields of the pattern used by Moshoeshoe and his adherents. These paintings, in black, are executed on an exfoliated area of rock surrounded by fragmentary paintings in dark red of an earlier period.

broke out on all fronts, and the situation was aggravated by the subsequent arrival of other displaced rivals including Basotho under Makwai, Batlokoa under Lehana, and Hlubi under a brother of Langalibalele.[102-106]

In 1864, Sir Walter Currie, accompanied by members of the Imperial army as well as the Frontier Armed and Mounted Police, visited Nomansland in an effort to settle the land claims. In addition, as was common among the armed forces at that time, they took advantage of the opportunities offered for big game shooting. (Figure 40)[107]

Despite intermittent visits from military authority, conditions in Nomansland continued to be chaotic. In 1872, a commission sent to investigate the cause of constant upheavals found the country in an indescribable state of confusion. Everywhere were traces of burnt kraals and devastated crops, with each community regarding its neighbour as a mortal enemy. Joseph Orpen was appointed British Resident in 1873 to prevent the various factions from exterminating one another, and Colonial magistrates soon followed to implement law and order.[108]

Nomansland gave way to East Griqualand, and the Bushmen gave way to everyone. Except in a few isolated pockets, they seem not to have survived the chaos as distinct social entities still preserving the traditions and practices of hunter-gatherers.[109]

The picture that emerges of the close association between Bushmen and Bantu in Nomansland in the mid-nineteenth century, and the two-way trade that existed between them, is well illustrated by an unusually complex rock-painting in the Muguswana Reserve on the Mcatsheni tributary of the Mkhomazi river. Although much of the subject matter has become too faded for certain identification, it clearly represents a scene in which Bushman encampments are being visited by Africans, and in which a mêlée of domestic stock is involved. Elements of scenery, a rare feature in the art of the Drakensberg, are suggested by paths that apparently lead to and from three separate Bushman camps, and along which various groups of people walk or animals are driven. (Figure 39)

The full sequence of events in this detailed picture is unfortunately impossible to reconstruct on a completely factual basis, but enlightened guesses can be made thanks to the evidence gathered by Henry Fynn. The Bushmen, it would seem, have returned from a successful stock raid, bringing with them cattle, horses and a few fat-tailed sheep. One of the drovers wears a European-type brimmed hat in association with decorative skin tassels at the knees. Africans have arrived at the Bushman encampments and have laid down their ox-hide shields before settling down to parley. The shields are of various designs: the long narrow pattern pointed at both ends which is typical of the Zulu fighting shield, the more oval variety used by the Pondo, and in one instance, the indented type adopted by the Basotho after 1820.[110] This mixture of ethnographic detail bears out the heterogeneous composition of the peoples with whom the Mountain Bushmen associated after the upheavals of the Mfecane wars.

Immediately below the central encampment, where dogs lie in attendance, two paths seem to join. Along the uppermost some cattle are being driven, including a bull with a halter on its head. Above, a troop of horses, also wearing halters, travel in the opposite direction. This may be taken to mean that the cattle and horses are being separated out, the cattle for the Bantu, while the horses are retained by the Bushmen. An unusual detail is the stallion mounting a haltered mare immediately below the road junction. Along the lower path, and walking uphill towards the central camp, are some figures followed by dogs. Two of these are naked and apparently of Bush type judging from the stature of one, while the other two are clad and carry what seem to be guns across their shoulders. The leader, swinging one arm forward in an exaggerated marching movement, wears a feather on his head, and sports three stripes, or bangles, on one arm. The camp on the far right from which this group is walking, is made up of three separate semi-circular huts or shelters, each with occupants. One of these seated

Figure 39 *Site E11*

This detailed scene showing the association between Bushman stock raiders and the Bantu to whom they bartered stolen cattle is one of the few in the Drakensberg that incorporates natural features or elements of scenery. People sit in skerms or shelters, weapons laid aside and dogs lying in wait, while they discuss, bargain and conclude a deal. The combination of various shield designs with bows is evidence of the heterogeneous mixture of peoples involved in the trade. At the upper centre is a marching figure, carrying a gun and powder horn. He is possibly a European as he wears a broad-brimmed hat, uniform trousers with buttons on the legs, and boots. A series of pathways, some of which appear to follow up and down mountains, are followed by groups of people, some with dogs, and files of horses and cattle. At the lower end of the composition are more horses, cattle and what may be fat-tailed sheep, but this part of the scene is unfortunately very fragmentary. It is also possible that there were more paintings to the left; this area of the rock face is badly stained by drip marks. The detailed contents and significance of this scene are more fully discussed in the text.

Figure 40 *Site Q8*

In 1864, members of the Imperial Army and the Frontier Armed and Mounted Police under Walter Currie visited Nomansland in an attempt to settle land claims. As was common among the armed forces at that time, they took advantage of the opportunities offered for big game shooting.

This scene on Belleview farm, painted at the base of the Cave Sandstone on a high spur overlooking the farmlands of the upper Mzimvubu, cannot be directly associated with the Commission of 1864, but it certainly portrays European members of the

armed forces firing at the Bushman's treasured eland herds. Cavalrymen of the Imperial Army habitually dismounted to fire, looping the reins over the arm. The Frontier Armed and Mounted Police adopted many of the habits of the Boers such as firing from the saddle, and horses were trained to stand when the reins hung loose. The harness on the horses includes high military-type saddles with cruppers, and military uniforms are suggested by the red jackets and black trousers outlined in red. (See Willcox 1956, Plates 45-47 for colour photographs of this scene.)

figures holds a bow. Another figure carrying a bow is shown among the group of four on the upper left, who, if the line they are walking along is indicative of a path, have just scaled a mountain. The leader of the party is a somewhat obese and highly steatopygous woman with beaded decorations on her legs. The figure immediately behind her, wearing a feathered head-dress and a long garment patterned with flecks, carries the bow. Bringing up the rear is another figure in a long kaross, carrying a bag or possibly a calabash. The villain of the story is a soldier on foot who marches resolutely along a path that leads above the camps where the bargaining is taking place. Ahead, this path drops down towards the encampment on the far right of the picture, which, in the shelter, is oriented towards the mountains. The soldier, if such he is, wears a slouch hat and carries a gun over his shoulder, with a powder horn swinging from his belt. The trousers or overalls appear to have buttons sewn down the leg-stripe, which poses a problem. This type of battle dress, like that worn by the British Hussars, went out of fashion about 1820, which is a little early to be associated with the painting.[111] The question is thus raised whether the 'soldier' depicted is European at all; he may possibly be Hottentot or Coloured, with whom discarded military uniforms became extremely popular. Nor were the Nguni immune from this vanity, for when Bishop Gray visited Natal in 1864, he recorded that the favourite dress of the Zulu in the Mkhomazi valley near Richmond, seemed to be a soldier's cast-off red coat. 'In place of a hat or head-dress, their woolly hair, which towers up to a great height, is cut into fantastic shapes, the most fashionable of which is that of a cocked hat, often very well executed.'[112] So much for being able to distinguish racial groups by the dress they wear! (Figure 52)

It is tempting to speculate whether this scene in the Muguswana Location, situated as it is at the foot of the Little Berg overlooking the Mkhomazi valley, was painted by a band of Bushmen from Nomansland when on a marauding expedition to or from the Bushman's river area. It is more likely, however, that Bushmen living on the upper reaches of the Mkhomazi were responsible, and like their compatriots on the Mzimvubu, they too had trading contacts among their Bantu-speaking neighbours.

References

1. *Natal No. 2*: 109-110.
2. *Natal No. 2*: 107-108.
3. C.S.O. 11(2), p. 197-200, 9/10/1846.
4. Fynn Papers. Fynn to Moodie, 17/3/1849.
5. Extracts from Fynn's diary, Fynn Papers, 1849.
6. C.S.O. 2296, No. 431, 28/12/1848.
7. See p. 44.
8. Fynn Papers, 13/1/1849, No. 21; Fynn to Moodie 30/1/1849.
9. Holt 1953; C.S.O. 19, p. 48, 28/4/1849.
10. C.S.O. 19, p. 50-56, 1849.
11. Fynn Papers. Notes accompanying evidence.
12. C.S.O. 19, pp. 13-40, 1849.
13. C.S.O. 19, pp. 13-49, 1849.
14. See p. 42, 46, 160.
15. S.N.A. 1/1, No. 29, 4/7/1849.
16. *Natal No. 3*: 78-81. See also p. 52.
17. *Natal No. 3*: 78-81.
18. C.S.O. 51 (1), No. 86, 18/1/1849.
19. *Natal No. 3*: 6.
20. *Natal No. 3*: 80.
21. Fynn Papers, 22/6/1849, Missionaries to Fynn.
22. Fynn Papers, 4/7/1849, Fynn to Moodie.
23. Fynn Papers, No. 100, 13/10/1851.
24. See p. 34.
25. I have visited only one painted site in the Mvenyane valley, on the farm *Kromellenboog*. Since the Thola Bushmen reputedly inhabited this valley, it is significant that the subjects painted include horned cattle.
26. The fact that separate bands of Bushmen occupied specific territories, and that some were closely allied whereas others were regarded as enemies, is of considerable interest to the archaeologist and student of rock art alike. For this reason, the statements upon which these territorial divisions are founded are given here in full.

I am indebted to J. Leeuwenburg for making copies of documents from the Cape Archives on my behalf. The original spelling has been altered to comply with the present orthography.

Cape Archives. G. H. 23, p. 408-411.
Statement of William Lochenberg. 29th March 1850.

My brother Hans Lochenberg who lives at Buntingville is the chief of a small tribe of Kaffirs, chiefly Fingos, and resides on the Tina river, on the other side of the Mzimvubu; between it and the Dabankulu mountain, and they have lived there I think about a year, but I know that Mdwebo lives sometimes at the Mzimkhulu, and at other times in the Ngeli Mountains. Bushmen generally follow the game. There is also a part of the Bhaca living between the Tina and Mzimvubu, under a chief called Mchithwa. There is also another small tribe of Kaffirs residing on the Tina near my brother's people called the Pondomise, under a chief called Mandela. There is also a small tribe of Tambookies under a chief called Joey [?] residing on the other side of the Tina, and between it and the Tsitsa river. The Tina rises out of a small range of mountains this side of Qahlamba, and turns into the Mzimvubu

I know a large tribe of Bushmen, Hottentots and runaway slaves called the Thola, living close to the side of the Qahlamba, above the Tina, and near the Mzimvubu. The name of the chief is Biligwana, and they are the Bushmen that steal not only from Natal, but from the Colony, and from my brother's people, Mdwebo's people and the other natives. These people live about three day's journey from this, on horseback, but the country is very broken.

Mr Fynn last year sent an expedition, composed of Faku's people, and took one hundred and eleven head of cattle from my brother's people, also thirty goats, and also a great many more from the Bhaca, but I do not know how many. Mr Fynn charged Mdwebo's people with being the thieves of Ogle's cattle from Natal. Upon this, Mdwebo offered Mr Fynn to point out the spoor of the stolen cattle, and the Bushmen who stole them. Mdwebo's people said there was a large track of the stolen cattle, leading to the Thola. The Thola have about two hundred men, and have plenty of horses and cattle, nearly all of which are stolen. Last year the Thola stole eight horses from Joey [?]. They were followed, and three Bushmen were killed. Mdwebo and the Thola are enemies, and I know that Mdwebo has all along and now is ready to furnish guides to point out all the stolen cattle and horses of the Bushmen who stole them.

Cape Archives. G. H. 8/23, p. 414-417.
Statement of Qinti. Palmerston, 13th April 1850.

I am the son of Mdwebo, the Bushman chief residing on this side of the Mzimvubu. We have resided there for two years, after moving from the Mkhomazi.

I know of another tribe of Bushmen called the Thola living some on this side and some on the other side of the Qahlamba [Drakensberg] mountains. The Thola are a much larger tribe of Bushmen than Mdwebo's. Mdwebo only has about fifteen men including his sons, but the Thola are a nation of people. The Thola live about four or five days' journey from this place. The Thola have many horses and cattle. Mdwebo and his people are at enmity with the Thola. We never go to hunt with them. The Thola hunt on the flats, under the Qahlamba. I also know of a small tribe of friendly Bushmen, relatives of ours, under Nqabayo, living at the Tina near the Umboonvena [? original not clear]. Many years ago there was another Bushman tribe, called the Mbaklu, living at the head of the Mzimvubu at the Qahlamba, but I do not know what has become of them. I have also heard that there are Bushmen at the Orange river. I know of no other Bushmen at present than Mdwebo's, the Thola and Nqabayo's.

I recollect the cattle being taken from the Bhaca and Lochenbergs' people by Mr Fynn. I recollect that after the cattle were taken, Hans Lochenberg [sent] to Mdwebo, and two of Mdwebo's people, namely Nqabayo and Xo Kana [?] went in consequence to Mandela. These two men are at the kraal at the Tina now. These men offered then to Mandela [of the Pondomise], that if Mr Fynn would send two men, they would point out the people who stole Ogle's cattle [from Natal]. Inasmuch as some of Nqabayo's men had seen the traces of the cattle from the Mzimkhulu leading to the Thola kraals. The track then was large and fresh. I know that Mdwebo will now give two or more men to show the spoor, and also to show the people who stole the cattle. The Thola Bushmen are still there, and can easily be found. I am sure that neither Mdwebo, Nqabayo, the Bhaca or Hans Lochenberg's people have anything to do with the thefts from Natal or anywhere else. They are all at enmity with the Thola, who are the thieves. We have only two horses and four head of cattle. I am sure that Mdwebo will give people to point out the thieves.

Cape Archives. G. H. 8/23, p. 406-408.
Statement of Mangana.

I live with and belong to Mdwebo at the Mzimvubu. I do not know Selijigy, but I heard from Nqabayo that Selijigy gave tobacco for the cow. I know the cow. She is black with a white back. I know that Nqabayo got the cow from Biligwana, a Thola Bushman. I was present when this cow was taken with many others from the Thola, when Nqabayo attacked the Thola in consequence of their stealing horses, and murdered an Englishman. This is long, but not so very long ago, and the cow was then a big heifer.

We live close to the Bhaca. The Bushmen do not belong to the Bhaca, but the Bushmen are connected with Mandela by marriage. I am sure that neither Nqabayo's Bushmen nor Mdwebo's people have ever stolen cattle from Natal. The Thola Bushmen are the people who steal. The Thola do not come into the lower country further than behind about the Ngeli Mountains.

Note: In the light of information later furnished by Silayi, a Thembu who had lived with Nqabayo's band for three years (Stanford 1910), the statements exonerating Mdwebo and Nqabayo from participation in the stock thefts are patently untrue. Nqabayo's Bushmen were, during the 1850s, actively engaged in raiding stock from farmers in the Wodehouse district of the eastern Cape, although no specific mention is made of their activities having extended as far as Natal. According to the evidence gathered by Fynn, the Mpondomise under Mandela, the Bhaca under Mchithwa, and the Bushmen under the protection of these chiefs (which included Mdwebo's band) were indisputably connected with the Natal thefts, as were the Thola Bushmen.

27. Recent excavations by P. L. Carter at Sehonghong shelter in Lesotho (X4), yielded at least 20 individual marine shells representing four different species common to the Indian Ocean. *Nassarius kraussianus* (Dunker) is found in salt marshes around estuaries and lagoons, and its distribution extends from Lourenco Marques to Saldanha Bay. *Turritella carinifera* (Lamarck) can be picked up on the open coast from Mocambique to Port Nolloth, and *Trachycardium rubicundum* (Reeve) extends from East Africa to Pondoland. The fourth species, *Cypraea tigris* Linnaeus, is rare in South African water, and is not found south of Pondoland. The sea-shells were recovered from the upper 40 centimetres of the deposit, and a date of 550 A.D. has been obtained for the 10-20 centimetre layer. These finds establish that trading contact between the mountain areas of Lesotho and the coast-line of the Indian Ocean had existed over a considerable period of time. It is of particular interest, therefore, that links between Bushman bands in these widely separated areas are confirmed by archival sources. (Personal communication P. L. Carter and J. C. Vogel, 1973. Radio-carbon Laboratory

number Pta 885. The identification of the shells was kindly undertaken by R. N. Kilburn of the Natal Museum.)

28. C.S.O. 19, p. 60, 8/5/1849.
29. Fynn Papers, 13/10/1851, Fynn to Moodie.
30. G. H. 1405, p. 212-216, 2/4/1850.
31. See p. 74.
32. G. H. 1405, p. 224-226, 29/3/1850.
33. Fynn Papers, 22/6/1849, missionaries to Fynn.
34. C.S.O. 51(2), Nos. 107, 108 & 109: 19, 24 & 25/4/1850.
35. C.S.O. 25(1), No. 44, 22/4/1850.
36. G. H. 1405, pp. 218-223, 2/4/1850.
37. Fynn Papers, No. 18, 22/9/1850.
38. Fynn Papers, No. 19, 25/9/1850.
39. Fynn Papers, statement of Qinti, 1/10/1850.
40. It is impossible to assess the exact location of these Bushmen from the available evidence. One of the most easterly branches of the Orange river is the Tsoelike, and the Leqoa tributary rises at a point parallel with the sources of the Mzimkhulu. Rock shelters abound in this area, and although paintings of horses and cattle are not common, they do occur.
41. *Natal Witness*, 23/8/1850.
42. *Natal Independent*, 11/7/1850.
43. Jenkins papers, diary, 8/7/1850.
44. G. H. 1322, Nos. 12 & 14, 23/7/1850 & 1/8/1850.
45. G. H. 1209, No. 89, 23/11/1850.
46. *Natal Independent*, 1/8/1850.
47. G. H. 1322, No. 15, 5/8/1850.
48. *Natal Witness*, 6/8/1850.
49. G. H. 129, No. 89, 23/11/1850.
50. Fynn Papers, 8/9/1850, Harding to Fynn.
51. C.S.O., 2296, 26/8/1850.
52. G. H. 1322, No. 15, 5/8/1850.
53. Fynn Papers, No. 59, 6/10/1850, Fynn to Harding.
54. Harding incorrectly states 1847, but this does not alter his argument.
55. Fynn Papers, No. 18, 22/9/1850.
56. Fynn Papers, No. 19, 25/9/1850.
57. Fynn Papers, 20/9/1850.
58. *Natal Independent*, 31/10/1850.
59. *Natal Witness*, 25/10/1850.
60. C.S.O. 2240, No. 757, 19/11/1851.
61. Africana Museum, Johannesburg, Notices of exhibitions of 'Earthmen' in Britain. Nos. 4385, 4386, 4387, 9806, 4389, 58/447.
62. *Proc. Native Affairs Commission*. Natal Govt. Gazette, 1852.
63. Fynn Papers, No. 60, 7/10/1850, Faku to Col. Govt.
64. G. H. 1209, No. 89, 23/11/1850.
65. *Natal No. 3*: 260.
66. Theal 1908 (5): 64.
67. Fynn Papers, 15/3/1850.
68. Fynn Papers, Nos. 86, 93, 94, 25/7/1851.
69. Fynn Papers, No. 161, 18/8/1851.
70. C.S.O. 26 (1), No. 12, 21/1/1851.
71. C.S.O. 27(2), No. 151, 2/1/1852.
72. J. Shepstone Papers, Box 4, p. 82.
73. *Natal Times*, 23/1/1852.
74. Fynn Papers, No. 66, ?/9/1851.
75. Fynn Papers, No. 96, 11/9/1851.
76. Fynn Papers, 1/10/1852.
77. Schweiger 1912, 1913.
78. Theal 1919: 65, 67.
79. Willcox 1963: 20.
80. Stanford 1910.
81. Hook 1908: 327.
82. Stanford 1910.
83. Willcox 1956: 34-7.
84. S.N.A. 1/18 No. 77, Speirs's Diary, 1858.
85. Hook 1908: 80.
86. S.N.A. 1/1/8 No. 77, Speirs's Diary, 1858.
87. Walker 1957: 286-8.
88. S.N.A. 1/1/9, No. 9, 12/2/1859.
89. S.N.A. 1/3/8, No. 272, 6/3/1859.
90. *Natal Mercury*, 5/7/1860.
91. In the Natal Museum there are two Hottentot bows and four arrows, larger than those of Bushmen, said to have been collected from Kokstad, East Griqualand, but the date is not specified. Catalogue No. 2573.
92. See Willcox 1963: 41 for debate on whether Hottentots were responsible for some of South Africa's rock art.
93. Dornan 1909.
94. Theal 1883, Vol. 3: xli (introduction).
95. C. P. Louw. Personal communication. Information obtained from Basotho residents of the Matatiele area.
96. Walker 1957: 284-286.
97. *Natal Mercury*, 22 & 29/12/1859.
98. C.S.O. 31/(2), No. 166, 30/5/1851.
99. Notices in *Natal Independent*, 1853.
100. *Natal Mercury*, 25/10/1860.
101. Kiewiet 1963: 418.
102. *Natal Mercury*, 4/10/1860.
103. G. H. 636, No. 46.
104. Fynn Papers, 30/6/1849.
105. Theal 1908(5): 67.
106. Walker 1957: 315.
107. Hook 1908: 128.
108. Theal 1908(5): 67.
109. See p. 104.
110. Tylden 1946.
111. Personal communication, G. Tylden 6/3/1968.
112. Gray 1864: 49.

Figure 41   *Site F2*

The horsemen in this group show mixed European and African characteristics. Most of the riders wear western-type brimmed hats yet, at top left, a skin cloak with long tail attached is shown. At centre, a figure on a small horse wears the flap-like leg decorations typical of Africans, and carries both gun and spear-like weapons. A marksman holding a gun to his shoulder and wearing a hat decorated with a large feather, has baggy European-type trousers and rides with his long legs hanging almost to the ground. By contrast, the naked legs of other riders are short and cling to the bellies of the mounts. The paintings are in black and orange, but due to exposure to long hours of direct sunshine, are now very faded.

Fort Nottingham and the Mpendle Location

Between 1852 and 1855 there was a distinct lull in Bushman activity against the farmers in Natal. At the time, this respite was attributed to the success of the buffer locations and to the fine of cattle imposed on Faku,[1] but it is more likely to have been a result of the inter-tribal upheavals in Nomansland which had direct repercussions on the organisation of the Bushman bands. After a brief period of disruption, however, it appears that Bushman alliances with Bantu-speakers who collaborated in and encouraged the thefts were re-established.[2] The actual catalyst for the resumption of activities against the Natal settlers is difficult to ascertain, but whatever the reason, the familiar pattern of raid and attempted retrieval was resumed at the beginning of winter, 1855. A herd of forty-one cattle kraaled near the Eland's river in the present Boston area were removed under cover of darkness, and a long and careful search disclosed that five or six horsemen had driven the cattle over a neck on the Nhlazane mountain, thence south-westwards to the upper reaches of the Mkhomazi. As in the past, the trail was marked by the carcases of cattle which had been stabbed, and one live beast was found that had strayed from the herd.[3] The Government, now concerned with a large influx of immigrants from Britain, do not appear to have regarded the raid very seriously, for no official action was taken.

Early in 1856, an outbreak of lungsickness in Natal prompted chief Lugaju to send a large herd of cattle to graze in isolation on the upper Mkhomazi in an attempt to avoid infection. This, no doubt, was too good an opportunity for the stock thieves to miss, and during a heavy thunder storm, six Bushmen on horseback and two on foot drove off no less than 340 cattle. The herdboys ran almost 30 miles to report the loss, and about a hundred Africans armed with assegais immediately followed the trail, continuing the chase across the Mzimkhulu and up into the mountains by moonlight. Hotly pursued, the thieves stabbed the majority of this vast herd to death because the animals were unable to keep the hectic pace. Lugaju's warriors were eventually forced back by hunger, fatigue and lack of knowledge of the country, having found nothing but a recently deserted Bushman's kraal where there were arrows and children's playthings lying around, as well as many cattle hides.[4, 5]

The Government, stung into action, sent spies to find out where the thieves were living. West of the Mzimkhulu, they followed the spoor along the crest of the sandstone escarpment for four days until it turned down among newly constructed kraals of the Mpondomise under Mandela. One of the scouts, who had been brought up in Nomansland, confirmed Fynn's evidence that Mandela's people had always lived on intimate terms with the Bushmen, intermarrying among them and participating in the stock raids.[6, 7] Despite this information, no action was taken, and the thefts continued.

In February, Langalibalele had a large herd of cattle taken from the foot of Ntabamhlope on the Bushman's river, and other Africans living in the Karkloof were raided. Prompt pursuit in both instances resulted in the animals being recovered.[8] Almost simultaneously all the stock from a farm on the Mngeni river was carried off, with the usual trail of dead and bleeding cattle marking the westward retreat. The farmers who pursued recovered a few animals from the middle source of the Mkhomazi, and reported traces of ten mounted robbers.[9-12] Following on appeals from the farmers, successive parties of a newly-formed volunteer force, the Natal Carbineers, patrolled the troubled area. Although they did not actually see any Bushmen, they located two recently occupied caves in the upper Mkhomazi, as well as 68 putrefying carcases of the animals previously taken from the Mngeni.[13-19]

Officials of the Natal Government felt convinced that the new spate of robberies was co-incident with Faku having at length been compensated in full for the previous fine imposed on him in connection with the Bushman robberies.[20] The inference was that even if Faku took no actual part in the depredations, he was at least able, through his petty chiefs, to check them effectually. Since Faku could apparently no longer be relied upon, it was decided to establish another military post as a protection against the Bushmen.[21] This was built by the 45th Foot (The Nottinghamshire Regiment) near Spioen Kop on the headwaters of the Mngeni river, at the place where John Shepstone had previously been stationed with the Native Police Corps. The post became known as Fort Nottingham.[22] The fort had hardly come into existence, however, when on a night in May, 120 cattle and eight horses were driven from a farm in the immediate vicinity. The theft was reported the following morning, and four Cape Mounted Riflemen with a guide set out in pursuit.

Two of the farmers whose horses were missing asked permission to borrow military mounts so that they could accompany the party, but were refused. Peeved but nevertheless undaunted, they obtained mounts from another farmer who joined them, and the three men followed on the trail several hours after the military detachment had left. The farmers knew the mountains well, so to make up for lost time, they continued riding by moonlight, and reached the top of the Little Berg (Kleinen Drakensberg in the report) early the following morning. Here they glimpsed six riders whom they initially supposed to be the military party, but soon realising they were the robbers, the farmers gave chase. The thieves were leading six horses in addition to those they were riding, but finding themselves closely followed, they abandoned their leads and galloped towards a nearby rock shelter. The Boers opened fire, and wounded two of the fugitives who fell from their horses. One of these, armed with a gun, turned round and fired a retaliatory shot before he and his comrade limped off into the mountains, leaving their mounts behind. The Boers were therefore left in possession of eight horses, two of them with saddles. Further search revealed nothing more than the robbers' campsite and the almost completely demolished remains of a fat cow near the fire.

The four dragoons arrived shortly afterwards, and thus re-inforced, the party continued the chase. At the Mkhomazi, the poor condition of the Boers' horses obliged them to retire, but the cavalry-men continued and crossed the river before halting at dark. During the night, their camp was attacked with gunshot and a hail of arrows, while the stolen stock could be heard bellowing near at hand. In order to keep the assailants at bay, the riflemen fired blindly into the shadows, soon exhausting their meagre supply of ten rounds of ammunition each. Although no-one was hurt during the attack, large numbers of arrows were found sticking into the saddles behind which the cavalrymen took shelter. No less than thirty of these were collected the following morning and taken back to camp on the Spioen Kop as souvenirs.[23]

Nearly two years later, at the end of January 1858, another theft was committed in the immediate vicinity of the Fort. A combined party of Cape Mounted Riflemen and farmers followed the tracks and found a fire where the thieves had spent the night with their booty. On the upper Mkhomazi a shelter was located in which there were stalls for horses, 'and all about the inside were rude drawings of horses, Bushmen fighting with Kaffirs etc. etc., elands' horns, baboons' jaw bones, and all kinds of rubbish, curiosities etc. some of which the pursuing party brought away with them.' This report

is of interest in that it contains the first specific mention of horse paintings in the upper Mkhomazi, and one can only lament that the 'etceteras' were not more fully described.

While the description is again too scanty for certain identification, the site can possibly be related to a spacious shelter on a small tributary of the Mkhomazana which is accessible to horses and is partly screened by creepers and a waterfall (site F 1). The floor of the shelter is relatively flat, with an ashy deposit containing fragments of bone, pot and stone artefacts, and 'curiosities' are still carried away by visitors from the nearby Sani Pass Hotel.[24] Although the paintings are now very faded, numerous horses are depicted, as well as dancing and fighting figures.

In an adjacent shelter upstream from the main site, there is another faded scene showing a group of horsemen, one of whom wears a feather in his hat and fires a gun from the saddle. (Figure 41.) The paintings are too weathered for certain identifica-tion, but the scene certainly represents a group such as the parties of cavalrymen, farmers, and African levies or servants whose pursuit of Bushmen led them into this valley during the years 1856 to 1858.

As a result of the renewed Bushman raids and the fruitless attempts to recover stolen property, the farmers presented a petition to the Natal Legislative Council requesting more effective protec-tion.[25] The general feeling was that the few troops at Fort Nottingham served little purpose, and that a volunteer commando given free rein would achieve far more satisfactory results. Much ethical discussion followed on whether or not individuals should be per-mitted to inflict punishment on the robbers, and there was also some dissension concerning the supposed headquarters of the Bushmen. Some said it was at the painted caves seen on the tribu-taries of the Mkhomazi (sites F1 and F2), others thought that this was merely a stopping place en route from their main residence on the upper Mzimvubu river. Although the increasing pressure from European farmers as well as from Africans in the Drakensberg locations may have resulted in the withdrawal of many Bushmen from the Natal side of the escarpment after the 1850s, the evidence presented by Sergeant Klaas and John Shepstone in 1848 and 1849 certainly pointed to permanent residence at that time, and there were still Bushman families, with women and children, living in the upper Mzimkhulu in 1862.[26, 27] That there could have been a scattered distribution of Bushman family groups not necessarily all involved in the stock thefts does not seem to have occurred to the authorities.

In any case the petition had little effect. In July of the same year, 1858, Robert Speirs from the farm *Brooklands* on the Mngeni was obliged to follow up his own stock losses because the officer in command at Fort Nottingham was absent when the theft was reported.[28] The information gleaned by Speirs during his sojourn in Nomansland, which implicated an increasingly heterogeneous mixture of peoples living among the Bushmen, has already been cited.[29] His evidence is also an early intimation that chief Moorosi of the Phuti in southern Lesotho was in league with the Bushmen and participated in the stock thefts.[30, 31]

Early in 1859, the farmers of the Upper Mngeni called a meeting because they heard with dismay that the troops at Fort Nottingham had been recalled and, not two days later, stock was stolen from an adjoining farm. Something must have happened to interrupt the thieves, however, for the cattle all strayed back with the exception of one cow. This was traced to a kloof leading into the Mkhomazi where, in the shelter of an overhanging rock, the remains of a feast was found with the small footprints of Bushmen all about.[32]

The farmers sent a deputation to the Government requesting that the troops at Fort Nottingham should be increased instead of recalled, and suggesting that the chiefs living at the base of the mountains in Nomansland should be held accountable for the stock thefts from Natal. They recommended that these Africans be given the liberty to destroy every Bushman kraal under the Drakensberg, by which means an effectual stop would soon be put to the harassing depredations.[33, 34]

The Government's reaction was to promise that, instead of military protection, they would establish a line of locations in positions which would check the robberies. This had proved successful north of the Mooi river, and it now remained to implement the same system to the south.[35]

In April 1859, a section of the people under Lugaju was removed from near Swartkop in the Pietermaritzburg district and placed on the north-eastern bank of the Mkhomazi river, an area now known as the Mpendle Location. Later, the followers of the famous hunter, chief Dumisa, who had himself learnt the secrets of his success from the Bushmen, were located to the south.[36] As time went on and the Bushman menace continued, protective kraals were established further and further up the Lotheni, Hlatimba and Mkhomazi valleys towards the mountains, and the present distribution of African occupied land in this area is a reflection of these early attempts to seal off the approaches of the Bushman marauders.

The establishment of the Mpendle Location did not meet with immediate success, for in October 1860, John Fumandaba, an employee of the Boston Saw Mills on the Eland's river, reported that forty-eight cattle had been taken during the night. Fumandaba immediately set out on foot to Lugaju's kraals, and there recruited the help of nine other Africans. Two Europeans, Mileman and Walker, followed on horseback soon afterwards, and with four more mounted men from Lugaju, they tracked the spoor.

A graphic account of the chase up the Mkhomazi valley was subsequently published in the local press by Mileman.[37] After first one and then the other pursuer taking up the cry 'Kona!' meaning 'Here is the spoor', they came to two very large rocks 'about the size of Pietermaritzburg Cathedral'. Under the side of one of these they found a quantity of eland biltong stored away, and could see the places where the Bushmen had slept and where their horses had been fastened to trees close by. After laying in a stock of the Bushmen's biltong for their own journey, the party followed along one of the tributaries of the Mkhomazi river. Twice they noticed that, as a deceptive ruse, the cattle had been turned and driven back on their tracks, and that the spoor then branched out again in the most unlikely and precipitous places.

At evening, the party crossed westwards over the Mkhomazi, but darkness forced even the determined Fumandaba, who had been crawling on his hands and knees to detect the hoof-prints in the half light, to halt. The pursuers' intention to continue the chase when the moon rose was thwarted by a dense mist, but at grey dawn they were on the tracks again, and cooked breakfast on a fire left by the Bushmen. Spurred on by the knowledge that the thieves could not be far ahead, they followed as fast as the foot party could walk, and were soon gratified by the sight of the cattle about five miles up the valley. Riding at full gallop up one of the spurs leading to the escarpment, the Europeans, each armed with a double-barrelled gun, and one of the mounted Africans with an assegai, caught up with the rustlers. There were five Bushmen on horseback who paused long enough to stab wildly all the cattle within reach, and who then galloped off, yelling defiance as they passed out of view.

As Mileman raced past the dead and dying cattle with blood gushing from the assegai wounds, and saw the haggard look of the remainder of the herd, overdriven, beaten, lame and cut, his 'soul burned with the hottest vengeance on the villains that had made such havoc'. However, when the pursuers arrived at the ridge over which the Bushmen had disappeared, they were somewhat deflated

Figure 42 *Site D1, upper Mkhomazi*
Two European horsemen carrying guns followed by a mounted African holding a knobbed stick.

by the prospect of the impossibly rugged country at the headwaters of the Mkhomazi. A mass of kloofs ran down both sides of a precipitous valley, uniting to form a gushing, boulder-strewn river. Throwing off saddles and bridles and abandoning their mounts, Mileman and Walker continued the scramble on foot, and caught sight of two of the Bushmen leading their horses, and picking their way along the top of a krantz. Shouting furiously, the Bushmen rolled rocks down on their pursuers, then disappeared over the mountains. Two Africans who had gone on ahead in an attempt to cut off their retreat arrived just too late, but reported seeing a total of eight Bushmen, six of whom were mounted. There was little doubt

of their racial identity, for the little men reached only to the horses' noses when on foot, and their language was full of clicks.

A search among the kloofs produced a saddled horse and a cow, which, together with the surviving cattle, were driven homewards. Returning via the two large rocks by which they had come, the Africans were convinced that another party of Bushmen had been back to the place in the interim. There were fresh blood stains on the grass, and a green reed, perhaps picked for an arrow shaft, was found. In addition, the stock of biltong had all gone, which suggests that, when out spying or actually raiding, the Bushmen left stores of food in strategic places for later use.

Figure 43 *Site D5, upper Mkhomazi*

An unusual composition of horsemen riding abreast. The riders are very indistinct, but at least one of them carries a gun.

Yet another raid which resulted in a hectic chase took place in 1862. Early one February morning, James Speirs galloped from his farm *Mount Park* on the Mngeni to tell neighbouring relatives and friends that seventy-three cattle and seventeen horses had disappeared from his kraals during the night. Lugaju's people in the Mpendle Location were immediately alerted, and the farmers were soon in the saddle. Later, members of a newly formed military volunteer corps who were drilling in Howick at the time, followed as a separate party. Circling round the shoulder of the Nhlazane mountain, they soon came upon stabbed animals, and ahead, the trail taken by the thieves was clearly marked by hovering vultures. Near the source of the Mngeni river, a Bushman's horse was found that had become bogged down in a swamp and abandoned, and the desperate pace set by the drovers was further reflected by the almost impossibly precipitous route they had taken when descending into the Nzinga valley. It was currently believed that in such places, a Bushman would go in advance smearing cow-dung over the ledges, and thus deceive the cattle into thinking they were following a trail already negotiated by one of their number. Darkness eventually called a halt to the chase, but at first light the pursuers were on the carcase-littered trail again, which they followed all day. At evening, the volunteer force saw smoke ahead and excitedly imagined they were close on the heels of the thieves, but their stealthy advance disappointingly proved the fire to belong to none other than the farmers who had gone on ahead. The combined party later found a partly eaten eland at the Lotheni river, followed by fifteen trek-oxen lying slaughtered within a few yards of one another. The following day, they met up with those of Lugaju's men who had been alerted, and who had actually caught up with the Bushmen at the point where the trek-oxen were killed. They told how the party of seven or eight thieves, after executing their wrath, had ascended a precipitous part of the Berg, and had by some 'magical dexterity' made the horses go with them. Each riding one horse and leading another, the Bushmen had shepherded the remainder of the mounts between them, killing two horses that were unable to keep up. Since most of the stolen cattle were already dead, the disheartened pursuers decided that further action would be fruitless unless by a fully equipped commando.[38, 39]

Ten days later, with official blessing, a combined party of twenty-five volunteer farmers and Natal Carbineers under the command of William Proudfoot assembled at Lugaju's kraal, where they were joined by eighteen Africans. After reaching the spot where the last of Speirs's oxen had been assegaied, traditionally a hill over-looking the Bodhla valley,[40] the party began climbing a spur of the Drakensberg, but were delayed two days by thick mist and cold rain before they could make the final ascent. It is uncertain which pass they negotiated; many years later, one of the party identified it as the Lotheni at the headwaters of that river, but it is more likely to have been the Hlatimba Pass as this is more practicable. If this was the point of ascent, the spoor would have followed the course of the Redi river in a north-westward arc as far as the present position of Mokhotlong or Molumong. Here there was a shelter where the thieves had apparently halted before continuing to the Orange river. Veering south by south-east, the pursuers entered 'what might properly be called the Bushman territory'. Five miles from the banks of the Orange they came upon nine crude huts made from the boughs of a few shrubs roughly tied together, with a handful of grass thrown on top — virtually the same description as the huts found in the vicinity of the Bisi river in East Griqualand sixteen years before.[41] Under each erection, holes scraped in the ground and strewn with a little grass seemed to have served as sleeping places. Children's toy assegais lying about and other indications suggested that the occupants had consisted of several families. A few miles beyond the huts was a rock shelter with recent signs of occupation, and three knocked up horses grazed nearby. Two of these were recognised as having come from Natal, and their backs had horrible sores from being ridden without proper saddles. Further eastwards the party surrounded and captured a troop of twenty-one well-conditioned horses, which included one from Natal.

By this time, the trail had led round in a great semi-circle towards the sources of the Mzimkhulu river, and the pursuers found themselves back near the edge of the escarpment not far south of where they had originally ascended. The spoor of the thieves became increasingly difficult to follow, and the party fanned out to cover the terrain more effectively. Suddenly a mounted Bushman was sighted. There was an instant rush to the saddle, and a wild chase ensued. The Bushman took to his heels when his horse was injured while galloping down a steep hillside, and protecting himself by continually jabbing backwards with his spear as he ran, he artfully made off across a swamp. This successfully bogged down his pursuers' horses, but Robert Speirs nevertheless succeeded in wounding the fugitive and catching him by the scruff of the neck. At this juncture, attention was diverted from the Bushman to one of the Carbineers, Thomas Hodgson who, in the excitement, had accidentally been shot in the thigh by a stray bullet. With no proper appliances to hand, the removal of the lead 'lopers' was a long and arduous task, and by nightfall, the patient was made as comfortable as possible in the lee of a rock, the only available protection in that bleak and desolate situation.

At sunset, the African scouts returned with the news that they had located the Bushman hide-out at the foot of the mountains, and to compensate for the delay caused by the accident, two-thirds of the force immediately set out with the intention of surrounding the robbers. In the dark, the guides failed to locate the path leading down the escarpment, so they sent back for the Bushman prisoner to show the way. He was a boy of about fifteen years who spoke no language other than his own, but with a riem round his neck, and despite his wound, he was made to lead the party down towards the source ravines of the Mzimkhulu river. The sun rose as they followed a path over a succession of steep ridges with streams flowing between, and on gaining the summit of one of these, a bold projecting bluff stood out beyond a deep and rugged chasm. In a shelter under the point of this bluff, they watched four Bushwomen and two children collect their belongings with unruffled deliberation, then disappear among the rocks. One of the women was the mother of the captured boy. Of the men there was no sign, much to the disappointment of the commando. The more adventurous of the party crossed over and explored the shelter,[42] but the majority returned to camp hungry and exhausted, their provisions having come to an end. After carting stones to erect a shelter round the wounded Hodgson, the main body of men set off for home. Robert Speirs, one of those detailed to remain with Hodgson, went to help the party down a precipitous pass at the source of the Mzimkhulu river, and at the same time he intended shooting something to make soup for the wounded man. While hunting, he wandered far down the Berg, and a sudden thunderstorm drove him to seek shelter in the cave which had been vacated by the Bushmen. Here he found a quantity of wood which enabled him to light a fire and to dry out his clothes. Continued rain induced him to stay there the night, and although no Bushmen made their appearance, a dog approached, but not close enough to be touched. Speirs reached camp on top of the escarpment the following morning to find it deserted. Hodgson was dead, and the stones that had sheltered him now covered his body. Although the position of his grave is no longer known, prominent twin buttresses which overlook the high swampy turf to the west, and the rugged headwaters of the Mzimkhulu river to the east, bear the name Hodgson's Peaks, a grand memorial to a tragic event.[43-45]

The remainder of the party having left, Speirs was stranded with neither provisions nor a mount, and endured harrowing privations until he finally reached Dumisa's kraals.[46] Once sufficiently recovered, he did his best to retain possession of the Bushman he had captured, but the Government placed the prisoner in the charge of Captain Proudfoot on the farm *Craigieburn* in the Riet Vlei area. It is said that he grew taller than the average Bushman because he was well fed, but despite the fact that he was a splendid horseman, he was quite unteachable for any useful service.[47]

Miss Jessie McArthur, a late resident of the Riet Vlei area, remembered seeing the boy tied to the leg of the kitchen table when he was meant to be assisting the cook.[48] He was also taken out on at least one expedition to assist with tracking down members of his own band, and when he came across signs of occupation in a cave, it is said he broke the pots, declaring all he wanted to do was catch

Figure 44 *Sites Q 4 and 5*
The rock shelters on Belleview *where the paintings illustrated in Figures 103, 104, 109 and 110 are located.*

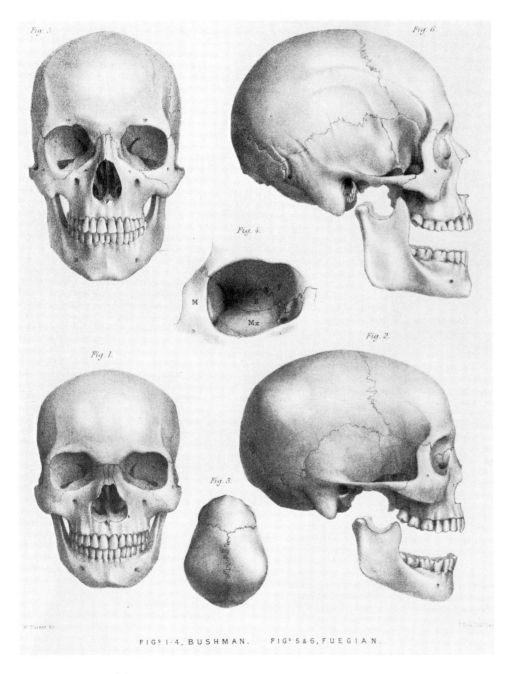

FIG^s 1-4, BUSHMAN.   FIG^s 5 & 6, FUEGIAN.

and kill his mother.[49] The sight of his mother making her way to freedom while he stood wounded and with a rope around his neck the morning after he was captured, seems understandably to have embittered him, but to his captors he was never more than 'a great rascal'. He took to drink 'and other evil ways'[50] and died not long after, probably the combined result of tuberculosis and sheer frustration.[51, 52] Some years later Dr. Peter Sutherland, with Proudfoot's permission, surreptitiously disinterred the body one moonlight night, bundling the bones into saddle bags, and donated the skeleton to the Edinburgh Medical School in 1881. The specimen is still there, labelled, 'Skeleton of a Bushman from Umzimkulu', with an additional note that the feet were missing at the time of presentation.[53, 54]

The Bushboy, then, who once roamed the secluded ravines of the upper Mzimkhulu, and galloped on the wind-blown plateau of high Lesotho, is now preserved on the collection shelves of an august institute of learning. He also holds the doubtful honour of being amongst the first Bushmen to have been subjected to a complete osteological examination. The published reports, being part of a comparative study by Sir William Turner, appeared in 1884 and 1886. Detailed measurements of the skull, together with illustrations, reveal the usual Bush characteristics — a short broad face, with flat features and a small chin. The dimensions of the pelvis, also illustrated, were in accordance with the small stature and proportions of the race, and the bones were generally light but substantial. This is the memorial of the Bushman who caused Hodgson's death; not the name of lofty peaks in his homeland, but a detached dissertation within the covers of a scientific report. (Figure 45.)

During the following months and years, the hit-and-run raids continued, but as always, the thieves eluded the pursuers. The

Figure 45

This page of illustrations from Sir William Turner's report on human skeletons collected between 1874–1876 bears the following captions:—
1. *Facial view of the skull of a Bushman from the mountain district at the source of the Umzimkulu river.*
2. *Profile view of the same skull.*
3. *Vertex view of the same skull.*
4. *Base and inner wall of the orbit of the same Bushman skull, showing a direct articulation between the orbital plates of the maxillary and frontal bones.*
5. *Facial view of the skull of a Fuegian.*
6. *Profile view of the same skull.*

troubled areas ranged from the Klip river district to the Mkhomazi river near Lundy's Hill, and on the intervening Bushman's river, the footprints of a great many Bushmen were reported to have been seen when some horses and a mule were lifted in November, 1863.[55, 56]

In 1865, the human barricade against the Bushmen entering Natal was completed when chief Thukelela requested the land between the Ngwangwana and Mzimkhulu rivers. This area had previously been settled by a party of Bhaca under Mdushane who had seceded from the chiefdom after the death of his father Ngcaphayi. Although it cannot be proven that Mdushane was as implicated with the Bushmen as were the Bhaca who remained on the Mzimvubu under his mother Mamjucu and brother Mchithwa,[57] he and his followers were notoriously lawless and disobedient. For this reason, the Government backed Thukelela's application, and subsequently furnished him with twenty stand of fire-arms so that he could pursue the armed and mounted Bushmen into the mountain fastnesses without fear.[58-60]

When the Bushman rustlers again made their appearance three years later, it was in the Thukela basin, and they entered and left Natal via the Mhlwasine pass. As a result, the resident magistrate of Weenen district recommended that this route should be blown up with dynamite, a suggestion which was apparently put into effect, for he subsequently wrote that the pass was no longer practicable.[61,62]

Then one night in December, 1868, the Bushmen found an opportunity to sneak down to a kraal between the Mzimkhulu and Mkhomazi rivers belonging to Mfongoswana, a headman under chief Sakhayedwa, son of Dumisa, and to retreat with seventy head of cattle. As soon as the theft was discovered, Mfongoswana and four men followed the spoor to a precipitous pass at the sources of the Mzimkhulu river. As the Africans were about to ascend the pass,[63] they were attacked by about ten Bushmen with fire-arms, bows and arrows, and who also rolled stones with good effect. One of the pursuers was wounded with gunshot while two others were struck by arrows, whereupon they all beat a hasty retreat. Back at the kraals, Sakhayedwa assembled a larger party of about fifteen men, at least some of whom were mounted, who resumed the chase up the pass. After following the trail across the high plateau for six days, they came across a deserted Bushman kraal, and a day's journey beyond this, they saw a new kraal which had been built on a hill overlooking the Orange river. Here they found three of the stolen cows and a young Bushgirl, whom they captured. Noticing a

horse grazing some distance away, a mounted member of the party incautiously went off to secure it when he was surrounded and attacked by five Bushmen who first wounded him in the head and then took his horse away. The remainder of the stolen cattle were followed for yet another half day beyond the Orange river, but the weather turned so bad that the pursuers were obliged to turn back without recovering any more of their property. It was noted that among the small Bushman footprints there were also the larger imprints of Basotho-type skin shoes.[64]

The captive Bushgirl was duly delivered to the magistrate at Richmond who in turn put her in the care of Dr. Callaway at Springfield mission. Although her age was judged to be about ten or eleven years, she was very small, 'not larger than a white child of three or four years old'. It was requested that the child be kept at the disposal of the Government because she could possibly prove useful in 'opening up communications with her relations', but no further mention of her can be found in the records. According to oral tradition among descendants of Dumisa's adherents, the name of the girl was Gqawukile.[65]

Subsequent appearances of mounted Bushmen in the vicinity of Sakhayedwa's kraals near the Pholela river resulted in the Africans of that area being granted permission to purchase guns.[66, 67] By 1870, armed Africans were located along the entire length of the Natal Drakensberg, and from this time onwards, stock raids attributed to Bushmen became the exception rather than the rule. (See Map No. 2)

References

1. *Proceedings of the Native Affairs Commission*, 1852.
2. Wright 1971: 190.
3. C.S.O. 78, No. 53, 13/6/1855.
4. *Natal Guardian*, 5/2/1856.
5. *Natal Mercury*, 1/2/1856.
6. S.N.A. 1/1/6, No. 86, 11/6/1856.
7. Willcox 1963: 24-5.
8. S.N.A. 1/3/5, No. 80, 19/2/1856.
9. S.N.A. 1/3/5, No. 80, 19/2/1856.
10. C.S.O. 84, Nos. 53 & 65, 27 & 28/2/1856.
11. G. H. 635, No. 46, 25/3/1846.
12. See also McKenzie 1967: 48.
13. *Natal Guardian*, 4, 11, 18/3/1856.
14. *Natal Mercury*, 7/3/1856.
15. *Natal Chronicle*, 4/6/1856.
16. *Natal Star*, 12/3/1856.
17. C.S.O. 84, No. 92, 12/3/1856.

Figure 46 *Site F2*

A shoal of fish and associated humans in dark red. This scene, on an extremely exfoliated area of rock, is very easily overlooked. It was first noticed only after repeated visits to the site. The faded area of paint at the back of the figure with arms outstretched is open to varied interpretations.

18. C.S.O. 85, No. 4, 24/3/1856.
19. Stalker 1912: 29-33.
20. See p. 63.
21. G. H. 635, No. 46, 25/3/1856.
22. Although nothing of the Fort can now be seen, the former position of the stables and barracks is commemorated by a stone cairn, and a bronze plaque reads:
   'On this site in 1856 the 45th Regiment, (1st Sherwood Foresters), was stationed to protect settlers from marauding Bushmen, those "children of the mist" known to the Zulus as Abatwa.'
23. *Natal Chronicle*, 4/6/1856; Hattersley 1936: 171-3.
24. This shelter, *Good Hope 1* (site F1), has recently been excavated by P. L. Carter. The top layers contained well-preserved bedding consisting of grass and small twigs, as well as the husks of edible bulbs of the *Watsonia* and *Cyperus* spp. A pierced sea-shell was also recovered.
   A date of 150 years B.C. was obtained for a charcoal sample at the 20-30 centimetre level of the deposit, which reached a depth of 100 centimetres. (Personal communication, P. L. Carter and J. C. Vogel, 1973. Laboratory number Pta 838).
   An interesting find was a bone fish-hook similar to others found in *Belleview 1* shelter, East Griqualand. Three fish are painted in the *Good Hope 1* shelter, while another scene in faded red in the partly recorded shelter at *Good Hope II* (site F2), shows more fish in association with humans. (Figure 46).
25. *Natal Witness*, 12/2/1856.
26. See pp. 42, 82.
27. *Natal Witness*, 19/2/1858; 26/3/1858; 2/4/1858; 2/7/1858.
28. *Natal Witness*, 2/7/1858.
29. See p. 67.
30. S.N.A. 1/1/8, No. 77.
31. Speirs's Diary 1858.
32. *Natal Mercury*, 8/2/1859.
33. S.N.A. 1/1/9, Nos. 8 & 6, 22 & 25/1/1859.
34. S.N.A. 1/1/8, No. 77, Speirs's Diary 1858.
35. S.N.A. 1/1/9, No. 191, 28/1/1859.
36. One of Dumisa's kraals occupied the present position of the Underberg village at the foot of Hlogoma mountain, where the hut circles could be seen until they were obliterated by the erection of the old hotel building, itself now ruined. (Information given by the late Lawrence Crocker of the farm *Cottesmere*, Underberg District.)
37. *Natal Witness*, 19/10/1860.
38. *Natal Chronicle*, 26/2/1862.
39. Ergates 1905.
40. Verbal communication, A. T. McClean, who obtained the information from Mfene Nyide, one of Lugaju's men.
41. See p. 30.
42. The precise locality of this shelter is not known, but the description could apply to one in the Mlambonje valley. There are no paintings at this site, although they do occur in smaller shelters nearby.
43. C.S.O. 146, No. 39, 25/3/1862.
44. Ergates 1905.
45. *Patriot*, Vol. 9, No. 7, July 1933.
46. According to local tradition, some of Dumisa's men found Speirs in an exhausted state in the lee of a large rock on the Mulungane mountain, near the present motor road where it crosses the Hlatikulu drift. Verbal communication, A. T. McClean, *Duart Castle*, P.O. Himeville.
47. Anderson 1888: 6.
48. Verbal communication, Canon J. B. Chutter, former rector of Drakensberg parish.
49. Anderson 1888: 6.
50. Bird Papers, P. C. Sutherland file, from notes furnished by Mrs Pope-Ellis, daughter of Dr Sutherland.
51. Turner 1884 & 1886, in H.M.S. Challenger Reports.
52. Ergates 1905.
53. Personal communication, Prof. G. J. Romanes, Dept. of Anatomy, Edinburgh Medical School.
54. Hattersley 1959: 126-144.
55. S.N.A. 1/3/13, Nos. 338 & 123; ?/10/1863 & 1/2/1863.
56. *Natal Witness*, 21/3/1862; 11/12/1863; 15/4/1864.
57. See p. 57.
58. S.N.A. 1/3/15, No. 174, 29/6/1865.
59. S.N.A. 1/3/19, No. 278, 27/2/1869.
60. S.N.A. 1/3/20, No. 276, 6/7/1870.
61. S.N.A. 1/3/18, No. 220, 3/7/1868.
62. S.N.A. 1/3/19, p. 205, 31/7/1869.
63. This was possibly the Mashai pass, a rough and stony route which ascends the escarpment immediately south of the Rhino's Horn.
64. S.N.A. 1/3/19, p. 258, Oct. 1868.
65. District records, Underberg magistracy.
66. S.N.A. 1/3/18, No. 256, 16/12/1868.
67. S.N.A. 1/3/19, No. 278, 27/2/1869.

The Final Raids

The last recorded Bushman raid against a European farmer in Natal was in July 1869, and the scale and organisation of the counter-measures exceeded anything previously embarked on under British rule.[1]

At about 11 o'clock one Sunday night, the enjoyment of a party of farmers on a week-end shoot near Fort Nottingham was rudely interrupted by the arrival of a messenger bringing news that all the cattle belonging to William Popham, of the farm *Meshlynn*, had been stolen. Chief Hlubi with some of his followers had already set out on the spoor, hoping that the European farmers would overtake them with whatever force and ammunition they could muster. Popham and his friends immediately rode back to his farm on the Mooi river to cast bullets and procure mealiemeal and fresh horses. At dawn, messengers were dispersed in various directions to mobilise other Africans in the area into action. Preparations completed, a small mounted party of five Europeans and two Africans made straight for the three known passes over the Drakensberg above *Meshlynn*, presumably those on the Bushman's river, and reached the northernmost route at two o'clock the next morning. After searching in vain for traces of the cattle when daylight came, they headed southwards to a point where they saw a stray beast, and soon struck a strong spoor. Following the trail round the spurs of the Mulungane mountain all day, they lost it again at the Mkhomazi river, having seen three stabbed animals on the route. At evening, they met up with a division of Hlubi's men who had also found slaughtered animals, but had similarly lost the spoor. More Africans arrived, including some from Lugaju's kraals, and all reported the same details. The combined party then methodically combed the area in an all-out effort to recover the tracks, commencing on the higher ground, then working down the valleys, but found only signs of old encampments marked by fires and horsedung. On the evening of the third day, they were joined by Hlubi himself, who had more positive news. Having also failed to follow the spoor beyond a certain point, he was cutting across-country when he unexpectedly came across tracks leading from several quarters and converging on the middle pass of the Mkhomazi. He reported the trail to be beaten like a waggon road, with some of the human footprints large like those of Bantu and others small like those of Bushmen, but the main party was apparently mounted and numerous. Because Hlubi had only two men with him and one gun, he decided that discretion was the better part of valour, and turned back. Popham and his party were bewildered by this information, for they had previously inspected the same terrain with no results whatever. Yet again the thieves had outwitted their pursuers. Their tactics seem to have been first to scatter the spoor by driving the booty in a series of small herds towards the upper Mkhomazi, and then, after further confusing the traces, to go into hiding. Watching their pursuers search the passes without success and then head downstream, they quickly rallied from their various points of concealment, and made good their escape over the mountain barrier. Being inadequately equipped, the pursuers realised it would be madness to continue the chase into an unknown country in the middle of winter.

Back home, Popham collected fresh mounts and did not rest until he had reported the full story first to the magistrate in Estcourt, and then to the seat of Government in Pietermaritzburg. Popham's total losses were one hundred and eighteen cattle and about thirty-five horses, while Basotho living near the Mooi river had lost another thirty horses and a bull.[2] Suspecting the thieves to be the same as those who had previously entered Weenen County via the Mhlwasine pass, Macfarlane, the magistrate at Weenen, pressed the Government to take decisive steps.[3] This was readily agreed to, and Macfarlane was appointed director of a full-scale expedition.

Twelve European volunteers, including a doctor, and 200 Africans, were divided into two detachments each under a European officer. The plan was to ascend the Drakensberg by way of separate passes, and after effecting a junction at the top, the combined parties were to follow the track of the stolen property to its destination. If this proved to be the headquarters of 'runaways and outlaws' known to inhabit the gorges of the Orange river, the expedition was instructed to arrest or disperse the robbers, but only to defend itself if attacked. If, on the other hand, the spoor led to settled peoples under a recognised chief, the expedition was to demand full restoration of, or compensation for, the missing stock. Again no force was to be used, and the finds were to be reported either to Col. J. H. Bowker, the newly appointed British Agent in Basutoland who had already promised his assistance, or to Captain Adam Kok in East Griqualand, depending on which side

— — —

of the Drakensberg the stock was found. As an additional measure, a third party consisting of Africans only, was sent southwards along the base of the Drakensberg to observe whether any of the stolen stock was received by tribes located there.[4]

Provisioned with cattle, biscuit and coffee, and armed with rifles, ammunition and signal rockets especially forwarded from Pietermaritzburg, the parties were eventually ready. The officers in charge were detailed to make sketch maps of the area they traversed, and again, strict injunctions were issued that the Africans, about half of whom were armed with guns, should be restrained from exercising unnecessary violence. Then, when the two main parties were on the brink of departure, a cutting wind from the south-west brought a severe snow-storm. It was reputedly the worst ever experienced in that locality, and lay eighteen inches deep on the flats. The southern detachment which had gathered on *Meshlynn* farm lost a large number of their commissariat cattle and several horses, and the unfortunate Popham was deprived of yet more stock. Of the hundred Africans who took shelter in huts and outhouses, three required medical treatment.

The northern detachment under Albert Allison, Captain of the Natal Carbineer force and Commandant of the Natal Mounted Police, was centred at Olivier's Hoek, and fared a little better in that the snow-fall in that area was less severe. As soon as the thaw set in, they ascended what is almost certainly the Mnweni Pass near Mponjwana Peak, where three cattle fell over a precipice concealed under snow. Once on the high plateau, Allison proceeded in a south-westerly direction to avoid broken country, and reported seeing Bush and Bantu footprints which suggested that spies had been out in that area since the snow-fall. After descending to the head-waters of the Orange river and continuing in a southerly direction, Allison struck the spoor of many horses. This soon developed into a beaten track, and led to a point where a halt of some days had been made. Sometimes the track followed along the river, sometimes over the hills, but became less and less distinct until it was lost. Thinking that this spoor was in any case too far north to have any connection with the recent robbery, Allison abandoned further

Figure 47

Hunting eland with dogs. The running hunter, painted in black with orange face and orange beads, carries a bifurcated stick and wears what are probably bladders on his head. The dog in front of him is also spotted with orange, and the eland it is chasing is outlined in black and filled in with a less dense black pigment. This site, near the junction of the Thala Boliba and the Orange, was located on a recent survey. It is not on the appended site list, nor is it plotted on the map.

search, and continued down the banks of the Orange where he expected to find the other party.

Meanwhile, after being considerably held up by the snow, James Giles, in command of the southern detachment, made his way over the rough country between *Meshlynn* and the upper Mkhomazi. Ascending what was probably the Illatimba Pass,[5] he reached the top of the escarpment on the 7th September, a week later than Allison. Giles immediately struck a well-defined spoor which, after making a southerly detour, entered a large valley leading to the north-west.[6] The spoor, however, became increasingly trifling, suggesting that the thieves had again split up into small parties, and when the pursuers found recent traces of horses near their camp, they had the uneasy feeling that Bushman spies had already detected their presence. An added disadvantage was that the grass had been burnt off since the raid, which not only baffled the trackers, but also deprived the expedition horses and cattle of nutriment. Having followed the course of the same valley for four days, they reached the Orange river, and Mpiko, the African headman accompanying

the party, pointed out a rock shelter where he had fought with Bushmen some years previously.[7]

While the party was trying to relocate the lost spoor of the stolen cattle, trackers brought the cheering news that traces of Allison's detachment, apparently several days' march ahead, had been detected on the opposite bank of the river. Although rockets fired into the air received no answer, the eventual union of the two parties was assured. Messengers went off to establish contact, and Allison decided on a rendezvous which he described as a cluster of thirteen Bushman huts built near a river junction. When passing this place on his southward journey, he had found the devoured remains of two small horses, and spies sent to report on a column of smoke seen ascending in the north-west, returned with a Bushman horse that had been abandoned.

Meanwhile Giles, in attempting to sort out the confusion of spoor, sent out scouting parties, and one returned saying that they had seen four Bushmen hunting eland with dogs. (Figure 47) That evening, the headman Mpiko set out with a posse of thirty-five men

89

Figure 48 *Site* X9

A Bushman stands holding the reins of his horse, while below, four warriors carrying spears and knobbed sticks march downhill. For convenience, the two groups of paintings have been moved nearer together than they appear on the rock face.

hoping to surprise the Bushmen round their fire, but after the moon set, darkness obliged them to halt on the trail. At daybreak, smoke issuing from a rock shelter not many miles away showed how narrowly they had missed their objective, but before they could surround the shelter, the six Bushman occupants emerged, quietly led their horses down the hill, and rode off without any apparent signs of alarm. (Figure 48). Mpiko and his men pursued all day in a south-easterly direction, but eventually gave up the chase and returned to the main party.

Allison, who had countermarched as soon as he received Giles's letter, linked up with the southward moving party at about midday on the 22nd September, and took command of the combined detachments. Because of the scattered spoor, he also sent out scouts in all directions. Some of these returned with horses, and the total of thirty-six included animals stolen from Popham and the Africans located on the Mooi river. The horses had apparently been driven to sheltered spots to graze on young spring grass, and although smoke from veld fires could sometimes be seen, there was never any sign of the Bushmen themselves. The spoor continued in a north-westerly direction, following a tributary of the Orange river, but after prolonged and strenuous exertion in exposed conditions, some twenty members of the expedition were now too weak to continue. Since supplies were also running low, Popham, with two other European volunteers and 50 Africans, returned home.

By this time the spoor, becoming increasingly difficult to follow, had led the expedition on a circuitous route through an intricacy of rivers and ravines, right over the Central Range of the Maluti mountains into the valleys of the Sinqunane or Little Orange river. Sometimes the party headed westward to avoid impassable gorges, and sometimes southward. Halting places were frequently passed where the robbers had slept, and the human footmarks, small and large, included imprints of skin shoes. At one of these places, the hide of a beast stolen from Popham was found, which confirmed that they were still on the right trail.

Then, on the evening of the 4th October, on an easterly tributary of the Sinqunane or Little Orange river,[8] scouts saw horses grazing beyond a deep ravine, and heard voices singing in the gorge beneath. The shelter, situated near a sharp curve at the intersection between two rocky streams flowing from the north-east and from the south, lay in a deep basin with precipitous sides, quite impassable to mounted men.

Despite heavy rain, a detachment was sent to outflank the position

90

Figure 49 *Site W23*
Hippopotamus, Tsoelike river.

to the southward, with instructions to conceal themselves until morning. Before daylight on the 5th, the rest of the men were mustered for duty, and were stationed to close the outlets of the river to the north-east and north-west, while others were posted on the heights above the shelter. When the main contingent entered the river bed to the eastward, the trap was complete, and a signal shot brought the concealed party into action. Although the African contingent had been repeatedly warned not to fire unless absolutely necessary, the shower of dreaded poisoned arrows and gunshot which immediately hailed them from inside the shelter caused a panic. According to one informant, three of the Bushmen had guns, but it was not only the males who defended themselves, for the women too, used bows and arrows with good effect.[9] A half-hour skirmish ensued, at the end of which there were sixteen or seventeen dead Bushmen and women, with no serious casualties among the attackers. Four or five Bushmen managed to escape over the rocks, and six children and two women were taken prisoner. One of the latter required treatment from the expedition doctor, her ankle having been shattered by a long shot. The objects of the expedition were thus successfully accomplished: the robbers were 'dispersed', and twenty-five horses were captured, amongst which were eight of

those stolen three months previously. The spacious rock shelter was strewn with animal bones, and a singularly shaped horn was recognised as having belonged to a cow stolen from a native in Natal the previous year.

From signs and a few words made use of by one of the Bush-women, Allison was induced to continue his journey southwards in the hopes of recovering more stock from a headman named Minnie-Minnie. After leaving the scene of the skirmish, the party no longer followed spoor, but soon struck a path used by Makwai on his way from western Lesotho to East Griqualand about three years previously. It was noted that the Orange river now ran due west, and other paths were found made by Basotho when hunting hippopotami. (Figure 49). Cultivated lands, huts and cattle began to appear, and Allison learnt that he was about two days' journey from the kraals of chief Moorosi of the Phuti who was reported to have two Bushwives, and who was himself described as being of Bush extraction.[10]

The 'live and let live' arrangement between the recent Basotho immigrants and the Bushmen was described in a statement taken by Allison from a man named Dinilapo:

Our law does not permit us to kill anyone unless they have committed some great offence. Bushmen are included in the law I refer to, ... I mean to say, their chief would be angry if I interfered with them without reason. Their chief is Moorosi. There are many Bushmen living amongst Moorosi's people. Bushmen live only a part of the year amongst the mountains; they are too lazy to work, and when picking time comes, some of them go off hunting until the work is over. They live half the time in the hills, the other half with Moorosi's people.

Moorosi, said Dinilapo, found the Bushmen useful for hunting eland, and one of his headmen, Minnie-Minnie, often went hunting with them. He had never heard of Bushmen stealing stock from Moorosi, but he knew they sold horses there.[11]

Rev. D. F. Ellenberger, who settled as a missionary among Moorosi's people in 1866, three years before the Allison raid, has recorded the history of the Phuti in some detail. Originating from the Zizi at the foot of the Natal Drakensberg, the Phuti had acquired a strong admixture of Bush blood, and for many years lived among the Bushmen on the Telle and Blikana rivers on the borders of southern Lesotho. Tiring of this way of life, Mokhoane and his son Moorosi went to join the Pondo, while the rest of the Phuti moved towards the Cape Colony. Unable to gain employment among the European farmers, they turned to cattle-stealing, and retreated with their booty to what is now the Dordrecht area. The Bushmen who occupied and exploited this terrain resented the intrusion and attacked the Phuti in a cave, showering them with poisoned arrows. After losing one of their number, the Phuti began to parley, and the Bushmen agreed to cease shooting provided that all the cattle were handed over. The chastened marauders followed their herds back to the Bushmen's camp, and there met Mokhoane and Moorosi who had returned from the Pondo. With Moorosi as an active participant, the Phuti continued to make extensive forays on stock in the Cape Colony, but trouble developed when the Bushmen claimed these as well. Preparations were made for battle, but instead of fighting, the two parties again agreed to parley. As a result, the Bushmen were given to understand that the Phuti, whom they had previously considered their servants, had now become their masters, and the Bushmen apparently went off quite satisfied with a present of only three cattle. From that time on, the Phuti and the Bushmen remained on amicable terms.[12]

Without being familiar with this history, Allison felt convinced from all he heard that Moorosi was in league with the Bushmen, and that he assisted or possibly even employed them to steal cattle.

Allison nevertheless decided that it would be impolitic to follow up the missing stock any further, because the guilty parties would have ample time to dispose of incriminating evidence. Preferring to leave Moorosi and his people under the impression that they were unsuspected, the expedition retraced its steps along the Orange river, and descended the Drakensberg at Qacha's Nek.

At the foot of the mountains, Allison succeeded in obtaining a Bushman interpreter, the servant of a Griqua waggoner, and took down a statement from one of the women prisoners. Dated the 19th October, 1869, and headed Makwai's kraal, west of the St John's river [Mzimvubu], it reads:

I know Minnie-Minnie, as I have told you he lives at the great Kraal (pointing west from Makwai's residence). He is a Basuto, he and his people come to hunt eland with us and we go to him. I mean to his kraal. My husband is there now, he has been there two months, he went with other Bushmen to visit there. There are many Bushmen living with the Basutos. They have huts there and pick the ground, they have also cows and sheep. My people live with Umpootozane the son of Mahale. Moorosi is the great chief. Masharka (of whom I spoke at the cave) is a Bushman. He is an old man and the captain of the Bushmen. Masharka lives with Umpootozane. I recollect upon the day of the fight, that two men escaped with guns, they were Bushmen and came from Minnie-Minnie. It is true that some of our people live in the hills, and some with Umpootozane. It is the custom of our people. We, that is my family, went from Minnie-Minnie to visit our friends in the hills about three months since. When I had been there a short time a lot of horses and cattle were brought there. I heard these horses and cattle come from there (pointing eastward). I cannot say how many there were. Basutos brought them there. There were Bushmen with the Basutos when the cattle came in. Those Basutos came from Umpootozane's. They came with Masharka, he was the captain. I don't know how many people. Some of them stayed at the cave, and some of them went away with the Bushmen to steal. When the cattle and the horses came there was much talk, and they were divided. A clump (I don't know how many horses or cattle) went away with the Basutos. They went with Masharka to Umpootozane's. The rest (I don't know how many) remained with the Bushmen. No cattle remained with the Bushmen. What I have said is true.[13]

Makwai himself told Allison that he had frequently lost horses since his arrival in East Griqualand three years previously, the greatest number being eighty in one night. He was sure the Bushmen were responsible for some of the thefts, and recognised four of his horses among those captured by the expedition.[14]

Allison continued his march north-eastwards along the foot of the Drakensberg, and arrived back at *Meshlynn* on the 27th October,

Figure 50

This aerial photograph of a stretch of the Orange river between Mashai and Matsaile in Lesotho gives some idea of the terrain into which the Bushmen were pursued. In the background are the snow-covered peaks of the Drakensberg, beyond which the escarpment falls abruptly to the farmlands of Natal and East Griqualand. The high peaks are basalt, while the Orange river and its tributaries have cut down to expose the underlying sandstone strata.

Photo: Pat Carter.

after two full months in the field. In the official reports, high praise was given the Africans serving on the expedition. Allison wrote:

> Throughout the march they have conducted themselves in the most exemplary manner — scantily clothed, and exposed at times to severe cold and storms, without cover of any kind except such temporary shelter as could only now and then be obtained, weary, and with their feet cut and bruised by the continual fording of rivers, marching by day and watching by night, these men have held on without a murmur through a march of more than six hundred miles, through a difficult and all but impassable country; an exhibition of courage, endurance, loyalty and obedience, not to be surpassed by the best disciplined troops.

One African had died on the return journey, while another, seriously ill, was left to recuperate at the kraal of Sakhayedwa who had also pursued a mixed party of Basotho and Bushmen to a point beyond the Orange river the previous year. The wounded Bush-woman, notwithstanding the hardships of the long march, made good progress and eventually recovered.

Many years later, Maurice Evans wrote that the two women captives and the six children who were taken as servants by members of the commando, all disappeared mysteriously and without warning at about the same time. Where they went was unknown, but it was assumed that they escaped back over the mountains to their old haunts.[15]

The Allison raid has become quite legendary and, like all legends, exaggerated. To Allison has been attributed the annihilation of the Bushmen under a headman named Soai when a final and determined stand was reputedly made by the last of his band at the Sehonghong shelter near Mashai. It seems, however, that in the course of time, the Allison expedition has become confused with later raids made by the Basotho against Bushman captains Soai and Sehonghong. Allison's fracas with the Bushmen took place near the junction of the Orange and Sinqunane rivers, well to the south-west of the Sehonghong shelter, and according to his prisoner, the leader of the band was named Mashake (Masharka), not Soai.[16] The accuracy of some Basotho oral history can be checked by comparing the official archival records of the Allison raid with the account related to Pastor Victor Ellenberger in 1935. His informant Azariele Sekese, did not himself participate in the raid, but only heard the story from others.[17] Although Sekese makes no mention of the name Soai, the connection with that chief was assumed by the missionary, who was undoubtedly influenced by other published accounts.[18]

It also came to be repeated, in future years, that when the Bushmen fled from Allison's attack, they mounted wild unbroken mares that had never before been ridden, and galloped them into the mountains.[19] A contemporary account published in the *Natal Mercury* by a correspondent who had apparently talked with members of the expedition on their homeward march, and which reveals much that was not reported in the official records, hints at the origin of this distortion.

> The Bushmen must be expert riders and hunters. Many of the mares were unbroken at the time they were stolen, but are now perfectly quiet. The remains of game were to be found all along their route. It is supposed they must use the lasso, as their riems, 20 to 30 yards long, were taken with the other spoil, arrows and etc. . . . . I hear that some of the Bushmen's caves are of immense size, and decorated inside with coloured drawings of hunting scenes and animals beautifully executed. One of the caves was large enough to admit of the whole commando — captured horses, the commando cattle, and three tents pitched — and yet seemed to be not half filled; and I hear that when the fires are lighted at night it has a very extra-ordinary appearance, the light reflecting on these coloured drawings of elands and etc.[20]

Shortly before the expedition under Allison, J. H. Bowker, British Agent in Basutoland, reported his findings on an arduous trek between East Griqualand and Maseru to the Governor of the Cape. Traversing part of the same southern terrain as that later covered by Allison, Bowker commented, 'There is not one acre of ground fit for anything but a baboon or a Bushman'. The scenery, however, was grand and rugged to a degree. After describing castellated gorges where the river seemed to tie itself in knots and then burst through between rocks piled high on top of one another, and which at times formed tall flanking pillars like shot-towers, he continued:

> We found some very good caves where we got shelter in the rain. Some of them were full of paintings of eland and other sorts of game, battles between Bushmen and Kaffirs, in which the spear and shield seemed somehow always to be giving way to the bow and arrow. History is often not very impartial, and I am afraid our little friends of the cave are no exceptions in their history as represented in the paintings. There was another very good group, a lot of women frightened by a naja serpent while getting water. They are represented as throwing away the water skins and egg-shells, and bolting in different ways. We sometimes came upon the tracks of the Bushmen, but saw none, although I have no doubt they saw us, but we kept a sharp look-out after the horses at night to prevent their shooting the horses. A very common practice with them is to creep up at night and wound two or three horses with poisoned arrows, knowing as a matter of course that the wounded animals will be unable to move in the morning and be left behind either dead or dying.

I find that there are about 200 men all told, and they say one or two Englishmen with them. The latter I almost was inclined to doubt, but all who knew anything about them stick to it. What a change it must be for such people if it is true. Their head-quarters, they say, are about the junction of the Great and Little Orange rivers, and it was near there where we saw their tracks.[21]

This corresponds exactly with the area where Allison caught up with and annihilated a group of Bushmen only six months later. When the Natal Government wrote to the authorities in Basutoland giving warning of their intended expedition, Wodehouse and Bowker promised to assist in the apprehension and punishment of the Bushman marauders, but Bowker felt it would be useless to do anything in a hurry. He was not afraid of attacking the Bushmen, he said, and would approach them from the direction of East Griqualand later in the year when there was grass available for the horses. He suspected that Lisawana's son was involved with the stock thefts, which suggests that the liaison between Lisawana and the Bushmen described by Speirs and Hulley eleven years previously, still persisted.[22]

In November 1869, Bowker wrote:

Should we go into the mountains after them [the Bushmen], we should be under the necessity of shooting. I therefore think it would be as well to hold on until we have a case against them from this side before extreme measures are resorted to, and this will not be long if the Natal patrols push them over towards this side of the Malutis.[23]

That same month, a Natal newspaper held the report:

Mr Bowker with a company of men, intends to start a patrol down the South Lesuto to see whether his orders have been obeyed, i.e. whether the Basutos have located themselves on certain spots indicated by him. In December next, the whole force will penetrate the Malutis as far as the Drakensberg, for the purpose of 'hunting Bushmen' — so graphically remarked one of the men. The Kafirs appear to be in great dread of Mr Bowker and the Police.[24]

It is uncertain whether these plans materialised, but for several years to come Natal continued to make representations against Moorosi and to press for redress for the stolen stock. Moorosi consistently denied all connection with the Bushmen who had committed the offence, and the final outcome of the case was a ruling by the resident magistrate in Basutoland that British authority could not intervene. At the time of the Allison raid, Moorosi had passed the initiative back to Natal by suggesting that clues to the thefts would probably be found on the eastern side of the Drakensberg, and he had offered his co-operation to make a further search there.[25] The matter was dropped, and Moorosi, with his Bushmen protégés, continued to find refuge in the inaccessible fastnesses of the Orange river system until 1879. Then, sparked off by one of his sons being convicted of horse theft, Moorosi finally fell foul of colonial rule. Retreating to his mountain fortress in the Quthing district, he and his people withstood concerted attacks from the Cape forces for seven long months. Only after pounding his walled defences with mortars, firing a total of 1 443 rounds of ammunition, awarding three Victoria crosses for bravery and losing several men in the affray, did the British finally succeed in dislodging Moorosi by scaling the krantzes with ladders. It was said that many Bushmen valiantly fought and died with the Phuti in the defence of their chief, whose body was found in a small rock shelter on the mountain which still bears the name *Mount Moorosi*.[26]

Many years later, in 1930, one of Moorosi's sons, Mapote, executed some rock paintings for Mrs. Walsham How at Qacha's Nek, having learnt the art with his half-Bush stepbrothers, from full-blooded Bushmen living under the protection of his father. Some of the Bushmen who dispersed after Moorosi's death subsequently re-assembled near Mohale's Hoek, where they, like other remnants of their people, soon hybridised with the Basotho and lost their identity.[27]

Back in Natal, the Bushman depredations did not immediately cease after the Allison raid, but gradually dwindled to a halt over the next few years. In fact, before Allison even reached *Meshlynn* on his return march, he heard that during his absence, ten horses had been taken from the Mpendle area, and that a party of eight Africans had unsuccessfully followed them over a pass south of Giant's Castle and thence into Lesotho.[28]

The following month, November 1869, another foray against Africans was traced back over the Mnweni Pass to the Orange river. On sighting the pursuers, the thieves made off with the horses, leaving a carnage of slaughtered cattle and one dead sheep.[29]

In March 1870, the thieves again used the Mnweni Pass to escape with twenty-five horses and a whole herd of cattle taken from Africans living near the Mnweni river. The familiar story was repeated: catching up with the thieves, the pursuers could do no more than helplessly watch their cattle cruelly speared, and the marauders gallop off over the mountains on the stolen horses.[30]

Bushmen apparently continued to frequent the ravines of the upper Thukela for several years to come, for in 1878, a party of these 'strange weird-looking creatures . . . hardly bigger than a child of ten' were encountered by a young English couple on honeymoon in the Mont-aux-Sources area.[31]

The last theft specifically attributed to Bushmen was reported by the Richmond correspondent of the *Natal Mercury* on 12th August, 1872. The story reads:

> About five weeks ago, during a snowstorm, a number of Bushmen made a descent from the rough kloofs about the Drakensberg, at the sources of the Mzimkhulu and Ngwangwana, upon a portion of Dumisa's tribe, under Sakayedwa, located on the upper Pholela, near the Berg, and drove away 17 horses belonging to the kafirs. Notwithstanding the rough weather, the Chief got a number of men together and followed on the spoor of the stolen horses. After a time, they came across six horses, which had probably knocked up and had been killed. After travelling along most difficult passes in the Berg, through snow and ice-covered rocks, and in places where there was barely room to get a horse along, they descended to a valley beyond the Drakensberg, to the sources of the Senqu river . . . . The rough, high table-lands were followed, when on the fourth day, after hard riding and exposure to cold, they espied what they anticipated was an encampment of Bushmen, indicated by a column of smoke. The ground lay nicely for entrapping the party. Scouts were sent, who gradually closed in upon them, when the work of death immediately commenced. The party consisted of only 5 men, 2 women and a girl, who were killed, and 2 women with infants, who were spared and brought back as captives. The reason for slaughtering them is stated to be no other than necessity. The Bushmen, instantly they saw their enemies approach, began to throw their poisoned arrows, and discharged a gun they had, but without any effect. There can be very little doubt that the whole party might have been captured, but then kafirs look upon Bushmen as a superior species of Baboon, and would glory in the chance of indiscriminate slaughter. The women are said to have fought most bravely. After the men were killed nothing would pacify them. It was unsafe to go within reach of their arrows and other weapons, so the bullets of Sakayedwa's men were sent to the fatal work for them and the girl also. The two women with infants were helpless and easily secured. Twenty horses were taken, ten being a portion of those already stolen: a number had been killed by cold.
>
> The country to which these singular people retire with their plunder, is described as very barren and fearfully broken. The Bushmen take shelter in caves and overhanging rocks, and in almost inaccessible krantzes. The country is marked on Hall's map as 'unexplored' . . . .
>
> The promptitude with which these men went to work, and the terrible example made, will tend to check in some measure these inroads. Hunger, no doubt, presses the Bushmen to do these daring deeds, or they would never venture out in the dreadful storms which assail the Drakensberg in winter. Could nothing be done to bring these unfortunate creatures — thorough outcasts of humanity: shot down as dogs whenever the opportunity offers — to live the quiet pastoral life of the kafirs? . . . . By educating a few of these people, in time they might become messengers of good to the last of the race of the once formidable and numerous Bushmen.[32]

But such sentiments, the first to be voiced that had any sympathy with the Bushmen, were already too late to save the race from extermination.

High on the Ngwangwana river in the south-western corner of Natal, a small and shallow shelter on a promontory of rock contains a few paintings of horsemen in red, black and white, one of them carrying a long-barrelled gun and powder horn. To one side is a very indistinct scene in faded black, but enough survives to show muscular Bantu, some carrying spears and one a shield, surprising a Bushman camp. (Figure 51). The shelter in which the Bushmen unsuspectingly lie and sit is suggested by a natural line in the rock, and a woman nearest the attacking Bantu raises her arms in alarm. One can only guess at the slaughter that ensued, but the tantalisingly fragmentary condition of the paintings leaves ample room for imagination.

Figure 51 *Site L9, Bushman's Nek.*

Large muscular Bantu carrying assegais, and one a shield, make a surprise attack on a Bushman encampment. That the Bushmen are in a shelter is suggested by a natural recess in the rock. The paintings, in black, are unfortunately very fragmentary. Horses and riders in black and white in the lower part of the group have been omitted from this rendering for the sake of clarity, and the figures on the right have been moved in closer than they appear on the rock face.

References

1. S.N.A. 1/3/19, p. 200-254, 1869.
2. S.N.A. 1/3/19, p. 209, 11/8/1869.
3. S.N.A. 1/3/19, p. 205, 31/7/1869.
4. S.N.A. 1/3/19, p. 206, 31/7/1869.
5. For useful discussion on the probable routes followed by Allison and Giles prior to joining parties, I am indebted to John Wright.
6. Judging from the directions given and the description of the tributaries which joined this river, a large one from the east and three successively from the north-east, it was probably the Mokhotlong valley.
7. This possibly refers to the same raid as that mentioned by Mfene Nyide, see p. 106.
8. Allison's sketch map, preserved in the Cape Archives, G. H. 9/8, marks the shelter on a tributary flowing into the Sinqunane from the north-east. The actual site may be near the junction of the Sinqunane with the Tinani and Lesubing tributaries, or possibly further south on the Kwebung or Motsekwa.
9. Ellenberger 1953: 254; Anderson 1888: 6.
10. Hook 1908: 271.
11. S.N.A. 1/3/19, p. 255, 19/10/1869.
12. Ellenberger 1912: 159-160.
13. S.N.A. 1/3/19, p. 256, 19/10/1869.
14. S.N.A. 1/3/19, p. 257, 19/10/1869.
15. Evans 1911.
16. Willcox 1956: 31-2; How 1962: 16-17, 21-22; Dornan 1909; Stow 1905: 229.
17. Personal communication, V. Ellenberger, 1959.
18. Ellenberger 1953: 253-5.
19. Tylor 1893; Evans 1911.
20. *Natal Mercury*, 4/11/1869.
21. Bowker to Wodehouse, 28/3/1869. Basutoland Records, Vol. 5 (Cape Archives), p. 126-9.
22. G. H. 595, No. 107, 2/9/1869; Basutoland Records, Vol. 5 (unpublished), Bowker to Wodehouse, 23/9/1869, p. 331-2; S.N.A. 1/1/8, No. 77.
23. Basutoland Records (Cape Archives); Bowker to Wodehouse, 12/11/1869, p. 381-2.
24. *Natal Witness*, 9/11/1869; How 1962: 58.
25. G. H. 596: p. 28-31, 30/10/1871; p. 136-7, 27/3/1872; G. H. 1324; No. 374, 10/12/1869.
26. Tylden 1945, 1952.
27. How 1962: 32, 12-14.
28. S.N.A. 1/3/19, p. 239, 23/11/1869.
29. S.N.A. 1/3/19, p. 239, 23/11/1869.
30. S.N.A. 1/3/20; No. 225 & 226, 16 & 20/3/1870.
31. Rogers 1937: 68; Willcox 1963: 22; see also Otto 1908.
32. *Natal Mercury*, 17/8/1872. The spelling of names and rivers in this report have been altered to conform to the present orthography.

Figure 52 *Site E11*

Detail of uniformed figure reproduced in Figure 39. (For discussion, see page 73).

Figure 53 *Site H2*

Figures sitting within constructed huts or skerms *on the left, and what appears to be a natural rock shelter in the centre. Skin bags with tassels hang from the ceilings of both types of dwelling. Above, steatopygous women carry sticks. They follow a male figure and another larger figure clad in a long kaross. This person wears the same knobbed head-dress observed in paintings of riders and stock raiders who are usually depicted naked. The paintings are in black.*

Photo: Pat Carter.

Figure 54

Sotho tribesmen hidden behind indented shields attempt to retrieve cattle from Bushmen who have drawn up a defence line against them. One of the Bushmen (lower left) has a knobbed head-dress similar to the Bushmen painted on Mpongweni Mountain (Figure 28), and others appear to have arrows in a fillet on their heads. A natural crack in the rock has been used by the artist to accentuate the division between attackers and defenders. This site, on the right bank of the Orange river opposite the junction with the Thala Boliba, was recorded during a recent survey, and does not appear on the map nor on the site list.

Oral Tradition

Although most of the people who had personal knowledge of the Mountain Bushmen are now dead, the recollections of white colonists and Bantu-speaking peoples whose way of life or interests brought them into contact with the last of the hunter-gatherers, help fill the many gaps in our knowledge. Since many of these recollections have not yet been recorded in print, this chapter summarises the traditions that have been handed down to the present generation.

Melikane, Sehonghong and Soai

By 1870, the Bushmen of the Orange River system had become caught between two fires. While they were being pursued by Dumisa and Sakhayedwa from the east, they were also being hounded by the Basotho from the west, and many of the rock paintings in the valley of the Orange river bear witness to this conflict. (Figure 54)

Jonathan, son of Chief Molapo, was particularly active in his persecution of the cattle thieves. According to varying traditions, the Bushman captain Melikane, whose name has been given to a river and a shelter in Lesotho as well as to a glen near the junction of the Kei rivers,[1-3] crashed to his death when he was caught gathering honey high on the face of a krantz. Another source claims this unfortunate chief to have been Sehonghong, who also has a river and a rock shelter named in his memory.[4] All accounts claim that the majority of the clan were ruthlessly exterminated, but Mrs How records the added detail that Sehonghong's son and another Bushman managed to escape on horses. Chased to caves in the Leqoa river valley, they put up a valiant fight before eventually being cornered and killed.

Among the last of the Bushman chiefs was Soai, a name which has become quite legendary. Under spellings such as Swai, Zweei, Stswaai and Tsuayi, his headquarters are variously given as a shelter in the Witzieshoek area,[5] Eland Cave north of the Mhlwasine valley near Cathedral Peak,[6] and a shelter overlooking the Mzimuti river in the Underberg district.[7] According to information collected by A. D. Whyte in 1910, Soai was driven from the Mzimuti shelter well after Bantu settlement of the area, and after severely trying the patience of the Basotho by incessant raids on their stock, most of his band was eventually exterminated in a large cave near Chief Thlakanolo's kraal. Chief Thlakanolo, now succeeded by his son, lived near the present site of the Sehonghong air-strip, which overlooks a deep ravine cut by the river of that name. Here, beneath a sheer amphitheatre-shaped krantz on a rock bluff, is the spacious Sehonghong shelter which is still pointed out by residents of the area as the place where the last Bushmen were killed. (Site X4, Figure 55)

Written accounts of the final stand made by Soai and his band against overwhelming odds differ in detail, but there is general agreement that the scene of the battle was the Sehonghong shelter.[8-10] According to a Mosotho informant, Rev. J Moteane, Soai himself was shot dead when found hiding in a deep pool in the nearby Orange river with only his nose above water. His body, adorned with bracelets of elephant ivory and a belt of beautifully worked beads, was subsequently dragged from the river and cut up for 'medicine'. When the men were all slain, the women and children were marched to Leribe, where some of them were still living at the beginning of this century. The majority, however, escaped back to their old haunts.[11]

The late Mr C. J. Laird, of Matatiele, recalled that when he was trading at Qacha's Nek in 1904, one of his Phuti customers arrived accompanied by a young man of small stature and very light skin colour. When Mr Laird enquired about his origins, the Phuti explained that he had found two small children alive in the Sehonghong shelter after the massacre of the Bushmen by Jonathan's men. They were a boy and a girl, and the Phuti man and his wife brought them up as their own children. Although he could not be sure, Mr Laird judged the age of the Bushman to be the early twenties. He never saw the girl.[12]

Immediately north of the Sehonghong shelter, the Mashai trading store of today displays the usual conglomeration of merchandise — saddlery, tobacco, cheap patent medicines, boots, pots, beads, detergents, paraffin, sacks of dry goods, and rows and rows of brightly patterned woollen blankets. For many years, the scene was made even more incongruous by a fragmentary human skull which peered down on prospective buyers from among these goods, a

Figure 55 *Site X4, Sehonghong*

This large rock shelter on a tributary of the Orange river is well concealed by the bluff of sandstone in the foreground. An idea of scale is given by the horseman and two walking figures at the top of the dyke to the right of the shelter.

According to tradition, the last band of Bushmen living an independent existence

in Lesotho, met their death at this site under their leader Soai. The shelter was visited in 1873 by Joseph Orpen in the company of a Bushman guide named Qing. Qing discussed the significance of some of the paintings with Orpen, and related the only recorded mythology of the Bushmen living in this region.

Photo: Pat Carter.

102

trophy that had been presented to the trader, Mr Crookes, along with other Bushman relics.[13, 14] Reputedly, this skull had been found in the nearby Bushman stronghold, and a wily profiteer sold pieces of it at half a crown a time for magical purposes. Mr Edgar Calder-Potts, present director of the trading concern, willingly lent the skull for inspection at the Anatomy Department of the Witwatersrand Medical School. Disappointingly, it proved to be nothing more than a witch-doctor's hoax, for the features were predominantly Bantu, not Bush.[15] It is nevertheless of interest that the superstitions attached to Bushman magical power persist to this day. Mrs Marion Walsham How has recorded the extremes to which a Mosotho resorted to obtain a sample of red paint found on the body of a dead Bushman many years before,[16] and several of the paintings in the Sehonghong shelter show areas where the pigment has intentionally been scraped off, presumably for use as medicine.[17]

Orpen, Qing and the Langalibalele rebellion

In November 1873, trouble flared up in Natal when Langalibalele's Hlubi refused to surrender the numerous unregistered guns they had acquired. When confronted by the Government forces sent to punish him, Langalibalele fled over the Drakensberg into Lesotho, where he was tricked by a patrol under Jonathan who first appeared friendly and then took him captive. The Natal forces, commanded by Captain Albert Allison who had pursued Langalibalele over the pass now known by his name, soon arrived on the scene at the Pitsang valley, and the rebellion was quelled.[18] This temporary association between the forces under Jonathan and Allison, both renowned for their activities against the Bushmen, perhaps explains why the attack on Soai at the Sehonghong shelter has been attributed to the combined efforts of these two men.[19] There is not, however, any official record of their having turned against the Bushmen on this occasion.

Meanwhile, Langalibalele's stand against the Natal government had called Joseph Orpen, then British Agent in Nomansland, into action. Detailed to enter Lesotho and intercept Langalibalele from the south, Orpen obtained the services of a Bushman guide who was employed as a hunter by Qacha, son of Moorosi. This young man, named Qing, had escaped extermination a few years earlier when remnants of his father's band had been attacked and killed, probably either by Allison or Jonathan. In addition to his own diminutive wife, Qing had inherited his brother's widow, and he spoke the

Phuti dialect as well as his own click language. While traversing the mountains on horseback Qing showed Orpen some rock paintings at Melikane (site X11) and Sehonghong (X4), and in the evenings when they were relaxed and smoking round the camp fire, he told Orpen some of the stories he had heard from his people.[20] Through an interpreter, Orpen wrote these down, an invaluable record in that they provide the only glimpse into the mythology of the Mountain Bushmen in existence.[21]

According to tradition, Qacha, Qing's employer, was himself obliged to seek protection from the Bushmen in later years. Found guilty of stock theft by the British Agent Col. Griffith, Qacha, with Molapo and Sehlabathebe, escaped punishment by hiding among the Bushmen on the Leqoa river. Here they were found some time between 1883 and 1885, when the Paramount Chief sent Makhaola Relocluadi to protect the borders of Lesotho against encroachment from Natal. As the number of Basotho immigrants increased under Sehlabathebe, who was created chief, the Bushmen fell foul of their usurpers, and the last of the Bushmen on the Leqoa and Tsoelike rivers are said to have been exterminated in about 1886.[22, 23] Many of the rock shelters along these rivers contain walled structures such as those described from other parts of Lesotho, and which have been attributed to close association between the first Basotho settlers and their Bushman predecessors.[24]

Another illustration of this interplay between two cultures can be found in a rock shelter high on a steep hillside overlooking the winding Orange river between Matsaile and Sehonghong (site X7). A few paintings, which include eland and cattle, survive on the friable sandstone, but the most notable features are the semicircular mud and stone partition walls. In the centre is a raised hearth similar to those found in Basotho huts today. Enquiry among the local inhabitants elicited the information that, in about 1880, conflicts in southern Lesotho forced a Mosotho named Seqhole to flee with his wife to the remote gorges of the Orange river. They found refuge with a Bushman family living in the shelter described above and now known as the Maliperi cave, where they remained until it was safe to return to their home area. As a token of gratitude, Seqhole named his own two daughters after the Bushman's daughters, Mokhala and Qhoasini, and these two Basotho women with Bushman names were thought to be still living in 1957. The Bushman family, it was said, 'disappeared' shortly after Seqhole left, but it was certain that no-one had lived in the Maliperi cave since the Bushmen had vacated it.[25]

The Transkei Bushmen

In addition to the Lesotho Bushmen, a few isolated family groups survived in the Transkei. Sir Walter Stanford wrote of a band who still clung to their haunts in a valley of the Great Kei between about 1874 and 1881:

> They were on friendly terms with the people of Mapaasa's tribe and spent a good deal of their time in winter with them. In summer, however, they were usually out among the rocks and precipices . . . .[26]

Major D. B. Hook, magistrate at Tsolo between 1884 and 1886, recorded an encounter with a Bushman band in his vivid, albeit disjointed narrative, *With Sword and Statute*:

> There is much beauty in the hills on the Buffalo river, with bush and cliffs, high mountains and ravines, where the only Bushmen known in Kaffirland dwelt in the 'krantz', living in their early primitive condition, practising as rainmakers to the tribes, revered and wooed as prophets.
>
> In a sauntering mood, I met them on the height, and caused amazement by the beard I wore — mistaken for a Boer. They were a scrap of pigmy life, pure and simple rock men by their flinty form and manner — jabber, laugh and capers. I told them I had been magistrate of Bushmanland, and that their race on the north-west border was fatter than they were, because there were many springboks! and they were amused. These little manikins could speak the Kaffir language. The women, little sharp-eyed imps, screamed with laughter at the beard![27]

In 1911 Maurice Evans wrote that a few genuine Berg Bushmen who had abandoned their predatory way of life were said to be still living in shelters on the Ntabankhulu mountains in the Tsolo district, and as recently as the early 1930s, Dr H. Anders was surprised at being addressed in a 'foreign' language when his car broke down one night on the steep Bushman's Cutting on Ntabamhlope. Two men were rowdily returning from a beer drink, and both knew phrases of what they called the Twa Bushman language. One of these men had a pure Bush mother, and the other, Poponi Mbekane, had been brought up among the Pondomise. His ancestors were therefore probably the Bushmen who had been living under the protection of Mandela.[28] Poponi said that a number of Bushman families had settled near the present Bushman's Cutting. His former band was known by the name *!ga-!ne*, and his dialect showed an affinity with the Bushman languages of the Gordonia and Vaal River areas in the Orange Free State.[29]

The Underberg area

In 1886, fourteen years after Sakhayedwa's success against the Bushmen who stole horses from the Pholela, the first European farmers moved into the Underberg district. This date also coincides with the date given for the final extermination of the Bushmen immediately over the Lesotho border in the Sehlabathebe area.[30] Stock thefts from the newly settled farmers nevertheless continued unabated, but were now attributed to Basotho rather than Bushman depredators.[31] One of the pioneer farmers, the late Mr Walter Crocker of the farm *Cottesmere* on the Ngwangwana river, had working for him a man Skebeza, who was one of those mustered under Sakhayedwa's headman Mdweli to follow the Bushmen over Bushman's Nek Pass. Camped on the trail at dark, and planning the attack, Skebeza was frankly terrified at the prospect of facing the dreaded poisoned arrows, and pessimistically remarked, 'We shall never see our wives again'. It being taboo for Zulus to mention women when out in battle, Skebeza was chased from the company, and was thereafter ostracised by his tribe as a coward.

In about 1905, a half-bred Bushman, small in stature and yellow in colour, presented himself at *Cottesmere* and asked for temporary employment. He stayed several months, and then disappeared as mysteriously as he had arrived. The late Mr Lawrence Crocker, son of Walter Crocker, remembered that he wore an animal horn attached to a belt round his waist, which he guarded jealously and never permitted anyone to know what it contained.[32]

A past magistrate of the Underberg district, Mr F. M. Meyer, recorded invaluable recollections from aged descendants of Dumisa's people who are now located in the Muguswana Reserve on the Mcatsheni river. According to traditions related by Dumisa's grandson, the late chief Mvimbela, Dumisa was not himself a hereditary chief, but gathered a strong following because of his prowess as a hunter and his immense physical strength and endurance. Once, when times were bad, Dumisa pretended he was dead, and was picked up by Bushmen who taught him many things. After this, he was able to succour the people who gathered under him, and he fed them on elephant flesh.[33, 34] Dumisa did not, however, feel any particular loyalty to his Bushman instructors in later years. After wandering about the countryside, hunting as he went, Dumisa was stationed at the foot of the Drakensberg by Theophilus Shepstone in order to clear the area between the Nzinga and the Ndawana rivers of Bushmen and wild animals, a condition he is said to have fulfilled with great efficiency.[35]

Figure 56 *Site E2*

Taking a rest from tracing the eland shown in Figure 97. Peasant farmers from the Mcatsheni Reserve deviate from the nearby bridle path to see what is going on. These people are the descendants of the famous hunter Dumisa who was stationed on the Mkhomazi to 'chase' Bushmen.

Photo: Pat Carter.

When Mvimbela was asked whether Dumisa had ever taken a Bush wife, he replied, 'No, they were animals. He did catch one female, and sent her to Pietermaritzburg.' This was probably the young girl captured from the Orange river by Sakhayedwa, Dumisa's son.[36] According to informant Mdala Majozi, her name was Gqawukile, and later, other Bushwomen were captured but escaped before they could be sent to the Capital.

Mr M. Houston, lately of the farm *Kilmun*, recollected having seen captured Bushwomen at kraals on the Ngwangwana river in what is now known as Location No. 1, when he was transport riding to the Underberg district during the period of early settlement. They subsequently mysteriously disappeared after lighting a fire, when it was presumed that a smoke signal had been sent and their compatriots had come to their rescue.[37]

Another descendant of one of Dumisa's followers, Joseph Kumalo, said that although he himself had not seen Bushmen, he had learned of them from his mother. They were wild, timid people who lived with the baboons and their language sounded like bird noises. They had no cattle and no houses, but lived in the krantzes where they killed animals with magic charms. Although small in stature, they were mighty sorcerers. One man, Mdeni Tshiza, captured a Bushwoman and made her his wife without paying *lobola*, or bride-price, but she later died in childbirth. This woman was very fond of her Bantu husband, and taught him how to make poison which enabled him to shoot much game, including an elephant, for his people to eat.[38] Although there may be some confusion in this account with the prowess attributed to Dumisa as an elephant hunter, it is interesting to note that some of Dumisa's men did take Bush wives. The late Hector McKenzie, of the farm *Seaforth* which borders on the Mcatsheni Location, was told of a man living in that Reserve who still had a Bushman bow, but this relic can unfortunately no longer be traced.[39]

Mr A. T. McClean of the farm *Duart Castle* in the Hlatimba valley, remembers an old African named Mfene Nyide who died in 1913 at an age of over 70 years. Mfene joined Lugaju in the Mpendle location as a young man, and was posted by the Natal Government to various valleys to 'chase' Bushmen. He took part in an expedition which surprised and killed Bushmen in the Mokhotlong valley, where the 'gluttonous little rascals' had gorged themselves on cattle stolen from Lugaju. Mfene recalled that this took place after the raid when Hodgson was killed, that is, after 1862.[40] When Mfene was on patrol with his men, they lived purely on the game they hunted, and always slept in protected places since they were never sure when the wily Bushmen would suddenly shoot at them with their poisoned arrows. Mfene and his family finally settled permanently in the Hlatimba valley, and began cultivating small fields with the hand hoe.

One day, calculated to be in approximately 1867, a party out hunting unexpectedly came upon a group of Bushmen sheltering under a painted rock now known as *Windy Palace* (site C11). The Bushmen immediately made off up the valley, and Mfene sent a hurried appeal to another headman in the Mkhomazi valley to call up his fighting men. The Bushmen fled over the Berg before any action could be taken, and Mfene never saw them again.[41]

From another source, Mr McClean learned of a strange small woman once seen playing with Bantu children outside a kraal, and trying to make friends. She seemed to be quite isolated from the rest of her community, and was asking for food. No-one knew what eventually happened to her — she simply 'disappeared'.

The Rev. Brother Otto Mäder, a Trappist missionary stationed on the Pholela at *Reichenau* towards the end of last century, wrote of a Zulu named Herman Gwala who had in his possession a medicine charm obtained from a Bushman shortly before 1893. Gwala also told of a Bushman tribe named Mzilikazi said to live, surprisingly, in the mountains beyond Ntabamhlope on the Bushman's river. He claimed they were known to the Zulu, with whom they occasionally mixed and whose language they spoke, as *aBantu aBahle*, meaning *The Good People*.[42] It is of interest that a rock painting of a horse and rider in the Giant's Castle area has been dated by the paper chromatography method to 100 years $\pm$ 20 years B.P.,[43] and this in conjunction with the finding of an exceptionally well-preserved hunting kit at Eland Cave in the Mhlwasine valley in 1926,[44] suggests that a few Bushmen may well have lingered on in the more remote valleys of the Drakensberg for much longer than is generally accepted.

When James William McClean settled on the farm *Morvern* on the ridge between the Hlatimba and Mkhomazi valleys in 1897, he heard from the local Africans of an old sick Bushman who still wandered about in the neighbouring kloofs. No-one objected to his being there, and sometimes gave him food when he begged for it. Once, while making a check on his stock after a snowfall, James McClean was riding along the brink of a gulley leading into the Mkhomazi river on the property now known as *Longlands*, when he glimpsed a wizened little figure sunning itself on a rock on the opposite side of the stream. It was the old Bushman. As soon as he realised he had been observed, the old man slipped back among the bushes and edged his way towards a nearby krantz, rather like a startled rock-rabbit. Locally known as 'The Recluse', he was seen, on occasions, until the early years of the twentieth century.[45]

He was the last of his race, eking out a pathetic and lonely existence in the haunts of his forefathers. He died unnoticed by anyone.

Figure 57 *Site B3*

In August 1965, a diminutive Mosotho woman with a strong admixture of Bushman blood washed the dishes and scoured the pots for a boisterous party of skiers enjoying a week-end of winter sports at the summit of the Sani Pass. Less than five feet tall, her pale flat features and hooded but alert eyes peeped out from beneath a cheap print head-scarf, and not even the voluminous skirt and child's gumboots could conceal an impressive steatopygea and tiny feet. Her name was Evelyn, and when her duties were done, I watched her patter through the slush to a stone-built hut with dung smoke oozing from below the thatched eaves. Beyond, Hodgson's Peaks glistened white in the wan sun, and the Natal farmlands stretched away into the blue haze thousands of feet below. A labouring vehicle with chains clanking on the wheels toiled its way up the zig-zagging pass to the concrete and plate-glass 'chalet' perched on top. A far cry, I thought, from the luxury of the present winter sports resort, to the scene of a century ago when Hodgson lay dying on the desolate mountain top, and one of Evelyn's forebears was wounded and dragged from his home with a rope round his neck because someone had stolen cattle from a farmer on the plains below.

Ironically enough, even though there are no longer full-blooded Bushmen to blame, the pattern of stock raid and retaliation that commenced one and a quarter centuries ago, continues unchanged. To quote but one example, on the 10th March, 1967, the *Natal Mercury* carried the following report:

> A posse of angry men — White and non-White — are taking the law into their own hands to strike back at rustlers operating in the Drakensberg Gardens area from across the Lesotho border.
>
> This week Mr R. S. . . . and his brother D . . ., both armed against ambush, went out with a group of mounted African farm hands and trackers to chase rustlers who had again struck on his farm and got away with several horses.
>
> Two of them were his but the rest belonged to his labourers who are just as angry about the raids as he is.
>
> "I have had enough of this, and so have other farmers in the district. We are going to have top level talks with the Government soon", he thundered.
>
> He told me that in the past few years he had lost about 300 sheep, 30 head of cattle and some horses.
>
> The posse was too late this time to recover the horses but Mr S. . . said that one had ridden into Lesotho a month ago and recovered 50 stolen sheep which had been hidden in a cave. This week the horse thieves were followed right to the Lesotho border where there were huge steps in the rocks.
>
> "I don't know how they got our horses up there — they must have dragged them."
>
> Mr S. . ., who is president of the Underberg Farmers' Association, said the raids had continued despite intensive police patrols.

There are always two sides to every question. All men resent being deprived of their personal property, but the factors which instigated the initial raids had their origin in an even deeper resentment — the resentment of a people who were deprived not only of their land, but also of their liberty and their self-respect.

References

1. Dornan 1909.
2. How 1962: 19.
3. Stow 1905: 199.
4. How 1962: 16.
5. Willcox 1956: 31.
6. Wells 1933.
7. Whyte 1910.
8. Dornan 1909.
9. Ellenberger 1953.
10. *Op cit.*, see Plate opp. p. 160.
11. Dornan 1909.
12. Verbal communication, Mr C. J. Laird, 1970.
13. How 1962: 26.
14. Verbal communication, Mr E. Calder-Potts, 1959.
15. Personal communication, Dr H. de Villiers, 1955.
16. How 1962: 34-5, 40-1.
17. See also Laydevant 1933: 362.
18. G. H. 1405, Memo 19, 14/12/1873.
19. Ellenberger 1953: 253-255.
20. See also p. 116.
21. Orpen 1874.
22. Verbal communication: Joas Tlali, headman of Paulus's village on the Leqoa river, 1959.
23. Oral history collected by the late Christoffel Louw, trader at Sehlabathebe and Matsaile in 1957.
24. Walton 1951; 1956 a, b.
25. Verbal communication, Lister Phokoane, Matsaile. 1957.
26. Stanford 1958: 45-6.
27. Hook 1908: 327.
28. See p. 57.
29. Anders 1935.
30. See p. 103.
31. Verbal communication, the late Mr D. D. Houston, *Silver Streams*, Upper Ngwangwana, 1957.
32. Verbal communication, the late Mr L. Crocker, son of W. Crocker, *Cottesmere*, Ngwangwana, 1960.
33. Cf. Mackeurtan 1930: 157-8.
34. Bulpin 1953: 45-6; see also p. 12.
35. District Record Book, Underberg Magistracy.
36. See p. 85.
37. Verbal communication, Mrs Hilda Clough, daughter of Mr M. Houston, 1960.
38. District Record Book, Underberg Magistracy, Mr F. M. Meyer.
39. Verbal communication, the late Mr H. McKenzie, *Seaforth*, 1958.
40. See also p. 89.
41. Verbal communication, Mr A. T. McClean, *Duart Castle*, 1958.
42. Otto 1908.
43. Denninger 1971; Willcox 1971.
44. Vinnicombe 1971.
45. Verbal communication, Mr A. T. McClean of *Duart Castle*, and the late Mrs R. May, daughter of J. W. McClean, Himeville, 1965.

Figure 58 *Site G3*

Figure 59

The Sani Pass at the head of the Mkhomazi valley.

Figure 60 *Site V12*

Moshebi shelter is to the left of the nose of rock in shadow on the sandstone bluff in the centre background. Below the shelter, and cutting across from one side of the picture to the other, is the road between Ramatseliso Nek and Sehlabathebe. The knoll on the skyline to the right is Letiba's Nek where a track crosses the mountains to the Orange river beyond. Recent excavations in Moshebi shelter yielded a lead musket ball in association with Later Stone Age artefacts in the upper levels. Underlying Later Stone Age hearths were dated to A.D. 1690 and 230 B.C. Middle Stone Age deposits in the shelter contained inadequate amounts of charcoal for dating, but at Ha Soloja shelter further upstream the Leqoa river, a date of greater than 43 000 B.P. was obtained for the lower levels of the Middle Stone Age. Photo: Pat Carter.

110

3   *Previous Investigations*

Archaeology

Archaeological interpretation in southern Africa is currently undergoing drastic revision. The entire nomenclature and chronology is being re-assessed and revised, therefore the outline given here can at best be regarded as provisional.

The prehistoric sequence in southern Africa has been divided into the 'Early', 'Middle', and 'Later Stone Ages',[1] each occupying a defined but overlapping period of time in the development of mankind. The 'Old Stone Age' dates back more than 2 million years, and is beyond the scope of this discussion. Until a few years ago, the 'Middle Stone Age' was thought to occupy the period between 35 000 and 8 000 years B.C., while the 'Later Stone Age' ranged from about 10 000 years B.C. to historic times.[2] However, recent radio-carbon dates of earlier than 20 000 B.C. for 'Later Stone Age' artefacts in widely separated areas, and 'Middle Stone Age' dates ranging back to 100 000 B.C., now suggest a far greater antiquity, but the precise nature of the assemblages associated with these dates awaits publication.[3]

The Bushmen were the most recent exponents of the 'Later Stone Age' in southern Africa, and among their technological accomplishments was the ability to chip and paint naturalistic representations on stone. The origins of this art, however, like the origins of the Bushmen themselves, are as yet unknown.

In the past, the industries of the 'Later Stone Age' associated with the rock art of southern Africa were described as 'Wilton' or 'Smithfield', each with subdivisions based on the typology of the stone tools. So-called variants of the 'Smithfield' complex were designated by the letters 'A', 'B', 'C' and 'N', but the relationship between these variants was never precisely determined.[4]

The validity of purely typological designations is now being severely questioned, and few archaeologists accept these terms as having any cultural significance.[5]

The confusion which existed in the historic terminology is reflected in the archaeological record of Natal and East Griqualand, for *all* variants of the 'Smithfield' complex have been described in association with painted shelters, although Smithfield 'B', 'C' and 'N' predominate.[6]

The 'Wilton' industries, characterised by the presence of small crescents, backed blades and occasionally tanged arrow heads, were formerly recorded in Natal only from the Oliviershoek area of the Natal Drakensberg and from the coast.[7] Recent excavations in East Griqualand and Lesotho have now added to this distribution, and have shown the so-called 'Smithfield C' and 'Wilton' to be part of the same techno-complex.[8] Bushmen are known to have made implements of Smithfield/Wilton type, for such were seen in the making by early colonists,[9] and a missionary in Lesotho has even been able to record the name of a particular Bushman who manufactured a thumb-nail scraper of Smithfield/Wilton form in about 1870.[10]

In the field of archaeology, Colonel J. H. Bowker and his brother T. H. Bowker were South Africa's first true antiquaries, their collections in the Cape dating back to 1855.[11] James Henry Bowker was also associated with the earliest records from Lesotho. In 1868, while acting as British Agent, he visited many shelters which showed evidence of Stone Age occupation and of recent cannibalism. The stone implements which lay strewn around were attributed to Bushmen although no-one had actually seen them in use.[12] Bowker sent a collection of artefacts together with part of a Bushman skull to Sir Joseph Hooker in Britain, and included a contemporary metal arrow tip for comparison with the earlier stone arrow points. Bowker also said that on revisiting places where he and his escort had previously camped, he found evidence of the Bushmen having fashioned arrow heads from the bases of discarded soda-water bottles. At a lecture to the Royal Anthropological Institute in London in 1884, H. W. Feilden exhibited such a glass implement from a rock shelter in Lesotho.[13]

While serving in the Frontier Armed and Mounted Police, Bowker heard of an aged Bushwoman living in the mountains of Lesotho who was able to manufacture bored stones. However, when she was brought to him, no amount of entreaty or offers of rewards elicited any action or information,[14] and her lack of co-operation led Bowker to the erroneous conclusion that bored stones were initially manufactured by an earlier race, and then re-utilised by Bushmen.[15] A more perceptive observation made by Bowker was that the implements found in shelters near rivers which contained fish differed from those in shelters far from the rivers, the latter being adapted to hunting rather than fishing.[14] It has thus taken a century to get back to where Bowker began. Instead of attributing different implements to different peoples as has been the recent archaeological vogue, Bowker was fully aware of what archaeologists currently refer to as 'inter-site variability.'

The first archaeological publication relating specifically to the survey area was made by E. M. Frames in 1898, when he reported and illustrated implements now designated 'Smithfield N' from a rock shelter on *The Curragh* in East Griqualand. He described the site accurately, and mentioned the presence of eight eland and a crude elephant painted in dark and light red.[16] Six of these eland are still visible, the others having been obscured by water seepage, but there is no longer any sign of the 'crude elephant'. Frames noted that much of the deposit had been thrown out by later Basotho inhabitants, and artefacts such as those illustrated by him can still be found scattered on the talus-slope. Until the late 1950s, small huts with semi-circular doorways could be seen against the back wall of the shelter, but they have since been demolished.[17]

William Bazley, one of Natal's early colonists, was a colourful character who first farmed unsuccessfully at Richmond, and later moved to the coast. At Port Shepstone, he blasted rocks in the harbour, quarried marble and constructed roadways.[18] Equipped with this experience he excavated a rock shelter at the turn of the century in Alfred County, the area of southern Natal adjoining Pondoland. Without giving a precise locality, Bazley describes a shelter 120 feet long and 20 feet wide, which he dug to a depth of 16 feet. A top layer of dusty soil three to four feet thick covered another four-foot layer containing ash, wood, charcoal and burnt human bones. Beneath this, loose stones overlay a three-foot deposit of firm soil containing cores and flake implements, below which there were more fallen slabs of rock. When these were removed, there was another five feet of debris which yielded scrapers, stone hammers, bored stones, chips and flakes. At this sixteen-foot horizon, a great roof-fall was encountered, but without further ado, Bazley blasted it away. Underneath, he found three skeletons, apparently of a family killed and crushed flat by the rock fall. A child lay between two adults whose heights were only four foot three inches and four foot seven inches respectively, which suggests that the unfortunate victims were Bushmen. At the same 16-foot level, the excavator claims to have found arrow heads and broken blades with thousands of scrapers of all sizes, some not larger than a finger nail, and cores, flakes and chips 'by the cartload'. Goodwin has pointed out that some of the illustrations show Middle Stone Age elements, and one can only grieve over the lack of method and documentation during this early period of Natal's archaeological exploration.[19]

Perhaps it is just as well that interest in archaeology seems to have lain dormant until the 1930s, when a group of enthusiasts in Durban re-commenced excavating and published several papers on archaeological topics.[20] Hybrid Bushman skeletons were uncovered on the Natal coast,[21] and an unpainted cave on the shores of Pondoland yielded worked bone and wooden implements in association with 'Smithfield' stone artefacts, together with well preserved layers of grass bedding.[22]

In 1932, W. E. Jones donated to the Natal Museum a Bushman skeleton found under the roots of a slow-growing olive tree in Zululand, in the vicinity of the Qudeni mountains where rock paintings have been reported.[23] The skeleton, buried in a flexed position, was associated with two carved bone ornaments, portions of a necklace of ostrich-egg discs, and fragments of pottery.[24]

Between 1934 and 1936, B. D. Malan, with assistance from Miss N. Kirk and Dr and Mrs W. Bauer, made a preliminary survey of archaeological sites in East Griqualand and reported an abundance of material.[25] An excavation in a painted rock shelter near Matatiele proved the deposit to have been disturbed, but the assemblage of typical 'Smithfield B' industry included a few pieces of crude 'Middle Stone Age' manufacture. Surface collections from shelters on *Belleview* indicated 'Smithfield B' and 'C' forms, but again, several waterworn 'Middle Stone Age' specimens were recovered, which Malan suggested were possibly collected and re-utilised by the later 'Smithfield' people.

A recent excavation of *Belleview Shelter* 1 has yielded a datable sequence which proves that the shelter was already occupied by 6 700 B.C. Although no 'Middle Stone Age' material was found *in situ*, another excavation at *Moshebi Shelter* only 6 kilometres away in eastern Lesotho, established the presence of a fully developed 'Middle Stone Age' occupation, and at *Ha Soloja*, upstream from *Moshebi's*, the 'Middle Stone Age' occupation dates back more than 43 000 years.[26] The former occupation of the high altitude areas of the Drakensberg by 'Middle Stone Age' peoples has therefore now been validated. (Figure 60)

In 1950, Dr O. Davies commenced an archaeological survey of Natal. He reported 'Smithfield N' sites in the Bushveld of the middle Thukela and Mooi river valleys and excavated a painted shelter at Natal Spa on the Pongola river near Paulpietersburg. In the disturbed upper layer he found 'Smithfield N' material, including an ostrich-egg bead; below this was an undisturbed deposit of somewhat indefinite affinities which Davies related to 'Smithfield A'.[27] Another shelter at Nqutu in Zululand yielded a pure 'Smithfield N' industry,[28] and from both sites a valuable identification of the faunal remains was made by Dr R. F. Ewer.

Between 1950 and 1960, Mr Gordon Cramb conducted an excavation at *Holley Shelter* near Wartburg, where very faded remnants of red paint are discernible on the shelter wall.[29] The surface stratum contained mixed 'Later' and 'Middle Stone Age' material, but below, a pure 'Middle Stone Age' industry is described. Carbon dates of 2 540 B.C. and 16 250 B.C. have been obtained for the lower layer, and although the latter date was at first regarded as anomalous,[30] more recent analyses from eastern Lesotho[31] and from *Border Cave* near Ngwavuma on the boundary between Natal and Swaziland,[32] lend credence to the early date of 'Middle Stone Age' material.

A painted shelter at *Rose Cottage* near Ladybrand in the Orange Free State[33] has produced successive layers of industries underlying the 'Later Stone Age',[34] and other excavations which suggest a possible association between paintings and the 'Middle Stone Age' have been summarised by Willcox.[35]

In western Lesotho, Pastor Paul Ellenberger has excavated a number of painted shelters which he claims provide evidence for associating the earliest appearance of rock art with 'pre-Later Stone Age' technology.[36] From Molapo, he records a long serpenti-form engraved line covered by a deposit in which there was a predominance of burins, which he suggests were the type of implement used for executing the engraving. An engraved paving stone excavated near Morija is also possibly of 'pre-Smithfield' date, and other 'pre-Later Stone Age' levels produced many burnt ochre concretions which are thought to have served for rock art as well as for ornamentation. By somewhat tenuous reasoning, Ellenberger has associated 'archaic' red monochrome paintings at *Jonathan Shelter* near Leribe with an industry which yielded an abundance of serrated points. Other monochrome paintings from Maphutseng are similarly linked with a 'pre-Smithfield' technology, but bichrome paintings, on the other hand, are associated with a later expression of the 'Smithfield'. Despite the early associations claimed for some of the art, Ellenberger nevertheless considers the majority of the paintings to be contemporaneous with the latest phase of the 'Smithfield/Wilton' complex. His paper, to be entitled *The beginning of pre-historic art in Basutoland* in which these associations will be outlined in greater detail, has unfortunately not yet appeared in print.[36] Ellenberger's evidence would seem to support the idea of a local evolution of painting techniques from simple to more complex styles within the Lesotho massif. My work immediately to the east of this area, and that of Pager to the north-east,[37] does not, however, lend support to the 'simple' or 'archaic' characteristics of the earliest art. Here paintings of eland in the lowest levels of superimposed panels are in the bichrome technique, suggesting that the earliest paintings still visible at the present time are comparatively well developed.

The whole problem, therefore, of whether or not there was a local evolution of rock art within the area, and whether or not the earliest appearance of the art can be associated with cultures earlier than the 'Later Stone Age', must await future clarification. The association of the great bulk of rock art with the 'Later Stone Age' is nevertheless beyond question.

My own surface collections from the area under survey come from 80 shelters, and amount to more than 1 500 artefacts; all of them would pass without comment in 'Smithfield B', 'C' or 'N' assemblages. Only one shelter was excavated during the survey period, the work being directed by Major T. H. G. Farnden, assisted by W. D. Gibbs and D. T. Allison, in 1961.[38] The site, a painted shelter on the farm *Sheltered Vale* in East Griqualand was selected because of the impressive range of superpositions. At least three painted sequences occur on the original rock face, which has flaked off in places to expose fresh rock surfaces. On the newly exfoliated areas have been painted two further sequences, making a total of five clear superpositions. Even if not much time elapsed between the direct superpositions, an appreciable period must have intervened between the exfoliation of the old painted surface and the painting of the new surface thus exposed. There was also the chance that a fallen fragment of the exfoliated paintings might be found in a datable context in the deposit, which would establish a minimum date for the older paintings. The deposit proved disappointing. The maximum depth was only 25 centimetres, and most of the finds were recovered from the surface dust. Below a sterile layer of 10-15 centimetres, more implements and flakes were lying in pockets in the bedrock. Very little difference was noted between the artefacts from the two layers, although the deeper specimens were coated with soil, whereas those near the surface were not. The finds included implements typical of 'Smithfield B'. There were also fragments of bone of which one was sharpened, fragmentary potsherds, three small glass trade-beads, and a piece of what was probably a stone pipe-bowl. There were no fragments of painted stone other than those left on the surface when specimens of paintings were chipped out for the Durban Museum in the 1930s. (Figure 72)

Farnden later made a collection of 'Smithfield N' artefacts in and around a painted site near Muden in the Umvoti district which he has compared with 'Smithfield N' material excavated by Willcox from the Main Cave at Giant's Castle in the Natal Highlands. The principal difference lies in the microlithic tendency of the Giant's Castle implements and the more robust nature of the material from Muden. While these industries may represent two separate phases of the 'Smithfield' complex, it is as likely that the differences are due to raw material or functional variability.[39]

Schoute-Vanneck and Walsh have suggested that 'Smithfield C' had yet another expression on the Natal Coast, where shell-collecting called for modified forms of the usual equipment required for up-country hunting.[40]

From the scatter of 'Smithfield B', 'C' and 'N' sites that have been reported in Natal, Pondoland and East Griqualand, it is obvious that the 'Smithfield' people, the latest of whom can definitely be associated with the Bushmen, once occupied the whole area. Their habitats ranged from rock shelters and open sites in the

Highlands, to shelters and open sites in the Midlands, Lowlands, and coastal belt. Movements of the hunter-gatherers were no doubt governed by seasonal factors, and wherever they went, they manufactured their tools for the most part from the nearest supply of raw materials. The tool kits found in the excavations therefore reflect the different purposes to which they were put in the various environments. Surface finds in the majority of painted shelters within the area have, to date, produced no cultural remains other than those of 'Smithfield' association, and in the Cape, paintings are indisputably proven to have been associated with 'Smithfield B' finds in the Middelburg and Colesberg districts.[41]

The dating of the paintings has been discussed in detail elsewhere,[42] but until there is a greater body of factual evidence, the archaeological associations of the earliest expression of art in the central mountain massif must remain an open question.

Ethnography and Rock Art

Between the years 1845 and 1851, much of the correspondence in the Natal Archives concerning action to be taken against the Bushmen cattle-raiders, was signed by the Honourable Donald Moodie, Colonial Secretary. It seems ironically incongruous, therefore, that during his leisure hours in Natal, this gentleman concerned himself with enquiries into the origins of the Bushmen based on translations from early Dutch documents, for which research, he wrote, very few of his associates cared a straw.[43]

In July 1855, Moodie read a lecture before the Natal Society[44] which was embodied in a paper published the same year, entitled '*A Voice from the Kahlamba: Origin of the Bushmen*'.[45] Dr W. H. I. Bleek, an eminent philologist from Germany who had arrived in Natal to work among the Zulu, encouraged Moodie in his studies, and a communication published in Pietermaritzburg drew attention to the confusion existing among savants in Europe concerning the Bushmen.[46] 'I fully believe', wrote Bleek, '. . . that contributions towards the ethnography of Africa will now command attention.' Unfortunately, the ethnography of the Khahlamba Bushmen did not, although Dr Bleek's personal interest in such a project was intimated in a long letter written from Pietermaritzburg between the 22nd and 30th April, 1856.

> During the first month of this year, the prolonged peace drew the Bushmen from their inaccessible hiding places in the Kahlamba Mountains to steal cattle[47] and directed my attention to them once more.

Figure 61 *Site F18*

*On the move: a general view of some of the marching figures on Ikanti Mountain.
Some are naked, others wear karosses. They nearly all carry equipment in the form
of hunting bags, quivers, arrows and bows or sticks. All the figures walk in one
direction, towards the escarpment. The scene possibly represents a seasonal migration.
A detail of the figures at upper right is reproduced in Figure 155.*

*The paintings are remarkably well preserved, and a photograph published in 1907
shows little or no deterioration since that time. In recent years, however, the site
has been included in a tourist itinerary, and is threatened by the misguided attentions
of an uninformed public.*

Photo: Pat Carter.

In the recesses of the Kahlamba mountains in the apparently inaccessible ravines named by Captain Gardiner, Giant's Cup,[48] must still remain interesting evidences of our race. Yet to pursue such ethnological studies with any success requires more freedom than I am able to command. In addition, one would also require considerable geographical information as the recesses of the Kahlamba are practically unexplored.[49]

One can only lament that this remarkable man was never afforded the opportunity to pursue his interest in the Mountain Bushmen. Had the same energy that he subsequently directed on the Xam Bushmen of the Cape been fostered and encouraged in Natal, a great deal more light would have been shed on the lore and mythology which inspired the paintings. Dr Bleek left for Cape Town, and no-one took his place in Natal. The *Voice from the Kahlamba* called in vain, for no-one stopped to question or to heed the answers. Bows and arrows inevitably succumbed to barrel and ball, and the identity of the few remaining Bushmen was soon lost in miscegenation with the surrounding Bantu.

In Cape Town, Dr Bleek finally decided to abandon a monumental grammatical work on the Bantu languages[50] in favour of recording the rapidly disappearing language and mythology of the Southern Bushmen.[51]

> We are still in the position, by prompt and energetic measures, to preserve [not only] a few 'sticks and stones, skulls and bones' as relics of the aboriginal races of this country, but also something of that which is most characteristic of their thoughts and their ideas.[52]

In 1873 Bleek presented the first report of his Bushman researches to the Cape House of Assembly.[53] During the same year J. M. Orpen, then British Resident in East Griqualand, managed to obtain from a young Bushman survivor in south-eastern Lesotho, some interesting information which was published with comments from Dr Bleek in the *Cape Monthly Magazine* of July 1874.[54] This Bushman, named Qing, actually guided Orpen to some painted sites, two of which, X4 and X11, are included in this survey. Although the explanations given by Qing are somewhat enigmatic, a definite correlation between Bushman mythology and at least some of their paintings was established for the first time. Through the influence of George William Stow, who had been recording rock art in the Eastern Cape since 1867,[55] Orpen made copies of some of the paintings shown him by the Bushman. These were published in colour at the same time as his article, and Dr Bleek appealed for further faithful copies, preferably backed up by photography. (Figures 223, 238).

Copies were made by various enthusiasts in the Cape, such as W. Piers and C. H. Schunke, and these were shown to Bushmen for explanation and comment.[52] A further set of copies given by Col. Durnford[56] to Sir Bartle Frere in Natal were lent for the same purpose,[57] but it is not known whether these copies are still in existence.

As a result of this wave of enthusiasm in the seventies, Sir Henry Bulwer, member of the Royal Anthropological Institute and Lieutenant Governor of Natal from 1875 to 1880, requested a farmer with artistic ability, Mark Hutchinson, to make copies of rock paintings from the Giant's Castle area of the Natal Drakensberg.[58] Hutchinson was assisted in this task by his son Graham, and the resultant facsimile copies are now housed in the Natal Museum, Pietermaritzburg, and the Library of Parliament, Cape Town.[59] Although these are the earliest surviving copies of rock paintings from Natal, a tantalising entry in the *Christy Collection* in the British Museum indicates that Hutchinson was not first in this field. The inventory, dated November 1869, reads:

> Presented by Gen. Lefroy. Copies of Bushmen paintings from Natal frontier. S. of Bushman's river, made by Col. A. Moncrieff.[60]

Unfortunately, when I went through the *Christy Collection* in 1965, these copies could not be located.

Also in the British Museum is a well-used Natal Bushman bow,[61] which was obtained from Mr J. Howell, Winburg. The following item on the catalogue[62] is a Bushman quiver and seven poisoned arrows sent by the same donor to the International Exhibition in 1862. Although it is not specifically labelled 'Natal', it probably belongs to the same hunting outfit as the bow.

James M. Howell, Lieutenant in command of the Natal Native Police Corps stationed at Bushman's river in 1849,[63] gave evidence on Bushman depredations at a Government commission of enquiry in Pietermaritzburg in 1852.[64] He subsequently became Landdrost of Winburg, and is therefore almost certainly the donor of the Bushman hunting kit.[65] It is also known from the writings of Captain A. W. Drayson that it was not uncommon for Bushman bows and arrows to be in the possession of Natal frontier farmers during the period of early settlement.[66]

Another pioneer in the field of recording rock art was Louis E. Tylor, nephew of Sir Edward Tylor who was then curator of the Pitt-Rivers Museum in Oxford. In 1893, at the request of his

Figure 62 *Site J18*

This elephant in black and grey, now very faded, was photographed by Brother Otto of Mariannhill in 1895. His photograph shows three hunters, one armed with long spears, attacking the elephant. These figures have now entirely disappeared, and the original elephant had a shapely sway back, swinging trunk and tusks which are no longer visible. To the right of the white horse, there are other mounted horses in black and red which have been omitted from this rendering.

Traced in 1954, assisted by Betty Mills.

117

uncle, Louis Tylor made copies of somewhat faded paintings in the vicinity of Wasbank. Then, on information supplied by a German doctor in Ladysmith, who had himself photographed some of the paintings, Tylor toiled his way by ox-waggon to the remote and inaccessible Giant's Castle area. Here he made an extensive search for paintings, locating more than thirty sites. He recorded eighteen of these and, under very adverse conditions, copied about eighty groups of paintings as faithfully as he could without the aid of tracing paper. From the letters written by Louis Tylor to his uncle at this time, fortunately preserved in the files of the Pitt-Rivers Museum, we learn that he was disappointed in his hopes of coming across other Bushman remains in the shelters. He found he had everywhere been preceded by Bantu of the Hlubi tribe who had been located in that area between 1849 and 1873 under their chief Langalibalele, to act as a buffer between the raiding Bushmen and the settler farmers.[67] Tylor ascribed the many animal traps and broken pots he came across to the Bantu, as well as crude attempts at imitating the paintings with charred sticks. European farmers too, who lived in the shelters while they hunted and grazed their sheep, had caused much damage by lighting fires, by scrawling signatures over the paintings, and by attempting to remove them. Tylor himself forwarded actual examples of paintings to the Pitt-Rivers Museum, where six slabs are on display.

While working in what is now known as Giant's Main Cave, Tylor was surprised by a chance visit from Hutchinson who had himself recorded paintings from the same shelter eighteen years previously when they were better preserved. It transpired, however, that Hutchinson's work had been limited entirely to the Main Caves, for he was unaware of the existence of any other sites. One of the groups copied by Hutchinson showing three horsemen riding abreast[68] had already deteriorated considerably in 1893, and in 1967 when I compared Tylor's copies with the paintings in the field, very faint indications of the horses' legs and tails could be made out only with the assistance of Tylor's accurate description of the relative positions of the paintings. Grave deterioration of many of the historic subjects depicted by the Bushmen is also revealed by comparing Tylor's copies with the present state of the paintings. None of Tylor's work was published until 1940, when Leonard Adam included one animal and a group of human figures in his book *Primitive Art*.[69] Because Louis Tylor's valuable work has been so long overlooked, many of the shelters assiduously recorded by him in 1893 have since been re-located and now bear the names of their more recent 'discoverers'.[70] (Figure 87)

While Tylor was investigating the Giant's Castle area, Brother Otto of the Trappist Mission at Mariannhill was taking a lively interest in rock paintings further south. As an artist skilled in reproducing and retouching religious paintings in Germany, he somewhat misguidedly applied quaint mediaeval theories to the development and purpose of the Bushman art he now found himself studying.[71] He removed some painted slabs from a shelter near the mission station at *Reichenau* in the Pholela valley, and deposited one of them, a red horse, in the museum at Mariannhill where it can still be seen. The other slabs painted in black and depicting fighting warriors, an antelope hunt and an unidentifiable animal, were taken to the Feldkirch Teachers' College in the Vorarlberg, Austria. An attempt to locate these paintings in 1964 proved unsuccessful. The Teachers' College was bombed during the second world war and was also requisitioned as a hospital. The remains of the museum collection are now reduced to litter in an attic, but there was no sign of any rock paintings.[72] I have also failed to locate the original site near *Reichenau* mission — it was probably somewhere on the adjacent Mahwaqa mountain.

Photographs illustrating a paper published by Otto and simply labelled as coming from the Drakensberg,[73] show a herd of cattle and an elephant hunt. A photographic copy of the latter is also in the Natal Museum and dated 1895. The originals of these scenes are on the farm *Sangwana* in the Underberg district, but the group of cattle is now disfigured by efforts to remove them with a chisel, and the hunting scene has greatly deteriorated. The elephant is very faint, and the human figures attacking it with long spears have disappeared altogether. The white horse above is nevertheless still visible. (Figure 62). Another photograph from a site on the neighbouring farm *Scotston* showing horsemen spearing an eland was later published in a guide book on Natal,[74] but since it bears the stamp 'Marianhill 1894' it was probably also taken by Brother Otto. This scene shows very little deterioration with time. In his article Otto mentions a tribe of Bushmen known as *aBantu aBahle* who lived near Giant's Castle, and on the accompanying map he marks the territory of an unnamed Bushman clan under Mzilikazi as ranging from just north of Giant's Castle as far as Mont aux Sources, and extending from the Orange river catchment well into the foothills of the Drakensberg. To the north-west the terrain included Tintwa mountain. It is known that Bushmen were still living in this area until a late date, for they are reported to have been seen near Mont aux Sources in 1878.[75]

Brother Otto was later transferred to a mission in the Kei river

Figure 63 *Site C5*

This scene showing men spearing fish from small boats or floats was first published in 1907. Since then, the paintings have faded considerably, but the area of exfoliation at centre right was already present at that date. The large fish on the left being speared by a man on the bank has four whiskers. It is probably either a barbel or a yellowfish with the whisker feature exaggerated. Both species are indigenous to the Orange river system, and to Natal waters north of the Mtamvuna. The scene measures 96 cm from left to right, the average length of the boats being 8 cm.

valley where he made copies of many paintings in that vicinity.[76] His work, about 139 sheets in all, is housed in the Museum at Mariannhill. The Rev. Albert Schweiger, who applied a romantic and fertile imagination to his interpretations of many of the paintings, succeeded Brother Otto in that area, first seeing the paintings in 1908. He published his rather eccentric views, with some interesting historical sidelights, in the *Catholic Magazine for South Africa* (1912), and in *Anthropos* (1913).[77]

In a geological paper published in 1898, F. F. Churchill drew attention to various shelters in the Bushman's River and Thukela areas of the Natal Drakensberg which had formerly been inhabited by Stone Age peoples,[78] and William Anderson, government geologist in Natal, followed this example. He mentioned sites in his reports of 1901 and 1904, but his *Third and final report of the geological survey of Natal and Zululand* (1907) contained photographs of rock paintings. Amongst these is the first publication of the now well-known scene of men spearing fish from boats on Mpongweni mountain in the Underberg district. Although the group was far clearer then than today, the photograph shows that the exfoliated area at the right of the shoal of fish was already present in 1907.[79] (Figure 63). The other photographs include records of the still well-preserved group of shaded polychrome eland on Mpongweni mountain and the marching figures on Ikanti mountain.[80] (Figures 61, 155). The fourth photograph, however, reveals a distressing deterioration of the *Good Hope* site on a tributary of the Mkhomazana river. Although progressive exfoliation of the paint from this particularly friable sandstone shelter has been evident even to those who have known the paintings during the past 20 years, there is a sharp contrast between the animated group of dancers as they were photographed 60 years ago, and the barely recognisable fragments of paint that is all that remains today. (Figure 64)

A subsequent report written in 1910 by a policeman based in Himeville throws further light on the fate of some of the paintings in this shelter. After complaining that much destruction had been wrought by young goatherds throwing stones at the paintings, he asked the then director of the Natal Museum:

> Are you in possession of any information that some of the paintings are frauds? Some of those on the Umkomazana appear to me to be done by ordinary coloured pencils, anyhow, some of them can be rubbed off the rock quite easily.[81]

The photographs published by Anderson, but not taken by him, are not the earliest from the Drakensberg to have appeared in print. In 1903, a photograph of a frieze of shaded polychrome eland with robed human figures from *Game Pass* shelter, Kamberg, illustrated an article in the *Natal railway guide and general handbook*,[82] and was later reproduced in *Scientific American*, 1915.[83] These paintings were to form the basis of a long controversy, because the cloaked figures were hailed as Babylonians or Phoenicians wearing Phrygian caps.[84] These exotic theories were later queried by Schofield, Davies, and Willcox, and have now been replaced by more homely analogies.[85]

In 1905 two of Hutchinson's tracings from the main caves at Giant's Castle were published in *The Natal Agricultural Journal and Mining Record*,[86] together with two photographs of paintings, which are not accompanied by any site information. One of these bears the evocative caption 'Arab Slave Gang', and is probably the group that was similarly described in later reports.[87] The scene is said to depict a tall dark man with a white head-dress and white robes, who, armed with a whip and a gun, is driving naked natives tied together in pairs. There is some confusion concerning the whereabouts of the site, the extant reports differing in detail, but it is reputedly near the junction between the Mhlangeni and Mkhomazi rivers.[88] I have not been able to re-find the site, therefore

the veracity of the slave story cannot be checked. Judging from the photograph, however, in which the details are admittedly not clear, the paintings merely represent a procession of white-faced hunters carrying the normal Bushman accoutrements, with a slightly larger figure dressed in a kaross bringing up the rear.

The following year, 1906, an ethnologist W. A. Squire wrote a well-balanced article entitled '*The Bushmen and their art*',[89] which was illustrated with paintings recorded by Mark Hutchinson and Brother Otto. He found no necessity to assign to the paintings any great antiquity, and suggested that most of those still visible in the Drakensberg had probably been executed during the first half of the nineteenth century. Squire pointed out that although the greater number of Bushman paintings apparently lacked significance, the pictograph was the parent of the alphabet and consequently lay at the root of education and culture. In expressing these views, Squire was advocating an approach to Bushman art that has only recently been expressed in more cogent detail.[90]

Underlying this burst of interest in rock paintings was a resolution passed in the Cape House of Assembly in May 1904, which recommended that steps should be taken to preserve Bushman paintings from decay and destruction. Appeals for information were sent out to all resident magistrates in the Cape Colony, and the resultant lists of sites were published in the *Votes and Proceedings of Parliament*, June and July 1906.[91]

The Natal Government was requested to take uniform action with the Cape to 'preserve these interesting memorials of a vanishing people', and it was also asked whether attention had ever been drawn to the 'wanton destruction' of rock paintings in that colony. In order to obtain urgent information on the subject, the Natal Colonial Secretary telegraphed the Magistrate at Estcourt, who in turn appealed to S. Barnes, ranger in the newly formed Giant's Castle Game Reserve, and to Graham Hutchinson of the farm *Boschfontein* near Balgowan. Hutchinson, who had first visited Giant's Main Cave in 1875 and had copied some of the paintings there, noted that much natural decay had taken place since that time. In addition, vain attempts had been made to remove paintings by chipping them out. Police who visited the caves on patrol, and the rinderpest guards who lived in the shelters during the 1897 epidemic, had also used the paintings as targets for revolver practice. Barnes complained that visitors to the site were writing their names on top of the paintings, sometimes in letters a foot long, and suggested that prohibitive notices should be erected.

1907

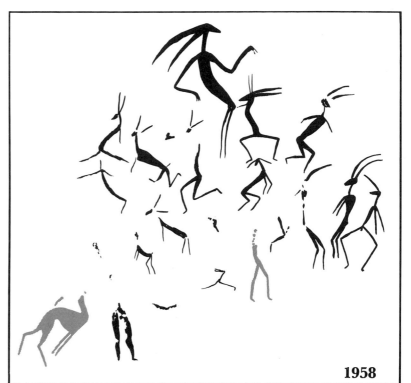

1958

1968

Figure 64 *Site F1*

In 1907, the photograph reproduced here appeared in a geological report. A tracing of the same scene in 1958 showed a considerable amount of deterioration to have taken place, although the group was still quite recognisable. Subsequently, the site was included on a tourist itinerary for visitors from the nearby Sani Pass Hotel, and ten years later, in 1968, the paintings were so fragmentary as to be barely discerned.

121

In order to control these acts of vandalism, the magistrate of Estcourt recommended that Ranger Barnes be given power to treat all people who visited the caves without his sanction as trespassers, a measure that was ratified by the Minister of Agriculture. This correspondence, dated May and June 1904, is preserved in the Natal Archives.[92]

Further impetus was given to protective measures by the newly formed South African National Society in Cape Town, which was visited by members of the British Association for the Advancement of Science in 1905. In his Presidential address, Dr A. C. Haddon urged that all relics of South Africa's past, for example the pictographs in the Bushman rock shelters, should be 'jealously preserved and guarded from intentional and unwitting injury'.[93] He also advocated that archaeological sites should be protected by law, a measure which was not introduced until 1911.

Sir Matthew Nathan, Governor of Natal from 1907 to 1909, did much to encourage the ethnographic section of the Museum in Pietermaritzburg, and towards the end of his tenure, he advocated the establishment of a Natal Branch of the South African National Society. Regional committees were set up in Durban and Pietermaritzburg, with the principal aim of preserving objects of historic interest and natural beauty. A request from the Governor for a detailed account of Bushman painting sites in Natal met with an enthusiastic response from the Society, and Mrs Nel MacKeurtan in Durban, and Dr E. Warren, director of the Museum in Pietermaritzburg, lent their energies to the cause.[94]

Notices were inserted in the local newspaper, and the assistance of magistrates, game keepers, forest rangers and the Natal Police was enlisted. They were requested not only to list the paintings in their respective areas, but also to comment on their state of preservation and suitability for removal to a museum, and to estimate the amount of fencing and number of cautionary notice boards required for their protection *in situ*. The sum of £200 was actually granted by Government towards these expenses, but because Union intervened, the money was never released. Reports were nevertheless collected from the entire length of the Drakensberg, as well as from other regions of Natal and Zululand. Particularly worthy contributions came from Forester R. E. Symons in the Giant's Castle area, and Trooper A. D. Whyte in the southern section of the Natal Drakensberg. Enthusiasts with an artistic flair committed many paintings to paper, and their facsimile copies were exhibited in the entrance hall of the museum in Pietermaritzburg.[95]

Because all accounts agreed that much damage to the paintings was being caused by exposure to weather, animals, and ruthless treatment by humans, the National Society appealed to Government to protect the paintings both by legislation and by granting funds towards preservation. Incentive to immediate action was lent by a rumour that a European collector was about to descend on Natal to obtain Bushman relics for overseas Museums. A letter dated January 21, 1910, and addressed to the Attorney General states:

> The Bushmen paintings and engravings are the sole record of a primitive and fast disappearing race, and their presence in Natal is of unique interest and value. It would therefore be greatly deplored if they should be allowed to be removed or mutilated by any unauthorised person. The Pietermaritzburg Committee of the Natal Branch of the National Society feel very strongly that some steps should be taken to prevent the removal of what should be regarded as the property of the Colony; and at a meeting held on January 18th, it was unanimously resolved that a letter should be sent to Government, earnestly praying that prompt and effective action should be taken.[96]

The Natal branch of the National Society was not the only one to make representations, and when the four Republics and Colonies were united in the Union of South Africa, the new government responded by introducing the Bushman Relics Protection Act of 1911. 'Bushman Relic' was defined to include paintings, engravings and the contents of caves, rock shelters, graves and middens. The Act prohibited the defacement or destruction of Bushman Relics as well as their removal or exportation without written permission. Further legislation in 1923 provided for the appointment of an Historical Monuments Commission, and in 1934 and 1937 additional refinements were introduced. These greatly increased the powers of the Commission, on whose recommendation the Minister of Education, Arts and Science was enabled to protect monuments, relics or antiquities without having actually proclaimed them as such. This made it possible to prohibit unauthorised removal, export, damage or destruction of all rock art, including sites not yet discovered,[97] and in 1969, legislation was passed authorising heavy fines and short-term imprisonment for such offences.[98]

Long before the existence of the Historical Monuments Commission, however, interest in the Bushman collections at the Natal Museum had waned. Slabs of painted rock were relegated to storerooms, copies of paintings were rolled up and put away in cupboards, and the valuable records compiled by the National Society were filed away and forgotten. Because of the lack of any co-ordinating body, this admirable foundation work which promised so well, has regrettably never been built upon.

With the establishment of the Archaeological Data Recording Centre in Cape Town however,[99] there is hope for the future. The Regional Centre for Natal and East Griqualand is at the Natal Museum where a full-time archaeologist has now been appointed. A long-term project which aims at fully recording and documenting all the rock art sites within the area has been initiated, and all interested persons are urged to co-operate in this effort to centralise information.

Whyte's Report

The report on rock paintings submitted by Trooper A. D. Whyte to the Natal branch of the South African National Society in 1910, deals with much of the area between the Mkhomazi and Ndawana rivers in the Underberg district, embracing valleys D to M of the present survey. After he had been promoted to the rank of Sub-Inspector, Whyte wrote a subsequent version of his 1910 report, and a copy of the latter, dated 1921, was filed in the Natal records of the Archaeological Survey in Johannesburg.[100] Fortunately the earlier statement, which is far fuller, is preserved in the Library of the Natal Museum, Pietermaritzburg, and there is additional information in the 1910 correspondence files of that Institution.

Acting on what appeared extraordinary instructions for a police-man, Whyte, accompanied by two African constables, set off on horseback from Bushman's Nek Police Post one April morning, with orders to locate all the Bushman paintings within the district. He took with him a pack horse, a small patrol tent, some provisions and a rifle, and thus equipped, systematically searched the Berg from south to north for four arduous months. He made interesting comments on the fauna encountered *en route*, and in all, located thirty-seven sites which he divided into ninety-six groups of paintings, comprising a total of 1 041 figures. He did not, he explained, visit every little side kloof, as this would have taken many more months, and he felt certain he had not located all the paintings.

Whyte was quite right; in the same area, fifty years later, I located 75 sites, and recorded a total of 4 468 figures. Even these numbers, however, are far from complete, for my survey did not include at least 17 of the sites mentioned in Whyte's report, the localities

of which are somewhat inadequately described. This does not necessarily imply that the paintings have disappeared since Whyte reported them; it simply bears out his observation that it is im-possible to look everywhere. Obviously the side kloofs and rock faces which I inspected did not always coincide with those seen by Whyte, and many gaps await exploration.

One of the most fruitful shelters located by Whyte overlooked the Mzimuti valley which, according to his informants, had been the headquarters of a Bushman Chief named *Tsuayi*, undoubtedly a variant of the name Sõai.[101] Besides many paintings, Whyte found an ashy deposit up to two feet thick, which contained great quanti-ties of broken clay pots, bones of eland and hartebeest, shafts of arrows, grinding stones, and other stones on which paint mixed with a greasy substance had been prepared. In addition, he collected human teeth, finger bones, vertebrae, and a lower jaw in good condition. Whyte forwarded these finds to his commanding officer in Bulwer, who in turn sent them to Dr Warren at the Museum in Pietermaritzburg.

The catalogue of the Natal Museum contains an entry, No. 2064, which reads:

> Bushman's bones, paints, palettes and stolen Basuto pottery fragments. Caves, Bushman's Nek, Natal. Presented by A. D. Whyte, N.P.

The following entry, No. 2065, obtained from the same shelter and the same donor, reads:

> Vegetable matter supposed to have been chewed by Bushmen.

Unfortunately, these interesting finds can no longer be traced in the stores of the Museum.

As a result of Whyte's recommendations, about twenty groups of paintings, some comprising more than one stone, were removed from various sites by an expert stone mason, R. Clingan, and deposited in the Natal Museum.[102] The provenance of each painted slab is unfortunately not clearly stated, and while it has been possible to relate some of the paintings to their original sites with the aid of Whyte's photographs and descriptions, others cannot be placed with any certainty.

A large slab from Bamboo mountain on which a successful stock raid and what is possibly a rain-making ceremony are depicted, is the only specimen brought in by Clingan now on public display. A photograph taken *in situ* before its removal in 1910 shows the original composition of the group now artificially divided in two,

the group was numbered from one upwards, thus A1/3(2) records valley and site number/tracing or photograph number (individual painting).

While many sites were already known to the local inhabitants and directions could be obtained on how to reach them, searches of potentially painted shelters along the hundreds of miles of sandstone krantzes within the area invariably resulted in more paintings being discovered. In this task I was greatly assisted by the energetic exertions of my brother and numerous friends and, at the close of the survey, a total of 308 sites had been located in contrast to the thirty-two sites recorded in the Archaeological Survey list of 1956.[127] Some of the new sites consisted of no more than a single fragmentary painting on an isolated boulder, while others were extensive shelters containing over 500 paintings. (Figures 70c, 74). Of the 308 sites located, 150 were fully recorded, seventy-nine partly recorded, fifty not recorded at all, and twenty had deteriorated to such an extent that no meaningful observations could be made. (Site List pp 355-361).

It is obvious from this summary that the objectives of the survey were not fully realised. It proved impossible to investigate thoroughly the whole of the terrain within the limited period of time, and the unprecedented number of sites located were more than could be adequately recorded by one person.

Where the state of preservation of the paintings permitted, a photographic record including a scale was made of each group in black and white as well as colour. In most instances, pictures were also taken to show the position and environment of the shelters in order to facilitate future location of the sites.

The bulk of the detailed recording was made by tracing. The medium preferred was a light-weight colourless polythene film which was placed directly over the original paintings, and attached to the rock face by means of masking tape. The outlines of the paintings were carefully followed with a fine brush dipped in Indian ink or water-colour paint mixed with a wetting agent. Where there was variation of hue and shading, the actual colours were blocked in. Before removal from the rock face, a vertical line was drawn on the polythene so that the group could be correctly orientated in the final reproduction, and the sheet was clearly labelled with the site name and number, and the date of the observations. The hues of the original paintings were then accurately matched against a specially prepared colour chart which has since been related to the Munsell soil colour chart, and the relevant

symbols were recorded on the polythene. The tracings were then transferred to durable paper previously tinted to approximate to the background colour of the rock. A granular effect was suggested by a combination of flat washes overlain by spraying or daubing with a soft scrubbing brush, sponge or textured cloth. The original polythene record, covered by the tinted paper, was then placed on a tracing box consisting of a sheet of glass supported above a strong light, and the details of the tracing thus projected through the permanent paper were again copied and the procedure of matching colours repeated. Because discrepancies easily occur in this double operation, the final sheet was compared with the photographs and, ideally, should have been taken back to the sites for final checking against the originals. This was not always possible, and some of my copies can therefore doubtless be faulted. I have nevertheless endeavoured to be as meticulous as possible and scrupulously to avoid personal interpretation. (For comparison between photographs and tracings, see Figures 15a, b, c; 31, 32; 67, 148, 149; 153a, b, 160, 161; 109, 110; 95, 247).

Subsequent to the field work, all the fully recorded sites comprising a total of 8 478 individual paintings, were analysed in detail.[127] The results of this analysis, and the bearing it has on the interpretation of the art, is discussed in the following chapters.

The field is still wide open to future research. Not only will the sites I have already located, recorded and analysed bear additional investigation, particularly with regard to detailed photography, but further sites will doubtless be discovered and new and improved techniques will, we may confidently hope, lead to a greater body of factual information and a better understanding of its significance.

References
1. Goodwin 1928.
2. Deacon 1966.
3. Vogel & Beaumont 1972; Beaumont & Vogel 1972.
4. Clark 1959: 205.
5. Inskeep 1967, 1969.
6. Albino 1947; Chubb 1932; Cramb 1952; Davies 1951, 1952; Farnden 1965, 1966; Lowe 1936, 1949; Malan 1955; Stein 1933; Willcox 1957.
7. Wilson 1955; Schoute-Vanneck & Walsh 1959, 1960. The implements described as crescents from a shelter near Champagne Castle are not, judging from the illustrations, acceptable as such (Albino 1947).
8. Carter 1970 a, c; Carter 1973; Willcox 1956 b. See also Ellenberger 1960 for reference to the 'Smithfield' and 'Wilton' being inextricably mixed, and the inference that the two 'cultures' were contemporaneous in that area. See Clark 1968: 321, for definition of 'techno-complex.'

(References cont. page 131)

Figure 66 *Site Q2*

At work tracing the giant eland shown in Figure 71. Transparent polythene sheeting is attached directly to the rock face with adhesive tape. The outlines and colouring of the original paintings are carefully traced with a fine brush dipped in water-based paint mixed with a strong wetting agent.   *Photo: Pat Carter.*

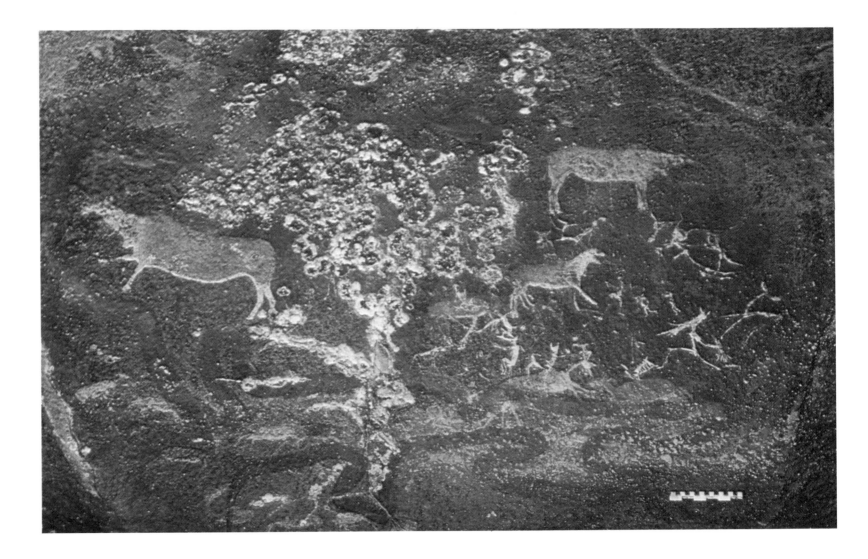

Figure 67a *Site W25*

These two illustrations placed adjacent to one another show the difference between a colour photograph of the actual rock face (left) and a reproduction of the same group of paintings using the tracing technique (right). Figure 148 is a black and white photograph of the same scene taken in situ, *and comparisons between the three illustrations give some idea of the advantages and disadvantages of the various techniques.*

Photo: Pat Carter.

Figure 67b *Site W25*

A tracing of the paintings photographed in situ *opposite. The composition, which is painted in the small rock shelter reproduced overleaf, includes eland, small antelope, humans, a long convoluted serpent, and bizarre skeleton-like figures in white. A fuller discussion of the contents is given on page 229, and in the captions of the black and white photographs reproduced in Figures 148 and 149. A chemical coating caused by water seepage has unfortunately disfigured the centre of the group.*

Figure 67c   *Sites W25 and W26*

Setsoasie River, a tributary of the Tsoelike, eastern Lesotho. The site of the wriggling snake and bizarre figures shown in Figs. 67a, 67b, 148, 149, is the small low shelter indicated by an arrow to the left of the path. The eland and strange animal surrounded by a dotted line are in a gallery shelter in the krantzes to the right. (Figs. 88, 214). Two human figures at bottom centre indicate scale.

Photo: Pat Carter.

9. Dunn 1873: 34; Kannemeyer 1890.
10. Ellenberger 1960.
11. Goodwin 1935; 1946: 18; Clark 1959: 24.
12. Bowker 1884.
13. Feilden 1884.
14. Gooch 1882.
15. Martin 1872.
16. Frames 1898.
17. Cf. Walton 1951; 1956a: Pl. 12.
18. *Natal Agric. Jnl. and Mining Rec.*, 1904: 595.
19. Bazley 1905; Goodwin 1946: 78.
20. P. Brien 1932; K. Brien 1935; Chubb & King 1932; Chubb & Schofield 1932; Cramb 1934, 1935; Schofield 1935.
21. Galloway & Wells 1934; Wells 1934.
22. Chubb & King 1934.
23. South African National Society files, 1910. Natal branch, Natal Museum.
24. Natal Museum, catalogue No. 2737.
25. Malan 1955.
26. Carter 1973.
27. Davies 1951, 26.
28. Davies 1952.
29. Cramb 1952, 1961.
30. Deacon 1966.
31. Carter 1973.
32. Beaumont & Vogel 1972.
33. Malan 1952.
34. Mason 1969.
35. Willcox 1956: 68-71.
36. Ellenberger 1960, & personal communication 14/12/1964.
37. See p. 139; Pager 1971: 354.
38. Farnden 1966.
39. Farnden 1965; Willcox 1957b. See also Clark 1959: 215; Willcox 1968a.
40. Schoute-Vanneck & Walsh 1961.
41. Hewitt 1931a; Sampson 1967.
42. See p. 145.
43. Spohr 1965b: 214; Moodie 1838.
44. *Natal Witness*, 20 & 27/7/1855.
45. Moodie 1855. Khahlamba, the present orthography, is the Zulu name for the Drakensberg.
46. *Natal Witness*, 9/11/1855. See also Spohr 1965b: 210.
47. This must have been the raid on Lugaju's stock on the upper reaches of the Mkhomazi river (see p. 77).
48. See pp. 16, 17.
49. Spohr 1965a: 41.
50. Bleek 1862-1869.
51. Theal, in Bleek & Lloyd 1911: xxxiv.
52. Bleek 1875.
53. Bleek 1873.
54. Orpen 1874.
55. Stow & Bleek 1930; 1953.
56. Col. A. W. Durnford, of the Royal Engineers, was in charge of dynamiting the Drakensberg passes in 1874 (Wright 1971: 179; Bulpin 1953: 244). It was possibly at this time that his attention was drawn to the rock-paintings in that area.
57. Lloyd 1889.
58. Tylor 1893.
59. Hutchinson 1883; Willcox 1963: 2.
60. Catalogue of the Christy Collection, British Museum.
61. Specimen CC 471. Christy Collection, British Museum.
62. Specimen CC 472. Christy Collection, British Museum.
63. See p. 51.
64. *Proceedings of the Native Affairs Commission, 1852.* Official publication. See also p. 77, Note 1.
65. Hattersley 1963.
66. Drayson 1858: 278.
67. See p. 51.
68. Willcox 1963: 83.
69. Adam 1940: Figs. 22, 23.
70. Vinnicombe 1966.
71. Otto 1908; Huss & Otto 1925; Dart 1925.
72. For assistance in my effort to trace the painted slabs, and for permission to search the attic of what is now the Bundes Lehrer und Lehrerinnen Bildungsanstalt, Feldkirch, I am indebted to Dr Phillipp Dünser, Director of that Institute, and also to the Brother in charge of the Christian Schools.
73. Otto 1908.
74. Squire 1906.
75. Rogers 1937.
76. Huss & Otto 1925.
77. Schweiger 1912, 1913; Dart 1925.
78. Churchill 1898.
79. Anderson 1901, 1904, 1907, 1911.
80. See also Willcox 1963: Plates XII, XIII, 18.
81. South African National Society files, Natal Branch, Natal Museum. Letter dated 11th April 1910; signature uncertain.
82. Natal railway guide and general handbook, 1903: 216.
83. Waterson 1915.
84. Dart 1924, 1925; Breuil 1948.
85. Schofield 1949; Davies 1950; Willcox 1956: 72-78; 1963: 43.
86. The Natal Agricultural Journal and Mining Record, 1905: 113.
87. Whyte 1910, 1921; Waterson 1915.
88. The name Mhlangeni now denotes an area on the Mkhomazi river, not a tributary. The Bisi stream runs through the Mhlangeni area, where there are three small painting sites, and where an aged Bushman survived until the turn of the century (see p. 106).
89. Squire 1906.
90. Lewis-Williams 1972.
91. Votes and Proceedings of Parliament, C. 4-1906; C. 419-1906.
92. G. H. Memo. 1628, Natal Archives.
93. Haddon 1905. Rept. Brit. Ass. Sci., (S. Afr.), 511-527.
94. G. H. Memo 1628, No. 3; G. H. Memo 1627, 18/5/1909.
95. Natal Descriptive Guide & Official Handbook 1911: 134.
96. Files of the Natal Museum, January 21, 1910.

97. Goodwin 1935; Lowe & Malan 1951: 3-6.
98. Malan 1970.
99. Leeuwenburg 1971.
100. Willcox 1956: 40-41.
101. See p. 101.
102. Natal Museum, Catalogue No. 2317.
103. Natal Descriptive Guide and Official Handbook 1911: 344.
104. See p. 268.
105. Natal Museum Nos. 2527, 2531, 2570.
106. Wells 1933.
107. Natal Museum No. 2530. Natal Museum Correspondence File: June, July, August, 1926. For full description and illustrations of the hunting kit see Vinnicombe 1971; Pager 1971: 31.
108. Stow 1905; Otto 1908; Tongue 1909; Moszeik 1910; Johnson 1910; Christol 1911; Schweiger 1912, 1913; Zelizko 1925; Burkitt 1928.
109. Frobenius 1931, 1937.
110. Wells 1933.
111. Chubb & King 1932.
112. Frobenius 1931: Table 103; Willcox 1956: 76; Breuil 1948.
113. Willcox 1956: 40; Pager 1962: 45; Lowe 1946.
114. Anderson 1907, 1911.
115. Battiss 1944.
116. Battiss 1948: 163, 194, 220.
117. Goodwin 1949.
118. Haynes 1954.
119. Malan & Kirk 1952.
120. Van Riet Lowe 1956.
121. Vinnicombe 1955.
122. Willcox 1956.
123. Willcox 1963: Plates 2, 3, 18, 20, 34, 35, 36, 37, xiii, xxii, xxiii.
124. Willcox & Friendly 1963; Willcox 1966, a & b.
125. Woodhouse 1964, 1965, 1966a, b; 1968b, c; 1969b; 1970b; Lee & Woodhouse 1970: Plates 42, 102, 107, 165, 171, 175, 180, 217, 235, 244, 246, 247, 248.
126. Vinnicombe 1960; 1967b.
127. Vinnicombe 1967a.

Figure 68

Bushman hunting kit found in Eland Cave, Mhlwasine valley, in 1926. The site lies within the Cathkin Park area of the Natal Drakensberg.

Left to right: Quiver *measuring 39 centimetres in length and 6,5 centimetres in diameter. It is made from a hollowed cylinder of light wood with a removable cap of hide. The quiver has no carrying strap, and was therefore probably transported within a skin hunting bag.*

Nineteen arrows. *The shafts are made from the culms of thatch grass,* Cymbopogon validus *or* Miscanthidium capense, *and the average length is 29 centimetres. Two of the arrows have single bone points, while the remainder have, or had small triangular points of metal inserted into a slit in the bone tip. Some of the arrows have link-shafts comprising a section of bone between the shaft and the tip, and secured with small sleeves of grass culms bound with sinew. A thick encrustation of poison on the tips of the arrows makes it difficult to see constructional details, but the arrows are all provided with a short barb attached just below the tip.*

Wooden spatula *for application of poison, 26 centimetres in length.*

Decorated rawhide sheath *for carrying a metal blade. The blade bound with leather thonging is shown to the right of the sheath.*

Small leather pouch *with thong, which contains a compact substance thought to be a component of the arrow poison.*

Curved metal blade *with bound leather handle.*

Below: Bow *measuring 89 centimetres, with very shallow curvature. The wood is fine-grained, and the bowstring comprises four strands of rolled and twisted sinew.*

Bowcase *measuring 91 centimetres, and with the same shallow curvature as the bow. The case is made from a single piece of stout hide joined by a seam sewn with leather thonging. An interior cylindrical core was used as a mould for the wet hide, which was tightly bound against the core with twisted cord. When dry the core was removed and the cord unwound, leaving the imprints of the binding clearly visible. The bowcase has a tightly-fitting cup-like lid, and the whole container has been coated with a thick resinous substance.*

For further details, see Vinnicombe 1971

Photo: Natal Museum.

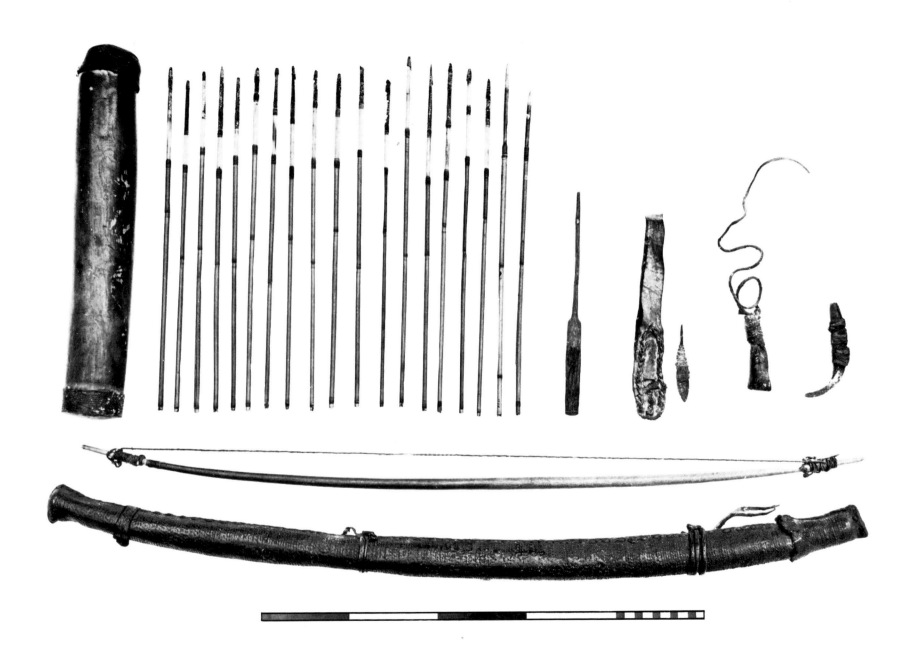

Photo: Patricia Vinnicombe

Figure 69a

A large rock shelter on the farm Eagle's Nest (site P1) commands an extensive view overlooking the border between Natal and East Griqualand. This terrain, formerly known as Nomansland, was occupied exclusively by Bushmen until the nineteenth century. The floor of the shelter is strewn with 'Later Stone Age' artefacts made from agate, chalcedony and indurated shale. The paintings illustrated in Figures 107, 121 and 204 are located at this site.

Figure 69b

The deep gorges of the Tsoelike river in eastern Lesotho are lined with innumerable gallery shelters of considerable size. Not all the shelters are painted, but all are currently used by Sotho herdsmen as kraals for their stock. This means that the paintings are rapidly becoming obliterated through being rubbed by greasy animal-bodies, or through being smeared with cow-dung by herdboys who also scratch the paintings with stones, scribble over them with charcoal, and light fires near the shelter walls.

Photo: Hans Witte

4   *Sites, Subjects and Sequence*

The Sites

All the rock paintings located during the survey were in sandstone shelters, some well protected from the weather, others on relatively exposed faces with but slight overhang. The sizes of the shelters varied from a floor area of more than 700 square metres to insignificant rock outcrops or fallen boulders barely able to afford protection to a single person in a crouched position. The majority of the shelters are on slopes with a northerly or easterly aspect and therefore have the sun shining directly on to the painted surfaces for at least part of the day. South-facing shelters do occasionally occur, but are usually somewhat cold and damp. Although paintings and scattered surface artefacts indicate use of the site, relatively few of the shelters show evidence of lengthy occupation. Most painted sites command an excellent view, overlooking extensive valleys or grassy plains, although there are exceptions and sites can occur in narrow concealed gulleys with an extremely limited outlook. Water is normally easily accessible, but where shelters are situated high on a spur with no water nearby, a steep walk to the stream-bed at the bottom of the valley is necessary. A direct correlation was found between the state of preservation of the paintings and the quality of the rock on which they were executed. Some of the sandstones are extremely friable, flaking or pulverising to the touch, whereas others are well silicified and highly resistant.[1] In the former shelters the paintings deteriorate at an alarming rate (Figure 64), whereas in the latter they are often remarkably well preserved where they have escaped the effects of water seepage and vandalism. Paintings are also occasionally executed on the friable shale deposits that occur at the base of some sandstone strata. Owing to the nature of the rock, these paintings are unlikely to survive for much longer. There is no apparent relationship between the situation, size or aspect of a shelter and the paintings within it, and the number of paintings at any given site varies from one to 565. (Figures 2, 69, 70c, 74)

Content

Three hundred and eight painting sites were located within the survey area up to the end of 1961, and of these 150 were fully recorded and the contents quantitatively analysed.[2] The individual paintings within these 150 sites totalled 8 478, giving an average of 57 paintings per shelter. The subject matter was divided into three categories, miscellaneous subjects comprising 4%, animals 43%, and human figures 53%. Despite the dominance of human over animal paintings, however, more shelters contain only animals (21 out of 150) as distinct from only humans (8 out of 150).

A large proportion (47%) of the total number of paintings were incomplete owing to poor state of preservation, and it must therefore be emphasised that caution is necessary in drawing definitive conclusions. The incomplete paintings which still retained sufficient detail to warrant inclusion in the analysis constituted 46% human, 52% animal, and 1% miscellaneous. It will be noticed that the numerical proportion here is reversed, more animals being poorly preserved than humans. Since there are also more animals than humans in the earliest layers of superimpositions, it may well be that the popularity of the human form was a relatively late development in the painting sequence.

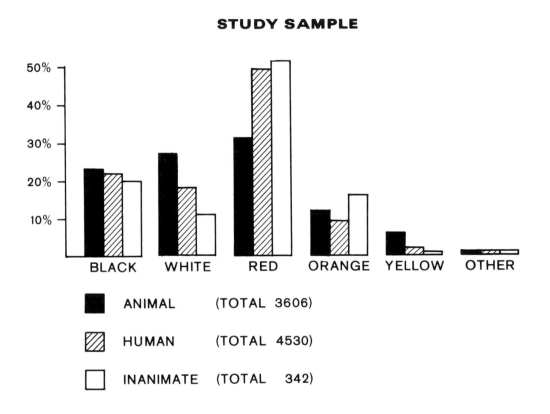

STUDY SAMPLE

Figure 70a: The use of colour in relation to subject matter

Red predominates throughout
Black is used equally on all subjects
White and yellow are used on animals more than on other subjects
Orange predominates on inanimate paintings
Colours other than the above are rarely used

STUDY SAMPLE

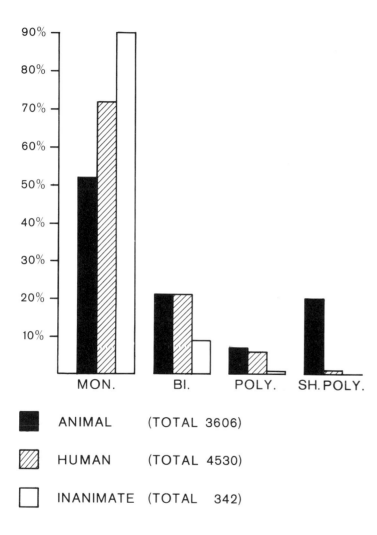

Figure 70b: Painting technique in relation to subject matter
Monochrome (mon.) paintings predominate throughout. Bichrome (bi.) and polychrome (poly.) techniques are used in similar proportions on both animal and human paintings. Shaded polychrome (sh. poly.) is used extensively in animal paintings, rarely in humans, and never in inanimate subjects.

In the sample of 8 478 paintings analysed, monochromes constitute 64%, bichromes 21%, polychromes 6%, and shaded polychromes 8%. Shades of red are the most popular colour, accounting for 40% of the colours used. Black and white are 22% each, orange 10%, yellow 4% and the less common colours such as brown 1%. A division of the subject matter into human, animal and miscellaneous shows a tendency to colour preference in the subject matter with reds still being the predominant choice throughout, but particularly for humans. (Figure 20a; Table 1, p 362). White is used more frequently on animal paintings than on humans, and yellow ochre and orange also predominate among animals while black is more or less equally distributed. The priority of colour choice in the miscellaneous subjects is red (51%), followed by black (20%) and then orange (16%). Orange finger smears, which were counted among the 'miscellaneous' paintings, are found throughout the area, and their prevalence accounts for the relatively high proportion of orange paint in the miscellaneous category.

The paintings vary in size from 1,3 centimetres (rhebuck fawn Figure 113), to 243 centimetres (mythological serpent and an eland, Figures 71, 143). The great majority of paintings, however, both human and animal, fall between 10 and 25 centimetres.

Superposition and sequence

Seventy-seven (51%) of the 150 fully recorded shelters contain superimposed paintings. Although it is impossible to ascertain the length of time that has elapsed between the painting of the different layers, some are apparently almost contemporaneous, whilst others, judging by the differences in preservation and the degree of exfoliation of the painted surface, must be separated by at least several generations.

In 31 (21%) of the shelters, more than 25% of the contained paintings involved are in direct superposition, 25 (17%) have between 10 and 25% of the paintings superimposed, and 21 (14%) contain less than 10%. The remaining 73 shelters (49%) show no evidence of a painting sequence.

Of the 31 shelters with more than 25% of the paintings superimposed, 5 shelters (Sites D13, F18, N2, Q4 and S1), each situated in a different valley, are of particular interest. In each case more than 200 paintings are present, and between 28% and 57% (average 45%) are superimposed. Sites with fewer paintings but a proportionately high concentration of superpositions (eg. F17, L28 and

137

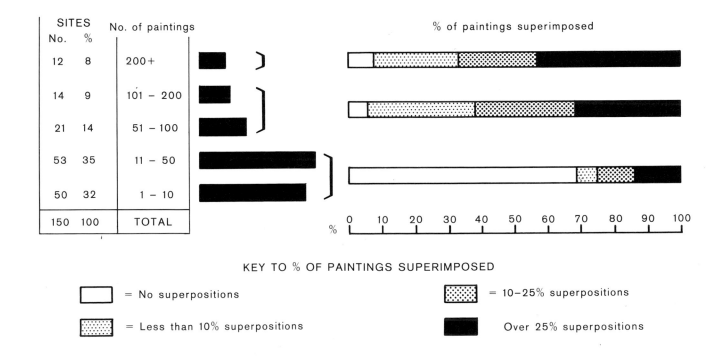

Figure 70c: Number of paintings per site, and the percentage of paintings superimposed

The sites with the greatest number of paintings have the greatest number of superpositions.
The sites with fewer paintings have a low concentration of superpositions.

W19), are also distributed in separate valleys. It would thus appear that each site with a large number of superpositions is surrounded by many smaller sites with few or no superpositions. This pattern clearly demonstrates that the Bushman artists selected specific shelters for repeated visits in order to paint and re-paint particular surfaces over a period of time. Since not all the superimposed shelters show evidence of repeated occupation, it would seem that the shelters were associated with special ritual or ceremonial functions that did not necessarily include regular habitation.

A study of the relationship between the various layers of paintings in an effort to recognise phases of development and thereby establish a chronological framework for relative dating proved disappointing in many respects. There was little correlation between subject matter, style and size, but some consistency emerged in the colour and application of the paints. Although as many as six layers of paintings were observed at certain sites, only four clearly recognisable but overlapping phases can be isolated in a general study. For convenience these will be referred to as Phases 1, 2, 3 and 4.

The earliest or Phase 1 paintings are mostly very fragmentary and little can be deduced as to their content and style. The colour commonly persisting is a very dark red or maroon which is seen more as a stain on the rock than a distinct application of paint. The paintings are usually too disfigured by weathering and subsequent over-painting to show whether or not any scenes or compositions were attempted, and because so few features can be recognised, most of the early paintings were eliminated from the numerical analysis although their presence was noted. The lack of distinguishing details may be partly due to the disappearance of fugitive colours, and it would be unwise to deduce from the available evidence that the early paintings were simple monochromes. Many of the paint masses still visible tend to occur in horizontal rather than vertical blocks, suggesting a predominance of animals in the subject matter rather than upright human figures. Breuil was able to distinguish the remains of large animal paintings underlying all other paintings at several sites in southern Africa, and the theory has been propounded that the paintings show a progressive decrease in size with time.[3] No clear evidence of this was observed in the survey area, and there is indeed one notable exception at a shelter on *Belleview* farm in East Griqualand. (Figure 71). Here a very large eland 85 centimetres high and 1,86 metres long (this measurement excludes the head and neck which are unfortunately missing) is superimposed on a smaller eland 72 centimetres long, and on numerous running hunters averaging 12 centimetres high. A second eland at the site, the head of which is also missing, is 2,43 metres long, but superpositions are absent. Admittedly these examples are in the later shaded polychrome technique and are probably of no great antiquity, but they nevertheless clearly demonstrate that increase in size cannot consistently be related to age.

Phase 2 paintings include clearer representations of humans and animals in various shades of red, sometimes with additional details in white, and specific compositions are recognisable. Dependent upon the state of preservation, the paintings appear either as a stain or as a thin film on the rock face, and sometimes both states can be observed in the same group. The white paint is frequently fugitive with the result that such features as heads and legs are often absent, resulting in 'hook-headed' humans and headless or legless animals. (Figs. 76, 182, 197, 207). The white paint sometimes leaves a bleached effect on the rock which is more visible in indirect and diffuse lighting, but which disappears entirely with dampening. There is some evidence that many of the paintings were first outlined and filled in with white, and that the other colours were painted on top, a procedure which seems to have persisted into the latest phase. This may explain the white lining visible in many of the red paintings, and, in instances where the white paint has since disappeared, suggests why some figures have spaces representing bands at the waist or knee. These ornamental details could have been executed in the negative as it were, by applying the red paint of the body round the waist or leg bands. In other examples, however, decorative white bands or beads were quite clearly applied on top of the red paint. (Figures 155, 193).

The third phase is marked by the full development of the shaded polychrome technique although indications of blended colours can also be detected in the second phase. In addition, elements of perspective are introduced in Phase 3. Some of the foreshortened paintings are highly experimental, whereas others are artistically very successful. Shaded methods of paint application and foreshortened attitudes are used almost exclusively for antelope paintings, eland and rhebuck being the favourite subjects on which much care and detail was lavished. Although human figures also show fine details such as facial markings, beaded bands and decorative thongs or tassels, their bodies and limbs are not foreshortened and are seldom shaded although exceptions to the latter do occur. (Figures 112, 197). The reason may simply be that the relatively small and broken planes of the human figure are not as readily adapted to a shaded technique as the larger, rounded bodies of antelope, although other more subjective reasons such as an unwillingness to portray

Figure 71   *Site Q2*

This giant bull eland in shaded polychrome is superimposed on a smaller bull, and on running hunters in red and white. The total length of the eland is 1,86 metres from the tip of the tail to the last fragments of visible paint which, as can be seen from the photograph, excludes the head and neck. The front legs can be seen very faintly above the scale, which is in inches and centimetres. The back of the eland follows the line of a projecting ledge of rock, which probably governed to some extent the elongated proportions of the animal. Near the brush of the eland's tail is a round depression made by the imprint of a nodule which has fallen out. The hole is encircled with dirty white paint, and this forms the head of a human figure with fat body and thin legs not visible in this photograph. The smaller eland at lower left has white lines zig-zagging between the tail and the rump, a detail also not clear at this reduction. To the left of the big eland shown here, there is a second even larger eland, unfortunately very fragmentary. Below the second eland, there is a painting of a bending over human enveloped in a large skin or kaross. (See Figure 235).   Photo: Pat Carter

140

human beings realistically cannot be ignored.[4, 5] Unshaded monochrome, bichrome and polychrome paintings continue to be contemporary with the shaded or modelled animals, and are often indistinguishable from those found in the second phase. Further confusion is caused by the fact that several layers of superposition, at times as many as three or four, occur within the shaded polychrome period, but I have been unable to detect any consistent pattern of development within the subdivisions of Phase 3. In many instances the superimpositions are apparently intentional and contemporaneous, and whatever other meaning they may have, certainly give a sense of depth and perspective to some of the groups. There is, however, also clear evidence that intentional overpainting or retouching of paintings occurred within the third or shaded polychrome phase, a practice which, judging from the differences in state of preservation, continued over several generations. (Figures 94, 104, 106). Much of the paint used during Phase 3 is very thick and distinct brushstrokes are visible. When this paint exfoliates there is no residual stain, that is, the pigments do not seem to have penetrated the rock background. In addition to the traditional reds, several colours appear with greater frequency in the shaded polychrome phase, notably black, orange, yellow and brown, and these tints, particularly when combined with white, create a wide range of subtle colours. The thick white paints, which are sometimes of the same consistency as oil paint, do not disappear when wetted. Black is often used for additional details such as facial features, horns, hooves, and part outlines, but like white, black is also a fugitive colour. (Figure 223)

During the fourth and final phase, shaded polychromes diminish although they persist, and many newly introduced subjects such as guns, brimmed hats and horses appear. (Figures 15, 40). There is a greater use of black, yellow ochre and bright vermilion or orange at the expense of the more traditional dark reds. The paints lack a binding medium and often appear rather powdery. Brush strokes are never visible and the paint deteriorates rapidly. It is therefore not uncommon to find the most recent paintings appearing less well preserved than the earlier. In case of superposition this can be particularly misleading when the underlying paintings are clearly visible through faded overlying paintings. The portrayal of eland during the fourth phase tends to revert to highly stylised bichromes and polychromes in yellow ochre or orange with white heads, necks and linings to belly and legs, and the foreshortening and more naturalistic poses often associated with the shaded polychromes give way to stiffer, more block-like representations. (Figure 205). Many

of the equestrian paintings, known from their subject matter to belong to the most recent phase, nevertheless display a great variety of highly spirited action, and the scenes are often of quite complex composition with a distinctly narrative character. Elements of scenery begin to be introduced such as paths or tracks, details which are not usually found among the earlier paintings. (Figures 31, 39). The late white pigments always disappear when dampened, and grey paintings become black. Particularly among cattle with multi-coloured hides, it appears that the silhouette of the animal was first blocked out in white and that the black or red hide markings and other details were then superimposed. When painted on white, the black pigment assumes a blue-grey appearance, but becomes black again if the paint is moistened and the white pigment thereby rendered invisible. On rare occasions, yellow ochre is superimposed on black or vice versa, when an unusual olive green effect is obtained. Within the survey area, however, there is no evidence for the actual use of either blue or green pigments. (Figure 124).

Paintings involved in direct superposition constitute 19% of the total analysed, the number of animals (848) being greater than the number of humans (753). Since human figures predominate in an overall count, the fact that animals predominate in the superpositions suggests a degree of selection on the part of the artists. It is of interest that although animal paintings outnumber humans in Phase 2 (12% compared with 5% human), as well as in Phase 3 (animal 52%, human 41%), the fourth and final phase shows a far greater accent on humans (53%) compared with animals (35%). There is no recognisable miscellaneous subject matter in Phase 2, 20% in Phase 3, and the majority, 80%, occurs in the latest period, Phase 4.[6]

The sample studied therefore reveals an increasing emphasis on the human figure at the expense of animal representations, an observation which may reflect predilection on the part of the artists, or which may be correlated with the marked decrease in game resulting from increased human population. On a numerical basis, Phase 2 superpositions constitute only 9% of the sample, Phase 3 constitute 47%, and Phase 4, 43%. (Table 1, p 362). While it is possible that the high percentage of superimpositions in Phase 3 reflects a period of intensified ritual activity, it is also tempting to relate the fluctuations of superposition percentages through time to changes in population density. A possible interpretation is that during the early period, Phases 1 and 2, occupation of the area was sparse or sporadic, while Phase 3 may be associated with in-

Figure 72 *Site S3.*   Sheltered Vale

This panel has so many layers of eland superimposed on one another that the rock face is quite smooth with paint. There are small antelope at the base of the panel, and at lower left, a skeleton-like creature bends towards the mass of eland. Above (centre left) there are two felines; one chases a hunter, and the other has claws and teeth bared. Above the felines, a large area of the panel was intentionally chiselled out when some paintings were removed to the Durban Museum over forty years ago. At the top, animal-headed figures wearing karosses are painted over and under eland.

One of the eland bodies has white bristles along the spine. The upside-down eland and associated figures at top right are reproduced in detail in Figure 99, and the three humans superimposed on eland at lower centre in Figure 98 (see also dust cover). A large slab of fallen rock at the foot of the palimpsest provides a convenient platform on which to sit or stand when painting. The right of the panel is near the drip-line, and is obliterated by water seepage.

Tracing made in 1960 with assistance from Lorna Peirson and Jean Hewlett.

142

creased population pressures necessitating a more permanent occupation of the mountain areas. Phase 4 paintings are of the historic period when the Bushman's traditional mode of life was challenged and overwhelmed. But despite ever-increasing encroachment on their hunting terrain, ever-increasing restriction of their movements, and ever-increasing pressure on their social and moral integrity, the available evidence indicates that painting, even though in a modified form, continued as an integral part of the Bushman's cultural expression right to the very end.

Dating

The internal evidence of the paintings, together with eye-witness accounts and oral tradition, firmly establishes a nineteenth century date for the Phase 4 paintings. Dating of all other phases is much less secure and will remain so until some form of chemical or radiometric dating can be applied to actual paint samples. Denninger has developed techniques based on the decay rates of certain amino acids contained in the albuminoid binding of some of the paints,[7-9] but unfortunately there is an increasing experimental error with time, and the technique is not applicable to material older than about 1 800 years.

Denninger has obtained a date between 1845 and 1885 for a painting of a horse from the Giant's Castle area, which accords well with historical records. Ages of approximately 200 to 300 years for shaded polychrome eland support the view that the technique of intentionally shading two or more colours was adopted in the central mountain region during the 18th century.[10] If an age in the region of 200-300 years is accepted for the Phase 3 or polychrome period, Phases 1 and 2 must be older. The greatest age obtained from paint analysis in the Drakensberg is approximately 800 years, that is about A.D. 1 150,[9] but the techniques used have not yet been fully accepted.

Archaeological evidence provides little additional information because of the difficulty of associating deposits on the floor of the shelter with paintings on the wall. It has been established, however, that paintings associated with the final expression of the 'Later Stone Age' and comparable with the Phase 4 paintings of the present survey, were executed after A.D. 1 680 at *Glen Elliot* shelter in the Northern Cape Province.[11] At *Sehonghong* shelter in Lesotho (Site X4), tanged arrow points such as appear in the paintings have

been dated to A.D. 450,[12] and in the same layer, exfoliated fragments of sandstone from the shelter wall showing indications of ochreous paint were found. This is certain evidence, therefore, that paintings were in existence at *Sehonghong* prior to A.D. 450, although it has not been possible to relate the fragmented exfoliations to paintings still visible on the rock face.

The earliest date so far obtained for the traditional 'Wilton/Smithfield' expressions of the 'Later Stone Age' in the area of the survey is 1 330 B.C., but at *Sehonghong* there is a micro-blade industry presumably associated with the use of the bow and arrow, dated to 11 050 B.C. This industry is also associated with fragments of red ochre, although ochre fragments are more concentrated in the upper 'Later Stone Age' layers. The occurrence of ochre below the microlithic industries is rare. Although the use to which the ochre was put is not known, the distribution of the fragments suggests that activities connected with paint were negligible prior to 11 000 B.C., and that such activity, although practised to some extent between 11 000 and 1 000 B.C., did not flourish until the period between 1 000 B.C. and historic times.

A date of 335 B.C. has been obtained for a naturalistically painted stone in an archaeological context on the Tzitzikama coast of the Cape Province, while another stone, displaying a schematic grid pattern in red, comes from a lower and therefore earlier horizon.[13] At *Matjes River* shelter, a painted burial stone was found in a 'Later Stone Age' deposit dated to between 3 400 and 5 800 B.C., but unfortunately, the precise associations of this find are questionable and therefore the age of the paintings remains uncertain.[14, 15] Recent evidence from South West Africa nevertheless lends support to the early occurrence of art in southern Africa. Four painted slabs from a shelter immediately north of the Orange river were overlain by a horizon dated to 12 400 B.C., while a layer below the paintings, containing artefacts typical of the 'Middle Stone Age', is calculated to be approximately 43 000 B.C.[16] The implication of these findings has not yet been fully assessed, as the whole chronology of the Stone Age in southern Africa is at present under drastic revision.[17]

The date therefore, for the beginning of rock art in southern Africa is still a matter for speculation, but it is not impossible that the earliest examples of representational depictions may originate in the period of transition between the 'Middle' and 'Later Stone Age'.

References

1. Van Riet Lowe 1949.
2. Vinnicombe 1967a.
3. Breuil 1949.
4. Willcox 1956: 57.
5. Cooke 1965.
6. See p. 147 for further discussion.
7. Denninger 1971.
8. Willcox 1971.
9. Pager 1971: 353-359.
10. Willcox 1955.
11. Sampson 1967, 1969.
12. Carter 1974.
13. Singer & Wymer 1969.
14. Louw 1960.
15. Inskeep 1961.
16. Wendt 1972.
17. See p. 111.

Figure 73 *Site U7*
A perspective painting of an antelope.
Photo: Pat Carter.

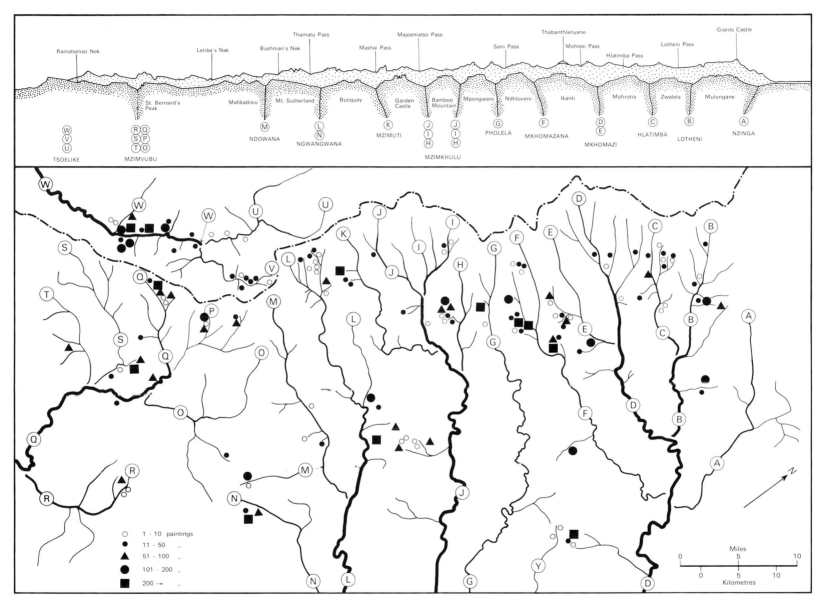

Figure 74, *Map No. 3.*

The number of paintings in each of the fully recorded sites is plotted according to the symbols shown in the key above. The sites that have not been recorded, or are only partly recorded, are not included. The site numbers are shown on map No. 4, back end paper.

145

Figure 75a *Site E2*

It is not known what this circular motif with radiating lines represents, although a trap or a drinking pool is suggested. Two small antelope (not shown here), approach the object at some distance to the left.

Figure 75b *Site W21*

These shield-like motifs, some outlined, some filled in, may represent the front apron worn by women. They are executed in a dry crayon-like medium. A similar object is associated with the serpents reproduced in Figure 143.

5 Inanimate and Non-Representational Subjects

Inanimate and non-representational paintings not included in the human or animal sections were jointly listed in a miscellaneous category, and constitute only 4% of the total subject matter. Of the total number of 342 miscellaneous representations, 90% are monochrome, 9% bichrome, 1% polychrome, and none shaded polychrome. Delineation tends to be simple with no great attention to detail. The most common colour used is red (51%), followed by black (20%), orange (16%) and white (11%), with yellow and other uncommon colours less than 1% each. Superpositions were recorded in 10% of the examples, the majority, 8%, being in the top or most recent layer, with 2% in the second layer, and none recognisable in the earlier levels. It seems, therefore, that the occurrence of these miscellaneous representations increased with the progression of time.

The most common non-representational paintings are intentional finger smears or blobs in bright orange paint, although sometimes red is used. They are often executed in pairs as though two fingers were dipped into the paint at a time, and then drawn down the rock face in short parallel lines. The strokes are usually more or less vertical, but may converge to form 'V's, and when on ceilings, disposition is random. Occasionally more complex designs incorporating crossed lines or strokes within rectangles are found, but these are rare. Apparently haphazard blobs are often seen superimposed upon other paintings, frequently eland, but where the smears occur in pairs or groups, it is usually on a separate area of rock within the painted shelter, and not infrequently on the ceiling. There are several sites at which finger marks occur in isolation, that is, not in association with any other paintings. Although my initial view was that these smears were no more than casual daubs made by passers by, their relative frequency[1, 2] now leads me to believe that they fulfilled a definite function, perhaps similar to hand-prints in the south-west Cape,[3, 4] and were possibly connected with a particular ceremony. Since they appear only late in the sequence, they may be associated with the final phase when external pressures obliged the Bushmen to relinquish more detailed paintings in favour of hurriedly executed blobs. On the other hand, it is possible that their origin was of longer standing, and that they were, for instance, the marks or 'signatures' made by initiates.[5] (Figure 76)

Other miscellaneous representations include red rope-like lines often embellished with white spots which are usually associated with sorcerer-type figures and eland. The lines often connect the figures with the animals, and may then meander within the group. (Figures 90, 95, 152). The interpretation of these lines remains a puzzle, but the motivation appears to be supernatural rather than practical, and their possible implication has been discussed elsewhere.[6] Another feature repeated at different sites is feathery white lines which lead upwards from the heads of human or therianthropic figures. (Figures 109, 110, 152). These too, suggest supernatural associations, and may perhaps be linked with the Bushman's concept of consciousness described by them as *thinking strings*.[7] Another belief is that a thin cord acts as a line of communication between the great 'Captain of the sky' and the Bushmen who specialise in rain-making,[8] a notion which would seem to be a visual concept of spiritual communication.

Fine parallel near-vertical lines in rows occur at several sites

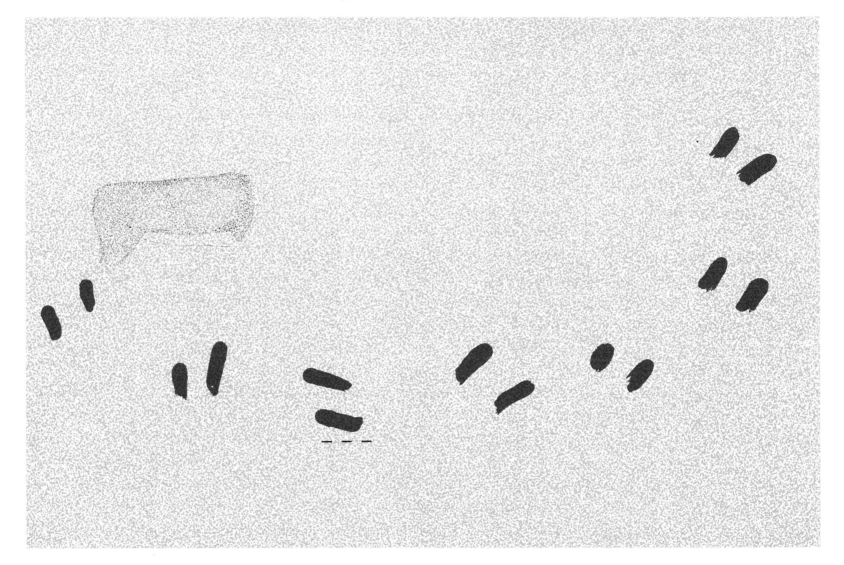

Figure 76 *Site M10*

Orange finger smears in pairs partly surround the faded body of an eland. Similar smears, often in pairs, are sometimes found on the ceilings of rock shelters.

and may represent some type of trap, barrier, or fence, or they may be sets of arrowshafts lacking in detail. Other inanimate subjects include boats, waggons and shelters or 'skerms' (small constructed huts) which should more properly be included among human artefacts in future analyses. Boats and waggons, which are uncommon subjects in the painted record, are discussed elsewhere,[9] while skerms or shelters are usually indicated by semi-circular or arched lines, open-ended at the base, and often human figures squat within. (Figures 53, 222). It is difficult to know whether these habitations are shelters or skerms represented in plan or in section; indeed, one painted group suggests both visual concepts in the same scene. Small tasselled bags hanging from the underside of the arched lines imply that the shelter is seen in section, while an adjacent partition, to which a cow is tethered, suggests a view in plan although the animals are in side elevation. (Figure 26). Rare elements of scenery, for example tracks or mountains, were also enumerated in the *miscellaneous* category. (Figures 31, 39).

The remaining miscellanea, such as apron-like objects both outlined and in silhouette, a circle with lines radiating outwards from the upper half, zig-zag lines, white rod-like shapes with red tips, and other unidentifiable shapes that are nevertheless deliberately delineated, are of such rare occurrence that they cannot in any sense be regarded as typical of the rock art of the area. (Figures 75a and b, 77).

In short, the subject of the great majority of paintings is usually readily identifiable, and schematic or non-representational designs apparently held little significance in the culture of the Mountain Bushmen. The subject matter is clearly based on recognisable objects from nature, and only rarely includes schematic signs devised by the human mind.

References

1. See also Moszeik 1910: 95.
2. Pager 1971: 54-5.
3. Willcox 1959.
4. Maggs 1967.
5. See also Vaughan 1962.
6. See pp. 323, 334, 336-340.
7. Bleek 1911: 87.
8. Schapera 1930: 198.
9. See pp. 18-21, 119, 125, 293-4.

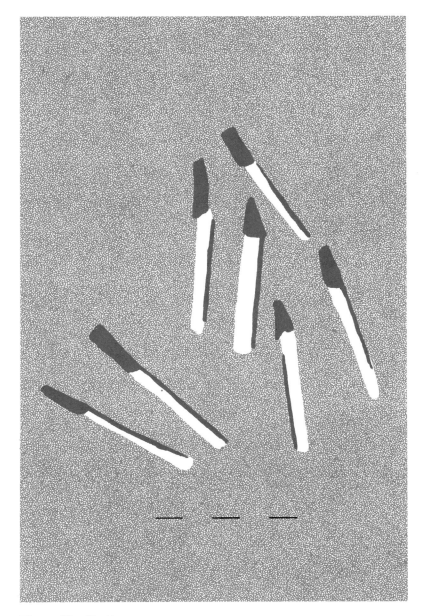

Figure 77 *Site F17*

These unidentifiable objects are part of a group of thirteen similar shapes associated with faded paintings of kaross-clad humans and a fragmentary animal.

Figure 78 *Site W23*
A fantasy animal with an element of humorous caricature.

6   *Animal Subjects*

In the analysis of 150 fully recorded sites, animal representations number 3 606, or 43% of the total paintings. Antelope are the most numerous of the wild animals depicted (77%), eland comprising 35%, the smaller antelope which include rhebuck 18%, and hartebeest 3%. Other specifically identifiable buck include reedbuck, oribi, roan antelope, wildebeest, and bushbuck, which together amount to only 1%. As high a proportion as 20% of the animals, although recognisable as antelope, are unidentifiable as to species. However, the body proportions of the majority of the unidentifiable antelope are either thick-set or relatively delicate, and therefore probably fall within either the eland or the rhebuck categories. Before deterioration of the paintings, the percentages for these two species were therefore almost certainly higher than those presented in the analysis, which is of necessity based on the present state of the paintings. It is doubtful whether any significant difference would be made to the relative proportion between eland and rhebuck even if the 'unidentifiable' antelope were clear enough for identification, that is, eland would still outnumber rhebuck by a considerable margin in an overall count.

With antelope forming 77% of the total wild animals portrayed, baboons constitute 2%, while felines, snakes, and birds or other winged creatures are 1% each. Fish, which appear in only four shelters within the survey area, were counted individually and are therefore as much as 16%, although if each shoal were listed as a single unit, fish would also constitute less than 1%. Other more rarely painted animals such as wild pigs or warthogs, antbears, elephant, rhinoceros, hippopotami, and the smaller mammals together make up only 2%. (Figures 9, 10, 49, 79, 109).

It is therefore clear that of the animals portrayed, antelope are the main focus of interest, yet paradoxically, available archaeological evidence from excavated living sites indicates a predominance of smaller mammals rather than antelope in everyday diet.[1] Smaller mammals appear rarely in the paintings, there being but two examples of jackals, one possible hare and no more than a dozen long-tailed short-legged animals which probably belong to the civet or mongoose family. Despite the prolific number of dassies or rock-rabbits (*Procavia capensis capensis*) in the Drakensberg region and the relative ease with which they can be snared or clubbed, paintings of dassies do not occur anywhere within the survey area. It is therefore evident that the paintings are not directly associated with the actual diet of the artists, nor do they represent a fair sample of the animals encountered in the normal course of daily living. In short, the paintings are neither a menu nor a check list.

Domestic animals, which constitute 23% of the total animals painted, can be directly associated with historical events, and the remainder of the animals, (9%), are those which are too fragmentary or too unrealistically executed for any identification to be made. (Figure 80 and Table 3, p 364).

The size of the paintings bears little relation to the actual size of the animals portrayed. A lion, for instance, may be the same size as an elephant, or a horse far smaller than an eland. Rhebuck paintings, however, are consistently smaller than eland, rhebuck ranging in size from 1,3 to 16 centimetres, while eland, which are among the largest antelope in reality, are represented in sizes from 8 to 243 centimetres.

The majority of animals are painted in red monochrome (52%) with bichromes forming 21%, polychromes 7%, and shaded polychromes 20%. It is apparent, therefore, that when animals were painted in more than two colours, the shaded technique was used more frequently than the simple juxtaposition of unshaded surfaces. Red (31%), white (27%), and black (23%) are the most frequently used colours, with orange forming 12%, yellow ochre 6%, and less common colours only 1%. Although antelope are occasionally painted in white or black monochrome, they are most commonly red, or red and white. Colouring is therefore not realistic, despite the fact that the true dun or brownish shades were known to the Bushman artists.[2]

The frequent use of red and white in antelope paintings is perhaps explained by a Xam Bushman myth which relates that their deity Kaggen gave bucks their colours by feeding them on different types of honey. The comb and cells were red according to Bushman belief, while the young bees produced a white milk-like liquid; some buck were therefore predominantly white, others red, while others were a combination of red and white.[3] In another Xam legend the body of a hartebeest was described as 'red',[4] while springbok had 'red' hair in winter which bleached to 'white' in the warmer sunny weather.[5] It is therefore of some significance that a Bushman, when shown a piece of red ochre, commented, 'It is red haematite, therefore I will draw a springbok with it.'[6] These records suggest that red and white were particularly significant symbols in Bushman animal lore, an observation borne out by the colour preferences expressed in the painted record. More precise particulars concerning the metaphorical associations of the colour symbols are unfortunately lacking. There are, however, indications in Bushman mythology, and in the ethnographic record, that the selectivity expressed in the animals portrayed may be related to Bushman social organisation as well as to their cosmological beliefs.[7]

In the more detailed analyses of animal paintings which follow, each of the most frequently recorded species is discussed in relation to habits and actual appearance compared with the way the animals were depicted by the hunter artists. An attempt is made to explain the possible motivation underlying the portrayal of each species. Although these hypotheses are necessarily speculative, they aim at provoking discussion based on a wider perspective than the currently popular but somewhat limited views on 'sympathetic magic' and 'art for art's sake.'[8]

References

1. Davies 1952; Deacon 1963, 1965; Parkington & Poggenpoel 1971; Sampson 1967.
2. Willcox 1956: 55.
3. Bleek 1924: 10.
4. Bleek 1911: 13.
5. Bleek 1933, B.S. 7: 312.
6. Bleek 1956: 206.
7. This aspect of the art is discussed in greater detail in the sections on different animals which follow.
8. Vinnicombe 1972a.

Figure 79 *Site FI*
A wild pig or warthog.

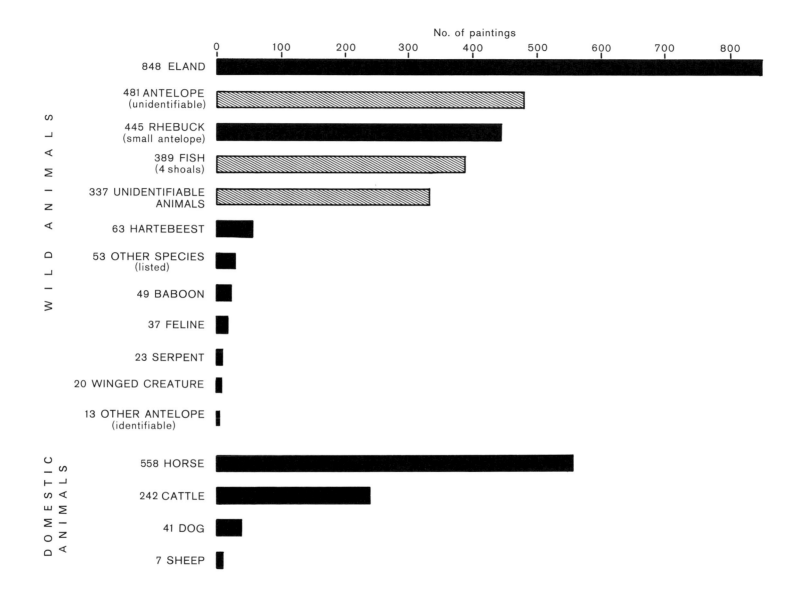

Figure 80: **Diagrammatic representation of numerical frequency of animal paintings**

The bars representing unidentifiable antelope, animals and fish (here listed as individuals and not as shoals) are shaded to avoid visual dominance.

153

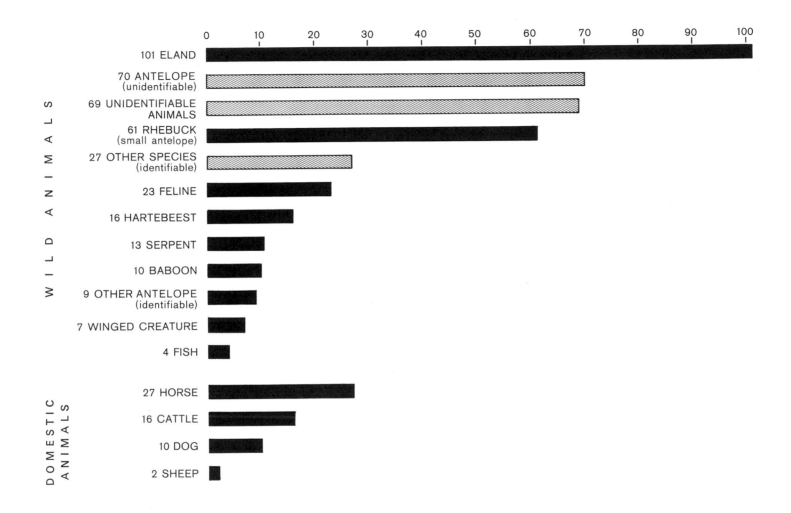

Figure 81: Distribution of animals in 150 recorded shelters

The classes of animals are plotted on a simple present or absent basis for each site. Domestic animals are shown separately from the wild, and bars representing unidentifiable animals are shaded to avoid visual dominance. 'OTHER SPECIES' (identifiable) combines numerically insignificant species such as elephant, rhinoceros, hippopotamus, antbear, hare, mongoose, etc., and this bar is also shaded so as not to dominate the more specific single categories. Fragmentary antelope paintings which cannot be identified with certainty are listed as 'ANTELOPE (unidentifiable)' — more correctly, order: Artiodactyla, family: Bovidae — although the majority were probably intended to represent eland and rhebuck. 'UNIDENTIFIABLE ANIMALS' are paintings which are too poorly executed or too poorly preserved for the class to be recognised.

Animals were recorded in 140 of the 150 shelters, humans in 128.

Domestic Animals

The paintings within the survey area show a marked emphasis on domestic animals when compared with other regions.[1] Of the 3 606 animals included in the analysis, 848 (23%) are domestic animals. Horses are by far the most frequently depicted, comprising 66% of all domestic animals, with cattle 28%, dogs 5%, and sheep less than 1%.

The popularity of the horse was already well established among the Bushmen of the eastern Cape as early as 1809. When on a tour of that area, Col. Collins reported:

> The practice of stealing horses, which is as yet unknown among the Bosjesmen of the Kareeberg and the neighbourhood of the Zak river, has for some years prevailed among those of Bamboos Berg and Zuureberg. They are indeed a much more valuable prize than cattle, as their possession insures them a subsistence, enabling them to overtake the eland, and other wild animals.[2]

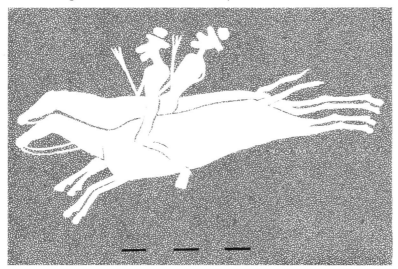

Figure 82 *Site G3*

Two horsemen race neck and neck, apparently enjoying a good joke. They wear brimmed hats, and carry three-pronged sticks in their hands.
The significance of this item of equipment is uncertain; it is often associated with horsemen, and may possibly represent a bundle of spears or arrows. (See p. 273 and Figures 26 and 53a)

The Bushman's preference for horses is reflected not only in the painted record, but is also endorsed by archival evidence. The Bushmen who raided stock from the Natal farmers frequently bartered cattle to their Bantu neighbours, but the horses were invariably retained for their own use.[3] A band of Bushmen encountered in East Griqualand in 1846 were riding mounts stolen from farmers in the Witteberg area of the Cape Province in 1837, as well as from Natal settlers in the Mkhomazi valley in 1840, and it is probable that the spoor of horses seen on the northern tributaries of the Mzimvubu in 1835, that is before the arrival of the Boers in Natal, may also be attributed to the Bushmen.[4] When the Boers trekked into Natal, therefore, they simply provided a convenient source from which the Bushmen living along the eastern mountain chain could obtain a commodity which had already become a popular addition to their hunting economy.

Of the 558 paintings of horses in the fully recorded shelters, 371 (49%) are mounted, and 153 (27%) show evidence of bridle, saddle, or other items of harness such as crupper or martingale. (Figures 15, 40). Not only did the Bushmen acquire European bridles and saddles whenever possible,[4] but also made their own. These were simple quilted leather cushions without any framework of wood or iron. A thick pad of dressed skin stuffed with animal hair provided the equivalent of a pommel. The stirrups were two flat pieces of wood with holes pierced in them through which cords of plaited horse hair were passed and fastened with knots underneath.[5]

Cattle paintings commonly show the patterned hide and lyre or crescent-shaped horns typical of the Sanga group. Some are hornless, but whether these depict polled animals, or result from using fugitive paint for horn details is uncertain. Polled animals, however, are not uncommon among Nguni breeds. Because the indigenous Hottentot, Tswana and Nguni cattle as well as the Africander breeds owned by the Boers, all belong to the Sanga group, it is unlikely that recognisable differences between Boer and Bantu-owned animals would be depicted by the Bushmen. Breeds of European origin, however, which were imported into Natal at a later date, tend to have longer, more slender legs than the indigenous stock.[6] In the paintings, great attention is drawn to the cloven hoofs of cattle, and spoor certainly played a very important role in the retaliatory raids. The cattle owners were pre-occupied with tracing the spoor of stolen animals to the haunts of the Bushmen, while the Bushmen were at pains to confuse the spoor to prevent their haunts being found.

Figure 83 *Site X9*

Drovers urge along crudely drawn cattle with exaggerated horns. One of the figures carries a bow, and is therefore presumably a Bushman. The paintings are in black, orange and white. The scene measures 52 cms from left to right.

156

Sex is also indicated more frequently in cattle paintings than in any other animal species depicted, bulls and cows being clearly differentiated. The spindles of cows' udders tend to be over-emphasised, and calves are often associated with the herd. Although it has not been established whether the Bushmen actually went in for stock-breeding as well as stock-herding, they doubtless soon learned the advantages of augmenting their diet with milk as well as with beef. (Figure 83).

Both horses and cattle are usually painted with the black, white or orange pigments typical of the most recent art.[7] Such details as the mane, tail, fetlocks and hooves of the horses are often picked out in contrasting colours, usually black, which can fade away completely and thus give the erroneous impression of short legs and no tail. (Figure 22). Both horses and cattle are sometimes shown wearing halters even when no rider is portrayed. (Figures 27, 39).

Dogs constitute 5% of the domestic animals in the painted record, and although dogs were certainly used by the Bushmen as an aid to hunting,[8] this activity is seldom painted. The scenes showing dogs hunting eland and dogs fighting baboons are notable exceptions. (Figures 47, 139). In the majority of cases, dogs are shown simply in the company of men or women, and they are usually painted with rather sharp noses and tails that curve upwards and forwards. (Figures 30, 84, 253). Gardiner observed the footprints of Bushmen accompanied by a dog on the upper Mzimkhulu in 1835,[9] and another Bushman dog was encountered in the same area in 1862.[10] Archival evidence confirms that the Bushmen of the upper Mzimvubu obtained dogs in exchange for stolen cattle,[11] and it is of interest that the percentage of dogs painted in the Mzimvubu shelters is higher than in the other valleys covered in this survey. (Table 4, p. 365).

Sheep occur at only two sites, on a tributary of the Mkhomazi, and on the Tsoelike in eastern Lesotho. (Figures 39, 85). In both cases they are fat-tailed sheep and they accompany cattle and horses. Fat-tailed sheep do not appear to have played nearly as significant a part in the lives of the historic Bushmen as did horses and cattle, although the archival evidence shows that they were stolen and eaten on occasion, and that they were also herded by the Thola Bushmen.[12]

It was undoubtedly the horse that had the greatest economic and social impact. In addition to revolutionising their hunting techniques, the horse provided both food and transport as the following Zulu tradition illustrates:—

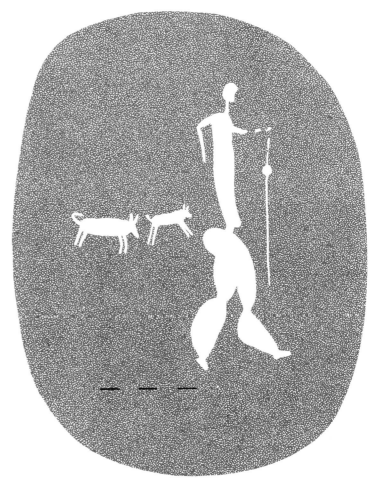

Figure 84 *Site W21*
Woman with weighted digging stick accompanied by dogs.

> It is said, when Abatwa are on a journey, when the game is come to an end where they had lived, they mount on a horse, beginning on the neck, till they reach the tail, sitting one behind the other. If they do not find any game, they eat the horse.[13]

The distribution of domestic animals among the paintings shows an interesting correlation with archival records. (Table 4). Of the 45 recorded stock raids south of the Bushman's river between 1840 and 1872,[14] 13 give no details of the area to which the thieves were traced, and 3 led towards passes in the vicinity of Giant's Castle. The remaining 25 raids were all traced towards the upper reaches of the Mkhomazi, Mzimkhulu, Mzimvubu and Orange rivers, precisely the areas where horse and cattle paintings are most frequently depicted.

The preponderance of domestic animals painted on the upper reaches of the Mzimkhulu suggests that this was the home base, so to speak, of the stock-raiding Bushmen, and that the territory they exploited extended to the Mkhomazi, the northern branches of the Mzimvubu, and the eastern tributaries of the Orange. It is known from written sources that Bushmen were living on the Natal side of the escarpment during the period of early European settlement, for signs of more than temporary residence were located in 1848, 1849 and 1858, and the fact that women and children were encountered on the upper Mzimkhulu in 1862 suggests a domestic rather than a marauding party.[15] It is also known that these Bushmen exploited both sides of the Drakensberg, for in 1848 horses and cattle raided from the Bushman's river were driven to the tributaries of the Orange,[22] yet the spoils of the same raid were later located on the upper reaches of the Mzimkhulu and Mkhomazi rivers.[16] The practice of moving backwards and forwards across the high escarpment certainly continued until at least 1862, when a young Bush boy on horseback was captured on the Lesotho plateau while his family occupied a shelter in the cave sandstone at the foot of the mountains.[17]

Archival records also confirm that the bands of Bushmen living on the headwaters of the Mzimkhulu, Mzimvubu, and Orange rivers had a certain amount of contact with one another, co-operating in the stock thefts and sharing the booty between them.[18] Even though they were probably autonomous bands under separate leadership, they were sufficiently co-ordinated to warn one another of impending attacks.[19]

With the introduction of increasingly stringent protective measures against depredations on the farmer's stock, the Bushman bands which permanently or intermittently occupied the Natal side of the escarpment withdrew eastwards and southwards, and after 1868, the stock thefts were traced over the escarpment and into Lesotho as far as the junction of the Great and Little Orange rivers. It is unlikely, therefore, that paintings on the Natal side of the escarpment are of post 1870 date, and the majority must have been executed prior to 1850. Paintings of domestic animals were already in existence on the upper reaches of the Mzimkhulu in 1849,[20] and on the basis of archival evidence, scenes depicting horse and cattle raids have been tentatively dated to events which took place in 1847 and 1848.[21] Because of the unique combination of accurate and graphic portrayal by the Bushman artists, together with detailed archival documentation, these paintings are among the very few that can be dated to within such narrow limits of time.[22]

Figure 85 *Site W21*
Fat-tailed sheep — ram, ewe and lamb. (See also Fig. 31)

References

1. Maggs 1967; Pager 1971; Smits 1971; Lewis-Williams 1972.
2. Moodie 1838.
3. See pp. 24, 92.
4. See pp. 18, 29.
5. Ellenberger 1912: 12; How 1962: 45.
6. Mason & Maule 1960: 21-48; Epstein 1971 (1): 467.
7. See p. 141.
8. Schapera 1930: 135-6. See also p. 89.
9. See p. 14.
10. See p. 83.
11. See p. 57.
12. See pp. 6, 61, 95.
13. Callaway 1868: 353.
14. Wright 1971: 196-202.
15. See p. 83.
16. See pp. 42-3.
17. See p. 83.
18. See p. 61.
19. See p. 61.
20. See p. 48.
21. See p. 48.
22. Since this chapter was written, I have, with the aid of students from the Universities of Birmingham and Cambridge, made a survey of 50 sites on the upper Orange river between Mashai and Matsaile. Of the total of 1 368 paintings, of which 709 are animals, there are 66 cattle, 32 horses, and 17 dogs. (N.B. This is a preliminary count). No paintings of sheep were located. Many of the cattle are associated with scenes of combat and figures carrying shields. (Figure 54).

The paintings provided striking evidence of contact between the Orange river in Lesotho and the Bushman's river in Natal. In a shelter near the top of the gorge below Matebeng trading store, there is a scene showing a mounted Bushman hunting eland, which is very reminiscent of the paintings in Steel's shelter in the Giant's Castle area. (Willcox 1956, Plate 37). In the Orange river shelter there is also a painting of a white squatting figure clearly associated with the remarkable figure in Willcox's shelter, which is adjacent to Steel's shelter (Willcox 1956, Plate 39). Another similar figure occurs in the Ndedema gorge, a tributary of the Thukela (Pager 1971, Figures 209, 212, 378). There is little doubt that the similarities between these figures are the result of close contact between the areas. Their unusual posture and other details such as skin apron hanging down, patterned body, facial features and weapons held aloft in one hand, could hardly have been independently invented on both sides of the escarpment. (Figures 86, 87).

Figure 86

A knob-headed horseman pursuing an orange and white eland, situated in a high shelter overlooking the Orange river near Matebeng. The style of painting and detail of head-dress is very similar to the horsemen pursuing eland in Steel's Shelter, Giant's Castle Game Reserve (see Willcox 1956, Plate 37).

A

B

C

Figure 87 (left)

Three unusual but similar figures from widely separated areas.

A. *Willcox's shelter, Giant's Castle Game Reserve, Bushman's River, Natal. Approximately 2/3 natural size. Based on a copy by Louis Tylor made in 1893, and reproduced with the authority of the Pitt-Rivers Museum, Oxford. The painting is still remarkably well preserved despite being in a relatively exposed situation (see also Vinnicombe 1966:157; Willcox 1956, Plate 39).*

B. *Sorcerer's Rock, Ndedema Gorge, Drakensberg, Natal. ½ natural size.*
Based on a copy by Harald Pager, and reproduced with his kind permission (see Pager 1971: 164, 165, 340). This figure is clearly male, and has the bar across the penis discussed on page 258 (op cit).

C. *Snap shelter, near Matebeng, Lesotho. Actual size.*
Located on a recent survey of the Orange river.
This painting is more poorly executed than the previous examples, and lacks facial details. In the rock shelter, there is a second cruder and more poorly preserved copy to the right, not reproduced here.

From archival sources, it is known that the Bushmen from these areas had a certain amount of contact with one another. It is possible that the artist responsible for Figure C retreated to the Orange river after seeing Figures A and/or B when stock raiding in the Bushman's river area. He may then have attempted to make a replica of the strange being. Conversely, the paintings may reflect a belief in a mythological character that was common to the Bushmen living on both sides of the escarpment.

Figure 88 *Site W26 (above)*

A herd of shaded polychrome eland, some with wrinkled necks, and one with head turned over shoulder. Close inspection of the eland at top right shows an extra forelimb and two additional but smaller hind-limbs, which suggests over-painting. Crouched behind the central eland is an ornately patterned human figure barely discernible at this reduction. To the right is a panel of superimposed paintings, eland on eland, and eland on humans, among which are several kaross-clad figures. Above the superpositions is the 'chained antelope' shown in detail in Figure 214. Unfortunately, many of the paintings at this site have been damaged by the careless scratching and scribbling of herdboys.

Photo: Pat Carter.

161

Figure 89

*According to Bushman belief, a legendary hero, Qwan-
tciqutshaa, lived in a place enclosed with hills and
precipices, and there was but one pass, and it was
constantly filled with a freezingly cold mist so that
none could enter into it. Qwantciqutshaa lived there
alone with his wife because other people wanted to
kill him, and all the elands that had died became alive
again. Some came in with assegais sticking in them,
which had been struck by those people who wanted
to kill him. And he took out the assegais, a whole
bundle, and they remained in his place.*

*One day his brother, when chasing an eland he had
wounded, pursued it closely through the mist, and
Qwantciqutshaa saw his elands running about, frightened at that wounded eland and the assegai that was
sticking in it.*

*Qwantciqutshaa came out and saw his brother, and
said — 'Oh My brother, I have been injured; you see
now where I am.'*

*And the next morning he killed an eland for his
brother, and told him to go back and call his mother
and his friends. He did so, and when they came, they
told Qwantciqutshaa how the people outside had died
of hunger; and they stayed with him, and the place
smelt of meat.*

From a legend told by Qing, a young Bushman from Lesotho.

162

Eland

(Taurotragus oryx)

The morning sun was just showing its rays above the horizon, and the fogs were rising up the mountains, when we were once more in the saddle. When we had ridden for nearly an hour, we suddenly saw, in the valley beneath us, an enormous herd of elands; they were scattered about grazing like cattle.[1]

Witnessed in the Drakensberg by Captain A. W. Drayson circa 1850.

'Where Kaggen is, elands are in droves like cattle.'[2]
Dictated by Qing, a Mountain Bushman from Lesotho, in 1873.

The eland is a large antelope of stately and somewhat benevolent appearance, and a gentle, docile disposition. It shows a greater propensity for domestication than any other animal in Africa, a potential which appears to have been realised by the Bushmen who themselves likened herds of eland to droves of cattle.

Eland are characterised by their ox-like massiveness. Both sexes are pale fawn or tawny in colour, becoming lighter underneath. They have a large pendulous dewlap fringed with darker hair, and in older animals the necks become wrinkled into folds. A ridge of dark hair extends along the crest of the neck and back, and, in addition, adult bulls have a growth of coarse hair on the forehead. The tail is tufted only at the end, and reaches to the hocks. Horns are present in both sexes, even in very young calves, and are relatively small by comparison with the bulky body proportions. They are spiral in the basal half, and project backwards in line with the profile of the face. Although black in colour, the horns often catch the sunlight and glint as though a silvery white.

Eland rest like cattle, either standing up or lying down, and their spoor is also like that of domestic cattle. The hooves of the front legs are appreciably larger than those of the rear, an adaptation to carry the weight of the deep chest, but eland are nevertheless light walkers, and the clefts expand very little unless the animal is driven to unusual exertion. (See Figure 212). Eland are both browsers and grazers, and can often be seen with their necks and heads stretched up to feed on leaves at a considerable height above them.

They are very selective in their feeding habits and therefore range over large tracts of country, walking with long easy strides. When disturbed, their usual pace is a heavy swinging trot, and they gallop only when hard pressed. Despite their ponderous proportions however, they can jump six feet or more, sometimes leaping into the air for no apparent reason.

Eland are keen-sighted and -scented, and are at all times difficult to stalk. When alarmed they always run against the wind, and although they can be deflected from one side to another if pursued, they never turn round and make off down wind. This habit is easily exploited by hunters. In addition, eland become fatter than other antelope, with a large accumulation of fat around the heart. They therefore easily become blown, and can be run down on horseback with relative ease. Once the Bushmen had acquired horses from European colonists, they soon utilised them in the chase, and there are some very spirited paintings showing their mastery of the technique of equestrian hunting. (Figures 5, 82, 252).

Concentrations of numbers in eland herds are largely seasonal. In the winter months they are scattered in small groups from one to twenty, the bulls always remaining by themselves and the cows and yearlings likewise. Periodically, however, they assemble into large herds, usually during or after rain. In the Drakensberg, where a total of some 6-800 eland survive, migrations are no longer possible because of restrictions imposed by settlement, but concentrations occur during spring immediately after the cows have calved. The mature bulls join the troops about the beginning of December when rutting takes place. Herds at this time of year number on an average from 120 to 150, but sometimes as many as 300 or more eland can be seen together in one place.[3]

It is very probable that seasonal movements and concentrations of Bushman bands followed a similar pattern to those adopted by eland, and in many respects, Bushman band structure is reflected in eland herd structure. Women and children equate with cows and calves, and their roles both in Bushman bands and in eland herds are separate and different from the roles of men and bulls. On occasions, however, the whole herd and the whole band amalgamate for particular purposes, when the propagation and cohesion of the animal herd and of the human society are assured.[4] The eland herd was possibly seen by the Bushmen as analogous or parallel to their own band structure, a structure that was the basis of survival.

Paintings of eland outnumber those of all other animals throughout the Drakensberg region,[5] and although their characteristics are as a rule faithfully portrayed, certain peculiarities and conventions of proportion and colour rendering are not true to life. There is a general tendency towards elongation of the head and neck, and although there are examples of monochrome eland in red or black silhouette, the bulk are painted in various combinations of red, yellow, orange, white or black, sometimes shaded to produce a remarkably sophisticated modelled effect. In most of the multi-coloured paintings black is used only for such details as eyes, hooves, tail-tufts and back-stripe. The body is usually painted in red with a lighter head and neck, and the belly, legs and tail are lined with white. (Figures 40, 90, 94). In their present state, many of the eland paintings appear legless and headless due to the fugitive nature of the white pigment. All that is now clearly visible is the red body, and sometimes the dark line extending up the ridge of the neck and the dark tuft on the forehead. It may also be due to vagaries of the paint that many eland paintings are without horns, yet even in examples where all other features painted in black or white are very clear, the horns are invisible. (Figures 96, 98, 111).

The majority of eland paintings show groups of animals in superimposed friezes or masterly compositions in a variety of restful poses. (Figures 97, 103-5). The activities most commonly depicted are walking, standing, lying down or running, in that order of preference, and relatively few are directly associated with hunting scenes. These vary from a lone hunter pursuing a single eland (Figure 92), to several hunters armed either with spears or bows and arrows chasing after a herd of eland or closing in on an individual animal. (Figures 93, 108). Often the hunters' faces are painted white, which would seem to be scarcely utilitarian, and in some detailed groups their bodies too are decorated with paint as though for a special ceremony rather than a routine activity. These somewhat unusual associations are confirmed by other scenes in which eland form the focal point around which extraordinary figures are gathered. A recumbent eland is shown with thongs tied round both fore and hind legs (Figures 109, 110), while another, with blood gushing from the nose, has thongs indicated on the rear legs only. (Figure 102). In some paintings eland are entwined with or encircled by a dotted line, or a series of dots may extend from their heads towards human figures. (Figures 90, 95, 104, 214, 237).

Another peculiarity noted is that one eland may be painted on top of another in such a way that the superimposed painting follows the outline of the original closely but not exactly. Often only a double line along the back of the eland can be detected, although sometimes there are two heads or more than the full complement of legs. In many instances the superpositions are bright orange or yellow ochre painted over earlier dark red paintings, which suggests a process of overpainting or renewal. (Figures 88, 94, 99, 104-6).

There are a total of 848 eland in the painting sample studied, as against 445 smaller antelope which are second to the eland in numerical importance. (Figure 80). Eland not only greatly outnumber all other animals depicted, but they are also visually preponderant because of marked size differentiation. Eland paintings are on an average 40 centimetres long, whereas the smaller antelope average only 10 centimetres. In one of the many painted sites on *Belleview* farm in East Griqualand, there are two exceptionally large eland measuring 1,86 and 2,3 metres long by 87 and 85 centimetres high. These measurements excluded the heads which are unfortunately missing as a result of exfoliation. In the same shelter a rhebuck measures only 16,5 centimetres, and humans 12 centimetres. (Figure 71). The relative proportions of eland and horses in scenes of equestrian hunting are also greatly exaggerated. One example is a group on the Tsoelike river in Lesotho which shows an eland bull measuring 18 centimetres, pursued by a mounted hunter whose horse measures only 8,5 centimetres. Even allowing, therefore, for the massive size of eland in the flesh, the paintings often exaggerate their bulk out of all proportion. The same applies to their numbers, for although eland were formerly plentiful throughout the Drakensberg region, they were not, judging from the early records, more common than other ungulates. Wildebeest and hartebeest, for instance, were reported in great herds,[6] yet together they represent only 3% of the total number of wild animals in the painted record. (Figure 80).

In addition to emphasising the numbers and size of eland, the artists treated this antelope more elaborately than other subjects. Techniques of shading and modelling, as well as of perspective and foreshortening, were used on eland more than on any other animal.[7]

The quantitative and qualitative dominance of eland among the paintings clearly reflects a high degree of preoccupation with this animal, and eland undoubtedly played an important role in the economy of the hunter-gatherers. The huge bulk of an eland bull, weighing in the region of 545 kilograms and dressing to about 363 kilograms, would have provided a camp of 20 Bushmen with enough meat for over a month, allowing an average of half a kilo of meat per person per day. A vaal rhebuck, on the other hand, weighing an average of 23 kilo and dressing to about 15 kilo[8] would

Figure 90 *Site M15a*

This enigmatic scene is painted in a small uninhabitable overhang in a gulley where other larger shelters show evidence of occupation.

At the top are three eland (body of eland on right not included here) which are associated with meandering dots. Below are a series of figures linked by a line with white dots on either side. In the centre, a large standing figure has one arm raised, and under the armpit is a funnel-shape linked to a long line. The male figure to the left holds two short sticks, one of which may be a fly-whisk. To the right are three figures with fragmentary facial features. One wears a long kaross, the other a short skin cape. Another figure with fingers outstretched at far left bends forward so that the shoulder cape falls free from the shoulders. At centre left another kaross-clad figure has hooves in lieu of feet, and carries a bundle of barbed arrows. The head, which is turned back over the shoulder, is decorated with quill-like spikes. Below is a faded bird-like creature associated with bowmen wearing antelope heads.

It is difficult to ascertain the temporal sequence of the large animal body. Although it appears faded, it was probably painted on top of and therefore later than the earlier but better preserved human figures.

165

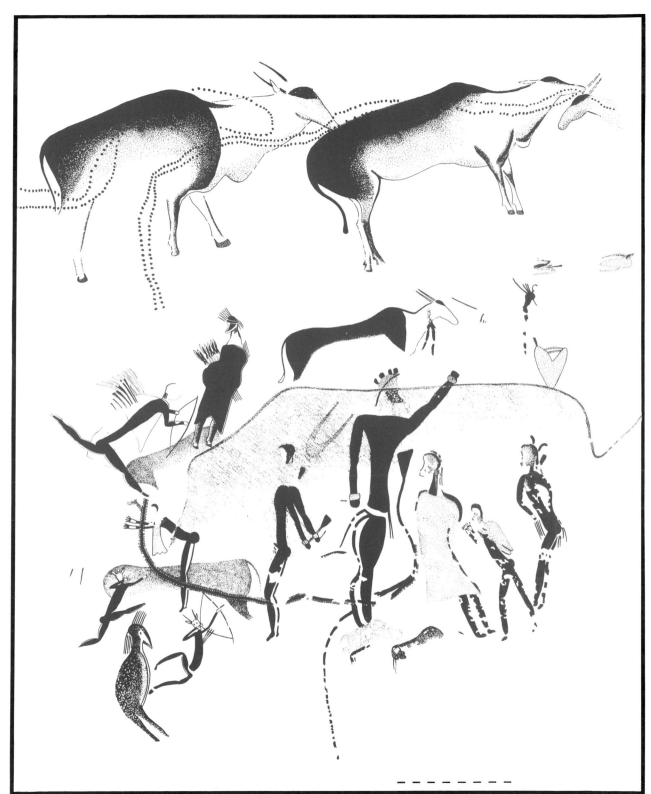

provide a camp of 20 with but two meagre meals. There is, however, convincing evidence that the emphasis placed on eland in the painted record was prompted not so much by economic motives as by social and metaphysical needs. Some would argue that the economic importance was primary and the social importance secondary, but whichever came first, Bushman cosmology focused more attention on eland than can adequately be explained by purely material needs.[9]

A study of recorded Bushman lore reveals an apparently widespread belief in the existence of an especially intimate relationship between their deity and a selected animal. The relationship is most clearly reflected in a series of creation myths which are similarly structured despite the fact that different animals are selected to express the relationship. Two gemsbok creation myths have been recorded by independent sources from the Heikum Bushmen in the Kalahari,[10] while eland creation myths were told by two Xam Bushmen from different areas of the northern Cape,[11] by a desert Bushman in Botswana[12] and a mountain Bushman in Lesotho.[13] Dr E. R. Leach,[14] who kindly read through the relevant mythology at my request, not only agreed that a common link existed in the creation stories of the two animals, but, more significantly, pointed to the existence of a special ritual relationship between man, animal and deity. The animal which expressed this ritual relationship was the eland in the south, and the gemsbok in the north where eland are not so plentiful.

The chief mythological figure of the Southern Bushmen, which includes those bands that inhabited the Cape Province, Orange Free State and Lesotho, has variously been spelt Kaggen, Qhang, 'Kaang, T'ang, Cagn or Ctaggen. Because of the different orthographies used to denote the initial click, Bleek, followed by Stow and Schapera, was of the opinion that the pronunciation of the name was identical among the various groups, although the concept of the Being varied somewhat from region to region.[15] Among the Xam Bushmen, Kaggen shared the same name as the Mantis, an insect with which their god has become identified, although it is not clear to what extent the identification of the name Kaggen with Mantis is actual or incidental.[16] The apparent similarity of words may be associated with a verbal pun, as Hahn observed that the Hottentot name for Devil or Harmful Being was Gaunab, the same as their name for 'mantis' but spoken in a different tone.[17] The mantis also has two names among the Kung Bushmen; one is the same as the word used for spirits or dreams, while the other is the

same as the name of their supernatural Being.[18] It is nevertheless evident from published mythology that the Bushmen did not necessarily conceive of Kaggen in the form of a mantis; Kaggen was principally human in form, but could change himself from human to animal at will.

Because of the relevance of Bushman beliefs to the preponderance of eland among the paintings, condensed versions of three of the eland creation myths are set out below.[19] The first was told by a Xam Bushman from the Katkop Hills in the Northern Cape.[20]

> Kaggen put the shoe of his son-in-law, Kwammanga, into a water-pool, and made an eland out of it, feeding it on honey. Kaggen's family wondered why he no longer brought any honey home, so his grandson Ni went out with Kaggen one day to discover the reason. While Kaggen went to call the eland from the reeds where it lived,[21] Ni pretended to be asleep, but was really watching through a peep-hole in his kaross. Kaggen called "Kwammanga's shoe!" and the eland came up and stood, while Kaggen moistened its hair and smoothed it with honey.

> Having discovered where the honey was disappearing to, Ni told his father Kwammanga, and together they plotted to kill the eland. While Kaggen was away, they cut honey, took it to the pool of water, called "Kwammanga's shoe!" and when the eland came leaping out of the reeds, Kwammanga shot it. The eland bounded off and lay down to die.

> Meanwhile Kaggen was looking for honey but each comb he went to was dry. He interpreted this as an omen that danger had come upon his home and that blood was flowing, so he returned. He went to the water and called the eland, but the eland did not come. Then he wept; tears fell from his eyes because he did not see the eland. When he looked for the eland's spoor, he found blood, then wept again. He covered his head with his kaross, and heart-sore with anger, he went home to lie down even though the sun was high in the sky.

> While Kaggen was lying mourning, the Meercats all went to cut up the dead eland. Then Kaggen roused himself, picked up his quiver, and ran along the eland's spoor. When he caught sight of the Meercats cutting up the eland,[22] he took out an arrow, for he meant to fight the eland's battle. But each time he shot, the arrow returned, passing close to his head so that he narrowly missed shooting himself. He tried to attack the Meercats with a knob-kerry, but a Meercat snatched it from him, beat him, and threw him on the eland's horns. The Meercats then made Kaggen carry wood for their fire, but he escaped further punishment by pricking the eland's gall which he saw on a bush; this covered him with darkness, and enabled him to escape. But then Kaggen could not see the ground, and he became tangled in the bushes. So he took off his shoe, and threw it into the sky where it became the moon, and lighted the earth so that he could see.[23]

Text continued on page 176

Figure 91

Top left: *Photograph of a bull eland trotting. Note the neck folds and tufted forehead; the heavy dewlap in this photograph has flapped back on itself, and does not therefore show clearly. The natural colouration of an eland is a uniform dun colour, with slightly lighter neck and linings to belly and legs.*

Photo: *Willi Dolder*

Bottom right: *Tracing of a bull eland trotting.*

The colouration is highly stylised, there being a marked colour division between red body, white neck, and white linings to belly and legs. This rendering of an eland is among the most realistically proportioned paintings yet found. They are usually more exaggeratedly elongated.

167

Figure 92 *Site S1*

A single white-faced hunter and an eland are the only paintings at this small river-side site in the Transkei. The Bushmen who lived in this area had to present the father of the girl they wished to marry with the breast and heart of an eland before they could take her. The length of the eland from tip of nose to tip of tail is 30 centimetres.

Figure 93 *Site X11   Melikane*

Hunters with white faces marked with stripes close in on an eland. The horizontal lines protruding from the back of the decorated figure on the right are possibly spare arrows carried in a body band. To the right of this group, a line of hunters, some of whom are illustrated in Figure 178, run towards the dying eland.

Figure 94   *Site M8*

Part of a frieze of paintings on Bonnievale farm, upper Ndawana. Shaded poly-chrome eland are superimposed on kaross-clad figures, one of which has cloven hooves in lieu of feet. The animal-headed figure with triple horns has an elongated ringed neck, and carries a bundle on its shoulders. The lower eland is superimposed on an earlier image, and at top centre, a smaller superimposed eland appears to share the same front leg as an earlier rendering of a larger eland.

Figure 95 *Site W32*

A shaded polychrome eland is connected by a spotted line to two figures. The one in a white kaross has hooves in lieu of feet, and the naked figure with beaded bandolier wears an unwieldy head-dress of wedge shapes protruding from a double band. Below the eland, which measures 36 centimetres from nose to tail, there is a horizontal figure with dark legs protruding from a light-coloured kaross. A paint smudge immediately below has not been reproduced in the tracing shown in Figure 237. Above the eland, an antbear-like animal crouches with tail tucked in and head bent down.

Figure 96 *Site V14*

This painted site on the Tsoelikane river is one of the few depicting a complete eland herd, including bulls, cows, yearlings and new-born calves. Standing above the eland are two white-faced humans, and at top left and top right curious part-animal figures are crouched. The paintings cover a slab of rock at the end of a recess where wild flowers cover the damp floor area.

Photo: Des Watkins.

172

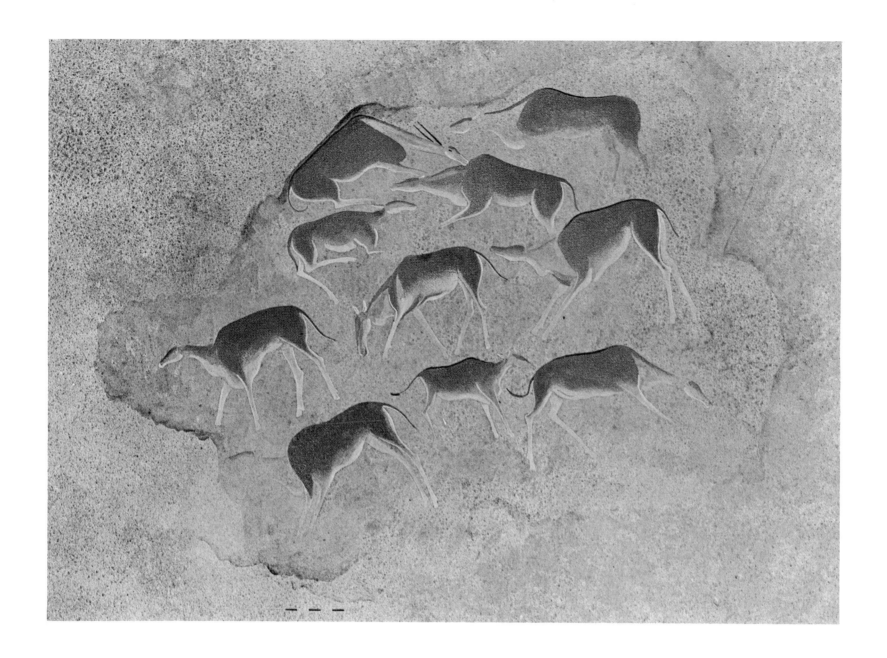

Figure 97 *Site E2*

A herd of eland composed to fit into a niche in the rock face. The originals are very faint; this reproduction is from a tracing made in 1959. (See also Figure 56).

Figure 98   *Site S3*

Two women with arms upraised face another figure wearing a white breech-cloth and beaded waist-band. The trio have small white faces, and are painted on top of at least two layers of eland. Another eland is superimposed on the left-hand figure.

174

Figure 99 *Site S3*, Sheltered Vale

A dead eland with heavy neck folds and bristling hair on the forehead has been painted on top of another upside-down eland — notice the double rump and two tails. The eland has also been superimposed on a kaross-clad figure with animal-like head. Above, a figure curiously patterned in red and white holds a stick. Another eland facing to the right (head and neck very faint) has been superimposed on the back of the eland with legs in air. (See also Figure 72).

The second version of the creation of the eland was told by Hankasso, a Xam Bushman from the Strontberg, about 200 miles east of the Katkop Hills. The two informants never met, therefore the myths can be regarded as independent testimonies.

> Kwammanga threw away part of his shoe, which Kaggen picked up and soaked in water at a place where reeds stood. Kaggen returned at intervals to watch the shoe grow into an eland. When it had grown, he trilled to it, making his tongue quiver as Bushmen do in springbok hunting, and he called to it, "Kwammanga's shoe piece!". The eland then walked up to his father, and Kaggen rubbed its ribs with honey. He repeatedly treated the eland in this way while it grew, and he wept, fondling it, and beautifying it with honeycomb. After one such occasion, the eland walked back to bask in the water, and Kaggen did not come back for a time. For three nights the eland grew, becoming like an ox. Then Kaggen returned early, as the sun rose, and called the eland. The eland came forth, and the ground resounded as he came. Then Kaggen sang for joy about the male eland, meanwhile rubbing it down nicely.
>
> Next morning, while the eland was grazing, Kaggen took his young grandson Ni with him to the water. They sat down in the shade of a bush, and Kaggen told Ni to go to sleep, covering his head. But Ni lay awake and saw the eland. Then young Ni went and told his father what he had seen, and while Kaggen was away, he guided his father, Kwammanga, to the place where the eland lived. Kwammanga knocked the eland down, and when Kaggen arrived on the scene he saw Kwammanga and the others cutting up the carcase. Kaggen was very angry because they had not waited for permission to kill the eland, and he wept for the eland. His heart did not feel satisfied about his eland, whom he alone had made.
>
> Kwammanga and Ni made Kaggen gather wood for them, for they wanted to cook and eat the meat. As he went gathering wood, Kaggen caught sight of the eland's gall, which he eventually pierced and burst. The gall broke, covering his head so that he could not see, and he groped about, feeling his way. While groping along, he found an ostrich feather and he brushed the gall from his eyes. Then he threw the feather up in the sky, telling it that henceforth it should be the moon and shine at night, to lighten the darkness for men till the sun rise.[24]

In 1873, J. M. Orpen collected a story of the creation of eland from a Bushman named Qing in the Qacha's Nek district of Lesotho, part of which area is included in this survey. Eastern Lesotho is about 340 miles from the Strontberg, and 540 miles from the Katkop Hills. (Map 1). Reports of the material collected by Bleek and Lloyd were not published until after 1874, therefore the information recorded by Orpen must have been independently collected.

> Kaggen, who was the first Being and a great chief, had a wife named Coti. As a result of a scolding from her husband, she conceived, and brought forth a strange child in the veld. She told her husband, who ran to see it, and with the aid of Canna (ground herbs?), he put questions to it.
>
> "Are you this animal? Are you that animal?" but there was no reply. Finally he asked, "Are you an eland?" and the reply was "Aaaa". Then he took the young eland and folded it in his arms, and put it in a gourd which he hid in a secluded kloof enclosed by hills and precipices, and he left it there to grow.
>
> Kaggen then attempted to kill the eland by throwing sharpened sticks at it, but each time he missed, so finally he went away to fetch arrow poison. During his three-day absence, his two sons Cogaz and Gcwi went out with young men to hunt, and they came upon the eland their father had hidden without knowing anything about it. After some difficulty, the newly grown eland was encircled and stabbed, the blood collected and the meat cut up. Before carrying the supplies home, however, they noticed Kaggen's snares and traps, and they were afraid, because they then realised the eland belonged to Kaggen.
>
> When Kaggen returned and saw blood on the ground where the eland had been killed, he was very angry with his youngest son Gcwi who had stabbed the eland, and after punishing him for his presumption and disobedience by pulling off his nose,[25] said "Now try to undo the mischief you have done, for you have spoilt the elands I was making fit for use." Gcwi was told to take some of the eland's blood which had been brought home in a paunch, and to scatter the blood by rubbing a churn-stick between the palms of his hands. The drops of blood first turned into frightful snakes which went abroad, then hartebeests which ran away, but Kaggen was dissatisfied with his son's creations. The blood was thrown out, the pot cleansed, and more blood emptied into it from the paunch. Fat from the eland's heart was added to the mixture and Kaggen's wife Coti now churned, while Kaggen sprinkled,[26] and the drops became bull elands which surrounded them and pushed them with their horns. Kaggen again said, "You see how you have spoilt the elands?" and he drove them away. Then they churned and produced eland cows, and they churned again to produce multitudes of elands and the earth was covered with them. Then Kaggen said to Gcwi, "Go and hunt them, and try to kill one; that is now your work, for it was you who spoilt them."
>
> Gcwi ran and did his best, but came back panting, footsore and worn-out. He hunted again next day but was still unable to kill any. The eland were able to run away because Kaggen was in their bones. Kaggen then sent his eldest son Cogaz to help turn the elands towards Gcwi by shouting, and when they came running close past him, he threw assegais and killed three bulls. Then Kaggen sent Cogaz to hunt, first giving him a blessing, and he killed two. Then his younger son Gcwi was sent again, and he killed one. That day game were given to men to eat, and this is the way they were spoilt and became wild. Kaggen said he had to punish his sons for trying to kill the thing he made, and he must make them feel sore.[27]

Qing gave neither the circumstances nor the manner in which the moon was created, but did say that Kaggen gave orders and caused the moon to appear.

Apart from the more obvious similarities between these three myths — Kaggen's creation and careful nurturing of the eland, the premature killing of the eland by younger members of Kaggen's family, and the sorrow and reproof that follow — there are suggestions of a more complex mystical significance.

In each instance, the victim (eland) is the child of the Creator, Kaggen. The betrayers are a son-in-law and grandchild in the first two stories, and sons in the third. The slayers of the eland are the same as the betrayers, and the victim (eland), has the same status vis-à-vis the Creator as the slayer. This structure is characteristic of true sacrifice, for in sacrificial rites many of the preliminaries are concerned with establishing a symbolic identification between the giver of the sacrifice (the slayer) and the victim (the sacrificial beast).[28]

In his monumental work on the South American Indians, Lévi-Strauss presents an elaborate argument in which honey represents menstrual blood or male semen, while Freudian symbolism links shoes with the female vagina.[29] If these symbols had a similar significance in Southern Africa, the shoe of Kaggen's son-in-law would symbolise Kaggen's daughter, and by feeding the shoe with honey Kaggen was having incestuous relations with his daughter. The product of this union, a young bull eland, was therefore Kaggen's daughter's son who shared the same relationship with Kaggen as his grandson Ni. Ni and the eland thereby became substitutes for one another, just as the ram became a substitute for Isaac in the Old Testament story.

In the Xam versions of the creation myths, Kwammanga and Ni rendered Kaggen impotent through slaying the eland, and temporarily reduced him to the status of a servant. This may be associated with a ritual in which hunting an eland brought the power of God into the service of man. If such an association between myth and ritual existed, it is probable that honey and gall, media associated with the creation of the eland and the creation of the moon, also played a symbolic part in the ritual sequence.[30]

It is also significant that the myth portrays the eland as being immune to attack from the creator Kaggen, but not from his sons. The blood of the eland murdered by them is then used as the basis for creating all other animals, including more eland. The son who

actually killed the first eland, a renowned hunter, was condemned to kill again, but he was unable to do so without the co-operation of Kaggen. His brother also had to be 'blessed' before he was able to hunt successfully. One of the basic tenets of the myth appears to be that, before being spoilt by the misdemeanours of mankind, eland were intended to be tame and close to man, like domestic animals. This leads to the suggestion, first made many years ago by Miss A. Werner, that eland were to Bushmen what the ox is to the pastoral Bantu — not only a food provider, but in a sense also a sacred animal.[31]

Among many African pastoralists, cattle literally give point and meaning to the life of the people. The so-called 'cattle-complex' which combines elements of social and economic structure, of political position and ritual, is everywhere reported as providing security, pleasure, and emotional satisfaction.[32] Describing the relationship between the Nilotic Nuer and their cattle, Evans-Pritchard writes:

> When ... we seek to estimate what their cattle are to Nuer and how they see them, we have to recognise that they are the means by which men enter into communication with God.[33]

Among the Zulu, too, there is a close association between cattle and man. One of the many metaphorical links was described by an informant in these words:

> A woman conceives and gives birth in the tenth lunar month. So does a cow. It conceives and gives birth in the tenth lunar month. So a cow is like a human.[34]

Eland also have a gestation period of similar duration to that of cattle and humans, and other similarities between the behaviour of eland and the behaviour of Bushmen have already been outlined.[35] If cattle are the very life-blood of Zulu society, then eland were similarly at the very heart of Bushman social structure.

That the Bushmen regarded eland as a personal and valued possession is reflected in another myth related by the Lesotho Bushman Qing.

> [Qwantciqutshaa] saw *his* elands running about and wondered what had startled them.[36]

The close association between the Bushman's creator deity and eland, and the similarity between eland and cattle, was further exemplified by Qing who, when asked where Kaggen was, replied:

> We don't know, but the elands do. Have you not hunted and heard his cry, when the elands suddenly start and run to his call? Where he is, elands are in droves like cattle.[37]

Kaggen, it was believed, was in the bones of eland, which is why they were able to run away from hunters. The Bushmen of western Lesotho believed that Kaggen gave to all animals a special mark — to this eland he gave a stump of a tail, to that a folded ear, and to another a pierced ear, and later Basotho settlers in the area appear to have taken over the belief that eland had an imaginary shepherd who lived in the Maluti mountains. This Being, never seen by human eye, was called *Unconagnana*, a name unmistakably borrowed from a click language.[38] The close man-animal relationships inferred from these observations lend further credence to the contention that the Bushmen did not regard eland purely as game, but considered them as comparable with a domesticated animal.

According to the Xam Bushmen of the northern Cape, Kaggen created the eland first among animals, followed by the hartebeest, and for this reason, Kaggen loved these antelope 'not a little, he loved them dearly'. The eland and the hartebeest had magic power, and enjoyed the special protection of Kaggen. Kaggen actually sat between the horns of eland, and when a hunter killed this antelope, Kaggen did not love them.[39]

The Basotho who settled among the Mountain Bushmen believed that a very dangerous viper lived between the horns of eland, hidden in the tuft of hair found on the foreheads of this antelope. Before stabbing an eland to the heart when it fell to the ground, they struck it with heavy blows on the head in order to kill the snake.[40] Khoisan peoples living further to the west also maintained that a snake lived on the forehead of all eland,[41] and in at least two scenes within the survey area, snakes are closely associated with eland paintings, one of which depicts a slaughtered animal. (Figures 67, 146).

Among the Xam, extremely intricate rules and taboos were bound up with hunting eland which closely identified the hunter with his prey, and these regulations to a great extent bear out the ritual aspect of the hunt.[42] The hunter who actually shot an eland was not allowed to cross its spoor but had to keep to one side. If the arrow-head was found lying on the ground after impact with the quarry, it was not touched directly by hand but was carefully picked up with a leaf and inserted into the quiver in such a way that the wind would not 'see' it. The arrow with which the eland had been shot was then laid alongside another arrow to imbue it with similar power. While waiting for the poison to take action, the hunter would return homewards, not hurrying and without enthusiasm for, from the moment of shooting onwards, he had a close bond with his quarry. Any action of his would affect the eland: '. . . [it would]

look as if it felt that its heart were not afraid, for the poison is killing its heart . . .' On nearing the camp, the man would avoid going directly to his people but would stand to one side lest he come into contact with the women and children. Only the senior men, the heads of the families, were allowed to approach and question him. The hunter would reply to the old men softly and as if in pain, making no direct reference to the eland he had shot. An old man would then carefully inspect the quiver, handling the arrows gently, to see what animal hair was stuck to the blood on the arrow shaft. Still no direct mention was made of the eland. One of the old men then rolled up the hunter's genital apron, tucking it into the waist belt, and told him that he must no longer urinate freely so that the eland would likewise not urinate freely. The poison would 'hold its bladder shut', and the eland would die.[43] The hunter, with one of the old men, slept apart from the camp in a specially prepared shelter well away from the children. He continued to act as if in pain, and the old man kept the fire going all night caring for him as though he were really ill.

Meanwhile Kaggen, the creator and protector of all eland, would examine the wounded eland which was writhing in pain. Kaggen would then follow the spoor of the man who had shot it, for he wanted to know who was responsible. After testing the bow-strings to see whether they were taut or slack, Kaggen would examine the quivers. When he found the eland's blood on an arrow-tip, he would pronounce 'This man shot the eland', and according to Bushman belief, 'Kaggen does not love us if we kill an eland'. Kaggen then proceeded to taunt the hunter and prevent him from sleeping by teasing him with pinches, pricks and bites. Sometimes he would make noises like a puff-adder hoping that the man would jump up so that the eland would also jump up. Even if Kaggen made a louse bite the hunter, he was not allowed to scratch, but could only wriggle his body gently. He was not allowed to catch or kill the louse, otherwise the blood upon his hands, with which he grasped the arrow when he killed the eland, would enter the arrow and 'cool' or nullify the action of the poison. If the hunter moved about or reacted to the taunts in any way, Kaggen immediately went to tell the eland, and by striking its horns, would make it come to life and eat and become well and strong again.

If the hunter ate at all, a special fire was lit at day-break, and special food prepared. He was not allowed to eat the flesh of certain animals, for instance swift springbok, for this would give strength to the movements of the wounded animal; he should rather eat the flesh of a slow-moving animal, especially of such as would

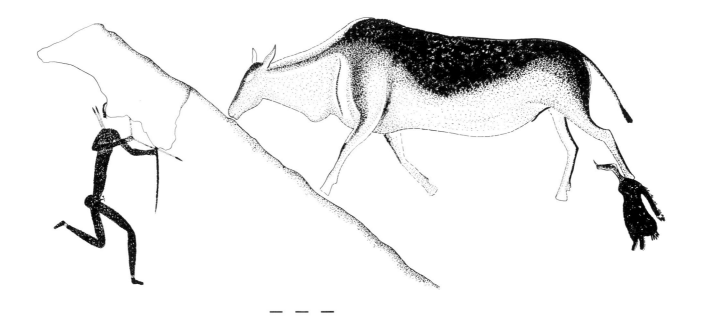

Figure 100 *Site W 33*

The Southern Bushmen believed that their creator deity had a special relationship with eland, and that he was with them as they lay dying. The curious creature with tusked snout, feathered arms and a tufted tail which crouches at the eland's hind leg may represent this special protecting spirit.

The hunter is painted in a slight recess in the rock. His head and part of his bow are unfortunately missing through exfoliation. Note the vestigial bar across the penis, which may signify a social and physical taboo imposed as a result of shooting eland. (See pages 258-9)

strengthen the action of the poison.[44] The Bushmen of the Strontberg were not permitted to eat at all, and had to sit to windward of the cooking fires so that they could not even smell the food. For if the eland were likewise to smell food, it would become strengthened and revitalised.

The following day the hunter would walk with a limp so that the eland would also limp and stumble and be unable to cover much distance.[45] He would point out the spoor of the wounded eland to the other Bushmen, but he himself remained behind with one of the old men. He was not allowed to join the other hunters at the carcase until the eland's heart had been cut out. The Bushmen believed that Kaggen was with the eland as it lay dying, and if the hunter's scent were to interfere before the eland was properly dead, the eland would become lean. Before the heart was excised, the eland's tail had to be cut off, and a man beat the eland with the tail. This ensured that the flesh would be fat. During this entire operation, no-one's shadow was to fall on the eland, for shadows too were harmful and would make the eland lean. One man then made an incision with a knife while the others looked away, for their eyes, by looking, may have affected the eland. Even then, the man who cut the flesh would not shout out, 'Look at the eland's fat!', but he would allude to it indirectly. Only when all the hunters had approached and seen the condition of the eland for themselves, were they able to say, 'Look! This eland's fat is such that people will not eat meat of this eland. For pure fat is what they will eat.'[46, 47]

The above information, given by Bushmen of the Katkop Hills and the Strontberg, unfortunately makes no reference to what the hunter had to do to placate his offended deity once the eland was dead. The Lesotho myths do, however, allude to an act of restitution. Kaggen, after punishing the son who killed his first eland, told him that he had to *try to undo the mischief he had done*.[48] Qing further related how a legendary chief, Qwantciqutshaa, '*killed an eland and purified himself and his wife*'. Qwantciqutshaa then told his wife to grind canna [herbs?] which were sprinkled on the ground, and all the elands that had died came alive again, some with assegais still sticking in their bodies. The same chief '*killed an eland and purified himself as the baboon had defiled him*'. The latter reference does not make it clear whether the hunter purified himself *because* he had killed an eland or whether, by performing certain rites *after* killing an eland, he was able to rid himself of other pollutions.[49] Irrespective of the precise function of these rites, the implication that the killing of an eland was followed by purification and a

ceremony *which brought the eland back to life* is of considerable significance. The possible role of painting in this ceremony can only be conjectural, but according to the myth, eland blood brought home in the paunch of the dead eland, and fat from the heart, were important symbols in the re-creation of eland. It is particularly significant that when an aged Mosotho who had formerly painted with Bushmen was asked to execute a painting using similar methods, he first requested the *blood of a freshly killed eland*. When this was not available, he mixed a substitute of ox blood with red ochre, and then said he would first paint an eland, because the *Bushmen of that part of the country were of the eland*. The fact that blood was amongst the media used by Bushmen for mixing paint has recently been confirmed by analytical tests,[50] and although the old Mosotho did not request fat as well as blood for his painting, fat was widely reported to be a component of Bushman paint by the early colonists,[51] and mortar stones containing pulverised ochre mixed with animal fat were found in painted shelters at the beginning of this century.[52] In the Cathedral Peak area of the Drakensberg where early Nguni settlers came into contact with surviving Bushmen, an informant stated that the Bushmen specifically used eland fat for mixing their paint,[53] and eland fat mixed with red ochre is still used in Kung marriage ceremonies in South West Africa.[54] With the aid of ultra-violet photography, fat has been detected in paintings in Zambia,[55] but similar methods have not yet been applied in South Africa.

Speculative additions to established evidence are of limited value unless they lead to an hypothesis that can be put to the test. Unfortunately, this is no longer possible — the artists are all dead. It nevertheless seems to me not improbable that many of the eland paintings, particularly those associated with over-painting and re-painting, are connected with an act of reconciliation and of reparation to atone for killing. By this means, dead eland would have been symbolically re-created in order to replace the life which had been taken, and thus to ensure their continued existence. One can sympathise with the psychological plight of the Bushman. He was doomed to continue hunting wild eland because his forebears had slain the first eland before the creation was complete, before eland had been sufficiently 'tamed' for man's use. Yet every time a hunter killed one of these animals especially loved and protected by Kaggen, he incurred the displeasure of his deity. The only solution to the unenviable situation was to make the dead eland come alive again. The eland myth recorded from Lesotho suggests that the hunter alone was incapable of effecting this re-creation, his initial attempts resulting in failure. Only when the conflicts

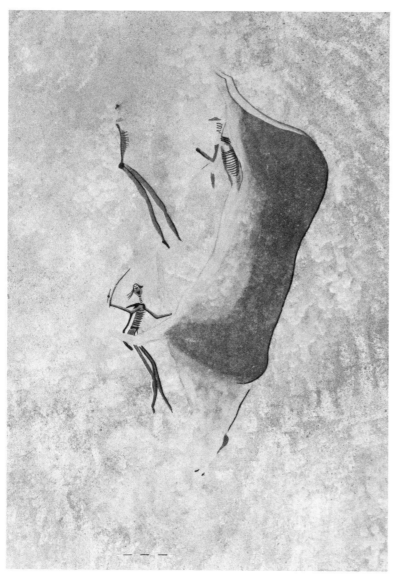

Figure 101 *Site B4*

An eland hanging head downwards is superimposed on skeleton-like human figures. One of these has unusual facial features (front view), stands cross-legged, and wears a black skin cape. The paintings are low down on a sloping part of the shelter ceiling, and are very easily overlooked.

were externalised and ritually symbolised in a social context were the drops of blood and fat from the heart of the dead eland successfully revitalised.

It seems reasonable to postulate that the Bushman artist played an important role in this propitiation ceremony, and by re-creating visible eland upon the shelter walls, Man the Hunter was reconciled with Kaggen the Creator, thereby restoring the balance of opposing forces that was so necessary for the well-being of the Bushman psyche. Through the eland, the Bushman established and maintained communication with his god. Through the eland, the eternal cycle of sacrificing life in order to conserve and promote life, was ritually expressed.[56]

References

1. Drayson 1858: 119.
2. Orpen 1874 & 1919: 142.
3. Rowland Ward 1892: 208; Shortridge 1934 (2): 610; Roberts 1951: 304; Abbott 1968 a, b.
4. Heinz 1966; Marshall 1960; Silberbauer 1965: 62-94.
5. Pager 1971: 327-9; Lewis-Williams 1972: 54-6.
6. See pp. 5, 203, 209.
7. See also Pager 1971: 328-330; Lewis-Williams 1972: 51-6.
8. The average live weight for eland has been conservatively estimated. The figures for both eland and rhebuck were obtained from Shortridge 1934 and Walker 1964. The dressed weights were obtained from a butcher.
9. See also Lévi-Strauss 1962: 34, 150; Fortes 1962: 66; Bulmer 1967.
10. Thomas 1950: 17-9; Schoeman 1957: 57-60.
11. Bleek 1924: 1-9.
12. Van der Post 1961: 235.
13. Orpen 1874; 1919: 143-5.
14. I am much indebted to Dr E. R. Leach, Department of Anthropology, University of Cambridge, for his comments dated 19/6/1965 and 15/6/1969, many of which are incorporated in the following text.
15. Bleek in Orpen 1974; Stow 1905: 117, 134; Schapera 1930: 180.
16. See Pager 1969 on Gusinde 1966.
17. Hahn 1881: 92.
18. Bleek 1935.
19. The gemsbok creation myths are not included because the distribution of gemsbok does not extend to the survey area.
20. Bleek 1875; 1924: 1-5.
21. It is of interest that the phrase *Eland of the Reed* in a Basotho praise poem symbolises childbirth (Norton 1921). According to the Bushman myth, Kaggen 'called the Eland from the middle of the reeds in which it stood. The Eland came out to eat, it went back again into the reeds when it had finished eating.' If a shoe symbolises the female vagina, and honey male semen, (see p. 177), then the association of childbirth with Eland in the Reeds is a logical metaphor.

22. Meercats in the context of this myth are probably a synonym for hunters. Meercats are a small carnivorous mammal, and live by killing animals in the same way that hunters live by killing animals. See also Vinnicombe 1972.
23. Condensed from Bleek 1924: 1-5. In this and the following myth related by Xam informants, the Bushman names Kaggen and Ni have been used in lieu of the English translations Mantis and Ichneumon.
24. Condensed from Bleek 1924: 5-9.
25. Dr E. R. Leach suggested that this may be a misplaced castration symbol. (Personal communication, 19/6/1965).
26. From the recorded text, it is not clear whether Kaggen sprinkled the blood itself, or whether he sprinkled the blood with something, possibly scented herbs, as in the recreation of dead elands performed by another legendary figure, Qwantciqutshaa. (See Orpen 1874; 1919: 148).
27. Condensed from Orpen 1874; 1919: 143-5.
28. Hubert & Mauss 1964.
29. Lévi-Strauss 1966 (3): 340.
30. Honey was also the medium through which Kaggen gave all the larger buck their colours (Bleek 1924: 10), and although reference to usage of gall in Bushman ritual is lacking, the gall of a specially slaughtered animal was smeared over the feet of the bride in Hottentot marriage ceremonies (Schapera 1930: 249). Because significant symbols often depend on verbal puns, a detailed knowledge of Bushman culture and linguistics would be necessary before a meaningful and reliable analysis of the mythology could be made. It is earnestly hoped that an ethno-mythologist will one day devote attention to the wealth of material collected by Bleek and Lloyd, as it is certain that a great deal of light could be thrown on the intricacies of Bushman thought by such a study.

    A preliminary analysis by the late Miss P. D. Beuchat and her students in the African Studies department of the University of the Witwatersrand, demonstrated a clear correlation in the relationship between the various animals in Bushman mythology and the actual kinship system expressed in Bushman social structure. (Personal communication, Beuchat 13/11/1968).
31. Werner 1907-1908, Professor van Riet Lowe echoed these sentiments in 1947 when he published two articles drawing attention to accumulating evidence that Bushmen possibly domesticated eland on occasion. In support of this suggestion, he cited the generally peaceful, homely, and ceremonial attitudes in which eland are depicted in rock paintings, as well as the close relationship between human figures and eland in scenes clearly not concerned with hunting.
    'I have therefore suggested that when the last of the Stone Age stock of this country first found their domain challenged by Bantu-speaking and other invaders, they were not in a Palaeolithic stage of development as is so widely believed, but rather in a Mesolithic or Proto-Neolithic stage and thus on the thresholds of significant developments.' (Van Riet Lowe 1947a, b).

32. Herskovits 1962: 62-8.
33. Evans-Pritchard 1956: 271.
34. Berglund 1972: 162.
35. See p. 163.
36. Orpen 1874; 1919: 147.
37. Orpen *op cit*: 142.
38. Arbousset 1852: 79.
39. Bleek 1924: 10-12.
40. Arbousset 1852: 79.
41. Hahn 1881: 81.
42. Bleek 1932: 233-249.
43. See also p. 259.

44. Bleek 1924; Schapera 1930: 139.
45. Elizabeth Marshall Thomas writes of similar behaviour among Bushmen in the Northern Kalahari. After wounding a buffalo, the hunters spent the night in the veld, eating nothing so that the buffalo would not eat and gain strength. They themselves moved around so as not to get stiff, but silently, so that the buffalo, not hearing them, would lie down and itself get stiff and sore. The following morning, they found a damp spot of the buffalo's urine containing black poison flecks. The hunter who shot the beast pushed a poisoned arrow into the spot of urine so that the buffalo would be unable to urinate again, and therefor unable to rid itself of more poison. (Marshall Thomas 1959: 192-3).
46. Bleek 1924: 10-12; Bleek 1932: 233-249. The emphasis placed on fat in this account suggests that fat was ritually important. In the creation myth, fat from the eland's heart was used to create more eland (Orpen 1874; 1919: 144), and eland fat is traditionally a component of Bushman paint (Wells 1933). Among Kalahari Bushmen, eland fat is a very highly valued gift (Marshall 1961: 242), and eland fat mixed with red ochre is used to decorate the bride in a Kung wedding ceremony (Marshall 1959: 355).
47. In addition to the Xam account of hunting eland, there are other eye witness accounts of Kalahari Bushman hunts that refer obliquely to a ritual concerning fat. After killing a zebra, the eldest of five hunters involved in the chase approached the carcase and made a deep cut in the buttock near the coccyx. The fat yellow flesh thus exposed made the Bushmen lick their lips and say things not understood by the western observer (Schoeman 1957: 26). Another description is of a successful elephant hunt, when the Bushmen were seen to throw handfuls of sand into the elephant's eyes, meanwhile 'muttering something that might be construed into thanks to the Good Spirit.' Then they opened a small part of the carcase to see if the beast was fat, 'their snake-like eyes sparkling joyfully at the result.' (Chapman 1868: 81).
48. Orpen 1874.
49. Orpen *op cit*. Arbousset records that the Basotho *purified* themselves before eating eland flesh because of the venomous juices with which they believed it to be charged (Arbousset 1852: 79).
50. Denninger 1971: Willcox 1971. My own practical experiments with pigments and media have shown that the addition of blood makes the paint appreciably more durable than a mixture without blood, which possibly explains why the red portions of eland paintings have outlasted the other colours in so many instances.
    In the southern Kalahari where there are no suitable rock surfaces for painting, a Bushwoman was observed to paint patterns on her face, thighs and shins with the blood of a freshly killed animal. No reason was obtained for this action.
51. Baines 1961; How 1962: 20; Kannemeyer 1890; Currlé 1913.
52. Moszeik 1910; Adam 1940: 93; letter in correspondence files of Natal Museum, Whyte to Bousefield, 3/11/1910.
53. York Mason 1933.
54. Marshall 1959: 355.
55. Clark 1954; Holliday 1961.
56. James 1962: 235. For further discussion of the ritual significance of eland in the rock art of southern Africa, see Vinnicombe 1972a, b and c.

Figure 102 *Site WI2*

Elongated humans gathered about an eland which appears to have thongs around the legs and blood gushing from the nose. Many of the figures stand cross-legged, they have cloven hooves in lieu of feet, and body painting which gives the effect of a split torso with horizontal riblike markings. The heads are crowned with a mop of hair or fur. Some of the figures wear waist-bands, one has a front apron, and another a three-pointed skin cloak hanging from the shoulder. The bows carried are also of

unusual design, having angular ends unknown in Southern Africa. One of the figures has a fly-switch over the shoulder, while another holds a similar object at his side. A bag with tassels and what is probably another fly-switch lies in the centre of the group. At upper right there are two seated figures, also with hooves, carrying similar weapons to those that are standing. One wears a cap with animal ears attached, and a bag lies next to them.

Figure 103 *Site Q4*

The friezes on this and the following page are on a narrow expanse of sandstone left exposed as a result of a large slab of rock having fallen from the ceiling of the overhang. They are painted so that they face one another across the fallen slab, which provides a convenient place on which to sit or lie while executing the paintings (see Figure 44).

At lower left, hunters with white faces which in some instances have faded completely, appear to stalk running and leaping eland. Above left, figures in ones, twos, and threes stand watching. At upper centre, a white male figure, his legs superimposed by an eland head, has markedly exaggerated sexual organs. To the right are other white-faced figures in groups of two and three, and at far right, male figures with white bodies decorated in orange and black have a bar across the penis. Two of these bars are decorated with tassel-like attachments. The figure at far right holds what may be a pipe or flute to his mouth. The right end of the frieze is orientated towards the interior of the shelter, and the dark colour of the rock background is probably due to smoke blackening.

Figure 104   *Site Q 4*

White-faced hunters, some in pairs, others in groups of three, run in the same direction as a herd of eland which are superimposed on eland facing in the opposite direction. A trio of figures with arms raised face the eland, while another pair crouch down holding lightly curved strung bows. Some of the hunters carry fly switches protruding from their backs, others have long tassels hanging from their bodies. Notice the head-dress and facial features of the figures on the left, and the patterning on the legs of the central hunter in the running trio. Among the eland, and in some cases overpainted by eland, there are curious anthropomorphic figures bending over in animal postures, and in some instances they have white claws in lieu of fingers. A dark red line meanders among the eland, and is apparently held by some of the bending figures. The two eland facing left immediately below the trio of running hunters with legs interlaced show evidence of over-painting. Note the additional forelimbs which are both smaller and fainter than the legs which overlie them. The scale is in 5 centimetre units.

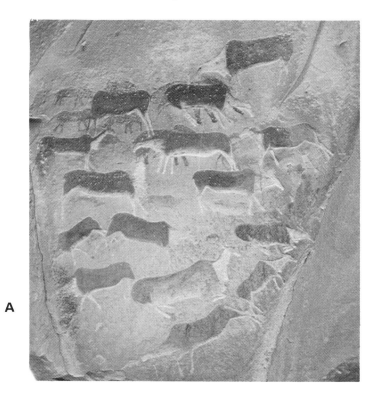

A

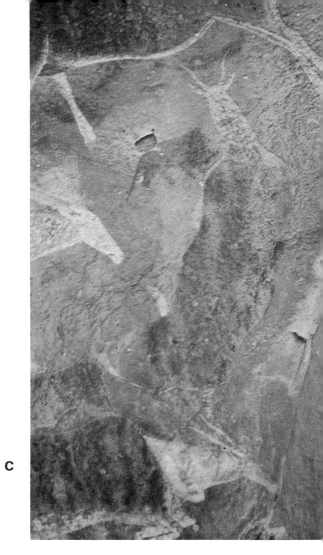

C

B

D

Figure 105 *Site B12*

A. *A beautifully preserved group of shaded polychrome eland superimposed on earlier paintings of elephant.*

B. *Detail of eland superimposed on monochrome elephant in dark red. Note the extra front limb on the central eland, a mistake which the artist has apparently attempted to erase. A correction can also be seen on the front hoof of the top right eland.*

C. *Detail of recumbent eland seen from the top. For similar top view representations, see Frontispiece and Figure 165.*

D. *Detail of eland extending its head towards an ant-eater or mongoose-like animal. There is a small white human below the neck of the eland.*

Photos: Patricia Vinnicombe.

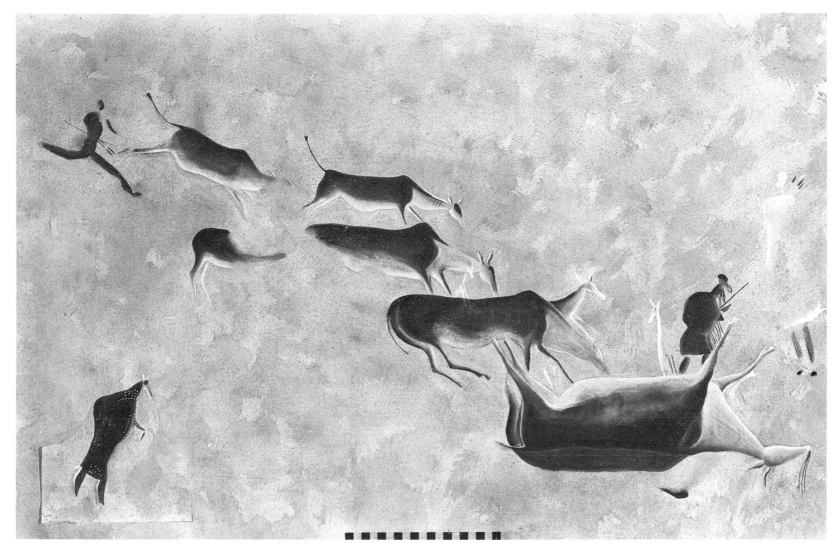

Figure 106   *Site K1*

*Eland cows, which are more slenderly built than bulls, are pursued by a hunter.
A dead eland with blood pouring from the nose has been superimposed on an earlier
eland with legs in the air — note double rump and two lines of the back. The dead
eland is painted on top of a kaross-clad figure with thongs hanging from neck and
torso. The antelope-headed figure at bottom left, which measures 17 centimetres from
tip of ear to bottom of leg, is in reality to the right of the dead eland, but has been
inserted here for economy of space.*

Figure 107 *Site P1*

At left and at right, strange winged creatures fly towards a herd of eland, some reclining, some standing. Notice the lines across the faces of the creatures at top left and centre. At bottom centre, there are two other unrealistic theriomorphs with stripes across the faces. They have tufted tails similar to the flying creatures, one has bars across the legs, and the other has claws. In the centre of the group there are what appear at first sight to be skin bags with carrying handles, and one has a bow and fly-switch protruding. On closer inspection, however, the bags are associated with eland heads, one of which has red streaks emanating from the nose, and there is also a leg, which converts the 'hunting bag' into an eland lying down and seen from the rear. Above this eland, or hunting bag, there is another curious white-headed figure with tail, and claws on the front limbs. At the lower left, a kaross-clad human stands with one foot inserted into an unidentifiable patterned object, oblong in shape with side projections. All the human figures are white-faced, and further to the left (omitted from this plate), there is another figure with bar across the penis. Dotted around the lower part of the scene are red finger smears.

Reproduced from a painted photograph.

188

Figure 108 *Site X8*

Caricature hunters with metal spears of exaggerated size close in on an eland. The colour demarcation of the eland in this group is unusual, in that the head, neck and belly, which are usually painted white, are here represented in black.

Figure 111   *Site L32*

Although the neck of the eland at upper left is no longer visible, the position of the horns indicates that the head is held high, and a human figure lying above its back gives the impression of having been tossed. Another figure holds the tail of the eland, while a third, standing in front, wards off a strange reptile. Below, a baboon-like creature with decorated human limbs grasps an object similar to that held by the

figure facing the reptile. These objects may represent fly-switches. The baboon-like creature wears 'flag' decorations on its head, as does the reptile, and the figure tossed by the eland is associated with similar motifs. A weapon with a triangular head pierces the reptile, and again, a similar weapon is seen protruding from the foreshortened antelope at lower left.

Figure 112   *Site C6*

White-faced hunters marching in a line are superimposed on an eland. The figures carry bows in hand (one balances his bow across the shoulders), and have quivers with arrows and what are probably fly-switches slung at their backs. A small figure appears to lead the way, while the rear figure has a bar across the penis.

Figure 113 *Site G3*

This pair of rhebuck with a small fawn lying down are among the paintings in the Natal Museum. The provenance is not clearly stated, but a quarried rock face on Mpongweni Mountain (site G3) marks the area where A. D. Whyte mentioned the presence of well-preserved rhebuck paintings in his 1910 report. (See p. 123) Fragments of painted rock bearing traces of other small antelope paintings were located on the shelter floor in 1960.

Rhebuck
and the smaller antelope

Paintings of the smaller antelope are second in numerical importance to eland, forming 18% of the animals recorded. Although they are occasionally depicted in red or white monochrome, the two colours are more usually combined and may be shaded or unshaded. The red and white coloration selected by the artists bears no relation to reality since the antelope are predominantly a fawn colour. As in paintings of eland, white is used as a lining for belly, legs, neck and ears, while the rump, back and shoulders are red. Sometimes mouth, eye, nostrils and hooves are indicated in black, but horns very seldom appear. The actual weights of the smaller antelope range from 20 to 60 kilograms as against an average of 900 kilograms for eland;[1] it is therefore understandable that paintings of the smaller antelope are dominated in size by eland. The smallest antelope recorded is a sleeping fawn only 1,3 centimetres long (Figure 113), while the paintings of adults average 10 centimetres.

Because of a general tendency to elongated proportions in the rock paintings, coupled with stylised use of colour and lack of horn details, it is not always easy to identify the smaller species of antelope with accuracy. Vaal rhebuck (*Pelea capreolus*) are the most common of the antelope encountered in the Drakensberg today, and account for the majority of smaller antelope in the paintings. Vaal rhebuck are more slenderly built than rooi rhebuck, also known as mountain reedbuck (*Redunca fulvorufula*), and although vaal and rooi rhebuck does may be confused because neither have horns, the rams are easily distinguished: the horns of the vaal are straight and point upwards, while those of the rooi are shorter and curve forwards. Since these distinguishing details seldom survive in the paintings, both species have been classified together for the purposes

of this study. Oribi (*Ourebia ourebi*), reedbuck (*Redunca arundinum*), blue duiker (*Cephalophus monticola*), bushbuck (*Tragelaphus scriptus*), and less frequently klipspringer (*Oreotragus oreotragus*) and steenbok (*Raphicerus campestris*), are also found in the Drakensberg region. Although none of these species has yet been identified with certainty among the fully recorded sites in the survey area, paintings of reedbuck and bushbuck have been found further north,[2] and there is an excellent rendering of a bushbuck ram in the Zwartmodder shelter near Matatiele. Their occurrence in the painted record is, however, rare, and the majority of specifically identifiable small antelope are rhebuck.

In habit rhebuck are not gregarious, and are usually seen in pairs or family groups. Although somewhat stilted in appearance when at rest, in action they leap and bound with effortless grace, their bushy tails thrown up to show the white underside. Vaal rhebuck often give themselves away by their alarm call, a series of unmistakable sharp coughing grunts. They usually run directly uphill when disturbed, then stand silhouetted against the sky, watching and grunting all the while. If they cannot follow the movements of the intruder, they may even approach more closely out of curiosity. Rooi rhebuck, on the other hand, often remain crouched like hares if they think themselves unseen, and permit one to approach very closely before bounding up with a startlingly shrill whistle at the last moment.[3] It is characteristic of both species that, after running a short distance, they always stop to look back. The early colonists believed that the only way to kill a rhebuck was by lying in wait while others drove it along runs,[4] and the Bushmen apparently also hunted by this method as well as by stalking and by taking advantage of the animal's curiosity. (Figures 196, 199, 202).

Rooi rhebuck venison is usually regarded as being more palatable than that of vaal rhebuck, and it is notable that the Bushman legends recorded from Lesotho make specific reference to rooi as opposed to vaal rhebuck. One of their mythological 'chiefs' named Qwantciqutshaa killed a rooi rhebuck and put the meat on a fire to roast, while on another occasion he had killed a rooi rhebuck and was skinning it when he was disturbed by elands

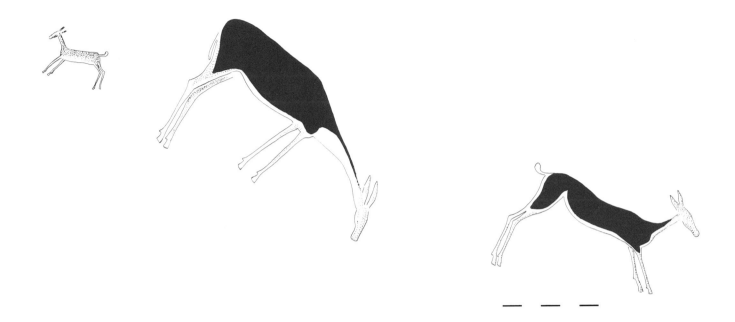

Figure 114 *Site W31, Setsoasie, Lesotho.*
Small antelope and their young.

running about. Qwantciqutshaa left the meat but took the skin, and when he returned home, asked a young girl to fetch water to wash the blood off his hands.[5]

In addition to the functional role of supplying meat and skins for clothing,[6] there is an implication in the Qwantciqutshaa myth that rhebuck were in some way connected with eland, and that an act of purification (washing of the hands) was performed after a rhebuck was killed. The ritual association between rhebuck and eland is strengthened by reference to two mythological figures, Haqwe and Canate, who were men with rhebuck heads. (Figure 223). They lived mostly under water, and tamed elands and snakes. These animal-headed figures were associated with the ceremonial curing dance the *Moqoma* or Dance of Blood,[7] and were also said to have been 'spoilt' (harmed?) at the same time as the elands.[5] The possible significance of these enigmatic remarks will be discussed later.[8]

The great majority of rhebuck paintings, like those of eland, are not associated with scenes of the chase, but unlike eland, they are not so frequently associated with man. Groups of rhebuck often appear in isolation and are shown in small family groups unconcernedly grazing, lying down at rest, curled up asleep, standing on the alert, or looking back over their shoulders. (Figure 116). Relationships between mother and young are most sensitively and delicately expressed: a newly born fawn with gangly legs is still apparently attached to its mother by the umbilical cord; a young fawn gambols by the side of its mother in a mock show of independence; the young stretch up their necks to suck from their mothers. (Figures 114, 115, 117). Fawns being suckled by their dams are shown at a number of different sites, and it is remarkable that, despite the many paintings of eland, eland calves are very seldom shown, and none in the act of sucking has yet been found.

The ethos and sense of poetry expressed in rhebuck mother-child

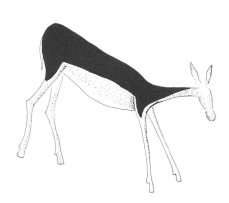
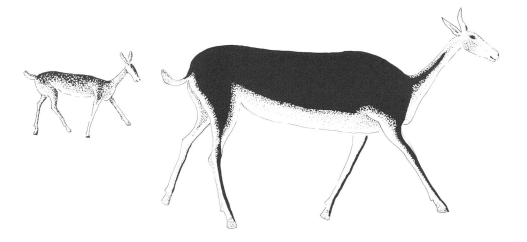

relationships is echoed by the Xam Bushman song in which spring-bok mothers sing to their children, soothing them to sleep:

> A-a-hn,
> O Springbok Child!
> Sleep for me.[9]

Another Xam description of springbok could equally be applied to paintings of rhebuck:

> The springbok mother is wont to do thus, as she trots along, when she has a springbok kid which is little, she grunts (because she protectingly takes along the child, she grunts as the child plays) . . .
> Their mothers say — "a, a, a,"
> The springbok kids say — "me, me, me,"
> while their mother says — "a, a, a" as they grunt.
> The springbok children say — "me, me, me,"
> while their mothers say — "a, a, a," as they grunting go forward.[10]

The paintings also reflect a sympathetic affinity between adult rhebuck, and it is not, in my opinion, fortuitous that the only clear rendering of mating animals yet recorded is of rhebuck.[11]

Scenes of mother-child and husband-wife relationships are notably rare among human paintings, and it is my contention that rhebuck symbolised this aspect of life for the Bushmen. Rhebuck, in short, represent the family unit. If, as I have suggested, eland symbolise the Bushman band, then rhebuck and eland paintings are expressing different but complementary aspects of Bushman social life.

The family is the primary and the most cohesive unit of Bushman society, while the band is the highest structural grouping. By far the strongest bonds Bushmen feel are those of the nuclear family — the bonds between parent and offspring, between siblings, between spouses — but it is through the band that individuals gain territorial rights and access to food resources.[12] Through the band,

Figure 115 *Site V13*

A new-born rhebuck fawn stands uncertainly on legs not yet under control. A line from the fawn's stomach may represent the umbilicus, or possibly a stream of urine. The paintings are on a narrow ledge of rock, the lower edge of which has broken away.

separate families are linked together by kinship bonds, and through the band, behaviour patterns are regulated and social control is exercised. But the individual and his family are nevertheless the stuff of which a band is made.[13] Harmony within the family is essential to harmony within the band. The family (rhebuck) is therefore essential to the effective working of the band (eland). In the myth recorded from Lesotho, man 'spoilt' the eland that Kaggen was making fit for use because he hunted them as wild animals before their creation was complete. Men with rhebuck's heads, men who had been initiated into a full understanding of Bushman cosmology through the Dance of Blood, could put matters right; they were able to 'tame' eland, to harness them, so to speak, for man's use.[5] As it would be impossible for band super-structure to function without the support of the nuclear family, so the relationship between man and eland could not be maintained without the support of rhebuck. Eland may have represented the highest moral and social order in Bushman society, but the rhebuck represented the basic family unit upon which that order was dependent.

References

1. Walker 1964: 1419, 1438, 1440, 1450.
2. Pager 1971: 20.
3. Shortridge 1934 (2): 515-9.
4. Mann 1959: 162.
5. Orpen 1874.
6. See p. 32 for reference to skins of small antelope being used as clothing.
7. See p. 314.
8. See p. 198.
9. Bleek & Lloyd 1911: 235; Bleek 1936b: 189.
10. Bleek & Lloyd 1911: 245-7.
11. Lee & Woodhouse 1970: Plate 21; Pager 1971: 20, Fig. 26. Fig. 39 in this book shows what is possibly a stallion mounting a mare, but this is a late painting.
12. Marshall 1960: 329, 340; Marshall 1965: 258.
13. Silberbauer 1965: 68-76; Heinz 1966: 48-50.

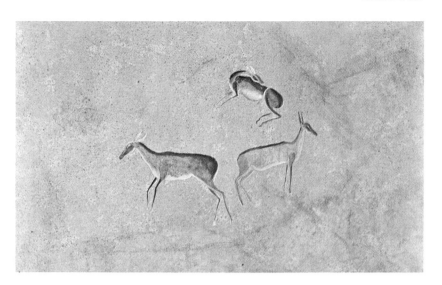

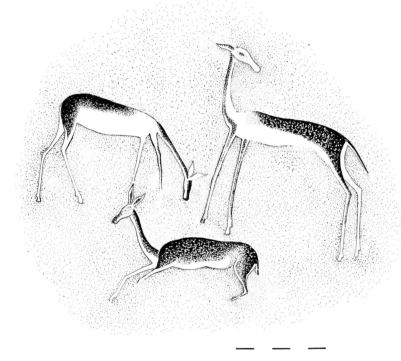

Figure 116 *Site U6*
Delicately painted rhebuck in a variety of restful poses.

Figure 117 (*see opposite*)

Above: *Rhebuck and their young. These paintings have been executed on top of earlier antelope which have been omitted from this rendering. Site U3.*

Below: *Bushwomen and children, Kalahari desert. Note the facial scarifications of the woman on the left, and the pendant on the forehead and nose of the woman on the right (see also Figure 166).*

Bushman family life is rarely shown in the paintings although rhebuck does with their young feature relatively frequently.

Figure 117

Single woman with child.

Photo: — Pat Carter.

Two women and child.

Photo: — L. Fourie, with the kind permission of the Museums of Man and Science, Johannesburg.

Figure 118 *Site W23*

A file of galloping hartebeest. For economy of space, the animal on the right has been moved closer in than it appeared on the rock face.

Cape or Red Hartebeest
(Alcelaphus caama)

The red hartebeest is an ungainly animal. It has a long narrow head made longer by a boney coronet from which the horns spring, first straight up, then upwards, outwards and forwards, then sharply back. It is a deep chestnut red, with a large white patch behind. It has an awkward rocking-horse-like gallop, but can move quite fast in spite of its ugly gait.[1]

The red hartebeest is now extinct in Natal in the wild state, once having been numerous. The size of the herds was governed by the nature of the country and the grazing, and varied from a few individuals to large numbers together. As recently as 1893, seven years after the first white farmers settled in the Underberg area, approximately 250 head of hartebeest still grazed on the plain then known as the Hartebeest Flats, lying between the Mzimkhulu and Ngwangwana rivers. By 1916, the numbers had been reduced to 16, and the last cow was killed by dogs in 1925. With encroaching civilization, many hartebeest retreated to the high grazing on top of the escarpment between the Sani Pass and Giant's Castle. In 1915, the numbers were estimated at between five and seven hundred, but a very severe snow-storm in the winter of 1918 completely wiped out the entire herd.[2] (Figures 1, 59).

The Bushmen usually portrayed hartebeest in small groups of from two to nine, seldom directly associated with hunting activities, and often in inactive poses including foreshortened views. The distinctive features accentuated by the artists are the long face of the hartebeest, the peculiar horns, the high withers as compared with the somewhat pinched rump, and the slender legs with small fetlocks and hooves.[3] The colours used on hartebeest are red, white and black, with red always predominating. Many of the hartebeest which appear as red monochromes today were probably originally bichrome, the white pigment having faded away. This accounts for the peculiar 'bite' out of the rump in some of the paintings, as this area would originally have been painted white to represent the marking typical of this antelope. (Figure 120). It is of interest that the Xam Bushmen always describe hartebeest as being red in colour: 'the Hartebeest ran forward, while his body was red',[4] and their mythology records that Kaggen once gave the Hartebeest some of the comb of young bees: 'That is why the Hartebeest is red, because the comb of young bees which he ate was red. So he became like the comb of young bees.'[5]

Hartebeest as well as eland had a special place in the affection of the Xam deity:

People say that Kaggen first made the Eland; the Hartebeest was one whom he made after the death of his Eland. That is why he did not love the Eland and the Hartebeest a little, he loved them dearly, for he made his heart of the Eland and the Hartebeest.

The Gemsbok was one whom he did not love so well, yet he was fond of the Gemsbok. For there are Hares which we see when we shoot Gemsbok, and those Hares do not stir, because they want us to kill them. We look at them because they are his Hares. He wants us to kill the Hares, in order that the Gemsbok may live.[6]

The fact that the life of specified antelope was in some way regarded as sacrosanct by the Bushmen is borne out by the above testimony; the Creator was concerned more with the preservation of their lives than with their destruction. Indeed, the close association between Kaggen and hartebeest which resulted in the re-creation of a dismembered hartebeest is told in dramatic form in one of the stories recorded from the Xam:

Kaggen pretended to be a dead hartebeest in order to trick some children into cutting him up and carrying him home. When the children did this, they were alarmed to discover that the flesh was animated, so they dropped the pieces and ran away. But the flesh sprang together, each piece joining itself on to the next, until the animal was whole again and became a man. In this form, Kaggen pursued the children who, fatigued and with 'burning hearts' decided to stay at home rather than hunt for food.[7]

The intimate relationship between Kaggen and the eland has already been discussed, but of the hartebeest, which held second place in his esteem, there is unfortunately very little information. What is preserved is nevertheless revealing:

The Hartebeest and the Eland are things of Kaggen; therefore they have magic power.

Kaggen is used to go with the Hartebeest when he walks about; Hartebeest's head resembles Kaggen's head, therefore it belongs to Kaggen. A woman who has a young child does not eat Hartebeest, nor does she spring over the Hartebeest's head, for Kaggen would press down the hollow of her child's head, and the child would die, if she did so.

So our parents used to tell the women who had young children to cut out a piece of the Hartebeest's foot between the toes, to thread it upon a sinew and make a charm and put it on the little

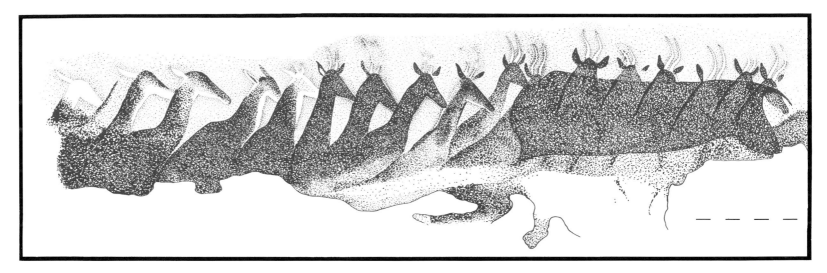

Figure 119 *Site V10*

A row of hartebeest heads has been overpainted by a later animal body. To the right, but not included in this reproduction, the superpositions become confused. The group includes other hartebeest, an eland, and running human figures. There are also a series of white strokes, some unusual cross-hatching, and curious leaf-like objects patterned with veins. Although the paintings are on a projecting ledge of rock the lower edge of which has exfoliated, the bodies of the hartebeest appear to have been intentionally left incomplete.

child. For these are things upon which Kaggen sits, and Kaggen would smell the thing's scent on the child and would not press in its head.[8]

Further magical properties were noted by Sparrman who observed that his Hottentots carefully collected a wax-like substance from a pore below the eye of a slain hartebeest, keeping it in a piece of skin as a rare and excellent medicine.[9]

In a site on the Tsoelikane river, there is a remarkable frieze of hartebeest heads painted in two sections on a narrow ledge of rock. They are associated with human figures on all fours and other unusual leaf-like objects and white lines of unknown significance. (Figure 119). The bodies of the antelope were apparently never included, the focus of interest being purely on the heads, which brings to mind that hartebeest heads 'belonged' to Kaggen because of the resemblance they bore to his own head. The only other isolated animal heads so far located among the paintings are those of rhebuck, but the significance of these is unknown.

While it is impossible from the fragmentary evidence available to determine the significance of hartebeest in the structure of Bushman values, and thus to deduce the motivation underlying the paintings, the rarity of hartebeest in hunting scenes is notable. The supernatural properties attributed to them by the Xam Bushmen of the Cape, and the close bond which linked their god Kaggen to the eland as well as to the hartebeest, cannot be overlooked. Although hartebeest constitute only 3% of the total number of paintings in the survey area, they are the third most popular antelope depicted (Table 3), and are also listed as the third species to be created by Kaggen in the eastern mountain region.[10] In Xam Bushman lore, it is stated that Kaggen loved the eland best, followed by the hartebeest and then the gemsbok. The subject matter preferences expressed in the area occupied by the Mountain Bushmen, to whom the gemsbok was unknown, suggest that Kaggen preferred first the eland (35%), then the rhebuck (18%), and thirdly the hartebeest (3%). The hartebeest would therefore hold a similar position to that of the gemsbok among the Xam, that is,

Kaggen had a special fondness for the hartebeest. Kaggen was intimately concerned with their protection and preservation even if he was not as closely identified with them as with his first creation, the eland.

References

1. Handley 1961.
2. Pringle 1963.
3. See Roberts 1951: 282, for descriptive notes on the hartebeest.
4. Bleek 1911: 13.
5. Bleek 1924: 10.
6. Bleek 1924: 12.
7. Bleek 1911: 3-17.
8. Bleek 1924: 10.
9. Sparrman 1786: 201.
10. Orpen 1874. The correlation between the myth in which hartebeest were the third animal to be created, and the quantitative analysis of the paintings which shows the hartebeest to be third in popularity, is likely to be no more than coincidence. The same myth states that snakes were created second, yet paintings of snakes appear sixth on the numerical list.

Figure 120

These paintings of red hartebeest are on a slab of rock in the Natal Museum that was removed from a site in the Bushman's Nek area in 1910. The light-coloured pigment used for painting the white rump of the hartebeest, as well as legs and horns, is very faded.

Figure 121 *Site P1*
A herd of hartebeest

Figure 122   *Sites P3, P4, P5*

The three painted shelters at the base of the sandstone exposure on Thule are marked with arrows. The overhang on the left (triangular-shaped shadow) could almost be classed as a cave, and is large enough to provide shelter for 1 000 sheep in winter snow-storms. The high sandstone face is pitted with holes which provide resting places for numerous birds, including a flock of the rare bald ibis, Geronticus calvus.

Photo: Pat Carter.

Figure 123 *Site W23*

This is the only site within the survey area where paintings of wildebeest or gnu have been positively identified.

Black Wildebeest or Gnu

(Connochaetes gnou)

Black wildebeest or gnu are somewhat idiosyncratic in appearance, having none of the grace associated with most antelope. They have bristly facial hair extending to the neck and chest which gives them a shaggy, unkempt look. In addition to an eccentric appearance, gnu are characterised by great curiosity and ritualised behaviour patterns. When disturbed, they prance about, paw the ground, probe the earth with their horns, and thrash their long white tails. If man approaches too close, they snort and dash off a short distance, then suddenly wheel about to face the intruder and resume their mannered antics. Gnu are gregarious animals, for they not only seek one another's company, but also frequently consort with zebra (commonly referred to as quagga by the early colonists), and with ostriches.[1, 2]

Wildebeest are extremely rare in the rock painting record. There is only one site within the survey area where they are certainly depicted (Figure 123), and one other where an animal that is possibly a wildebeest is pursued by two horsemen. (Figure 124). Both scenes are in black monochrome, and belong to the latest painting phase.

The lack of wildebeest paintings is curious in that this animal was formerly among the most prolific of the game animals in the area, and furnished Natal's pioneer settlers with abundant meat as well as hides for thongs and whips. Black wildebeest were, in fact, so identified with the history of the province that they were incorporated in the Natal coat-of-arms. Hunters have recorded that they became so tired of shooting wildebeest, that for sport they chased them on horseback and killed them with spears.[3] Indeed, overhunting and interference with grazing patterns resulted in the wildebeest becoming extinct in Natal and East Griqualand, although some have recently been re-introduced into the Drakensberg game reserves.

The original distribution of wildebeest certainly extended into the mountain region, for Gardiner records having come across several small groups when traversing the headwaters of the Mzim-khulu river in September 1835. Later in his journey, on the northern tributaries of the Mzimvubu, there were 'herds of gnu in all directions', in one of which he counted thirty-seven.

> On riding towards them they often stand and snort for some time, and then suddenly plunge, kick up, and lash their tails, and in an instant are off at full gallop, making the dust fly as they sweep over the hills . . . .
> When seen at full gallop with their heads down, their long white tails floating in the wind, and the necks and forelegs thickly covered with long shaggy hair, they have a most ferocious appearance.[4]

Continuing over the open downs skirted by mountains which are typical of East Griqualand, Gardiner counted seventy-six gnu from the spot where he stood, but remarked that there must have been many more in the neighbourhood.

In March 1864, Major Hook, when hunting on the Cedarville Flats in East Griqualand, shot forty wildebeest in one day as well as several hartebeest, wild boars and lions.[5] All the early settlers with whom I have spoken testify to the great herds of wildebeest that formerly roamed the plains of East Griqualand; in fact, the original name for the Cedarville Flats was Wildebeest Vlachte.[6]

The Bushman hunters, too, are known to have exploited this animal to the full. An aged Mosotho informant remembered Bushmen hunting wildebeest between Qacha's Nek and Matatiele,[7] and on the western side of Lesotho, Arbousset[8] described how Bushmen drove a herd of gnu towards an ambush they had previously erected. Slices of flesh from a slaughtered animal were roasted in an oven excavated from an ant-hill, and a brush made from gnu hair was used to mop up the fat and juice. One of the familiar phrases recorded from among these Bushmen was 'See! The gnus! Run and turn them!', and when praying to their Supreme Being they pleaded:

> Kaggen, lead me to a male gnu . . .
> Kaggen, bring a male gnu under my arrows.[9]

In addition to providing meat, wildebeest furnished the raw material for a number of artefacts. A Mosotho woman saw Bushmen making a spoon from the horns of gnu with which they ate thick meat soup, while another informant saw Bushmen painting pictures on the rocks at Sehonghong shelter (Figure 55) with brushes made of hair from the tail of a gnu.[10] This fact was corroborated by a Thembu named Silayi, who stated that the Bushmen of the Transkei painted with brushes made from hairs taken from the tail or mane of a gnu.[11] Later horse hair was used.

Figure 124 *Site G3*

An animal that possibly represents a wildebeest is pursued by two horsemen wearing brimmed hats. The painting at top is an example of the blue effect obtained by mixing black and white pigments, or by over-painting white with black. (see p. 141)

Taking into account the extensive use made of wildebeest, the almost total avoidance of this animal in the paintings is difficult to explain except on grounds of ritual avoidance or taboo. A search of the myths and legends recorded by Bleek and Lloyd hints at one possible explanation.[12] The story *Why the Wildebeest has a Light Tail*, makes it clear that wildebeest were regarded as a great hindrance when hunting quagga, the flesh of which was highly esteemed. According to this legend, not only did the wildebeest interfere with the hunter's bow-string and arrow-heads to make his aim inaccurate and ineffectual, but they would also go in among the quagga, pretending to be one of them with a white tail made of dried grass. When the quagga were driven towards concealed bowmen, the wildebeest would run in front and trample upon the hunter's screen of bushes, or even upon the hunter himself, thus ruining any chance of procuring the desired prey.

It would seem, then, that even if the wildebeest was hunted and utilised for numerous purposes, its behaviour also symbolised hindrance and interference, or that which thwarted plans and sapped strength. Above all, the wildebeest was an animal which resorted to subterfuge; it lived among other animals under false pretences. The significance of these qualities in terms of human relations is more fully discussed later; it suffices to suggest here that certain categories of kin were symbolically likened to wildebeest, and that both were subject to rules of avoidance.

The fact that selected animals are still the subject of strict avoidance rules among extant Bushmen is borne out by recent investigations in the Kalahari desert. Gwi adolescents of both sexes are subject to strict taboos on eating the meat of large male buck,[13] and among the Ko, there is a wide range of meat avoidances associated with age groups.[14] A major part of Ko puberty ceremonies is devoted to acquainting the candidates with the restrictions imposed upon them, and the consumption of meat is entirely forbidden during the period of ceremonial seclusion. At prescribed times after initiation, some of these prohibitions are lifted, and special ceremonies are performed to release the affected persons from the taboos to which they are subjected. Two girls being released from a hartebeest taboo were treated with a piece of meat from the animal they were henceforth permitted to eat. The meat was pounded together with herbal charms, and the mixture was ritually passed around the girl's head, under her left arm-pit, and then rubbed between the breasts. The ceremony for males is somewhat different, but is also associated with the potent medicines believed by the Bushmen to emanate from sweat.

Rock-paintings showing women standing with arms raised to expose an arm-pit may perhaps be a similar type of ceremony (Figures 98, 125), and it is quite possible that at least some of the animal paintings were executed as a means of instructing initiates and enforcing the meat taboos which regulated their pattern of living.

Increase in age among the Ko Bushmen is associated with a progressive relaxation of taboos, but there are certain categories of carnivorous animals, as well as rabbits and ducks, that may never be eaten by women at any time. The steenbok, too, is completely taboo to all males below the age of thirty, and all females below the age of forty.[14] The question as to why particular animals are singled out for avoidance could no doubt be answered by the Ko themselves, but in the absence of direct information, it is of interest that Laurens van der Post describes special qualities attributed to steenbok by an unnamed group of Kalahari Bushmen.[15] Despite the fact that they hunt and snare steenbok, which are among the most numerous of the antelope in the Central Kalahari Game Reserve,[16] the Bushmen believe that this graceful, solitary little buck is protected by a special 'magic'. An old Bushman, when questioned about this 'magic', contrasted the characteristic behaviour of steenbok with that of other buck. Steenbok do not run when danger threatens, but hide until the last moment. Even when they eventually dart away, they stop after a short run to look back. Steenbok often return to the place they vacated, as they are notoriously tenacious of their territory.[17] In the combined words of Van der Post and the Bushman:

> The steenbok would stand there all the time "looking so nicely and acting so prettily" that the person who had come hunting it would begin to feel "he must look nicely at the steenbok and act prettily too". The person who stood watching would suddenly find there was "a steenbok person" behind him who "feeling he was looking nicely at the little buck, wanted him to act nicely and prettily too". When the person who had come to kill the steenbok fitted the arrow to his bow and aimed to shoot, the steenbok person behind him "pulled his arm and made him miss". Yes, that was the magic of the steenbok; it had a steenbok person to protect it.[15]

The Kung Bushmen, who are neighbours of the Ko, believe certain animals to be endowed with a supernatural quality termed *n!ow*, but according to the Kung, steenbok have positively no *n!ow* at all.[18] The correspondences or differences of quality attributed to this small antelope by the various Bushman groups are difficult to ascertain, but it is of particular interest that despite the fact that steenbok are hunted, the Bushmen invest this animal with an 'essence' or 'power' which is suggested, at least in part, by the

Figure 125 *Site W23*
A figure with arm raised is inspected by a companion wearing a knobbed head-dress.

appearance and behaviour of the animal.[19] These special qualities are in turn metaphorically related to human behaviour in general, and among the Ko, to avoidance relationships in particular. There are well documented parallels therefore, to support the suggestion that among the Mountain Bushmen, wildebeest may have been one of the animals singled out for taboo and avoidance. Alternatively, as in the case of steenbok among the Kung, the wildebeest may have been entirely lacking in qualities such as *n!ow*, which would have eliminated it from any positive role in the ritual hierarchy. In both instances, the net result would have been expressed by acts of avoidance rather than positive acts of commission

Soxa is another concept prevalent among the Heikum Bushmen which is relevant to systems of avoidance. *Soxa* relates only to the meat of specified animals which has to be shared according to prescribed rules and which is subject to avoidance under certain conditions; if the *soxa* rules are broken the efficacy of arrow poison would be impaired, and future hunting would be unsuccessful.[20] It will be remembered that according to the Xam legend, wildebeest also had a detrimental effect on hunting:

> [The Wildebeest] came to blunt the tips of the . . . arrowheads. He untied the . . . bowstring, he strung on his own entrails . . . The Wildebeest ran in front . . ., and he saw the . . . screen of bushes. He ran up to it, he went and stamped on it, crushing the hunter[21] as he trod it down.[22]

Social avoidances symbolised by animals or by meat and other taboos are by no means limited to Bushman culture,[23, 24] and although the metaphorical structure has not yet been properly analysed, it is significant that the praise poems of the Zulu, which refer to a great number of game animals, also completely avoid mention of wildebeest as well as zebra.[25] Zebra were certainly among the animals which migrated into the Thukela basin from the Orange Free State during winter,[26] and herds were also found in East Griqualand.[27] As yet, however, no zebra paintings have been recognised in the survey area, and from the entire Drakensberg, only one fragmentary picture of a zebra is known. This is at Giant's Castle, where it occurs in the same shelter as one of the rare wildebeest paintings.[28] Paintings of ostriches too, are notably rare, despite the fact that beads of ostrich-egg have frequently been found in excavations.[29] Since ostriches, zebra and wildebeest often consort together in herds, these animals may, in the minds of the Bushmen, have been linked in the expression of social avoidances.

The behaviour between individuals within Bushman bands is characterised by avoidances based on age, sex, kin and name relationships. Examples can be observed in such behaviour as who an individual Bushman may or may not marry, next to whom he may or may not sit, who he may address by name, to whom he may hand things or make gifts, with whom he may joke and express familiarity. Even within the joking relationship, which is the most relaxed of their behaviour patterns, there are many subtle nuances of conduct that are or are not condoned. Parents-in-law are the object of the strictest avoidance relationships, particularly between those of the opposite sex. A daughter-in-law avoids her father-in-law, while a son-in-law avoids his mother-in-law, and these avoidances are extended to all those with whom the in-laws are on terms of familiarity. In particular, anything pertaining to sexual matters is absolutely taboo. The Bushmen not only respect but actually fear the persons with whom they are on avoidance terms, and the etiquette of proper behaviour is taken seriously even by the very young.[30]

It is of particular interest that each individual among the Kung is taught and can recite an ancestral list of names to which kinship terms are linked. Although the Bushmen questioned did not know exactly how the list was compiled, they said 'the old people' knew, and in following the teaching of their forebears, they knew how to regulate their behaviour towards each named person according to the prescribed homonymous pattern.[31] Name relationships are another important factor in the social system of the Kung, for they believe name and personality to be closely connected. When one is specifically named *after* a person, as opposed to having the same name *as* a person, one partakes of that person's entity in some way and to some degree.[32] If it is accepted that pre-literate societies tend to classify animals according to their own social conceptions,[33] it is tempting to interpret the 'animal incantations' referred to by Bleek[34] as analogous to the ancestral list of names which governs the behaviour of Kung individuals. The 'animal incantations' of the Xam Bushmen consisted of the names of different animals recited in succession, and different versions were given by different Bushmen.

Whether the ancestral list of names which regulates social relations among the Kung, and the successive recitation of animal names among the Xam can be linked or not, the fact remains that there are many examples of avoidance in Bushman social relations which reflect the structure of their society. While I do not necessarily suggest a direct equation between, for instance, wildebeest and mother-in-law, or zebra and mother-in-law's brother, the ethnographic record, supported by documented mythology, suggests that there may have been an analogous association between wildebeest and social avoidance categories in the minds of the Southern Bushmen. The nature of a wildebeest leads it to interfere with hunting practices; the nature of a mother-in-law leads her to interfere in domestic affairs; and since the very nature of a Bushman is to avoid friction at any cost,[35-37] the social solution was to avoid the qualities expressed by wildebeest. The taboo applied not only to wildebeest themselves, but also to the animals with which wildebeest were on terms of familiarity; hence the avoidance of paintings of wildebeest as well as of their companions, the zebra and the ostrich.

References

1. Walker 1964: 1448.
2. Shortridge 1934: 463-7.
3. Roberts 1951: 279.
4. Gardiner 1836: 347-8.
5. Hook 1908: 127.
6. Sanderson 1860: 338.
7. How 1962: 39.
8. Arbousset 1852: 351.
9. Arbousset 1852: 367.
10. Ellenberger 1953: 87, 148.
11. Stanford 1910.
12. Bleek 1924: 58.
13. Silberbauer 1965: 61.
14. Heinz 1966: 137-142.
15. Van der Post 1961: 36, 52-3.
16. Silberbauer 1965: 36.
17. Walker 1964: 1452.
18. Marshall 1957a: 235.
19. See also Douglas 1972.
20. Fourie 1925: 55-6.
21. In order to avoid confusion, I have referred to the 'mouse' in Bleek's translation as 'hunter' in this text.
22. Bleek 1924: 58.
23. Bulmer 1967; Tambiah 1969.
24. Douglas 1966, 1972a, b.
25. Cope 1968.
26. See p. 6.
27. Hook 1908: 336, 343.
28. Wildebeest Shelter, Giant's Castle Game Reserve. Both the zebra and the wildebeest were first recorded by Louis Tylor in 1893. The original tracing is housed in the Pitt-Rivers Museum, Oxford.
29. Wells 1933; Willcox 1957b; Carter 1970c; Pager 1971: 15.
30. Heinz 1966: 167-180; Marshall 1957b.
31. Marshall 1957b: 14.
32. Marshall 1957b: 22.
33. Douglas 1972.
34. Bleek 1875: No. 57.
35. Heinz 1966: 189.
36. Silberbauer 1965: 67.
37. Marshall 1961.

Figure 126 *Site W19*
A figure with arms clasped across chest turns her head away from a companion.

Figure 127 *Site W23*

A Bushman hunter at right takes aim at a feline while his companions flee in alarm. Notice the short bows and spare arrows carried in the hand. Some arrow heads are triangular, suggesting metal, while others are elongated, suggesting bone. Two of the figures have what appear to be broad-bladed spears with short handles thrust into a band at the waist. All the hunters save one wear the knobbed head-dress observed on paintings of riders and stock-raiders. (See Figures 26, 28, 54, 86.)

214

Predators:
a symbol of aggression

The sample of 3 551 animal paintings studied includes 37 representations of large felines, of which most are specifically recognisable as lion and leopard. Other species of predators are rarely depicted.

At a site overlooking the Tsoelike river in Lesotho (site W23), wild dogs are shown attacking a hunter, and a black-backed jackal is featured in a small shelter on the Leqoa. Further examples of what may be jackals occur at two other sites on the headwaters of the Mkhomazi river (sites F7 and F13), and small carnivorous mammals belonging to the meercat or mongoose families appear sporadically but never in any detail. The small carnivores were not, apparently, particularly significant in the imagery of the Bushman artist; he was far more preoccupied with the larger and more aggressive species that were a threat to his life.

Lions and leopards are now extinct within the Drakensberg region, but were once the natural predators of the game and the humans that inhabited the area. Paintings of felines occur at 14% of the fully recorded shelters, yet in number they total only 1% of the wild animals depicted. This indicates that although individual felines were not represented in great numbers, the theme is consistently repeated at shelters throughout the area.

The paintings are predominantly in red and white or yellow and white bichrome, and less frequently in shaded polychrome or black monochrome. Usually the lions and leopards are shown in pursuit of hunters whose terror is self-evident (Figures 127, 131), or they are isolated singly or in pairs and not apparently engaged in any particular activity. One scene depicts a predator amidst a troop of terrified baboons, in another two lionesses follow a trail to what may be a trap, and in a third a pair of leopards are apparently eating their prey, although the object of their attentions is now somewhat indistinct and is possibly an earlier painting. (Figures 129, 132, 135). Two unusual compositions show a group of people gathered round

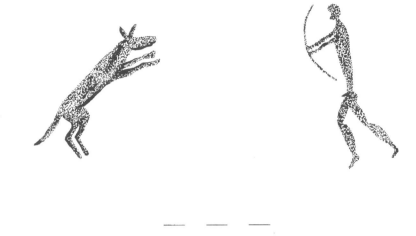

Figure 128 *Site W23*

A hunter holds a wild dog at bay. It was apparently one of a pack, for remains of similar animals, too faded for certain record, are included in the original composition.

an animal with cat-like characteristics; in both cases the humans appear to be performing antics round rather than directly attacking the animal. (Figures 130, 133).

The Xam Bushman folklore collected by Bleek and Lloyd clearly indicates that lions occupied a prominent position both in the world of fable and in astrological mythology. The Pointers to the Southern Cross were named 'Male Lions', while Alpha, Beta and Gamma Crucis were 'Lionesses'. These Lions were the subject of complicated legends which included adventures with other personified animals such as a blue crane, a crow, a tortoise and a hare, but the relation, if any, of these events to celestial phenomena is not clear, nor is it known whether paintings were in any way connected with the elements of sidereal worship practised by the Southern Bushmen.[1]

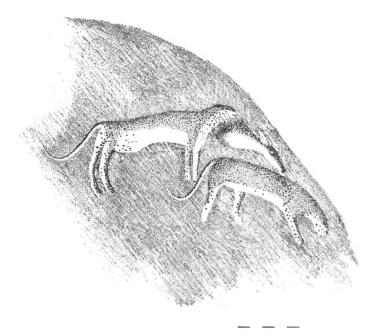

Figure 129 *Site W8*

These leopards are painted in a niche of rock low down on the shelter wall. It is uncertain whether the antelope head is intended to represent prey, or whether it is part of an earlier painting.

Despite the folk stories often portraying the lion as a vanquished party whose strength does not necessarily make him the equal of other cleverer animals,[2] in daily life the lion was obviously greatly feared. A legend in which a tortoise exhorts a lion to attack an encampment at night describes in dramatic detail the depredations to which Bushmen were sometimes subjected:

> O Lion, let us go ... seeking Bushmen's huts, that we may steal up to them ... Thou shalt take out for us that big man, he will be fat ... Ye will gently steal up ... One man lies listening with his ears, he is listening at night; he does not sleep, for he sleeps peeping out of his eyes, he is listening ... to the night's dangers ... He lies listening whether a beast of prey is walking about at night, it smelling seeks a thing which it can kill ... It will steal up to the hut ... then it snatches up the man, it runs off with the man, it runs penetrating the night, it runs into the night's blackness,

while other men call behind its back, while it runs away carrying off the man ... (While [the Lion] thus goes into the night, other people are throwing at his back with fire ... for they feel the other [man] is disappearing into the night, while the Lion holds him in his mouth, inside the Lion's mouth. The Lion runs biting him, the Lion runs along biting him to death. As the Lion runs off with him, [the man] opens his mouth, and the Lion feels that he is going along screaming. Therefore the Lion bites him to death, that he may be quiet, for other people would run after the Lion, if they heard the [man screaming].) ... It runs along, it goes and stops, it lies down, it walks on, as it goes carrying, as it goes carrying the man into the bushes. It talks, carrying the man into the bushes' middle, it puts the man down in the bushes' middle, it eats the man's flesh, it devours the man's fat.

> Other people walk in fear of the Lion, for they feel that the Lion may again come to them ...[3]

Although no paintings of attacks on encampments have been found within the survey area, Victor Ellenberger has recorded two splendid scenes in western Lesotho. One of these from Maphelase[4] shows a lion approaching a cowering group of people in a hut or skerm, while in a cruder section of the scene a lion is actually entering a skerm. Another painting from Theko Khotso, Thaba Bosiu, also depicts a lion entering a shelter. The surrounding spoor indicates that it has already made a thorough reconnaissance, and an escaping human figure flees for its life.

Among the Ko Bushmen, lions and leopards are classified as 'large biting animals' as opposed to antelope which are 'large non-biting animals',[5] and it is clear from both the painted and written record that aggression was regarded as one of the main characteristics of carnivores.

The Xam Bushmen had many avoidance rules relating to predators which had to be strictly observed.[6] The lion was never to be mentioned directly by name because it was believed that certain flies that 'belonged' to lions would tell the lion whenever it heard a Bushman mocking or 'playing with' its name. The lion would then retaliate when least expected. A child should never chase away a pestilential fly by forcibly expelling breath through the nostrils, for again the fly would go and tell the lion that the child had insulted it by insinuating that the lion had a bad smell. The beast of prey would delay action until the child was bigger and would provide a better meal:

> Therefore it happens when we are grown-up, we come unexpectedly upon a lion which is lying down. Then our mouth is black with fear, with terror, with alarm. Our mouth is not light on account of our terror.[7]

Figure 130   *Site T1*

A group of figures gathered around an animal with a mane, claws and long tufted tail. Some of the people are armed, and could be interpreted as attacking the animal, while others nonchalantly sit facing one another or stand cross-legged. Behind the feline there is an animal-headed figure, and at the top left, another horned figure carries arrows or spears over the shoulder. The paintings are in black, orange and white. The felid measures 20 centimetres from nose to tip of tail.
Traced in 1959, assisted by Jean Hewlett.

If lion footprints were seen by children, they were not to inspect the spoor closely, but were to walk on as though nothing had been noticed. When reporting the spoor to their parents, they should simply hold up a hand with all fingers extended in representation of claws, or they could mention the lion only by using certain indirect names such as 'hair' or 'lighting in', the significance of which was understood by all.[8]

Lions, it was believed, were able to turn themselves into other animals in order to deceive the Bushmen. They could be wild cats during the day so that their footprints would not be recognised, but become lions at night in order to drag people from their sleeping places. Or else the lion could transform itself into a hartebeest which the Bushmen would want to hunt. Then suddenly when the hunters were in front of it, the hartebeest would turn into a lion — 'Then terror nearly kills us when we see it is a lion.'[9] Sorcerers, too, could adopt the guise of lions, and could even grow lion's hair when exorcising harmful things from the body of a patient.[10] It was also believed that strange happenings, or the presence and calls of certain animals, could act as a warning that lions were about. If a predator was suspected of being in the vicinity, camping places were carefully selected and a fire was kept burning all night — 'the fire's smell will make it think that some-one is awake.'[11]

When Bushmen came across a lion's kill, they were not to carry all the meat home, but were to leave the head and the backbone. If something was not left for the lion it would return to punish them for their greed.[12]

In view of the number of rules and prohibitions connected with predators in Bushman belief, the possibility of similar concepts being connected with paintings of predators is very real. For instance, if a lion was seen in the vicinity, the image may have been represented on the rocks in lieu of mentioning it by name, or, if someone inadvertently offended a lion, it may have been thought that subsequent disasters could be avoided by executing or commissioning a painting. The scenes of people gathered round but not attacking felines may be associated with sorcerers whose familiars were lions, or sorcerers who 'grew lion's hair on their backs' and bit with their teeth.[13] It is probable, however, that the associations were more abstract: 'When he wants to kill us . . . a lion is a thing which . . . makes things happen which we do not understand.'[14] Medicine men would take 'lions' out of people in order to cure them, and 'cats' too, could bring illness and cause harm.[15] These records of Xam Bushman attitudes towards the larger carnivores suggest that lions and leopards were associated with harm as opposed to benefit, with disease as opposed to health, insecurity not security, malevolence rather than benevolence, with death as opposed to life. The essence symbolised by carnivores — the large biting animals — was the opposite of the essence symbolised by herbivores — the large non-biting animals. Antelope were regarded as a constructive force in Bushman symbolism. Lions and leopards were destructive.[16]

References

1. Bleek 1875: No. 26.
2. Bleek 1929.
3. Bleek 1936, B.S. 10: 169-172. The section in parenthesis comes at the end of the story related by the Bushman, but for clarity the sequence has been altered here.
4. Ellenberger collection, Musée de l'Homme, Paris, No. 56, 138.
5. Heinz 1973, personal communication.
6. Bleek 1932, B.S. 6: 47-63.
7. Bleek 1932, B.S. 6: 60.
8. Bleek 1932, B.S. 6: 57, 61.
9. Bleek 1932, B.S. 6: 62-3.
10. Bleek 1936, 10 (2): 131, 132.
11. Bleek 1932, B.S. 6: 52.
12. Bleek 1932, B.S. 6: 55-7.
13. Bleek 1935, B.S. 9: 1-2.
14. Bleek 1932, B.S. 6: 59.
15. Bleek 1935, B.S. 9: 2-3.
16. See also Lévi-Strauss 1968: 224.

Figure 131 *Site XII*
The hunter hunted.

Figure 132 *Site U11*

The uppermost of the two lionesses follows a trail of white spots towards unidentifiable paintings which possibly represent a trap. Above left are faded human figures with accoutrements lying around. The lower lioness is 23,5 centimetres long from nose to tip of tail.

Photo: Hans Witte

Figure 133 *Site F1*, Good Hope.

A feline with claws extended and what is probably blood pouring from the nose is surrounded by figures performing various antics. A stick with a spiked knob has apparently been thrown at the feline, and the figure confronting the animal, as well as the figure above, carry small pouch-like objects with two tassels. Some of the humans have knobbed head-dresses, others wear horns or feathers on their heads. In the centre of the group, a fragmentary painting in black with bristly red projections may be the remains of another feline. Here, too, there is a knobbed stick across the extended foreleg, and red streaks that may be blood. The entire group is surrounded by dashes of orange paint, which are difficult to interpret. They may represent rain. (See Figure 240).

This tracing was made in 1956. Since then, the paintings have suffered much deterioration, partly due to the soft sandstone on which they are executed, and partly due to repeated wetting and fingering by the many visitors from the nearby Sani Pass Hotel.

Figure 134   *Site X9*
'Ye are ugly! Your foreheads resemble overhanging cliffs!'

Cape Chacma Baboon
(Papio ursinus)

My parents used to say to me, that the baboons were once
people at the time when we who are people were not here . . .
Their parts resemble humans, for they feel that they are people . . .
That is why the baboon still understands like a man. That is why
the baboon still speaks, he sounds like a man.
(Dictated by a Xam Bushman from the northern Cape[1])

The close resemblance between man and monkey as defined
in these observations by a Bushman from the northern Cape,
was no doubt clearly appreciated by stone-age hunters long before
the propagation of Darwin's theories, even if the Bushman's ideas
on evolution are the reverse of those propounded today.

Baboons live in large troops in the mountainous districts of South
Africa, and were doubtless often in competition with the Bushmen
for plant foods. Although principally vegetarian in diet, they have
been known occasionally to capture and eat young animals. In
appearance, baboons are a dark brown colour, with a protruding
muzzle and prominent supra-orbital ridge. They have a characteristic swaggering gait, with distinctive tails raised upward from the
base before curving over, downwards and backwards. Baboons
sleep in rock shelters or on rocky ledges at night, foraging for food
during the day. Young males are usually stationed to keep a look-out
for intruders from a high point, and upon their giving the alarm
bark, the whole troop makes off and seeks refuge. When on the
move, the babies are carried by their mothers, the very small ones
clinging to the breast and the larger ones to the back of the parent.
Their greatest natural enemy is the leopard, which usually attacks
them at night in their sleeping places. In a fight, the long canines
of old male baboons are formidable weapons for piercing and
rending. When attacked by dogs, baboons have been known to
turn on them and tear the dogs to pieces with their teeth while
holding them down with their hands and feet.[2] (Figures 137, 139).

Baboons represent only two per cent of the wild animals shown
in the rock paintings, but their characteristic appearance and habits
are faithfully portrayed, usually in black monochrome.

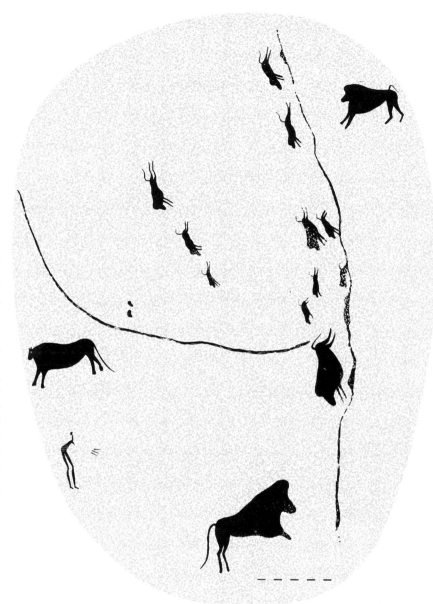

Figure 135 *Site X9*

*The greatest natural enemy of the baboon is the leopard. In this scene, unfortunately
very faded, baboons run terrified down a vertical line painted on the rock, which may
represent a cliff face or some other feature of the landscape.*

223

Figure 136 *Site K1*

A baboon standing in the upright position is shown holding sticks. The line partly surrounding the animal possibly represents a shelter.

224

From their mythology, it is clear that Bushmen attributed to baboons many human qualities, even thinking that if a baboon was shot with an arrow, the animal was able to retaliate by throwing the poisoned missile back. Another example of the baboon's ability to manipulate weapons is given in the anecdote of the man who derided baboons by saying, 'Ye are ugly! Your foreheads resemble overhanging cliffs!' Angered, the baboon broke off sticks and feigned attack.[3] Again, a young woman who grumbled about the crookedness of her digging stick was said to have offended a baboon who, thinking she was mocking the crookedness of its tail, threw stones at her.[4] While these stories may be to some extent exaggerated, recent studies of baboons suggest that they are capable of remarkable manual dexterity and intelligence,[5] a fact that in no way escaped the attention of the Bushman hunters. (Figure 136).

Two very similar myths concerning baboons were told by a Bushman from the Strontberg south of the Orange river, and a Bushman from eastern Lesotho. Since the latter is nearer the area of this survey, a condensed version is related here:

> Kaggen sent his son Cogaz to cut sticks to make bows. When Cogaz came to the bush, the baboons caught him. They called all the other baboons together to hear him, and asked who sent him there. He replied that his father had sent him to cut sticks to make bows. But the baboons said; "Your father thinks himself more clever than we are; he wants those bows to kill us, so we'll kill you!" So they killed Cogaz, and tied him up in the top of a tree. They danced around the tree singing a baboon song with a chorus ending, "Kaggen thinks he is clever."
>
> Kaggen was asleep when Cogaz was killed, but when he awoke he told Coti his wife to give him his charms, and after putting some in his nose, he said, "The baboons have hung Cogaz." So he went to where the baboons were, but when they saw him approaching, they changed their words to omit the words about Kaggen. A little girl baboon complained, "Don't sing that way, sing the way you were singing before!" Kaggen asked the baboons to sing as she wished, and while they sang and danced as before, Kaggen fetched a bag full of pegs. Then, approaching the baboons from behind as they were dancing and raising a great dust, he drove a peg into each one's back. Giving it a crack, he sent the baboons off to the mountains to live on roots, beetles and scorpions as a punishment. Before that baboons were men, but since then they have tails, and their tails hang crooked.[6]

According to Bushman belief, baboons are very sensitive to derision and insult. One therefore had to take great care not to offend them, and it was considered bad luck to talk or even refer directly to baboons when on the way to hunt game. Baboons were credited with the power to render hunting grounds barren, and because of their highly developed ability to sense danger, were believed to possess supernatural qualities. Baboon hair, for instance, was worn tied up in sinew and used as a curative charm.[7]

A group of paintings on the farm *Belmont* in the Mount Currie district of East Griqualand vividly depicts a vicious fight between baboons and dogs, some of the latter being restrained on leashes by their owners. (Figures 137, 139). Although the motive underlying this scene could be regarded as direct illustration of an event, remarks made by one of Dr Bleek's informants suggests that a straight-forward interpretation need not necessarily be correct.

> We who are Bushmen are accustomed to do this when the dogs chase baboons and drive them away from the mountain. A baboon sits on a boulder, thinking that the dogs will not catch it if it deceives them. It will wait until the dog comes up to it, it will catch the dog and tear off the dog's skin. When we see that a baboon has seized a dog, we say, "It is a girl's dog that you have seized there."[8] When the baboon hears us say that . . ., it does not seize the dog again . . . We deceive it, because we do not want it to tear off the dog's skin. It believes us when we speak to it . . .
>
> Father used to tell me that when I had killed a baboon, I must take an arrowhead and cut fine lines round the points of my bow. For father used to say, that the baboon's teeth were what it was putting on my bow . . . (With the hyena it is the same. When we kill a hyena, we also put little lines, in order to take the hyena's curse off our bows, for we want the hyena's actions not to be on our bows) . . . For father used to tell me, that the baboon's death would live in our bows, if we did not cause it to leave them.[9]

If it was necessary to engrave lines on a bow in order to remove a curse on hunting as a result of the death of a baboon, one wonders whether, in a community where painting was an important aspect of cultural expression, the delineation of this animal on the rocks may in some way have immobilised the evil that would otherwise afflict the hunter.[10] As evidenced by their mythology, the dividing line between man and animal was not very deep in Bushman thought;[11] so too, the dividing line between secular and ritual art may not always have been clearly distinguished.

References

1. Bleek 1931: 175-177.
2. Roberts 1951: 10.
3. Bleek 1911: 255.
4. Orpen 1874.
5. Bolwig 1959, 1961.
6. Condensed from Orpen 1874.
7. Bleek 1931: 167-179.
8. The female sex is regarded with some disdain by Bushman males. Heinz 1966: 146-148.
9. Bleek 1931: 172-174. The text within brackets is a footnote in the original text.
10. See also Griaule 1950: 70.
11. Rheinhallt & Doke 1931.

Figure 137 *Site O1*

A man runs to thrust a spear into a baboon which has caught a dog by the tail. Below, a spear has been thrust into a baboon's back. (See also Figure 139).

225

Figure 138 *Site L15*

A troop of baboons. Two of the females carry their young on their backs. The paintings are now in the Natal Museum, having been removed from a site in the Bushman's Nek area in 1910.

Figure 139 *Site O1*

Dogs and hunters armed with spears attack baboons. Two of the dogs are on leashes.
The paintings in Figure 137 are from the same site.

Figure 140   *Site I3*

This snake with an antelope head is 1,52 metres long. The spotted body is painted in such a way that it disappears behind a natural feature in the rock face, and emerges only to disappear again into a crack below a ledge. The tail re-emerges to curl back on itself. To the right and below, other fragmentary remains of snakes can be seen and, out of the picture, a fat spotted snake with spreading black horns slithers from below a rock ledge.

Opposite is a tracing of the head of the snake shown in the photograph. The colours are red and white, with some details emphasised in black.

Serpents:
regeneration and rain

'And the snake came out of the water and raised his head, and looked warily and suspiciously around, and then he glided out of the snake's skin and walked . . . .'

From a legend told by Qing, a Mountain Bushman from eastern Lesotho.[1]

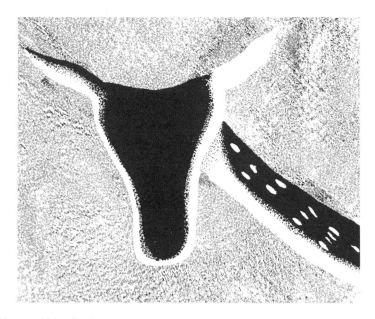

Figure 141 *Site I3*

Many varieties of snakes, both venomous and harmless, abound throughout the regions formerly inhabited by the Mountain Bushmen. Among the most lethal are the adders, the largest of which is the puff-adder, *Bitis arietans* (Merrem), a beautifully patterned, sluggish snake that can strike sideways, with venom that forms yellow flakes when dry. The night adder, *Causus rhombeatus* (Lichtenstein), is a more slender reptile, with a venom that becomes thick and toffee-like on exposure to air. The Berg adder *Bitis atropos* (Linnaeus), though small in size, can nevertheless be very dangerous, but perhaps the most aggressive of all the snakes common to the Drakensberg are the hooded rinkhals, *Hemachatus haemachatus* (Lacépède), and spitting cobra, *Naja nigricollis* (Reinhardt).

The deadly black mamba, *Dendroaspis polylepis* (Günther), and green mamba, *D. angusticeps* (A. Smith), tend to be limited to the coastal bush, as is the python, *P. sebae* (Gmelin), although in former times this large serpent, which grows to between fifteen and eighteen feet in length, was found further inland than it is today.[2]

Among the rock paintings in the survey area there are twenty-three snakes, forming less than one per cent of the indigenous animals portrayed. Some of these are so fragmentary that few details survive, but in most cases the paintings do not appear to be realistic depictions of any particular species. There is little attempt to represent skin-patterns accurately, the decoration consisting usually of arbitrary spots or stripes, and the fangs are rarely shown. The paintings are more often imaginative creations with ears, tusks or horns (Figures 141, 145), and are sometimes associated with elaborate scenes of uncertain interpretation. An example of such a scene is the huge wriggling snake whose contortions cover the rock face of a low shelter on the Setsoasie tributary of the Tsoelike river in eastern Lesotho (site W25). The serpent is superimposed upon paintings of eland and smaller antelope, and is associated with skeleton-like figures with bizarre animal heads or masks. These horrifying creatures, both male and female, show varying combinations of massive jaws, horns, tusks, teeth and protuberant eyes. (Figures 67a and b, 148, 149). The interpretation of these fictitious beings is a puzzle, but it is noteworthy that paintings of snakes associated with grotesque figures have also been found in western Lesotho.[3]

In most instances, the dimensions of the snake paintings are exaggerated out of all proportion to the other subjects with which they are associated. If the convolutions of the serpent in the Setsoasie shelter were to be straightened out, the measurement would be 4,3 metres. While this would be commensurate with the actual

Figures 142a and b   *Site J10, Lammermoor, Underberg.*

Above: *Eight naked men appear to haul a tapering object which is at least 2,74 metres long, almost the total length of the overhang in which it occurs. Human figures, small antelope and eland are scattered above and below the object, and on the exfoliated area of rock (right) hunters with dogs have been painted in yellow ochre at a later period. (See Figure 30). All the other paintings are in dark red and white.*

Below: *Detail of the men tugging at the reptile.*

recorded lengths of *Python* spp., the largest painted eland in the Setsoasie shelter is only 38 centimetres long whereas in reality eland measure about 2,74 metres from nose to root of tail. Similarly, two large snakes in the *Khomo Patsoa* shelter, one of which has horns or ears and what may be a forked tongue, are about 2,44 metres long, whereas associated humans and an eland are only 55 centimetres. Another painting on the farm *Lammermoor* in the Underberg district (site J 10) shows a group of men on an average only 12,7 centimetres high tugging at a vast object which extends at least 2,74 metres across the rock face. Although the tapering, upturned end of this unfortunately very fragmented painting looks remarkably like the bow of a boat, the shape is identical to the tails of the snakes at *Khomo Patsoa*. (Figures 142, 143). The *Lammermoor* painting therefore probably represents a mythical serpent which, if multiplied in proportion to the human figures holding its tail, would be over 30 metres in length!

The myths and legends related by Qing, a Bushman from Lesotho, make frequent reference to snakes. They were 'frightful things' which could cause destruction, they were evil and repulsive, and yet they could seduce women, change their skins and become human. The Bushman's creator-deity Kaggen sent a son to fetch the snakes who had abducted his daughter, 'and he struck them with his stick, and as he struck each the body of a person came out,

Figure 143   *Site W21, Khomo Patsoa, Lesotho.*

Two long serpents, one with horns, ears and a forked tongue, are superimposed on earlier kaross-clad figures. The upturned tapering tails closely resemble the object painted on Lammermoor *reproduced opposite. The scale is in 10 centimetre units.*

and the skin of the snake was left on the ground, and he sprinkled the skins with canna [a herb?], and the snakes turned from being snakes and they became his people'.[4]

A painting in Mahahla's shelter, East Griqualand, shows a large writhing serpent with open mouth, horned snout and a hood or ear. Above it is a group of women with exaggeratedly fat thighs and wearing brief genital aprons. A white-faced figure walking away from the serpent on the left carries a stick, while other cruder figures are grouped above and to the right of the serpent's head. The association of this painting with the abduction myth can only be conjectural, but the juxtaposition of mythical serpents with exaggerated female features, considered by the Bushmen to be sexually attractive, is suggestive of such an interpretation.

Although no analysis has yet been made of the role played by snakes in Bushman life and thought, the painted records as well as recorded mythology suggest that their metaphorical associations were both complex and multifarious. It is nevertheless relevant that snakes did contribute, even though indirectly, to the economy of the Mountain Bushmen, for snake venom was one of the ingredients used in the preparation of their arrow poison.[5] A sample of poison labelled 'Drakensberg' and held by the Natal Museum,[6] is stated to consist of the juice of aloes and various herbs mixed with snake venom, but there is unfortunately no further documentation accompanying the specimen. In addition to killing snakes and removing the whole poison gland for incorporation in the arrow poison, the Bushmen also knew how to extract venom from the fangs of live snakes, and used this as an inoculant against snake bite.[7] There are also indications that other precautions were sometimes taken, for one of Qing's stories describes how young men bound rushes round their limbs and bodies to prevent themselves from being bitten when they went to rescue Kaggen's daughter, who had been taken in marriage by the Chief of the Snakes.[8]

A Bushman from the eastern Cape who was exhibited in London in 1847 entertained spectators with a pantomimic enactment of the capture of a serpent, holding up a stuffed specimen by way of illustration. Regrettably the procedure is not more fully described; the reporter simply commented, 'This fellow would make a capital melodramatic actor'.[9]

Although the evidence is meagre, there are suggestions that snake 'sorcerers' existed among some Khoisan peoples, but there is no information as to whether these 'sorcerers' were also responsible for the preparation of the arrow poison.[10] Among living

Figure 144 *Site Q 4*

A row of women with white faces and exaggerated thighs are superimposed on what appears to be a faded snake. Below, a well-preserved snake rears up from a ledge in the rock, and details on the head (opposite) show an eye, open mouth, hood or ears, *and a white tusk protruding from the nose. A figure with a 'hook head' and carrying a stick walks away from the snake.*

Photo: Pat Carter.

Kalahari Bushmen, there are no such poison 'specialists', and the preparation and application of poison to their arrows is a routine task completely devoid of fuss.[11] There are, however, many examples of rites and observances performed to ensure the efficacy of poison *after* it has been applied to the arrows, and *after* it has been shot into the animal.[12] Activities relating to the *use* of the poison are therefore hedged about with injunctions and prohibitions, not the manufacture of the poison itself. One early record nevertheless claims that the preparation process was accompanied by weird chants and songs which were supposed to enhance the efficacy of the poison,[13] and there is an oblique reference to the Mountain Bushmen giving part of the meat of an eland killed in the hunt as a sacrifice to a tree from which the poison was obtained.[14] This suggests some form of ritual attitude towards the source of poison, but whether snakes in their role of poison-providers would have been accorded similar ritual treatment is not known. The fact that some snakes are painted with antelope heads and horns may possibly reflect a symbolic connection between hunting and snake venom. Qing, the Bushman informant from Lesotho, said that burnt snake powder was used as charm medicine to strengthen participants in the ritual Dance of Blood, and men with rhebucks' heads who lived under water and who had been 'spoilt' (harmed or affected?) by the dance were able to 'tame elands and snakes'.[15] It has been suggested that paintings showing humans 'playing with eland' may be associated with a ritual performed around eland after they had been stupefied by poison;[16] if this were so, then the eland would have been 'tamed' or subdued through the action of snake poison. This interpretation certainly helps explain the otherwise enigmatic remarks made by Qing. (Figures 140, 146, 223, 234).

Further association between snakes and antelope horns, particularly the horns of eland, is reflected in the belief that a special snake lived between the horns of all eland, and before eland meat could be consumed, it had to be 'purified' of the venomous juices which it contained.[17] The association between eland horns and a particularly potent force may be one of the reasons why the horns are often omitted from eland paintings, and it is also significant that Bushmen within the survey area used an eland horn in a ceremony to bring rain.[18]

Among the present Basotho it is still widely held that malicious snakes of immense proportions, sometimes with horns but more often with a light shining from their heads, inhabit the deeper pools of the rivers. The close association of snakes with water, a belief commonly held throughout Africa, is referred to in several

Figure 145 *Site Q4*
A tracing of the head of the snake photographed opposite.

instances in the myths related by Qing. Of particular significance is the story in which the return of snakes to a certain area dooms the whole country to be filled with water.[19] The Xam Bushmen specifically cited cobras and puff-adders, as well as tortoises, as being 'rain animals'; the rain put them aside as meat and 'owned' them. For this reason, they were greatly feared and respected.[20] In the drier regions of South Africa where surface water is scarce, the Khoisan peoples believed that every source of water had a resident snake, and Hahn records that the Hottentot word for 'snake' and 'rain' come from the same root, meaning 'to flow.'[21] Snakes seen in low precipitation areas were also thought to be a good omen for rain.[22] A painted scene copied by Stow from the Sand Spruit in Lesotho shows a marvellously patterned 'rain animal' with a snake hanging from its muzzle, and the association with water is further emphasised by fish swimming towards the animal.[23]

Figure 146 *Site N2*

At lower right, a hunter has laid down his weapons and skin carrying bag in order to dismember a dead eland which lies on its back, stiff legs in the air. Another figure sits above the head of the carcase, and bends towards the thorax with skin bag in hand, possibly to collect blood. A second seated human is dealing with what may be the entrails of the animal, while a row of smaller figures watch or wait at the left.

Above, a long snake with forward-curving horns wriggles towards the dead eland, and a small male figure with exaggerated genitalia seems to fly or float downwards from the right. Further to the right, and not included in this photograph, a group of kaross-clad people approach, while a strange seated figure with snout-like face looks on.

Photo: Pat Carter.

Another belief commonly held by Bantu-speaking peoples is that the bodies of particular non-poisonous snakes house the spirits of deceased ancestors.[24] That this concept was also shared by some Bushmen is borne out by mythology recorded from the Kung in South West Africa. If a certain non-biting, timid snake was seen to roll over on its back, it intimated death in the family:

> A snake which is near a grave, we do not kill, for, [it] is our other person, our dead person, the dead person's snake. And we do not kill [it]; for [we] respect it . . . . Another day, [if] we see a lizard, we follow the lizard's spoor; [if] the lizard has gone to the earth [grave?] of our other person, we respect the lizard, [we] do not kill the lizard, [we] let the lizard alone. When we see an antelope, an antelope [which is] near our other person's place, that place where our other person had died, we respect the antelope; for, the antelope is not a mere antelope. Its legs [?] seem [?] small, it is the person who has died, and is a spirit antelope.[25]

It is significant that both snakes and lizards shed their skins annually, and the leaving behind of the old self to become a new body is an obvious symbol of transformation and re-incarnation.

The phases of the moon were also equated with regeneration and life after death; from an object left with only a back-bone after fighting with the sun, the moon was able to develop a large stomach and come alive again. The Kung compared their Deity with the moon: 'The Moon is thy person, for ye, thou and the Moon, do not die outright, but we die outright', and the Xam prayed directly to the Moon, 'Thou shalt give me thy face, [with] which thou, when thou hast died, thou dost again, living return . . . .'[26] The metaphorical connection between the monthly regeneration of the moon and the annual renewal of a snake's skin is implicit in the Kung myth which states: 'The sun rose, and the Moon was not the Moon, but was a little snake and lay on the ground'.[27]

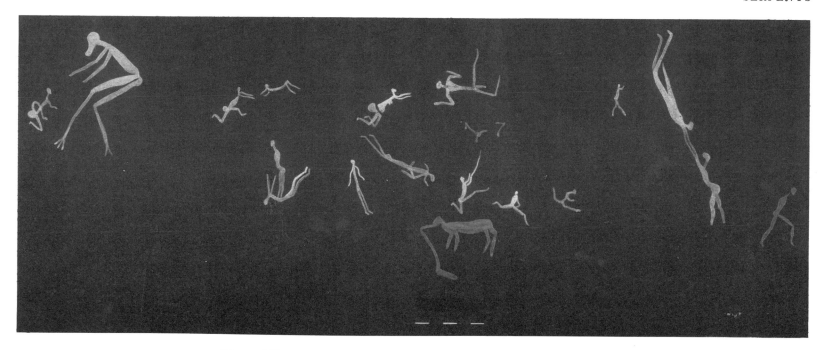

Figure 147 *Site I₂*
Ethereal figures float through the air or perform acrobatics.

High on the Mlambonje tributary of the Mzimkhulu river, there is an inconspicuous shelter containing paintings predominantly of snakes, and on two separate visits to the site, we saw a live puff-adder among the rocks nearby.[28] Although some of the painted snakes are very fragmentary, others are clearly imaginative creations. A particularly fat spotted serpent with widely spreading horns slithers from a crack in the rocks, while another, with the head of an antelope, is painted so that the body emerges from either side of a natural promontory on the shelter wall. A small shelter at a higher level on the same hillside has a somewhat ethereal scene painted in white on a very dark background. (Figures 140, 147). The interpretation of this group can only be conjectural, but the subject matter certainly includes dead human figures. One of these lies on its back with blood running from the head, while another human figure stands or emerges from its chest. On the left, a figure with animal head and clawed feet seems about to pounce on a smaller mortal grovelling at its feet. Other figures can only be described as apparently floating through the air, and on the right, a standing, earth-bound human grasps the arms of a 'spirit' — 'our other person, our dead person'. The association of this site with the other containing paintings of snakes may be fortuitous, but the combined effect certainly produces an extraordinarily eerie atmosphere.

On the farm *Kilrush* in Mount Currie district, East Griqualand, there is an unusual scene in which a group of hunters, some holding skin bags, are gathered round the carcase of an eland. A human with elongated neck and exaggerated male genitalia seems to float or fly down towards the dead eland from the right, while a snake with forward-curving horns wriggles towards it from the left. On the far right is a seated therianthropic figure with streaks of red paint issuing from the nose, but it is difficult to know whether this figure is part of the same scene as the dead eland. The association of ideas in this composition is indeed obscure to the modern viewer, but no doubt to the Bushmen it conveyed a wealth of meaning through the juxtaposition of significant symbols. (Figure 146).

Figure 148   *Site W25*

A convoluted serpent winds its way over paintings of small antelope and other figures. Bright orange and white eland face in opposite directions at top left and top right and, at centre right, an eland has been painted over an earlier rendering of the same animal, resulting in two heads and additional limbs. Surrounding it are bizarre skeleton-like figures in white with gross heads, some predominantly anthropomorphic, others theriomorphic. The centre of the panel has unfortunately been obliterated by a mineral exudate which overlies the paintings. (See also Figures 67a and b, 149).

Photo: Pat Carter.

We no longer know whether the Bushmen painted grotesque serpents in connection with poison or rain-making cults, whether they were used as a means of enforcing moral codes in the instruction of initiates, or whether they were in some way associated with death and re-incarnation. It is, however, unlikely that the representations of serpents were sheer figments of the imagination without further meaning; the significance of their symbolic associations in Bushman culture are undoubtedly to be sought in cosmological beliefs as yet imperfectly understood.

References

 1. Orpen 1874 & 1919: 148.
 2. Fitzsimons 1962; Stow 1905: 202.
 3. Christol 1911: 13.
 4. Orpen 1874; 1919: 146.
 5. Shaw, Woolley & Rae 1963; Schapera 1925: 199.
 6. Natal Museum Catalogue No. 2398.
 7. Alexander 1838: 83; Bazley 1904: 511, 595; Willcox 1956: 32.
 8. Orpen 1874 & 1919: 145.
 9. *Illustrated London News*, 12 June 1847.
10. Hahn 1881: 77.
11. Shaw, Woolley & Rae 1963.
12. See p. 303.
13. Dornan 1925: 96.
14. How 1962: 44.
15. Orpen 1873 & 1919: 151-152. See also p. 432.
16. Woodhouse 1971: 346.
17. Arbousset 1852: 79; Hahn 1881: 81.
18. *Natal Independent*, 16/1/1851; see also p. 52.
19. Orpen 1874 & 1919: 145.
20. Bleek 1933, B.S. 7 (3): 303.
21. Hahn 1881: 105.
22. Alexander 1838 (1): 115.
23. Stow 1930: Pl. 67a.
24. Bryant 1949: 353-63.
25. Bleek 1911: 429-33.
26. Bleek 1911: 51-3, 57; Bleek 1935: 278-9.
27. Bleek 1935: 278-9.
28. See also Morris 1965: 16.

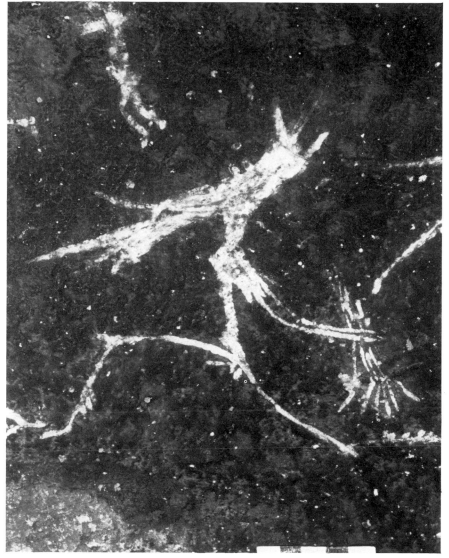

Figure 149 *Site W25*

Photographic detail of Figure 148. This bizarre male figure has protuberant eyes, jaws and tusks. There are orange stripes across the head, which has animal ears and thin straight horns. The arms, held back, carry a bundle of objects which are like putting clubs in shape, but which may represent fly-whisks. The knees are spiked and the lower limbs have barb-like projections.

Photo: Pat Carter

Figure 150   *Site W28*

This unusual composition in dark red and white shows a flock of birds in association with antelope. The birds on the right with red necks and legs may represent vultures, but others are more like guineafowl or partridge. The birds with long wings on the left are not recognisable in nature, nor can the objects at centre bottom or lower left be identified with certainty.

Winged Creatures:
intermediaries between earth and sky

There are 20 representations of winged creatures in the survey area, comprising less than 1% of the animals in the study sample. Only two of the paintings are recognisable as to species and may be tentatively identified as a Secretary bird (*Sagittarius serpentarius*) and a Blue Crane (*Tetrapteryx paradisea*). They are in black silhouette and probably belong to the most recent phase of paintings since they are associated with fragmentary cattle. (Figure 151b). At two other sites indistinct paintings in white suggest flying birds simply represented by two adjacent semi-circles, but these may be the remnants of paintings from which other colours have since disappeared. (Figure 151a). On the Setsoasie river in Lesotho, a flock of birds are shown distributed around three bichrome buck, and although some of the birds superficially resemble partridge, guinea-fowl and vultures, others with long drooping wings are apparently not intended to represent actual birds, but simply bird-like creatures. (Figure 150). It is, in fact, to this category of non-realistic creatures that most of the winged paintings belong, for many of them display therianthropic and other unusual details. The heads may be filled with white paint similar to human 'hook-headed' forms, or they may show some characteristics common to antelope. Limbs are usually stubby and sometimes display claws; tails are often indicated by a few quill-like strokes; and the wings, which are thrown back, usually have feathery protrusions. In most scenes, these winged creatures are associated either with human figures or large antelope, especially with eland.

a. Top Left: *Site P1*
Paintings in dark red, light red and white which may represent birds in flight.

b. Right: *Site L37*
Two birds in black silhouette which may be a Blue Crane and a Secretary Bird.

239

Figure 152 *Site:* Klipfontein, *Albert district, Cape*

Eland, bowman, kneeling figures and mythological creatures with wings.

Traced by Harald Pager from a painted slab in the Archaeological Research Unit, Wits. Univ., Johannesburg.

The distribution of these winged creatures is by no means limited to the survey area, for examples have also been recorded to the south where they are referred to as 'flying buck'[1], and to the north where they have been named 'ales'.[2] In the north-eastern Cape the compositions are particularly complex, showing various forms of buck-headed winged creatures linked to hunters or to dead and dying figures.[3] Another excellent example originates from the farm *Klipfontein* in the Albert district, and is now preserved on a painted slab in the Archaeological Research Unit, Johannesburg.[4] This scene shows three figures with outstretched arms, one of which has a buck's head, crawling along a spotted line. Another line emanates from the head of the central figure and extends upwards towards two exquisitely detailed 'flying buck' with fine red streaks hanging from their mouths and feathery extensions above their heads. In front of the crawling or crouched figures, there is a break in the spotted line where a bowman shoots upwards at a recumbent eland. The spotted line re-forms in front of the hunter, and above is a

therianthropic figure with relatively small horizontal body, the hind legs of a beast, and arm-like wings ending in feathery protrusions stretching upwards and backwards. A line from this figure leads again to the eland being shot by the hunter. There would seem to be a clear association here between the death of the eland, the therianthropic representation, the human figures with arms flung back, and the winged creatures. (Figure 152).

A postulated interpretation of the winged creatures is that they represent some form of spirit connected with death,[5] and Bushman lore does, indeed, lend support to the association between wings and spirits.

The line of reasoning is that spirits are linked with the wind, and wind in turn with a bird. A Xam informant stated:

> We, who are human beings, we possess wind; we make clouds, when we die. Therefore, the wind does thus when we die, the wind makes dust, because it intends to blow, taking away our footprints, with which we had walked about . . .[6].

240

When men killed things, they also made a wind which blew up dust. Some made a cold wind, others a warm wind, and people could recognise the winds as belonging to specific hunters. The wind was 'one with the man', and was also connected with the stars. Hankasso claimed that his own wind had 'no equal in pleasantness as it is the north wind, for it feels warm when it blows the east wind away, after I have killed an ostrich.'[7]

A Bushman song has the words:

My younger brother's wind feels like this
When he seems to have killed a lion.
Father's wind feels like this
When a lion seems to have killed him.[8]

It is clear from these quotations that the Bushmen believed that a special 'wind' was created both when a person died and when certain animals were slain.

According to another legend:

The Wind was formerly a man. He became a bird. (Therefore he is tied up in stuff. The skin is that which we call stuff). And he was flying, while he no longer walked, as he used to do.[9]

The informant's brother-in-law claimed he had seen the wind in the form of a bird when he was a child. [10]

Among the Bushmen of the North-West Kalahari, *Gauwa* is the word used for 'a person who has died', or more precisely, the ghost of a dead person. The Naron speak of the wind as a man, and of *Gauwa* as a bird accompanying him:

the Wind has *Gauwa* with him and walks no more, rises up, from the earth rises, into the sky goes and thus flies . . . The Medicine man sees the bird walking with the wind. The bird is *Gauwa*.
Gauwa says, "I make the Wind and thus go!"

The wind is called *Gauwa* when it is strong and howls, and *Gauwa* is also associated with thunder, lightning and shooting stars.[11, 12] Among the Southern Bushmen too, a whistling wind was believed to forbode death:

. . . . the wind cries as the people are going to cry when someone dies . . . when the wind sounds as if it cries, it is sending its crying on the wind.[13, 14]

In addition to the association of spirits with wings and flight, there are several legends in which Kaggen, the chief mythological being of the Southern Bushmen, manages to escape from dangerous situations by growing wings; 'He quickly got feathers; he flew away.'[15-17]

Some of the paintings within the survey area depict what are quite definitely human beings with wings, while others have unrecognisable bodies and heads, with short legs that are sometimes clawed. In one scene on the farm *Eagle's Nest* these winged creatures are associated with eland and hunters in an unusual composition, in another, on the adjacent farm *Thule*, with a line of eland approaching a somewhat confused group including winged humans (one with a very elongated ringed neck), a strange white figure with grid patterns on a muzzle-like face, and people carrying or holding hunting equipment. (Figures 107, 153). The winged creatures, it will be noted, follow in the same direction as the line of eland which lead toward the human group.

According to a Xam informant, certain animals had a premonition of death and behaved in a strange way, seeking out rather than avoiding human habitations:

. . . the springbok had . . . known when father's heart fell . . .;
. . . they came along approaching the hut where father lay dead . . .
"The springbok appeared to be moving away and the wind really blew following them. They were running before the wind. It was really father's wind, and you can feel yourself how it is blowing. You know that whenever father used to shoot game, his wind blew like that."[18]

It is perhaps no co-incidence that both the *Eagle's Nest* and *Thule* sites are particularly exposed to wind, and an expansive sandstone face at *Thule*, pitted with numerous cavities, is an ideal nesting place for a multitude of birds, including a colony of the rare Bald Ibis (*Geronticus calvus*). As the birds noisily awaken at dawn and fly off from their inaccessible perches to go foraging far afield, returning to roost again at dusk, one can well imagine the Bushmen associating this unusual amphitheatre-like setting with the home of the wind.

He became a bird . . . and he dwelt in a mountain's hole. He early awaking goes out of it, he flies away, again he flies away. And he eats about, about, about, about. He again returns. And he, again, comes to sleep in it.[9]

If we accept the association between spirits, wind and birds, many of the painted scenes which include representations of winged humans, winged buck and other therianthropic winged creatures are likely to be symbolically connected with the death of both humans and animals. That the act of painting was, on occasion, directly associated with burial is demonstrated by the numerous painted grave stones excavated from rock shelters along the southern Cape coast and from the Little Karoo and Albany districts of the Cape Province.[19] Although no representations of therianthropic

Figure 153a *Site P5*

This composition of figures is painted to the left of the file of eland reproduced in Figure 154. In the centre is a seated figure with a long ringed neck and wing-like arms thrown back. Above and right, a muscular running figure has more definite wings. Feathery protrusions are clearly visible in the tracings at right. Details of the five figures at centre left are reproduced in Figure 17.

Figure 153b *Site P5*

A tracing of the winged figures photographed at left. Note the detailed arrows held by the seated hunters.

winged creatures have been found in Bushman graves, the art tradition associated with the Cape burials shares many common features with the Drakensberg paintings. One clear example of this is the Coldstream grave stone which depicts three white-faced hunters with the horizontal lines across the cheek also recorded from the Drakensberg and other areas.[20, 21] It is noteworthy that some Bushmen are said to have painted their faces with black and white stripes as a sign that a death had occurred in their encampment,[22] and some of the 'flying buck' and other winged creatures are similarly decorated with lines across their faces. (Figures 107, 152).

Lévi-Strauss, who has done so much to elucidate the thought processes of the pre-literate mind, has drawn frequent attention to the series of logical connections that come into play to unite mental relations. And in the thought processes of man in general, not only the Bushman in particular, birds occupy an intermediary position between the supreme spirit (sky) and human beings (earth).[23] That winged creatures should be used as a symbol of mediation between life and death, between the physical and the spiritual, would seem to be an inherent tendency of the human mind.

242

References

1. Lee & Woodhouse 1964: 1968.
2. Pager 1971: 342-3.
3. Lee & Woodhouse 1970: Plates 189, 201, 202, 209, pp. 135, 137.
4. Catalogue no. 23/45.
5. Lee & Woodhouse, *op. cit.*
6. Bleek & Lloyd 1911: 397.
7. Bleek 1932, B.S. 6 (4).
8. Kirby 1936a, B.S. 10 (4): 233.
9. Bleek & Lloyd 1911: 107.
10. Lloyd 1889, No. 48.
11. Schapera 1930: 194.
12. Bleek 1928a: 46.
13. Lloyd 1889: No. 313.
14. Bleek 1932, B.S. 6 (4): 330-1.
15. Bleek 1875: No. 8.
16. Bleek 1924: 15-21, 30-4, 45-6.
17. Fock 1969.
18. Bleek 1932, B.S. 6 (4): 329.
19. Rudner 1971.
20. Haughton 1926.
21. Woodhouse 1968a, 1970.
22. Dornan 1925: 144-6.
23. Lévi-Strauss 1969: 152, 153.

Figure 154 *Site P5*

a. Above: *A file of eland, one with a bird flying below its stomach, walks towards a herd of smaller eland. Bringing up the rear is a flying creature with white face and stubby hind legs with claws. Further left, and out of this picture, is the group of figures including winged humans reproduced in Figure 153.*

b, c. Below: *Close-up photographs of the flying creatures reproduced above.*

Photos: Pat Carter.

Figure 155 *Site F18, Ikanti Mountain*

A detail of the scene reproduced in Figure 61. Two of the figures are clad in short karosses, open at the front to allow freedom of movement. A man at lower centre appears to have highly exaggerated genitalia with a bar across the tip, and the kaross-clad figure in front of him has clearly delineated toes. Details of caps or hair, and beads on neck, arms, waist and legs show clearly, the humans being painted in dark red, and the decorations in white. Some of the figures carry arrows in hands, others have arrows protruding from the back with no sign of a quiver, and others with quivers or hunting bags apparently have the arrows concealed. Bows or sticks are also seen protruding from backs. The figure second from left sits down, and holds a quiver with carrying straps and a decorative band near the opening. Behind, earlier paintings of humans and a small antelope in faded red can be discerned.

Photo: Pat Carter.

244

7   *Human Subjects*

Paintings of humans, being 53% of the total sample studied, predominate over animals by a small margin (Figure 80, Table 1), a finding which is supported by quantitative studies in other areas of southern Africa.[1] It is therefore obvious that the portrayal of humans and human activities was as important, if not more important, than the animals on which they preyed. In other words, culture as opposed to nature was an important aspect of the art.

Colour. A total of 4 530 individual figures were analysed, and of these 72% are monochrome, 21% bichrome, 6% polychrome, and less than 1% shaded polychrome. (Figure 70b). Red is the colour predominantly employed, followed by black, white, orange and yellow ochre. Colours such as brown or grey occur so rarely that they are statistically insignificant. (Figure 70a).

Size. Humans are most frequently depicted in sizes ranging from 5 to 20 centimetres, although paintings smaller than 5 centimetres also occur, and less frequently larger sizes up to 60 centimetres. No human figure greater than 60 centimetres high was recorded. Some correlation between size and whether the paintings were naked or kaross-clad was noted, and the significance of this finding is considered elsewhere.[2]

Sex. Where sex could be determined by the presence of genitalia or mammae, males predominated, being 9% of the total, with females only 2%. A considerable number of the figures nevertheless display the steatopygia, steatomeria and lumbar lordosis typical of Khoisan females; only very marked and therefore indisputable examples were counted in the analysis, and these formed 8% of the total.

As it is probable that a large number of the steatopygous figures are intended to represent women, the proportion of male to female figures recognisable on purely physical grounds would be more or less equal. If, however, cultural accessories such as bows, quivers, arrows and assegais were taken to signify men, then the ratio of male to female would be greatly increased. Female accessories such as weighted digging sticks are relatively rare by comparison with items of male hunting gear. (Table 2). The paintings do, therefore, reflect a distinctly masculine bias.

Because only 11% of the total number of figures show sexual differentiation by drawing attention to pudenda or breasts and because the sexual act itself is very rarely represented, it is unlikely that the paintings are associated with a developed fertility or sex cult. Among the male figures, however, there are a number which show highly exaggerated genitalia, the significance of which is not easy to interpret. This feature may possibly stress the link between male sexuality and hunting,[3] but it may be of some relevance that *Tokoloshe*, a mischievous and improper dwarf which figures in Nguni lore, is also said to have gargantuan sex organs. *Tokoloshe* is especially feared by women because he is believed to indulge in rapacious sexual advances,[4] and scenes which could bear this interpretation are occasionally shown in the paintings. (Figures 157, 158).

Among the Australian Aboriginals, certain cults represented their principal mythical figure with an exaggerated penis because he was the 'husband and creator' of all, while other distortions of the genitalia acted as warnings against the infringement of sexual laws.

Figure 156 *Site B3*
Steatopygous women with children.

246

Figure 157 *Site A5*

A rape scene. On the left, a man with highly exaggerated sexual organs pursues a woman. In the centre, she has apparently attempted to defend herself, having picked up a stick, but to no avail. On the right, she flees in distress.

Paintings of exaggerated pudenda and of couples in the sexual act were not intended to be amusing or lecherous, but were meant as a fearful deterrent to sex offences in the teaching of youths during initiation.[5] Although there is little positive evidence to attribute similar motives to the South African paintings, the possibility cannot be excluded.

Children, though rarely painted, are sometimes shown carried on their mothers' backs or held by squatting figures, and occasionally, a small walking figure is seen among a group of steatopygous women. (Figures 156, 26). Bush children usually accompany the women on food collecting excursions, the younger being carried while the older walk, and in view of the fact that children are in almost constant association with their mothers,[6] it is remarkable that children do not figure more prominently in the art. The painted evidence shows women to be most frequently portrayed in the motion of clapping hands with outstretched fingers, presumably to the accompaniment of singing, and the second activity stressed is that of carrying, but not necessarily using, digging sticks. It seems, therefore, that the roles of providing food and music were regarded by the

painters, who were probably predominantly men, as being the most significant activities associated with femininity, while motherhood, although acknowledged, is incidental. Again, culture predominates over nature.

Clothing.   The majority of human beings included in the quantitative analysis appear to be naked (59%), while a scanty covering in the form of breech-cloths and front or back aprons can be seen in less than 1%. It is probable, however, that many of the apparently naked figures also wore some form of apron, as this relatively inconspicuous detail does not show in the paintings, particularly those in silhouette.[7] Male figures displaying clear genitalia obviously wear no covering garment whatever, but in some instances it is not easy to differentiate between a penis and a front apron. (Figure 253). As high a proportion as 22% of the human figures are so faded or fragmentary that forms of dress cannot be determined with certainty, but the majority doubtless belong to the naked or scantily clothed category. The figure of 59% for this group is therefore almost certainly a low estimate.

Figure 158   (*below*)

a. *Site L30*
Two figures lying face to face. The line above possibly represents a shelter or skerm.

b. *Site S3*
Two figures in close proximity.

c. *Site W6*
Male figure with exaggerated genitalia.

d. *Site F19*
The upper figures in this group show protuberant genitalia. The lower pair sit face to face and apparently embrace one another with their legs.

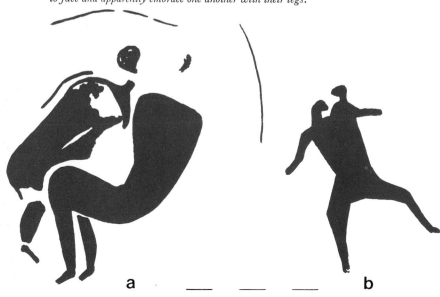

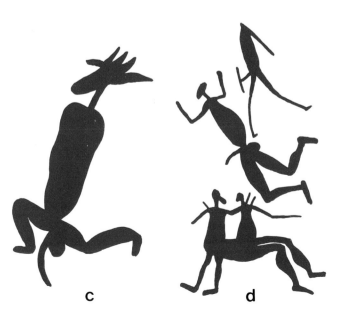

a   b   c   d

The few breech-cloths depicted were probably similar to those worn by the present Kalahari Bushmen, that is, a three-cornered piece of skin with two ends tied round the waist and the third drawn up between the legs and tied behind. This dress is typical of the males, while the women wear a small apron hanging in front and sometimes a larger skin behind. The front apron may be a semi-circular piece of leather, or may consist of a number of bead or leather tassels attached to a belt.[8] Both forms are found in the paintings, as well as what appears to be a complete skirt or soft leather wrapping hanging from the waist to above the knees and decorated with beads. (Figures 3, 98, 224). Occasionally walking or running figures are shown with two strands or projections hanging from between the legs. These may be thongs suspended from the waist, or may be an exaggerated depiction of female labia. (Figures 157, 195). Sometimes male figures are also shown wearing a long rear apron or skin flap hanging down as far as the backs of the knees and typically ending in two or three points, but this is not a common form of clothing, the buttocks usually being left uncovered. Front tassels or thongs of exaggerated length are sometimes shown in association with dancing figures and it has been recorded that Bushwomen in the Orange Free State sometimes wore long aprons made from ostrich-egg beads which hung from their waists to their feet.[9] (Figures 181, 218).

The most common form of clothing shown in the paintings is coverings of skin, which may be short capes hanging from the shoulders, or longer skins that envelope the body and hang to just above or just below the knees. (Figures 61, 90, 230). Whether long or short, these coverings are generally known as *karosses*, and the lower edges usually end in two or three points which are sometimes decorated with white tassels or animal tails. The points, which form a scalloped edge, probably result from the way in which the hides were pegged out to dry. The karosses may either be made from the single skin of a large animal or from a number of smaller skins sewn together. A few of the coverings have additional decorations in the form of diagonal or chevron-like patterns or spots, and some are fringed with fur or with thongs suspended from the lower edge. (Figures 237, 247). It is uncertain whether these garments were intentionally fashioned as rough tunics, or whether they were simply fastened round the shoulders like a cape. The latter method is in common use among extant Kalahari Bushmen, an advantage being that the skins then serve the dual purpose of clothing during the day and blanket at night.

Body painting, which could be interpreted as a form of clothing, is discussed more fully as an ornament. Some paintings show the lower half of the leg in a different colour from the rest of the body and while this may be a distinctive form of body decoration, it is possible that leggings are represented. (Figures 203, 223). A legend related by a Lesotho Bushman refers to leggings made from rushes which were worn as a protection against snake-bite,[10] but it is doubtful whether these were in common use.

Footwear in the form of sandals is suggested at one site in Lesotho where hunters pursuing an eland have black linings to the soles of their feet. (Figure 159). Although Bushmen in the desert regions sometimes wear sandals to insulate their feet from the hot sand, footwear is generally unnecessary in the highland grassland regions except during snow and freezing conditions. In certain areas of Lesotho, however, there are concentrations of thorny 'Duiweltjies' or 'Dubbeltjiedorings' (*Emex australis*) which are a great hazard to unprotected feet,[11] and doubtless the Bushmen living in thorn-infested areas would have taken precautions.

Apart from the post-European era when some articles of western dress are featured (Figures 14, 15, 52), it is clear from the painted record that no items of clothing need be ascribed to exotic influence. Skin aprons and skin karosses, although also worn by Bantu-speakers, are typical of all the Khoisan peoples of southern Africa.[12]

It has been recorded that there were formerly three different groups of Bushmen in Lesotho, classified according to their clothes. Those who wore no covering at all were known as the *Maqabanga*, while the *Magolong* wore a breech-cloth of buck skin, and the *Mapeshoane* a girdle of rock-rabbit pelts.[13] The distribution of clothing types in the paintings does not, however, distinguish between these three groups on a territorial basis in the eastern mountain regions, as both naked and clad figures are often depicted side by side in the same shelters. (Figure 155). The only written description of Bushman attire to the east of the escarpment comes from John Shepstone who encountered a band of hunters in what is now East Griqualand in the spring of 1846. He wrote:

> There were no made karosses amongst them, that is skins sewn together; the only covering they had were the simple skins of the small antelopes of the country.

The skins were worn suspended from the neck.[14] It is nevertheless unlikely that clothing as scanty as a single small skin was worn throughout the cold winter spells, and doubtless the longer and more substantial garments shown in the paintings reflect the need for seasonal protection against cold.

Figure 159   *Site X11   Sehonghong*

Men carrying hunting bags containing various items of equipment trail an eland. Black lines under the soles of some of the hunters' feet suggest footwear. The three strokes on the belly of the eland possibly represent a wound.

An old Mosotho living near Sehonghong who had known a Bushman survivor of the band which formerly occupied the shelter, maintained that this scene illustrated Bushmen using 'magic' on the eland's spoor. There is a strong tradition among Bantu-speaking peoples that the Bushmen were able to control the movements and behaviour of eland by placing strong 'medicine' in the imprints left by their hooves.

Figure 160   *Site Q 3*

An unidentifiable beast with floppy ears, whiskers, short legs and straight tail held erect pursues hunters with antelope heads. Above centre and at lower left there are figures seen from the front displaying what may be elongated labia. Various types of head-gear are worn — an animal cap with ears attached, peaked caps, a flat-topped cap like a mortar-board and hair or thongs hanging down to the shoulder, seen from the front

and the side. The large figure, top left, also wears a skin kaross, and walking away from the group, another figure clad in a light-coloured kaross has a bag slung over the shoulders. Outlined paintings such as the antelope at lower centre and the human at lower left, are unusual in the Drakensberg. They may originally have been filled with transient pigment.

As a warning against too naturalistic an interpretation of the kaross-clad figures, there are indications that not all these paintings are mundane representations, but are more likely to have mythological or supernatural associations. Reference to Figure 170 will show that the majority of figures wearing long karosses are appreciably larger than those which are naked or scantily clad, an observation which is confirmed by field research in other areas of the Drakensberg.[15] These findings suggest that kaross-clad figures were of more than average significance to the Bushmen. In addition to being accentuated in size, many of the kaross-clad figures show other unusual features. They often walk in stately procession carrying large bundles on their backs; they have exaggeratedly prognathous heads which are sometimes clearly animal; and their thick legs, which may be hairy or decorated with button-like knobs, often terminate in hooves or flat stumps rather than feet. Broad beaded bands are worn just below the knee, and their necks and shoulders are frequently ringed with a wide decorative collar.[16] (Figures 94, 228, 230, 237). While perfectly ordinary kaross-clad figures performing normal daily tasks also exist among the paintings, the artists show a marked tendency to associate long karosses with extraordinary rather than commonplace features.

Headgear.   Some form of headgear is shown on 29% of the figures whose heads can still be seen, or 18% of the total number of humans. On the evidence of the paintings, therefore, the majority of people

Figure 161 *Site Q 3*

A photograph of the original paintings shown as a tracing on the opposite page.

Photo: Pat Carter.

went about bare-headed. Of the 847 items of headgear shown, 18% are caps which either stand up in a peak or fit closely against the skull. Some of the latter could possibly represent hair depicted in a different colour from the head, therefore interpretation of these details should be cautious. There are 176 examples of either a flap or a series of thongs hanging down at the nape of the neck, and occasionally ending in knobs. Barrow encountered Bushmen among whom 'a few had caps made of the skin of asses, in form not unlike helmets; and bits of copper, or shells, or beads, were hanging in the neck, suspended from their little curling tufts of hair.'[17] Bush-women in South West Africa and Angola too, have been observed to unroll their tight peppercorn curls, mix them with fat, and then draw them out to tassels about five inches long.[18] In addition to lines painted hanging down from the head, there are also lines depicted radiating upwards and outwards. While some of these may represent spare arrows carried in a headband, or tufts of grass worn as a camouflage, others may be porcupine quills thrust into the hair for decorative purposes, or a band of bristly fur worn round the head. Other head-dresses give the impression of a triple-peaked leather crown reminiscent of those worn by Ovambo and Herero women.[19] (Figures 18, 28, 87, 102, 160, 225).

Another recurrent decoration found in the paintings is a single knob, or more occasionally two or three knobs, worn on the back of the head. This head-dress is usually associated with the later Bush-men who raided stock and rode horses. (Figures 26, 28, 212). The knob may be the result of shaving the head and leaving only a tuft of hair on the crown which was then smeared with fat and powdered aromatic herbs,[20] or it may be a separate attachment. The Lesotho Bushmen used to wear animal bladders fastened to their hair, and later to the grass hats the Basotho taught them to make.[21]

Brimmed hats became very popular among the historic bush-men, and judging from early photographs and illustrations of Khoisan and Bantu-speaking peoples, it was an article of European clothing widely adopted and imitated. Among the examples of headgear depicted, 14% are brimmed hats, many of them worn by horsemen. (Figures 15, 41, 163). Although some of these paintings undoubtedly represent Europeans who also wear boots, jackets and long trousers and carry guns, others are certainly non-European, for the riders have bare legs, wear skin decorations attached below the knee, and often carry assegais. Sometimes naked stock-drovers are also shown wearing hats. (Figures 27, 31, 82). During the 1850s,

251

Figure 162   *Masarwa Bushman hats, Botswana*
The hat on the left is made from matted grass seeds, that on the right from vegetable fibre covered with spider webs.

Photo: British Museum.

Henry Francis Fynn, who took evidence on stock theft in the Mzimvubu area, thought it worthwhile to note that a party of Coloureds who were supposedly implicated with the Bushmen, could be distinguished by the fact that they wore hats. Since it is recorded that the Bushmen traded cattle with these people in exchange for dogs and tobacco, it is possible that hats, too, were in demand as items of barter.[22] An excavation of a painted shelter in the Cathedral Peak area yielded a felt hat of the early European period in a layer immediately below the surface, but this may have been of Bantu rather than Bushman association.[23] When European-made brimmed hats could not be obtained, the Bushmen no doubt resorted to making their own, as evidenced by two examples of Masarwa Bushman hats collected in Botswana and presented to the British Museum in 1910.[24] One is made from a framework of vegetable vine, probably *Clematis* sp., which has then been covered over with what appear to be cobwebs, and decorated with ostrich

feathers set at a jaunty angle. The second has a framework held together with the inflorescences of 'Klitsgras' (*Setaria verticillata*), and matted into these are hairs from the pappus of the 'Kapokbossie' (*Eriocephalus pubescens*) which together form a felt-like fabric.[25] A piece of woven trade cloth is used as the hat band, and again, a feather gives the finishing touch to this ingenious creation. (Figure 162).

Body Ornament.   There are 940 examples of body ornament on the 4 530 paintings of humans in the sample study. The most popular form of decoration is a band worn on the legs, either just below the knee or at the ankle (29%). While some of these bands may be simple strips of skin or sinew, others may be made from plaited grass or strings of beads. Some examples suggest a combination of materials as the bands are broad and decorative, and occasionally have additional flaps of skin or tassels of hair hanging down over

Figure 163 *Site K1*

Horsemen accompanied by dogs. Both riders carry spears and wear brimmed hats, one of which is decorated with a long feather.

the calf. Second in popularity is a body band (18%) usually worn around the waist, but also seen as a bandolier slung across the torso. The waist-bands vary in width from a thin strip to a substantial belt on which beads are often shown as small white dots. Necklaces comprise 15% of the sample, and are represented as rows of beads or solid bands which sometimes extend right up the neck like a wide collar, while headbands form 7%. Bracelets, worn either above the biceps or at the wrist constitute 12% of the body ornaments. It is recorded that some Bushmen wore hunting trophies in the form of a series of arm-rings made from the hide of large game animals on their left wrists,[26] but where left and right sides can be distinguished in the paintings, decorations are represented on either arm. There is also no obvious consistency in the association of leg, body, arm, neck or headbands in any given type of figure, although a more sophisticated analysis may reveal significant patterns. Combinations of all kinds seem to occur, and figures may be

adorned with all the decorations listed, or may show no decorations whatever.

Body painting in the form of spots, vertical or horizontal lines across the torso, and meandering or zigzag lines on the limbs represent 6% of the decoration, and legs painted white from the knee down 3%. White faces are a common feature, and often show two, three or even four fine lines radiating outwards across the cheek. Occasionally the lines are vertical, or there may be a short series of bars fringing the forehead. Some Bushwomen bound greatly valued sea-shells to the centre of their foreheads or wore rings made from ostrich-egg elegantly suspended from a headband.[27] Others decorated themselves with a cord passed through a perforation in the nostril, then draped across the cheek and tied at the back of the head.[28] Although the practice of whitening faces has not, to my knowledge, been reported among Bushmen, it is common among Pondo, Xhosa and Bhaca initiates as well as among novice witch-doctors. White paint symbolises purification, is a defence against evil influences, and indicates heightened powers of perception.[29] An analytical study of ritual symbols among Ndembu hunters in Zambia reveals the immensely complex significance of colour, particularly white and red, in their ceremonies,[30] and a recent interpretation of red, black and white colour symbolism in terms of Zulu cosmology is a classic demonstration of the multi-dimensional scope of metaphorical thinking.[31] The possibility of similar associations in the thought processes of the Bushmen cannot be ignored. Miss Bleek saw a Bush medicine woman dot herself with white ash before uttering incantations[32] and the use of red ochre in Bushman rituals associated with puberty, marriage and death are well documented.[33] (Figures 112, 165, 166).

Many forms of facial and body painting as well as permanent tattooing have been recorded among the Khoisan peoples. Naron women often decorate themselves with tattoos at the corners of the eyes and with diagonal cuts across buttocks and thighs. They smear charcoal and red ochre mixed with fat around their eyes, mouth and cheekbones when preparing for a dance, and young girls ready for marriage do likewise.[34] Some women are tattooed by their husbands at the time of marriage, for instance with a line running from one cheek-bone to the other across the forehead, or with a short series of strokes extending from the hair-line down towards the eye-brows.[35] At the puberty ceremony for Gwi girls, who are usually already married before this age, similar tattoo marks are made on the faces of both husband and wife during which their bloods are intermixed. This act has a powerful symbolism, and is believed to link

Figure 164 *Site H8*

Steatopygous women with decorated thighs. The two figures leading the procession carry spears over their shoulders, while those behind carry sticks, one of them knobbed. The woman in the centre has a child on her back.

the couple together in a harmonious relationship. The designs do not follow any prescribed pattern, but one illustration shows three pronounced vertical bars on the forehead, and three across the cheek.[36] (Figures 117, 164, 167).

During the last century, Bushwomen on the western Lesotho border were described as having their faces and breasts speckled with red and yellow ochre and white clay,[37] and Cornwallis Harris encountered a 'bewitching maid' with a red painted nose, triangular red ochre patches on her cheeks, and meander patterns on her chest and upper arms.[38] Similar meander patterns were photographed on the thighs and shins of a Bushwoman in the Gemsbok Park who smeared her body with the blood of a freshly killed animal and then drew patterns with her fingers so as to expose the skin. She also painted radiating lines across her cheeks, but no reason for this action was obtained. Another woman using blood and ash painted a circular design on her forehead surrounded by dots, with more spots on her cheeks and around her mouth.[39] It is of note that a sorcerer-like figure painted in association with a dead eland in the Lotheni valley has, in addition to body markings, a

very extraordinary face with a red diamond shape around the mouth (Figure 101), and another small shelter near Qacha's Nek camp just south of the survey area, contains a remarkable collection of figures with distinctive facial markings. While the ethnographic record suggests that some body patterning among extant Bushmen may be purely decorative,[40] the practice was, on occasion, clearly associated with ritual symbolism.

Scarifications and other forms of decoration are also widely used by medicine men in the treatment of ailments.[41] In the 18th Century, Cape Bushmen were encountered whose faces had been coloured with red clay and black lines made from the ash of a certain nut considered to be a preventive against stiff joints, while other marks are made to bring good luck and to ensure success in hunting.[42] Southern Bushmen used to rub cuts with a mixture of fat and charcoal from a particular plant as a remedy for headaches, and when about to hunt, they treated their fingers, arms and foreheads with the same plant to ensure accurate aim. The power attributed to this plant was particularly potent, as a legend tells of the tribulations and final unconsciousness suffered by a man who went to dig it

Detail of upper part of Figure 165.

Detail of central part of Figure 165.

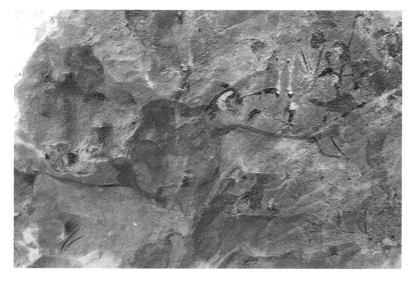

Figure 165   *Site Q20*

This complex scene is painted on the uneven ceiling of a rock-shelter on Swartmodder *and due to erosion of the original ground level, is now out of reach.*

A herd of delicately painted shaded polychrome eland are shown in a variety of poses, including foreshortened front and rear views (lower left). At lower right is an eland lying down as seen from the top, an unusual perspective similar to the eland reproduced in the frontispiece and in Figure 105.

In the centre, three eland in lateral view are closely associated with steatopygous women with whitened faces (see details at right and Figure 166). Some stand close behind eland, others bend towards eland with arms extended, and many of the women carry fly-whisks or staffs which apparently have some ceremonial significance.

Photo : Pat Carter.

255

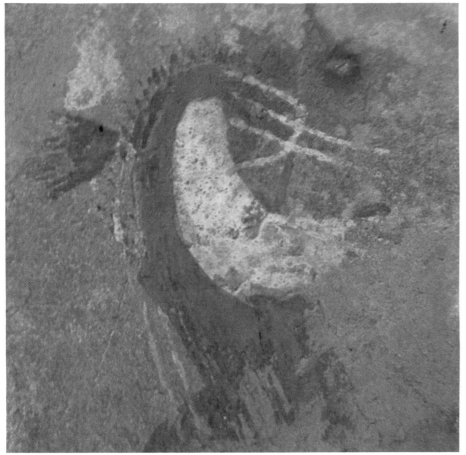

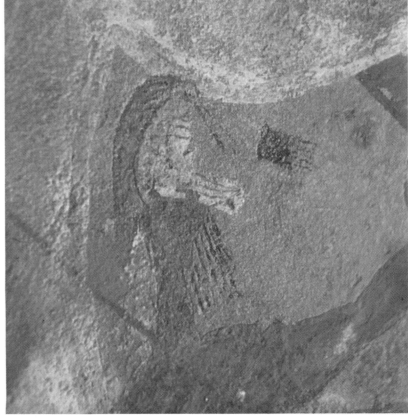

Figure 166 *Site Q20*

a. Above: *Details of the white painted faces of female figures associated with eland shown in Figure 165. At left, the concave face has a white strand looped across the forehead, with two long pendants hanging down in front. Attached at the back of the head, where short lines probably indicating hair project upwards, there is a decorative black tassel, and hair or thongs hang down the nape of the neck.*

b. At right: *The white face is decorated with red stripes across the cheek and forehead, and a tassel as well as two black pendants hang in front of the forehead (see Figure 117 for parallels among living Bushmen). There are also strands of hair or thongs hanging around the neck.*

Photos: Pat Carter and Patricia Vinnicombe

c. Lower right: *Black girls in Lesotho are painted white for participation in a puberty ritual. They wear plaited grass devices decorated with pendulous tassels at the back of their heads. While they dance, they have laid down the symbolic staffs that are an integral part of the ritual paraphernalia.*

Photo: Bert Woodhouse

256

up without understanding the proper ritual procedure which had to be followed. In order to revive him, rescuers blew smoke from the burning root into his nostrils, spat into his eyes, and cut his chest with an arrow-point to let blood. Long cuts were also made down the man's legs and on his thighs, and charcoal from the plant was rubbed into all the incisions. When he returned to camp, he was not allowed to sit to windward of his wife, nor to share the same hut with her, because he had 'new cuts'.[43]

Special scarifications are associated with boys' puberty rites after they have proved their ability as food providers by shooting a certain number of buck. These may be vertical incisions between the eyebrows, or on the cheek bones or shoulders. Although most extant Bushmen have forgotten the significance of these symbols, Miss Bleek was of the opinion that they were tribal marks connected with religion.[44] Other tattoos are made when a boy shoots his first bird or buck, part of the flesh or bone of which is burnt to a cinder, powdered, and rubbed into the incisions.[45] Among the Ko Bushmen in Botswana, both boys and girls have their faces painted to resemble the face of the gemsbok during puberty rites, and a small shield made from the brow-skin of this antelope plays an important part in the ceremonies.[46] J. F. Maingard elicited the information that other typical scarifications were connected with the 'gemsbok play' enacted at initiation, and he himself was struck by the singular importance of gemsbok in the social and communal life of the Bushmen in the southern Kalahari.[47] In my view, the white painted faces and marks across the cheeks so often represented in the rock paintings are probably similarly concerned with ritual procedures rather than with pure ornamentation. These marks are found not only on humans, but also occasionally on eland, small antelope and winged creatures. (Figures 107, 247, 249). In other instances lines are shown on the faces of anteaters which approach eland (Figures 95, 109, 237), anteaters being associated with medicine men by the Basotho. The similarities in facial decoration painted on man as well as animal suggest a close ritual relationship, and since most of the scenes in which this phenomenon occurs incorporate eland, I believe this to be further evidence of the metaphorical identification between Bushmen and eland in the southern mountain areas, just as Bushmen are identified with gemsbok in the more arid regions to the north.[48]

Another 'adornment' probably associated with puberty and hunting rites was recorded on 38 of the 405 paintings showing male genitalia. It consists of a single or double bar drawn across the penis

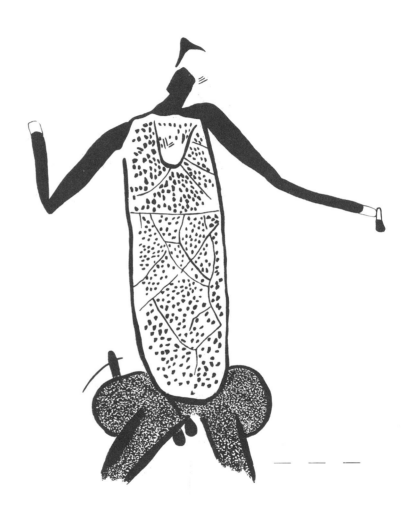

Figure 167 *Site W30*

This curiously patterned figure, the face of which was painted in transient pigment, has white hands and holds a small pouch or bag. Despite the marked steatopygia, it is masculine, with the bar across the genitalia noted among other paintings. The legs are unfortunately missing, and the red and white paintings with which it is associated (not reproduced here) are very indistinct.

and the bar is occasionally decorated with a tassel or similar ornament hanging from a cord. (Figs. 103, 168-9). Although this practice has been referred to as 'infibulation' in the literature, 'infibulation' implying the attachment of a ring or clasp to the male prepuce to prevent coitus from taking place, African ethnographic parallels lend little support to this suggestion. Penis sheaths, on the other hand, are widely used, and have been recorded among most Bantuspeakers as well as among Hottentots;[49] but their use by Bushmen has never been noted. If the Bushmen adopted the custom from their Hottentot and Bantu neighbours, they apparently added their own modifications, for typical penis sheaths are simple caps made from skin, wood or plaited vegetable fibre. The Bushman device, on the other hand, is usually represented as a rigid bar at right angles to the penis, and at a little distance from the tip. During the first quarter of this century, Mr A. T. McClean of the farm *Duart Castle* in the Mpendle district saw Bantu youths wearing a split mealie-stalk clipped on to the prepuce prior to circumcision, and the Bushmen may have had a similar habit connected with puberty rites. In the Kalahari, circumcision has only been recorded among acculturated Bushmen in the service of Bantu peoples,[50] but in the eastern region where their contact with the Nguni had extended over 500 years,[51] there is some evidence that the Bushmen participated in the circumcision ceremonies of their neighbours.

Dornan records that a certain Sotho circumcision song includes reference to the 'clever Bushman' who first taught them to perform the rite in a 'good manner'.[52] A fuller translation by Ellenberger reads:

> The astute Bushman uncovered what was hidden . . .
> The oxen crushed him whilst he was sitting on the ground . . .
> They started a quarrel on this score, insisting that we should pay them amends . . .
> We refused emphatically but . . .
> they had the upper hand and started their work . . .
> with whispers [i.e. quietly] and without outward demonstrations and songs.[53]

Pastor Ellenberger's interpretation of this song is that following an accident at a circumcision ceremony in which a Bushman was trampled and killed by an ox, a quarrel arose as a result of which a sanction was imposed on all the Sotho cattle owners, a sanction which entailed obligatory circumcision. By right of prior occupation, the Bushmen were the legitimate 'owners' of Lesotho, and just as the Sotho branded their cattle to make known their ownership, so the Bushmen 'branded' or circumcised the Sotho settlers as a mark that they 'owned' the newcomers.

Figure 168 *Site WII*
These figures with exaggerated genitalia and bar across the penis are reproduced actual size.

Father S. S. N. Norton, formerly a missionary in Lesotho, has also claimed that the Bushmen held precedence in Sotho circumcision lodges, and a Mosotho centenarian affirmed that the Bushmen had taught the Sotho their current method of circumcision.[54]

However, whether the Mountain Bushmen practised circumcision only on the Sotho or on themselves as well, the bar across the penis found among their rock paintings suggests a sexual or physiological significance, although a purely decorative motive cannot be ruled out. The practice may be related to puberty rites with or without circumcision, or it could denote a temporary taboo on intercourse or urination in connection with hunting procedure or other ritual activities. Kalahari Bushmen are very discreet in their reference to sexual matters,[55] and it is on record that a young Kung hunter would not speak of sex in front of women because this would 'weaken his power to hunt', whereas an older man could do so because he was past the age when many of the sex taboos applied to him.[56] Examples of such taboos are also found among the

Heikum Bushmen in South West Africa. A man who shot an eland or a giraffe, for instance, could not have intercourse with his wife when he returned to camp, and as an additional precaution against this, he had to sleep in the same quarters as the unmarried boys. Intercourse, it was believed, would interfere with the efficacy of the arrow poison, and the animal would not die.[57] A related practice was apparently adopted by the Cape Bushmen, although intercourse as such is not mentioned. After a hunter who had wounded an eland returned to camp to wait for the poison to take effect, an old man rolled up the hunter's front apron, and by tucking it into his waist belt, left the genitals exposed. The hunter was then instructed

> not to pass water freely, for if he did so, the eland would also pass water freely; if he passed water with difficulty, then the eland too would not pass water freely. For if he acted so, then the poison would hold and kill the eland, for the poison would hold its bladder shut, and it would not open to pass water.

The older men then made a separate hut for the hunter which children were not allowed to approach, and a patriarch slept with the man who shot the eland. The hunter was thereby set apart from his wife and family.[58] Although no mention is made of any actual device being attached to the penis, the phrases 'pass water with difficulty' and 'hold its bladder shut' imply a metaphorical barrier. The paintings showing a bar across the penis may therefore symbolise a prohibition rather than depict an actual practice, and this, in my view, is the most plausible explanation of the so-called 'infibulation' phenomenon.[59] It is also significant that most of the male figures displaying this genital device carry hunting equipment, and further support is lent to the ritual interpretation by the fact that many 'infibulated' hunters have the whitened faces already discussed.[60] (Figures 100, 103, 112, 169, 237).

Fine thongs hanging from various parts of the body are another decoration recurrently portrayed. If these were ornaments of beads or cords, one would expect to find them associated principally with women who are more partial to such ornamentation than are men among extant Bushmen,[61] or in dance scenes when additional finery is worn. Paradoxically, this is not the case, and it is usually figures in action and often carrying hunting equipment that display this feature. Although some of the thongs could represent decorative tassels on hunting bags, their excessive length would hardly be practical when stalking or chasing game, and it is of interest that many of the thongs or 'streamers' appear to emanate from under the arms. Possibly, therefore, perspiration rather

Figure 169 *Site C6*

Hunters with painted faces and carrying bows, quivers and arrows, have exaggerated sexual organs. The figure with excessively long torso and short legs (right), has an addendum to the tip of his penis, while the smaller figure facing him, with a face darker than the rest of his body, has a double bar across the penis.

than actual decoration is symbolised. Perspiration and its associated odour was regarded as a powerful agent by the Bushmen, and references to its supernatural properties are numerous. Perspiration could heal (Kaggen anointed his child's eye with the perspiration of his armpits and then placed it in water in order to make it grow 'like that which it had formerly been');[62] perspiration could harm ('it is his scent they fear for the eland . . . When anything lies dying, if our scent comes to it, our scent makes it lean')[63] and perspiration could transfer properties from one object to another ('One man anoints another, putting his hands under his armpits into the perspiration. And the other gets it on to his face, where the first man anoints him, that he may become like the first man.')[64] The importance of perspiration in connection with medicine dances and the initiation of sorcerers is discussed elsewhere,[65] and paintings showing figures with one arm raised and another apparently thrusting a hand towards the armpit may also be concerned with rites employing the use of perspiration. (Figures 98, 125, 171).

Sometimes shorter projections are shown emanating from the necks of figures, and again it is tempting to interpret these not as literal adornments, but rather as figurative thought processes. According to the Cape Bushmen, the thinking powers of man, or literally 'thinking strings', were to be found in the sides of their throats;[66] a belief possibly originating from an awareness of the jugular pulse during moments of stress, tension or intense concentration. (Figures 201, 228, 232).

It is of interest that Pager has independently advanced the suggestion that lines emanating from the mouths of some hunted animals, as well as from 'antelope men' and winged creatures or *alites*, may signify not purely physical matter such as blood or saliva, but possibly life itself escaping from the body.[67]

Whilst a great number of the decorative devices shown in the paintings may be taken as literal representations of ornamentation, some of the features are almost certainly symbolic representations of abstract ideas. The numerical data on human paintings and their associated artefacts should not, therefore, be used purely for the elucidation of ethnographic details.

References

1. See Lewis-Williams 1972: 50 for comparative figures.
2. See p. 250.
3. See p. 287.
4. Krige 1936: 354.
5. Arndt 1962.
6. Silberbauer 1965: 77; Marshall 1960: 341.
7. See also p. 247.
8. Bleek 1928a: 8.
9. Arbousset 1852: 354.
10. Orpen 1874: 5.
11. Dunn 1931: 36; Smith 1966: 204. Since writing this section on footwear it has been brought to my notice that a Bushman sandal made of leather was found during excavation of Giant's Main Cave prior to developing it as a Site Museum. This proves, therefore, that the Berg Bushmen did wear sandals on occasion.
12. For discussion, see Willcox 1956: 72-78.
13. Ellenberger 1912: 9.
14. See p. 30.
15. Pager 1971: 341; Lewis-Williams 1972: 53.
16. It is of interest that the Kung Bushmen in the Kalahari believe in mythical 'Gemsbok People' who often wear strings of beads round their necks. See Marshall Thomas 1959: 146.
17. Barrow 1801: 276.
18. Bleek 1928a: 12; 1928b.
19. Tyrrell 1968: 11, 15, 152; Bleek 1928b; Hahn 1928.

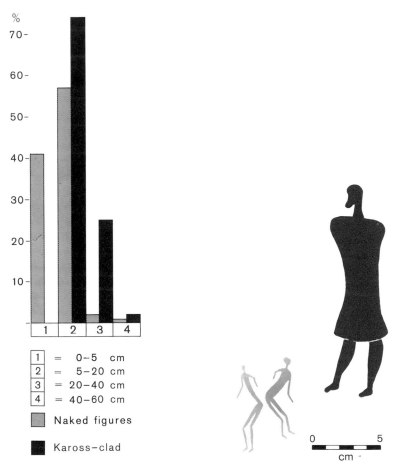

%

1	=	0-5 cm
2	=	5-20 cm
3	=	20-40 cm
4	=	40-60 cm

▨ Naked figures

■ Kaross-clad

Fig. 170: Relative size of naked and kaross-clad figures
The diagram is based on a sample of 12 sites containing a total of 604 naked figures and 102 figures wearing karosses. Only complete paintings are included, that is, figures in which both heads and legs are preserved. Seated figures are excluded.

The illustration is from the site C9 in the Hlatimba valley. The figures, in dark red, are superimposed on an eland in the original composition.

20. Arbousset 1852: 354.
21. Ellenberger 1912: 9.
22. See p. 57.
23. Wells 1933.
24. Christy Collection, No. 125.
25. I am indebted to Dr O. A. Leistner, seconded to the Royal Botanic Gardens at Kew in 1965, for the identification of the plants used in the manufacture of these hats.
26. Alexander 1838 (2): 19.
27. Dunn 1931: 36.
28. Arbousset 1852: 354; c/f Tyrrell 1968: 94.
29. Tyrrell 1968: 159, 169, 172, 179, 191, 196-8.
30. Turner 1962b.
31. Sibisi 1972: 125-127, 158-211.
32. Bleek 1928b: 114.
33. Marshall 1959: 355; Silberbauer 1965: 86; Marshall 1959: 234; Roos 1931.
34. Bleek 1928a: 10.
35. Bleek 1928b.
36. Silberbauer 1965: 85.
37. Arbousset 1852: 354.
38. Harris 1841: 262.
39. Dart 1937: Plates 78 & 86, No. 6.
40. Marshall Thomas 1959: 42.
41. Schapera 1930: 215.
42. Barrow 1801: 288; Bleek 1928: 10; Bleek in Stow 1930: Plate 29; Stow 1905: 49; Schapera 1930: 70.
43. Bleek 1935: B. S. 9: 153.
44. Schapera 1930: 122; J. F. Maingard 1937; Bleek 1928a: 10; 1928b: 114.
45. Schoemann 1957: 27; Marshall Thomas 1959: 197.
46. Heinz 1966: 117-129.
47. Maingard 1937.
48. See p. 166.
49. Bryant 1949: 134-6; Singer & Jopp 1967; Jeffreys 1968; Willcox 1972; Ucko 1969.
50. Schapera 1930: 71.
51. Cf. Sparrman 1786 (2): 27; Arbousset 1852: 364.
52. Dornan 1909.
53. V. Ellenberger, personal communication, 8/12/1964.
54. V. Ellenberger 1953: 63; personal communication, 8/12/1964.
55. See also p. 212.
56. Marshall Thomas 1959: 70.
57. Fourie 1928.
58. Bleek 1932, B.S. 6 (3): 235.
59. See also Breuil's views expressed in Willcox 1972.
60. See p. 257.
61. Marshall 1961; Bleek 1928a; 10.
62. Bleek 1911: 27.
63. Bleek 1932, B.S. 6 (3): 238.
64. Bleek 1924: 50.
65. See pp. 311, 314, 320.
66. Bleek 1875, No. 4; Bleek 1924: 28-30; see also pp. 347, 352.
67. Pager 1971: 341.

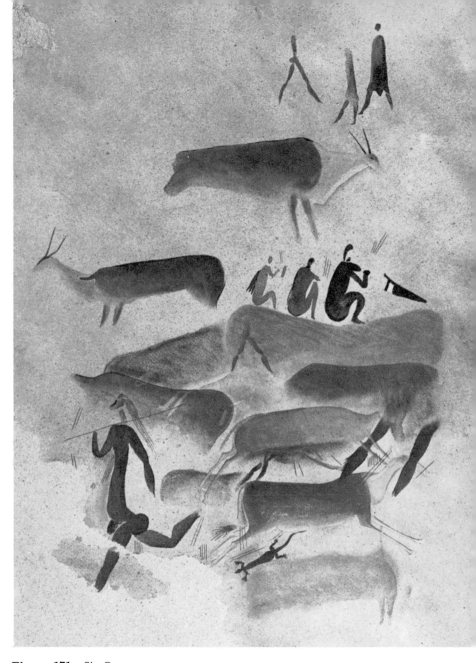

Figure 171 *Site C13*

A confusion of superimposed antelope and associated humans. The naked figure running at lower left has long emanations from the head and from under the arm. A lizard (lower centre), a rare representation among the paintings, is superimposed on a faded animal.

Figure 172 *Site Q4*

Hunters with whitened faces carry long bows. The shafts of the arrows, painted in transient pigment, have faded away completely, leaving only the arrow tips visible.

Weapons and Equipment

	%		
78	14	QUIVERS	
125	22	BOWS	
364	64	ARROWS	
567	100		

STUDY OF 150 SITES

	%		
340	15	QUIVERS	
494	22	BOWS	
1414	63	ARROWS	
2248	100		

Bows, arrows and associated quivers, the traditional weapons of the Khoisan people, are the most frequently depicted artefacts among the rock paintings. Together forming 55% of the total of 4 033 artefacts, arrows constitute 35%, bows 12%, and quivers or long bags 8%. Although some Bantu-speaking tribes such as the Zizi are also known to have used bows and arrows, their adoption was a result of close association with the Bushmen. Maingard, using documentary, philological and technological evidence, has argued that all the non-Bushman races south of the Limpopo adopted the use of the bow from the Bushmen.[1] There is little reason, therefore, to regard the peoples painted in association with these weapons as other than Khoisan. (Figure 173).

The most common type of bow depicted has a simple, gently curved stave usually little more than half the length of a human. If the average height of the male Bushman be taken as 155 centimetres[2] then the length of the bow would be about 90 centimetres. This accords with measurements given for bows used by other Southern Bushmen,[3] and with those of a Bushman bow found in a Drakensberg rock shelter in 1926 together with a complete and well preserved hunting kit now housed in the Natal Museum.[4] Some of the painted bows, however, are relatively much shorter than the above, being approximately equivalent in length to the torso of the carrier, while others are as long as the hunter himself. (Figures 28, 68, 172). It must therefore be assumed either that the relative proportions between human figure and bow were not always accurately portrayed, or that different types of bow were deliberately depicted. While proportions in the rock art record are often distorted, Stow recorded that long bows and short bows were used by different Bushmen, those of the Stormberg, Orange and Caledon favouring the shorter variety while those north of the Vaal river and further westward used a much longer bow.[5] Increasing encroachment by pastoral peoples forced Bushmen from several different regions to

Fig. 173: Frequency of appearance of hunting equipment.
The study of 567 weapons from 20 sites and the total sample of 2 248 weapons from 150 sites reflect a similar pattern.

seek refuge in the Lesotho mountain massif during the 19th century,[6] and this fact alone would account for diverse methods of weapon construction.[7]

In addition to simple lightly curved bows, a few paintings show sharply curved ends similar to Venda bow-staves. Others are asymmetrically curved, one side of the stave being bent more acutely than the other, with the string attached at some distance from the tip. (Figures 102, 233). As far as I know this pattern is not paralleled by any other bows in Africa;[8] but as a caution against taking the bow designs represented in the paintings too literally, it should be noted that the human beings associated with these bows of unusual design also display anomalous characteristics. Not only are they highly elongated and mannered in their gestures, but many of the figures stand cross-legged with animal hooves in lieu of feet. It may be, therefore, that the bows are similar creations of the mind, possibly associated with mythology.

In order to assess the inter-relationship between items of hunting equipment carried by individual figures, a detailed study was made of 20 painting sites[9] containing a total of 1 426 humans. Of these, 195 figures (17%) are shown carrying bows, arrows and quivers or long bags in various combinations. There are 125 clear portrayals of the bow, 78 long bags or quivers, and 119 figures carry a total of 364 arrows. Of the 125 bows, 89 (72%) are shown carried in the hand, usually held in a vertical position in front of the body, although sometimes running figures carry them horizontally across the body at about waist height. (Figures 112, 172, 178). In only 13 examples out of the 125 is the bow shown in the act of being drawn, and in paintings where left and right arm are clearly indicated, the bow is held in either hand. (Figures 103, 178, 202). A noticeable feature of many of the bows is the very shallow arc of the stave, almost as though the string had been relaxed and the bow was not carried taut and ready for action. (Figures 103, 104). The specimen found in the Drakensberg near Cathkin Peak displays similarly shallow curvature, the greatest distance between string and stave being but 3 centimetres.[10] The string is nevertheless quite taut and is securely attached at both ends with no easy means of adjusting the tension, and all extant Bushmen carry their bows strung and ready for action. The Drakensberg hunting kit includes a bow case made of sewn hide stiffened and made water-proof by a resinous substance. The greatest diameter of the case is only 5 centimetres, and it is gently curved to coincide with the shape of the bow. Although the paraphernalia carried by some figures in the painted record may include similar bow-cases, no certain identifications have yet been made. It is nevertheless probable that bows were at times protected in an all-purpose carrying bag, for as many as 31 of the 78 hunters associated with long bags in the study sample show no evidence of bows. (Figure 175). Since moisture renders bow-strings made from sinew lax and useless[11], the Bushmen inhabiting the high-precipitation valleys of the Drakensberg must have found some form of protection for their bows essential during the rainy season. (Figure 68).

Because of the limited curvature of many of the bow-staves, it is often not easy to decide whether bows or ordinary sticks are intended

Figure 174 *Site G3*
A slender figure with fuzzy hair-style or furry cap wears a knob on the head, and carries a knobbed stick as well as a bow.

in the paintings, particularly when the bow-string is absent. In the great majority of cases, the strings are painted with a white-based pigment, which is less permanent than the reds usually used for the staves. When only part of the bow is shown, for instance slung over the shoulder or protruding from a long bag, identifications are especially difficult. For the purposes of the present analysis, any rigid weapon other than an arrow shown carried in the hand or protruding from the back with no suggestion of a curve, is recorded as a stick, while those with a curve are listed as bows irrespective of the presence or absence of a string. It is very likely, however, that the criterion of a recognisable curve as the distinctive feature of a bow is often misleading, particularly if the rough rock on which many of the paintings are executed be taken into consideration. As an example of probable misidentification, it was noted that 10 of the 31 figures carrying hunting bags or quivers but no bow, are listed as carrying 'sticks'. It may be, therefore, that as high a proportion as 32% (10 out of 31) of the weapons recorded as 'sticks' in the overall analysis in fact represent bows. However, 16 of the 125 bowmen do carry sticks in addition to bows, and these were no doubt used for throwing or hitting, although pointed sticks for digging cannot be ruled out. Two of the sticks are knobbed. (Figure 174).

Of the 125 figures clearly carrying bows, 32 (26%) are shown with about half the weapon protruding from their backs, and 20 of these are associated with clearly visible quivers or long bags. This suggests that the Mountain Bushmen, like the present Kalahari Bushmen, also carried their bows over the shoulder. They either thrust the arm between stave and string, or insert half or more of the bow into a skin bag which is in turn slung over the shoulder. Sticks, fly-whisks and more commonly arrows may also protrude from these bags, and since arrows are associated with both quivers and general purpose hunting bags, it is at times difficult to distinguish between them. In the present analysis, no attempt has been made to differentiate between quivers and hunting bags, and all elongated containers shown slung across the body, protruding from behind the shoulders, or lying in isolation, are listed jointly. According to this classification, a total of 78 long bags or quivers are shown in association with the sample of 196 figures. Of these, 68 are carried on the back, 8 are lying beside seated figures and 2 are in the hands of sitting figures. Whilst the presumed hunting bags are roughly conical in shape, the presumed quivers are narrow and elongated. In the paintings, however, strictly cylindrical quivers are rarely depicted, although the tubular, parallel-sided design was widely used by the Southern Bushmen and is still found among Kalahari Bushmen.[12] It is significant that the quiver included in the hunting kit found in the Drakensberg is also of this cylindrical design. The Drakensberg specimen, hollowed from a section of wood and fitted with a skin cap, is but 39 centimetres long and $6\frac{1}{2}$ centimetres in diameter. It can therefore contain little more than the 20 arrows associated with it, together with other small items such as a wooden spatula for applying poison to the arrows, a small leather bag of what is possibly a poison mixture, and two metal blades partly bound with thonging. The quiver shows no attachment that would enable it to be suspended from the shoulder as a separate article, which suggests it was carried in a larger bag containing additional items of equipment, or else was left at camp and not necessarily carried on hunting excursions. A Xam Bushman, in relating a hunting legend, stated: 'the quivers are left at home;

Fig. 175: Methods of depicting hunting equipment.
The data represented by these bar diagrams are from a sample study of 20 sites containing a total of 364 individual arrows and 125 bows.

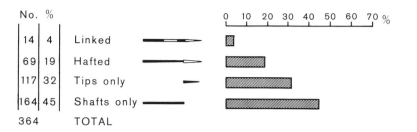

METHOD OF DEPICTING ARROWS

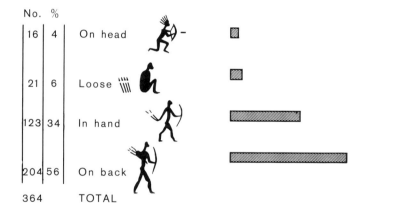

METHOD OF CARRYING ARROWS

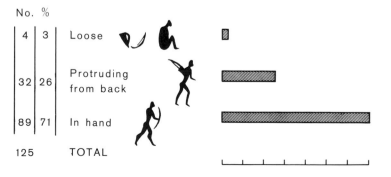

METHOD OF CARRYING BOWS

bags are what they kept a few arrows in. When it rains, then they take the quivers'.[13] This may be the reason why the larger conical-shaped bags with a wide opening tapering to a narrow base are more frequently illustrated among the paintings than the simple cylindrical quivers. (Figure 177).

It is not possible to ascertain from the paintings whether the long conical containers were cut and sewn to a specific pattern, or whether they were complete animal skins similar to the hunting bags in common use among the present Kalahari Bushmen.[14] Although the skin bags are soft and shapeless when empty, they are made rigid by the insertion of bow, stick and/or quiver, and do then assume a roughly conical outline.[15] The regular pattern of many of the containers shown in the paintings, sometimes with ornamental tassels or thongs and occasionally decorated with bands or spots around the opening, indicate that the artefact was made with more care and attention than bags consisting simply of complete animal skins. (Figure 171). It is significant that just over half the quivers or hunting bags in the sample study (40 out of 78) are not associated with paintings of arrows although 20 of the 40 show bows, which suggests that the arrows were often completely concealed within the bags. (Figure 175).

Figure 177 *Site B4*
Figures at rest, some holding hunting bags, others reclining near their equipment.

Figure 176 *Site E4*
Elongated figures carry long bags suspended by double thongs from their shoulders.

The bulk of the arrows actually visible in the paintings are shown protruding from the backs of the associated figures (56%), although as many as 31 of the 56 figures carrying arrows in this way have no visible quivers or long bags. Possibly these hunters were using the smaller cylindrical quivers which, because of their compact design, would not necessarily be visible in a silhouette painting. Evidence from paintings in Lesotho nevertheless suggests an alternative explanation. (Figures 127, 178). Here several bowmen appear to carry spare arrows thrust into a band on the upper arm or into a band around the body. The arrows do not protrude upwards and backwards from the shoulder as is common in other paintings, but lie at an angle across the thorax, the tips pointing backwards. That spare arrows were in fact carried in this manner on occasion is borne out in a drawing by Christol.[16]

Of the 195 human figures associated with archery in the study sample, 119 carry a total of 364 arrows. The average number of arrows per person is therefore just over three,[17] although some of the figures display from 6 to 9. Other figures not included in the detailed study carry from 20 to 30 visible arrows. (Figure 173). This would suggest that 3 arrows was a practical number to have readily available, while the balance were stored out of view within the quiver or long bag. The total number of arrows carried by any individual must have varied enormously, and it is likely that during the Bushmen's latter years, when bows were used for warfare as well as for the chase, the number of arrows required greatly increased. Orpen, for example, recorded that as many as 102 arrows were counted in a single quiver when a surprise attack was made on a Bushman camp in the Orange Free State.[18] Sometimes the arrows were stuck into a headband or fillet in order to have them easily accessible,[19] and although no rock-paintings within the survey area indisputably depict this usage, there are scenes of bowmen in action with spikes radiating upwards from their heads. These may well represent arrows although in no instance are the points clearly represented. (Figures 15, 28, 54). 56% of the total of 364 arrows in the sample are carried on the back, 34% are held in the hand, 6% are lying loose and are usually associated with seated figures, and 4% are possibly inserted in a headband.

The present state of preservation of the paintings shows 164 of the 364 arrows as simple shafts with no additional details (45%), while in 200 (55%) the heads are picked out in a contrasting colour. Because of the common use of a fugitive white pigment for the shaft, the tips, which are usually painted red, often appear in isolation (32%), while the remaining 23% are bichrome, or even polychrome where link shafts are shown. This division is, however, meaningless, as there is little doubt that arrows now represented only by points were originally the same as the arrows with shafts and heads in different colours. Conversely, some of the 45% of arrows now seen as simple shafts were no doubt originally embellished with points in fugitive pigments that are no longer visible, (Figure 175) which would increase the number of hafted specimens yet further. Clear illustrations of arrows with link-shafts number 14, or 4% of the sample; these are usually in two or more colours, and again the points often appear separated from the shaft due to the use of evanescent pigment. A more comprehensive count based on a larger sample would probably raise this figure marginally, as numerous examples of link-shafts can be seen in sites not included in the detailed study. (Figure 103). Occasionally quite clear bulbs

or nodules are shown at the intersection between link-shaft and point. Their function is uncertain although they possibly represent flight weights. Barbed heads, although rare, are also portrayed, and sometimes the arrow points are partly outlined in a contrasting colour which could suggest an application of poison. (Figure 178). The arrowheads are usually represented as simple tapering points probably fashioned from bone, although some broaden out into spear-like blades suggesting metal heads, as do the tanged points which are sometimes very exaggerated in size.[20] (Figures 127, 223a).

The 19 arrows found with the Cathkin Park hunting kit all measure from 30 to 41 centimetres in length. The shafts are made from culms of coarse grass, *Cymbopogon validus* or *Miscanthidium capense*, and in each case the notch for the bow-string is cut immediately below a node which is further strengthened by a sinew binding. The head or distal end of the shaft is cut just short of a node so that the pithy interior of the grass can admit a bone shaft or point without obstruction. The arrows are of two basic designs which include combinations of simple or linked shafts and bone or metal tips. In some, the bone shaft is all in one piece with the truncated end slotted for the insertion of a small metal tip. In others, the bone is in two sections linked by a small tube of grass no more than a centimetre in length and reinforced with sinew. The average length of the distal section of bone is shorter than the proximal, the function being to provide added weight and balance to the light and relatively flimsy shafts. The present Kalahari Bushmen intentionally manufacture their arrows so that the shaft will break off at the link once the quarry is shot. This prevents the point from being pulled out if the animal brushes against obstacles or bites at it with its teeth.[21]

Two of the arrows with link-shafts have simple tapered bone points while the remainder all have metal points. These are very small segments of iron with no tangs and a rounded tip only 6 millimetres long and 6 millimetres wide, the flattened base of which is fitted directly into a slit in the bone shaft. No gum is visible in the slot, but the whole exterior is thickly coated with poison. The 17 complete arrows all have a single barb attached about 12 millimetres from the tip. Because of the encrustation of poison not much of the barb protrudes and it is impossible to see whether they are made from quills, bone splinters or thorns. The barbs are about 12 millimetres long and were attached to the bone point by means of a sinew binding before the poison application. Neither the barbs nor the small metal heads are at all obvious. It is not surprising, therefore, that such details should be omitted from the majority of paintings in which the total length of the arrow is often little more than 32 millimetres; the relative size of the arrowhead would therefore be reduced to a mere pinhead.

The various types of arrow found in the Cathkin Park quiver, bone tipped, metal tipped, with and without compound link-shafts, suggest that the Mountain Bushmen, like those from other regions, used different arrows for different types of game. It has also been claimed that the Bushmen of the same locality used a variety of poisons, each fulfilling a specific purpose.[22] Inspection of the Cathkin Park arrows nevertheless shows the points all to be coated with what is apparently the same poison, although chemical analysis would possibly reveal differences. The poison is a very thick blackish substance at present cracking and crumbling, and is applied all over the point of the arrow down to a distance of about 5,7 centimetres. It is possible, therefore, that the colour differentiation in many of the arrow paintings depicts the poison application and not necessarily a hafted tip. (Figure 178).

Two other bone-pointed arrows from the Little Bushman Pass, Drakensberg, were presented to the Natal Museum by Gilbert Randles in 1914 (*Catalogue No.* 2251 and 2252). These show similar details to those from Cathkin Park, but there is no link-shaft, the bone points being inserted directly into the grass culm forming the shaft. One of the specimens[23] has a white latex-like coating over the tip, and the junction between point and shaft displays a shiny black substance. While this is possibly an application of poison, it is quite unlike the dark, thickly encrusted poison on the Cathkin arrows. (Figure 68).

Yet another cache of arrows ascribed to the 'Bosjesmen' and said to have been found in a cave in the Drakensberg is housed in the Natal Museum.[24] They are 7 in number, 3 being incomplete, and were presented by Miss Henderson in 1896. Unfortunately no additional information is recorded. These arrows are very much larger and heavier than the specimens from Cathkin Park, their length being between 59 and 78 centimetres, while the weight varies from 18,5 to 31,8 grams. The average weight of the Cathkin set is but 7 grams. The shafts of the Henderson arrows are made from Berg bamboo, *Arundinaria tessellata*, with heavy metal heads inserted directly into the bamboo which is strengthened with a coarse sinew binding. The heads vary in shape; one has swallow-tail barbs, another a flattened spear-like head with no barbs, a third a similar head with barbed shaft, while the fourth has a rounded end with long multi-barbed shaft. There is no evidence of poison on any of the arrows. The notches on the butt ends of the shafts are much deeper than those on the Cathkin arrows, but the area immediately above the notch is similarly strengthened with sinew to prevent splitting. Two of the Henderson specimens show incised and blackened decorations above the notch, in one four fine parallel lines have been carved around the circumference of the bamboo shaft, in the other parallel bands separate two distinctive zig-zag patterns. These may be ownership marks, although no such distinguishing features are observable on the Cathkin specimens. Three of the Henderson arrows, those with incomplete heads, are feathered down one side of the shaft. No clear evidence of feathering has yet been recognised among the paintings but sometimes the notch is shown in a rather exaggerated form. (Figure 178). Because the precise provenance and association of the Henderson arrows is doubtful, they must be regarded with caution as they may have belonged to Bantu-speakers allied to the Bushmen rather than to the Bushmen themselves. Whoever the original owners were, it is nevertheless certain that the added weight of all-metal arrowheads increased the weight of the arrows considerably, which must in turn have required a far heavier bow to put them to flight. Mr A. T. McClean of the farm *Duart Castle* in the Mpendle district has in his possession a 'Bushman' bow and set of arrows thought to originate from the Estcourt district. No further information is available, but the arrows are very similar to those found by Miss Henderson in a Drakensberg rock shelter, and the bow is correspondingly far larger and heavier than the Cathkin specimen, with a thicker bow-string and a greater curvature of the stave.

The materials used for the arrow-shafts are all indigenous to the montane belt of the Drakensberg. *Arundinaria tessellata* is locally common on streambanks and is found as far up valleys as the lowermost basalt cliffs. *Miscanthidium capense* is frequently dominant on stream-banks and along margins of scrub and forest up to an altitude of about 6 600 feet, while *Cymbopogon validus* favours similar situations including cliff ledges and moist gulleys up to 9 000 feet.[25] The collection of these grasses could not have presented much difficulty to the Mountain Bushmen, but the materials for bow-staves and ingredients for arrow-poisons were not so easily procured. Although no definite identification of the wood used for the Cathkin bow can be made without sectioning the stave, it is close-grained and light in colour, and both Professor A. W. Bayer and Dr O. Hilliard suggested white iron wood, *Vepris undulata* (*V. lanceolata*) which is found principally in the coastal and midland forested zones. Other woods possibly suited to bow-making are *Grewia occidentalis* and *Halleria lucida*, the distribution of which is less restricted as they grow in selected areas from the Drakensberg to

Figure 178a *Site X I I*

Part of a line of eleven hunters who run towards the recumbent eland shown in Figure 93. The detail in the weapons carried is remarkable. The arrows have compound link-shafts, the heads and shafts of some are barbed, and the tips of others appear to be coated with poison. In some examples the nock in the shaft is clearly shown. Two of the figures carry spare arrows thrust into a band on the upper arm, and the arrows seen protruding from their backs may similarly be carried in a body band. There is no suggestion of a quiver. The hunters have white painted faces with one, two or three bars across the cheek, and they all have hair or thongs hanging from the back of the head. (See also overleaf.)

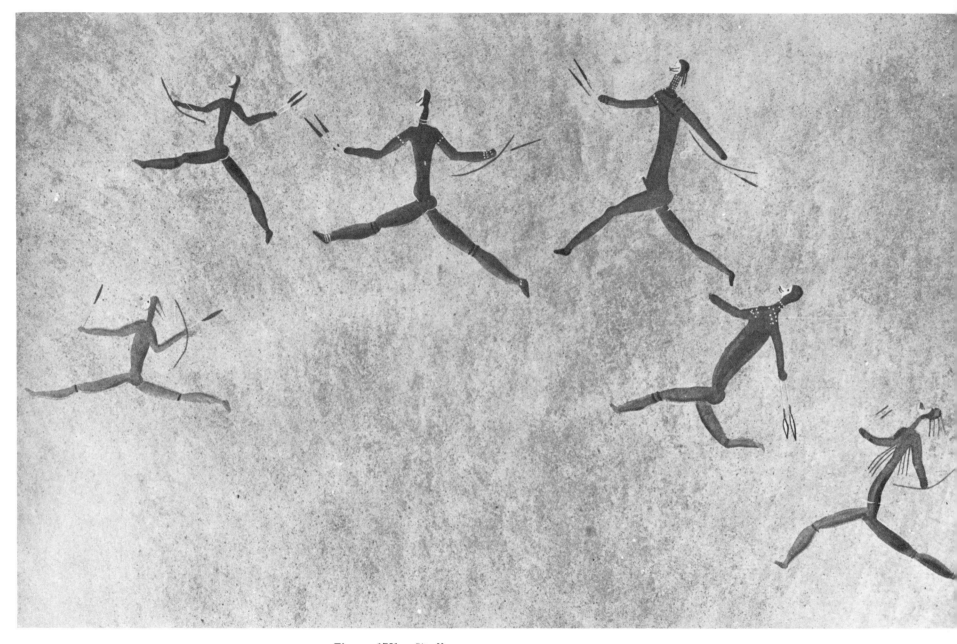

Figure 178b *Site X11*

These white-faced hunters are a continuation of the paintings shown overleaf and in Figure 93.

the sea. It must therefore have been necessary for some of the Bushmen, particularly those living in the Lesotho highlands, to make periodic excursions to forested areas to procure suitable wood for bow-staves as well as for throwing and digging sticks. Indeed, legends collected from a Lesotho Bushman allude to this fact: Kaggen sent Cogaz to cut sticks to make bows. When Cogaz came to the bush the baboons caught him, and there is also mention of young boys being sent to collect digging sticks for the women.[26] Another myth states that Kaggen 'went to his nephew to get arrow poison, and he was away three days', which suggests that considerable distances were travelled to obtain this commodity.[27]

Among the plant poisons widely used by the Bushmen were *Acokanthera oblongifolia* and *Acokanthera oppositifolia* (*A. venenata*).[28] *A. oblongifolia* occurs only in the coastal vegetation of Natal and the Eastern Cape Province whereas *A. oppositifolia* is typically confined to midland and lowland valley bushveld. Very occasionally, however, it can also be found in the tall grassveld, and even more rarely in hot, dry situations on north-facing slopes immediately at the foot of the Cave Sandstone in the highland sourveld.[29] Both Ellenberger and How[30] state that the Lesotho Bushmen used, among other ingredients, poison collected from a tree that grows in Natal. Silayi, a Thembu who lived among Bushmen in the north-eastern Cape, said the poison used on their arrows was prepared by the chief from the root of a shrub mixed with the bark of a tree. Although he knew the shrub (which suggests it grew locally), he did not know the tree from which the bark was obtained. The poison mixture was boiled together in a clay pot until it became a black-looking jelly, the whole process taking several days to complete.[31] Other records describe the wood of *Acokanthera* being pounded into a rough powder or divided into slivers, and then boiled in a clay vessel together with a little water until a dark glutinous liquid was obtained. This was then mixed with fresh juice drawn from the stem of a *Euphorbia* tree which was believed to enhance the toxicity of the arrow poison. A sample of arrow poison labelled 'Drakensberg' and presented to the Natal Museum in 1918[32] is stated to consist of various 'herbs' mixed with the venom of snakes and aloe juice. The sample adheres firmly to a plate of glass on to which it must have been poured when in a thick viscous state. The mixture has a dark, shiny appearance, and in addition to other small pieces of vegetable matter, it contains five Euphorbia thorns, probably from the species *Euphorbia pseudocactus*, the distribution of which is limited to the hot, dry valley bottoms of the Thukela river and its principal tributaries.[33] In a study of arrow poisons used in Tanzania, Raymond

noted that although *Acokanthera venenata* grew only in one locality in the Southern Province, it was well known to the natives of surrounding districts who came to purchase it. The poison was also peddled to other districts, and the sales extended in all directions to a radius of 150 to 200 miles.[34] References to the collection of arrow-poison already quoted strongly suggest that similar trading patterns existed between Natal and the hinterland.

Acokanthera poisons are more toxic during the dry winter seasons than the wet summers, and they remain unimpaired for two to three years if protected from sun and rain.[35] Sometimes the prepared arrows were covered with soft hide or animal membrane to keep the poison soft and in good condition. This demonstrates the necessity of water-proof quivers or bags for the safe and economic storage of arrows, and also explains the present dried and cracked condition of the poison on the Cathkin arrows. If the small skin bag included in the Cathkin hunting kit indeed contains poison, it is noteworthy that it bears no resemblance whatsoever to the black glue-like poison on the arrows. The contents of the skin envelope is a tightly packed light-coloured substance, which could conceivably be powdered bark which would have to be boiled before being applied to the arrows with the wooden spatula also carried in the quiver. Although it is claimed that some poisons were prepared in secrecy, the majority were apparently mixed and distributed with the minimum of fuss and ceremony. Elaborate rites were nevertheless performed before and after hunting to ensure the potency of the poison.[36]

Spears, although not an essential for hunting, were normally used for delivering the *coup de grace* to animals either wounded by poisoned arrows or caught in snares.[37] They constitute 4% of the artefact sample, and are not so commonly depicted as are bows (12%), arrows (35%) or hunting bags (8%). In the paintings the barbed heads are usually somewhat exaggerated in size which again suggests the use of iron. Indeed, the painted record reflects an increased use of this weapon after contact with Bantu-speakers and Europeans, as many of the scenes showing the use of spears include domestic animals. When hunting animals on horseback, the spear virtually replaced the use of bow and arrow. (Figures 5, 108, 252). It is noteworthy that women, too, are sometimes portrayed carrying a spear over the shoulder, usually in scenes where steatopygous characteristics are exaggerated and dress is elaborate. (Figures 164, 224). This somewhat unusual association of the female with a male weapon may perhaps be linked with a courtship or marriage ceremony in which the young Bushwoman shows approval of her suitor by

Figure 179 *Site W5*
Hunters with barbed spears.

accepting his hunting gear;[38] or a girl's puberty rite in which male weapons play a symbolic role.[39]

Sticks are another accessory to hunting, and form a high proportion of the total artefacts portrayed (26%), although as many as a third of this number may be intended to represent bows.[40] The sticks are most commonly about half the length of the figure with which they are associated, although great variations in size occur. Some are excessively long, even longer than the figures carrying them, while others, often associated with dancing groups, are so short as to appear more of a ceremonial baton than a utilitarian weapon. (Figures 222, 233). Approximately 5% of the sticks are knobbed, and these are often illustrated in scenes of personal combat. (Figure 33a). Throwing sticks are still commonly carried by Bantu-speaking peoples, and by hurling them so that they move though the air in a horizontal plane with a whirring rotary movement, startled birds and small mammals are often felled.

Weighted digging sticks are also associated specifically with Khoisan peoples, and were used principally by the women to unearth roots and tubers. These form only 1% of the total artefacts depicted, while carrying bags or pouches constitute 4%.[41] (Figure 195). Occasionally forked or multi-pronged sticks are shown, which might have been used for securing portions of honeycomb,[42] (Figure 182), but no actual scenes of bees or honey-collecting have yet been found within the survey area. Several such scenes, which include the use of ladders, have been recorded from the tributaries of the Thukela river to the north.[43]

So-called 'fly-switches' (1%) are an additional item of equipment encountered in the painted record. Made from grass or the tail of an animal such as a jackal, hyena, or gnu, they were used by Khoisan peoples not only for keeping pestilential insects at bay, but also as a type of handkerchief to mop up perspiration. On occasion they were used to convey signals and also played an important part in certain dances.[44] Paintings of hunters sometimes show them carrying a type of 'fly-switch' among their gear (Figures 30, 104, 112), but these could be plumes or brushes consisting of bunches of feathers tied to sticks which were used as an aid to driving game.[45] The feathers were specially treated with a noxious scent disliked by animals, and the 'brushes' were stuck into the ground in strategic positions to divert the game and thereby channel it to places where the hunters were hiding.[46] Other paintings of a mythical or ceremonial character show human figures extending similar 'brushes' towards eland. (Figures 165, 247). Although the precise intention of

Figure 180 *Site J13*

The upper figures, wearing short skin karosses and with bags or bundles on their backs, carry long sticks over their shoulders. The karosses of the lower figures were painted in fugitive white pigment, and are now barely discernible.

shoulder, the prongs pointing backwards. (Figure 29). I have not yet found a convincing explanation of this perplexing item of equipment. It could conceivably represent a bunch of spears held in the hand, the blades forming the 'prongs',[52] or the object may be a specially designed riding goad, or even a gun with a decorative or waterproofing device thrust into the barrel.

There are at least 49 depictions of guns in the total artefact sample studied, and most of these are carried by horsemen, usually over the shoulder or held in front of the saddle. Others are shown in the act of being fired, and are mostly of the long-barrelled flint-lock design. (Figures 15, 40, 41).

Other artefacts of non-Khoisan origin are shields and battle-axes which are the traditional weapons of the Bantu. The design of the shields can be ascribed to the Sotho, Barolong, Pondo and Zulu peoples, while the battle-axes, only four of which are at all distinctive, are probably also of Zulu origin.[53] Most of the shields and battle-axes can be dated to post 1820, and the variety of designs represented confirms the mixed composition of peoples with whom

these scenes is not known, the 'brushes' possibly contain substances not intended to frighten game, but rather to subdue or tame them. In Xam mythology, 'rain-animals' were subdued by the use of scented herbs: ('If the bull had smelt *buchu*, it would have been calm and gone quietly without struggling');[47] and the bull which abducted a girl of the 'early race' was put to sleep through being rubbed with *buchu*.[48] The Lesotho myths tell of a snake which was beguiled by the use of charms and scented herbs, while both dead eland and Kaggen's son were made to come alive again by the use of a similar charm, *canna*.[49]

Among the less common artefacts recorded in the paintings are long flexible fishing spears often associated with small boats or floats.[50] One of the spears recorded from the survey area is forked and barbed (Figure 206), but none shows the detachable harpoon heads known to have been used by the Bushmen in historic times, and which are illustrated in a fishing scene recorded from western Lesotho.[51]

Another unusual weapon featured in the paintings is commonly associated with riders on horseback. It is a rod or stick terminating in three prongs, and is usually shown held upright in front of the saddle, prongs upwards, although it sometimes rests over the

Figure 181 *Site P4*

A bowman aims a flight of arrows towards an unidentifiable animal, while four hunters wearing distinctive skin aprons and carrying metal battle-axes run in to the kill. Nguni and Sotho farmers are known to have employed Bushmen to assist them in hunting, and this scene possibly represents such combined action.

the Mountain Bushmen were in contact during the latter part of their history. (Figures 36–39, 181).

Only a small proportion of the artefacts depicted in the paintings (2%), has been listed as 'unidentifiable'. This includes objects of peculiar shape often associated with human figures which also display unusual characteristics. (Figures 101, 233). Small decorated rods and other special cult objects are known to be used in puberty and initiation ceremonies by the Ko Bushmen in the Kalahari,[54] and among the Bushmen further south, particular 'rods' were associated with ritual curing dances.[55] Although the precise function of some of the artefacts shown in the paintings is no longer understood, they may similarly be connected with ritual or ceremonial activities.

References

1. Maingard 1932.
2. Dart 1937.
3. Kirby 1936; Maingard 1937.
4. Vinnicombe 1971, see also Figure 68.
5. Stow 1905: 68.
6. Dornan 1909.
7. See also p. 268 for discussion on increased bow size in relation to heavy metal arrow tips. In some instances, therefore, increase in bow size may have been related to increased contact with metal-using peoples.
8. Leakey 1926; Maingard 1932.
9. The sites analysed in the detailed study were B1, B3, B4, B6, C6, C12, C13, C14, C15, C16, D3, E2, F4, F5, F6, F17, G3, K1, N2.
10. Vinnicombe 1971.
11. Orpen 1908: 465; Campbell 1815: 200.
12. For descriptions and/or illustrations of quivers, see Stow 1905: 70; Sparrman 1786 (I): Pl. 2; paintings by Angas 1846 & Bains 1865 in The Fehr Collection, Cape Town; Silberbauer 1965: 58; Schapera 1930: Pl. 10.
13. Bleek 1924: 59.
14. Silberbauer 1965: 59.
15. Stow 1930: Pl. 10: 140; Schapera 1930: Pl. XI.
16. Christol 1911: 4; see also How 1962.
17. The average number of arrows per person based on the detailed study of 195 figures is corroborated by the total sample which works out at 3,1 arrows per person, that is, 453 figures carry 1 414 arrows.
18. Orpen 1908: 477.
19. Stow 1905: 71.
20. Recent finds of tanged arrowheads fashioned from chalcedony in Eastern Lesotho indicate that paintings of barbed arrow-heads in the Drakensberg need not necessarily imply metal. The stone tips are nevertheless small, on an average 17 millimetres long by 12 millimetres wide (Carter 1970a).
21. Logie 1935; Silberbauer 1965: 55.
22. Stow 1905: 75.
23. Natal Museum No. 2251.
24. Catalogue No. 78.
25. Killick 1963.
26. Orpen 1874, see also p. 224.
27. It has been recorded that Bushmen could not only cover 50 miles in a day but keep up the pace day after day (Dunn 1931: 7). At a conservative estimate therefore, the distance travelled on this occasion was possibly over 50 miles each way, and even then the nephew may have traded with an intermediate party who had obtained the poison from still further afield.
28. Schapera 1925; Shaw, Woolley & Rae 1963.
29. D. Edwards: pers. comm. 29/9/1969; E. Moll, pers. comm. 26/9/1969; Acocks 1953.
30. Ellenberger 1953: 133; How 1962: 44.
31. Stanford 1910.
32. Natal Museum Catalogue No. 2398.
33. Edwards 1967.
34. Raymond 1947.
35. Watt & Breyer-Brandwijk 1962; Raymond 1947.
36. Schapera 1925; Raymond 1947; Shaw, Woolley & Rae 1963; see also pp. 300-304.
37. Silberbauer 1965: 59; Schapera 1930: 133.
38. Metzger 1950: 53; Fourie 1925-6: 60.
39. Silberbauer 1965: 85; Heinz 1966: 122.
40. See p. 264.
41. See p. 280.
42. Dunn 1931: 25.
43. Pager 1971: 351.
44. Chapman 1868: 91; Sparrman 1786 (2): 36; Stow 1905: 49; Bleek 1924: 60-64.
45. Bleek 1911: 359.
46. Willcox 1963: 26.
47. Bleek 1933, B.S. 7 (4): 382.
48. Bleek 1911: 197.
49. Orpen 1874: 7, 8.
50. See also pp. 119, 125.
51. Ellenberger 1953: 109; Vinnicombe 1965.
52. See illustration in Gordon-Brown 1914: 113.
53. Tylden 1946; Tylden: personal communication March 1968.
54. Heinz 1966: 119, 122, 129.
55. Arbousset 1842: 353; Stow & Bleek 1930: explanation of Plate 2a.

Figure 182 *Site Q4*

Figures carrying pronged sticks, one of which is forked at both ends. These may have been used to secure combs of honey, or to catch snakes. The white face and neck of the person on the right has completely faded away. (See also Figure 144). For convenience, the paintings illustrated here have been moved closer together than they appear on the rock, and superpositions have been omitted.

Figure 183 *Site G3*

Women with carrying bags slung on their backs and weighted digging sticks in hands. Wedges are inserted on the underside of the bored stone weights in order to keep them secure.

Food Gathering

Figure 184 *Site W8*
The work of the Bushwoman is not easy.

The quantity of wild vegetable which had been dug in the mountain to be used as food also showed it to have been more than a temporary abode.[1]

These words, written by John Shepstone in March 1849, described a rock shelter recently vacated by Bushmen in the vicinity of the upper Mzimkhulu river in the Drakensberg, and suggest that the Mountain Bushmen, like hunter communities in other temperate parts of the world, relied for their livelihood on plant-foods to an even greater extent than on meat.[2]

On Mpongweni Mountain, and overlooking the catchment of the Mzimkhulu river, the exact area visited by Shepstone, there is a charming painted group of four pendulous-breasted women returning from a food-gathering expedition. Three have bulky food bags on their backs, and in their hands they carry weighted digging sticks.[3] (Figure 183).

Bushman digging sticks, known as *kibi*, were about one metre long and consisted of hard wood sharpened at one end, often weighted with a centrally-pierced stone that was threaded on to the stick like a giant bead. Sometimes the points of the sticks were strengthened by fire-hardening or by the addition of an animal horn. The bored stones, used as a weight to give added momentum in hard ground, were secured on the lower half of the digging stick by means of a short wedge inserted from the underside. The size of the holes in these stones suggests that the sticks most commonly used had a diameter of about 2,5 centimetres. Weights of individual stones vary considerably, but from published data, it is possible to calculate an average weight of about 1,5 kilogrammes (3,3 lbs.).[4] They were made from any suitably rounded stone, usually a close-grained sandstone, and were perforated by picking with a long pointed flake, first from one side of the axis and then the other, until the two holes met in the centre. The aperture was then made more regular by using a tapered stone reamer with a rotatory action. To obtain symmetry the outside surface of the stone was often pecked all over, then at times rubbed smooth again.[5,6] The hours of labour involved in the preparation of a digging stone, known to the Southern Bushmen as '*Tikoe*' or '*Strong hand*', was sometimes all in vain when, in the final stages, an impatient or misdirected blow broke the stone in half before the hole was completed. Occasionally, too, the stone would break during digging, or, if the wooden stick became wet, it was liable to swell and burst the weight. Such a stone, broken in half, was found lying on the southern slopes of Mpongweni Mountain where it was doubtless dropped by an exasperated Bushwoman while out foraging.[7] A complete stone, apparently dropped or left at a temporary camp site, was picked up on arable flats in the nearby Pholela valley.[8] The locality of both these finds is within a day's collecting range from the paintings depicting food-gatherers returning from their labours.

It is clear from Bushman stories collected by the Bleeks that the process of digging for 'veldkos' was far from easy, and often resulted in sore and blistered hands.[9] (Figure 184). Although this was principally a feminine task, men also participated when conditions for hunting were poor, but their digging sticks were usually not weighted with a stone.[10]

In the paintings it is obviously impossible to differentiate between ordinary throwing sticks and digging sticks without weights, but the weighted sticks are usually associated with figures which,

Legends collected from the Lesotho Bushman named Qing indicate that women took a part in the manufacture or maintenance of their own digging sticks (Kaggen's wife took her husband's knife and used it to sharpen a digging stick), and that they complained if the sticks were not up to standard (a number of little boys were sent to get sticks for women to dig ants' eggs, but one of the women grumbled, saying the stick she received was crooked while those of the others were straight).[12] Since trees have a very limited distribution in Lesotho, special trips over considerable distances must have been made to gather suitable wood, so it would not have been possible to replace inadequate or broken sticks without delay. However, despite the preference for straight sticks, it is notable that among the paintings a number of supposed digging sticks are distinctly curved at the lower end. Possibly this type of stick, with or without the addition of a curved horn, served a special purpose, or they might even represent a slightly bowed musical instrument with resonator attached.[13] Some of the sticks are disproportionately long and may depict rods for poking into rodents' burrows or subterranean ants' nests. (Figure 186).

Figure 185   *Site F6*

A kaross-clad figure carries a weighted digging stick across the shoulders, and a bag with tassels on the back.

even if breasts as such are not clearly shown, display the marked steatopygia and steatomeria typical of Bushwomen. The figures are also usually devoid of clothing other than scanty aprons, suggesting that food-gathering was predominantly a summer occupation. (Figures 183, 187, 195). On occasions, however, kaross-clad figures are also shown carrying digging sticks (Figures 185, 193), which supports the hypothesis that vegetable products, though not so readily available during the cold winter months, were an essential component of Bushman diet throughout the year.

The digging sticks are usually shown carried in one hand which is held out in front of the body, or they are balanced over the shoulder. Occasionally they lie by the side of shelters or huts, or alongside seated groups, and although there are examples of women in digging positions, that is, bending over or squatting, the depiction of digging sticks *in use* is rare in the painted scenes. Carrying-straps attached to the shaft of the digging stick are clearly shown in paintings in the Ndedema gorge to the north,[11] but this detail is either absent or not preserved in the area of this study.

Figure 186   *Site B5*

Woman with long stick curved at the lower end.

Figure 187 *Site W8.*
A party of women with digging sticks accompanied by dogs.

Figure 188 *Site S3*

A woman about to dig up a bulbous plant, with weighted digging stick in hand, and tasselled collecting bag suspended from her shoulders. The painting, in orange-red, is on display in the Durban Museum, and is one of several slabs of rock said to have been removed from the farm Vielsalm *(Site S3), in East Griqualand.*

In two painted groups food-gatherers are shown accompanied by animals almost certainly intended to represent dogs, and in one a hare is possibly depicted. (Figures 84, 187). This suggests that dogs sometimes accompanied the women on foraging expeditions, and no doubt small mammals, when these could be captured, were a welcome addition to the contents of the bag carried back to camp.

Although 47 digging sticks (1% of the total artefacts) are depicted in sites included in the present painting analysis, botanical subjects clearly recognisable as such are very rarely found. This curious absence of plants associated with food-gathering has been noted throughout the rock paintings of the Republic of South Africa,[14] although in Rhodesia they are more common. The reason for this is difficult to ascertain, but it is noteworthy that although the Southern Bushmen attributed magical properties to particular plants,[15] their mythology gives no hint of any vegetable associations with their deity. Among the Kung Bushmen of the northern Kalahari, on the other hand, there are such references as 'Xue's son was a *bobo* plant, and he was a *sao* plant. . . . And Xue heard, and he was a *naxane* fruit',[16] while the Naron believed that in olden times trees

as well as animals were people.[17] Drawings made by two young Kung boys represent Xue as various trees bearing edible fruits and berries which closely resemble some of the Rhodesian paintings.[18] In addition to directly phytomorphic conceptions of their deity, some Bushmen perform special rituals related to food-gathering. Kung women, for instance, herald the ripening of veld foods in the summer season with a special ceremony which, though executed without fuss or audience, is considered very important. The purpose is to protect the women from the harmful effects of certain 'powerful' foods and to integrate the life force of the plants with the life force of the people.[19] It is possible, therefore, that a greater religious significance was attached to specific plants by the Bushmen north of the Tropic of Capricorn than by those who lived on the open grassland further south.

Among the slabs of painted rock displayed in the Durban Museum and said to have been removed from the farm formerly known as *Vielsalm* in Mount Currie district (sites S2 and S3), there is a singular illustration of plant life. A steatopygous woman, body leaning forward so that her breasts and tasselled collecting bag swing free, runs with digging stick in hand towards a solitary bulbous plant with lanceolate leaves. One is left to guess whether this was an especially rare medicinal find or whether it was a tasty addition to everyday vegetable fare, but there is no mistaking the woman's eager intention. (Figure 188).

Skin collecting bags were an essential adjunct to food-gathering, and are depicted in the paintings in two basic forms. They appear either as single skins suspended sling-fashion from the shoulder, with the bulk of the produce hanging at the back, or as sewn bags with a rounded base and a carrying-handle. The latter are often decorated with tassels at the sides or thongs that hang like a fringe underneath. The bags, usually slung like a bandolier across one shoulder, are carried so that they hang either at the back, side or front of the body. Only rarely are they carried in the hand. (Figures 189, 190). Often they are simply lying, with other accoutrements, beside seated or standing figures. Some scenes depict what are almost certainly sandstone shelters or small huts with tasselled bags hanging from the roof. (Figures 53, 219). The most detailed of these groups shows the bags suspended from forked branches where the food was no doubt stored beyond the reach of children and dogs. Against the shelter walls are rounded objects that may represent grinding stones used in the preparation of food. (Figures 24, 26). From records left by those who saw shelters recently vacated by the Drakensberg

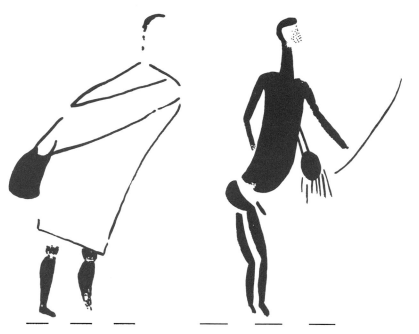

Figures 189 and 190

Left: *Site Q3*

Figure in a light-coloured skin kaross carrying a skin bag slung diagonally over the shoulder.

Right: *Site G3*

Figure with a 'hook head' and light-coloured face carries a tasselled skin bag hanging from the shoulder and swinging in front of the body. In paintings such as this, it is difficult to determine whether male genitalia or a front apron made of skin are represented.

Bushmen, it is evident that their utensils included pots and calabashes as well as European trade goods when these could be obtained.

Among the paintings in the area surveyed there are but few scenes that may be said to illustrate food preparation, although several groups show seated figures with bags and other apparatus lying strewn around, including handled objects of uncertain identification. (Figs. 192, 194, 215). A comparatively popular representation is just two figures sitting facing one another, apparently enjoying a gossip. One can well imagine Bushwomen returning to their shelter after a successful day's collecting, bags bulging with a variety of foods, and then settling down to pound or grind their less digestible finds whilst having a friendly chat. (Figure 191).

Although it is not yet possible to reconstruct the exact vegetable content in the diet of the Mountain Bushmen, very informative analyses are being made of plant remains found in excavations in the Eastern Cape,[20] and more recently in Eastern Lesotho.[21] In the absence of comparable data for the Drakensberg region, I thought it worth while to make a preliminary collection of information on edible plants known to the local Nguni, some of whom still retain a fund of knowledge that may be indirectly inherited from their Bushman predecessors.[22] (Table 5; pages 366-7).

During the dry winters in the Highveld, the leaves of most herbaceous plants become frosted, and only the underground portions are available throughout the year. Many of these are edible. Most common are the small tubers of various species of *Cyperus*,

Figure 191 *Site I1*

Two figures sitting facing each other, apparently enjoying a chat. This is a motif repeated at a number of sites. The figure on the right is possibly wearing a cap made of fur.

known as 'Uintjie' in Afrikaans, 'Monakaladi' in Sesotho, and 'nDawo' in Zulu, which the Bantu-speaking peoples eat raw or roasted. *Oxalis semiloba* and *Oxalis latifolia*, in addition to having prolific spherical tubers at all seasons, produce sweet succulent bulbils in late summer, and the pink flowers and trifoliate leaves have a fresh, tart taste when eaten raw. Locally known as 'Sour Flower' or 'Suring', they are very thirst-quenching and can also be used as a salt substitute in cooking. The corms of several species of *Watsonia*, though rather bitter in taste and therefore not popular as food among the present Nguni, are relished by baboons and guinea-fowl and possibly become more palatable when ground and cooked with other ingredients. In a small shelter on the upper Ngwangwana river where a profusion of these plants grows (Site L13), no less than seventeen upper grind-stones and three lower were found lying scattered around.

Several of the larger species of *Hypoxis* or 'Kaffirtulp' have large corms which are also edible when roasted or boiled, as are the root-stocks of *Kniphofia* species ('Red Hot Pokers'). The wiry *Kohautia amatymbica* and *Wahlenbergia denudata* have a series of linked bead-like tubers which penetrate deep into the ground, known to the Nguni as 'Mgungwe Mnyama' (black tubers) and 'Mgungwe Mhlope' (white tubers). It requires a lot of hard digging to obtain these in sufficient quantities for a meal, but a heavy rainfall helps substantially by softening the ground. More easily gathered are the underground rhizomes of the common swamp reed, *Phragmites australis*, which have a sweet flavour. The roots of *Cussonia paniculata*, the 'Kiepersol' or 'Cabbage Tree', taste somewhat like raw turnip, while the leaves are evergreen and can be cooked as spinach. This plant, typically found growing near the sandstone krantzes, also bears fruit, red when ripe and black when dry, which is edible at both stages.

Other fruits and berries are more seasonal, most of them ripening in late summer or autumn. The most tasty of these, *Rubus ludwigii* and *Rubus rigidus* belong to the bramble family and last only for a month or two. Wild currants, *Rhus dentata* and *Rhus discolor*, can be eaten raw or ground with other foods to make them less astringent. In the secluded ravines of the Drakensberg, where patches of natural forest survive, several varieties of trees produce edible fruits, notably *Scolopia mundii* (Red Pear), *Grewia occidentalis* with a four-lobed berry, and *Halleria lucida*, commonly known as 'Kinderbessie' or 'Wild Fuchsia'. The fruit of the latter is astringent when eaten raw, but is made more palatable by baking in hot ashes.

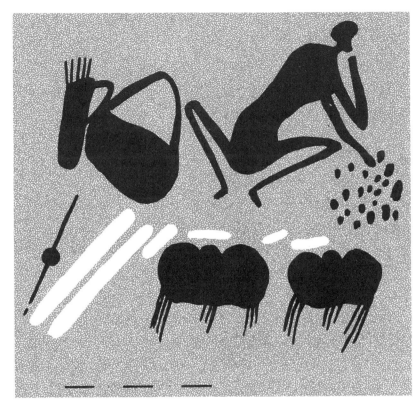

Figure 192 *Site U3*

Mealtime — an unusual subject for the Bushman artist. The spherical black objects suggest bulbs or tubers. Lying around the squatting figure are a weighted digging stick, a quiver with arrows protruding, and a bag with carrying handle. Below are what appear to be bags or bundles with thongs hanging from the underside, although they may possibly represent cumulus clouds and falling rain. The long white objects are also of uncertain interpretation.

The ground creeper *Citrullus lanatus* yields a round melon-like fruit, the pips surrounded by a gelatinous flesh with a flavour resembling cucumber. Known as 'Tangazana' by the local Nguni, they are not easy to detect among the screening veld grasses. Even more inconspicuous is *Pygmaeothamnus chamaedendrum*, a small plant that grows flat on the ground and produces a distinctively flavoured medlarlike fruit late in the summer. The 'Inkberry' bush, or *Phytolacca heptandra*, a semi-weed that may not have been so common before the spread of cultivation, produces abundant berries which are very unpleasant when green, but become more palatable later in the season. In addition to eating the berries, the Nguni cook the young shoots of this plant like asparagus and use the leaves as spinach, but the swollen roots, despite their strong resemblance to sweet potatoes, are poisonous in quantity. The shoots of *Asparagus africanus*, and the young leaves and rhizomes of the white-flowered arum lily *Zantedeschia aethiopica*, make an excellent cooked vegetable rich in starch. Other sources of edible leaves which can be cooked as greens are *Hypochaeris radicata* and *Rumex woodii*, the latter being tolerably frost resistant.

Reports from early travellers and missionaries confirm that the Bushmen were not averse to eating leaves, both cooked and un-cooked. Alexander describes a Bushman child attending to 'a small conical-shaped earthen pot which, full of some green leaves, was cooking on the fire',[23] while Posselt, reporting from a mission station near the Kei river, scathingly remarks:

> These animal-like human beings, a sort of gnome of dirty-yellowish colour, always came out of their hiding places towards the evening and paid us late visits. Like goats, they were continuously chewing leaves, which each of them carried in considerable amounts . . . . Amongst them, there was an old, shrivelled creature, full of lice, who chewed his leaves more eagerly than the rest. He rather resembled an old, decrepit billy goat. He was the captain".[24]

The blooms of several varieties of flowering plants are also edible, for example the bright yellow spring daisy, *Gazania krebsiana* and the trumpets of *Gladiolus dracocephalus*. The lanceolate leaves of the latter plant are rolled into a ball by the Bantu and chewed to quench thirst; the flavour is sharp but refreshing. The furry stems of the everlasting *Helichrysum latifolium* are peeled and then eaten raw, young specimens being quite crisp and sweet. Good sweet nectar is obtained by sucking the bright flame-coloured flowers of *Watsonia* and various *Aloe* species, as well as the stamens of Berg *Protea*.

After the spring thunder storms, mushrooms are often plentiful, and later in the season other edible fungi such as the large fleshy *Termitomyces* can be found growing in the veld.

Firewood for cooking and for warmth during the winter nights is now obtained largely from introduced trees, but before extensive European settlement, the indigenous 'Suikerbos' or 'Sugarbush' (*Protea* spp.) was a good slow-burning source of fuel. These decorative evergreen bushes with stiff pink blooms characteristically dot the slopes of the Little Berg at an altitude of between five and seven

Figure 193 *Site F12*

A kaross-clad figure with arm raised stands in front of a collecting bag and a weighted digging stick. Decorative knee bands are indicated by spaces rather than by the direct application of paint.

thousand feet. As the altitude increases, trees and shrubs capable of providing firewood disappear altogether, but some of the scrubby alpine heaths and plants such as *Helichrysum trilineatum* burn readily when green because of their high oil and resin content. The Bushmen who lived on the escarpment doubtless augmented their meagre wood supply with dried animal dung, as is the custom among present-day Basotho.

Although the local Nguni, who are predominantly tillers and herders, probably know of but a fraction of the natural vegetation formerly exploited by the hunter-gatherer Bushmen, the information that can be gleaned from them lends some realism to the seasonal routine that was formerly the lot of the Mountain Bushwoman. Future archaeological excavation and identification of botanical remains, as well as further enquiry among the local inhabitants, should add greatly to this still very incomplete picture.[25, 26]

References

1. C.S.O. 49 (1), No. 73, 28/3/1849.
2. Lee 1968b.
3. Site G3, Figure 183.
4. Goodwin 1947. The average diameter of the perforations has been calculated from measurements given by Goodwin for bored stones from the Natal and East Griqualand Highlands, but because of the paucity of data, the average weight has been determined from Goodwin's entire South African sample. The few known weights from the Drakensberg are less than one kilogram which suggests that the digging stones from this area may be smaller than the average.
5. Dunn 1931: 79-80.
6. Stow 1905: 67-8.
7. Picked up by the author and now in the Natal Museum.
8. Found while ploughing by Mr G. McDougal, owner of the farm *Scafel.*
9. Bleek 1924: 50-4.
10a. Lloyd 1889: No. 187.
10b. See also Ellenberger, 1953, dust jacket.
11. Pager 1971, Figs. 343, 362.
12. Orpen 1874.
13. Kirby 1931a & b; 1935.
14. There are a few exceptions. See Stow 1930: pl. 51; unpublished tracing by V. Ellenberger housed in Musée de l'Homme, Paris, showing the bulb and flower of *Brunsvigia* Spp. (Candelabra flower), from a small shelter on the eastern aspect of Thaba Bosiu, near Rafutho's, Lesotho.

15. Bleek 1935: 150-153.
16. Bleek 1935: 266, 268.
17. Bleek 1928.
18. Bleek 1911: 404-7.
19. Marshall Thomas 1959: 155-6.
20. Deacon 1963.
21. Carter 1973.
22. My principal informants were Lea Mguni and Mkiki Zondi, of Underberg, while my brother, John Vinnicombe, was largely responsible for collecting and pressing the plants. Dr Olive Hilliard of the Herbarium at the Bews Botanical Laboratory, University of Natal, very kindly undertook the identification of the specimens, a list of which is appended (see pp. 366-367).
23. Alexander 1838: 282.
24. Posselt, Pfitzner & Wangemann 1891. I am indebted to Harald Pager for drawing my attention to this reference, and for translating it from the German. A recent excavation by P. L. Carter in *Sehonghong* shelter, Lesotho, has produced wedges of expectorated fibre, some of which show clear imprints of teeth. No identification has yet been made of the vegetable components of this chewed matter.
25. I am indebted to Drs D. J. B. Killick and C. Turner for reading and commenting on an earlier draft of this chapter.
26. Since the above was written, Amy Jacot Guillarmod has added considerably to the information on edible plants in her publication *Flora of Lesotho,* 1971. Lehre: Verlag von J. Cramer.

Figure 194 *Site Q 4*

A row of figures, some seated, some standing, associated with decorated bags, quivers and a bow.

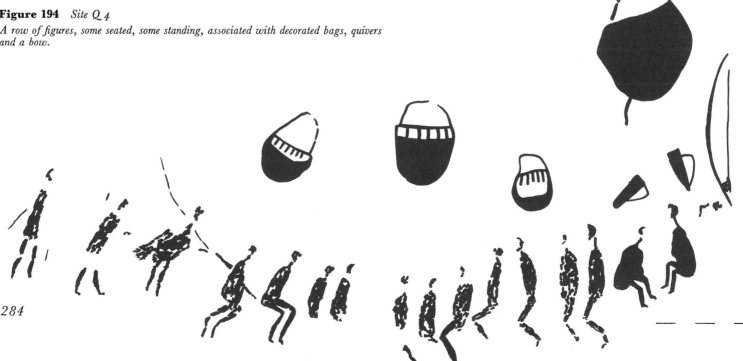

Figure 195 *Site W8*

Women with skin collecting bags swinging from their backs carry weighted digging sticks in arms held stiffly in front of them. They appear to wear a rear apron consisting of a double thong (see also Figures 157, 184, 186, 187, 191).

Figure 196   *Site VII*
Three hunters approach a small antelope which has stopped to look back.

Hunting

The ability to hunt is extremely important to Bushmen for both practical and social reasons. As boys, they are expected to prove themselves proficient before being initiated into manhood, and they are also required to demonstrate their ability as food providers before taking a wife.[1-4]

When a Kung Bushman kills his first large animal (birds or small mammals do not count), he is qualified for the most important ceremony in his life — the Ceremony of the First Killing. The ceremony is performed twice for each boy: for the first male animal he is scarified on his right side and for the first female on his left side.

> Charred meat and fat, turned to magic by the ceremony, are rubbed into the several lines of vertical cuts on his face, arms, back and chest to give him the will to hunt, good sight, and accurate aim, also to enable him to find the animal and protect himself from being seen by the animal. The ceremony is both a solemn celebration and a magic force to increase and strengthen the boy's power to hunt. It also carries with it the right to marriage . . . .[5]

Marriage does not necessarily follow immediately upon this ceremony; years may elapse, but again, at the time of the wedding, the boy must bring the bride's parents an animal that he himself has killed.

> The parents of a girl want a boy to be responsible, kind to their daughter and, above all, a good provider — which means a good hunter. They want him to make his arrows straight, to shoot swiftly and accurately, to be able to run down an eland, and most of all, they want a son-in-law whose heart says to him, "Why am I sitting lazily here in the werf? Why do I not get up and go hunting?" and who, in obedience to his heart, and the group's desire, and the magic which has been rubbed into his scarifications in the Ceremony of the First Killing, gets up and goes.[6]

Lorna Marshall has drawn attention to the ceremonial link between hunting, virility and marriage, marriage involving not only procreation, but the inception of a family which is the most cohesive unit in Kung society. Hunting, to the Kung, is therefore strongly linked with the primary sources of physical life: sex and

Figure 197 *Site C6*

A pair of figures running neck and neck, with legs widely extended, is a theme repeated at several sites along the Drakensberg. The two rear figures of the trio who follow more sedately in this group have a double bar across the penis.

food. Hunting is also a male prerogative, therefore sex and the power to provide are linked with men rather than with women.[7]

In the painted record, hunters are often shown with markedly protuberant genitalia, and although a semi-erect penis is a physical characteristic of Bushman males, the paintings often exaggerate this feature to a considerable degree. (Figures 158c, 168–9). In marked contrast to the paintings, present-day Bushmen show a great sense of modesty and decorum, and the exposure of genitalia or other direct expressions of sex are considered highly improper.[8] The typical dress of a Bushman hunter is a belt with a soft skin breech-cloth slung between the legs which completely covers the genitalia. Although there is no way of being certain that Bushman males adhered to this dress convention in the mountain areas where paintings occur, Christol illustrates a Bushman from the Orange Free State borders who wears a genital apron or sling, and Professor Van Riet Lowe found Bushman survivors in the same area in the 1920s who were similarly dressed.[9] It is possible, therefore, that the paintings of naked hunters are not a realistic portrayal of customary dress or undress, but rather that they express in symbolic terms the association between hunting and the male sexual principle.

There are recurrent scenes among the paintings, usually isolated from other groups, in which a lone hunter is seen pursuing an animal, usually an eland. The hunter carries, but is not necessarily using, his bow and arrow, and he is often shown with a white painted face.

287

Figure 198 *Site C6*
Groups of figures shown running in unison, with legs interlaced.

It is recorded that Bushmen living immediately south of the survey area had to present the father of their bride-to-be with the heart and breast of an eland as part of the marriage contract.[10] It seems probable, therefore, that paintings of lone hunters and eland may in some way be connected with male initiation or marriage ceremonies which require proof of each individual's hunting proficiency. (Figure 92). Once the individual has acquitted himself, however, hunting is normally a more co-operative effort and is carried out by a group of men varying in number from two to five.[11] Only on very rare and special hunts are more men included.[12] A high degree of silent understanding and co-operation between the hunters is essential if the hunt is to be a success, and often two men establish a permanent hunting bond which has deep social significance. The relationship can become so strong that the families of the two hunters may adopt a fictitious kinship which supersedes any real kinship, and all the obligations of siblinghood and incest taboos are strictly observed.[13] In a sense, the men and their families become one. This spirit of unity and close co-operation is, I think, often expressed in the paintings by two or more hunter figures in close proximity to one another, often in identical but exaggerated running poses, or with legs interlaced to form a criss-cross pattern. (Figures 104, 197–8). A similar convention for showing inter-relationships between hunters can be found in many shelters over a wide area[14] and for this reason the pattern is, in my opinion, symbolic of an idea rather than descriptive of an incident.

In addition to the more esoteric role of both hunting and painting, there is a wealth of practical detail contained within the pictorial record which clearly relates to specialised hunting methods and can be taken as realistic descriptions of how the hunters set about finding and immobilising their prey. The most common hunting activity represented is stalking. Since the Bushman's bow is small and inaccurate over long distances, great reliance is placed on stalking animals to within close range. Many paintings show hunters stealthily approaching game with bows and arrows in hand, bodies almost horizontal, and legs bent in a crouched position. Others creep up on hands and knees, and sometimes the head of the buck is turned suspiciously. (Figures 196, 199). Most animals are inherently inquisitive, and provided they are not startled, will actually draw nearer to an object with which they are unfamiliar rather than run away. The Bushmen exploited this habit, and could also cleverly imitate the sounds of animals, for instance, the cry of the young, which would attract attention from the mother.[15] The hunter would stalk his quarry using what natural cover was available, but where this was absent, he would resort to carrying small bushes or wearing a fillet of grass on his head.[16, 17] The use of animal disguises, particularly an ostrich skin, is recorded both in the literature and in the paintings,[18-20] and within the survey area there are four curious figures with human-like legs protruding from animal bodies. None, however, carry weapons, and none are definitely hunting or attacking an animal. (Figures 228, 235). In each instance the figures are associated with eland, and in my view are more likely to represent sorcerers or supernatural beings rather than hunters in disguise.

Figure 199 *Site F6*
A hunter creeps up to an inquisitive small antelope.

Figure 200 *Site Q 4*

The hind legs of this antelope, as seen from the front, are abnormally splayed. It is difficult to assess whether this is the result of difficulty in portraying perspective, or whether it intentionally represents the effects of poisoning.

Once an animal has been wounded, the hunters wait for the poison to take effect, sometimes not tracking down the quarry till the following day. Generally speaking, the smaller the animal, the quicker the action of the poison; larger game like eland, gemsbok and buffalo take from one to three days to die.[21-23] When following the spoor, the hunters interpret all the details such as where the animal has rested, urinated, or rubbed itself, with uncanny accuracy. They can tell from the signs when their quarry begins to weaken, and hope to come upon the carcase before scavengers make a meal of it. Sometimes they close in on the animal as soon as it collapses, finally killing it with spears.[24, 25] Formerly, some other method must have been used, as it is thought that very few Bushmen had spears prior to contact with Bantu-speakers.[26] This is borne out by the painted record; spears are most frequently associated with late paintings, while earlier hunting scenes show the use of bow and arrows only. (Figs. 103-4, 108, 212). Sometimes the painted animals appear to be incapacitated in some way: they either lie down, or have hunched backs with splayed legs and heads hanging low.[27] Most poisons used by African hunters are cardiotoxic and produce characteristic effects such as slowing of the heart rate, laboured

breathing, slight vomiting and gradual loss of muscular control.[28] These symptoms may well be portrayed in some of the paintings. (Figures 93, 200).

Once the animal has been killed, it is skinned and cut up, care being taken to collect the blood which is carried away in the paunches or bladder. Very little other than the gall is thrown away, even the sinews being kept for making cord. The meat is divided according to certain prescribed rules, and if there is more than can be portered by the hunters themselves, a message is sent back to camp for others to come and assist.[29, 30] Sparrman has given a comic description of the way meat was sometimes carried:

> The Hottentots cut out large slips of buffalo flesh whole and entire, with holes in the middle wide enough for them to put their heads and arms through, and loaded themselves with it in this manner before, behind and on every side of them; the meat all the while dangling about their bodies in a manner ludicrous enough though not much adapted to create an appetite in the spectator. In this way, their hands being entirely disengaged excepting that each man carried a stick, they clambered up the brow of the hill that overhung the vale, and thus walked towards the waggon, whither one might trace them all the way by the blood.[31]

Figure 201 *Site Q 5*

An antelope head lolls from one of the tasselled bags carried by kaross-clad humans armed with long sticks. The heads of the figures can no longer be seen, but they appear to have had lines or thongs hanging from the neck.

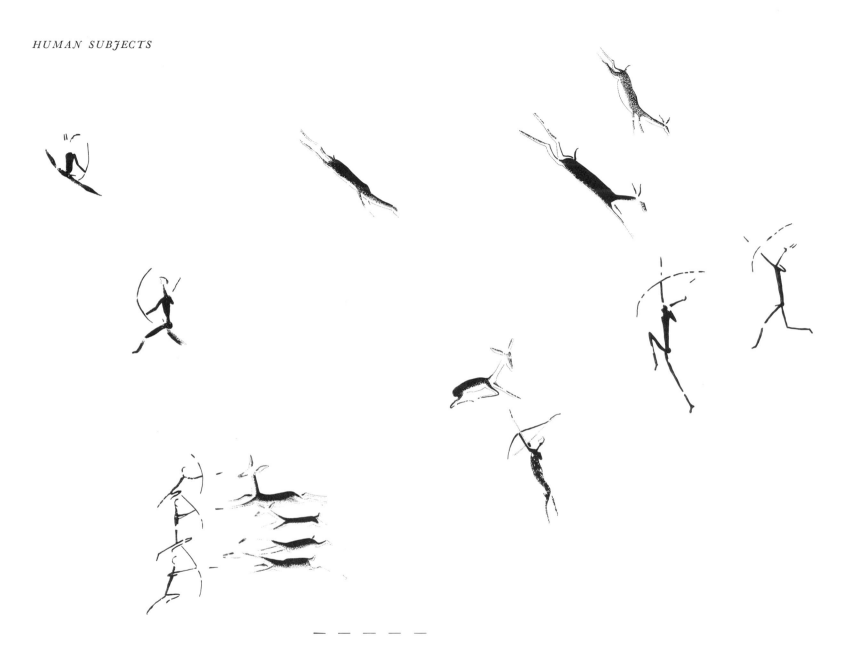

Figure 202   *Site Q1*

Small antelope are driven towards hunters with bows at the ready.
The group at lower left has been moved further into the picture for economy of space.
The paintings are in dark red and white.

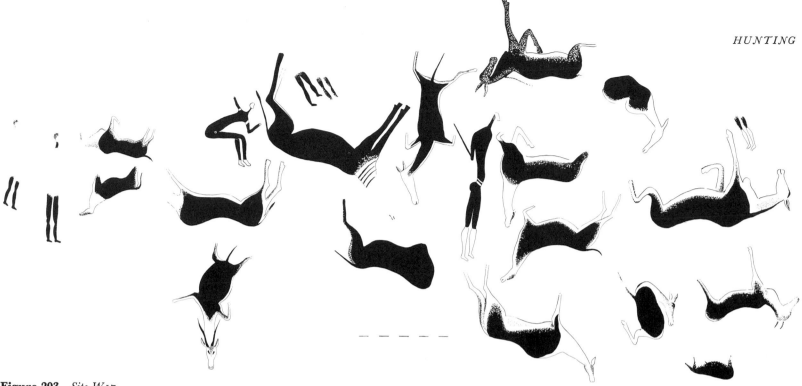

Figure 203 *Site W17*

All the animals represented here appear to be dead, some with legs spread-eagled and viewed from above. The human figures on the left, showing heads and legs only, were probably originally painted with white karosses. A more complete figure near *the centre leans over towards the hindquarters of an animal with wrinkled neck (probably an eland), while another standing figure with a stick has a white face, and legs whitened from the knee downwards. The paintings are in dark red and white.*

Some of the large untidy bundles shown in the paintings may well represent such loads of meat. Only small antelope are carried back to camp whole, and this method of conveying the kill is also shown in the paintings. The legs were presumably held in pairs over the shoulder, as the heads usually dangle downwards with the body forming a bundle on the back. (Figure 201). Large antelope actually being dismembered are shown lying on their backs, legs in the air, with a small human figure crouching on the thorax or bending over the carcase. In one of the scenes, the butchers are equipped with skin bags, and one man appears to be calling over his shoulder to other figures approaching. Unidentifiable shapes lying around are possibly the internal organs and entrails of the slaughtered eland. (Figures 146, 211).

At times the game is not cautiously stalked, but is driven towards concealed hunters and then despatched either with bows and arrows or by spearing. (Figure 108). A legend told by the Mountain Bushman Qing describes how Kaggen sent his son to turn the elands towards him, and he threw assegais and killed three bulls.[32] A painted group on the farm *Berridale* shows a line of small antelope running towards an opposing line of hunters with bows at the ready, and in a continuation of the scene to the right, more buck bound directly towards expectant hunters. Although no-one is seen actually to drive the buck, the action leaves little doubt that this was in fact being done. (Figure 202).

It has also been suggested that certain paintings of numerous antelope all lying in different positions depict the aftermath of a drive in which the desperate animals were induced to leap to their death over a precipice.[33] Such a scene may also be represented in a shelter on the Tsoelike river. (Figure 203). Unfortunately, the associated human figures are very faded, but the spread-eagled attitude of some of the buck is typical of a carcase looked down on from above.

Figure 204 *Site P1*

A file of small antelope in orange pigment head downhill towards linear objects of uncertain interpretation. They may represent barriers set up to deflect the antelope towards concealed hunters, or they may be nets hung up in the path of the animals in order to ensnare them. There are orange finger smears to the left and right of the group.

Sometimes obstructions were set up to make the animals move in a certain direction. Arbousset describes a row of clods being erected at the entrance to an angle formed in the mountains, and how a herd of black wildebeest grazing on a nearby plain was turned towards this trap. Taking fright at the heaps of earth, they ran off in single file towards a ravine where the hunters were concealed. Only one wildebeest was despatched on this occasion, and slices of the flesh were cooked in an oven dug into an ant-hill.[34] Barrow saw stones piled one on top of another in rows with openings left for the game to pass through and where the hunters could conveniently lie in wait. In this way walls continued across plains and mouths of defiles for several miles. Sometimes rows of sticks with ostrich feathers tied on the ends were used in lieu of barricades.[35, 36] Circular hides about three feet high and built of stone were also erected in narrow passes and other strategic positions,[37] and similar structures can still be recognised in parts of the Karoo.[38] The Cape Bushmen, too, used temporary screens made of bushes, but these were sometimes trampled by stampeding game.[39] Although no clear examples of such hides have been found among the paintings

in the survey area, a very good example has been recorded from western Lesotho.[40] Barriers are sometimes suggested by a series of painted strokes or blobs which are near or partly surround the animals, but in no instance are associated hunters shown. (Figures 76, 90, 204).

Trapping and snaring was another widely used hunting method, and among present Kalahari Bushmen accounts for more meat than shooting with the bow and arrow. Their snares are usually laid in the form of nooses made of sinew or plaited fibres. Among the Naron trapping is a seasonal occupation, wet weather having a detrimental effect on the action of the fibre rope, and it is possible that the same applied to Mountain Bushmen during the summer rains.[41] Arbousset met Bushmen near Morija in western Lesotho who sold him cord made of twisted grass which they used for snares, placing them in defiles or across bogs. He specifically mentions that game was lured into marshy places as they could be killed more easily there.[42] Basotho who lived among the Bushmen have been able to give some additional information on snares: 'These cords are made with hairs and the tail of a gnu or zebra, or with the fibres of a plant, solidly plaited and rolled; . . . . They make snares from the mane of the blue wildebeest, into which the game puts its feet or neck'; and 'They secure the grey gazelle by means of nets or cords hung in such a way that the beast gets caught in it'.[43] At a site on the farm *Eagle's Nest* in Mount Currie district, a single file of small antelope are painted heading downhill towards some lined objects which may well represent such nets made of cord strung across their path. (Figure 204). Another somewhat faded painting on the ceiling of a shelter on *Scafel* in the Underberg district shows a hunter spearing an eland, the hind leg of which is apparently held by a rope (Figure 205), and another eland on *Belleview* has a double cord entwined between its hind legs, then rather curiously zig-zagging between the tail and the hindquarters. (Figure 71). It is not at all clear whether these lines represent an actual snare or whether they have some other significance, and the interpretation of scenes in which lines meander between eland is equally uncertain. (Figure 90, 104).[44]

Other types of traps were deep holes covered over with sticks and grass which were often dug near rivers to capture hippopotami,[45] and Chapman gives gruesome details of large pits approached by funnel fences into which great quantities of game were frightened with firebrands.[46] Other than the painting on the Bokberg of a hippopotamus hunt in which the animal is surrounded by strokes

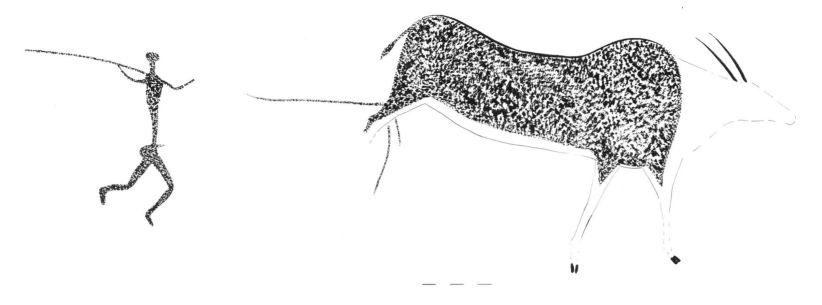

Figure 205 *Site G1*

This eland, painted in red and white on the ceiling of a shelter, appears to be held by a rope, while a hunter runs up from the rear with a spear in his hand. Such representations, which may depict snaring or trapping, are rare in the painted record. The eland is superimposed on an earlier antelope which has been omitted from this rendering.

which could possibly represent a trap (Figure 242), such pits are not recognisable among the paintings in the survey area. Considering the amount of trapping and snaring that must have been done, it is surprising that this method of catching game is so rarely illustrated.

Fishing was also practised by the Mountain Bushmen and provided another valuable source of protein. In 1873 Qing, the young informant from eastern Lesotho, remarked that the Bushmen of that area could no longer spear fish and had forgotten how to build 'stone crossings' over rivers. It is not clear whether this statement refers to stepping stones or whether the building of stone weirs for fish-trapping is implied.[47] The spearing of fish is corroborated by the paintings, as there are three scenes showing this method of fishing within 56 miles of one another as the crow flies. However, another perplexing detail unfortunately not referred to by Qing is that the fish appear to be speared from small one-man floats or boats, no parallels for which can be found in the literature. The

habitual construction and use of indigenous craft south of the Limpopo is unknown, although bundles of reeds or wooden logs were formerly used for crossing rivers.[48] While the craft shown in the paintings could conceivably be no more than reed floats, the use of anchors suggests a somewhat more developed structure.[49] The headwaters of the Natal rivers and the upper Orange river system, though navigable for only short stretches, were noted for good fishing long before the introduction of trout,[50-52] and the fish portrayed in the paintings have been identified as indigenous freshwater species. Jubb is of the opinion that seasonal spawning runs of Cyprinidae are depicted (*Barbus* spp.) and that another painting in the Underberg district represents a screened trap placed to catch Cyprinids while leaping over barriers during their determined and spectacular migration upstream.[53] This small group, painted in a shelter high on Bamboo Mountain and overlooking a tributary of the Mzimkhulu, is orientated in such a way that the fish swim

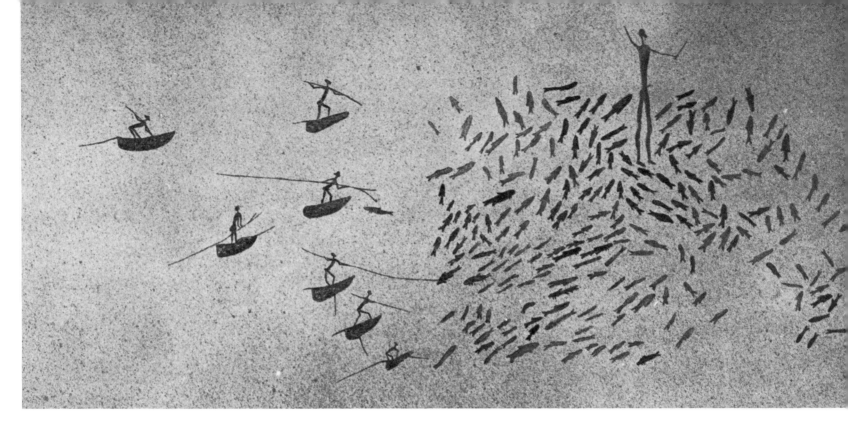

Figure 206 *Site WII*

Men in boats spearing fish, painted in black silhouette on the Tsoelike river, eastern Lesotho. The elongated figure standing in the shoal of fish is in brick red, and is not necessarily connected with the fishing scene. Two of the fishermen on the left of the group carry forked leisters, one of them barbed, while the third figure from the right (opposite page) has a spear which is hafted at the tip. The boat or float on which this figure stands is steadied by an anchor. Some of the boatmen (far left and far right) appear to manipulate punting poles, while their long fishing spears balance along the length of the craft. The total length of the scene from left to right is 59 centimetres. (See also Figures 63, 65, 207, 208).

Figure 207 *Site WII*

Photograph of part of the Tsoelike fishing scene showing the extent to which the paintings have been defaced by scratches and charcoal imitations by Sotho herdboys. Above can be seen the elongated bodies of eland. The legs, necks and heads, originally in white, have disappeared.

Photo: Pat Carter.

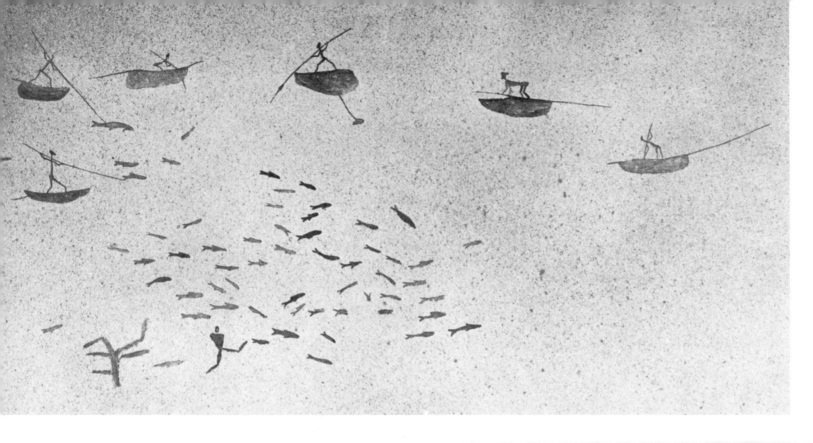

Figure 208 *The Tsoelike river in mid winter.*

On the right is the rock shelter where the fishing scene was found (Site W11). A large fall of rock from the ceiling of the overhang provides a convenient bench on which to sit while working on the paintings. A tracing is in progress. The sheet of polythene on the rock face marks the exact position of the paintings.

Photo: Pat Carter.

295

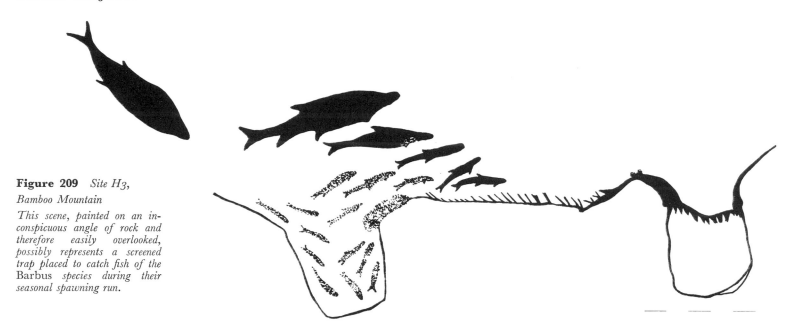

Figure 209 *Site H3,*
Bamboo Mountain

This scene, painted on an in-conspicuous angle of rock and therefore easily overlooked, possibly represents a screened trap placed to catch fish of the Barbus *species during their seasonal spawning run.*

towards the head of the valley, which supports the spawning run theory. (Figure 209). Fishing scenes showing the use of conical basket-traps have been located in western Lesotho,[54] and Bushman fishing equipment found lying on the banks of a southern tributary of the Orange river at the end of the 19th Century included neatly made basket traps and wooden harpoons. Some of these were pointed with bone and attached to cords made from grass.[55] Although no certain harpoons are illustrated in the paintings from the survey area, one of the long flexible spears associated with fishing from craft has a hafted point, while another, forked and barbed, is more suggestive of a leister. (Figure 206). All the fish paintings within the study area are in black silhouette save two of a group of three at *Good Hope* which are orange, and which are executed below similarly coloured horses. The scene on Mpongweni mountain is also situated below horse paintings (Site G3, Figure 63), and since the state of preservation of the fishing group is comparable with other scenes including domestic animals at the site, it is unlikely that the boat paintings are of any great antiquity. Another faded spearing scene is reported on the Tsoelike river downstream from the present survey area,[56] and other illustrations, some showing the use of fishing lines, have been recorded from the Cape, Orange Free State and western Lesotho.[57-59] Recent excavations on the farm *Belleview*

in East Griqualand near the Lesotho border have produced fish bones from a Later Stone Age shelter deposit, as well as very finely carved bone hooks,[60] and Ellenberger records that the Lesotho Bushmen caught fish with hooks made of ivory.[61]

During the last decades of the Bushmen's existence in the central mountain area, their adoption of the horse completely revolutionised hunting techniques.[62] The rock paintings in the southern Drakensberg adjacent to the farmlands settled by the early Natal colonists, from whom at least 560 horses were stolen between the years 1840 and 1870, include numerous illustrations of equestrian hunting. Eland are the usual object of attack, and after pursuing them on horseback until they were blown, the hunters despatched them with spears. As was the practice with European hunters, the Bushmen no doubt drove the eland to within close range of their camps whenever possible in order to avoid carrying the meat long distances.[63, 64] The horses themselves were often used as pack animals for carrying meat, a fact borne out by archival references as well as the paintings. (Figures 20, 21, 210). One of the most vivid scenes depicting hunting on horseback is on the Tsoelike river in eastern Lesotho. Here a herd of ten eland are involved, of which seven have been or are being slain. Mounted

Figure 210   *Site J21*

Part of a scene showing horses and cattle being driven towards an encampment. In among the domestic animals is an eland brought back by mounted horsemen, presumably to be slaughtered near home base. One of the horses, led by a figure wearing a feathered head-dress, carries a load of meat on its back. To the left of this group and not reproduced here, are four more cattle and ten horses, some of which are wearing halters. The paintings are in bright orange, brown, red, black and white.

297

Figure 211   *Site W23*

Slain eland are being dismembered, and a horse loaded with strips of meat is led away. Another horse (centre) waits patiently for its turn, weight distributed on three legs only. The objects at top right are of uncertain interpretation — they may be part of the entrails, although one of the shapes looks remarkably like a gun. (See also Figure 212 which is to the right of the above in the rock shelter).

hunters wearing the knobbed head-dress typical of the later Bushmen pursue the eland, and one very heavy old bull is singled out for attack. The splayed hoof-marks and imprint of the ergots in the spoor indicate its distress. The cleft of an eland's hoof is usually very compact, while the ergots, two cartilaginous projections immediately above the hoof, do not make contact with the ground unless the animal is hard pressed. One rider has thrust a spear into the rump of the eland leaving a trail of blood alongside the spoor. Another hunter has abandoned his horse and runs up on foot, spears in hand, to assist in the kill. Ahead of the bull, other eland have already been slain, and lie with their legs in the air. Some are in the process of being dismembered, severed limbs and entrails lying nearby,

and the exposed ribs indicate that the flank meat has already been flayed off. One man leads away a horse well laden with meat, a hump showing on the animal's back, and strips of flesh hang down below the belly. Another horse patiently awaiting a load stands in a typical resting posture with weight taken on three legs only. Odd unidentifiable shapes lying around may represent the internal organs of the slain eland, although one object looks remarkably like a gun.

Guns were certainly possessed by Bushmen in the nineteenth century, and the advantages of these introduced weapons were soon recognised. More than anything else, one of Dr Bleek's old informants, who had been imprisoned for stock theft, wanted a gun as a reward for teaching the language and lore of his people.

Figure 212 *Site W23*

Eland hunted on horseback. One particularly heavy bull has left a trail of blood and splayed footprints. A horseman thrusts a spear into the rump of the fatigued animal, while another hunter has abandoned his horse and runs with spears in hand to assist in the kill. Water seepage down the rock face after heavy rain is erasing the paintings.

For starvation was that on account of which I was bound, — starvation's food, — when I starving turned back from following the sheep . . . . For, a gun is that which takes care of an old man; it is that with which we kill the springbok which go through the cold [wind]; we go to eat, in the cold [wind]. We do, satisfied with food, lie down [in our huts] in the cold [wind]. It [the gun] is strong against the wind. It satisfies a man with food in the very middle of the cold.[65]

This eulogy of the virtues of the white man's weapon implies that successful hunting with the bow and arrow was, by contrast with the gun, very much dependent upon weather conditions. In addition to wind affecting the flight of the arrow, rain or heavy dew stretches the sinew bowstring, which then has a tendency to snap when it dries out.[66, 67] It is unknown to what extent hunting was a seasonal occupation among the Mountain Bushmen, but it has been noted that the Hadza, for example, hunt more in the dry season than in the wet, largely because of the deleterious effect of rain on the bowstring.[68] Since a waterproof bowcase, the only one of its kind yet described in southern Africa, was found in a rock shelter in the Drakensberg,[69] it can be assumed that hunting during the summer must have been frequently interrupted by the sudden thunder storms which occur in the mountains, and the bitter winds characteristic of some winter months would also have been a serious obstacle.

The hunting technology of the Bushmen was, therefore, affected by many factors beyond their control, with the result that the procedure of the hunt was governed by numerous rites and prohibitions aimed at ensuring success. However, even when all external factors combined favourably, an intimate knowledge of the temperament and behaviour of the animals on which he preyed was a greater asset to the Bushman hunter than technical proficiency.[70]

The Bushman's profound understanding of animal behaviour was drawn on not only to develop skilled hunting techniques, but also to identify himself in an almost symbiotic association with his quarry. The elaborate procedure connected with eland hunting is outlined elsewhere[71] and there are many other examples of the complex relationship which existed between hunter and victim.

Prior to going springbok hunting, for instance, preparations did not consist merely of the commonplace and practical details of checking hunting equipment, locating a herd and then deciding on the best tactics. Even if hunger was pressing, it was deemed useless to set out unless various omens indicated that the hunt would be successful. The Kalahari Bushmen often throw discs of eland hide as a form of divination,[72] but this practice is thought to be adapted from their Tswana neighbours who throw bones. The Southern Bushmen simply had inward presentiments described by them as 'letters in their bodies' which they believed foretold future events. If a herd of springbok was approaching and the omens were good, the hunter would experience a vibration in his feet similar to the rustling of springbok hooves. He would sense a tapping on his ribs because of the black hairs on the flanks of the springbok, and he would himself feel the black stripe on the springbok's face as well as the black marks round its eyes. He would have a sensation in his head similar to that of having horns chopped off after the kill, and it would feel as though blood dripped and trickled down the calves of his legs, just as it did when he carried a dead springbok back to camp.[73] In short, the hunter identified himself so closely with his quarry that in anticipation he became that animal, feeling how it looked and experiencing what it felt.

If the occurrence of springbok in the southern and western regions be equated with rhebuck in the eastern mountains, an area not frequented by springbok herds, then many of the rhebuck paintings do, I believe, reflect the empathy between hunter and quarry that is evidenced in the lore of the Xam Bushmen.[74]

The Bushmen maintained that it was necessary at all times to show 'respect' to game, for the game would not die if it was not respected. Prior to hunting, it was forbidden to eat the flesh of any fleet animal, because:

> The game we have shot acts in the same manner as the thing we have eaten. We only eat food which will strengthen the poison, that the poison may kill the game. We especially do not eat springbok flesh, because the springbok does not a little go. Even if it be night, it is used to walk about. The springbok is wont to

do thus: when the sun has set for it in one place, the sun arises for it in a different place. The game we shoot would do the same — it would let the day break while it did not sleep.[75]

Other preparations deemed essential by the hunters included rubbing special ash into cuts on their arms and on their hand between the thumb and first finger. This was the place where the arrow lay when drawing a bow, and the charm ensured that the arrow would 'fly well' and the aim be straight. When a herd of springbok was sighted from a hill-top, the hunters would quickly burn a stick of charm medicine carried especially for the purpose in a body band, and would point the stick towards the springbok to make them 'run gently'. After extinguishing the flame, the hunters would mark their own faces with the charcoal, drawing a line down the centre of the forehead and nose, then sideways over the right nostril to the middle of the cheek. Only then, while sitting sharpening their arrows, would they discuss the tactics to be adopted during the hunt.[76]

Animals displaying unusual features usually had supernatural properties attributed to them, and it was forbidden to hunt these animals under any circumstances. For instance, should an albino springbok be killed, it was believed the springbok would disappear altogether.[77] The Kung believe that some gemsbok are mythical 'gemsbok people', and if a hunter were mistakenly to shoot one of these 'people', who is quite indistinguishable from a real gemsbok, he would become very ill and die.[78] Other antelope may be 'spirit antelope' which embody the souls of the dead, and these also have to be 'respected'.

Certain animals such as springbok, lions, baboons, gemsbok and eland could convey forebodings of misfortune by strange behaviour, and many other chance phenomena like body aches or howling wind were interpreted as ill omens. A girl undergoing seclusion during puberty rites was thought to exude particularly potent influences. She was not allowed to eat game killed by young men for fear that the saliva she put into the meat would enter the bow, causing the inside of the bow to become 'cool'. Through the hands of the hunter which held the bow, the arrow would also be affected: the poison would in turn become 'cool' and the animals would not die.[79] The moon too, could 'cool' or nullify the action of arrow-poison. The moon was therefore not to be looked at while tracking game, and the moon could also affect the movements of a wounded animal: 'The moon travels far; day breaks while it is still going along, and the game would do the same'.[80]

Sneezes were always suppressed as they were thought to 'curse' hunting grounds, and bad aim could be attributed to such circumstances as the death of a friend.[81] If hunters missed their aim, they brought ill luck to themselves, but this could be counteracted by the performance of a special ceremony. The women would make incisions on the affected hunter's shoulders with a sharp arrow-head, and after sucking the cuts, would spit the blood into a springbok horn. The blood was then poured on top of burning *buchu*, a fragrant herb, and by holding the arrows in the smoke, good fortune could be restored. The hunters' heads were also shaved in paths leading from the temples straight backwards, which, it was believed, would make the springbok run straight towards them.[82]

A hunter responsible for killing a springbok was not allowed to touch the meat with his hands, 'because our hands are those with which we held the bow and arrows when we shot the thing'. Any blood accidentally spilt was carefully lifted up together with the earth or bushes on which it lay, and was put down opposite the hut entrance of the man who made the kill. The bones, too, were not to be thrown about, but had to be carefully piled in the same place as the blood, and the contents of the rumen were also emptied on the heap of bones. The shoulder blades were treated with especial deference; these had to be put away in the hut to prevent dogs from crunching them.[83] All this was done to ensure that the hunter would not miss his aim in future.

In the division of meat, the man who shot the springbok was always given the upper bones of the foreleg from which his child could suck the marrow. The tip of a springbok tongue, on the other hand, was never to be eaten by children, and children were not allowed to play on a springbok's skin. Likewise, women were forbidden to eat meat from the shoulder because they had to show 'respect' for the men's arrows. If any of these taboos were broken, the springbok could enter that person's flesh and cause illness. Finally, when the sharing and eating and related observances were over, the hunter's wife was responsible for curing and softening the springbok skin which she would make into bags. These were then bartered for valued items such as more poisoned arrows, black powder for anointing the head, and red ochre with which to rub their bodies.[84, 85] Red ochre was also used to mark arrows as a sign of ownership,[86] and in an archaeological context, traces of red paint have been found on small stone crescents which formed the point or barbs of arrows before the introduction of iron.[87]

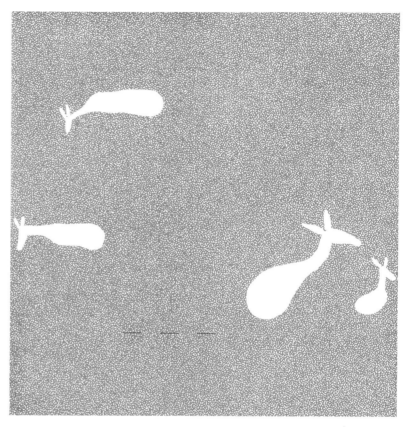

Figure 213 *Site S3*
Small antelope with their young. No attempt has been made to portray the legs.

Similar customs connected with slain animals were described by Chapman during his travels in the mid nineteenth century. Sand was thrown in the eyes of dead elephants which Chapman thought to be an expression of thanks, and certain parts of the animal were allowed to be eaten only by certain people. The elephant's eyes were always burnt to a cinder, and the point of the trunk cut off and broiled; this ensured power over elephants in the future, and was said to be a preventive against being charged. Similarly, when a rhinoceros was shot, the Bushmen threw a handful of dust on the animal's tail and spat in its eyes before touching it, and these actions were interpreted as a means of ensuring future good luck.[88]

Figure 214 *Site W26*

An unidentifiable antelope which may be an eland has a line across the neck suggesting a rope. From the nose, a dotted line leads round the bottom of the legs and up to the buttocks. Protruding from the shoulders of the animal is a quiver or hunting bag containing what may be arrows and flywhisks. A smear of red paint at the nose of the antelope suggests blood or some other exudate. (See also Figure 88).

302

Even after the incorporation of the gun into their technology, superstitions persisted among the Khoisan peoples. For instance, in order to induce cowardice in their enemies, they burnt and pounded a crow's heart which was fired into the air, and when out raiding, they carried special roots in their bullet pouches in the belief that these charms would render enemy bullets or arrows ineffectual while their own would be made more powerful. If a bullet did not cause immediate death to an animal, a handful of sand from the footprints of the game was thrown into the air, and this would cause the animal to die.[89]

Some Kalahari Bushmen are said to make first offerings of the chase to their Supreme Beings,[90] and in South West Africa all the tribes have or had customary practices connected with hunting, the details of which vary from band to band. Among these is the concept of *soxa*, a form of taboo whereby all meat killed with the bow and arrow may not be eaten until the leader of the group has tasted it, and even then certain categories of people may eat only prescribed portions. The man who shot the animal receives the ribs and shoulder blade of one side, and he is not allowed to touch any other meat; were he to do so, the poison would weaken and refuse to act and he would have no success in hunting. If women partake of any meat other than that prescribed for them, their action would likewise interfere with the action of the poison, and animals would not die when shot. *Soxa* applies only to the larger game such as steenbok, duiker, springbok, hartebeest, gemsbok, kudu, wildebeest and giraffe, and *soxa* animals vary from band to band. The eland, admittedly a comparatively rare visitor to the area inhabited by the Xom-Khoin, is absolutely *soxa* to that language group; that is, they believe the meat to have a harmful effect on everyone, therefore they will not kill an eland under any circumstances.[91]

Among the Kung, the custom of meat-sharing also applies only to the larger game animals. Smaller mammals and chance finds such as tortoises, lizards, snakes, grasshoppers, birds and birds' eggs, belong to the person who shoots, snares, finds or catches them. He may keep these for himself, or may share them as he chooses.[92] The larger antelope are believed to be endowed with a mystic power or essence called *n!ow*, whereas the smaller animals are not. Men too, are born with a particular *n!ow*, and when a hunter kills a large antelope, a complicated interaction of the *n!ows* takes place which may affect the forces in the world about them.[93, 94]

It is significant that in the painted record, large game animals predominate almost to the complete exclusion of the smaller mammals, and it may well be that paintings, too, were bound up

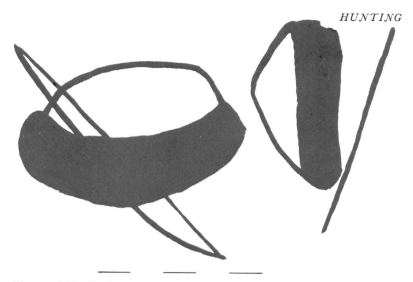

Figure 215 *Site D3*

Hunting bags with a bow and a stick. The paintings are not apparently associated with any humans.

with intricate concepts such as *soxa* and *n!ow*. *Soxa* applies only to meat shot with the bow and arrow, and the fact that the smaller mammals which have no *n!ow* are normally snared, clubbed, or speared, perhaps explains their absence from the paintings. *Soxa* is very much concerned with ensuring potency of the poisons and accuracy of aim in hunting with the bow and arrow, and this may be an added reason for the preponderance of painted figures shown carrying, but not necessarily actively using, their bows and arrows. A cult concerned predominantly with the use of the bow and arrow would also explain the absence, or near absence, of paintings showing snaring and trapping.[95]

Since the acts and prohibitions connected with eland and springbok hunting among the Cape Bushmen were obviously closely related to the concept of *soxa* practised in the Kalahari, it is perhaps not unjustified to suggest that the concept was wide-spread. If this were so, then the frequent occurrence of eland and rhebuck among the paintings of the eastern mountain massif would suggest that these antelope were particularly strongly connected with *soxa*-like rituals. Black wildebeest, on the other hand, which hardly appear among the paintings and yet were common antelope within the area, were possibly not included in the *soxa* category at all, and were thereby eliminated from any prescribed ritual procedure.[96]

The observances described above confirm that hunting to a Bushman was not merely a technical act concerned with obtaining food, but a ritual performance in which were embodied certain expressive and symbolic elements. As with all rites, these observances are not necessarily rational or practical, and their significance is not immediately apparent to the outsider. Although the participants themselves usually know the meaning of their own symbols and acts, they do so intuitively, and can rarely express their understanding verbally. This is doubtless one of the reasons why so little information on the motivation underlying their actions has been obtained from Bushmen themselves, but detailed anthropological analyses based on observations over a wide field all draw attention to the psychological and social function of such acts.

> A person performing the rite ... derives therefrom a definite feeling of satisfaction, but it would be entirely false to imagine that this is simply because he believes that he has helped to provide a more abundant supply of food for himself and his fellow tribesmen. His satisfaction is in having performed a ritual duty, we might say a religious duty .... In the performance of the rite he has made that small contribution, which it is both his privilege and his duty to do, to the maintenance of that order of the universe of which man and nature are interdependent parts. The satisfaction which he thus receives gives the rite a special value to him ....
>
> To discover the social function of the ... rites we have to consider the whole body of cosmological ideas of which each rite is a partial expression .... The *social* importance of food is not that it satisfies hunger, but that a ... large proportion of the activities are concerned with the getting and consuming of food, and that in these activities, with their daily instances of collaboration and mutual aid, there continuously occur those interrelations of interests which bind the individual men, women and children into a society ....
>
> ... We have here the primary basis of all ritual and therefore of religion and magic, however these may be distinguished. The primary basis of ritual ... is the attribution of ritual value to objects and occasions which are either themselves objects of important common interests linking together the persons of a community or are symbolically representative of such objects .... The negative and positive rites of savages exist and persist because they are part of the mechanism by which an orderly society maintains itself in existence, serving as they do to establish certain fundamental social values.[97]

Bushman art, like Bushman hunting, was more than a technical act which gave material and aesthetic satisfaction. The paintings were, in my opinion, integrally concerned with the symbolic and ritual regulation, maintenance and transmission of the values and sentiments on which the structure of their society depended.

References

1. Bleek 1928a.
2. Bleek 1928b.
3. Metzger 1950.
4. Dornan 1917: 86.
5. Marshall 1959: 351.
6. Marshall 1959: 349.
7. Marshall 1959: 351, 354; Marshall 1960: 340.
8. Marshall 1959: 339.
9. Christol 1911: 4; Goodwin & van Riet Lowe 1929, Fig. D. opposite p. 188.
10. Stanford 1910; Willcox 1956: 35.
11. Marshall 1961: 236; Fourie 1928.
12. Silberbauer 1965: 47.
13. Silberbauer 1965: 91.
14. See also Battiss 1948: 225.
15. Bleek 1931: B.S. 5 (2).
16. Dunn 1931: 32.
17. Stow 1905: 88.
18. Stow 1905: 88.
19. Stow 1930: Pl. 21.
20. Alexander 1838 (2): 145.
21. Bleek 1935: B.S. 9, 153.
22. Stanford 1910.
23. Marshall 1960: 331.
24. Marshall, J. Film: "The Hunters".
25. Silberbauer 1965: 49.
26. Schapera 1930: 133.
27. See also Coles and Higgs 1969: Fig. 37a, b, c.
28. Watt and Breyer-Brandwijk 1962: 63.
29. Marshall 1961: 236-7.
30. Marshall Thomas 1959: 47-50.
31. Sparrman 1786 (2): 129.
32. Orpen 1874.
33. Willcox 1963: Pl. 8.
34. Arbousset 1852: 351.
35. Barrow 1801: 284.
36. Stow 1930: Pl. 51.
37. Alexander 1838 (2): 7.
38. Palmer 1966: 74.
39. Bleek 1935: B.S. 9.
40. Smits, Personal communication 1969.
41. Bleek 1928a: 15, 57.
42. Arbousset 1852: 346.
43. Ellenberger 1953: 124.
44. See also Ellenberger 1953: 154.
45. Barrow 1801: 284.
46. Chapman 1868: 81.
47. Orpen 1874.
48. Kirby 1952.
49. Clark 1960; Vinnicombe 1960b.
50. Anderson 1888: 9.

51. Struben 1920: 19.
52. Hook 1908: 76.
53. Jubb 1967: 83-87; Vinnicombe 1961.
54. Smits 1967.
55. Barrow 1801: 300.
56. Smits, Personal communication, 1968.
57. Ellenberger 1953: 109.
58. Schoonraad 1962.
59. Vinnicombe 1965.
60. Carter 1970a.
61. Ellenberger 1912: 8.
62. Moodie 1838: Collins Report 3 & 4.
63. Harris 1841: 68.
64. Sparrman 1786: 210.
65. Bleek & Lloyd 1911: 315-317.
66. Orpen 1908: 465.
67. Campbell 1813: 147.
68. Woodburn 1962: 269.
69. Vinnicombe 1971.
70. Silberbauer 1965: 47.
71. See pp. 178-180.
72. Marshall, J. 1958.
73. Bleek & Lloyd 1911: 331.
74. See also p. 379.
75. Bleek & Lloyd 1911: 271.
76. Bleek 1935, B. S. 9: 146.
77. Bleek 1932, B. S. 6 (3): 249.
78. Marshall Thomas 1959: 146.
79. Bleek & Lloyd 1911: 77.
80. Bleek & Lloyd 1911: 67.
81. Bleek 1932. B. S. 6 (3 & 4): 248, 325.
82. Bleek 1932, B.S. 6 (3): 248.
83. See also Willcox 1963: 48.
84. Bleek & Lloyd 1911: 275.
85. Lloyd 1889, No. 232.
86. Bleek 1911: 363.
87. Hewitt 1921.
88. Chapman 1868: 56, 79, 159.
89. Hahn 1881: 82, 84, 90.
90. Schapera 1930: 185, 187.
91. Fourie 1928.
92. Marshall 1961: 236.
93. Marshall Thomas 1959: 161.
94. Marshall 1957a.
95. See also pp. 292-293.
96. See p. 212.
97. Radcliffe-Brown 1952: 144-152.

Figure 216 *Site G3*
Actual size.

Dances, Mime and Music

Similarity and union are the aim of music; difference and distinction that of ceremony. From union comes mutual affection; from difference, mutual respect.
It is the business of the two to blend people's feelings and give elegance to their outward manifestations.
Let music attain its full results, and there will be no dissatisfactions in the mind; let ceremony do so, and there would be no quarrels.

Texts of Confucianism: Yo Ki or Record of Music.[1]

Dances, mimes and singing games of various kinds still figure prominently in the life of Kalahari Bushmen. Some of the dances are of a distinctly ritual character, while others are more spontaneous performances which give the impression of having no deeper significance than the expression of pure pleasure.[2] To date, however, most of the non-ceremonial dances and mimes have simply been described in terms of technique or artistry, with little attempt to analyse the concepts and behaviour which underlie the expression.[3]

Many Bushman dances are based on episodes in the lives of animals, when the hunter's inborn talent for mimicry and imitation is vividly displayed. It would nevertheless be gross over-simplification to regard all these dances merely as light-hearted enactments of observed behaviour. It is now well established that many illiterate peoples express their thought metaphorically through representing the animal world in terms of social relations; they see in animal behaviour oppositions and correlations, exclusions and inclusions, compatibilities and incompatibilities relative to their own set of values.[4,5] Moreover, mimetic performances in other parts of Africa have been shown to express not only an individual's experience on behalf of the community, but also to re-affirm the solidarity of the social group.[6] There is little doubt, therefore, that the Bushmen attach far greater significance to their animal dances than is apparent to observers for whom mime is no longer an integral part of social expression.

Although the values expressed are now lost to us, there are several vivid dance scenes represented among the rock paintings. One such group in a magnificent setting high up on Mpongweni mountain shows a central baboon-like figure which may well illustrate a Baboon Dance similar to those described in the literature: '. . . the performers imitated all the actions and droll grimaces of rival baboons, springing, gambolling, and running about on all fours, chattering and grimacing like a troop of excited simiadae'.[7] Additional details recorded from among the Khomani Bushmen in the Gemsbok Park may throw further light on the painted group:

This dance is carried out in the usual circular style, the dancers following one another around forming an ellipse rather than a circle in the sand.. . . As the dance warms up, one of the women. . . will from time to time leave the group of clappers, cross the ring and approach the principal baboon dancer with obvious sexual movements, to which the man . . . responds with contortions in imitation of the baboon. On returning to the group of women and girls clapping, the woman will go through the usual process of looking for vermin in their heads, on their bodies, and as she gets worked up, even on their aprons. All this goes on while the rest are dancing with various contortions in imitation of the baboons.[8]

The women on the left of the Mpongweni painted group, one with her body decorated with red and white spots, another with a baby on her back, are perhaps performing a de-lousing mime. Another on the upper right, also carrying a baby and with a small bag in her hands, dances across towards them. The women, showing typical steatopygia, wear bun-like hair arrangements or decorations, with a band across the head. (Figure 217).

Describing Bushmen seen in western Lesotho in 1836, Arbousset records that the women adorned themselves for merrymaking by speckling the face and breast with red and yellow paint and white clay. On their forehead was a narrow band of thread hung with rings made of ostrich-egg shells, while their hair, usually shaved

Figure 217 *Site G3 (opposite)*

The central figure in this dancing scene on Mpongweni mountain appears to represent a baboon. Many of the figures in action carry sticks, and wear feathers or horns on their heads. A woman at the upper right has a bun-like hair arrangement, and carries a baby on her back and a small bag in her hand. At the lower left, another woman with a baby on her back stands clapping, and watches three others indulging in what may be de-lousing activities. The body of the woman on the far left is speckled with dots of orange and white paint. The total length of the group from left to right is 26 centimetres.

save for a round tuft on the crown, was plastered with ochre, fat and powder from an aromatic wood, a little bag full of which they constantly carried.[9, 10]

Another Bushman dance, which Stow suggested might appropriately be named the Dance of Acrobats, can also be paralleled by painted groups in the area surveyed. It is described as follows:

> In hopping and jumping about in a ring, it appeared as if all their efforts were directed to place themselves in every possible position and contortion, the leader taking his place in the centre, and occasionally joining in the posture-making going on around him, while the dancers moved in a circle, writhing, twining and twisting their bodies in whatever droll and uncommon attitude their fancy suggested, now balancing themselves on their hands and throwing their legs upwards until their heads were in the position of a clown's looking through a horse-collar at a circus, now standing on their heads, and again balancing and walking upon their hands with their legs thrown high in the air, in true acrobatic style. The changes from one posture to the other were rapid and continuous, and the entire circle was ever in ceaseless motion.[11] (Figures 218, 227).

One such acrobatic ballet painted in the same shelter as the Baboon Dance shows a highly steatopygous figure, presumably a woman, holding a bow in outstretched hands. The string of the bow has unfortunately been pencilled by subsequent visitors to the shelter, which makes it impossible to determine the authenticity of this detail. The bow itself is nevertheless far more curved than the normal hunting bow which is only slightly arched. It is possible, therefore, that this is a representation of a musical bow.[12] Against this interpretation is the fact that both hands hold the stave; the string is not being vibrated, nor is the mouth applied to one end of the instrument to obtain variations of tone. The bow may simply be a symbol used in the dance, but all interpretations must of necessity be cautious because of the pencilled embellishments.

Bushman dances are usually held at night round a special dance fire. Music in the form of clapping and singing is provided by the women who usually sit or stand to one side, while the men, who also sing, supply additional rhythm by wearing rattles on their legs and torsos. The men are the principal dancers, although women may join in from time to time.[13] Dances often take place at full moon, or following on a good meal after a successful hunt. The motivation of one such spontaneous display of pleasure is well expressed in a prayer song recorded from among the Kung Bushmen in South West Africa, when a hunter donned his dancing rattles, headband and feather, and then exhorted the women to support him by 'singing well'. The satisfaction resulting from having sufficient meat to eat is described in such poetic terms as 'our hearts are shining' and 'my heart is awake' as opposed to 'my heart is sad from hunger' when there is no meat. But despite the physical basis for the pleasure, the song makes it clear that the principal reason for the dance is to explain to their god *Gauwa*[14] how happy they are that he had helped them. In other words, the basic motivation of the dance was concerned with the spiritual rather than the material.[15]

Many of the dances illustrated in the paintings show the participants wearing feathers, and the outstretched fingers of the clapping women are faithfully portrayed, a detail that also shows clearly in photographs of Kalahari Bushman dances. (Figures 219-222).

While some dances were no more than informal occurrences within a family group, others of a more ceremonial character were celebrated at special gatherings. One such important annual event was held to celebrate the breaking of the rains: 'They are . . . particularly joyful at the approach of the first thunder-storm after winter, which they consider so infallible a token of the summer having commenced, that they tear in pieces their skin coverings, throwing them in the air, and dance for several successive nights'.[16] Not only would the commencement of the rains have been an important seasonal event in the calculation of time, but it also marked the end of a lean period, heralded the warmer weather, and brought succulent spring grass which attracted the game. Doke mentions that the Khomani Bushmen held a dance in honour of the new grass,[17] and a religious dance known as the *Gei* was performed by various Khoisan groups when the constellation *Pleiades* first appeared over the horizon, or if a heavy thunder storm with lightning was approaching.[18] Bushmen north of Mafeking performed an all night ceremonial dance known as the *Khu* which was associated with rain,[19] as was the rain dance of the Kung so vividly reported by Elizabeth Marshall Thomas:

> The singing was very hard, very fast, and as the dancers swung around the circle dancing harder and faster, it suddenly began to rain. It was like a miracle. It was the first rain of the year . . . . The people had not danced to bring the rain; they had known that rain was coming and had danced to use its strong medicine.[20]

Part of the girl's puberty ceremony among the Gwi is to ceremonially introduce her to the band's territory and the edible plants it contains. The girl is then taken on an ecstatic run by the younger

Figure 218 *Site X9*

An animated dance showing figures leaping and somersaulting. The participant at top centre wears a tail and may be imitating a baboon. On the far left, a figure carries a small bag. A majority of dancers have feathers on their heads, and carry knobbed sticks. Fringes are worn around the calves, and bands of beads decorate thighs, waists and chests. Particularly long strands of beads or thongs hang from the waist of the figure at upper left. The paintings are in orange and white, and the scene measures 42 centimetres from left to right.

women of the band, which is said to express a 'rainstorm' and joy at 'getting wet'. This ceremony is believed to bring the girl good fortune, and to attract good falls of rain to her in the future.[21]

During the last century, Hahn several times witnessed a ritual in which Khoisan girls who had reached the age of puberty actually ran about naked in the first rain-storm of the year. This ceremony, enacted in the dramatic setting of flashing lightning and roaring thunder, was believed to ensure fertility, and was considered so important that even young converts would absent themselves from the mission stations at this time of year in order to have their bodies washed by the 'waters of the thunder-clouds'.[22]

Some of the exuberant dances depicted in the paintings possibly echo in visual form the electric tension and mounting feeling of climax which precedes the first storm of spring, a tension which is dramatically released as the first large drops of rain splash on the dry, sun-drenched earth.

Another important ceremonial dance widely described among Bushmen is a trance performance associated with protective medicine and the curing of ailments, both physical and psychological, actual or potential. An example of early reportage is that given by Chapman who in 1849 encountered a large gathering of Bushmen in present-day Botswana. Thirty young men participated in the dance, while about sixty women decked in beads formed a singing and clapping chorus. The men, adorned with plumes of black ostrich and eagle feathers on their heads, beads on their bodies, a fan consisting of the tail of a gnu in their hands, and rattles tied on their legs, indulged in 'all sorts of uncouth antics, gestures and gymnastic evolutions and contortions. The principal dancer, who seemed to command general admiration, commenced like a reasonable being, but ended like a man in a frenzy, gesticulating with hands and feet while he lay on the ground'.[23]

From such descriptions the dance sounds somewhat bizarre, which indeed it probably is, but thanks to recent anthropological investigations among living Bushmen, the significance and function of these trance performances is becoming better understood.

These special curing or protective dances have their own special style, the men dancing in a circular rut, stamping around and around, hour after hour, now clockwise and now anti-clockwise. Within the circumference of the circle sit the women, shoulder to shoulder, facing inwards towards the central dance fire.[24] They have been described as looking like 'a flock of birds crouched on the ground, their karosses like hunched, folded wings, and their

heads up alertly'.[25] Their function is to clap and sing. The men dance in a line, one close behind the other, with knees bent and bodies carried with little motion, leaning forward. The steps are very precise. They are minute in size, advancing only two or three inches, but they are strongly stamped, and ten or twenty dancers dancing together produce a loud thud. (Figure 221). The women clap loudly and sharply, and the men readily acknowledge that the success of the dance is dependent upon the perseverance and sustained enthusiasm of the women.[26]

The dances are accompanied by special songs which the Bushmen believe are sent to them by messengers from their god, usually when they are asleep. Each band has its own medicine song, named after things that are vital and strong: the giraffe, rain and gemsbok medicine, the ratel, fire and gemsbok medicine, or the sun, dove and gemsbok medicine. 'Almost every band has the gemsbok medicine, for magically, the gemsbok are very important animals.'[27] The dances named after animals do not, however, attempt to imitate the behaviour or locomotion of the animal, nor do they produce magic to control these animals in hunting; it is simply that their strength is imparted to the medicine.[28]

The principal purpose of medicine dances is to cure sickness and drive away evil, but they also serve as an outlet for pent-up emotions and tensions, and unite the members of the band in an act of protection. The 'medicine' is contained within the bodies of the medicine men, and is warmed to potency by the exercise of dancing and by the dancing fire. The Kung believe that by actually touching the affected person with both hands, the medicine man is able to draw sickness, real or potential, out of that person and into his own body. With a piercing, quivering yell he then shrieks the evil into the darkness, back to the spirits of the dead who brought it. Eventually, the medicine man reaches a state of frenzy. The shrieking becomes more frequent and violent, hot embers from the fire are trampled or handled, and burning sticks and insults are hurled at the spirits to keep them away. Finally, the medicine man falls down in an unconscious or semi-conscious state, described by the Kung as 'half-death'. During this deep trance, the medicine man's spirit leaves his body and goes to meet the spirits of the dead. It is therefore a dangerous time. The women must sing and clap ardently to protect him from harm, and other medicine men attend him. His body must be kept warm, and as an added protection, they rub him with sweat from their arm-pits.[29] Sweat is the most important of the trance symbols, for it is the palpable and visible expression of medicine on the surface of the body. The production and transmission of sweat is the key element in the curing ritual.[30]

A similar dance prompted by slightly different concepts is performed by the Gwi Bushmen of the central Kalahari.[31] The Supreme Being of this group of Bushmen, Nodima, who is visualised as predominantly anthropomorphic, is the giver of all life, but he is also able to punish anyone with death for evil-doing, the sign being that the corpse will bleed from the nose. The Lesser Being, Gawama, who is polymorphic and is manifested particularly in the crocodile, is decidedly harmful.

The most widely employed technique of confounding the evil-doing of Gawama is the exorcising dance. Among the Gwi, these are the Gemsbok and the Iron dances, which are performed in a similar manner to the Kung medicine dances. The women are thought to be most susceptible to the invisible evil-containing missiles sent by Gawama, and by dancing around them, the men are able to absorb the evil into their own bodies, which finally induces a trance. In this state, fire and glowing coals can be handled without injuries being sustained. When the exorcist has collapsed completely, he is revived by his fellows who execute a fast, shuffling dance at his feet and head. This, it is believed, starts expelling the evil from his body. In addition, his limbs and trunk are massaged with sweat from under the arms of the other participants.

Initiates are taught to dance by the more experienced men, and when a pupil has shown he is able to enter a state of trance, he is marked with incisions. These are made across the pupil's chest, laterally across the shoulders, and longitudinally on the anterior of the thighs, the incisions being deep enough to bleed. Perspiration from the head and armpit of the instructor is then rubbed into the cuts. This is believed to transfer the medicine to the pupil.

In instances of specific illness, blood-sucking and herbal medicines will be combined with the dance. 'Bad things' identified with a thin sinew or pieces of grass can be sucked out of patients through an incision in the skin overlying the site of pain. Other illnesses are caused by 'bad things' that sit too deep in the body to be extracted by sucking and cannot be removed.

The Medicine Dances are extremely vigorous and tiring, not only from the amount of physical energy expended by all participants, but also from the intense degree of emotional involvement. If the dance is to succeed, very close co-operation between the singing, clapping women and the dancing men is necessary.

The performers give everything that is in them, losing themselves completely in the unity of the group and, at the end of the night's dancing, are emotionally and physically drained. There is a marked feeling of peace and well-being . . . . Not only does such a night of dancing have a cathartic effect on the band by purging members of tensions and repressed emotions, but the sense of joint achievement of a successful dance has a significant unifying effect on the band.[32]

Lee's analysis of Kung Bushman trance performances also draws attention to the co-operative aspects of the dance, which is characterised by a lack of secrecy and a high degree of mutual aid. Much of the complex trance behaviour is directed to the training of young men, for although the Bushmen believe that medicine was given by God in the beginning, since then it has been maintained by transmission from man to man. Novices tend to have violent and dramatic reactions when they enter the state of trance, but after years of practice, they usually learn to refine their technique until they are able to function with controlled intensity. Lee stresses that the Bushmen seek for benevolent powers *within* the social body, while the blame for malevolence is projected to forces *outside* the social body. 'Such a conception of health and disease serves to bind together the living in a common front against hostile external forces'.[33]

Often the Medicine Dances continue throughout the night, for there is a special potency in those that are danced at dawn. The numbers participating dwindle as the night wears on, only the strongest seeing the performance through to the end.

The dawn wind lifted and blew away the smoke and dust and made the people shiver. The light showed the dancers moving stiffly, the singers hunched together for support and warmth, and revealed dusty, dirty faces and dirty teeth. Dust had made mud in the corners of our mouths and eyes.

Only about ten women were singing in the circle now, and they all sat together at one spot, leaving a lot of space around the fire; only four men danced and they moved slowly in their track, burdened by their rattles. They too, stayed close together so that most of their huge track was bare.

When the sun was over the horizon, the dance stopped. The women ended their song abruptly, stood up, shook the dust and straw from their clothing, and walked away. They did not speak to one another because they were too tired. The men talked for a moment as they sat down, stretched, untied their rattles, before walking off two by two toward their werfs. Soon all that remained was the dance track, a deep circular rut in the ground, the big heap of dead white ashes, and the dusty bushes and trees.[34]

Figure 219 *Site F6, Ndhloveni Mountain. A line of male dancers, bodies leaning forward and legs bent at the knee, stamp with small steps towards a group of seated women who are clapping and singing the dance rhythm. This dance is apparently identical to the Medicine Dances among living Bushmen in the Kalahari desert (see below and opposite).*

Figure 220 *Kung Bushmen in the Kalahari. Boys and women caper between the more serious dancing of the men. Children learn to dance from a very early age. The women wear long skin karosses, and the skin slings used for carrying babies and veldkos. The boys have dancing rattles twined round their ankles, and dance with sticks in imitation of their elders. Notice the ostrich-egg ornaments and the outstretched fingers of the women clapping and singing.*

Photograph by kind permission of Lorna Marshall, Peabody Museum.

Figure 221 above

The Medicine Dance of the Kung Bushmen in the Kalahari desert. The seated women clap and sing while the men dance around them, sometimes cutting through the circular track made in the sand. Notice the typical dance posture of flexed hips and knees. In the background, to the left, a semi-circular grass hut or skerm *can be seen.*

Photo by kind permission of Lorna Marshall, Peabody Museum.

Figure 222 left   *Site F6.*

A painted scene on Ndhloveni Mountain.

Men armed with bows dance towards a group of clapping women who have left their weighted digging sticks outside their skerms *or shelters. The two lower dancers carry short sticks or reeds which were associated with the Medicine Dances of the Mountain Bushmen (see p. 314). On the rockface, there are other figures extraneous to the dance scene which have been omitted from this copy.*

313

This scene, described by Elizabeth Marshall Thomas near Nama Pan in South West Africa, could doubtless also have been witnessed in a different setting in the Drakensberg little over a century ago. Such a dance has, indeed, been recorded by the Bushmen themselves in a painted shelter high on Ndhloveni mountain in the Underberg district. (Figure 222). Here one sees a procession of eight men in the typical dancing posture approaching a group of clapping women seated on the ground.[35] In another dance scene from Ndhloveni mountain, the men are shown carrying bows while the women, providing the usual accompaniment of singing and clapping, have laid aside their weighted digging sticks and are seated near their werfs or small grass huts. A similar type of hut, semi-circular in section, is still used in the Kalahari and can be seen in the background of Figure 221.

Qing, a Bushman of the Qacha's Nek district in eastern Lesotho, told a story which referred to 'dancing and making a great dust', and he also gave details of the Mountain Bushman's version of the Medicine Dance.

> Kaggen[36] gave us the song of this dance, and told us to dance it, and people would die from it, and he would give charms to raise them again. It is a circular dance of men and women following each other, and it is danced all night. Some fall down, some become as if mad and sick; blood runs from the noses of others whose charms are weak, and they eat charm medicine, in which there is snake powder. When a man is sick, this dance is danced round him, and the dancers put both hands under their armpits, and press their hands on him, and when he coughs, the initiated put out their hands and receive what has injured him — secret things.[37]

When questioned about rock paintings in a shelter on the Melikane river in his home area (Figure 223), Qing described a group of rhebuck-headed figures as 'men who had died and now lived in rivers, and were spoilt[38] at the same time as the elands and by the dances of which you have seen paintings'. Of other paintings showing tailed humans and animal-headed figures, he said, 'They are people spoilt[38] by the (Moqoma) dance because their noses bleed'. Orpen, who recorded this information, did not note the name of the dance in Qing's language, but said the Basotho called it *Moqoma*, a name meaning *blood from the nose*.

The Bushmen of western Lesotho also believed that their ancestors derived instructions concerning the *Moqoma* or *Dance of Blood* directly from Kaggen himself, and in times of famine, war, scarcity or sickness, the dance continued throughout the night in his honour.

They gambol together till all are fatigued and covered with perspiration. The thousand cries which they raise, and the exertions which they make, are so violent that it is not unusual to see some-one sink to the ground exhausted and covered with blood, which pours from the nostrils . . . . When a man falls . . ., the women gather around him, and put two bits of reed across each other on his back. They carefully wipe off the perspiration with ostrich feathers, leaping backwards and forwards across his back. Soon the air revives him; he rises, and this in general terminates the strange dance; the employment of the two bits of reed, already mentioned, is the point which seems to me most obscure. I can give no further explanation of it than that they constantly have recourse to it in cases of severe sickness, and that they say it exerts a salutary effect on the sick person; I could almost fancy that there may be mixed with it something of religious rite . . . .[39]

Dr Bleek showed a copy of the same paintings from the Melikane river which had been commented on by Qing to a Xam Bushman informant from the Cape. (Figure 223). He gave the following explanation of the buck-headed figures clad in long karosses and carrying sticks, two of which are crossed.[40]

> The thing (held by the first man on the right) is like the thing which people take when they are practising sorcery, for they mean to let other people, who are dying of sorcery, smell it, those (learners) who are not strong enough yet. This will help them to practise sorcery, for these things are in the things with which they strengthen their senses.
>
> For these are not people who are like other Bushmen . . . . For these are sorcerers who have things whose bodies they own . . . .[41]

These combined testimonies suggest that, among the Southern Bushmen, specific rods or reeds were connected with protective and curing medicines, and that there was a definite triadic association between sorcerers, humans with animal characteristics, and the ceremonial Dance of Blood.

Because Qing was the only Bushman ever questioned about rock paintings in the area of this survey, it is important to follow up as fully as possible every clue he left. Although his comments are at first reading highly enigmatic, they can be considerably amplified and clarified when looked at in the light of the Xam Bushman beliefs recorded by Dr Bleek and his sister-in-law Miss Lucy Lloyd.

From information supplied principally by Diakwain, it is apparent that, among the Xam, there was only one word for both medicine man and sorcerer, whether the object of the worker in magic was helpful or harmful. It is therefore difficult to translate the Bushman term accurately, there being no duality of meaning

Figure 223 *Site XII*

Inset: *Copy of the antelope-headed figures from Melikane made by Joseph Orpen in 1873. Although the copy is not particularly accurate it clearly shows that the figures had black horns at that date.*

A more recent tracing made in 1959 shows no trace of the horns whatever. The sticks held by the lower figures are pale pink in colour, and do not show up clearly in this rendering. The animal-headed figures are superimposed on the hindquarters of a
large eland painted at an earlier period. Above are black hunters, one with barbed metal spear and another with bow and heavy-tipped arrows, who aims at a second superimposed eland. At far right is a highly elongated figure (40 centimetres high) with long front apron, very small head, and arms held up with fingers extended. The legs from the knee downwards are painted in a different colour from the rest of the body.

315

in English terminology, and this limitation should be borne in mind during the following discussion. Although the term 'medicine man' is normally used for the worker whose object is beneficent, those who specialised in dealing with the supernatural among the Xam could be either men or women. It was the task of those who cured to ward off the evil of those who caused sickness, and the spirits of both were forever striving for supremacy.

It was believed that the spirits of medicine men were able to leave the physical human body during sleep, and could then enter the body of an animal such as a lioness, a jackal or a little bird. In this form, the medicine men could prowl or fly about without being recognised, watch everything that was going on, and then return to the human body without anyone knowing they had been away. Medicine men thus had knowledge of events and circumstances unknown to anyone else. This ability was further strengthened by a highly developed sense of smell which could be used to detect mischief. A patient with a complaint was literally sniffed, or 'snored', as Diakwain expressed it. Through their noses, sorcerers could absorb harmful things which could be anything from an owl to a butterfly, or even little sticks, bits of wood or invisible arrows from other sorcerers. These objects were then forced out of the nose by 'sneezing', an act that was often accompanied by bleeding. This blood was then rubbed on the patient as a protection against future harmful attacks. If an animal was 'snored' out, the medicine man often became like that animal, roaring and biting like a lion, or hooting like an owl. The services of medicine men were sometimes paid for, for instance, with a gift of a knife, and if they were not adequately rewarded, sung to, rubbed with fat, or given scented herbs to calm them, their power was weakened. In this weakened state they could grow hair and become a beast of prey, then as sorcerers, destroy instead of cure.[42] The dividing line, it would seem, between what was helpful and what was harmful, was both slender and unstable. There was no absolute good or bad. The qualities were interchangeable and dependent upon circumstances.[43, 44]

'When a sorcerer dies', said Diakwain, 'his heart comes out in the sky and becomes a star'. A falling star signified a sorcerer of evil or illness; 'When ... his heart falls down from the sky, it goes into a water-pit ... which is alive, as is also the sorcerer'.[45]

Here perhaps lies the explanation of Qing's 'men who had died and now lived in rivers', and who were 'spoilt by the (Moqoma) dance because their noses bleed'. It seems that, when initiated into the art of sorcery, one man could become endowed with a power for good, and another with a power for evil. The latter were possibly those who were 'spoilt' and who, in the form of therianthropic figures (half human, half animal) lived under water when they died.

According to Qing, the secrets of sorcery, as well as the significance of certain myths and beliefs, were known only to 'the initiated men of that dance', and once again information recorded from Diakwain confirms the close association between dancing, instruction and initiation. When shown a copy of a procession of painted figures from a shelter in the Tarka district of the Cape Province, he said:

> They seem to be dancing, for they stand stamping with their legs. This man who stands in front seems to be showing the people how to dance ... so he holds the dancing stick. ... The people know that he is one who always dances first, because he is a great sorcerer .... He wants the people who are learning sorcery to dance after him. For he is dancing, teaching sorcery to the people .... For when a sorcerer is teaching us, he first dances the *Ken* dance, and those who are learning dance after him as he dances ....
>
> When a sorcerer is teaching us, when his nose bleeds, he sneezes the blood from his nose into his hand, he makes us smell the blood from his nose, for he wishes its scent to enter our gorge, that our gorge may feel as if it were rising .... And when his blood has made our gorge rise, our gorge feels cool, as if water which is cold were in it. For however hot a place may be, the blood from a sorcerer's nose feels like cold water. Because he is a sorcerer, he is cold.
>
> Therefore when a sorcerer makes us smell the blood from his nose, we shudder away ....; we shiver all over .... Therefore a man who is a sorcerer will not lay down his kaross, even if it is hot, because he knows that the place will not seem hot to him, for his inside is cold .... For the doings of sorcery are not easy.[46, 47]

It is possible that this association of cold with the 'doings of sorcery' may explain the fact that a significant number of therianthropic figures among the paintings are depicted wearing long skin karosses.[48]

Of another painted scene from the Queenstown district showing steatopygous figures wearing animal masks and decorative bangles and streamers, Diakwain said:

> The things which the people here have put on are caps which they have made for themselves of young gemsboks' heads. They have cut the horns out; they mean to tread the *Ken* with them. At the time they do the *Ken* they wear such caps. The rings they have put on are the *Ken*'s rings. ... [49]

Figure 224 *Site X9*

Steatopygous women carrying knobbed sticks and spears walk in from left and right to join a central group of dancers. Two women stand with arms outstretched while between them, figures leap and somersault. Several of the women wear short beaded skirts, and the dancers use feathers as a head-dress or as tails stuck into a waist band. Some of the figures have been moved in closer than they appear on the rock face.

Figure 225 *Site G2*

A hairy figure with spread-eagled legs towers over white-faced humans sitting with hands held together and fingers extended. They wear skin karosses, and hair or thongs hang down at the nape of their necks. The large figure, possibly an imaginary spirit conjured up at a trance performance accompanied by singing and clapping, appears to have hooves in lieu of feet, as does the smaller figure lying in a flexed position above it. These paintings are executed on a very pitted surface of the boulder near which Captain Allen Gardiner halted his waggons and pitched camp in the upper Pholela valley in 1835. (See Figure 11).

This description of the *Ken* can perhaps be paralleled by photographs of the Eland Bull Dance performed by Khomani Bushmen in the Gemsbok Park, in which men and women wearing horns attached to their heads, and who discard all clothing save beads and headgear during the course of the dance, are seen in the stamping posture typical of the Medicine Dances.[50]

The Eland Bull Dance is usually held as part of the female initiation ceremony, and among the Naron is danced every night until the girl's menstruation has finished. The 'eland bulls' are two old men who imitate the eland with karosses pulled down over hunched shoulders. The Nusan Bushmen, who hold a similar ceremony, wear a bird's beak on the head instead of horns.[51] The Eland Bull Dance, which is undoubtedly erotic and in some descriptions overtly sexual,[52] is essentially a rite of transition associated with female pubescence and fertility. The music accompanying the dance is sung in an unusual scale, and the tune is the same among all Kalahari Bushman bands irrespective of language group or geographical situation.[53]

Boys' initiation among the Naron is also accompanied by a special dance, the *Gi*, at which a supernatural being is thought to appear. The descriptions of this 'being' include such details as a flat head, red eyes, black body, long broad tail, wings and claws. In the past, some of the participants may have dressed up to make the 'being' more convincing, but when Miss Bleek witnessed the performance, realistic visual symbols were not employed. The 'Ostrich Dance' is also performed at Naron initiation, when the men wear ostrich feathers or the head and beak of the black and white stork as head ornaments.[51]

Gemsbok have also been closely associated with puberty rites among several of the Kalahari Bushman clans. The boys' initiation into manhood is called by some 'the gemsbok play', and Schoeman describes how a captured gemsbok calf is sometimes incorporated into a ceremony that ensures skill in hunting. For the girls, a bonnet made from a gemsbok stomach is placed on the initiate's head in order to ensure strength and stamina during motherhood.[54] Among the Ko, who also perform the Eland Bull Dance, a girl's face is painted to resemble the face of a gemsbok on the fifth day of her seclusion, and for the boys too, gemsbok face-patterns play an important role. At both male and female initiation ceremonies small shields made from the hide of a gemsbok's forehead are shot at with a bow and arrow.[55] The Kung Bushmen say it is obvious that gemsbok are 'magic' animals because of the black medicine

markings on their faces,[56] and bearing in mind the importance of gemsbok in the naming of their Medicine Dances, observations made by J. F. Maingard on the Khomani Bushmen are particularly pertinent:

> The gemsbok pervades every aspect of their lives, the centre around which hinges all their philosophy, all their habits and customs. The Bushman's horizon, one might say, is bounded by the gemsbok.[57]

It is therefore clear, from the ethnographic record, that animal symbolism plays an important part in the expression of Bushman values, values which are reiterated and reinforced at ceremonial dances such as those concerned with initiation, healing and protection from harm.

Among the Southern Bushmen, the eland appears to have been the dominant symbol used[58] and there is a hint in Qing's remarks that eland were indeed connected with the mysteries of the Dance of Blood. '[The people with rhebok heads] were men who had died and now lived in rivers, and were *spoilt at the same time as the elands* and by the dances of which you have seen paintings'.[59] Since eland definitely had supernatural associations among the Southern Bushmen,[60] it is possible that their curing dances may have been named after eland rather than gemsbok. If, by inference, eland could be said to form the focal point of their philosophy, habits and customs as did gemsbok among the Khomani, this would be an additional explanation for the importance accorded to eland in their paintings.

Dancing to the Bushman, therefore, was not only a source of pleasure and a channel for the release of tensions and pressures; dancing could influence the forces of good and evil, thus humans, animals and natural phenomena were inextricably involved. Through the medium of dances, the Bushman passed his deepest secrets and beliefs concerning the universe from one member of the band to another, and from one generation to the next. An old Bushman from the Cape once remarked, with a kind of pious awe, that dances were to the Bushmen what prayer is to white people, and that his people would look upon it as irreverent if one only danced for entertainment.[61]

Dancing was an integral part of the Bushman way of life. It was one of the media through which he expressed his emotions, consolidated his relationships, communicated his values and maintained his equilibrium; painting was no doubt another.

References

1. Legge 1885: 98.
2. Schapera 1930: 202-204.
3. Merriam 1965: 461.
4. Lévi-Strauss 1962: 152-164.
5. Radcliffe-Brown 1958: 116.
6. See Goody 1962: 107, 129.
7. Stow 1905: 117-8; from Sparrman 1786: 356.
8. Doke 1936: 469.
9. Arbousset 1852: 354.
10. Schapera 1930: 67.
11. Stow 1905: 118; from Sparrman 1786: 356.
12. Kirby 1931a.
13. Schapera 1930: 202-4.
14. Gauwa: the lesser god of the Kung Bushmen.
15. Marshall 1962: 247.
16. Barrow 1801: 283; see also Stow 1905: 112.
17. Doke 1936.
18. Hahn 1881: 58.
19. Schwarz 1926.
20. Marshall Thomas 1959: 152.
21. Silberbauer 1965: 86.
22. Hahn 1881: 87-8.
23. Chapman 1868: 91.
24. Lee 1968: 37.
25. Marshall Thomas 1959: 255.
26. Marshall 1962: 248.
27. Marshall Thomas 1959: 130.
28. Marshall 1962: 249; Lee 1968: 39.
29. Marshall 1962: 250-1.
30. Lee 1968a: 44.
31. Silberbauer 1965: 95-99.
32. Silberbauer 1965: 98.
33. Lee 1968: 46, 51.
34. Marshall Thomas 1959: 255.
35. Mrs Lorna Marshall, to whom a copy of this painting was sent, writes that the beginning of a dance period is commenced in this way by young men who dance strongly towards the women. Personal communication 15/4/1969.
36. Kaggen — the creator god of the Southern Bushmen.
37. Orpen 1874.
38. One cannot help feeling that the word 'spoilt' used in Orpen's text has suffered from translation; 'spoilt' in the sense of 'harmed' would perhaps be more appropriate.
39. Arbousset 1852: 353-4; see also Stow 1905: 119.
40. See also Woodhouse 1968b.
41. Bleek 1935, B.S. 9: 14.
42. Bleek 1935, B.S. 9: 2, 21, 23.
43. Cf. the concept of *N!ow*, Marshall 1957a: 232-10.
44. Lee's analysis of the Kung Bushman trance performances shows certain differences from the concepts outlined in Bleek's material on the Xam. Although Lee records that the Kung believe that a few of the very powerful curers did, in the past, have the ability to transform themselves into lions who would then search for human prey, he argues that the Kung now assign to trance performers an essentially benevolent, positive and socially constructive role. Other differences of concept are that the key symbols and metaphors in the Kung trance complex are *boiling*, *fire*, *heat* and *sweat*, whereas the Xam in the south appear to have associated medicine men with *cold*, as well as with *sweat* and *blood*. (Lee 1968: 43, 46; Bleek 1935, B.S. 9: 13.)
45. Bleek 1935, B.S. 9: 24, 27, 28.
46. Stow & Bleek 1930: Pl. 2A.
47. Bleek 1935, B.S. 9: 11-12.
48. See p. 323.
49. Stow & Bleek 1930: Pl. 13, 14.
50. *Bantu Studies* 1937: Pl. 93.
51. Bleek 1928: 24.
52. Drury & Drennan 1926-7.
53. England 1967.
54. Schoeman 1957: 19-28; Maingard, J. F. 1937.
55. Heinz 1966: 122, 131.
56. Marshall Thomas 1959: 129-30.
57. Maingard, J. F. 1937.
58. See pp. 163, 164.
59. Orpen 1874.
60. See pp. 166, 176-181.
61. Moszeik 1910: 85.

Figure 226 *Site B5 (right)*

A woman sits with a baby on her back while another woman, facing her, has arms extended.

Figure 227 *Site G3*

At left and right, steatopygous women clap and sing while dancers wearing feathers in their hair and carrying sticks indulge in energetic contortions. The scene, painted in black and orange, measures 42 centimetres from left to right. (For colour reproductions, see Willcox 1963, Plate 35; Lee and Woodhouse 1970, Figure No. 171).

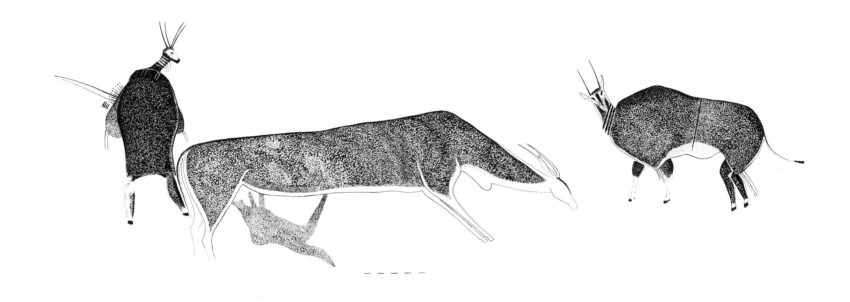

Figure 228   *Site F17*

Close to the rear of a highly stylised and elongated eland is a kaross-clad figure whose legs terminate in hooves. The animal-like head supports a double set of thin straight horns or porcupine quills, and the long ringed neck has short lines hanging from the throat. The figure carries a large bag or bundle, as well as a strung bow, arrows and fly-whisks. At the head of the eland is a curious figure with a line down the centre of the body dividing in half what appears to be an animal skin. The protruding legs have hooves, yet the shape of the rear limbs is distinctly human. The antelope head with thin tapering horns is turned to face the observer. The neck is striped, and thong-like lines hang near both front and hind legs. To the right of the group, and not reproduced here, are two other fragmentary kaross-clad figures, one of which also has an antelope head and carries a large bundle decorated with thongs or tassels. (See also Lee and Woodhouse 1970, Figures 42 and 175).

Hunting-Sorcerers and Rainmakers

There are a total of 155 human figures with animal attributes within the survey area. Of these, 41 have animal hooves, 15 have animal heads combined with hooves, and 106 have animal heads. Roughly half of these therianthropic figures are naked or scantily clad, while the other half wear long skin cloaks or karosses. The legs of the cloaked figures are typically thick and stump-like, and even where no hooves can be seen, there are often indications of a fetlock. It is probable, therefore, that the details of actual hooves have now disappeared through the use of fugitive colours. Similarly, the heads of many of the figures are no longer clear, and there was no doubt a greater correlation between animal heads and animal hooves than is at present evident.

The heads that are clearly animal are usually those of antelope, either eland or rhebuck, and may be with or without horns. Other figures with animal hooves have prognathous heads with snout-like faces that may be marked with lines radiating outwards across the cheek. They often wear broad beaded collars extending high up the neck, and have extraordinary headgear that may resemble a 'coronet' of feathers, or a 'helmet' with thongs or flaps hanging at the rear. The 'helmets' are sometimes embellished with a vizor-like band across the face, or have a short rod projecting backwards with a tassel suspended from the end. (Figures 94, 230–2). Red spots, possibly representing blood, are sometimes shown falling from noses, and fine streamers may emanate from necks or from under armpits. Other figures have feathery white strokes leading upwards from the head, or are associated with rope-like lines, frequently dotted with white, which connect them to an animal. (Figures 90, 109). Occasionally small fangs or tusks protrude from snouts, and while these could represent pieces of wood or porcupine quill worn through the cartilage of the nose, a form of adornment reported among some Bushmen,[1] they are more likely to have a mythological explanation. (Figures 232, 247). In addition to animal heads and hooves, these

Figure 229 *Site W19*

An animal-headed figure with exaggerated male organs, cloven hooves and a monkey or baboon on its back is confronted by two birds.

Figure 230 *Site S2*

A procession of cloaked figures much damaged by exfoliation of the rock. Long karosses are worn with the typical uneven hemline due to the method of pegging skins out to dry. The figures have hooves in lieu of feet, and some of the legs are hairy. Bobbles are worn on the calves and beaded bands at the knee. Where details of heads survive, *the necks are heavily decorated, faces are long and snout-like, and tassels on short sticks are worn protruding from the back of the head. The figures are superimposed on earlier bichrome antelope. (See also Figure 231).*

curious beings sometimes display other therianthropic features such as hairy legs and bodies, or arms terminating in claws. Legs are often decorated with broad beaded bands worn just below the knee, or with button-like knobs that follow the outline of the lower limbs. (Figure 230). The kaross-clad figures always walk sedately, sometimes in procession, and carry large bundles on their backs. They are also frequently superimposed on eland, or have eland painted on top of them.[2]

The naked or scantily clad figures with animal attributes can be divided into three main categories. A minority are associated with dancing scenes, and here the figures are probably not truly therianthropic, but are dressed up to represent animals. (Figure 217). Other figures with animal heads are interspersed among paintings without any apparent scenic relationship, but since they seldom carry hunting equipment and do not appear to hunt the animals with which they are associated, it is doubtful whether masks are intended. The third and largest category of near-naked figures with animal characteristics are painted in a very distinctive style, and although not all the figures in each scene are consistently therianthropic, they are clearly not concerned with secular or mundane activities. These figures are all markedly slender and elongated with characteristic postures and body markings. A 'split-bodied'

effect is given by a vertical strip of white paint bisecting the torso which is often crossed by a series of horizontal rib-like bars in black. In well preserved examples, additional flecks of white or black paint are dotted over the body. The figures usually wear a broad waistband from which an apron is sometimes suspended, and occasionally a skin cloak hangs from the shoulders. There is seldom any indication of buttocks or genitalia. The long thin legs often terminate in elegantly pointed cloven hooves instead of feet, and the stance is invariably cross-legged or bandy-legged, or the limbs are widely spread in highly exaggerated positions. All the postures, even when bodies or legs are bent at acute angles, have a theatrical air, with the long thin necks inclined to one side and the arms often bent towards the thorax in the manner of an opera singer. In most examples the heads are fragmentary, but where details survive, the faces were painted with a fugitive light-coloured pigment. The head-gear is usually black, and gives the impression of a rather wild, fuzzy hair-style or furry cap. Sometimes vestigial wide-spread horns are suggested. When present, weapons also show unusual features. The bows are of a design not encountered among other paintings,[3] and the figures sometimes carry ornamental switches or baton-like sticks ending in spiked knobs. (Figures 101, 102, 233, 234, 236).

Figure 231 *Site S2*

A photographic detail of two heads of the procession of fragmentary cloaked figures shown in Figure 230. Note the red lines falling from the snouts, the visor-like bars of white across the foreheads, and the tassels or plumes projecting backwards from the crown of the head.

Photo: Moira Soffe.

325

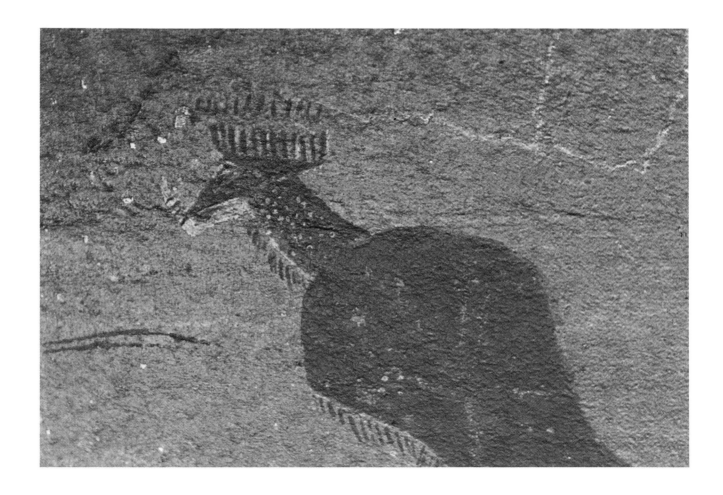

Figure 232 *Site A3*

Detail of kaross-clad figure from Cyprus. The antelope head has a striped tusk protruding from the snout, and is crowned by a double row of upward-pointing spikes. The kaross is apparently fringed, and there are also fringelike lines hanging from the spotted neck.
                                                                    Photo: Pat Carter

Figure 233 *Site W19*

A curious figure with horned animal head and cloven hooves sits cross-legged, knees drawn up to the chest. A tusk protrudes from the whiskered snout, and the torso is painted to give the impression of being split down the centre with horizontal black ribs. A spotted cape hangs from the shoulders. To the right is an anthropomorphic figure with similarly decorated torso which stands cross-legged and has hooves instead of feet.

This figure carries a short-handled object in one hand, and has a bow, hunting bag and two fly-whisks slung across the shoulders. Between the seated and standing figures is what may be a black skin bag shaped somewhat like a fish. To the left are two other anthropomorphic figures with grotesque white heads. (See also Figures 67, 102).

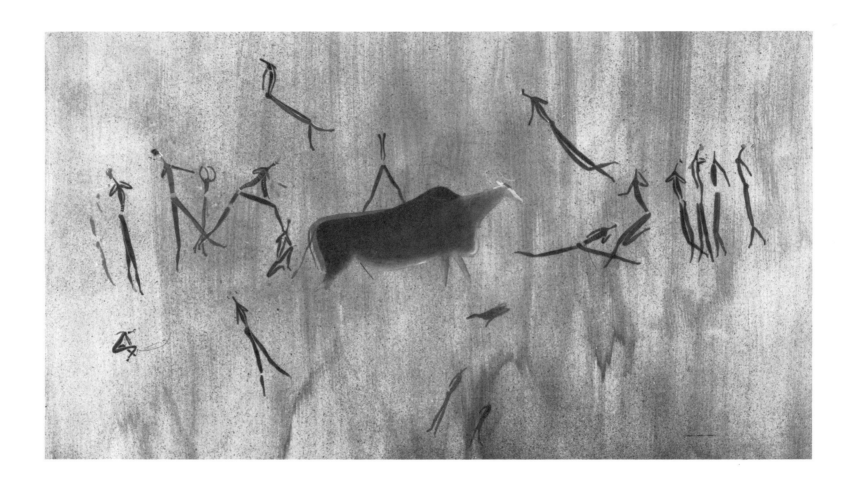

Figure 234 *Site W22*

Elongated figures with 'split bodies', some standing cross-legged and others with arms held towards the chest in theatrical poses, perform antics round an eland. The eland has been painted on top of an earlier, more faded image of the same animal. At left, a seated human with a bow has hooves in lieu of feet, and although this detail is not clear in the other figures, many of them have fetlocks rather than heels.

The compositions and content of these paintings are likewise out of the ordinary. In one group, the 'split-bodied' figures perform antics round a faded eland which shows evidence of overpainting, and in other scenes they are associated with dead eland. (Figures 102, 234). A shelter in the Tsoelike valley contains a complex figure with an animal head showing mouth, small tusk, nostrils, eyes and horn. The legs are drawn up towards the chest with the knees almost at shoulder level, and the forelegs, which are crossed over in front of the thighs, terminate in elongated cloven hooves. Despite the predominantly animal features which include a tail, this mythological creation has the traditional 'split-bodied' patterning of the human figures with which it is associated, and it also wears a skin cape. (Figure 233). At *Game Pass* in the Kamberg, north of the survey area, there are other examples of 'split-bodied' figures with hairy or crossed legs and cloven hooves. They wear horns or helmet-like headgear, and are also closely associated with an eland.[4] Sometimes the figures are grouped together in pairs, and there is a striking similarity between two such compositions, one in the Lotheni valley and the other in the Kamberg. (Figure 236). Similar 'cross-legged' figures were recorded by Stow in the Witzieshoek area bordering on northern Lesotho,[5] and by Ellenberger in western Lesotho,[6] where Smits also reports several examples.[7] Although it might be inferred that consistently unusual characteristics repeated at different sites could represent the work of a single artist, the wide distribution of these figures argues against such an interpretation. It is more likely that these highly stylised figures demonstrate a widely held mythological concept, and that different artists belonging to the same cultural tradition were responsible for the paintings. This would account for the slight variations in style even though the details remain constant.[8]

The motivation underlying the paintings of human figures with theriomorphic characteristics will probably never be satisfactorily understood, but in my view, literal interpretations — such as that the animal-headed figures represent masked hunters in disguise, and that the hairy-legged paintings with hooves instead of feet are humans wearing skin leggings[9] — do not convincingly explain all that can be observed in the painted record. Apart from the celebrated scene copied by Stow in which a hunter conceals himself under the skin of an ostrich in order to approach his quarry more closely,[10] I have seen no clear illustrations of 'disguised' or therianthropic figures actually participating in a hunt. Within the survey area there are two representations of figures with human legs protruding from bulky animal bodies which could be interpreted as forms of disguise,[11] and although one of them carries hunting weapons, it is not in any way attempting to shoot at the eland with which it is associated. (Figure 228). The second figure, without weapons, is painted below an almost life-sized shaded polychrome eland, the largest yet found in the survey area. (Figure 235). Both of these 'disguised' figures are in the crouched or horizontal position, that is, they do simulate the stance of an animal, whereas most examples of therianthropic figures wearing skins are upright and walk sedately. Where animals are associated, they are usually eland, and the relationship between figure and animal never gives any impression of aggression or attack. The scenes appear to be concerned more with Bushman beliefs and attitudes than with the factual depiction of an event.

From what little survives of the mythology of the Southern Bushmen, it is clear that in addition to those members of the band who specialised in the power to cure ills, there were also those who claimed power over animals, and others over weather. For want of better terms, these may be referred to as Medicine, Game and Rain sorcerers. The concepts associated with Game and Rain sorcerers have considerable bearing on the interpretation of therianthropic paintings.

Although Bushman social organisation is not totemic in the strict sense of the word,[12] there is clear evidence that they used animals as symbols of relationship.[13] Stow claimed that each band of Bushmen in the eastern Cape had a special shelter where their particular totem was conspicuously depicted.[14] There was, for instance, a Snake, Elephant, Eland or Rhinoceros shelter, and in western Lesotho, various antelope, including the Blesbok, were said to be held sacred by the Bushmen.[15] The Masarwa of the Sansokwe river further north called themselves the Zebra, Eland or Duiker clan, while another group in contact with settled peoples were known as the Goat clan.[16] In the Kalahari, extant Bushman bands distinguish themselves according to the emblems of their Medicine Dances. Thus there are the giraffe, rain and gemsbok medicines; the ratel, fire and gemsbok; or the sun, dove and gemsbok. Gemsbok are invariably included in the naming of the dances because the Bushmen regard them as magically very important.[17] Among the neighbouring Tswana peoples each tribe has its own particular song and dance which is an integral part of their totem, and in order to find out a man's totem, one asks, 'What do you dance?'[18] It is not impossible that Bushman dances reflect similar symbolism.

Figure 235 *Site Q2*

This curious figure, with human legs and a human arm protruding from a large skin kaross, is painted below the fragmentary remains of a very large eland measuring 2,43 metres. There is no indication of a head on the figure, but two rods with lines hanging from them stick out of the skin in the region of the neck. A mineral deposit is encroaching upon the painting.

Photo: Pat Carter

A remark which identifies the Bushmen of southern Lesotho with eland is particularly relevant to my own study area. An aged Phuti who had painted among Bushmen in his youth was asked to demonstrate the techniques used. After making the necessary preparations, he said he would first paint an eland, because the Bushmen in that part of the country, were 'of the eland'.[19]

Examples of what may be called individual or personal totemism can also be detected in information given by the Xam Bushmen. There are such references as: 'The Chameleon is our father's man. Therefore my mother used to tell me not to kill it, for my father would be very angry, and would not give me any food in consequence'. The chameleon in this instance could also be asked for rain, and was able to foretell when rain was coming. It was said of another Bushman, the father-in-law of the informant: '. . . he had Mantises, he was a Mantis's man'; and yet another possessed locusts and rain, and was described as 'a Rain's man'.[20] In addition to these examples of a personal association with selected animals among Bushmen who claimed no special supernatural powers, there were game and rain sorcerers to whom these relationships were particularly important. By a process of close identification tantamount to 'ownership', they were able to exercise control over game and over rain: '. . . you believe that I really own springbok, that I am a springbok's sorceress'; and 'the people sounded as if they believed that he really owned rain'. Other sorcerers were said to 'have things whose bodies they owned', which may refer to sorcerers who were believed to appear in animal form.[21] It was generally held that sorcerers were able to control the behaviour of game and to 'bewitch' animals either to the hunter's advantage, or his disadvantage. They could make animals aware of the hunter's presence and so escape, or conversely could lead them directly to the hunter's bow. If spirit sorcerers were suspected of working against a hunter, they were asked in prayer form to 'change their thoughts'. Communication with the spiritual world was established by beating the ground with a stone, sometimes a perforated digging stone.[22]

Among the Xam Bushmen, both males and females could practise as sorcerers, and at the site *Swartmodder* in the Matatiele district, highly steatopygous women, and a therianthropic figure with hunting equipment, are associated with a beautiful group of shaded polychrome eland painted on the ceiling of the shelter. (Figure 165). One of Bleek's informants recounted how an aged female game sorceress was able to turn herself into a lioness in order to visit relatives incognito to see what they were doing. Her methods of controlling game included the actual capture of a springbok with

peculiarly short horns which she castrated and kept tied up. At times, she would let her animal loose among the wild springbok and use it as a decoy to lead the herd towards concealed hunters. One day a relative unwittingly killed the decoy animal. There were serious repercussions. The hunter's brother immediately fell ill after eating some of the springbok's flesh, and further catastrophe was only averted by the timely action of the hunter's wife. Realising that the castrated springbok was not like other springbok, she cut off the animal's head and made a cap of it, and presented it to the sorceress in order to appease her wrath. With good relations restored, the family continued to request game from the old woman. She used to lend them her 'springbok's head cap' in the belief that the wild herds would still follow the dead springbok wherever it went.[23]

Another informant gave this description of a particular sorcerer: '[He] was a springbok sorcerer, he had springbok, he used to cut off the springbok head. He also cut off the scalp, he thus sewed a scalp cap, which looked like a thing's ears when he put it on.' He described the cap by holding up thumb and little finger with the three middle fingers bent downwards.[24] Similar caps are illustrated in the rock-paintings, both with and without horns, (Figures 102, 247), but to date only one scene located within the survey area shows the wearers of such caps or antelope heads to be actually hunting. (Figure 90). Even if the caps happened to serve as a camouflage, their prime function seems to have been mystical rather than practical.

The Bushmen believed that game sorcerers were particularly prone to become 'spirit people' when they died, and their apparitions could take on many forms. 'They change themselves into a different thing. At one time when we looked at it, it was not like a person; for it was different-looking, a different thing. The other part of it resembled a person.'[25] This description, in conjunction with the fact that certain sorcerers were thought to possess bodies other than their own, certainly suggests a combination of human and animal traits. Bushman deities, too, were often conceived of as both human and animal.[26] The Naman thought of their Supreme Being as human in shape with *ribs drawn over the flesh*, and with feet the length of arms. He could nevertheless assume animal form at will, and when in this state was invulnerable.[27] One of the names for a ghost or spirit among the Khoi was 'fawn-feet',[28] and an informant described a spirit in the form of a skeleton: 'no flesh, a white bone alone I saw'.[29] Spirits could also look like 'a little child . . . seeming as if it sat with its legs crossed over each other'.[30]

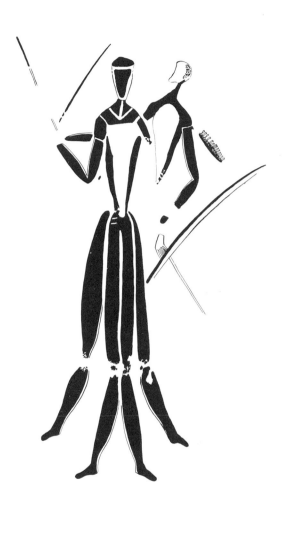

Figure 236

Similar pairs of figures from widely separated sites.
Left: *The Krantzes, Kamberg.*
Centre: *Site B10, Xamalala Location, Lotheni.*
Right: *Site U12, Leqoa river, eastern Lesotho.*

It is indeed tempting to associate the cross-legged figures in the paintings that have antelope hooves in lieu of feet and rib-like markings across their bodies, as representing these 'spirit people', and in particular, the spirits of game sorcerers.

Even after sorcerers had died, their spirits could be appealed to for help:

> When they died their thoughts, with which they had been sorcerers and worked magic, continued .... Therefore mother used to beg from her sorcerers who had owned game, when ... she beat the ground [with a stone], then she spoke with them ... Mother did not see them, yet she talked with them, for mother felt sure that they would hear ... as she struck down with the stone she said, "O my spirit people, do you no longer think of me? It seems as if you had turned your backs on me, that you do not seem to think as you used to do, at the time when you still had bodies; you used to talk as if you really loved me. But it seems as if you had in dying taken your thoughts away from me".[31]

The idea that game sorcerers actually 'possessed' the animals over which they exerted power is especially relevant to painted compositions in which buck are either bound with thongs or appear to be connected by a thong to a human figure. 'It was a springbok that did not stand outside, but one that was loosed from a thong, a springbok that did not wander about, but was used to stand tied up.'[32] The actual role of paintings in the practice of game control must remain conjectural, but if it is accepted that some of the therianthropic figures represent game sorcerers either in the flesh or in spirit form, the ethnographic evidence makes it clear that the role of the game sorcerer was to exert power over game through close identification with game. The paintings no doubt echo this concept. (Figures 90, 95, 102, 104, 109, 214, 237, 247, 249).

The Kung Bushmen of the Kalahari believe that a certain power or essence known as *n!ow* closely links the birth, life and death of all men with that of certain game animals. Man and selected game animals are in turn linked with the weather: wind, heat, cold, and rain. At the moment of birth, every child is believed to acquire *n!ow*, and from that moment on, the child is connected with certain forces in the world around him. The effects of *n!ow* can be very complex, particularly when women bear children, and when men kill the larger antelope. As the fluid of the womb falls upon the ground when the child is born, and as the blood of the antelope falls upon the ground when the antelope is killed, the interaction of the *n!ows* takes place. And the effect of one *n!ow* upon another brings a change in the weather. In this way a mother may bring rain or drought when she bears a child, and a hunter may bring rain or drought when he kills an antelope. *N!ow* is intangible, mystic and diffuse, and the Kung Bushmen themselves do not fully understand its workings. They do not know how or why *n!ow* affects the weather, but they know that it does. By careful observation of weather changes in association with their own activities, each person is able to discover the limits of his own *n!ow*.[33] The Xam Bushmen of the Cape had a similar concept. They believed that both men and animals created a wind when they died, which in turn influenced weather conditions.[34] It is this belief, then, which provides the second link in the chain connecting man, animal and rain.

Because the well-being of the hunter-gatherer Bushmen was very largely dependent upon an adequate rainfall, it is hardly surprising that they sought to gain control over the elements. Their reputation as successful rainmakers was indeed widespread, and the service of Bushman weather specialists was much sought after not only by the band or tribe of which they were a member, but also by their Bantu neighbours.[35] As in other forms of specialisation, particular members of the band acquired their knowledge of rain-making by apprenticeship to older, experienced practitioners. The general belief among the Xam Bushmen seems to have been that rain was closely associated with specific animals such as snakes and tortoises, and the 'rain-animal' itself was variously imagined as looking like eland, hippopotami, or other unidentifiable spotted animals resembling cattle or buck.[36] Rain could be induced to fall by capturing one of these animals and dragging it over the land, or by cutting up the carcase and distributing portions of meat over the area where moisture was required. Information told to Bleek suggests that this was done quite literally:

> If rain does not fall, they [the Bushmen] cannot see the wild onion leaves, for these things are bulbs which they dig up and eat .... That is why they want the water's people to make the rain fall for them, that they may dig and feed themselves when rain falls on the wild onion leaves, for these are what they eat, the Bushman's food. So they beg the water's medicine men to make rain to fall for them ... and these promise that they will really make rain fall for them. Then they go and sling a thong over the water-bull's horns, they lead it out, they make it walk when they have slung the thong over its horns. They make it walk along and kill it on the way, that the rain may fall. They cut it up, and rain falls at the place where they threw it down.
>
> Then the rain does fall, they compel it; where the water's flesh is put down, there rain falls following them as they return home; the rain falls behind them, they come on first.[37]

Figure 237 *Site W32*

In the centre of the scene is a shaded polychrome eland, above which crouches an anteater-like animal with stripes on its face and thongs hanging from the neck. A red line with white dots extends from the eland's nose towards two extraordinary figures, the lighter coloured Being having cloven hooves in lieu of feet, and a tusk protruding from the muzzle-like face. The darker standing figure, the face of which has faded away, wears a curious head-dress, and carries a triangular object on a short stick. The decorated arms have hairy or bristly projections, and the penis has a long thin rod-like line hanging from the tip. The genitals of the fragmentary figure at right are similarly marked. The paintings in the upper part of the scene are unfortunately poorly preserved, but appear to represent crouched animal-headed figures in tasselled skin karosses. Below and to the left of the central eland are two horizontal figures in faded karosses, the limbs protruding as dark stump-like objects. The heads are missing, but beaded tassels and other angular lines were probably part of their ornate head-dresses. Another red line spotted with white links these prone figures with three kaross-clad beings at left. The two better-preserved figures have antelope heads, and the lines falling from the nose of one probably indicate some form of exudate, real or symbolic. Notice the fringed garments or bundles carried by these therianthropic beings. A procession of some twenty-three kaross-clad figures, only a few of which are included in this reproduction, extend to the left. Only the heads and legs are now visible, transient paint having been used for the skin garments.

Paint smears and smudges which confuse the composition have been omitted from this tracing. (See also Figure 95, and Lee & Woodhouse 1970, Figure 107).

Figure 238 *Site XII*

This rain-making scene from a site originally known as Mangolong, was copied by J. M. Orpen in 1873. Since then, the site has become better known as Sehonghong, and the connection between the two has only recently been discovered.[71] *The paintings have often been reproduced because they are among the few which were commented on by the Bushmen themselves. It was said that rain sorcerers had caught a rain-animal, and were leading it over the land with a thong so that rain would fall in its wake. In the original lithographic reproduction of the scene, short strokes surrounding the animal which had been recorded by Orpen were omitted in error.*

In one of the stories the rain or water-bull was attributed with the characteristics of a hippopotamus, although the mention of 'horns' is somewhat confusing. The sorcerers lay in wait at the water-bull's hole, knowing that it would return there after grazing at night:

> They will wait its return to put a thong over its head as it comes, for they want to catch it and lead it away. So they try to approach quietly . . . .
>
> A man who is an old rain medicine man and knows how people work with the rain-bull will lead, the men whom he teaches will follow. They hold the end of the thong to help him when he has thrown the noose over the water-bull's horns; when he draws the thong tight on the bull's head, they will pull it back and not let it enter the water.[38]

The story was told of a medicine man who used a weak thong which allowed the bull to escape. A more experienced rain-maker pointed out that he should have used *buchu*, a sweet-smelling herb, 'for if the bull had smelt *buchu*, it would have been calm and gone quietly without struggling'.

The painted scene first copied by Orpen from the Sehonghong shelter in Lesotho shows figures carrying decorative objects in one hand and leading a hippopotamus by a thong in the other. The whole group is surrounded by short strokes which were unfortunately omitted from the original lithographic reproduction. The strokes were included in Orpen's copy, and can still be seen on the rock although the group is now very faded. (Figures 238–9). Qing, the young Bushman who was with Orpen when the copy was made, curiously described the animal as a *snake*, an anomaly perhaps explained by the fact that snakes were also closely associated with water and rain.[39] Qing said the men who were catching the animal were holding out charms to it, and securing it with a long *riem* or thong made of hide. Rather bafflingly, the men were also said to be under water, and the strokes were things growing under water. However, since the Bushman language has but one word for both water and rain,[40] an alternative translation could read that they were all in the *rain*, and the strokes represented things growing in the *rain*. One of Bleek's Xam informants gave a rather more coherent description of the scene: Bushmen were charming the animal, attaching a rope to its nose, and then leading it over as large a tract of country as they could so that the rain would similarly fall over a wide area. The informant described the objects carried by the sorcerers as charmed *buchu* contained within boxes made of tortoiseshell and ornamented with dangling thongs. The strokes in the painting indicated rain.[41]

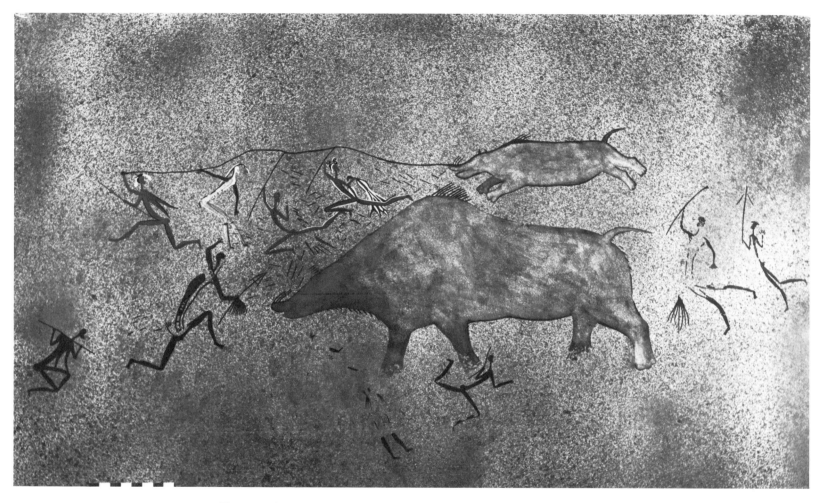

Figure 239 *Site XII*

A recent tracing of the rain-making scene first recorded by J. M. Orpen in 1873 (see opposite). The paintings are now very indistinct, and are difficult to photograph. Although there are many inaccuracies in Orpen's copy, the content of the scene is the same, and the interpretation is therefore not affected. Four men lead a young hippopotamus by a thong attached to its nose, while a larger hippo-like animal is driven and deflected by other figures carrying spears.

Figure 240   *Site H2*

A 'rain-bull' is led by a thong towards a Bushman encampment where tasselled skin bags hang on the shelter wall. A rain sorcerer extends a tufted stick towards the rain-bull, probably a charm to 'calm' the animal, while two other decorated sorcerers follow behind. These men bend forward, and drops of blood fall from their noses.
When this long frieze was removed to the Natal Museum in 1910, the slab of rock cracked in several places. A modern repair above the head of the rain-animal has obliterated some of the red 'rain' strokes which are visible in a photograph taken before the painted slab was quarried. (See Figures 24–26.)

An interesting observation was made by Dunn when travelling immediately north of the Orange river in 1872, that is, before the publication of Orpen's paper with Bleek's accompanying remarks. Dunn saw a stone on which there was an engraving of a hippopotamus being dragged across the dry veld by several Bushmen who held a rope attached to the nose of the effigy. The sergeant of police who accompanied Dunn, and who had an intimate knowledge of the Bushmen, thought the performance was connected with rain-making. He commented that magic played a big part in Bushman life, and since the hippopotamus was closely connected with water yet could also exist on land, the Bushmen, by association of ideas, felt they could induce rain to follow a replica of the water-loving animal into the drought-stricken country.[42] This record indisputably demonstrates that representational art was, on occasion, incorporated in rain-making rites.

The clearest of the Drakensberg rain-making scenes shows a male animal resembling an elongated hippopotamus being led towards a Bushman encampment. Small red strokes around the group suggest falling rain. The leading figure holds out a tufted object on the end of a stick towards the animal. The two men who follow behind are spotted with decorative paint, and have what is apparently blood falling from their bowed heads.[43] (Figure 240). It is of note that a Xam rain-sorcerer who could summon clouds which were 'unequalled in beauty', and who could also manufacture lightning, was said to have 'sneezed' while he was at work, and 'blood poured out of his nostrils'.[44] The details of the painted scene therefore accord well with Bushman descriptions of rain-making ceremonies. In addition to the significance of nasal blood in other ritual contexts, the use of body paint and scarifications among sorcerers has already been noted,[45] as well as the fact that an experienced sorcerer leads the rain-bull while the initiates he is teaching follow.[46]

A rock shelter in the Skelegehle valley, a tributary of the Mkhomazi, has two paintings of hippopotamus-like animals. One, in red monochrome and with open mouth showing a tongue, is part of a complex superimposed panel, while the other, in faded white, is painted on a ledge high above the panel. (Figures 243, 245). Both hippopotami are male and are superimposed on earlier paintings of humans, and both have an elongated, 'split-bodied' figure near them. The white hippo-like animal is pursued by a running figure, and is confronted by another which is unfortunately very faded. There are red strokes on the body of the animal, and above its

Figure 241 *Site P2*

An animal with a hippo-like rear end and elephant-like trunk is connected by a line to a human figure. A series of strokes fall from the head of the animal.

back a series of strokes form a vertical column. To the left is a streak, forked at the top, which is suggestive of lightning.

On the farm *Eagle's Nest* (site P2), there is another curious painting of an animal with a series of strokes emanating from its head. The rear of the animal resembles that of a hippopotamus, but the head is more like an elephant with a long trunk-like protrusion. The 'trunk' ends in a nozzle-like swelling, and a zig-zag line above the animal ends in a similar 'nozzle'. Another line leads from the head of this beast towards a human figure who has red streaks falling from his head, and who is linked to another line leading upwards. (Figure 241).

Other paintings of hippopotami in the survey area are not obviously connected with rain-making scenes. A shelter on the Bokberg in Mount Currie district contains no less than five hippopotami, including a cow and calf being attacked by hunters with long assegais. (Figure 242). Another hippopotamus in black silhouette on the Tsoelike river in Lesotho represents the characteristics of this large amphibious animal very faithfully, but is not, apparently, part of a scenic composition. (Figure 49). It is, indeed, surprising to find these paintings of hippopotami in the high altitude areas where river beds are rough and the water comparatively swiftly flowing, but large-scale hunting did eventually force hippopotami to seek refuge in abnormal habitats.[47] It is significant, therefore, that both the shelters where hippopotami are naturalistically portrayed, also have representations of horses, which suggests that the paintings are probably late.

Eland as well as hippopotami were associated by the Bushmen with rain, and it has been observed that eland usually concentrate into large herds during or after the first rain of the season.[48] A legend tells how the rain in the form of an eland was shot with disastrous results,[49] and an illustration of a 'rain-bull' by one of Bleek's informants resembles an eland in shape and bulk.[50] Paintings showing eland tied up or eland connected to strange figures by rope-like lines, may therefore be associated with rain-making rites as well as with game-sorcerers. (Figures 95, 102, 109, 214, 237).

Rain specialists among the Xam were attributed with the power to disperse as well as to create rain, and the Drakensberg Bushmen were apparently able to do the same. Louis Tylor's waggon driver told how Bushmen in the Giant's Castle area could continue to sit round an open fire with clear sky above them even in the midst of a hailstorm,[51] while another report claimed that Bushmen who had raided stock from the Bushman's river repelled their attackers by summoning a torrent of rain through the medium of an eland horn.[52] Supporting evidence for the use of horns in rites connected with rain can be found among other Bushman groups. The mythological hero of the Kung in the Kalahari was said to have made 'rain, sky rain, until it poured much upon the women. Then he forbade it: "Rain, vanish, hi, hi, hi", and was silent, then blew upon a buck's horn and sang. And the rain disappeared'.[53] The Xam Bushmen in the northern Cape burnt horn in order to disperse rain. It was believed that the unpleasant smell rose into the sky and counteracted the ominous-looking green storm clouds whose potential violence was dreaded.[54] Heavy or damaging storms were regarded as masculine and were represented by the rain-bull,

and mist was thought of as breath from its nostrils. When Bushmen heard a rain-bull come thundering, they would light fires in the hope that the bull would take fright and retreat.[55] A rain-cow, on the other hand, represented gentle rain:

> I will cut a she-rain which has milk, I will milk her, then she will rain softly on the ground, so that it is wet deep down in the middle . . . by cutting her I will let the rain's blood flow out, so that it runs along the ground.[56]

Soft rain falling uniformly from a cloud was called the rain's hair, or was identified with the strings hanging from a collecting bag. Columns of rain, on the other hand, were thought of as the rain's legs — 'a rain's leg is when it does not rain everywhere'. And the rain's scent, like that of all other animals, was specifically identified: 'The people say that there is no scent as sweet, hence the people say that it is fragrant'.[57]

The rain was nevertheless quick to take offence, with the result that many acts and avoidances had to be observed in order to avert catastrophe. Young girls and unmarried men, particularly those undergoing seclusion and initiation into adulthood, had to be especially careful; respect had to be shown to elders, silence had to be observed at the onset of rain, and certain foods such as tortoises and other things that 'belonged' to the rain could not be eaten for fear that everyone would be struck by lightning or carried away in a whirlwind and turned into frogs. Frogs were not to be killed lest drought ensue, and stones could not be thrown into ponds in case the rain became angered. In order to placate the rain, red haematite and *buchu* (a sweet-scented herb) could be strewn on the water's surface, for these were things that the rain loved very much.[58] Certain pools were associated with dead sorcerers whose hearts were thought of as falling stars which entered the water, and it was from these pools that water-bulls were fetched during rain-making rites.[59] This belief throws some light on Qing's enigmatic comments on the paintings from Melikane and Sehonghong: the sorcerers, who were given specific names, were described as *men who had died and now lived in rivers*. They were envisaged as having animal heads, and they had the power to 'tame' (subdue or control?) elands and snakes, both animals being identified with water and rain.[60] (Figures 223, 238-9).

When the Xam requested particular weather, old men of the band first addressed the dead men who were with the rain, and then they spoke to the rain itself. Dead people were thought to ride the rain like a horse — they owned the rain, and the thongs with which they held it were like a horse's reins.[61]

Figure 242 *Site R6*

Hunters armed with spears surround a hippopotamus and calf which have been immobilised by many wounds. The young hippopotamus has been overpainted by a horse. Other later paintings of mounted hunters pursuing eland have been omitted from this rendering to avoid confusion.

Figure 243 *Site E7*

A hippo-like bull animal with mouth open to show the tongue is superimposed on human figures. Above and to the left, eland in bright orange and yellow ochre are superimposed on humans in dark red, the white pigment on the eland having faded so that the underlying paintings show through. Below the 'hippo' is a split-bodied figure in action, and to the left are several small antelope.

Photo: Pat Carter.

Figure 244 *Site E7*

The rock shelter in the Skelegehle valley in which the hippo-like animals in Figures 243, 245 appear. The grassy slopes in the foreground have been burned black by a veld fire.

Photo: Pat Carter

Figure 245 *Site E7*

A white hippo-like animal is pursued and headed off by two figures carrying sticks. A man running behind, with clearly defined toes, wears a rectangular front apron, and a swallow-tail rear apron. The animal is superimposed on faded red humans. To the right, a fragmentary animal body, only part of which is reproduced here, is overlain by a red figure with white hands and face, and a white strip down the centre of the torso. Above the hippo-like animal, and on its body, strokes of red paint suggest falling rain, but the 'rain-animal' interpretation of the scene can only be suggested with caution. The 'thong' across the nose of the animal may be no more than the tail of the faded animal on the right.

One informant said:

> Father called on [my great-grandfather] when he wanted rain to
> fall; although he was no longer with us, yet father used to beg
> him for rain. For father believed that, being a rain-medicine man,
> he would hear father when he called.
> Father said ". . . you used to say to me, that when the time
> came that you were dead, if I called upon you, you would hear me,
> you would let rain fall for me." And when father spoke thus,
> the rain clouds came gliding up, the rain did not pass over,
> for the rain clouds covered the sky.[62]

Thus rain-sorcerers, like game-sorcerers, could be called on for
assistance whether they were alive or dead.

If rain clouds came up and then dispersed again, the lack of
success was said to be because the thong with which the rain-bull
was being led had broken, or that someone had contradicted or
offended the rain-sorcerer.[63] Several stories refer to disapproval
registered by rain-makers because their services were sought only
when the band was in need, after which they were neglected and
forgotten.[64] On one occasion, a Bushman asked a sorcerer who
appeared in the guise of a lion to make rain:

> O beast-of-prey, you must please really listen to us, for the
> place here is not pleasant, for it is dry, for the bushes are dry;
> the place is not pleasant, because it is white, for the bushes are
> withered. Please let it be wet, that the bushes may grow beautiful.
> For a place is beautiful when it is sprouting, when the mountain
> tops are green.[65]

Unmoved by the poetry of this request, the rain-maker rebuked
him:

> 'You beggar! you come and talk of danger because the bushes
> are dry.'

An astute Bushman who obviously had some insight into the
artifices of rain-making commented that medicine men only seized
the rain-animal and 'threw down its ribs' when the wind was in
the north — 'that wind is the rain wind. Then the clouds come
out.'[66] Hahn records that rain-sorcerers among the Khoi had great
practical knowledge of meteorology, and that they also claimed
power over clouds by binding them.[67]

A sorcerer whose name was 'Rain's New Grass' was said to
summon clouds by playing a rhythm on his bow-string, and it is
known that certain songs and dances were specifically associated
with rain.[68] Another renowned sorcerer who was mortally wounded
by a Boer commando, passed on what information he could to
a young Bushman selected to inherit the secrets of rain-making.
The rites included a song described as a 'string' which called
the rain-bull, but because of increasingly unsettled circumstances,
the chosen man apparently never practised the art. He explained
the break in tradition in these words:

> For things continue to be unpleasant to me; I do not hear the
> ringing sound [in the sky] which I used to hear. I feel that the
> string has really broken, leaving me. Therefore when I sleep, I
> do not feel the thing which used to vibrate in me, as I lay asleep.
> For I used, as I lay asleep, to hear something which sounded as
> if a person called to me. (This would be the sorcerer speaking to
> him, and asking "whether thou dost lead out the Rain-bull".)[69]

The man for whom 'things continued to be unpleasant' composed
a lament in memory of the dead rain-maker:

> People are those
> Who broke for me the string.
> Therefore,
> The place became like this to me,
> On account of it,
> Because the string was that which broke for me.
> Therefore,
> The place does not feel to me,
> As the place used to feel to me,
> On account of it.
> For,
> The place feels as if it stood open before me, because the
> string has broken for me.
> Therefore,
> The place does not feel pleasant to me,
> On account of it.[70]

This remarkably poignant song reflects the way in which the
Bushman's social cohesion and ritual functions were fragmented
by the pressures exerted upon him by encroaching civilization.

The Bushman's 'string' has been irrevocably broken, and
although we can no longer feel and comprehend the vibrations nor
hear and interpret the ringing sounds that were his cultural
inheritance, the paintings can still convey some of the magic and
mystery that technological progress has otherwise totally destroyed.

References

1. Barrow 1801, 276; Bleek 1928b.
2. See also Lewis-Williams 1972: 58, 59.
3. See p. 227.
4. Lee and Woodhouse 1970: Pl. 51; Willcox 1956: Pl. 44.
5. Stow 1930: Pl. 72.
6. Ellenberger collection, Musée de l'Homme, Paris.
7. Smits, personal communication, 1970.
8. For discussion on similarities in paintings see Goodwin 1949; Malan 1958; Schoonraad 1963; Keenan-Smith 1964.
9. Woodhouse 1964; 1966b; see also Pager 1971: 340.
10. Stow 1930: Pl. 21.
11. Woodhouse 1964, 1965.
12. Schapera 1930: 85.
13. Radcliffe-Brown 1952: 117-132; Lévi-Strauss 1962.
14. Stow 1905: 32, 33.
15. Arbousset 1838: 364.
16. Dornan 1917; 1925.
17. Marshall Thomas 1959: 129-130.
18. Dornan 1925: 281.
19. How 1962: 38.
20. Bleek 1933, B.S. 7 (4): 388, 391; Bleek 1935, B.S. 9 135, 143.
21. Bleek 1935, B.S. 9: 15, 28, 43.
22. Bleek 1935: 35, 36. Beating seems to have been associated with request prayers in the minds of the Bushmen, for there are other records of a drum being beaten in order that bees and therefore honey might be abundant. (Bleek 1911: 353). Bushes were beaten with a stick to make the wind blow to assist in springbok hunting, or sticks were struck upon each other and sandals beaten together to ensure that the sun should shine normally after an eclipse. (Bleek 1932: 14; 1933: 391). A rain-maker was said to 'strike a bow-string' in order to conjure up clouds, (Bleek 1938: 390) and there are also recent accounts of rock paintings being struck with a stone in order to bring rain. (Burkitt 1928: 119-120; Culwick 1931).
23. Bleek 1935: 43.
24. Bleek 1935: 144.
25. Bleek & Lloyd 1911: 367.
26. Silberbauer 1965: 96.
27. Schapera 1930: 368.
28. Hahn 1881: 74.
29. Schapera 1930: 368.
30. Bleek 1911: 367.
31. Bleek 1935: 35.
32. Bleek 1935: 43.
33. Marshall Thomas 1959: 161-2; Marshall 1957a.
34. Bleek 1932: 338; see also pp. 240-242.
35. Stanford 1910; Hook 1908: 327; Silberbauer 1965: 127; Wilson 1969: 106.
36. Bleek 1911: 132; Lloyd 1889: No. 50; Stow 1930: Pl. 67a.
37. Bleek 1933: 375. An earlier translation reads somewhat differently, 'water-bull' being replaced by 'water-cow'. (Stow 1930: Pl. 34.).
38. Bleek 1933: 379.
39. Orpen 1874; Bleek 1933: B.S. 7.
40. Bleek 1929.
41. Bleek in Orpen 1874.
42. Dunn 1931: 46.
43. See p. 43.
44. Bleek 1911: 115.
45. See pp. 253-257.
46. Bleek 1933: B.S. 7 (4): 379.
47. Stow 1905: 228.
48. Shortridge 1934: 611.
49. Lloyd 1889: No. 50.
50. Bleek 1911: Pl. 31, p. 224.
51. Tylor 1893.
52. See p. 52.
53. Bleek 1935: 269.
54. Bleek 1911: 199; Bleek 1932, B.S. 6 (4): 339.
55. Bleek 1933: 307, 308.
56. Bleek 1933: 309.
57. Bleek 1911: 193; Bleek 1933, B.S. 7: 305, 310.
58. Bleek 1933: 298-301.
59. Bleek 1935: 28, 31.
60. Orpen 1874: 2, 10; see also p. 314.
61. Bleek 1933: B.S. 7: 305.
62. Bleek 1933: 382-384.
63. Bleek 1933: 386.
64. Bleek 1933: 377.
65. Bleek 1933: 388.
66. Bleek 1933: 387.
67. Hahn 1881: 83.
68. See p. 308.
69. Bleek 1936a: 134.
70. Bleek 1911: 236.
71. Smits, L. G. A. 1973. Rockpainting sites in the upper Senqu valley, Lesotho. *S. Afr. archaeol. Bull.* 28, 109 & 110: 32-38.

Figure 246 *Site F12*
Naked figure with antelope head.

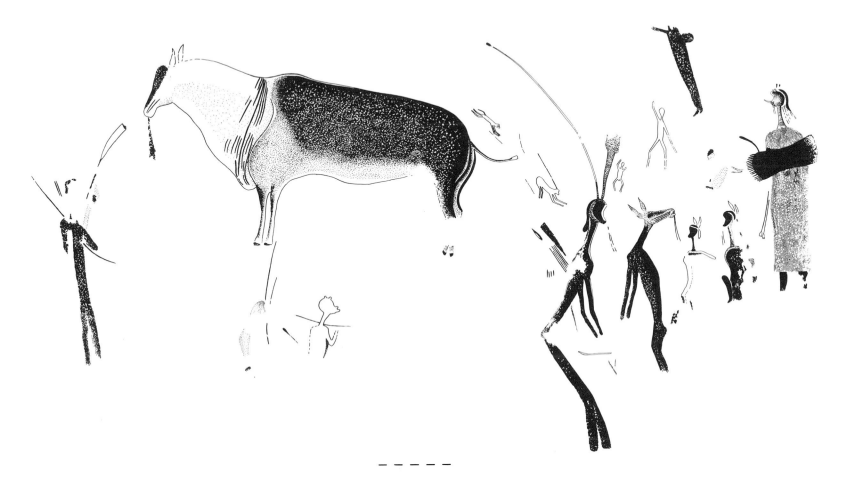

Figure 247   *Site U1b*

This faint and fragmentary group in a shelter overlooking the Leqoa valley shows an eland, apparently bleeding from the nose, with a hunter extending a rigid wand-like object towards its head. At right is a spotted kaross-clad figure with a tusk protruding from its snout. Streaks of red paint fall from its head, as well as from the heads of two other figures in the centre of the scene. One of these has an antelope head, while the other has a concave face with a flap hanging down the nape of the neck. A long white streak ending in a red blob extends upwards from the crown of this figure, while another funnel-like emanation is unfortunately not clearly preserved. Two fragmentary seated figures wear caps with animal ears, and below the eland, an incomplete figure painted in thick dirty white pigment has protruding pouted lips. Also in white are two small baboon-like animals, one with a streak from the head, which run downwards at the rear of the eland.

8 *Thinking Strings*

Conscious and Subconscious Perception

I would altogether talk to thee, while my thinking strings still stand.

(Dictated by a Xam Bushman from the northern Cape
who was dying from wounds inflicted by a white farmer).[1]

One of the most striking facts that emerges from an objective and quantitative study of the rock paintings is that they are not a realistic reflection of the daily pursuits or environment of the Bushmen. Specific subjects or activities selected for preferential treatment recur again and again at different sites over a wide area. Conversely, other subjects which were commonplace but essential components of the lives of the Bushmen are excluded from the painted record. Examples of this selectivity are the repeated connection of human figures with bows and arrows which are shown more frequently as a technological adjunct rather than a weapon of the chase; while activities such as trapping and snaring, though an important means of procuring food, are ignored. Plants, also an important source of food, are hardly featured at all. Women are rarely shown in the role of motherhood but are associated with music-making and digging sticks which are represented more as an abstract symbol of food-gathering than as a practical instrument for digging. In the animal record, the large herbivorous ungulates predominate to the virtual exclusion of the smaller food mammals; and within the herbivorous ungulates, there is a marked preference for eland and rhebuck as opposed to an avoidance of black wildebeest which were very common in the area. In addition to the selective element in the subjects portrayed, there is a marked adherence to certain conventions of posture, proportion and colour division. The majority of human figures conform to characteristic head, limb and buttock shapes with arms and legs in formalised attitudes, while the colour division in animals, particularly the red body and white extremities of eland, is repeated so often as to be accepted as the hall-mark of Bushman art.[2, 3] Despite a wide variety of detail, the subject matter is relatively restricted; the artists were not imitating nature, but were selecting patterns or basic formulae from nature which they repeated time after time.

The presentation of numerical data in support of the selective and repetitive characteristics of the art is nevertheless relatively meaningless unless the rationale underlying the preferences is understood. Although the reasons suggested must of necessity remain hypotheses which can never be put to the test since the authors of the art are long since dead, to ignore further probing of the question would result in an approach that was both stagnant and sterile. Some attempt to negotiate the impasse is surely warranted, and despite the tantalisingly perfunctory nature of many of the written sources, there are sufficient clues in the literature to enable one to correlate at least some aspects of the art with the Bushman's mode of thinking.

It should be stressed that the recording of the paintings and subsequent analysis of the data was carried through without preconceived ideas on the interpretation of the material. Admittedly I was influenced by, and tended to accept without question, the current views on motivation. The following are examples from authoritative works:

Europeans often raise the question, for what purpose were the paintings made, and are apt to think that the only possible answers are for magic purposes or for decoration. Knowledge of the lazy, improvident Bushman character makes the first answer seem highly improbable. It is difficult to imagine one of these people who live only for the hour and take no thought for the morrow, practising art till he had gained sufficient proficiency to make a picture that would be effective as a magical means of inspiring confidence in his fellow-men. That would be absolutely out of keeping with the thoughtless, care-free cast of mind of the race. Whenever there is plenty and the sun shines they are happy. Anxiety for the future never worries them.

Decoration too, seems unlikely as an explanation of the paintings, not in keeping with the nature of the artists nor with the manner in which the pictures are strewn haphazard over the rocks and each other. Those who know the people and have seen the great quantities of artistic work they have left, cannot help feeling that only from love of painting would they have painted so much, only from a spirit of emulation would they have covered the same rock faces over and over again. That now and then an artist may have used the skill acquired to make a magic picture seems possible. A few of the paintings bear such an interpretation, but only one here and there; the bulk of the work makes no such suggestion.[4]

. . . pre-Bantu art is restful in the sense that it seems to have been enjoyed by people who had little, if anything to fear and knew how to use their leisure. Not only do their paintings depict the animals and birds they hunted, but also themselves, their weapons and clothes and their ceremonies — especially dancing. They were obviously a care-free and happy people with a fine sense of humour and caricature.[5]

It is obvious that an art as highly developed as is the whole of this complex of paintings and drawings must have had beginnings which can no longer be traced . . . . Sympathetic magic may have been one of the contributory factors, but it does not seem to be the motive behind the realistic art south of the Sahara as we see it now, except, possibly, in some of the very early static ungrouped figures of antelope.

Since animals are only painted in or near their own specialised habitat, and many of the scenes depicted appear to be of actual occurrences, while scarcely any paintings of the "bread and butter" animals are ever found, it is reasonable to suggest that most of the paintings and drawings were executed only for pleasure or as a record. If the idea behind the rock paintings was just to kill, surely one simple position would be sufficient for the purpose. Many scenes must be pictorial representations of actual happenings; not magic before the event, but a record of tragedy, a successful hunt or something of importance in the life of the people . . . . The whole of the realistic art appears to have been based on the simple principle that some people liked to paint and have the ability to do so, whilst others can admire, control, and of course, criticise . . . . The development of this art . . . shows that this was in the main "art for art's sake", an endeavour by the artist to record scenes and events . . . but more often a scene of beauty remembered for its aesthetic qualities.[6]

As to his [the Bushman's] motives, whatever part magical intent may have played in the early development of Eur-African rock art, there is little to suggest it in the South African paintings. Some work may have had historical intention or have been done to illustrate a tale but in general the art gives strongly the impression of being *art pour l'art* executed for the pleasure of the artist in the work and the reciprocal pleasure of the beholder . . . .[7]

. . . . The impossibility of language performing the function of art is especially clear in connection with Bushman art, for it is not conceptual — not thought expressed in paint — but perceptual visual imagery fixed with paint.[8]

If my approach was influenced by preconceived views, therefore, the preconception was that the behaviour which motivated the paintings was predominantly pragmatic and technical, though coupled with an aesthetic awareness. As the analysis progressed, however, and the marked preferences and omissions in the subject matter became obvious, I grew increasingly conscious of the limitations and inadequacy of the essentially practical approach to interpretation. The popular theories of sympathetic magic on the one hand, and art for art's sake on the other, appeared to be confusing, contradictory, and generally to lack conviction.[9] These theories also ignored the most potent force underlying all Bushman activity, that is, the Bushman's own interpretation of the facts that governed his struggle for survival.

Dr Fourie, a medical research worker in South West Africa who had a perceptive insight into the minds of the Bushmen, wrote that the lives of all Bushmen were surrounded with multitudinous magico-religious beliefs and practices. 'Every sphere of activity in life is influenced by some superstition or other which, as a rule, finds expression in certain avoidances or in ceremonial and other rites and practices.'[10] It seemed to me highly unlikely that painting should be the one activity to be excluded from this influence. I was therefore led more and more to the view that a significant proportion of the art must have been prompted by reasons that can best be termed potent or communicative.[11] That is, the Bushmen did not paint simply what they saw but selected what was symbolically important to them. Following on this approach came the realisation that the numerical analysis of the paintings could be regarded not merely as a random assemblage of data, but as an ideological structure which reflected a set of values. The evidence suggested that these values were centred principally round the eland, followed by the rhebuck, with other animals and objects incorporated in descending order of importance. After searching the literature on Bushmen with this interpretation in mind, I presented a synopsis of the relevant material to Dr E. R. Leach of the Department of Anthropology, University of Cambridge, who confirmed that the mythology of the Southern Bushmen pointed to a strong ritual relationship having existed between man and eland.[12] The positive identification of ritual with the subject-matter preferences expressed in the paintings opened up a wider field of thought, and induced me to consult theoretical works on anthropology. Here I found cogent evidence of the existence among other peoples of the very concepts I was struggling to formulate and express. It is therefore true to say that I have not simply selected attractive anthropological viewpoints and related these to the paintings, but rather that the selectivity evidenced by the paintings themselves led me to seek an explanation. The most convincing explanation, to my mind, lay in the anthropological approach in general, and the theory of ritual in particular.

The concepts which underlie ritual attitudes are perhaps best expressed in the words of Radcliffe-Brown:

> There exists a ritual relation whenever a society imposes on its members a certain attitude towards an object, which attitude involves some measure of respect expressed in a traditional mode of behaviour with reference to that object . . . . The ritual attitude may vary from a very indefinite one to a definite and highly organised one . . . . A social group such as a clan can only possess solidarity and permanence if it is the object of sentiments of attachment in the minds of its members. For such sentiments to be maintained in existence they must be given occasional collective expression . . . . All regular collective expressions of social sentiments tend to take on a ritual form . . . . And in ritual . . . some more or less concrete object is required which can act as the representative of the group . . . . In a great number . . . of the societies where man depends entirely or largely on the hunting of wild animals and the collection of wild plants, whether they have any form of totemism or not, the animals and plants are made objects of the ritual attitude. This is done frequently . . . in mythology, in which animal species are personi-

Figure 248   *Site P3*
A human figure wearing horns extends a stick towards the head of a bull eland with wrinkled neck.

fied and regarded as ancestors or culture heroes. It is done also by a mass of customs relating to animals and plants. This system of ritual and mythological relations between man and natural species can best be studied in non-totemic peoples . . . . In such societies we find that the relation between the society and the natural species is a general one, all the most important animals and plants being treated as in some way sacred (either in ritual or in mythology) and some being regarded as more sacred than others . . . . The ritual attitude . . . constitutes a relation between the whole society and the sacred species . . . .

Any object or event which has important effects upon the well-being (material or spiritual) of a society, or any thing which stands for or represents any such object or event, tends to become an object of the ritual attitude . . . . The seasonal changes that control the rhythm of social life, the animals and plants that are used for food or other purposes, these enter into and become an essential part of the social life, the social order . . . . For primitive man the universe as a whole is a moral or social order governed not by what we call natural law but rather what we must call moral or ritual law. The recognition of this conception, implicit but not explicit, in ritual and in myth is, I believe, one of the most important steps towards the proper understanding not only of what is called 'primitive mentality' but also of the phenomena that we group vaguely around the term religion.[13]

Turner, a prominent exponent of the relationship between ritual, symbolism and religion, has demonstrated that any type of ritual forms a system of great complexity. The multiple links combining the parts into a system are re-inforced by the constant repetition of symbolic acts, the repetition emphasising the images, meanings and models for behaviour that constitute the landmarks of a culture.

> Ritual is a periodic re-statement of the terms in which men of a particular culture must interact if there is to be any kind of coherent social life. More important is its creative function — it actually creates, or re-creates, the categories through which men perceive reality — the axioms underlying the structure of society and the laws of the natural and moral orders. It is not here a case of life being an imitation of art, but of social life being an attempted imitation of models portrayed and animated by ritual.
>
> Ritual is not a meaningless inheritance from a dead past, but something that meets contemporary needs. The form of the ritual is consistent with the form of the society. And the conflicts of that society are the same as those dramatised and symbolised in its ritual. Because people are deeply concerned emotionally about such conflicts, they are moved when they see them ritually portrayed. And when they are ritually resolved, they feel emotional catharsis.[14]

That paintings are associated with this ritual attitude is borne out by the selective, conventionalised and repetitive nature of the subject matter, as well as by the fact that subjects are apparently juxtaposed and superimposed according to prescribed rules.[15] Through the act of painting and re-painting eland for instance, the mental conflict involved in destroying a creature that was prized and loved by their deity — of killing in order to live yet at the same time incurring the displeasure of their Creator — was, I believe, ritually symbolised and resolved. The emotional catharsis experienced by Bushmen after participation in the ritual Medicine Dance has been stressed by all authors on the subject,[16-18] and the fact that paintings were emotionally significant to the Bushmen was poignantly demonstrated by Stow a century ago. He showed a folio of rock-painting copies to an old Bushman couple in the Jammerberg who still tenaciously clung to their haunts after the rest of their band had been exterminated or dispersed. They expressed continual delight, and with twinkling eyes explained all they saw, enthusiastically and emphatically claiming them as an inheritance of their culture. On seeing some dances illustrated by the paintings, the old woman was reminded of tunes she had sung when a young girl, and moving her head and body to the rhythm, began to sing. Her husband became visibly affected, and pleaded with her not to revive memories of the past as it made his heart too

sad. But, unable to resist the spell, he finally joined in with the singing, and momentarily man and wife were transported to the time when their traditions had been significant. Looking at another painting representing a number of Bushmen with bows in their hands and arrows filleted around their heads, the old woman commented that it was a special dance for huntsmen. Again she began singing the rhythm, and the powerful effect of the paintings, together with the accompanying music, induced the old man to don a coronet of barbed arrows and dance to the tune.[19]

This incident clearly demonstrates the connection between paintings, music, dance and ritual in the minds of the Bushmen, and is a pointer to the fact that all aspects of a culture interact. In order, therefore, to understand the paintings, one must understand the way the Bushmen related to their environment as a whole.

It is now established that human beings everywhere select elements from their surrounding environment, and endow these elements with a significance which reflects a wider cosmology.[20]

Radcliffe-Brown was one of the first to realise the symbolic importance of the categories through which men perceive reality, and amongst hunting peoples in particular, the categories are predominantly animal:

> The resemblances and differences of animal species are translated into terms of friendship and conflict, solidarity and opposition. In other words, the world of animal life is represented in terms of social relations similar to those of human society.[21]

In an essay on totemism, Lévi-Strauss takes these views a stage further:

> The animals . . . cease to be solely or principally creatures which are feared, admired or envied: their reality permits the embodiment of ideas and relations conceived by speculative thought on the basis of empirical observation . . . . Natural species are chosen not because they are "good to eat" but because they are "good to think".[22]

Metaphor, Lévi-Strauss concludes, is a primary form of discursive thought.[23]

Turner has demonstrated that it is not necessary for a symbol to be verbally explained for it to be comprehended; its significance is often understood at pre-conscious or even unconscious levels. Symbols of ritual are 'storage units' into which are packed the maximum amount of information. Thus every type of ritual represents a storehouse or powerhouse of traditional knowledge. Ritual symbols are not a mere system of referents, but a source of power.[24]

As reflected in their hunting, dance and exorcising rituals, and

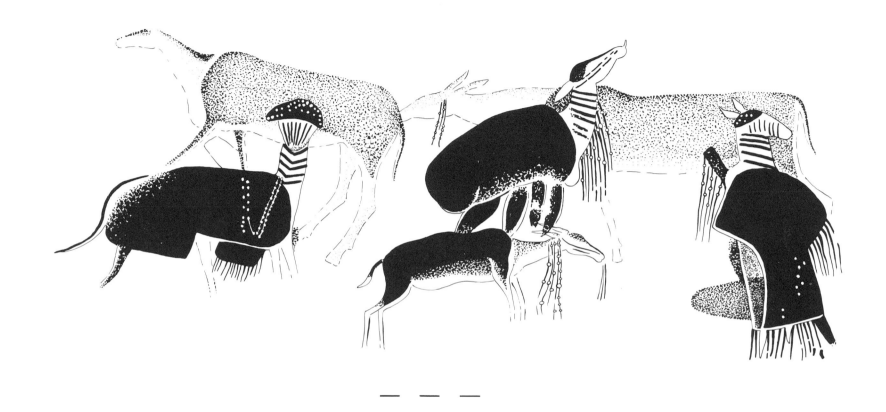

Figure 249 *Site U3*

Part of an intricate group of paintings somewhat confused by superpositions on a small side-stream of the Leqoa river. At lower centre is a small antelope with beaded streamers falling from the neck. Above, a crouched figure with human legs and antelope head has similar streamers falling from a banded neck. Note the facial marks extending from nose to ear of this animal. A small tusk or tooth protruding from the snout is a feature also shown in Figures 100, 232–3, 247. To the left is an animal-headed figure wearing a beaded cap and a kaross decorated with tassels. This figure also has stripes on the head and neck, and beaded thongs or 'streamers' hang from a quiver-like object projecting from its back. To the right is a similar figure in a horizontal posture. A tail and fragmentary legs suggest predominantly animal characteristics, with striped face and neck and beaded cap seen from the front. These paintings are superimposed on two eland, one of which also has 'streamers' or blood issuing from the head.

in the practice of game and rain control, Bushman symbolic acts could bring blessing and avert catastrophe if properly used and respected, but could also be dangerous agents of forces working against them if misused or offended. The precise function and meaning of art in Bushman society may never be fully understood, but in painting selected animal species in relation to human activities, in adhering to basic conventions and repeating certain features in accordance with prescribed rules, the Bushman artists were clearly saying far more than meets the eye. While their art serves as an incidental visual aid to archaeology, the paintings are telling us not only about the hunting methods, weapons and equipment used by a stone-age community, not only about the introduction and development of new techniques of paint application and of relative age and chronology, but they are also concerned with the crucial values of a society whose ultimate unity depended upon its orientation towards an invisible power. These channels of invisible force, the consciousness of which the Bushmen described as 'thinking strings',[1] were linked with and expressed through the medium of their most potent symbol, the eland. The eland was in turn seen in relation to other animals, and these relationships were correlated with human behaviour; each aspect of life was integrated with all other aspects. The symbolism in this complex web of correlations and interconnections is as yet imperfectly understood, but I should like to propose some tentative lines of thought which may either be accepted, re-structured or rejected in the light of further evidence.

The repeated association of men with hunting equipment and women with digging sticks seems, in essence, to illustrate a connection between man and technology rather than between man and a direct quest for food. In the minds of the Bushmen, however, the proper working of these technological adjuncts was dependent not so much upon skill in manipulating the equipment, as upon the strict observance of specific injunctions and prohibitions.[25] In my view, the bulk of the paintings are similarly concerned with these positive acts of commission and negative acts of omission, acts which can in turn be related to social patterns either of integration or of avoidance.

The connection between hunting and male prestige in the context of social organisation[26] is suggested by the simple means of visually associating hunting weapons with male sexuality rather than by painting dramatic exploits in the chase, and sexual prohibitions may be indicated by a bar across the penis. The important but separate role of women in society is represented not by obvious mother-child

relationships, but by the potent influence women can have on the supernatural powers through the medium of rhythmic clapping and singing. While the differences between male and female roles are emphasised, the importance of co-ordination and co-operation is also expressed in group compositions, and by the interconnection of separate limbs and bodies to create a single functional pattern. Fear, anxiety, disruption, aggression and hostility appear to be symbolised by the larger carnivores, lions and leopards. Winged creatures are the intermediary between human beings and the supernatural, between earth and sky. Serpents, among a host of other attributes, symbolise regeneration, and regeneration is in turn linked with water. The absence of wildebeest, zebra, and ostriches, animals which consort together, may be associated with social avoidances which are directed towards certain categories of kin and affines, as well as to those with whom the kin and affines are on terms of familiarity. Therianthropic figures embody relationships between man and animals, between those who kill and those who are killed, thus emphasising the dependence of one set of values on another. These are but some of the endless permutations and combinations possible with a selected set of metaphorical criteria each of which in turn has several referents.

While paintings of humans are numerically dominant, the animal categories most frequently and most carefully represented are the eland and the rhebuck. In symbolic terms, the non-gregarious rhebuck appears to represent the basic unit of Bushman social organisation, the family, and the paintings embody all the tender, sensitive, and emotional ties that are associated with intimate family life. Eland, on the other hand, are herd animals which periodically amalgamate into large groups, a pattern which is reflected by the periodic amalgamation of Bushman bands. The band, although made up of individual family units, is a cohesive but fluid community which is linked together by marriage, kinship ties, territorial control, and a sense of friendship, fellowship and interdependence. The frame of reference within the band is supplied by a kinship system which prescribes certain patterns of behaviour and imposes mutual obligations and rights; the behaviour of each individual is ordained by a system which regulates with whom he may fraternise and whom he should avoid.[27, 28] It is significant that eland paintings too, are characterised not only by dominance in number and in size, but by the systematised rendering of proportion, action and colour division, and by the fact that they are superimposed and juxtaposed in relation to other subjects according to a set pattern.[29]

The eland epitomised more than the regulated unity of the Bushman band: it served also as a link between the material and spiritual worlds. The eland was the medium through which the oppositions of life and death, of destruction and preservation, were resolved. The eland was connected with the practical here and now as well as with the less tangible concepts of fertility, regeneration, eternity. The eland was the focus of the Bushman's deepest aesthetic feelings and of his highest moral and intellectual speculations.[30] The Mountain Bushmen were known to be people 'of the eland',[31] and in sharing the eland's name, they partook of the eland's entity.[32] As the wind was one with the man,[33] so man was one with the eland.

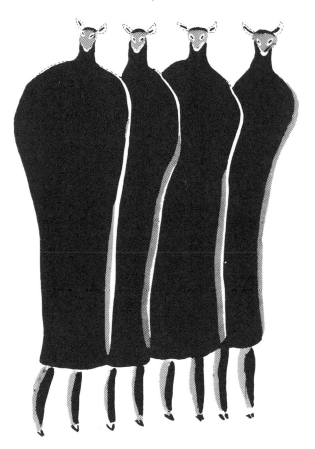

Figure 250   *Site N2*

References

1. Bleek 1911:87.
2. Pager 1971:325.
3. Lewis-Williams 1972:64.
4. Bleek in Stow 1930: xxiv.
5. Van Riet Lowe 1956:7.
6. Cooke 1969:148.
7. Willcox 1963:84.
8. Willcox 1956b.
9. Vinnicombe 1972a.
10. Fourie 1928:104.
11. Leach 1966.
12. See also p. 166.
13. Radcliffe-Brown 1952:123-130.
14. Turner 1968:4-6, 239.
15. Lewis-Williams 1972.
16. Silberbauer 1965.
17. Lee 1968a.
18. Marshall 1969; see also p. 311.
19. Stow 1905:103.
20. Leach 1970:40.
21. Radcliffe-Brown 1958:116.
22. Lévi-Strauss 1969:161-2.
23. Lévi-Strauss 1969:175.
24. Turner 1968:78 and introduction.
25. See also Goody 1962:109.
26. Heinz 1966:149.
27. Silberbauer 1965:62-7.
28. Heinz 1966:60.
29. Lewis-Williams 1972.
30. Lévi-Strauss 1973:23.
31. How 1962:38.
32. Marshall 1957b:22-3.
33. Bleek 1932: see also p. 241.

Figure 251 *Site G3*
Running figure wearing short kaross and carrying crossed spears.

APPENDIX I: SITE LIST

KEY: * Fully recorded sites.
      † Part recorded sites.
      ‡ Nil recorded sites.
      § Sites too faded for record.

The names of privately-owned properties appear in *italics*, followed by the registered farm numbers in brackets.

A. NZINGA, Mpendle District, Natal.

† A1. *Castle Howard* (No. F.P. 35, 36, 37).
† A2. *White Rocks* (No. 10079).
† A3. *Cyprus* 1 (No. 11461).
† A4. *Cyprus* 2.
† A5. *Cyprus* 3.

B. LOTHENI, Mpendle District, Natal.

Mulungane Mountain
* B1. *The Bushes* 1 (No. 8990), Hlatikhulu Drift.
‡ B2. *The Bushes* 2. Faded eland on boulder.
* B3. *The Bushes* 3. Castle Rock.
Lotheni Valley
* B4. Pickett's shelter (Kwa Pikide), Forestry Reserve.
* B5. Boulder below and S.W. of B4, Forestry Reserve.
* B6. Head of valley, near path to Kamberg, Forestry Reserve.
* B7. Horse paintings, Forestry Reserve.
* B8. Masihlenga stream, Nature Reserve.
* B9. Throttling shelter, Nature Reserve.
† B10. Cross-legged shelter, Xamalala Location.
‡ B11. Lion shelter, Xamalala Location.
† B12. *Bundoran* (No. 9183). Elephant and Eland shelter.

C. HLATIMBA, Mpendle District, Natal.

§ C1. *Duart Castle* 1 (No. 9426), Mohrotia Mountain, behind farmstead.
§ C2. *Duart Castle* 2. Mohrotia Mountain (above C1).
* C3. Rhebuck on boulder, Mohrotia Mountain, Forestry Reserve.

* C4. Bichrome eland below Lizard shelter (C13), Forestry Reserve.
† C5. Robbers' cave, Mohrotia Mountain, Forestry Reserve.
* C6. Eagle Krantz, Forestry Reserve.
§ C7. Faded eland and humans (above C6), Forestry Reserve.
§ C8. Skin pegged out, Forestry Reserve.
* C9. Horse-shoe rock, Forestry Reserve.
† C10. Verandah cave, Forestry Reserve.
* C11. Windy Palace, Forestry Reserve.
* C12. Black cave, Forestry Reserve.
* C13. Lizard shelter, Forestry Reserve.
* C14. Boulder near stream, Forestry Reserve.
* C15. Hunters and rhebuck (above C14), Forestry Reserve.
* C16. *Duart Castle* 3 (No. 9426). Charcoal drawings and human figure.
'* C17. *Duart Castle* 4. Fragmentary polychrome eland.

D. MKHOMAZI, boundary between Mpendle, Underberg and Pholela Districts, Natal.

* D1. Horses opposite Mission, *Tavistock* (No. 11691), Mpendle District.
* D2. Never-ending shelter, Forestry Reserve.
* D3. Swimming-pool shelter, Forestry Reserve.
* D4. Shelter north of *Twin Streams* road, Forestry Reserve.
* D5. Chinese horses, Forestry Reserve.
‡ D6. Stream north of first zig-zag, Mohlesi Pass, Forestry Reserve.
‡ D7. Ntuba 1, Forestry Reserve.
‡ D8. Ntuba 2, Forestry Reserve.
‡ D9. Ntuba 3, Forestry Reserve.
‡ D10. Bisi Stream 1, Mhlangeni, Bantu Location.
‡ D11. Bisi Stream 2, Mhlangeni, Bantu Location.
‡ D12. Bisi Stream 3, Mhlangeni, Bantu Location.
* D13. *Grafton* 1 (No. S. 88, 89, 90), Pholela District.
* D14. *Grafton* 2. Lower shelter.
‡ D15. *Grafton* 3, Near waterfall.

E. MCATSHENI & SKELEGEHLE, Underberg District, Natal.

* E1. Single buck, Forestry Reserve.
* E2. Liche ya Batwa, Forestry Reserve.
* E3. Shelter below E2, Forestry Reserve.
* E4. Grindstone shelter, Forestry Reserve.
* E5. Shelter-from-the-stormy-blast, Forestry Reserve.
* E6. Brambley shelter with sitting figures, Forestry Reserve.
* E7. Firelight shelter, Forestry Reserve.
§ E8. Upstream from E7, Forestry Reserve.
§ E9. Further upstream from E7, Forestry Reserve.
* E10. Muddy puddle site, Forestry Reserve.
* E11. Soldier on path, Mcatsheni Reserve, Bantu Location.

F. MKHOMAZANA, Underberg District, Natal.

* F1. *Good Hope* 1 (No. 7168), Forestry Reserve.
† F2. *Good Hope* 2.
* F3. Shaly overhang, Forestry Reserve.
* F4. Matins shelter, Forestry Reserve.
* F5. Superman pitted rock, Forestry Reserve.
* F6. Crazy-paving shelter, Forestry Reserve.
* F7. Pink shaly shelter, Forestry Reserve.
‡ F8. Isolated buck on boulder, Forestry Reserve.
‡ F9. Small isolated painting on boulder, Forestry Reserve.
‡ F10. Group of figures on boulder, Forestry Reserve.
§ F11. Ikanti marching men on boulder, Forestry Reserve.
* F12. Pinnacle rock, Forestry Reserve.
* F13. Hartebeest rock, Forestry Reserve.
* F14. Faded figures above Lamont and Weiring, Sani Pass, Forestry Reserve.
* F15. Buck on boulder, Forestry Reserve.
* F16. Eland high up, Forestry Reserve.
* F17. *Snowhill* (No. 8974, F.P. 72).

* F18. Ikanti 1. Marching men, Forestry Reserve.
* F19. Ikanti 2. Delicate buck, Forestry Reserve.
* F20. Ikanti 3. Frieze of eland, Forestry Reserve.

Y. LURANE, Pholela District, Natal.

* Y1. *Sunset* 1, (No. 11822). Marunga Mountain.
§ Y2. *Sunset* 2, Top Farm. Shelter opposite Y1.
‡ Y3. Faded site lower down Lurane, (No. 8436).
‡ Y4. Large shelter with few paintings, (No. 8436).

G. PHOLELA, Underberg District, Natal.

* G1. *Scafel* (No. F.P. 211, 8519). Paintings on roof.
† G2. Boundary rock, Forestry Reserve.
* G3. Mpongweni north, Forestry Reserve.
‡ G4. Below Mpongweni north, Forestry Reserve.
§ G5. *Sunset* (No. 11822). Shelter above homestead.

H. MZIMKHULWANA, Underberg District, Natal.

* H1. *Goshen* (No. 8977).
* H2. Whyte's shelter, Bamboo Mt., Forestry Reserve.
* H3. Ox-waggon and fish-trap, Bamboo Mt., Forestry Reserve.
* H4. Black figures, Bamboo Mt., Forestry Reserve.
‡ H5. Crude big eland, Bamboo Mt., Forestry Reserve.
* H6. Chatting figures, Bamboo Mt., Forestry Reserve.
* H7. Large shelving rock, Bamboo Mt., Forestry Reserve.
† H8. Mpongweni south, Forestry Reserve.

I. MLAMBONJE, Underberg District, Natal.

* I/1. The gossips and buck, Forestry Reserve.
* I/2. Trapeze artists, Forestry Reserve.
* I/3. Snake shelter — "Alcoholics Anonymous", Forestry Reserve.
‡ I/4. Eland across from I/3, Forestry Reserve.
‡ I/5. Polychrome eland, Forestry Reserve.
‡ I/6. White buck, Forestry Reserve.
‡ I/7. Red figures on roof, Forestry Reserve.

J. MZIMKHULU, Underberg District, Natal.

* J1. Below Swiman, Drakensberg Gardens, Forestry Reserve.
† J2. The lion hunt, Forestry Reserve.
† J3. Varnished shelter, Forestry Reserve.
* J4. *Restmount* (No. 10664, F. P. 341).
* J5. Garden Castle, Spotted animal, Forestry Reserve.
‡ J6. Underberg Commonage.
§ J7. Underberg Commonage.
† J8. *Scotston* (No. 8540, F. P. 157).
† J9. *The Rocks* (No. 12450).

J10–J20. Ekamanzi tributary of Mzimkhulu.

* J10. *Lammermoor* 1 (No. 8422, F.P. 130). Men tugging reptile.
* J11. *Lammermoor* 2. Hartebeest.
* J12. *Lammermoor* 3. Tall figure.
† J13. *Lammermoor* 4. "Red Indians".
‡ J14. *Coralynn* (No. 8423, F.P. 131). Faded eland.
* J15. *Dartford* 1 (No. 7603). Hunter.
* J16. *Dartford* 2. Bright eland.
§ J17. *Dartford* 3. Too faded for record.
† J18. *Sangwana* 1 (No. 8658). Elephant shelter.
† J19. *Sangwana* 2. Baboon shelter.
‡ J20. *Lammermoor* 5 (No. 8422, F.P. 130). Bone's shelter.
† J21. *Kilmun* (F.P. 133).
‡ J22. *Glenside* (No. 7867).

K. MZIMUTI, Underberg District, Natal.

* K1. Soai's shelter, Forestry Reserve.
* K2. Langalibalele shelter, Forestry Reserve.
* K3. Site on path to *Crystal Waters*, Forestry Reserve.
‡ K4. Cloaked figures, Forestry Reserve.
§ K5. *Castle Gardens* (No. 8948, F.P. 238).

L. NGWANGWANA, Underberg District, Natal.

‡ L1. River-at-base, Bushman's Nek, Forestry Reserve.
* L2. Faded buck, Bushman's Nek, Forestry Reserve.
* L3. Sign spots, Forestry Reserve.
* L4. Feline painting, Forestry Reserve.
* L5. Downstream from L4, Forestry Reserve.
* L6. Immediately below Helmet Rock, Forestry Reserve.
* L7. Faded eland on boulder at stream junction, Forestry Reserve.
* L8. Stow-away shelter, Forestry Reserve.
* L9. White horse shelter, Forestry Reserve.
* L10. Eland group in tributary to south, Forestry Reserve.
† L11. Human paintings in smaller shelter near L10, Forestry Reserve.
* L12. Thamathu Pass, Forestry Reserve.
‡ L13. Buck in tributary E.N.E. of old Police Post, Forestry Reserve.
‡ L14. North of Forester's Road, Bushman's Nek, Forestry Reserve.
‡ L15. Sedhludhlube Hill, Bushman's Nek, Forestry Reserve.
§ L16. *Elton* (No. 9795, F.P. 317).
‡ L17. *Berg View* (No. 7821).
‡ L18. *Waterford* (No. 11675).
§ L19. *Penwarn* 1. (No. 7566, F.P. 187). Paintings on promontory.
† L20. *Penwarn* 2. Horsemen on band of krantzes.
§ L21. *Penwarn* 3. Band of krantzes — very faded.

‡ L22. *Penwarn* 4. Tegwaan's nest on upper ledge.

‡ L23. *Penwarn* 5. Eland on high rock face.

‡ L24. *Penwarn* 6. Eland in blackened shelter.

§ L25. *Ideal View* (No. 9143, F.P. 169).

† L26. *XL Farm* (No. 8911, F.P. 192).

† L27. *Lowlands* 1 (No. 8063, F.P. 166). Elongated hunter and finger smudges.

* L28. *Lowlands* 2. Calf-drinking scene.

† L29. *Lowlands* 3. Faded elongated hunters.

† L30. *Lowlands* 4. 'Infibulated' man.

* L31. *West Ilsley* 1 (No. 8536). Faded buck under boulder.

* L32. *West Ilsley* 2. The Slug, behind homestead.

† L33. *West Ilsley* 3. Small procession of figures.

† L34. *West Ilsley* 4. Tubby figure with hair.

§ L35. *West Ilsley* 5. Faded black painting, Otto's Cave.

§ L36. *West Ilsley* 6. Paintings at bottom lands.

† L37. *Coralynn* 1 (No. 8423, F.P. 131). Horses and eland.

‡ L38. *Coralynn* 2. Bamboo Valley.

‡ L39. *New England* (No. 7552, F.P. 196). Sandhleni Mt. Paintings and artefacts.

M. NDAWANA, boundary between Underberg and Mount Currie Districts, Natal and East Griqualand.

* M1. *Curragh* (No. GE 4,35).

* M2. *Belfast* (No. GE 4,23).

‡ M3. *Excelsior* 1 (No. 9570, F.P. 34). Orange finger marks and implements.

† M4. *Excelsior* 2. Paintings below bridge.

† M5. *Redversdale* 1 (No. 10558, F.P. 352). Hunters and skin bag in sidestream.

† M6. *Redversdale* 2. Faded figures and bichrome eland.

† M7. *Bonnievale* 1 (No. GE 4,16). Border guards.

† M8. *Bonnievale* 2. Eland and robed figures.

* M9. *Beersheba* 1 (No. GE 4,18). "Fin Tragique".

* M10. *Beersheba* 2. Habitation site.

† M11. *Alicedale* 1 (No. GE 4,40). Paintings behind bushes.

† M12. *Alicedale* 2. Eland near waterfall.

‡ M13. *Alicedale* 3. Habitation site.

‡ M14. *Alicedale* 4. Faded paintings near habitation site.

† M15a. *Alicedale* 5. Paintings with spotted rope.

  b. *Alicedale* 6. Marching figures near M15a.

† M16a. *Alicedale* 7. In valley south of above.

  b. *Alicedale* 8. Orange finger smudges near M16a.

† M17. *The Wilds*, ex *Middle Valley* (No. F.P. 253).

N. GONGUNUNU, Mount Currie District, East Griqualand.

* N1. *Kilrush* 1 (No. GE 4,25). Waterfall site.

* N2. *Kilrush* 2. Main shelter.

* N3. *Kilrush* 3. Small shelter N.E. of Main shelter.

O. KROMRIVIER, Mount Currie District, East Griqualand.

* O1. *Belmont* 1 (No. GE 3,8). Baboons and dogs fighting.

† O2. *Belmont* 2. Faded paintings.

§ O3. *Belmont* 3. Beyond record.

P. MAFIKADISIU, Mount Currie District, East Griqualand.

* P1. *Eagles Nest* 1 (No. GE 12,43). Flying birds and hartebeest.

* P2. *Eagles Nest* 2. Elephant and Hyena.

* P3. *Thule* 1 (No. GE 37,16). Ibis cave.

* P4. *Thule* 1a. Yellow eland between P3 and P5.

* P5. *Thule* 2. Winged man and 'cloak-signalling.'

Q. MZIMVUBU, Mount Currie and Matatiele Districts, East Griqualand.

* Q1. *Berridale* (No. GE 12,44). The beast
and the rhebuck drive.

* Q2. *Belleview* 1 (No. GE 12,41). Giant
eland.

* Q3. *Belleview* 2. Squatting figures and
jumping buck.

* Q4. *Belleview* 3. Mahahla's shelter.

* Q5. *Belleview* 4. Moshek's shelter.

* Q6. *Belleview* 5. Solitary robed figure.

* Q7. *Belleview* 6. Little white buck.

† Q8. *Belleview* 7. Soldier shelter.

* Q9. *Middle Valley* (No. GE 4,4). Behind
St. Bernard's Hotel.

* Q10. *Koppies Kraal* (No. GE 4,3).

* Q11. *Nooitgedacht* (No. GE 3,9).

* Q12. *The Meads* 1 (No. GE 3,2). Removed
to Natal Museum.

§ Q13. *The Meads* 2. Insignificant paintings
opposite Q12.

‡ Q14. *Belleview* 8 (No. GE 12,41). Horse-
raid shelter.

‡ Q15. *Belleview* 9. Front-facing buck.

† Q16. *Belleview* 10. Ghost and lioness shelter.

† Q17. *Kruiskop* (No. GE 3,31).

* Q18. *Highbank* ex *Vaalbank* (No. GE 3,45).

† Q19. *The Crown* ex *Koningskroon* (No.
GE 3,26).

† Q20. *Swartmodder* (No. GE 5,17).

R. RIET RIVER, Mount Currie District,
East Griqualand.

* R1. *Forres* 1 (No. GE 3,39). Bi-chrome
eland and hunter.

* R2. *Forres* 2. Solitary human figure.

* R3. *Forres* 3. Messy shelter.

† R4. *Forres* 4. Red-coats.

† R5. *Bokfontein* (No. GE 3,24). Paintings
behind homestead.

† R6. *Bokfontein*, on Bokberg. Hippo and
waggon shelter.

* R7. *Pleasant View*, Upper Mzimhlava
(D. 8, A. 112).

‡ R8. *Forres* 5. (No. GE 3,39). Fragmentary
eland.

† R9. *Forres* 6. Charging buffalo.

‡ R10. *Forres* 7. Hartebeest, horse, humans.

S. UMTAI, Mount Currie and Matatiele
Districts, East Griqualand.

* S1. Mzongwana Location. Lone buck and
hunter.

* S2a. *Veryan* ex *Vielsalm* (No. GE 18,37).

b. *Veryan* ex *Vielsalm*. Small shelter south
of S2a, facing W.S.W.

* S3. *Sheltered Vale* 1, ex *Vielsalm* (No. C58,
185).

* S4. *Sheltered Vale* 2, ex *Vielsalm*.

‡ S5. Upper Umtai, Mzongwana Location.
Four detailed humans.

‡ S6. Upper Umtai, Mzongwana Location.
Buck-headed figures.

‡ S7. Upper Umtai, Mzongwana Location.
Squatting bowman.

T. MNGENI, Matatiele District, East Griqualand.

* T1. Pamlaville, Mzongwana Location.

U. LEQOA. Qacha's Nek District, Lesotho.

† U1a. Faded horses and cattle, confluence
of Ha Edward and Leqoa.

b. Therianthropic figures and eland.

* U2. Jackal shelter, below Sehlabathebe
store.

† U3. Side-stream 1, N.E. of Ha Paulus.
Animal-headed humans.

‡ U4. Side-stream 2. White paintings.

‡ U5. Side-stream 3. Crouching figures.

* U6. Patrick's little buck.

† U7. Front-facing animal.

† U8. Eland frieze.

* U9. Artefacts-in-plaster shelter.

‡ U10. Lone prancers, opposite Ha Paulus.

† U11. Lioness shelter, Ha Paulus.

† U12. Michael's shelter, Ha Soloja.

V. TSOELIKANE, Qacha's Nek district, Lesotho.

* V1. Eland and rhebuck.
† V2. Upper herd-boy shelter. Fragmentary paintings.
† V3. Sooty-flea site.
* V4a. Criss-cross procession.
   b. Buck.
* V5a. Polychrome eland.
   b. Three rhebuck.
* V6. Lying-down herd.
* V7. Wriggly lines.
* V8. Dunged eland.
* V9. Goat-milking site.
† V10. Hartebeest heads.
† V11. Big shelter, small paintings.
† V12. Moshebi shelter.
† V13. Little white buck upstream of Tsoelikane ford.
† V14. Eland herd.

W. TSOELIKE, Qacha's Nek district, Lesotho.

* W1. Above Moshebi School.
† W2. Section shelter.
‡ W3. Big shelter next to W2, fragmentary paintings.
* W4. Lower built-in shelter, below W2.
* W5. Barn shelter.
† W6. The Twisters, above deserted kraal.
* W7. Herd-boy's buck.
* W8. Sick man's shelter.
† W9. Plastered shelter.
‡ W10. Eland high above river.
* W11. Fishing site.
* W12. Cross-legged shelter, near fishing scene.
‡ W13. Faded paintings opposite W12.
§ W14. Faded paintings below Khabana Letsie Village.
† W15. Lion hunt towards tin house.
† W16. Lion hunt below Slaughter shelter.
* W17. Slaughter shelter.

† W18. Thirsty shelter; above Trussed-up shelter.
* W19. Trussed-up shelter.
§ W20. Faded eland; opposite Trussed-up shelter.
* W21. Khomo Patsoa.
* W22. Cross-legged performers round eland, Tsoelike.
* W23a. Hippo shelter.
   b. Low shelter behind keystone, upstream from Hippo shelter.
‡ W24. Across Setsoasie, near path.
* W25. Wriggly snake shelter, Setsoasie.
† W26. Chained buck shelter, Setsoasie.
‡ W27. Dirty walled-in shelter, Setsoasie.
† W28. Bird shelter, Setsoasie.
† W29. Faded black man near Setsoasie stream.
* W30. Body-patterned shelter, Setsoasie.
* W31. Doe with fawn, Setsoasie.
† W32. Ant-eater shelter, Tsoelike.
† W33. Kaggen with eland, Tsoelike.

X. ORANGE RIVER SYSTEM, Mokhotlong and Qacha's Nek districts, Lesotho.

* X1. Below Malepeba's village, Mokhotlong river.
† X2. Faded paintings, Tlokoeng.
* X3. Grazing eland, Tlokoeng.
† X4. Sehonghong shelter.
† X5. Qudu shelter.
† X6. Sehonghong — Matsaile track, near Orange river.
* X7. Seqhole's shelter (Malipere), Matsaile Hill.
* X8. Makhenckeng 1. Caricature hunters.
* X9. Makhenckeng 2. Feathered dancers.
§ X10. Orange River boat crossing, Matsaile.
† X11. Duma-Duma, Melikane.
‡ X12. Upstream from Duma-Duma, Melikane.

Z. OUTLYING AREAS.

† Z1.   Wilson's Cutting, upper Uvongo, near Paddock, Port Shepstone District.

† Z2.   *The Falls* (No. 8477). Upper Uvongo, near Paddock.

† Z3.   *Thornton* (No. 2243) near Muden.

† Z4.   Hell's Gate, Oribi Gorge. Ex *Highlands* (No. 8613). Paddock, Port Shepstone District.

† Z5.   *Penrith*, ex *Baboon Spruit* (No. 6727). Near Paddock.

† Z6.   *Rockfontein* (No. 5310). Near Eastwolds, Ixopo district.

‡ Z7.   *Waterfalls* (No. 5700). Battle-axe shelter, near Paddock.

‡ Z8.   Powerline shelter.

† Z9.   'Giraffe' shelter.

Figure 252 *Site J8*
Two horsemen with spears attack an eland.

APPENDIX II: PAINTING ANALYSIS

TABLE 1

SUBJECT, STYLE, COLOUR and SUPERPOSITION

SUBJECT	Human		Animal		Miscellaneous		Total	
No. of representations	4 530	53%	3 606	43%	342	4%	8 478	100%
STYLE								
Monochrome	3 279	72	1 875	52	307	90	5 461	64
Bichrome	941	21	798	21	34	9	1 773	21
Polychrome	290	6	239	7	1	1	530	6
Shaded polychrome	20	1	694	20	—	—	714	8
TOTAL	4 530	100%	3 606	100%	342	100%	8 478	99%
COLOUR								
Black	1 262	22	1 405	23	76	20	2 743	22
White	1 027	18	1 654	27	43	11	2 724	22
Red	2 845	49	1 850	31	193	51	4 888	40
Yellow	151	2	370	6	5	1	526	4
Orange	507	9	741	12	59	16	1 307	10
Other	4	1	16	1	3	1	23	1
TOTAL	5 796	100%	6 036	100%	379	100%	12 211	99%
SUPERPOSITION								
Layer 1 (Upper)	398	53	303	35	8	80	709	43
Layer 2 (Middle)	315	41	450	52	2	20	767	47
Layer 3 (Lower)	40	5	104	12	—	—	144	9
TOTAL	753	99%	857	99%	10	100%	1 620	99%

TABLE 2

HUMAN PAINTINGS

(For definitions of listed categories, see Vinnicombe 1967a).

SEX		No	%
Male		405	9
Female		86	2
Indeterminate . .		4 039	89
TOTAL		4 530	100%

SCENE		No	%
Hunting		375	8
Dancing . . .		204	5
Fighting . . .		115	3
Other . . .		249	5
Uncertain . .		3 587	79
TOTAL		4 530	100%

DRESS		No	%
Naked . . .		2 665	58
Apron . . .		188	4
Cloak . . .		104	2
Short kaross . .		208	5
Long kaross . .		340	7
European . . .		17	1
Other . . .		3	1
Fragmentary . .		1 005	22
TOTAL		4 530	100%

ARTEFACTS		No	%
Bow		494	12
Arrows . . .		1 414	35
Quiver . . .		340	8
Stick . . .		1 031	26
Digging-stick . .		47	1
Assegai . . .		142	4
Bag		149	4
Fly-switch . .		54	1
Shield . . .		27	1
Other . . .		254	6
Unidentifiable . .		81	2
TOTAL		4 033	100%

HEADTYPES		No	%
Round etc. . . .		1 536	34
Concave . . .		655	14
Hook . . .		526	12
Animal . . .		121	3
Other . . .		88	2
Fragmentary . .		1 604	35
TOTAL		4 530	100%

HEADGEAR		No	%
Knob . . .		98	12
Hat		121	14
Cap . . .		150	18
Horns . . .		49	6
Feathers . . .		113	13
Horns or feathers . .		21	2
Lines down . .		176	21
Lines up . . .		49	6
Other . . .		70	8
TOTAL		847	100%

DECORATIONS		No	%
Head . . .		70	7
Neck . . .		139	14
Body . . .		173	18
Arms . . .		115	12
Legs . . .		276	28
Penis . . .		38	4
Other . . .		167	17
TOTAL		978	100%

TABLE 3

ANIMAL PAINTINGS

ANTELOPE	No	%
Eland	848	35
Rhebuck etc. . . .	445	18
Hartebeest . . .	63	3
Reedbuck . . .	4	
Wildebeest . . .	3	
Roan antelope . .	2	1
Bushbuck . . .	2	
Oribi	2	
Unidentifiable antelope .	481	20
TOTAL	1 850	77%

OTHER SPECIES	No	%
Baboon	49	2
Feline	37	2
Small carnivore . .	17	
Pig or warthog . .	10	
Elephant	5	
Hippopotamus . .	5	
Jackal	3	
Antbear	3	2
Wild dog . . .	3	
Hyena	2	
Rhinoceros . . .	1	
Buffalo	1	
Hare	2	
Lizard	1	
Fish	389	15
Serpent . . .	23	1
Winged	20	1
TOTAL	571	23%
TOTAL WILD ANIMALS .	2 421	100%

DOMESTIC ANIMALS	No	%
Dog	41	5
Cattle	242	28
Horse	558	66
Sheep	7	1
TOTAL	848	100%

	No	%
ANTELOPE	1 850	51
OTHER WILD SPECIES .	571	17
DOMESTIC ANIMALS .	848	23
UNIDENTIFIABLE ANIMALS	337	9
TOTAL ANIMALS . .	3 606	100%

TABLE 4

PAINTINGS OF DOMESTIC ANIMALS

in relation to areas to which stock raided from Natal was traced.

	Mkho-mazi-	Mzim-khulu	Mzim-vubu	Orange	Total
No. of painted shelters	51	42	27	30	150
No. of shelters with domestic animals	8	14	5	5	32
% of shelters with domestic animals	16%	33%	19%	17%	21%
Source to which raids were traced	10	6	5	4	25
No. of animal paintings	862	1 226	726	792	3 606
No. of domestic animals	135	548	33	132	848
Domestic animals as % of total animals	16%	45%	5%	17%	23%
No. of horses	98	369	17	74	558
Horses as % of domestic animals	73%	67%	52%	56%	66%
No. of cattle	22	167	9	44	242
Cattle as % of domestic animals	16%	31%	27%	33%	28%
No. of dogs	12	12	7	10	41
Dogs as % of domestic animals	9%	2%	21%	8%	5%
No. of sheep	3	—	—	4	7
Sheep as % of domestic animals	2%	—	—	3%	1%

Note: A recent survey of 50 painted sites in the upper Orange valley has added considerably to the number of domestic animals listed here.
(See Domestic Animals, p. 157-161)

TABLE 5

SPECIES	COMMON NAME	METHOD OF PREPARATION	Sept.	Oct.	Nov.	Dec.	Jan.	Feb.	March	April	May	June	July	Aug.
				Spring			Summer			Autumn			Winter	
fruits & seeds														
Rhus dentata Thunb.	Wild currant (Nana bessie)	Berries eaten raw or mixed with milk					X	X	X	X				
Cussonia paniculata E. & Z.	Cabbage tree (Kiepersol)	Berries eaten raw; red when ripe, black when dry						X	X	X	X			
Halleria lucida L.	Wild fuchsia (Kinderbessie)	Berries astringent when raw. Made more palatable by baking in hot ashes						X	X	X				
Rubus ludwigii E. & Z.	Wild raspberry (Wildebraam)	Berries eaten raw when red					X							
Rubus rigidus Smith	Bramble (Braam)	Berries eaten raw when red						X						
Rubus pinnatus Willd.	Bramble (Braam)	Berries eaten raw or cooked							X					
Citrullus lanatus (Thunb.) Mats.	Wild melon (Tangazana)	Fruit eaten raw; cucumberlike flavour							X	X	X			
Scolopia mundii Warb.	Red pear (Rooipeer)	Berries eaten raw						X	X	X				
Haemanthus magnificus Herb.	Snake lily (Gifwortel)	Red berries eaten raw							X	X				
Phytolacca heptandra Retz.	Inkberry (Inkbessie)	Berries eaten raw							X					
Pygmaeothamnus chamaedendrum Robyns	(Bobbejaanappel)	Berries eaten raw when ripened to a brown colour							X					
Eragrostis curvula (Schrad.) Nees	Weeping Love-Grass (Bergsoetgras)	Seeds pounded into flour and cooked like porridge					X	X	X	X	X			
greens														
Cussonia paniculata E. & Z.	Cabbage tree (Kiepersol)	Evergreen leaves cooked and eaten as spinach	X	X	X	X	X	X	X	X	X	X	X	X
Zantedeschia aethiopica (L.) Spreng.	Arum Lily (Varkblom)	Young leaves and petioles cooked; rich in starch			X	X	X	X	X					
Asparagus africanus Lam.	Wild asparagus (Wildeaspersie)	Young shoots cooked	X	X	X									
Rumex woodii N.E.Br.	(Tongblaar)	Leaves eaten raw or cooked as spinach		X	X	X	X	X	X	X	X	X		
Phytolacca heptandra Retz.	Inkberry (Inkbessie)	Young leaves and shoots cooked as vegetable		X	X	X								

SPECIES	COMMON NAME	METHOD OF PREPARATION	Spring			Summer			Autumn			Winter		
			Sept.	Oct.	Nov.	Dec.	Jan.	Feb.	March	April	May	June	July	Aug.
greens *continued*														
Oxalis semiloba Sond. *Oxalis latifolia* H.B. & K.	Sour Flower (Rooisuring)	Flowers and leaves eaten raw. Substitute for salt in cooking		X	X	X	X	X	X					
Helichrysum pilosellum (*L.f.*) Less.	Yellow Everlasting (Sewejaartjie)	Furry stems peeled then eaten raw		X	X	X								
Ranunculus multifidus Forsk.	Buttercup (Botterblom)	Leaves cooked or infused as a drink		X	X	X	X	X	X	X				
Gazania krebsiana Less.	Buttercup (Botterblom)	Flowers and leaves eaten raw	X	X										X
Gladiolus dracocephalus Hook. f.	Wild gladiolus	Flowers eaten raw. Leaves rolled and chewed		X	X	X	X	X	X					
Protea spp.	Sugarbush (Suikerbos)	Calyx sucked for nectar				X	X	X	X	X	X			
Watsonia spp.	Watsonia	Blooms sucked for nectar				X								
Aloe spp.	Aloe	Blooms sucked for nectar											X	X
underground organs														
Cussonia paniculata E. & Z.	Cabbage tree (Kiepersol)	Roots eaten raw or cooked; taste like turnip	X	X	X	X	X	X	X	X	X	X	X	X
Asparagus africanus Lam.	Wild asparagus (Wildeaspersie)	Roots eaten raw; sweet flavour	X	X	X	X	X	X	X	X	X	X	X	X
Phragmites australis (Cav.) Trin. ex Steud.	Common reed (Vinkriet)	Roots eaten raw or cooked, sometimes infused as drink	X	X	X	X	X	X	X	X	X	X	X	X
Oxalis semiloba Sond. *Oxalis latifolia* H.B. & K.	Sour Flower (Rooisuring)	Bulbs eaten raw or baked	X	X	X	X	X	X	X	X	X	X	X	X
Kohautia amatymbica E. & Z.	?	Tubers eaten raw or baked	X	X	X	X	X	X	X	X	X	X	X	X
Wahlenbergia denudata A.DC.	?	Tubers eaten raw or baked	X	X	X	X	X	X	X	X	X	X	X	X
Cyperus esculentus L.	Watergrass (Uintjie; nDawo)	Bulbs eaten raw or baked	X	X	X	X	X	X	X	X	X	X	X	X
Cyphia longifolia N.E. Br.	(Bergbarroe)	Bulbs eaten raw or baked	X	X	X	X	X	X	X	X	X	X	X	X
Watsonia spp.	Watsonia	Bulbs ground and cooked	X	X	X	X	X	X	X	X	X	X	X	X
fungi														
Termitomyces	(Khowe)	Eaten cooked				X	X	X	X					
Psalliota	Mushroom	Eaten raw or cooked	X	X										

ABBREVIATIONS USED FOR OFFICIAL MANUSCRIPTS

NATAL ARCHIVES
PIETERMARITZBURG

C.S.O. = Colonial Secretary's Office.

Volumes 1, 3, 5, 6, 11, 12, 14, 15, 19, 20, 21, 25, 26, 29, 36, 37, 38, 41, 43, 44, 45, 49, 51, 70, 72, 75, 78, 79, 84, 85, 87, 88, 91, 98, 99, 102, 107, 119, 123, 136, 146, 148, 152, 191, 198, 345, 363, 2236, 2238, 2239, 2240, 2246, 2248, 2295, 2296, 2297, 2303, 2309.

G.H. = Government House.

Volumes 177, 325, 595, 780, 1209, 1321, 1322, 1323, 1324, 1405, 1628, 1629.
(Since the completion of this research, the Government House volumes have been re-numbered).

S.N.A. = Secretary for Native Affairs.

Volumes 1/1/1, 1/1/2, 1/1/3, 1/1/6, 1/1/8, 1/1/9, 1/1/19, 1/3/1, 1/3/5, 1/3/7, 1/3/8, 1/3/10, 1/3/13, 1/3/15, 1/3/16, 1/3/18, 1/3/19, 1/3/20, 1/8/9, 1/8/10, 1/8/19.

The Bird Papers, Fynn Papers, John Shepstone Papers, and Theophilus Shepstone Papers are housed in the Natal Archives.
Other archival sources are listed in full in the references.

OFFICIAL PUBLICATIONS

Natal No. 1 = South African Archival Records,
Notule Natalse Volksraad, 1838-1845.
Cape Town. 1958.

Natal No. 2-4 = South African Archival Records,
Records of the Natal Executive Council, 1846-56.
Cape Town, 1960-3.

Other official publications are listed in full in the references.

Bibliography

ABBOTT, C. W. 1968a. *Observational research on the eland Taurotragus oryx.* Unpublished report. Faculty of Agriculture, University of Natal.

ABBOTT, C. W. 1968b. *Eland in the Thabanyama-Injasuti area of the Drakensberg.* Unpublished report. Faculty of Agriculture, University of Natal.

ACOCKS, J. P. H. 1953. Veld types of South Africa. *Bot. Surv. S. Afr. Mem.* **28**. Dept. Agric., Pretoria.

ADAM, L. 1940. *Primitive Art.* Harmondsworth: Pelican Books.

ALBINO, R. 1947. Note on the excavation of a rock shelter at Champagne Castle, Natal. *Ann. Natal Mus.* **2** (1): 157-160.

ALEXANDER, J. E. 1838. *An expedition of discovery into the interior of Africa.* London: Henry Colburn.

ANDERS, H. 1935. A note on a South Eastern Bushman dialect. *Z. für Eingeborenen-Sprachen* **25** (2): 81-9.

ANDERSON, A. A. 1887, 1888. *Twenty-five years in a wagon,* 2 vols. London: Chapman & Hall.

ANDERSON, W. 1901. Report on the geology of the lower Tugela district, Victoria County, Natal. *Rep. Geol. Survey Natal & Zululand* **1**: 79-95. London: West, Newman & Co.

ANDERSON, W. 1904. *Rep. Geol. Survey Natal & Zululand.* London. West, Newman & Co.

ANDERSON, W. 1907. *Third & final report of the Geological Survey of Natal and Zululand*: 153-160. London: West, Newman & Co.

ANDERSON, W. 1911. Notes on the geology of the Drakensberg range, in *Natal descriptive guide and official handbook* ed. A. H. Tatlow: 351. Durban: South African Railways.

ARBOUSSET, T. 1852. *Narrative of an exploratory tour of the north-east of the Cape of Good Hope,* transl. by J. C. Brown. London: John C. Bishop.

ARNDT, W. 1962. The Nargorkun-Narlinji cult. *Oceania* **32** (4): 288-320.

BAINES, T. 1961. *Journal of residence in Africa,* ed. R. F. Kennedy. Cape Town: Van Riebeeck Society.

BARROW, J. 1801. *Travels into the interior of Southern Africa, 1797-1798.* London: Cadell & Davies.

BARTER, C. 1852. *The dorp and the veld,* or six months in Natal. London: William S. Orr & Co.

BATTISS, W. 1944. Prehistoric fishing scenes. *S. Afr. J. Sci.* **41**: 356-360.

BATTISS, W. 1948. *The artists of the rocks.* Pretoria: Red Fawn Press.

BAZLEY, W. 1905. Exploration of a Bushman's cave in Alfred County, Natal. *Man* **5**: 10-11.

BEAUMONT, P. B. & VOGEL, J. C. 1972. On a new radiocarbon chronology for Africa south of the equator. *Afr. Stud.* **31** (2): 65-89, & 31 (3): 155-182.

BEAUMONT, P. B. 1967. The Brotherton Shelter. *S. Afr. archaeol. Bull.* **22** (85): 27-30.

BERGLUND, A. I. 1972. *Zulu ideas and symbolism.* Unpublished Ph.D. thesis submitted to the University of Cape Town.

BLEEK, D. F. 1924. *The mantis and his friends: Bushman folklore.* Oxford: Blackwell.

BLEEK, D. F. 1928a. *The Naron,* a Bushman tribe of the Central Kalahari. Cambridge: University Press.

BLEEK, D. F. 1928b. Bushmen of Central Angola. *Bantu Stud.* **3** (2): 105-125.

BLEEK, D. F. 1929. Bushman folklore in Africa. *Jl. de l'institut internationale des langues et civilizations africains* **2**: 302-313.

BLEEK, D. F. 1931-1936. Customs and beliefs of the !Xam Bushmen. *Bantu Stud.*

BLEEK, D. F. 1931. Pt. 1: Baboons. *Bantu Stud.* **5**: 167-179.

BLEEK, D. F. 1932. Pt. 2: The lion. *Bantu Stud.* **6**. 47-63.

BLEEK, D. F. 1932. Pt. 3: Game animals. *Bantu Stud.* **6**: 233-249.

BLEEK, D. F. 1932. Pt. 4: Omens, windmaking and clouds. *Bantu Stud.* **6**: 323-342.

BLEEK, D. F. 1933. Pt. 5: The rain. *Bantu Stud.* **7**: 297-312.

BLEEK, D. F. 1933. Pt. 6: Rainmaking. *Bantu Stud.* **7**: 375-392.

BLEEK, D. F. 1935. Pt. 7: Sorcerers. *Bantu Stud.* **9**: 1-47.

BLEEK, D. F. 1936a. Pt. 8: More about sorcerers and charms. *Bantu Stud.* **10**: 131-162.

BLEEK, D. F. 1932b. A survey of our present knowledge of rock-paintings in South Africa. *S. Afr. J. Sci.* **29**: 72-83.

BLEEK, D. F. (Ed.) 1934/35. !Kun mythology. *Z. für Eingeborenen-Sprachen* **25**: 261-283.

BLEEK, D. F. 1936b. Special speech of animals and moon. *Bantu Stud.* **10**: 163-199.

BLEEK, D. F. 1956. *A Bushman dictionary.* New Haven, Conn: American Oriental Soc.

BLEEK, W. H. I. 1862-1869. *A comparative grammar of South African languages,* pts 1 and 2. London: Trübner & Co.

BLEEK, W. H. I. 1873. Report of Dr Bleek concerning his researches into the Bushman language. *Cape Parliamentary Paper*, Cape Town.

BLEEK, W. H. I. 1875. A brief account of Bushman folklore and other texts. *Cape Parliamentary Paper*, Cape Town.

BLEEK, W. H. I. and LLOYD, L. C. 1911. *Specimens of Bushman folklore*. London: George Allen & Co. Ltd.

BOLWIG, N. 1961. An intelligent tool-using baboon. *S. Afr. J. Sci.* **57** (6): 147-151.

BOLWIG, N. 1959. A study of the behaviour of the chacma baboon, Papio ursinus. *Behaviour* **14**: 137-163.

BOURQUIN, W. 1951. Click-words which Xhosa, Zulu and Sotho have in common. *Afr. Stud.* **10** (2): 59-81.

BOWKER, J. H. 1884. Other days in South Africa. *S. Afr. J. Phil.* **3** (2): 68-73.

BOXER, C. R. 1959. *The tragic history of the sea, 1559-1622*. Hakluyt Soc. 2nd ser., 132. Cambridge: University Press.

BREUIL, H. 1948. South African races in the rock paintings. *Trans. R. Soc. S. Afr.* Robert Brown Commemorative Vol: 209-216.

BREUIL, H. 1949. Remains of large animal paintings in South West Africa, older than all other frescoes. *S. Afr. archaeol. Bull.* **4** (13): 14-18.

BRIEN, K. 1935. The Late Stone Age in Natal. *S. Afr. J. Sci.* **32**: 500-505.

BRIEN, P. G. 1932. Coastal archaeological sites near Durban. *S. Afr. J. Sci.* **24**: 742-750.

BROOKES, E. H. & WEBB, C. de B. 1965. *A history of Natal*. Pietermaritzburg: University of Natal Press.

BRYANT, A. T. 1929: *Olden times in Zululand*. London: Longmans.

BRYANT, A. T. 1949. *The Zulu people as they were before the White Man came*, 2 vols. Pietermaritzburg: Shuter & Shooter.

BULMER, R. 1967. Why is the cassowary not a bird? A problem of zoological taxonomy among the Karam of the New Guinea Highlands. *Man* **2** (1): 5-25.

BULPIN, T. V. 1953. *To the shores of Natal*. Cape Town: Howard Timmins.

BURKITT, M. C. 1928. *South Africa's past in stone and paint*. Cambridge: University Press.

CALLAWAY, H. 1868. *Nursery tales, traditions and histories of the Zulus*, vol. 1. Natal: John A. Blair, Springvale.

CAMPBELL, J. 1815. *Travels in South Africa* ... London Missionary Soc.

CAMPBELL, J. 1822. *Travels in South Africa* ... second journey, 2 vols. London Missionary Soc.

CARTER, P. L. 1970a. *An interim report of an archaeological survey in Eastern Lesotho, Southern Natal and East Griqualand*. Unpublished circular.

CARTER, P. L. 1970b Late stone age exploitation patterns in southern Natal. *S. Afr. archaeol. Bull.* **25** (98): 55-58.

CARTER, P. L. 1970c. Moshebi's Shelter: Excavation and exploitation in eastern Lesotho. *Lesotho* (Maseru) **8**: 1-10.

CARTER, P. L. 1973. The dating of industrial assemblages from stratified sites in Eastern Lesotho. *Man*: in press.

CHAPMAN, J. 1868. *Travels in the interior of South Africa*, 2 vols. London: Bell & Daldy.

CHRISTOL, F. 1911. *L'Art dans l'Afrique australe*. Paris: Berger-Levrault.

CHUBB, E. C. & KING, B. G. 1932. Remarks on some stone implements and strandloper middens of Natal and Zululand. *S. Afr. J. Sci.* **29**: 765-769.

CHUBB, E. C. & KING, B. G. 1934. A new variation of Smithfield culture from a cave on the Pondoland coast. *S. Afri. J. Sci.* **29**: 768-769.

CHUBB, E. C. & SCHOFIELD, J. F. 1932. Rock engravings at Otto's Bluff, Natal, *S. Afr. J. Sci.* **29**: 678-680.

CHURCHILL, F. F. 1898. Notes on the geology of the Drakensbergen, Natal. *S. Afr. J. Phil.* **10** (3): 419-426.

CLARK, D. L. 1968 *Analytical archaeology*. London: Methuen.

CLARK, J. D. 1959. *The prehistory of Southern Africa*. Harmondsworth: Pelican Books.

CLARK, J. D. 1960. A note on the early river-craft and fishing practices in South East Africa. *S. Afr. archaeol. Bull.* **15** (59): 77-79.

COLES, J. M. & HIGGS, E. S. 1969. *The archaeology of early man*. London: Faber and Faber.

COOKE, C. K. 1964. Bowmen, spears and shields in Southern Rhodesian rock art. *Cimbebasia* **10**: 2-8.

COOKE, C. K. 1965. Evidence of human migrations from the rock art of Southern Rhodesia. *Africa* **35** (3): 263-285.

COOKE, C. K. 1969. *Rock art of Southern Africa*. Cape Town: Books of Africa.

COPE, T. (Ed.) 1968. *Izibongo*, coll. by J. Stuart and transl. by D. Malcolm. Oxford: Clarendon Press.

CORY, G. E. 1926. *The rise of South Africa*, vol. 4. London: Longmans, Green & Co.

CRAMB, J. G. 1934. Smithfield implements from a Natal coastal site. *Trans. R. Soc. S. Afr.* **22** (3): 205-223.

CRAMB, J. G. 1935. Early stone age in Natal. *S. Afr. J. Sci.* **32**: 488-493.

CRAMB, J. G. 1952. A middle stone age industry from a Natal rock shelter. *S. Afr. J. Sci.* **48** (6): 181-186.

CRAMB, J. G. 1961. A second report on work at the Holley shelter. *S. Afr. J. Sci.* **57** (2): 45-48.

CULWICK, A. T. 1931. Ritual use of rock paintings at Bahi, Tanganyika Territory. *Man.* **31** (41): 33-36.

CURRLÉ, L. 1910. The odyssey of our Bushman boy. *Trans. R. Soc. S. Afr.* **2** (1): 13.

CURRLÉ, L. 1913. Notes on Namaqualand Bushmen. *Trans. R. Soc. S. Afr.* **3** (1): 113.

DART, R. A. 1923-1926. A note on Jan the Bushman. *Bantu Stud.* **2**: 107-9.

DART, R. A. 1924. The ancient mining industry of Southern Africa. *S. Afr. geogr. J.* **7**: 7-13.

DART, R. A. 1925. The historical succession of cultural impacts upon South Africa. *Nature* **115**: 425-429.

DART, R. A. 1937. The physical characters of the ?Auni and ‡Khomani Bushmen. *Bantu Stud.* **11** (3): 173-246.

DAVIES, O. 1950. Foreigners in South African archaeology. *Theoria*, University of Natal.

DAVIES, O. 1951. Archaeology of Natal, in *Natal Regional Survey vol. 1*: 1-29. London: Oxford University Press.

DAVIES, O. 1952. *Natal archaeological studies.* Pietermaritzburg: Natal University Press.

DEACON, H. J. 1963. Scott's Cave: A Late Stone Age site in the Gamtoos valley. *Ann. Cape Prov. Mus.* **3**: 96-121.

DEACON, H. J. 1969. Melkhoutboom Cave, Alexandria district, Cape Province; a report on the 1967 investigation. *Ann. Cape Prov. Mus.* **6**: 141-69.

DEACON, H. J. 1972. A review of the post-Pleistocene in South Africa. *S. Afr. archaeol. Bull., Goodwin Ser.* **1**: 26-45.

DEACON, J. 1965. Cultural material from the Gamtoos valley shelters (Andrieskraal I). *S. Afr. archaeol. Bull.* **20** (80): 193-200.

DEACON, J. 1966. An annotated list of radio-carbon dates for sub-Saharan Africa. *Ann. Cape Prov. Mus.* **5**: 5-84.

DENNINGER, E. 1971. The use of paper chromatography to determine the age of albuminous binders and its application to rock paintings. *S. Afr. J. Sci.*, special issue no. 2: 80-84.

DE VILLIERS, H. 1968. *The skull of the South African Negro.* Johannesburg: Witwatersrand University Press.

DOKE, C. M. 1936. Games, plays and dances of the Khomani Bushmen. *Bantu Stud.* **10** (4): 461-471.

DOKE, C. M. & VILAKAZI, B. W. 1948. *Zulu-English Dictionary.* Johannesburg: Witwatersrand University Press.

DORNAN, S. S. 1909. Notes on the Bushmen of Basutoland. *S. Afr. J. Phil.* **18**: 437-450.

DORNAN, S. S. 1917. The Tati Bushmen (Masarwas) and their language. *Jl. R. anthrop. Inst.* **47**: 37-112.

DORNAN, S. S. 1925. *Pygmies and Bushmen of the Kalahari.* London: Seeley, Service & Co. Ltd.

DOUGLAS, M. 1957. Animals in Lele religious symbolism. *Africa* **27**: 46-57.

DOUGLAS, M. 1970. *Purity and Danger.* Harmondsworth: Penguin Books Ltd.

DOUGLAS, M. 1972a. Deciphering a meal. *Daedalus, Boston, Mass.* **101** (1): 61-81.

DOUGLAS, M. 1972b. Self-evidence. *Proc. R. anthropol. Inst.*: 27-43.

DRAYSON, A. W. 1858. *Sporting scenes amongst the Kaffirs of South Africa.* London: Routledge & Co.

DRURY, J. & DRENNAN, M. R. 1926/27. The pudendal parts of the South African Bush race. *Med. Jl. S. Afr.* **22**: 113-117.

DUNN, E. J. 1873. Through Bushmanland, pt. 2. *Cape Monthly Mag.*: 31-42.

DUNN, E. J. 1931. *The Bushman.* London: Charles Griffith & Co. Ltd.

EDWARDS, D. 1967. A plant ecological survey of the Tugela river basin. *Bot. Surv. S. Afr. Mem.* **36**. Dept. Agric., Pretoria.

ELLENBERGER, D. F. 1912. *History of the Basuto, ancient and modern*, transl. by J. C. Macgregor. London: Caxton Publishing Co.

ELLENBERGER, P. 1960. Le quartenaire au Basutoland. *Bull. Soc. prehist. fr.* **57**: 439-475.

ELLENBERGER, V. 1953. *La fin tragique des Bushmen.* Paris: Amiot Dumont.

ENGLAND, N. 1967. Music among the Zu/wa-si of S. W. Africa and Botswana. *Jl. Internat. Folk Music Council.* **19**: 58-66.

EPSTEIN, H. 1971. *The origin of domestic animals of Africa*, vol. 1. New York: Africana Publishing Corporation.

ERGATES, 1905. Bushmen's stock raids in Natal. *Natal agric. J.* **8**(2): 113-123.

EVANS, M. 1911. Cave hunting in the Drakensberg, in *Natal descriptive guide and official handbook*, ed. A. H. Tatlow. Durban.

EVANS, R. J. 1971. A draft scheme for computer processing of rock art data *S. Afr. J. Sci.*, special issue No. 2: 73-79.

EVANS-PRITCHARD, E. E. 1956. *Nuer Religion . . .* Oxford: University Press.

FARNDEN, T. H. G. 1965. Notes on two Late Stone Age sites at Muden, Natal. *S. Afr. archaeol. Bull.* **20** (77): 19-23.

FARNDEN, T. H. G. 1966. Excavation of a Late Stone Age shelter at New Amalfi, East Griqualand. *S. Afr. archaeol. Bull.* **21** (83): 122-124.

FEILDEN, H. W. 1884. Stone implements from South Africa. *Jl. R. anthrop. Inst.* **13**: 162-174.

FITZSIMONS, V. F. M. 1962. *Snakes of Southern Africa.* London: Macdonald & Co. Ltd.

FOCK, G. J. 1969. A rock engraving of 'Flying Buck'. *S. Afr. archaeol. Bull.* **23** (92): 145-146.

FORTES, M. & DIETERLEN, G. (Eds.) 1960. *African systems of thought.* London: Oxford University Press.

FORTES, M. 1962. Ritual and office in tribal society, in *Essays on the ritual of social relations*, ed. M. Gluckman: 53-58. Manchester: University Press.

FOURIE, L. 1925/26. Preliminary notes on certain customs of the Hei-//om Bushmen. *Jl. S.W. Afr. Sci. Soc.* **1**: 49-63.

FOURIE, L. 1928. The Bushmen of South West Africa, in *The Native tribes of S.W. Africa*, ed. C. H. L. Hahn. Cape Town: Cape Times Ltd.

FRAMES, E. M. 1898. Stone implements found in a cave in Griqualand East, Cape Colony. *Jl. R. anthrop. Inst.* **28**: 251-257.

FROBENIUS, L. 1931. *Madsimu Dsangara:* Südafrikanische Felsbilderchronik, 2 vols. Berlin, Zurich: Atlantis-Verlag.

FROBENIUS, L. & FOX, D. C. 1937. *Prehistoric rock pictures in Europe and Africa.* New York: Museum of Modern Art.

FYNN, H. F. 1950. *The diary of Henry Francis Fynn.* Pietermaritzburg: Shuter and Shooter.

GALLOWAY, A. 1935/36. Some prehistoric skeletal remains from the Natal coast. *Trans. R. Soc. S. Afr.* **23**: 277-295.

GALLOWAY, A. & WELLS, L. H. 1934. Report on the human skeletal remains from the Karridene site. *Trans. R. Soc. S. Afr.* **22** (3): 225-233.

GARDINER, A. F. 1836. *Narrative of a journey to the Zoolu country in South Africa.* London: William Crofts.

GOOCH, W. D. 1881. The stone age of South Africa. *Jl. R. anthrop. Inst.* **11**: 124.

GOODWIN, A. J. H. 1928a. An introduction to the Middle Stone Age in South Africa. *S. Afr. J. Sci.* **25**: 410-418.

GOODWIN, A. J. H. 1928b. Sir Langham Dale's Collection. *S. Afr. J. Sci.* **25**: 419-426.

GOODWIN, A. J. H. & VAN RIET LOWE, C. 1929. The Stone Age cultures of South Africa. *Ann. S. Afr. Mus.* **27**: 1-289.

GOODWIN, A. J. H. (Ed.) 1935. A commentary on the history and present position of South African prehistory with full bibliography. *Bantu Stud.* **9**: 293-417.

GOODWIN, A. J. H. 1946. *The loom of prehistory.* Handbook Ser. 2. Archaeological Soc. Cape Town.

GOODWIN, A. J. H. 1947. The bored stones of South Africa. *Ann S. Afr. Mus.* **37** (1): 1-20.

GOODWIN, A. J. H. 1949. A fishing scene from East Griqualand. *S. Afr. archaeol. Bull.* **4** (14): 51-70.

GOODY, J. 1962. *Death, property and the ancestors* ... London: Tavistock Publications.

GORDON-BROWN, A. 1941. *The narrative of Private Buck Adams, 1843-1848.* Cape Town: van Riebeeck Society.

GRAY, R. 1849. *Visitation tour through the Cape Colony in 1848.* London: Soc. for promoting Christian Knowledge.

GRAY, R. 1851. *A journal of the Bishop's visitation tour through the Cape Colony in 1850.* London: Soc. for Promoting Christian Knowledge.

GRAY, R. 1864. *Journal of a visitation of the Diocese of Natal in 1864.* London: Bell and Daldy.

GREENBERG, J. H. 1966. *The languages of Africa.* Bloomington: Indiana University.

GRIAULE, M. 1950. *Arts of the African native.* London: Thames & Hudson.

GUILLARMOD, A. J. 1971. *Flora of Lesotho.* Lehre (Germany): Verlag von J. Cramer.

GUSINDE, M. 1966. *Von gelben und schwarzen Buschmännern:* 69-74. Graz: Akademische Druck.

HADDON, A. C. 1905. Presidential address, sect. H: Anthropology. *Rept. Brit. Assn:* 511-527.

HAHN, C. H. L. (Ed.) 1928. *The native tribes of S.W. Africa.* Cape Town: Cape Times Ltd.

HAHN, T. 1881. *The supreme being of the Khoi-Khoi.* London: Trübner & Co.

HANDLEY, G. L. 1961. Extinction of the Red Hartebeest in Natal. *Natal Wild Life* **2** (2): 6-8.

HARDING, J. R. 1950. Paintings of robed figures in Basutoland. *S. Afr. archaeol. Bull.* **5** (20): 133-136.

HARDING, J. R. 1968. Interpreting the 'White Lady' rock-paintings of South West Africa: some considerations. *S. Afr. archaeol. Bull.* **23** (90): 31-34.

HARRIS, W. C. 1841. *The wild sports of Southern Africa.* London: William Pickering.

HATTERSLEY, A. F. 1936. *More annals of Natal.* Pietermaritzburg: Shuter & Shooter.

HATTERSLEY, A. F. 1959. *Oliver the Spy and others.* Cape Town: Maskew Miller.

HATTERSLEY, A. F. 1963. The reminiscences of James Michiel Howell, *Quart. Bull. S. Afr. Libr.* **18** (1): 34-38.

HAUGHTON, S. H. 1926. Note on a burial stone. *Trans. R. Soc. S. Afr.* **13**: 105-106.

HAYNES, M. 1954. Some rock paintings in the Stormberg Mountains. *Africana Notes and News* **11** (5): 167-168.

HEINZ, H. 1966. *The social organisation of the !Ko Bushmen.* Unpublished M.A. thesis submitted to the University of South Africa, Pretoria.

HERSKOVITS, M. J. 1962. *The human factor in changing Africa.* New York: Knopf.

HEWITT, J. 1921. On several implements and ornaments from Strandlooper sites in the Eastern Province. *S. Afr. J. Sci.* **18**: 454-467.

HEWITT, J. 1931a. Discoveries in a Bushman cave at Tafelberg Hall. *Trans. R. Soc. S. Afr.* **19**: 185-196.

HOLLIDAY, C. S. 1961. The application of ultra-violet light photography to prehistoric rock art. *Bull. S. Afr. Mus. Ass.* **7** (8): 179-184.

HOLT, B. 1953. Nicolaas Lochenberg. *Africana Notes and News* **11** (1): 3-9.

HOOK, D. B. 1908. *With sword and statute.* London: Greaves, Pass & Co.

HOW, M. W. 1962. *The Mountain Bushmen of Basutoland.* Pretoria: J. L. Van Schaik Ltd.

HUBERT, H. & MAUSS, M. 1964. *Sacrifice: its nature and function.* London: Cohen & West.

HUSS, B. & OTTO. Bro. 1925. The origin of the Bushman paintings at the Kei river. *S. Afr. J. Sci.* **22**: 49-503.

HUTCHINSON, M. 1883. Notes on a collection of facsimile Bushman drawings. *Jl R. anthrop. Inst.* **12**: 464-465.

ISAACS, N. 1836. *Travels and adventures in Eastern Africa*, vols. 1 & 2. London: Edward Churton.

INSKEEP, R. R. 1961. The present state of archaeology in South Africa. *Bull. S. Afr. Mus. Ass.* **7** (10): 225-229.

INSKEEP, R. R. 1967. The Late Stone Age in Southern Africa, in *Background to evolution in Africa*, ed. by W. W. Bishop & J. D. Clark: 557-580. Chicago: University Press.

INSKEEP, R. R. 1969. The archaeological background in *The Oxford history of South Africa*, ed. M. Wilson & L. Thompson: 1-39. Oxford: Clarendon Press.

JAMES, E. O. 1962. *Sacrifice and sacrament*. London: Thames & Hudson.

JEFFREYS, M. D. W. 1968. The penis-sheath, the Basenji & Bezoar. *S. Afr. J. Sci.* **64** (8): 305-318.

JOHNSON, J. P. 1910. *Geological and archaeological notes on Orangia*. London: Longmans, Green & Co.

JOHNSON, R. T., RABINOWITZ, H. & SIEFF, P. 1959. Rock paintings at Katbakkies, Koue Bokkeveld, Cape. *S. Afr. archaeol. Bull.* **14** (55): 99-103.

JUBB, R. A. 1967. *Freshwater fishes of Southern Africa*. Cape Town: Balkema.

KANNEMEYER, D. R. 1890. Stone implements of the Bushmen ... *Cape Illust. Mag.* **1**: 120-130.

KEENAN-SMITH, D. 1964. Correspondence: Similarities in paintings. *S. Afr. archaeol. Bull.* **14** (73): 20.

KIEWIET, C. W. de. 1963. The period of transition in South African policy, 1854-1870, in *The Cambridge history of the British Empire*: 400-438. Cambridge University Press.

KILLICK, D. J. B. 1963. Plant ecology of the Cathedral Peak area, Natal Drakensberg. *Bot. Surv. S. Afr. Mem.* **34**. Dept. Agric., Pretoria.

KING, L. C. 1951. *South African scenery*. Edinburgh: Oliver & Boyd.

KIRBY, P. R. 1931a. The mystery of the grand gom-gom. *S. Afr. J. Sci.* **28**. 521-525.

KIRBY, P. R. 1931b. The gora and its Bantu successors. *Bantu Stud.* **5** (2): 89-109.

KIRBY, P. R. 1935. A further note on the gora and its Bantu successors. *Bantu Stud.* **9**: 53-60.

KIRBY, P. R. 1936a. A study of Bushman music. *Bantu Stud.* **10** (4): 205-252.

KIRBY, P. R. 1936b. The musical practices of the ?Auni and ‡Khomani Bushmen. *Bantu Stud.* **10** (4): 373-431.

KIRBY, P. R. 1952. The swimming log of the Hottentots. *Africana Notes and News* **9** (4): 107-123.

KRIGE, E. J. 1936. *The social system of the Zulus*. Pietermaritzburg: Shuter & Shooter.

LANHAM, L. W. & HALLOWES, D. P. 1956. Linguistic relationships and contacts expressed in the vocabulary of Eastern Bushmen. *Afr. Stud.* **15** (1): 45-8.

LAYDEVANT, F. 1933. The praises of the divining bones among the Basotho. *Bantu Stud.* **8** (4): 341-373.

LEACH, E. R. 1966. Ritualization in man. *Phil. Trans. R. Soc.* (B) **251**: 403-408. Organised by Sir Julian Huxley.

LEACH, E. R. (Ed.) 1967. *The structural study of myth and totemism*. London: Tavistock publications.

LEACH, E. R. 1970. *Lévi-Strauss*. London: Fontana/Collins.

LEAKEY, L. S. B. 1926. A new classification of the bow and arrow in Africa. *Jl R. anthrop. Inst.* **56**: 259-300.

LEE, D. N. & WOODHOUSE, H. C. 1964. Rock paintings of 'flying buck'. *S. Afr. archaeol. Bull.* **19** (75): 71-74.

LEE, D. N. & WOODHOUSE, H. C. 1968. More rock paintings of flying buck. *S. Afr. archaeol. Bull.* **23** (89): 13-16.

LEE, D. N. & WOODHOUSE, H. C. 1970. *Art on the rocks of Southern Africa*. Cape Town: Purnell & Sons.

LEE, D. N. 1972. Bushman folk-lore and rock paintings. *S. Afr. J. Sci.* **68** (7): 195-199.

LEE, R. B. 1968a. The sociology of !Kung Bushman trance performances in *Trance and possession states*, ed. R. Prince: 35-63. Proc. 2nd Ann. Conference R. M. Bucke Memorial Soc., Montreal.

LEE, R. B. 1968b. !Kung Bushmen subsistence: an input-output analysis, in *Man the hunter*. ed. by R. B. Lee & I. De Vore. Chicago: Aldine.

LEEUWENBURG, J. 1971. The history of rock art recording at the South African Museum, the later establishment of the Rock Art Centre, and the development and aims of the Centre. *S. Afr. J. Sci.* Special Issue no. 2: 98-100.

LEGGE, J. A. (Transl.) 1885. *The Sacred Books of China: The texts of Confucianism*. ed. F. M. Müller. Oxford: Clarendon Press.

LEROI-GOURHAN, A. 1965. *Prehistoire de l'art occidental*. Paris: Lucien Mazenod.

LEVINE, M. H. 1957. Prehistoric art and ideology. *American Anthropologist* **59**: 949-964.

LÉVI-STRAUSS, C. 1966. *Mythologiques: Du miel aux cendres*. Paris: Plon.

LÉVI-STRAUSS, C. 1966. *The savage mind*. London: Weidenfeld & Nicolson.

LÉVI-STRAUSS, C. 1968a. *Structural anthropology*. London: Allen Lane.

LÉVI-STRAUSS, C. 1968b. *Mythologiques: L'origine des manières*. Paris: Plon.

LÉVI-STRAUSS, C. 1969. *Totemism*. London: Merlin Press Ltd.

LÉVI-STRAUSS, C. 1973. Structuralism and ecology. *Soc. Sci. Inf.* **12** (1).

LEWIS-WILLIAMS, J. D. 1972a. The syntax and function of the Giant's Castle rock-paintings. *S. Afr. archaeol. Bull.* **27** (105-106): 49-65.

LEWIS-WILLIAMS, J. D. 1972b. The Drakensberg rock paintings as an expression of religious thought. First international symposium on prehistoric religions. Valcamonica, Italy, *In press.*

LLOYD, L. C. 1889. *A short account of further Bushman material collected.* London: D. Nutt.

LOGIE, A. C. 1935. Preliminary notes on some Bushman arrows from South West Africa. *S. Afr. J. Sci.* **32**: 553-559.

LOUW, J. T. 1960. Prehistory of the Matjes River Rock Shelter. *Navors. nas. Mus., Bloemfontein* **1**.

LYE, W. F. 1967. The Difaqane: The Mfecane in the Southern Sotho area, 1822-24. *J. Afr. Hist.* **8** (1): 107-131.

LYSTAD, R. A. (Ed.) 1965. *The African World:* a survey of social research. London: Pall Mall Press.

McKENZIE, G. 1967. *Delayed action.* Pietermaritzburg: Shuter & Shooter.

McKENZIE, P. 1946 (?) *Pioneers of Underberg.* A short account of the settlement: 1-22. Pietermaritzburg: L. Backhouse.

MACKEURTAN, H. G. 1930. *The cradle days of Natal, 1497-1845,* London: Longmans Green.

MAEDER, F. 1884. *Leselinyana la Lesotho* (Morija), October, 1884.

MAGGS, T. M. O'C. 1967. A quantitative analysis of the rock art from a sample area in the western Cape. *S. Afr. J. Sci.* **63** (3): 100-104.

MAINGARD, L. F. 1932. History and distribution of the bow and arrow in South Africa. *S. Afr. J. Sci.* **29**: 711-723.

MAINGARD, L. F. 1937. The weapons of the ?Auni and the ‡Khomani Bushmen, in *Bushmen of the Southern Kalahari,* ed. J. D. Rheinhallt-Jones & C. M. Doke: 277-283. Johannesburg: University of Witwatersrand Press.

MAINGARD, J. F. 1937. Notes on health and disease among the Bushmen of the southern Kalahari. *Bantu Stud.* **11** (3): 285-295.

MALAN, B. D. 1955. A preliminary account of the archaeology of East Griqualand. *Archaeol. ser.* **8**. Union of S.A. Dept. of Educ., Arts & Sci.

MALAN, B. D. 1958. Similarities in paintings. *S. Afr. archaeol. Bull.* **13** (50): 71.

MALAN, B. D. 1970. Remarks and reminiscences on the history of archaeology in South Africa. *S. Afr. archaeol. Bull.* **25** (99 & 100): 88-94.

MALAN, B. D. & KIRK, N. 1952. Cover of *S. Afr. archaeol. Bull.* **7** (27).

MALAN, B. D. 1958. Investigation of causes of deterioration of pre-historic rock paintings and methods of preservation: a preliminary report. *Bull. S. Afr. Mus. Ass.* **6** (14): 373-376.

MANN, R. J. 1859. *The Colony of Natal.* London: Jarrold & Sons.

MARKS, S. 1972. Khoisan resistance to the Dutch in the seventeenth and eighteenth centuries. *J. Afr. Hist.* **13** (1): 55-80.

MARSHALL, J. 1958. Huntsmen of Nyae Nyae, pt. 2. *Nat. Hist.* **67**: 376-395.

MARSHALL, J. Film: The Hunters. Peabody Museum Film Study Center, Harvard University.

MARSHALL, L. 1957a. N!ow. Belief concerning rain and cold. *Africa* **27** (3): 232-240.

MARSHALL, L. 1957b. The kin terminology system of the !Kung Bushmen. *Africa.* **27** (1): 1-24.

MARSHALL, L. 1959. Marriage among !Kung Bushmen. *Africa* **29** (4): 335-365.

MARSHALL, L. 1960. !Kung Bushman bonds. *Africa* **30** (4): 325-355.

MARSHALL, L. 1961. Sharing, talking, and giving: relief of social tensions among !Kung Bushmen. *Africa* **31** (3): 231-249.

MARSHALL, L. 1962. !Kung Bushman religious beliefs. *Africa* **32** (3): 221-252.

MARSHALL, L. 1965. The !Kung Bushmen of the Kalahari desert, in *Peoples of Africa,* ed. J. L. Gibbs: 241-278. U.S.A.: Holt, Rinehart & Winston, Inc.

MARSHALL, L. 1969. The medicine dance of the !Kung Bushmen. *Africa* **39** (4): 347-380.

MARSHALL THOMAS, E. 1959. *The harmless people.* London: Secker & Warburg.

MARTIN, P. D. 1872. Stone implements and shell caves. *Cape Monthly Mag.* **5** (25): 53-55.

MASON, A. Y. 1933. Rock paintings in the Cathkin Peak area, Natal. *Bantu Stud.* **7** (2): 131.

MASON, I. L. & MAULE, J. P. 1960. The indigenous livestock of Eastern and Southern Africa. *Commonwealth Agric. Bureau of Breeding & Genetics. Tech. Comm.* **14**.

MASON, R. J. 1969. Tentative interpretations of new radio-carbon dates for stone artefact assemblages from Rose Cottage Cave O.F.S. and Bushman Rock Shelter, Transvaal. *S. Afr. archaeol. Bull.* **24** (94): 57-9.

MERRIAM, A. P. 1965. Music and the dance, in *The African world,* ed. R. A. Lystad: 452-468. London: Pall Mall Press.

METZGER, F. 1950. *Narro and his clan.* Windhoek: John Meinert Ltd. S.W.A.

MOODIE, D. 1838. *The record.* A series of official papers relative to the treatment of the native tribes of South Africa, pt 1, 1649-1720. Cape Town: A. S. Robertson. Reprinted Cape Town 1960: Balkema.

MOODIE, D. 1855. A voice from the Kahlamba ... origin of the Bushmen. See *Natal Witness,* 20 & 27/5/1855.

MORRIS, R. & D. 1965. *Men and snakes.* London: Hutchinson.

MOSZEIK, O. 1910. *Die malereien der Buschmänner in Südafrika.* Berlin: Dietrich Reimer.

MURRAY, N. L. 1933. Skeletal remains from rock shelters in Cathkin Park, Natal. *Bantu Stud.* **7**: 201-215.

NATAL REGIONAL SURVEY VOL. I. 1951. London: Oxford University Press.

NIDDRIE, D. L. 1951. The climate and weather of Natal, in *Natal regional survey* vol. I: 42-66. London: Oxford University Press.

NORTON, W. A. 1921. Sesuto praises of the chiefs. *S. Afr. J. Sci.* **18**: 441-453.

ORPEN, J. M. 1874. A glimpse into the mythology of the Maluti Bushmen. *Cape Monthly Mag.* **9**. Reprinted *Folklore* 1919 **30**: 139-156.

ORPEN, J. M. 1908. *Reminiscences of life in South Africa from 1846 to the present day, with historical researches*, vol. 1. Durban: P. Davis & Sons.

OTTO, Br. 1908. Buschmann-malereien aus Natal. *Anthropos* **3**; 1047-1049.

OTTO, Br. 1921. A plea for more method. *Bantu Stud.* **1** (1): 4-7.

PAGER, H. 1962. Summary in *Madsimu Dsangara* by L. Frobenius. First printed 1931. Graz, Austria: Akademische Druck u. Verlagsanstalt.

PAGER, H. 1969. Review of Gusinde 1966. *S. Afr. archaeol. Bull.* **24** (2): 75-77.

PAGER, H. 1971. *Ndedema*, a documentation of the rock paintings of the Ndedema gorge. Graz, Austria: Akademische Druck u. Verlagsanstalt.

PALMER, E. 1966. *The plains of Camdeboo*. London: Collins.

PARKINGTON, J. & POGGENPOEL, C. 1971. Excavations at de Hangen. *S. Afr. archaeol. Bull.* **26**: 3-36.

PHILLIPSON, D. W. 1969. Early iron-using peoples of Southern Africa, in *African societies in Southern Africa*, ed. L. Thompson: 24-45. London: Heinemann.

POSSELT, K. W., PFITZNER, E. & WANGEMANN, D. 1891. *Wilhelm Posselt der Kaffermissionar*. Berlin: Buchhandlung der Berliner evangelischen Missionsgesellschaft.

POTGIETER, E. F. 1955. *The disappearing Bushmen of Lake Chrissie*. Pretoria: van Schaik.

PRINGLE, J. A. 1963. The Red Haartebeest of Natal. *Natal Wild Life* **4** (1): 4-6.

RADCLIFFE-BROWN, A. R. 1952. *Structure and function in primitive society*. London: Cohen & West.

RADCLIFFE-BROWN, A. R. 1958. *Method in social anthropology*, ed. M. N. Srinivas. Chicago: Copyright 1958 by the University of Chicago. Published 1958. Composed and printed by the University of Chicago Press, Chicago, Illinois, U.S.A.

RAYMOND, W. D. 1947. Tanganyika arrow poisons. *Tanganyika Notes Rec.* **23**: 49-65.

RHEINHALLT JONES, J. D. & DOKE, C. M. 1931. Editorial notes: Customs and Beliefs of the /Xam Bushmen, pt. 2. *Bantu Stud.* **5** (2): 167-179.

ROBERTS, A. 1951. *The mammals of South Africa*. South Africa: Central News Agency.

ROGERS, G. M. 1937. *I . . . alone. The story of an English-woman's 60 adventurous years in South Africa, 1876-1936*. Pietermaritzburg: Shuter & Shooter.

ROOS, T. 1931. Burial customs of the !Kaū Bushmen. *Bantu Stud.* **5**: 81.

RUDNER, J. 1971. Painted burial stones from the Cape. *S. Afr. J. Sci.*, special issue no. 2: 54-61.

SAMPSON, G. & M. 1967. Excavations at Glen Elliot Shelter, Colesberg District, N. Cape. *Navors. nas. Mus., Bloemfontein* **2** (5 & 6).

SAMPSON, G. 1972. The Stone Age industries of the Orange river scheme and South Africa. *Navors. nas. Mus., Bloemfontein Mem.* **6**.

SANDERSON, J. 1860. Notes to accompany sketch maps of the Zulu and Amatonga countries, and of the country between Aliwal North and Natal. *Geogrl. J.* **32**: 335-339.

SCHAPERA, I. 1925. Bushman arrow poisons. *Bantu Stud.* **2**: 199-214.

SCHAPERA, I. 1930. *The Khoisan peoples of South Africa*. London: Routledge & Kegan Paul Ltd.

SCHAPERA, I. (Ed.) 1934. The present state and future development of ethnographical research in South Africa. *Bantu Stud.* **8**: 219.

SCHARF, B. R. 1970. *The sociological study of religion*. London: Hutchinson University library.

SCHOEMAN, P. J. 1957. *Hunters of the desert land*. Cape Town: Howard Timmins.

SCHOFIELD, J. F. 1935. Natal coastal pottery from the Durban district: a preliminary survey. *S. Afr. J. Sci.* **32**: 508-527.

SCHOFIELD, J. F. 1949. Four debatable points. *S. Afr. archaeol. Bull.* **4** (15): 101-102.

SCHOONRAAD, M. 1962. Rock painting depicting prehistoric fishing found near Maclear. *S. Afr. J. Sci.* **58** (5): 141-143.

SCHOONRAAD, M. 1963. Further similarities in paintings. *S. Afr. archaeol. Bull.* **18** (70): 66.

SCHOUTE-VANNECK, C. A. & WALSH, R. C. 1959. The shell middens of the Ingane river mouth, Natal South Coast. *S. Afr. archaeol. Bull.* **14** (54): 43-45.

SCHOUTE-VANNECK, C. A. & WALSH, R. C. 1960. The Tongaat variant of the Wilton Culture. *S. Afr. archaeol. Bull.* **15** (58): 29-35.

SCHOUTE-VANNECK, C. A. & WALSH, R. C. 1961. The Umlaas variant of the Smithfield C Culture. *S. Afr. archaeol. Bull.* **16** (64): 137-143.

SCHWARZ, E. L. 1926. The Northern Kalahari. *S. Afr. geogr. J.* **9**: 27-36.

SCHWEIGER, P. M. A. 1912. Bushman caves at Keilands. *Cath. Mag. S. Afr.* **23** (253): 103-109; (254): 152-159; (255): 204-208; (256) 251-255; (257): 302-304.

SCHWEIGER, P. M. A. 1913. Neu entdeckte Buschmannmalereien in der Cape Provinz, Südostafrika. *Anthropos* **13**: 652-669.

SCHWEITZER, F. R. & SCOTT, K. J. 1973. Early occurrence of domestic sheep in sub-Saharan Africa. *Nature* **241** (5391): 547.

SCOTT, J. D. 1957. Vegetation, in *Natal Regional Survey*, vol. 13: 25-42. London: Oxford University Press.

SHAW, E. M., WOOLLEY, P. L. & RAE, F. A. 1963. Bushman arrow poisons. *Cimbebasia* **7**: 2-41.

SHORTRIDGE, G. C. 1934. *The mammals of S.W. Africa . . .*, vol. 2. London: William Heinemann Ltd.

SIBISI, H. 1972. *Health and disease among the Nyuswa - Zulu*. Unpublished Ph.D. Thesis submitted to the University of Cambridge.

SILBERBAUER, G. B. 1965. *Bushman Survey*. Gaberones: Bechuanaland Govt.

SINGER, R. & JOPP, W. 1967. The earliest illustration of Hottentots: 1508. *S. Afr. archaeol. Bull.* **22** (85): 27-30.

SINGER, R. & WYMER, J. 1969. Radiocarbon date for two painted stones from a coastal cave in South Africa. *Nature* **224** (5218): 508-510.

SMITH, C. A. 1966. *Common names of South African plants*. Pretoria: Government Printer.

SMITS, L. G. A. 1967. Fishing scenes from Botsabelo, Lesotho. *S. Afr. archaeol. Bull.* **22** (86): 60-72.

SMITS, L. G. A. 1971. The rock paintings of Lesotho, their content and characteristics. *S. Afr. J. Sci.*, special issue no. 2: 14-20.

SPARRMAN, A. 1786. *A voyage to the Cape of Good Hope, 1772-1776*, 2 vols. London: Robinson, Pater-Noster Row.

SPOHR, O. H. 1965a. *The Natal diaries of Dr W. H. I. Bleek*. Cape Town: A. A. Balkema.

SPOHR, O. H. 1965b. Notes from letters and pamphlets about Donald Moodie, W. H. I. Bleek and the Record. *Africana Notes & News* **16** (15): 204-216.

SQUIRE, W. A. 1906. The Bushmen and their art, in *20th century impressions of Natal*: 206-211. Natal: Lloyds Greater Britain Publishing Co.

STALKER, J. 1912. *The Natal Carbineers, 1855-1911*. Pietermaritzburg and Durban: P. Davis & Sons.

STANFORD, W. E. 1910. Statement of Silayi, with reference to his life among the Bushmen. *Trans. R. Soc. S. Afr.* **1** (2): 435.

STANFORD, W. 1958. *The Reminiscences of Sir Walter Stanford, 1850-1885*, ed. J. W. Macquarrie. Cape Town: Van Riebeeck Society.

STEIN, H. B. 1933. Stone implements from Cathkin Peak area. *Bantu Stud.* **7** (2): 161.

STEVENSON-HAMILTON, J. 1954. *Wild life in South Africa*. London: Cassell & Co.

STORY, R. 1958. Some plants used by the Bushmen in obtaining food and water. *Bot. Surv. S. Afr. Mem.* **30**. Dept. Agric., Pretoria.

STOW, G. W. 1905. *The native races of South Africa*. London: Swan Sonnenschein & Co. Ltd.

STOW, G. W. & BLEEK, D. F. 1930. *Rock paintings in South Africa*, from parts of the Eastern Province and Orange Free State. London: Methuen & Co. Ltd.

STOW, G. W. 1953. *Cave Artists of South Africa*, coll. D. F. Bleek. Cape Town: A. A. Balkema.

STRUBEN, H. W. 1920. *Recollections of adventures*: Pioneering and development in South Africa, 1850-1911. Cape Town: Maskew Miller.

SUMMERS, R. (Ed.) 1959. *Prehistoric rock art of the Federation of Rhodesia and Nyasaland*. Salisbury: National Publications Trust, Rhodesia and Nyasaland.

TAMBIAH, S. J. 1969. Animals are good to think and good to prohibit. *Ethnology* **8** (4): 423-459.

TEN RAA, E. 1971. Dead art and living society: a study of rockpaintings in a social context. *Mankind* **8**: 42-58.

THEAL, G. Mc C. 1883. *Basutoland Records* **3**. Cape Town: Richards & Sons.

THEAL, G. Mc C. 1908. *History of South Africa since 1795*, 5 vols. London: Swan, Sonnenschein.

THEAL, G. Mc C. 1919. *Ethnography and condition of South Africa before 1505*. London: Allen & Unwin.

THOMAS, E. W. 1950. *Bushman stories*. Oxford: University Press.

TOBIAS, P. V. 1964. Bushman hunter-gatherers: a study in human ecology, in *Ecological studies in Southern Africa*, ed. D. H. S. Davis: 67-86. Den Haag: Dr W. Junk.

TOERIEN, M. J. 1961. The skulls from the Holley Shelter. *S. Afr. J. Sci.* **57** (2): 48-50.

TONGUE, M. H. 1909. *Bushman paintings*, with preface by H. Balfour. Oxford: Clarendon Press.

TURNER, V. W. 1962a. Chihamba the white spirit, a ritual drama of the Ndembu. *Rhodes-Livingstone Pap.* 33, Rhodesia.

TURNER, V. W. 1962b. Three symbols of passage in Ndembu circumcision ritual, in *Essays on the ritual of social relations*, ed. M. Gluckman. Manchester: University Press.

TURNER, V. W. 1962c. Themes in the symbolism of Ndembu hunting ritual. *Anthrop. Quart.* **35** (2).

TURNER, V. W. 1966. Colour classification in Ndembu ritual, in *Anthropological approaches to the study of religion*, ed. M. Banton: 47-84.

TURNER, V. W. 1967. *The forest of symbols*: aspects of Ndembu ritual. Ithaca, New York: Cornell University Press.

TURNER, V. W. 1968. *The drums of affliction*. Oxford: Clarendon Press.

TURNER, W. 1884. The crania. *Challenger Reports, Zoology* **10** (29): 2-17.

TURNER, W. 1886. The bones of the skeleton. *Challenger Reports, Zoology* (47): 13-22.

TYLDEN, G. 1945. C.M.R. uniforms in pictures. *Africana Notes and News* **2** (2): 48-51.

TYLDEN, G. 1945. Morosi's mountain. *Libertas* **6** (1): 10-13.

TYLDEN, G. 1946. Bantu shields. *S. Afr. archaeol. Bull.* **1** (2): 33-37.

TYLDEN, G. 1950. The Cape Coloured regular regiments, 1793-1870. *Africana Notes and News* **7** (2): 37-59.

TYLDEN, G. 1952. Three mountains. *Africana Notes and News* **9** (2): 36-47.

TYLDEN, G. 1957. Shoulder fire-arms in Southern Africa, 1652-1952. *Africana Notes and News* **12** (6): 198-218.

TYLOR, L. E. 1893. Unpublished correspondence in files of Pitt-Rivers Museum, Oxford.

TYRRELL, B. 1968. *Tribal peoples of Southern Africa*. Cape Town: Books of Africa.

UCKO, P. J. 1969. Penis sheaths: a comprehensive study. *Proc. R. anthropol. Inst*: 27-67.

UCKO, P. J. & ROSENFELD, A. 1967. *Palaeolithic Cave Art*. London: Verona Press.

VAN DER POST, L. 1961. *The heart of the hunter*. London: Hogarth Press.

VAN RIET LOWE, C. 1936. The Smithfield 'N' Culture. *Trans. R. Soc. S. Afr.* **23**: 367-372.

VAN RIET LOWE, C. 1946. Cover design for *S. Afr. archaeol. Bull.* **1** (3).

VAN RIET LOWE, C. 1947a. A ground axe from Natal. *Trans. R. Soc. S. Afr.* **31**: 325-331.

VAN RIET LOWE, C. 1947b. More Neolithic elements from South Africa. *S. Afr. archaeol. Bull.* **2** (8): 91-96.

VAN RIET LOWE, C. 1949. Rock paintings near Cathedral Peak. *S. Afr. archaeol. Bull.* **4** (13): 28-33.

VAN RIET LOWE, C. & MALAN, B. D. 1951. *The monuments of South Africa*. Pretoria: Government printer.

VAN RIET LOWE, C. 1956. The distribution of prehistoric rock engravings and paintings in South Africa. *Archaeol. Ser.* **7**. Union of S.A. Dept. of Educ., Arts & Sci.

VAUGHAN, J. H. 1962. Rock-paintings and rock gongs among the Marghi of Nigeria. *Man* **62** (83): 49-52.

VINNICOMBE, P. 1955. Early African art. *The Listener* **53** (1354): 229.

VINNICOMBE, P. 1960a. The recording of rock paintings in the upper reaches of the Umkomaas, Umzimkulu and Umzimvubu rivers. *S. Afr. J. Sci.* **56** (1): 11-14.

VINNICOMBE, P. 1960b. A fishing scene from the Tsoelike river, South Eastern Basutoland. *S. Afr. archaeol. Bull.* **15** (27): 15-19.

VINNICOMBE, P. 1961. A painting of a fish trap on Bamboo Mountain, Underberg district, Southern Natal. *S. Afr. archaeol. Bull.* **16** (63): 114-115.

VINNICOMBE, P. 1965. Bushman fishing as depicted in rock paintings. *Sci. S. Afr.* **2** (12): 578-581.

VINNICOMBE, P. 1966. The early recording and presentation of rock paintings in South Africa. *Stud. Speleol.* **1** (4): 153-162.

VINNICOMBE, P. 1967a. Rock painting analysis. *S. Afr. archaeol. Bull.* **22** (88): 129-141.

VINNICOMBE, P. 1967b. The recording of rock paintings — an interim report. *S. Afr. J. Sci.* **63** (7): 282-284.

VINNICOMBE, P. 1971. A Bushman hunting kit from the Natal Drakensberg. *Ann. Natal Mus.* **20** (3): 611-625.

VINNICOMBE, P. 1972a. Motivation in African rock art. *Antiquity* **46**: 124-133.

VINNICOMBE, P. 1972b. Myth, motive and selection in southern African rock art. *Africa* **42** (3): 192-204.

VINNICOMBE, P. 1972c. *The ritual significance of eland (Taurotragus oryx) in the rock art of Southern Africa*. First international symposium on prehistoric religions, Valcamonica. Italy. *In press*.

VOGEL, J. C. & BEAUMONT, P. B. 1972a. New radio-carbon dates for South Africa. *Nature* **237** (5349): 50-51.

WALKER, E. A. 1957. *A history of southern Africa*. London: Longmans, Green & Co.

WALKER, E. A. 1963. The formation of new states, in *The Cambridge history of the British Empire*: 325-364. Cambridge University Press.

WALKER, E. P. 1964. *Mammals of the world*, vol. 2 Baltimore: Johns Hopkins Press.

WALTON, J. 1951. Early Ba-Fokeng rock shelter dwellings at Ntlo-Kholo. *African Stud.* **10** (2): 83-86.

WALTON, J. 1956a. *African Village*, Pretoria: J. L. van Schaik Ltd.

WALTON, J. 1956b. Early Ba-Fokeng settlement in South Africa. *African Stud.* **15** (1): 37-43.

WARD, R. 1892. *Horn measurements and weights of the great game of the world*. London: at "The Jungle", 166 Piccadilly.

WATERSON, D. 1915. The Bushmen of the Mooi River, Natal. *Scient. Am.* **112** (9): 191.

WATT, J. M. & BREYER-BRANDWIJK, M. G. 1962. *The medicinal and poisonous plants of Southern and Eastern Africa*. Edinburgh & London: E. & S. Livingstone Ltd.

WELLS, L. H. 1933. The archaeology of Cathkin Park. *Bantu Stud.* **7** (2): 113-129.

WELLS, L. H. 1934. A further note on human skeletal remains from the Natal coast. *Trans. R. Soc. S. Afr.* **22** (3): 235-243.

WENDT, W. E. 1972. Preliminary report of an archaeological programme in South West Africa. *Cimbebasia* Ser. B, **2** (1): 1-61.

WERNER, A. 1907-1908. Bushman paintings. *Jl R. Afr. Soc.* **7**: 387-393.

WESTPHAL, E. O. J. 1963. The linguistic pre-history of Southern Africa: Bush, Kwadi, Hottentot & Bantu linguistic relationships. *Africa* **3**: 237-265.

WHYTE, A. D. 1910, 1921. Unpublished reports on Bushman Paintings. Correspondence files of the Natal Museum, Pietermaritzburg.

WILLCOX, A. R. 1955. The shaded polychrome paintings of South Africa, their distribution, origin and age. *S. Afr. archaeol. Bull.* **10** (37): 10-14.

WILLCOX, A. R. 1956. *Rock paintings of the Drakensberg*. London: Max Parrish.

WILLCOX, A. R. 1956b. The status of Smithfield C reconsidered. *S. Afr. J. Sci.* **52** (11): 250-252.

WILLCOX, A. R. 1957a. The classification of rock paintings. *S. Afr. J. Sci.* **53** (16): 417-419.

WILLCOX, A. R. 1957b. A cave at Giant's Castle Game Reserve. *S. Afr. archaeol. Bull.* **12** (47): 87-97.

WILLCOX, A. R. 1959. Hand imprints in rock paintings. *S. Afr. J. Sci.* **55** (11): 292-297.

WILLCOX, A. R. 1963. *The rock art of South Africa*. Johannesburg: Wageningen Press.

WILLCOX, A. R. 1966a. Who made the rock art of South Africa and when? *S. Afr. J. Sci.* **62** (1): 8-12.

WILLCOX, A. R. 1966b. Art on the rocks. *S. Afr. Panorama*, Sept. (22): 19-23.

WILLCOX, A. R. 1966c. Sheep and sheep-herders in South Africa. *Africa*, **36** (4): 432-438.

WILLCOX, A. R. 1968a. A survey of our present knowledge of rock paintings in South Africa. *S. Afr. archaeol. Bull.* **23** (89): 20-23.

WILLCOX, A. R. 1971. Summary of Dr Edgar Denninger's reports on the ages of paint samples taken from rock paintings in South and South West Africa. *S. Afr. J. Sci.*, special issue no. 2: 84-85.

WILLCOX, A. R. 1972. So-called 'infibulation' in rock art. *S. Afr. archaeol. Bull.* **27**: 83.

WILLCOX, A. R. & FRIENDLY, W. 1963. Africa's Bushman art treasures. *Natn. geog. Mag.* **123** (6): 849-865.

WILSON, A. L. 1955. Wilton material on the Natal slopes of the Drakensberg. *S. Afr. archaeol. Bull.* **10** (37): 20-21.

WILSON, M. 1969. The hunters and herders, in *The Oxford history of South Africa*, ed. M. Wilson & L. Thompson: 40-74. Oxford: Clarendon Press.

WOOD, J. G. 1874. *The natural history of man: Africa*. London: Routledge & Sons.

WOODBURN, J. 1962. The future of the Tindiga. *Tanganyika Notes Rec.* 58-59: 269-273.

WOODBURN, J. 1972. Ecology, nomadic movement and the composition of the local group among hunters and gatherers: an East African example and its implications, in *Man, settlement and urbanism*, ed. P. J. Ucko & R. Tringham. London: Duckworth & Co. Ltd.

WOODHOUSE, H. C. 1964a. The prehistoric painters of South Africa. *Bantu Educ. Jl.* **9** (9): 455-459.

WOODHOUSE, H. C. 1964b. The cunning Bushman hunters. *Sci. S. Afr.* **1** (8): 303-4.

WOODHOUSE, H. C. 1965. Prehistoric rock painters of South Africa. *S. Afr. Panorama* **10** (1): 10-13.

WOODHOUSE, H. C. 1966a. Prehistoric hunting methods as depicted in the rock paintings of Southern Africa. *S. Afr. J. Sci.* **62** (6): 169-171.

WOODHOUSE, H. C. 1966b. How Bushmen saw other men's beasts. *Farmer's Weekly*, Dec. 28: 48-49.

WOODHOUSE, H. C. 1967. Animal-headed human figures in the rock paintings of Southern Africa. *S. Afr. J. Sci.* **63** (11): 464-470.

WOODHOUSE, H. C. 1968a. The Cold Stream burial stone: painting of a prehistoric painter. *S. Afr. J. Sci.* **64** (9): 341-344.

WOODHOUSE, H. C. 1968b. The Melikane rock-paintings: sorcerers or hunters? *S. Afr. archaeol. Bull.* **23** (90): 37-39.

WOODHOUSE, H. C. 1968c. History on the rocks. *Personality*. Feb. 1: 55-57.

WOODHOUSE, H. C. 1969a. The Cold Stream burial stone. *S. Afr. J. Sci.* **65** (4): 127.

WOODHOUSE, H. C. 1969b. Rock paintings of Southern Africa. *Afr. arts* **2** (3): 44-49.

WOODHOUSE, H. C. 1970a. Three widely distributed features depicted in the rock paintings of people in southern Africa. *S. Afr. J. Sci.* **66** (2): 51-55.

WOODHOUSE, H. C. 1970b. Beersheba shelter, in *Standard encyclopaedia of Southern Africa*. Cape Town: Nasou Ltd.

WOODHOUSE, H. C. 1971. Strange relationships between men and eland in the rock paintings of South Africa. *S. Afr. J. Sci.* **67** (6): 345-348.

WRIGHT, J. B. 1971. *Bushman raiders of the Drakensberg 1840-1870*. Pietermaritzburg: University of Natal Press.

ZELIZKO, J. V. 1925. *Felsgravierungen der Süd Afrikanischen Buschmänner*. Leipzig: F. A. Brockhaus.

Figure 253 *Site L34*
Man, woman and dogs, painted in dark red.

Index

Page numbers in *italics* refer to captions
Numbered notes appear in brackets after the page number, e.g. 37(n. 43)